INDIA: A HISTORY

South Asia boasts one of the world's longest, richest and most rewarding histories. It crowds the past with a teeming diversity of civilisations and packs the present with a kaleidoscope of regional and cultural entities. John Keay discerns the continuities and highlights the glories while here presenting, in a single volume, the first truly comprehensive and thoroughly readable history of modern-day India, Pakistan and Bangladesh for thirty years.

A cradle of civilisation, the subcontinent is today the cockpit of one of its most explosive disputes. From the myths of an impossible antiquity to the masterpieces of classical glory, from the boasts of obscure dynasts to the chronicles of Islamic conquest, and from the triumphs of liberation to the recriminations of partition, Keay recounts a five-thousand-year epic in which conflict underwrites achievement and kings defer to saints.

The monuments, tombs, temples and palaces are paraded in context and their significance explained. Revelations from recent scholarship prompt unexpected insights. And a new slant is given to those conventional tides of inward incursion and outward dissemination – Alexander the Great's débâcle, the all-Asia diffusion of Indian culture, the Islamic, Mughal and British conquests, and the twentieth-century diaspora of south Asian society.

Beginning with the Flood and ending with the Bomb, *India: A History* combines narrative delights with social, economic and cultural analysis. Provocative and authoritative, it confirms John Keay's reputation as one of the foremost writers on the subcontinent.

JOHN KEAY is the author of three acclaimed histories: *The Honourable Company*, about the East India Company; *Last Post*, about imperial disengagement in the Far East; and the two-volume *Explorers of the Western Himalayas*. His books on India include *India Discovered*, *Into India* and *The Great Arc: The Dramatic Tale of How India was Mapped and Everest was Named*. John Keay is married with four children, lives in Scotland and is co-editor with Julia Keay of the *Collins Encyclopaedia of Scotland*.

INDIA

A HISTORY

JOHN KEAY

HarperCollins*Publishers* London
HarperCollins*Publishers* India

For Tara

HarperCollins*Publishers*
77–85 Fulham Palace Road,
Hammersmith, London w6 8jb

HarperCollinsPublishers India Pvt Ltd
7/16 Ansari Road, Daryaganj, New Delhi, 110 002

The HarperCollins website address is:
www.**fire**and**water**.com

This paperback edition 2001
3 5 7 9 8 6 4

First published in Great Britain by HarperCollins*Publishers* 2000

Copyright © John Keay 2000

Maps and tables by Jillian Luff

John Keay asserts the moral right to
be identified as the author of this work

ISBN 0 00 638784 5

Set in PostScript Linotype Minion by
Rowland Phototypesetting Ltd, Bury St Edmunds, Suffolk

Printed and bound in Great Britain by
Omnia Books Limited, Glasgow

CONTENTS

List of Illustrations   vii
List of Maps   xi
List of Charts and Tables   xiii
Introduction   xvii

1 The Harappan World: c3000–1700 BC   1

2 Vedic Values: c1700–900 BC   19

3 The Epic Age: c900–520 BC   37

4 Out of the Myth-Smoke: c520–c320 BC   56

5 Gloria Maurya: c320–200 BC   78

6 An Age of Paradox: c200 BC–c300 AD   101

7 Gupta Gold: c300–500 AD   129

8 Lords of the Universe: c500–700   155

9 *Dharma* and Defiance: c700–c900   180

10 Natraj, the Rule of the Dance: c950–1180   202

11 The Triumph of the Sultans: c1180–1320   231

12 Other Indias: 1320–1525   262

13 The Making of the Mughal Empire: 1500–1605   289

14 Mughal Pomp, Indian Circumstance: 1605–1682   320

15 From Taj to Raj: 1682–1750   348

16 The British Conquest: 1750–1820   383

17 Pax Britannica: 1820–1880   414

18 Awake the Nation: 1880–1930   448

19 At the Stroke of the Midnight Hour: 1930–1948   484

20 Crossing the Tracks: 1948–   509

     Source Notes   535
     Bibliography   545
     Index (incorporating Glossary)   559

ILLUSTRATIONS

Bronze 'dancing girl' from Mohenjo-daro in Sind province, Pakistan, c.2000 BC. (© *Clive Friend*)

Mohenjo-daro, the 'Mound of the Dead'. (© *Clive Friend*)

Sunrise at Dashashwamedh Ghat on the Ganga (Ganges) at Varanasi (Benares). (© *Clive Friend*)

A scene from the *Ramayana* by an early-nineteenth-century artist. (*Courtesy of The Bridgeman Art Library*)

The Ashoka column atop Feroz Shah Khalji's fort in Delhi, inscribed in the third century BC. (© *Clive Friend*)

The Lion capital from Sarnath (near Varanasi). (© *Clive Friend*)

The rock at Shahbazgarhi (Panjab province, Pakistan) bearing Ashoka's Edicts. (© *Clive Friend*)

Bactrian coins of a Bactrian Greek king of the second century BC, and of Kanishka, the great Kushan king of uncertain date. (© *Clive Friend*)

Relief panel from one of the gateways to the Great Stupa at Sanchi, first century BC. (© *Clive Friend*)

Bracket carved as a *yakshi* on one of the Sanchi gateways. (© *Clive Friend*)

Seated Buddha of the Gandhara school, second century AD. (© *Clive Friend*)

Seated Buddha from Sarnath, fifth century AD. (© *Clive Friend*)

Fresco of a Bodhisattva in Cave 1 at Ajanta, Maharashtra, fifth century AD. (© *Clive Friend*)

The eighth-century Shore Temple at Ellora in Mamallapuram near Madras. (© *Clive Friend*)

The late-eighth-century Kailasa temple in Maharashtra, cut from solid rock for the Rashtrakuta king Krishna I. (© *Clive Friend*)

Man Singh palace in Gwalior fort, Madhya Pradesh, 1486–1516. (© *Clive Friend*)

Qutb Minar, Delhi. *(© Clive Friend)*

Lingaraja temple, Bhuvaneshwar, Orissa, c.1100. *(© Clive Friend)*

Interior dome of Adinatha (Vimal Vasahi) temple, Mount Abu, Rajasthan, eleventh–twelfth century. *(© Clive Friend)*

Tughluqabad Fort, Delhi, 1321–5. *(© Clive Friend)*

Daulatabad (Devagiri, Deogir) Fort, Maharashtra. *(© Robert Harding Picture Library)*

Hoysaleshwara temple at Dorasamudra (Halebid), Karnataka, mid-twelfth century. *(© Clive Friend)*

Babur and his son Humayun, sixteenth-century miniature. *(Courtesy of The Bridgeman Art Library)*

Akbar hunting tigers, from the *Akbar-nama*, c.1590. *(Courtesy of The Bridgeman Art Library)*

Akbar giving an audience, from the *Akbar-nama*. *(Courtesy of Victoria & Albert Museum/The Bridgeman Art Library)*

Rejoicing over the birth of Salim (Jahangir) at Fatehpur Sikri, from the *Akbar-nama*. *(Courtesy of Victoria & Albert Museum/The Bridgeman Art Library)*

Taj Mahal, Agra, from across the Jamuna river, 1630–52. *(© Clive Friend)*

Equestrian portrait of Shah Jahan, seventeenth century. *(Courtesy of Victoria & Albert Museum/The Bridgeman Art Library)*

Ali Adil Shah II of Bijapur, Deccani miniature of c.1660. *(Courtesy of The Barber Institute of Fine Arts, University of Birmingham/The Bridgeman Art Library)*

St Mary's Anglican church, Fort St George, Madras, 1679. *(© M. Amirtham/ DPA/Images of India)*

Sir Henry Havelock relieving the British besieged in Lucknow in 1857, from an illustration by Howard Davie of c.1910. *(Courtesy of Mary Evans Picture Library)*

The Golden Temple (Hari Mandir) at Amritsar, eighteenth century and later. *(© Ilay Cooper/DPA/Images of India)*

Statue of the Jain saint Gomateshwara, Sravana Belgola, Karnataka. *(Courtesy of Archaeological Survey of India)*

Relief medallion from the Bharhut stupa, originally in Madhya Pradesh. *(Courtesy of Archaeological Survey of India)*

The Great Stupa (no. 1) of Sanchi, near Vidisha in Madhya Pradesh, first century BC. *(Courtesy of Archaeological Survey of India)*

Relief panel from the Amaravati stupa, originally in Andhra Pradesh, second–third century A D. (© *The British Museum*)

Relief panel from the Amaravati stupa. (*Courtesy of Archaeological Survey of India*)

Relief panel from the Amaravati stupa. (*Courtesy of Archaeological Survey of India*)

Exterior of cave temple (no. 2), Badami, Karnataka, late sixth century A D. (*A. White © Robert Harding Picture Library*)

The Jyotirlinga group of temples, Aihole, Karnataka. (*Courtesy of Archaeological Survey of India*)

The Rajarajeshwara temple at Tanjore, Tamil Nadu, early eleventh century. (*Courtesy of Archaeological Survey of India*)

Sculptural panel from the Chenna Kesava temple, Belur, Karnataka, twelfth century. (© *Clive Friend*)

Jahaz Mahal ('Ship Palace'), Mandu, Madhya Pradesh, late fifteenth century. (*Courtesy of Archaeological Survey of India*)

Jaya Stambha ('Victory Tower') at Chitor(garh), Rajasthan, 1457–68. (*Courtesy of Archaeological Survey of India*)

The tomb of Humayun in Delhi, completed 1565. (*Courtesy of Archaeological Survey of India*)

The tomb of Itimad-ud-Daula in Agra, completed 1628. (*Courtesy of Archaeological Survey of India*)

Gol Gumbaz ('Great Tomb') of Muhammad Adil Shah II in Bijapur, Karnataka, c.1659. (*Courtesy of Archaeological Survey of India*)

The City Palace, Udaipur, Rajasthan, from 1567. (*Courtesy of Archaeological Survey of India*)

Robert, Baron Clive of Plassey, engraving after a portrait by J. Drummond. (*Courtesy of Mary Evans Picture Library*)

Warren Hastings, first British governor-general of India, from a painting by Sir Joshua Reynolds. (*Courtesy of Mary Evans Picture Library*)

Lakshmi Bai, Rani of Jhansi. (*Courtesy of The Nehru Memorial Museum and Library*)

The Indian National Congress at Allahabad, December 1888. (*Courtesy of The Nehru Memorial Museum and Library*)

George Nathaniel, Lord Curzon. (*Courtesy of Mary Evans Picture Library*)

'Lal-Bal-Pal' – Lala Lajpat Rai, Bal Gangadhar Tilak and Bipin Chandra Pal. (*Courtesy of The Nehru Memorial Museum and Library*)

Gandhi leading the April 1930 Salt March. *(Courtesy of The Nehru Memorial Museum and Library)*

Protestors on the streets of Calcutta during the Quit India movement of 1942. *(Courtesy of The Nehru Memorial Museum and Library)*

Jawaharlal Nehru and Muhammad Ali Jinnah at the Simla Conference, 1945. *(Courtesy of The Nehru Memorial Museum and Library)*

Indira Gandhi. *(© FM/DPA/Images of India)*

Rajiv Gandhi at the cremation of his mother, Indira Gandhi, 1984. *(© DPA/Images of India)*

MAPS

South Asia – Physical xv
South Asia Today xvi
The Harappan world c1900 BC 11
Northern India at the time of the Buddha (c400 BC) 45
Alexander the Great's invasion, 327–6 BC 74
India under Ashoka 93
The Karakoram route 116
Peninsular trading stations in the first century AD 122
Western India c150 AD (with Shatavahana cave-sites) 126
Gupta conquests 138
Harsha's probable empire c640 AD 165
Chalukyas and Pallavas in the seventh century 173
India and south-east Asia in the seventh to twelfth centuries 178
The Arab conquest of Sind in the eighth century 184
The Kanauj triangle: Rashtrakutas, Palas and Gurjara-Pratiharas 198
The land of the Shahis c1000 AD 204
The Ghaznavid empire under Mahmud of Ghazni c1030 210
The Chola kingdom c1030 and the expeditions of Rajendra I 217
Avanti/Malwa: the incarnations of a proto-state 228
Chahamana defeat and Muhammad of Ghor's conquests 1192–1200 236
Eastern India c1200 243
The peninsular incursions of Ala-ud-din and Malik Kafur,
1296–1312 253
Delhi old and new 273
The stillborn states: India in the fifteenth century 280
The campaigns of Babur, Humayun and Sher Shah 297
The Bahmanid kingdom and its successor sultanates 303
Expansion of the Mughal empire, 1530–1707 314
Rajasthan under the Mughals 346
The Deccan and the south in the reign of Aurangzeb 349
Successor states of the Mughal empire 369

European trading stations c1740   378

The peninsula in the eighteenth century (the Anglo–French and Anglo–Mysore Wars)   380

The British in Bengal, 1756–65   389

British India in 1792, after the Third Mysore War;   401

British India in 1804, after Wellesley's acquisitions   401

The Anglo–Maratha Wars 1775–1818   412

British India in 1820, after the Maratha Wars   417

British India in 1856, after Dalhousie's annexations   417

The north-west in the nineteenth century: British expansion into Panjab, Sind and Afghanistan   421

Northern India during the Great Rebellion 1857–8   441

The partition of the Panjab, 1947   507

CHARTS AND TABLES

The peaks and troughs of dominion xxii–iii
The Mauryas: probable succession 321–181 BC 87
The imperial Guptas: probable succession 135
The Chalukyas and the Pallavas: the rival successions 175
The rise and fall of the Cholas of Tanjore 224
Avanti/Malwa: the incarnations of a proto-state 229
The Delhi sultanates. 1: The 'Slave' Dynasty, 1206–90 246
The Delhi sultanates. 2: The Khalji Dynasty, 1290–1320 250
Muslim conquest to Mughal empire: the dynasties of the
 Delhi sultanate 264
The Delhi sultanates. 3: The Tughluq dynasty, 1320–1413 266
The Great Mughals 329
Intermarriage of Great Mughals with the family of
 Itimad-ud-Daula 333
The Sikh Gurus: the chosen successors of Guru Nanak 344
The royal house of Shivaji (Bhonsle Chatrapatis) 358
The later Mughals 365
Succession of the Peshwas of Pune 409
British governors-general 434
British viceroys 460
Countdown to Independence 478
The Nehru-Gandhi dynasty 522
The post-Independence leadership 525
India's general elections 1947–99 527

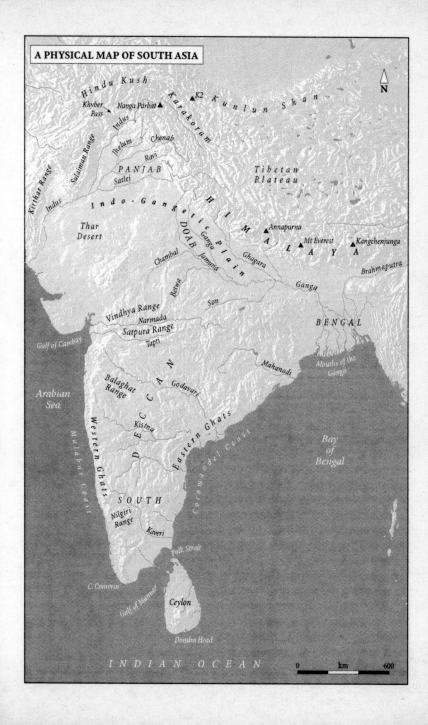

A PHYSICAL MAP OF SOUTH ASIA

N

Hindu Kush

Khyber
Pass

Nanga Parbat ▲

▲ K2

Karakoram

Kunlun Shan

Indus

Chenab

Jhelum

Chenab

Ravi

Kirthar Range

Sulaiman Range

PANJAB

Satlej

Indus

*Tibetan
Plateau*

Thar
Desert

Indo-Gangetic Plain

DOAB

Ganga

Jamuna

H
I
M
A
L
A
Y
A

Annapurna ▲

Mt Everest ▲

Kangchenjunga ▲

Ghagara

Chambal

Betwa

Son

Ganga

Vindhya Range

Narmada

Satpura Range

Tapti

Gulf of Cambay

BENGAL

Brahmaputra

Balaghat
Range

Godavari

Mahanadi

Mouths of the
Ganga

Arabian
Sea

D
E
C
C
A
N

Kistna

Western Ghats

Eastern Ghats

Malabar Coast

Bay
of
Bengal

SOUTH

Nilgiri
Range

Kaveri

Coromandel Coast

Palk Strait

C. Comorin

Gulf of Mannar

Ceylon

Dondra Head

I N D I A N   O C E A N

0   km   600

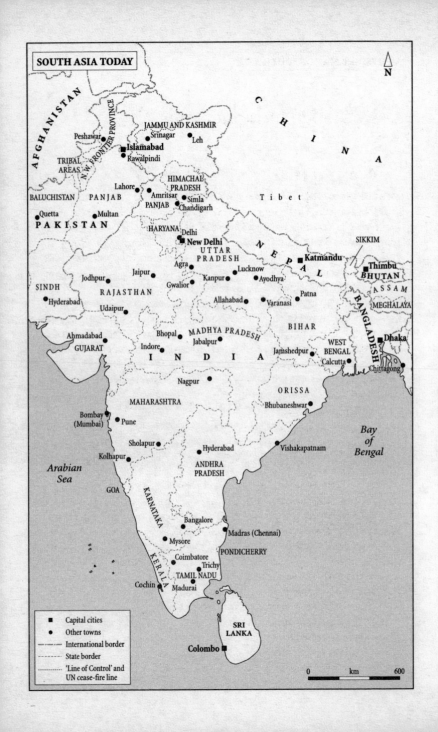

SOUTH ASIA TODAY

AFGHANISTAN

Peshawar
N.W. FRONTIER PROVINCE
TRIBAL AREAS
BALUCHISTAN
PANJAB
Quetta
Multan
PAKISTAN
SINDH
Hyderabad
Ahmadabad
GUJARAT

JAMMU AND KASHMIR
Srinagar
Leh
Islamabad
Rawalpindi
HIMACHAL PRADESH
Lahore
Amritsar
Simla
PANJAB
Chandigarh
HARYANA
Delhi
New Delhi
UTTAR PRADESH
Agra
Lucknow
Jodhpur
Jaipur
Kanpur
Ayodhya
Gwalior
RAJASTHAN
Allahabad
Varanasi
Patna
Udaipur
Bhopal
MADHYA PRADESH
BIHAR
Indore
Jabalpur
Jamshedpur
INDIA
Nagpur
MAHARASHTRA
ORISSA
Bombay (Mumbai)
Pune
Bhubaneshwar
Sholapur
Hyderabad
Kolhapur
ANDHRA PRADESH
GOA
KARNATAKA
Bangalore
Madras (Chennai)
Mysore
PONDICHERRY
Coimbatore
Trichy
KERALA
TAMIL NADU
Cochin
Madurai

CHINA

Tibet

NEPAL
Katmandu
SIKKIM
Thimbu
BHUTAN
ASSAM
MEGHALAYA
BANGLADESH
Dhaka
WEST BENGAL
Calcutta
Chittagong

Bay of Bengal

Arabian Sea

Vishakapatnam

SRI LANKA
Colombo

N

Capital cities
Other towns
International border
State border
'Line of Control' and UN cease-fire line

0   km   600

INTRODUCTION

HISTORIES OF INDIA often begin with a gripe about the poverty of the available sources. These sources were once thought so inadequate as to make what is certainly one of the world's longest histories also one of its more patchy. 'Prior to the thirteenth century AD,' wrote Professor R.C. Majumdar in the 1950s, 'we possess no historical text of any kind, much less such a detailed narrative as we possess in the case of Greece, Rome or China.'[1] Majumdar cited the thirteenth century because that was when northern India, succumbing to Muslim rule, attracted the attention of partisan writers keen to chronicle the triumphs of Islam. But given a good four thousand years of earlier pre-Islamic civilisation, it followed that for more than 80 per cent of attestable Indian history there were no histories.

'It is difficult to give a rational explanation for this deficiency,' continued Majumdar, 'but the fact admits of no doubt.' Rational explanations apart – and there have been many, most supposing an Indian indifference to treating antiquity as an academic discipline – this dearth of ready-made chronicles and memoirs weighed heavily on the historian. It handicapped his reconstruction of past events and hobbled his presentation of them in an acceptable narrative. His gentle readers were forewarned. A rough ride was in prospect.

Happily the situation has improved considerably over the last half-century. No unsuspected ancient chronicles have come to light but much new research has been undertaken and other disciplines have made important contributions. I have therefore stressed in the pages which follow those feats of discovery and deduction, the fortuitous finds and the painstaking analysis, whereby the documentational void has been gradually filled. While spiking the narrative with some lively debate, this explorational approach also has the advantage of mitigating my presumption in venturing, gownless, onto the campus sward. History based on histories looks to be the province of professionals; but where so much of the past, even its chronology, has to be teased from less articulate objects like coins and charters, or pieced together from random inscriptions, titbits of oral tradition, literary compositions and religious texts, and where such researches are then usually consigned to specialist publications and obscure monographs, there surely must be need for an overview.

Reconstructing the past from such reluctant materials can be intensely exciting, but it is not easy. The ingenuity of those scholars who from rocks and runes, bricks and rubrics, have wrested one of the oldest and richest civilisations constitutes something of an epic in itself. It deserved to be told, and in a previous book I had endeavoured to do so in respect of mainly nineteenth-century scholarship.[2] But this is an ongoing epic of research which is itself part of India's history. As well as being directly responsible for revealing those distant personalities and events by way of which, like stepping stones, the historical narrative progresses, it also betrays much about the age to which the stepping stones supposedly led. More personally, since what we know has been derived so largely from research and so little from testimony, it seemed perverse not to credit the discoverers while appropriating their discoveries. What follows, therefore, is both a history of India and to some extent a history of Indian history

I liked the idea that the variety of disciplines involved in this work of discovery – archaeology, philology, numismatics, phonetics, art history, etc. – seemed to admit the need for a generalist, and I hoped that the heavy ideological and religious distortions to which the findings have sometimes been subject might be countered by the reticence of a confirmed sceptic. Better still, thirty years of intermittent wandering about the subcontinent, reading about it and writing about it, could now be construed as other than pure indulgence. D.D. Kosambi, the most inspirational of India's historians, reckoned that for the restoration and interpretation of India's past the main qualification was a willingness to cover the ground on foot. He called it 'field work'; and so it is.

The fields which Kosambi mainly quartered, and the inhabitants whom he questioned, belonged to a very small area around Pune (Poona) in Maharashtra. Freer to travel and drawn to more spectacular sites, I wanted to construct a history which took particular account of the country's extra-ordinary architectural heritage. Lord Curzon, the most incisive of British India's Viceroys, hailed India's antiquities as 'the greatest galaxy of monu-ments in the world'. To all but scholars steeped in the glories of Sanskrit literature it is the architectural and sculptural wonders of India which provide the most eloquent testimony to its history. They stimulated its first investigation by foreign antiquarians, and they continue to whet the curi-osity of millions of visitors. A history which acknowledged the prominence of India's buildings and provided a political, economic and ideological context for them looked to be useful.

Monuments also go some way towards compensating for that deficiency of historical texts. Of the Chola kings of Tamil Nadu, for instance, we would be poorly informed but for the great Rajarajeshwara temple, sublimely moored amidst acres of cloistered paving, which they built and maintained in eleventh-century Tanjore. From its inscriptions we learn of the Cholas' remarkable expeditions and of their lavish endowments; we even gain some insights into the organisation of their kingdom. But equally instructive is the sheer scale of their monument and the grandeur of its conception. Here, clearly, was a dynasty and a kingdom of some significance. To construct and endow India's largest temple, the Cholas must have commanded resources beyond those of their traditional wet-rice patrimony in the delta of the Kaveri river. In fact, were the temple devoid of inscriptions and were there no other clues as to its provenance, historians would surely have coined a name for its builders and have awarded them a dominion of either trade or conquest.

Buildings and sculptures so magnificent have done more than stimulate history-writing; they have sometimes hijacked it. Political and economic certainties being scarce while artefacts and literature, mostly of a religious nature, are plentiful, Indian history has acquired something of a religio-cultural bias. Whole chapters devoted to the teachings of the Buddha, the mathematical and musical theories of ancient India, or Hindu devotional movements are standard fare in most Indian histories. They are not without interest or relevance, and they conveniently bridge centuries for which the political record is deemed deficient or unbearably repetitive. But it might be hard to justify comparable digressions into, say, Greek drama or scholastic exegesis in a history of Europe.

The implication seems to be that Indian history, indeed India itself, has always been a place apart in which culture and religion often outdid armies and administrations in influencing the course of events. I remain unconvinced. Religious and cultural identities are important; but as a source of political differentiation and conflict they are not much in evidence in pre-Islamic India, were often exaggerated thereafter, and only became paramount during the last decades of British rule. Historically it was Europe, not India, which consistently made religion grounds for war and the state an instrument of persecution.

Whilst paying homage to architecture in particular, this is not, then, a cultural history of India, let alone a history of Indian cults. If it has a bias, it is in favour of chronology, of presenting such information as is available in a moderately consistent time sequence. This might seem rather elementary; but chronology is often a casualty of the interpretative urge which underlies much Indian history-writing. Whole centuries of no obvious distinction are cheerfully concertina-ed into oblivion, while their few ascertainable productions are either anticipated in an earlier context or reserved for inclusion under some later heading. If, as many authorities now concede, the *Arthasastra* of Kautilya, a manual of statecraft by the Indian Machiavelli, was not compiled in the fourth–third centuries BC, then our whole idea of the nature of authority during the great 'imperial age' of the Maurya kings (c320–180 BC) needs revision. Likewise if Kalidasa, 'the Indian Shakespeare', did not coincide with the next 'imperial flowering' – and only circumstantial evidence suggests that he did – then the 'golden age of the Guptas' (c320–500 AD) begins to look somewhat tarnished.

Analysis thrives on a synchronism of evidence which, in such cases, is often hypothetical or contrived. Indeed Indian history is altogether perverse when it comes to clustering. A curious feature of that 'galaxy of monuments' is that comparatively few are located around major power centres. Nor can many certainly be credited to pan-Indian dynasties like the Mauryas and the Guptas. The exceptions are the newer cities of Delhi and Agra on which Sultans, Mughals and British all lavished their patronage. But at earlier power centres like Pataliputra (at Patna in Bihar) or 'imperial' Kanauj (near Kanpur in Uttar Pradesh), tangible evidence of the great empires which their Maurya, Gupta or Vardhana rulers claimed to control is scarce. Instead, for the earliest temples one must travel more ambitiously to Sanchi or Ellora, Kanchi or Badami, places hundreds of kilometres away in central India, the Deccan and the south.

The traditional explanation for this poor correlation between dominion and architectural extravagance held that Muslim iconoclasts demolished whatever temples and palaces adorned the earlier capitals of northern India. This may have been the case, especially with richly endowed religious centres like Varanasi (Benares) and Mathura (Muttra), but the fact remains that those temple clusters which do survive, as also the great palaces and forts of a later date, are attributable not to high-profile and supposedly all-India rulers like the Guptas or Harsha-vardhana but to lesser (because more localised) dynasties and to the merchants and craftsmen who lived under their protection.

These lesser dynasties, which flourished throughout India during the first and much of the second millennium AD, we know mainly from inscriptions. Unfortunately the inscriptions are couched in such oblique language, the claims they advance contain so much repetition and poetic exaggeration, and the kings and dynasties they mention are so numerous and so confusing, that most histories pay them scant attention. With perhaps twenty to forty dynasties co-existing within the subcontinent at any one time, it would be an act of intellectual sado-masochism to insinuate this royal multitude into a tender narrative, and I have not attempted to do so. But trusting to the reader's indulgence, I have tried to convey the flavour of their inscriptions and to isolate those dynasts whose claims on our attention are substantiated by other sources or by still gloriously extant memorials.

Without some treatment of this long dynastic fray, gaping holes appear in the record. Compression and selection are the historian's prerogative, but it is not self-evident, as per several current histories of India, that remote centuries may be ignored because 'recency has a decided priority'.[3] My own experience as an intermittent correspondent and political analyst suggests exactly the opposite. Since most of today's headlines will be on tomorrow's midden, 'recency' is a deceptive commodity which the historian might do well to approach with caution. In this book, far from sharpening the focus as history blends into the foreground of current affairs, I have intentionally blurred it. Affairs still current are affairs still unresolved.

In contriving maximum resolution for the present, there is also a danger of losing focus on the past. A history which reserves half its narrative for the nineteenth and twentieth centuries may seem more relevant, but it can scarcely do justice to India's extraordinary antiquity. Nor, simply because the British and post-colonial periods are better documented and more familiar, are they more instructive. There lurks in contemporary-centrism an arrogance no less objectionable than that in Euro-centrism, Occidento-centrism or Christo-centrism. To my mind such selective editing diminishes history. In pillaging the past for fashionable perspectives on the present we deny the delightful inconsequence, the freak occurrences and the human eccentricities which enliven what is otherwise a somewhat sombre record. Honest dealing with the time-scale, as with the spatial environment, is not without its rewards.

If time is the locomotion of history, place could be the gradient against which it is pitted. Dynamic, the one hurtles forward; inert, the other holds it back. Not for nothing are unspoilt landscapes invariably billed as 'timeless'. Boarding at random an overnight train, and awaking twelve hours later to a cup of sweet brown tea and a dawn of dun-grey fields, the traveller – even the Indian traveller – may have difficulty in immediately identifying his whereabouts. India's countryside is surprisingly uniform. It is also mostly flat. A distant hill serves only to emphasise its flatness. Distinctive features are lacking; the same mauve-flowered convolvulus straggles shame-lessly on trackside wasteland and the same sleek drongos – long-tailed blackbirds – festoon the telegraph wires like a musical annotation. It could

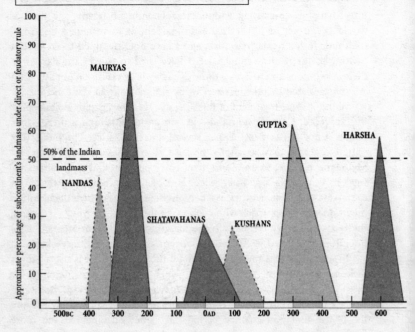

THE PEAKS AND TROUGHS OF DOMINION

be Bihar or it could be Karnataka, equally it could be Bengal or Gujarat. Major continental gradations, like west Africa's strata of Sahara, sahel and forest or the North American progression from plains to deserts to mountain divide, do not apply. The subcontinent looks all of a muchness.

There are, of course, exceptions; in India there are always exceptions, mostly big ones. The Himalayas, the most prominent feature on the face of the earth, grandly shield the subcontinent from the rest of Asia; likewise the Western Ghats form a long and craggy rampart against the Arabian Sea. Both are very much part of India, the Himalayas as the abode of its gods, the Ghats as the homeland of the martial Marathas, and both as the source of most of India's rivers. But it is as if these ranges have been pushed to the side, marginalised and then regimented like the plunging V of the south Asian coastline, so as to clear, define and contain the vast internal arena on which Indian history has been staged.

An instructive comparison might be with one of Eurasia's other subcontinents – like Europe. Europe minus the erstwhile Soviet Union comprises about the same area as the Indian subcontinent (over four million square

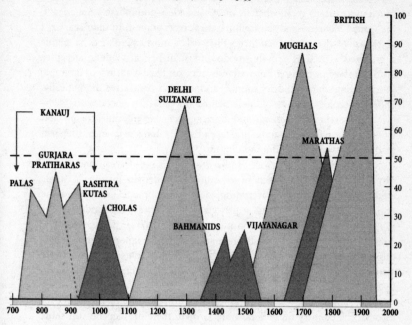

A diagrammatic chronology for the major dynasties giving approximate indication of their territorial reach

kilometres). But uniform and homogeneous it is not. Mountain chains like the Alps and the Pyrenees, plus a heavily indented coastline and a half-submerged continental shelf, partition the landmass into a tangle of semi-detached peninsulas (Iberia, Scandinavia), offshore islands (Britain, Ireland) and mountain enclaves (Switzerland, Scotland). The geographical configuration favours separation, isolation and regional identity. Corralled into such natural compartments, tribes could become nations and nations become states, confident of their territorial distinction.

But if for Europe geography decreed fragmentation, for India it intended integrity. Here were no readily defensible peninsulas, no snowy barriers to internal communication and few waterways which were not readily crossable for much of the year. The forests, once much more widespread than today, were mostly of dry woodland which afforded, besides shelter and sanctuary to reclusive tribes and assorted renunciates, a larder of exotic products (game, honey, timbers, resins) for the plains dwellers. Only in some peripheral regions like Kerala and Assam did this sylvan canopy become compacted into impenetrable rainforest. Wetlands also were once much more extensive. In what are now Bangladesh and Indian West Bengal, the Ganga (Ganges) and the Brahmaputra rivers enmesh to filter seawards in a maze of channels which forms the world's most extensive delta. Semi-submerged as well as densely wooded, most of Bengal made a late entry onto the stage of history. But wetlands, too, supplied a variety of desirable products, and during the dry summer months they contracted dramatically. Different ecological zones complemented one another, encouraging sym-biosis and exchange. Nomads and graziers, seers and pilgrims, traders and troops might pass freely across the face of such a congenial land. It seemed ready-made for integration and empire.

Climate decided otherwise. 'India is an amalgam of areas, and also of disparate experiences, which never quite succeeded in forming a single whole;'[4] only the British, according to Fernand Braudel, ever ruled the entire subcontinent; integration proved elusive because the landmass was too large and the population too numerous and diverse. But surprisingly, considering Braudel's emphasis on environments, he ignores a more obvi-ous explanation. Settlement was not uniform and integration not easily achieved because what geography had so obligingly joined together, hydrography put asunder.

India enjoys tropical temperatures, yet during most of the year over most of the country there is no rain. Growth therefore depends on short seasonal precipitations, as epitomised by the south-west monsoon which sweeps unevenly across nearly the whole country between June and Sep-tember. The pattern of rainfall, and the extent to which particular land-scapes can benefit from it by slowing and conserving its run-off, were the decisive factors in determining patterns of settlement. Where water was readily available for longest, there agriculture could prosper, populations grow, and societies develop. Where not, stubby fingers of scrub, broad belts of desert and bulging plateaux of rock obtruded, cutting off the favoured areas of settlement one from the other.

Like lakes, long rivers with little fall, especially if their flood is prolonged by snow-melt as with the Ganga and the Indus, serve the purpose of conserving water well. Much of northern India relies on its rivers, although the lands they best serve, as also their braided courses and even their number, have changed over the centuries. Depending on one's chosen date, Indian history begins somewhere on the banks of north India's litany of great rivers – either along the lower Indus or amongst the 'five rivers' (*panj-ab*, hence Panjab, or Punjab) which are its tributaries, or in the 'two rivers' (*do-ab*, hence Doab) region between the Jamuna (Jumna) and the Ganga, or along the middle Ganga in eastern Uttar Pradesh and Bihar.

North India's mighty river systems ordained much the most extensive of these well-watered zones of agricultural settlement; and though these zones were several, in the course of the first millennium BC they tended to become contiguous, thus creating a corridor of patchy cultivation and settlement from the north-west in what is now Pakistan to Bihar in the east. Here commercial exchange, cultural uniformity and political rivalry got off to an early start. The corridor became a broad swathe of competing states, cherishing similar ideals, revering common traditions and inviting claims of paramountcy. For empire-builders like the Mauryas, Guptas and Vardhanas, this was where the idea of Indian dominion began.

Elsewhere surface reservoirs supplemented rivers as a useful means of water conservation if the terrain permitted. In the deep south, weeks after Tamil Nadu's November rains have ceased, what looks from the air like chronic flooding proves to be a cunningly designed patchwork of fields with their sides so embanked as to form reservoirs, or 'tanks'. When, after carefully managed use and the inevitable evaporation, the water is nearly exhausted, the tank can itself be planted with a late rice crop. Since the peninsula lacks the vast alluvial plains of the north and has to accommodate hills like the Western Ghats, zones favourable to agricultural settlement were here smaller although numerous and, in cases like the Kerala coast, exceptionally well watered.

In other regions geology did its best for moisture conservation by trapping water underground. From wells it could then be laboriously hauled to the surface for limited irrigation. For the intervening zones of greatest aridity, this sub-surface water was the only source available during most of the year. And since about half the subcontinent receives less than eighty centimetres of rain per year, these arid zones were large. By supposing a continuity between the western deserts of Sind/Rajasthan and the drier parts of central India plus the great Deccan plateau of the peninsula, a broad north–south divide has sometimes been inferred. In fact the terminology here is too vague (even the Deccan is more a designation of convenience than a natural feature). Moreover, considerable rivers traverse this divide: the Chambal and Betwa, tributaries of the Jamuna, afford north–south corridors between the Gangetic plain and the peninsula. And slicing across the waist of India, the west-flowing Narmada forms a much more obvious north–south divide; indeed it figures historically as something of an Indian Rubicon between the north and the peninsula. Micro-zones with excellent water conservation also dot both Rajasthan and the Deccan; in historical times they would sustain a succession of the most formidable dynasties.

As with the forests and wetlands, the dry-lands were not without their own sparser populations, typically herdsmen and warriors. As barriers, dry regions are hardly as formidable as the seas and mountains of Europe. But as boundaries and frontier zones they did have something of the same effect, encouraging separation, fostering distinction and, in time, confronting ambitious rulers with the great Indian paradox of a land that invited dominion full of lesser rulers who felt bound to resist it.

The socio-cultural dimension to this climate-induced paradox would be even more enduring. Indeed it largely accounts for the strength of 'regional' sentiment in the subcontinent today. In those favoured, because well-watered, zones where settlement became concentrated, surplus agricultural production encouraged the development of non-agricultural activities. Archaeologists are alerted to this process by the distribution of more standardised implements, weapons and styles of pottery. These things also help in the identification of the favoured areas – most notably, and at different times, that great trail across the north from the Indus to the Gangetic basin, plus Gujarat, Malwa and the Orissan littoral in mid-India. In the south a similar diversification is inferred, although here the archaeological display-case remains somewhat empty. Save for a few Stone Age productions, south India's history has to wait until jump-started by a remarkable literary outpouring at the very end of the first millennium BC.

As crafts and trades prospered, specialisation encouraged congregation, and congregation urbanisation. Within the same favoured enclaves, ideological conformity, social stratification and political formation followed. The models for each – for an effective religion, a harmonious society and a legitimate state – married local elements and imperatives with a set of norms derived from the propagandised traditions of an Indo-Aryan people who had emerged in north India by 1000 BC. These Indo-Aryans were probably outsiders and, as well as a strong sense of community centred on elaborate rites of sacrifice, they possessed in the Sanskrit language an exceptionally versatile and persuasive medium of communication. Had India been as open and uniform a land as geography suggests, no doubt Sanskrit and its speakers would speedily have prevailed. They did do so over much of north India, but not speedily and not without compromise. Further afield, in west, east and central India and the Deccan, the process somewhat misleadingly known as 'Aryanisation' took even longer and involved so much compromise with local elements that hybridisation seems a fairer description. From it emerged most of the different languages and different social conformations which, heightened by different historical experiences, have given India its regional diversity, and which still distinguish the Bengali from the Gujarati or the Panjabi from the Maratha.

The pantheon of spirits and deities worshipped in each zone, or region, typified this process of hybridisation, with Indo-Aryan gods forsaking their original personae to accommodate a host of local cults. Thus did Lord Vishnu acquire his long list of *avatars* or 'incarnations'. In parts of India this process of divine hybridisation is still continuing. Every year each village in the vicinity of Pudukottai in Tamil Nadu commissions from the local potter a large terracotta horse for the use of Lord Ayanar. Astride his splendid new mount, Ayanar will ride the village bounds at night, protecting the crops and warding off smallpox. But who is this Ayanar? None other than Lord Shiva, they tell you. The pan-Indian Shiva, himself an amalgam of various cults, looks to be only now in the process of usurping the Tamil Lord Ayanar. But it could be the other way round. To the people of Pudukottai it is Ayanar who is assuming the attributes of Shiva.

As with gods, so with the different languages spoken in India's zonal regions. In its earliest form Marathi, the language now mainly spoken in Maharashtra, betrayed Dravidian as well as Sanskrit features. At some point a local form of early Dravidian, a language family now represented only in the south, is thought to have been overlain by the more prestigious and universal Sanskrit. But the precedence as between local indigenous elements and Sanskritic or Aryan influences is not clear. Did Sanskrit speakers domiciled in Maharashtra slowly absorb proto-Dravidian inflexions? Or was that too the other way round?

A more clear-cut example of Aryanisation/Sanskritisation is provided by the many attempts to replicate the topography featured in the Sanskrit epics. By word of mouth core elements of the *Mahabharata* and *Ramayana* had early penetrated to most of India. By the late centuries of the first millennium BC, even deep in the Tamil south they knew of the Pandava heroes who had fought the great Bharata war for hegemony in the Ganga-Jamuna Doab and of Rama and Lakshmana's expedition from Ayodhya to rescue the Lady Sita. Clearly these stories had a universal appeal, and in a trail of still recognisable place-names their hallowed topography was faithfully adopted by far-flung rulers anxious to garner prestige. The trail of 'Ayodhyas', 'Mathuras', 'Kosalas', 'Kambojas' and so on would stretch way beyond India itself, most notably into areas of Indian influence in south-east Asia. And like that hybridisation of deities, it continues. In Karnataka a Kannada writer complained to me that, despite the best efforts of the state government in Bangalore to promote the Kannada language, villagers still persisted in Sanskritising the names of their villages in a bid for greater respectability, then lobbying the Post Office to recognise the change.

As well as renaming local sites and features, some kings actually tried to refashion them in accordance with the idealised models and layouts of Sanskrit literary tradition. The Rashtrakuta rulers of eighth- to tenth-century Maharashtra evidently conceived their sculpted temple-colossus at Ellora as a replica of the Himalayas. It was named for Shiva as Lord of Mount Kailas (a peak now in Tibet) and was provided with a complement of Himalayan rivers in the form of voluptuous river deities like the Ladies Ganga and Jamuna. In a bid to appropriate the same sacred geography the great Cholas went one better, and actually hauled quantities of water all the way from the Ganga, a good two thousand kilometres distant, to fill their temple tanks and waterways around Tanjore. Thus was authenticated their claim to have recreated the north Indian 'holy land' in the heart of Tamil Nadu.

Geography, like history, was seen as something which might be made to repeat itself. In tableaux like that of the Taj Mahal the Mughal emperors strove to realise the Islamic ideal of a paradise composed of scented verdure, running water and white marble. Later, in leafy hill-stations, the British aimed at recreating their own idealised environment of green gables and lych-gated churchyards connected by perilous pathways and fuchsia hedges; new names like 'Annandale' and 'Wellington' were added to the map; existing nomenclatures were bowdlerised and anglicised.

Now they are being vernacularised. This is a confusing time for both visitors to India and those who write about it. With the process of revision far from complete, the chances of finding spellings and appellations which are recognisable and acceptable to all are slim. At the risk of offending some, I have continued to call Mumbai 'Bombay', Kolkota 'Calcutta' and Chennai 'Madras'; to non-Indians these names are still the more familiar. On the other hand I have adopted several spellings – for instance 'Pune' for Poona, 'Awadh' for Oudh, 'Ganga' for Ganges, 'Panjab' for Punjab – which may not be familiar to non-Indians; they are, however, in general use in India and have become standard in South Asian studies.

For anyone ignorant of both Sanskrit and Persian, transliteration poses another major problem. Again, I lay no claim to consistency. For the most part I have kept the terminal 'a' of many Sanskrit words (Rama for Ram, *Ramayana* for *Ramayan*, etc.) and used 'ch' for 'c' (as in Chola) and 'sh' for most of the many Sanskrit 's's (Vishnu for *Visnu*, Shiva for *Siva*, Shatavahana and Shaka for *Satavahana* and *Saka*). The knowledgeable reader will doubtless find many lapses for which the author, not the type-setter, is almost certainly responsible – as indeed he is for all the errors and omissions, the generalisations and over-simplifications, to which five thousand years of tumultuous history is liable.

The Harappan World

c3000–1700 BC

THE BREAKING OF THE WATERS

IN HINDU TRADITION, as in Jewish and Christian tradition, history of a manageable antiquity is sometimes said to start with the Flood. Flushing away the obscurities of an old order, the Flood serves a universal purpose in that it establishes its sole survivor as the founder of a new and homogeneous society in which all share descent from a common ancestor. A new beginning is signalled; a lot of begetting follows.

In the Bible the Flood is the result of divine displeasure. Enraged by man's disobedience and wickedness, God decides to cancel his noblest creation; only the righteous Noah and his dependants are deemed worthy of survival and so of giving mankind a second chance. Very different, on the face of it, is the Indian deluge. According to the earliest of several accounts, the Flood which afflicted India's people was a natural occurrence. Manu, Noah's equivalent, survived it thanks to a simple act of kindness. And, amazingly for a society that worshipped gods of wind and storm, no deity receives a mention.

> When Manu was washing his hands one morning, a small fish came into his hands along with the water. The fish begged protection from Manu saying 'Rear me. I will save thee.' The reason stated was that the small fish was liable to be devoured by the larger ones, and it required protection till it grew up. It asked to be kept in a jar, and later on, when it outgrew that, in a pond, and finally in the sea. Manu acted accordingly.
>
> [One day] the fish forewarned Manu of a forthcoming flood, and advised him to prepare a ship and enter into it when the flood came. The flood began to rise at the appointed hour, and Manu

1

entered the ship. The fish then swam up to him, and he tied the
rope of the ship to its horn [perhaps it was a swordfish], and thus
passed swiftly to the yonder northern mountain. There Manu was
directed to ascend the mountain after fastening the ship to a tree,
and to disembark only after the water had subsided.

Accordingly he gradually descended, and hence the slope of
the northern mountain is called Manoravataranam, or Manu's
descent. The waters swept away all the three heavens, and Manu
alone was saved.[1]

Such is the earliest version of the Flood as recorded in the *Satapatha
Brahmana*, one of several wordy appendices to the sacred hymns known
as the Vedas which are themselves amongst the oldest religious compositions in the world. Couched in the classical language of Sanskrit, some
of the Vedas date from before the first millennium BC. Together with later
works like the *Brahmanas*, plus the two great Sanskrit epics, the *Mahabharata* and the *Ramayana*, they comprise a glorious literary heritage
whence all knowledge of India's history prior to c500 BC has traditionally
been derived.

Brief and to the point, the story of Manu and the Flood served its
purpose of introducing a new progenitor of the human race and, incidentally, explaining the name of a mountain. Such, however, was too modest
an interpretation for later generations. Myth, the smoke of history, is seen
to signal new and more relevant meanings when espied from the distance
of later millennia. In time the predicament of the small fish liable to be
devoured by larger fish became a Sanskrit metaphor for an anarchic state
of affairs (*matsya-nyaya*) equivalent to 'the law of the jungle' in English.
Manu's flood, like Noah's, came to be seen as the means of putting a stop
to this chaos. And who better to orchestrate matters and so save mankind
than Lord Vishnu? A minor deity when the Vedas were composed, Vishnu
had since soared to prominence as the great preserver of the world in the
Hindu pantheon and the second member of its trinity. Thus, in due course,
the Flood became a symbol of order-out-of-chaos through divine intervention, and the fish (*matsya*) came to be recognised as the first of the nine
incarnations (*avatara*) of Lord Vishnu. Myth, howsoever remote, serves the
needs of the moment. So does history, in India as elsewhere.

Some historians have dated the Flood very precisely to 3102 BC, this
being the year when, by elaborate computation, they conclude that our
current era, the *Kali Yug* in Indian cosmology, began and when Manu
became the progenitor of a new people as well as their first great king and

law-giver. It is also the first credible date in India's history and, being one of such improbable exactitude, it deserves respect.

Other historians, while conceding the importance of 3102 BC, have declared it to be not the date of the Flood but of the great Bharata war. A Trojan-style conflict fought in the vicinity of Delhi, the war involved both gods and men and was immortalised in the Sanskrit verse epic known as the *Mahabharata*, the composition of whose roughly 100,000 stanzas constituted something of an epic in itself. This war, not the flood, was the event that marked the beginning of our present era and must, it is argued, therefore belong to the year 3102 BC. Complex astronomical calculations are deployed in support of this dating, and an inscription carved on a stone temple at Aihole in the south Indian state of Karnataka is said to confirm it.

But the Aihole memorialist, endowing his temple 1600 kilometres from Delhi and nearly four thousand years later, may have got it wrong. According to the genealogical listings in the *Puranas*, a later collection of 'ancient legends', ninety-five generations passed away between the Flood and the war; other evidence based on sterner, more recent, scholarship agrees that the war was much later than the fourth millennium BC. This greatest single event in India's ancient history, and the inspiration for the world's longest poem, did not occur until 'c1400 BC' according to the *History and Culture of the Indian People*, a standard work of many volumes commissioned in the 1950s to celebrate India's liberation from foreign rule and foreign scholarship.

Nevertheless, 3102 BC sticks in the historical gullet. Such are the dismal uncertainties of early Indian chronology that no slip of the chisel is going to deny the historian the luxury of a real date. Corroboration of the idea that it may, after all, apply to a Flood has since come from the excavations in distant Iraq of one of Mesopotamia's ancient civilisations. There too archaeologists have found evidence of an appalling inundation. It submerged the Sumerian city of Shuruppak, and has been dated with some confidence to the late fourth millennium BC. In fact, 3102 BC would suit it very well.

This Sumerian inundation, and the local Genesis story in the *Epic of Gilgamesh* which probably derived from it, is taken to be the origin of the legend of the Flood which eventually found its way into Jewish and Christian tradition. Yet in many respects the Sumerian account is more closely echoed in the Indian version than in the Semitic. For instance, just as in later Hindu tradition Manu's fish becomes an incarnation of the great god Vishnu, so the Sumerian deity responsible for saving mankind is often represented in the form of a fish. 'It is the agreement in details which is so striking,' according to Romila Thapar.[2] The details argue strongly for some common source for this most popular of Genesis myths, and scholars like Thapar, ever ready to expose cultural plagiarism, see both Manu and Noah as relocated manifestations of a Sumerian prototype.

The tendency to synchronise and subordinate things Indian to parallel events and achievements in the history of countries to the west of India is a recurrent theme in Indian historiography and has rightly incurred the wrath of some Indian historians. So much so that they sometimes go to the other extreme of denying that any creative impetus, any technological invention, even any stylistic convention, ever reached India from the west – or, indeed, the West. And in the case of the Flood they may have a point. Subject to the annual deluge of the monsoon and living for the most part on the flat alluvial plains created by notoriously errant river systems, the people of north India have always had far more experience of floods, and far more reason to fear them, than their neighbours in the typically more arid lands of western Asia.

Floods, though now associated more with the eastern seaboard of the Indian subcontinent and Bangladesh, still annually inundate vast areas of the Ganga and Indus basins. They have always done so. One such Gangetic flood, dated by archaeologists to about 800 BC, destroyed the town of Hastinapura which, after the great Bharata war, had become the capital of the descendants of Arjuna, one of the war's main protagonists. Since the flooding of Hastinapura is also recorded in Sanskrit textual tradition, and since the same tradition says that the town was then under its seventh ruler since the war, an approximate date for the war itself of about 975 BC has been postulated.

Thus, for the titanic struggle recorded in the *Mahabharata*, we already have three dates: 3102 BC, c1400 BC and c950 BC. A couple of millennia one way or the other is a long time even in prehistoric terms. India's history, though undoubtedly ancient, leaves much room for manoeuvre. A mistranslated word from one of the many voluminous, difficult and defective texts wherein, long after their composition, the Vedic verses were eventually written down, can create havoc. Similarly a chance discovery of no obvious provenance can prompt major revisions.

Another flood, later than the Sumerian one but much earlier than that at Hastinapura and so perhaps a serious contender for the one which Manu survived, is thought by some to have once inundated the plains of the lower Indus in what is now Pakistan. Geologists date it to some time soon after 2000 BC, and believe that it may in fact have been a succession of inundations. Whether they were the result of climate change, of tectonic action lower down the river resulting in damming and the formation of inland lakes, or simply the cumulative effect of annual siltation is not clear. But whatever the cause, the floods were bad news for those agriculturalists who had pioneered a highly productive economy based on growing cereals in the fine soil alongside the river. Managing the river's seasonal rise so as to enrich and irrigate their fields was the key to their success. An annual surplus had generated wealth, encouraged craft industries and fostered trade. Settlements had become cities. Along the lower Indus and its tributaries had grown up one of the world's first urban societies, a contemporary of those on the Nile and the Euphrates and a rival for the tag of 'the cradle of civilisation'.

Then, soon after 2000 BC according to the archaeologists, came the floods. If they did not actually overwhelm this precocious civilisation, they certainly obliterated it. In time, layer after layer of Indus mud, possibly wind-blown as well as water-borne, choked the streets, rotted the timbers, and piled high above the rooftops. The ground level rose by ten metres and the water table followed it. Meanwhile the river resumed its regular flow and found new channels down which to flood. On top of the cities, now consigned to oblivion beneath tons of alluvium, other peoples grazed their goats, sowed their seeds and spun their myths. A great civilisation was lost to memory.

Not until nearly four thousand years later, in fact in the early 1920s, was its existence even suspected. It was pure chance that Indian and British archaeologists, while investigating later more visible ruins at Mohenjo-daro in Sind and at Harappa in the Panjab, made the prehistoric discovery of the twentieth century. They called their find the 'Indus valley civilisation', and drew the obvious comparisons with those of Egypt and Sumeria. Indeed they thought that it might be an offshoot of the latter. Later, as its sophisticated and surprisingly uniform culture became more apparent, the Indus valley civilisation was accorded distinct status. And when the extent of its cultural reach was found to embrace a host of other sites, many of them well beyond the valley of the Indus, it was renamed after one of these sites as the Harappan civilisation.

Suddenly India's history had acquired a rich prehistoric pedigree of archaeologically verifiable antiquity. Here, it seemed, was a worthy companion to that Sanskrit literary heritage of equally impressive, though maddeningly uncertain, antiquity as comprised by the Vedas and associated texts – the *Brahmanas* and *Puranas* as well as epics such as the *Mahabharata*. Perhaps these two very different sources, the one purely archaeological and the other purely literary, would complement one another. An ancient and immensely distinguished civilisation would thus be revealed in multi-dimensional detail.

The Harappan finds included buildings, tools, artefacts, jewellery and some sculpture. Intimate details about Harappan housing, diet and waste disposal came to light. Maritime trade with Sumeria was attested and led to some cross-dating. The Carbon 14 process produced comparative dates accurate to plus or minus a century or so. Amongst the Harappans there was even what looked like a system of writing: some four hundred characters were identified, each, it was deduced, representing a single word; and they read from right to left. Sanskritists were soon clear that this was not Sanskrit, the language of the Vedic heritage. But it might be some kind of proto-Dravidian, the parent of south India's languages, while the script did suggest similarities with Brahmi, the earliest Indian script hitherto identified and read. It seemed only a matter of painstaking study before the Harappan language would also be understood and the secrets of its civilisation revealed.

Unfortunately this script, despite the best endeavours of international scholarship and despite the code-cracking potential of computers, remains undeciphered. Totally lacking, therefore, is any intelligible record of the Harappans written by themselves. Who were they? What did they worship? Had they established a recognisable state or states? They tell us nothing. How did they come to be there? And what became of them in the end? We don't know. Here was history complete with approximate dates, cities, industries and arts, but absolutely no recorded events. Here too was a society with a distinct and extensive culture but, barring some not very helpful bones, no people, indeed without a single name.

Names, on the other hand, were precisely what that Sanskrit literary tradition of the Vedas provided – in mind-boggling abundance. Kings and heroes, gods and demons, places and peoples, tumble from the Vedas, *Brahmanas*, *Puranas* and epics as if ready-made for the compilation of a historical index. Although no single site, no potsherd or artefact, can certainly be identified with the people who composed these verses, and although their chronology remains shrouded in that maddening uncertainty, we know that they called themselves *arya* – hence 'Aryan' – and we know of their lifestyle, their social organisation, their beliefs and their innumerable antecedents and descendants. Here, in short, was a people proudly obsessed with the past, who defined themselves in terms of lineages reaching back through the generations to Manu, and whose records might therefore provide for the enigmatic Harappan civilisation precisely the human detail that it so notably lacked.

Would that it were so. In fact, as will be seen, though the two civilisations – the Harappan and the Aryan – overlapped in geography and possibly also in chronology, no shred of coincidence certainly connects them. India's history starts with the apparently irreconcilable. Only in the last few years have sustainable connections between its Harappan and Aryan constituents been tentatively proposed. These connections, though tantalising, remain few and far from conclusive. India's history as currently understood must be seen as beginning with two woefully unconnected cultures.

This state of affairs may, however, serve as a warning. Despite the pick-and-preach approach of many nationalist historians, geographical India is not now, and never has been, a single politico-cultural entity. In fact, its current three-way division between Pakistan, India and Bangladesh, far from denying some intrinsic unity, is a notable simplification of its traditional plurality. Analogies should be drawn, if at all, not with Egypt or with Greece but with regional constructs of a similar size like the Middle East or Europe. And just as in the Middle East those early civilisations in Egypt and Mesopotamia flourished simultaneously yet quite independently, or just as later in Europe the Byzantine and Carolingian empires could both claim pre-eminence without necessarily coming into conflict, so it is in India.

Sadly, though, this is not a situation which makes for fluent narrative history. In a global landmass as vast and varied as the South Asian subcontinent an orderly linear progression from one cultural flowering to another, one dynasty to another, or one empire-builder to another will prove elusive. Only a still far from certain chronology, and not any sequential progression, demands that the Harappans and their archaeology take precedence ahead of the Aryans and their literature.

A VERITABLE EMPIRE

To anyone familiar with the Egypt of the Pharaohs, the warren of dun diggings which is an excavated Harappan site may seem unimpressive. It is hard not to sympathise with the first archaeologist to survey Mohenjo-daro. 'I was greatly disappointed,' wrote Mr D.R. Bhandarkar in his report. He was visiting the largely desert province of Sind in the winter of 1911–12 as Superintending Archaeologist of the Western Circle of the Archaeological Survey of India. 'Mohenjo-daro', he noted, meant 'the Mound of the Dead Men'. There was one big mound and six smaller ones. And in words that must subsequently have haunted him, the Superintending Archaeologist dismissed the lot as 'not representing the remains of ... any ancient monument'.

> According to local tradition, these are the ruins of a town only
> two hundred years old ... This seems not incorrect, because the
> bricks here found are of the modern type, and there is a total lack
> of carved terra-cottas amidst the whole ruins.[3]

Wrong in every detail, this statement must rank amongst archaeology's greatest gaffes.

Today's less qualified visitors, though willing to forgive the absence of 'carved terra-cottas', tend to bemoan that of more obvious features. For at Mohenjo-daro no pyramids or ziggurats, no sculpted towers or mighty henges frown over the deep and dusty thoroughfares. On first acquaintance it is as if the most extensive of the Harappan sites was never really a city at all, merely the footings and foundations of one.

This, though, is decidedly not the case. Deep in 'the Mound of the Dead Men' there was once activity and industry. Behind the extant façades of blank, featureless wall families lived, craftsmen plied their trades and vendors sold their wares. If there was an absence of eye-catching memorials it was not, as will appear, through any lack of civic pride or direction. It may tell us something about the nature of authority in the Harappan state and the organisation of its society; more certainly it indicates the limited materials available to the city's builders.

Four thousand years ago stone was as scarce in the lower Indus region as it is today. Even the local timber, though more plentiful than now, and possibly able to meet the need for roof joists, seems not to have been sufficiently well-grown for major construction purposes. Instead, it was used as fuel to fire brick kilns. The Harappans built almost entirely in brick, both sun-baked and kiln-fired, and the excellence of their firing is well attested by the survival, albeit underground, of so many structures in such a comparatively friable material. In assuming their bricks to be 'of a modern type', Bhandarkar was unwittingly paying the Harappan brickmakers a generous compliment.

Brickwork, however, has its limitations, as the Harappans were no doubt aware. Large areas can be easily enclosed and conveniently partitioned; groundplans of some of the Mohenjo-daro houses compare favourably with those of today, while larger individual structures, presumably public buildings, cover areas equivalent to half a football pitch; some walls, obviously for defence, are as thick as thirteen metres. On the other hand bricks, unlike dressed stone, must be kept small for good firing and are therefore less suitable for towering elevations and long-lasting monuments. Sun, salt and wind play havoc with a mortar of mud; weight stresses cause bowing and buckling. Few if any buildings at Mohenjo-daro were of more than two storeys. Even supposing the Harappans had aspired to the monumental extravagances of their Egyptian contemporaries, it is hard to see how they could have achieved them.

Of unremarkable profile, then, the mud-and-rubble mounds of the Harappan cities and settlements nevertheless made an impression on Bhandarkar's successors in the Archaeological Survey. Happily ignoring his report, R.D. Banerji and Sir John Marshall resumed explorations at Mohenjo-daro in the late 1920s. Ernest Mackay and Sir Mortimer Wheeler continued their work and also re-examined Harappa, a collection of mounds in the Panjab whence in the nineteenth century bricks similar to those at Mohenjo-daro had been removed by the wagonload as ballast for a 160-kilometre section of the Lahore–Multan railway line. After Independence and the Partition of the subcontinent in 1947 B.B. Lal, J.P. Joshi, S.R. Rao, M. Rafique Mughal and a host of others extended operations to numerous other sites with outstanding results. What amazed all these pioneers, and what remains the distinctive characteristic of the several hundred Harappan sites now known, is their apparent similarity: 'Our overwhelming impression is of cultural uniformity, both throughout the several centuries during which the Harappan civilisation flourished, and over the vast area it occupied.'[4]

The ubiquitous bricks, for instance, are all of standardised dimensions, just as the stone cubes used by the Harappans to measure weights are also standard and based on a modular system. Road widths conform to a similar module; thus streets are typically twice the width of side lanes, while the main arteries are twice or one and a half times the width of streets. Most of the streets so far excavated are straight and run either north–south or east–west. City plans therefore conform to a regular grid pattern and appear to have retained this layout through several phases of rebuilding. In most cases the ground plan consists of two quite separate settlements, one apparently residential and commercial ('the lower town'), and the other elevated on a massive brick platform ('the citadel') and endowed with more ambitious structures. 'The citadel' invariably lay to the west of 'the lower town'. Clearly Harappan settlements were not just India's first cities and townships but its first, indeed the world's first, planned cities and townships. Town-planning not being conspicuous in the subcontinent's subsequent urban development, they have been hailed as the only such examples until, in the eighteenth century A D, Maharajah Jai Singh decided to lay out his 'pink city' of Jaipur in Rajasthan.

Harappan tools, utensils and materials confirm this impression of obsessive uniformity. Unfamiliar with iron – which was nowhere known in the third millennium BC – the Harappans sliced, scraped, bevelled and bored with 'effortless competence' using a standardised kit of tools made from chert, a kind of quartz, or from copper and bronze. These last, along with gold and silver, were the only metals available. They were also used for casting vessels and statuettes and for fashioning a variety of knives, fish-hooks, arrowheads, saws, chisels, sickles, pins and bangles. As for the potters' production of dishes, bowls, jars, flasks and figurines, it was all that one would expect of master brickmakers – well made, competent if restrained as to decoration, and predictably uniform as to design. In short, the uniformity in technology 'is as strong as in the town-planning, and so marked that it is possible to typify each craft with a single set of examples drawn from one site alone'.[5]

What made all this consistency even more remarkable was the area throughout which the Harappans sustained it. With Mohenjo-daro and Harappa nearly six hundred kilometres apart, it was immediately obvious that the 'Indus valley' civilisation was more extensive than its contemporaries – Egypt's Old Kingdom and Mesopotamia's Sumeria. The Indus valley, however, has proved to be only the core area. Subsequent to the discovery of its two principal sites (Mohenjo-daro in Sind and Harappa in the Panjab) the Harappan civilisation has been steadily expanding by more than a province a decade. In Pakistan further sites have been found, not only in Sind and Panjab (where at Fort Derawar on the desert frontier with India a third major city stood), but as far away as the Iranian frontier in Baluchistan and in the North-West Frontier Province. India itself, not to be outdone, now boasts an important cluster of sites in Gujarat, another in Rajasthan, and more scattered settlements in the states of Panjab, Haryana, Uttar Pradesh, and Jammu and Kashmir. Lately, hundreds of kilometres away to the north-west, what seems to be a Harappan settlement, or 'colony', has been identified at Shortughai near the river Oxus (Amu Darya) on Afghanistan's Russian frontier. From Lothal, a small but important settlement in Gujarat which may have been a port, to Shortughai in the mountains of Badakshan, where the Harappans probably obtained supplies of lapis lazuli, is a distance of over sixteen hundred kilometres; and east–west from Alamgirpur on the upper Ganga to Sutkagen-dor on the Makran coast is hardly less.

Naturally such a bonanza of new sites has prompted some revisionism. The uniformity of Harappan culture, necessarily dented by local adaptations to the desert, upland and maritime extremities of such a vast area, is no

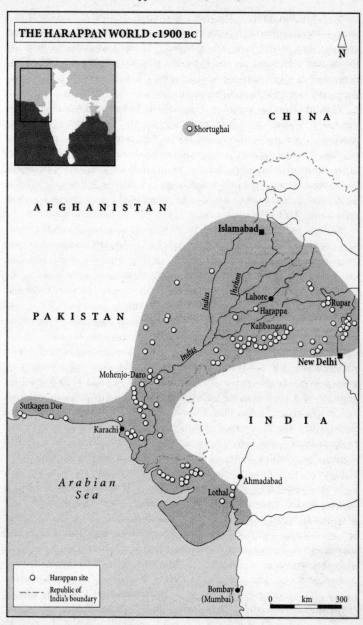

THE HARAPPAN WORLD c1900 BC

N

○ Shortughai

C H I N A

A F G H A N I S T A N

Islamabad ■

P A K I S T A N

Indus

Jhelum

Lahore ●
Harappa
Kalibangan

Rupar

New Delhi ■

Indus

Mohenjo-Daro ●

Sutkagen Dor

I N D I A

Karachi ●

*Arabian
Sea*

Ahmadabad ●

Lothal

Bombay ●
(Mumbai)

○   Harappan site

       Republic of
       India's boundary

0   km   300

longer taken for granted. Theories based upon it about the existence of a strong central authority, a pervasive administration and a heavily regulated and stratified society have also suffered. The easy assumptions made on the basis of a few partially and imperfectly excavated sites are dubbed 'old platitudes' as a new generation of scholars and field workers gingerly sifts the incontrovertible from the fanciful.

One mystery has certainly been solved. Pioneers like Marshall were puzzled how such a sophisticated culture could have sprung up from nowhere. Unaware of any other Bronze Age cultures in the region, not impressed by the Indian characteristics of Harappan architecture and arte-facts, and wrongly assuming dates of about 3500–3000 BC, they duly looked to the west for an explanation, and suggested that the Indus valley civilis-ation must be a colony or offshoot of Mesopotamian or even Mycenaean civilisation. This idea is now quite untenable. At numerous sites to the west of the Indus in Baluchistan and Afghanistan, as well as in the Indus valley itself, sufficient pre-Harappan and Early Harappan settlements have been found to establish a local progression from hunter-gatherer to urban dweller by way of all the various stages of pastoralism, agricultural settle-ment, technological advance and cultural refinement. No such consensus exists about the Late Harappan and post-Harappan periods, but it is now possible to assign most Chalcolithic (Bronze/Stone) Age sites in the region to one of these categories and to give approximate dates for each.

Designated by their find sites and principally distinguished by their pottery styles, the pre-Harappan peoples of c3000 BC had already pro-gressed to building houses and tilling the land. They had some knowledge of metals and had access, through trading links, to other precious materials and manufactures. Some time around 2600 BC – the dating varies from site to site – the appearance of typically Harappan styles in pottery and tools announces the Early Harappan phase. Brick-built houses assume a regular design with a courtyard and rooms off it. Figurines anticipate later Harappan styles. Towards the end of the millennium, say 2300 BC, this Early Harappan style gives way to the Mature Harappan phase, in which appears the full inventory of Harappan artefacts – standardised bricks and pots; regular streets above a network of well-made sewerage ducts; typical terracottas; a notable production of decorative artefacts including beads, faïence and shell work; more copper and bronze hardware; and a plenitude of the mysterious seals (as well as the impressions made by them) whereon that enigmatic script features prominently. In some cases, to produce the typical grid layout of streets, sites were apparently cleared and then rebuilt. Other sites were briefly deserted before being rebuilt. Still others suggest a continuance of non-Harappan or pre-Harappan styles, particularly in ceramics, side by side with the Mature Harappan. It is thus far from clear what relationships – of tribute, migration, conquest, intermarriage or cultural attraction – underlay the transition to greater standardisation.

Even worse inconsistency characterises the Late Harappan phase. Around 1900 BC Mohenjo-daro was gradually abandoned, possibly because of those floods and the associated salination of the soil. Kalibangan, an important town in Rajasthan, suffered a similar fate, but probably from desertification and the drying-up of the Ghaggar river. Elsewhere there is evidence of declining authority and of population decrease, possibly as a result of migration from the central settlements. Yet in some peripheral areas like Gujarat, Haryana and the Panjab, the decline is less marked and there may even have been an increase in activity and population.

Dispersal or dilution are evident from the prevalence of non-Harappan pottery styles, impoverishment and disruption from the gradual disuse of the script and from the disappearance of the more fanciful manifestations of Harappan culture, including that obsessive standardisation. On the other hand, craft skills and agricultural expertise survived. The spinning and weaving of cotton, for instance, in which the Harappans seem to have been the world's pioneers, must have been gradually disseminated throughout India, since by the mid-first millennium BC it was commonplace. The finer textiles were by then an important item of trade and would remain so ever after, enticing to India Roman, Arab and eventually European merchants.

A similar case might be made for the ox-drawn wagon, which was as much a cliché of the Harappan world as it is of the Indian subcontinent today. Again, the Harappans may have been the first in the world to use wheeled transport. Numerous toy carts in terracotta and bronze testify to their pride in this technological breakthrough, and the generous street widths of their cities were presumably dictated by the consequent traffic.

Provisioning cities the size of Mohenjo-daro, with its estimated thirty to fifty thousand inhabitants, necessitated not only effective transport, both by river and road, but also a reliable rural surplus, a large labour force, and some means of crop storage. It has been conjectured that the largest structures at Mohenjo-daro, Harappa, Kalibangan and possibly Lothal may have been granaries, although their internal arrangements, consisting of carefully aligned brick plinths, await a satisfactory explanation.

The only public building whose function is beyond dispute is the great bath at Mohenjo-daro. The size of a modest municipal swimming pool, carefully sealed with bitumen, and with steps down at each end, it was clearly designed to hold water and to be used for bathing. Quite probably the ablutions, or immersion, were of some ritual significance. The bath forms the inner sanctum of an elaborate building, although there is no clear evidence that, as with later temple tanks, it was a place of worship. In fact, we have no idea what part religion played in the lives of the Harappan people. No site has certainly been identified as a temple, and most suppositions about sacrificial fires, cult objects and deities rest on doubtful retrospective reference from the Hindu practices of many centuries later. Such inferences may be as futile as, say, looking to Islamic astronomy for an explanation of the orientation of the pyramids. In short, 'these theories are all fanciful and do not bear scrutiny.'[6]

A much-cited example, depicted on some of the Harappan seals, is that of a big-nosed gentleman wearing a horned head-dress who sits in the lotus position with an erect penis, an air of abstraction and an audience of animals. He may indeed be an early manifestation of Lord Shiva as Pashu-pati, 'Lord of the Beasts'. But myth, as has been noted, is subject to frequent revision. The chances of a deity remaining closely associated with the same specific powers – in this case, fertility, asceticism and familiarity with the animal kingdom – for all of two thousand years must raise serious doubts, especially since, during the interval, there is little evidence for the currency of this myth. Rudra, a Vedic deity later identified with Shiva, is indeed referred to as *pasupati* because of his association with cattle; but asceticism and meditation were not Rudra's specialities, nor is he usually credited with an empathy for animals other than kine. More plausibly, it has been suggested that the Harappan figure's heavily horned headgear bespeaks a bull cult, to which numerous other representations of bulls lend substance.

Similar doubts surround the female terracotta figurines which are often described as mother-goddesses. Pop-eyed, bat-eared, belted and sometimes mini-skirted, they are usually of crude workmanship and grotesque mien. Only a dusty-eyed archaeologist could describe them as 'pleasing little things'.[7] The bat-ears, on closer inspection, appear to be elaborate head-dresses or hairstyles. If, as the prominent and clumsily applied breasts suggest, they were fertility symbols, why bother with millinery? Or indeed mini-skirts?

These and other 'folk' products, including numerous toys, scarcely merit comparison with the finest of Harappan sculptures. Indeed the latter are so fine and so exquisitely modelled that, 'for pure simplicity and feeling' nothing comparable was produced 'until the great age of Hellas'.[8] They are, however, extremely few: Sir Mortimer Wheeler records just eleven 'more or less fragmentary' stone statuettes and one bronze figure. They are also extremely small, indeed just a few centimetres high. This combination of rarity and pocket-size invites doubts as to their provenance. They could easily have come from somewhere further afield. Two perfectly modelled miniature torsos were found at Harappa – one decidedly male, the other probably female; both have socket holes by which their missing arms were attached. On this evidence they have been convincingly related to a similar technique used by artists of the contemporary Namazga culture which was discovered by Soviet archaeologists in the Ashkabad region of Turkmenistan. Namazga equivalents have also been cited for the formidable bearded figure in an embroidered toga, of which there are two examples, and even for the most famous of all Harappan works of art, the bronze 'dancing girl'.

Although probably not dancing, the 'dancing girl' is unquestionably 'a pleasing little thing'. Naked save for a chunky necklace and an assortment of bangles, this minuscule statuette is not of the usual Indian sex symbol, full of breast and wide of hip, but of a slender nymphet happily flaunting her puberty with delightful insouciance. Her pose is studiously casual, one spindly arm bent with the hand resting on a *déhanché* hip, the other dangling so as to brush a slightly raised knee. Slim and attenuated, the legs are slightly parted, and one foot – both are now missing – must have been pointed. She could be absent-mindedly surveying her wardrobe, except that her head is thrown back as if challenging a suitor, and her hair is somehow dressed into a heavy plaited chignon of perilous but intentionally dramatic construction. Decidedly, she wants to be admired; and she might be gratified to know that, four thousand years later, she still is. If there is one piece of Harappan fine art that one is reluctant to yield to the Namazga culture it is the 'dancing girl'.

Happily her local credentials are not insignificant. For one thing her features, including full lips and broad nose, are distinctly proto-Australoid, a type not usually associated with the Central Asian culture of Namazga. Skeletons unearthed in the Indus valley, however, attest that the Harappan people were of several different racial types, amongst them that, related to Australia's native people and still represented in parts of India, of proto-Australoid cast. Furthermore, although most of the surviving Harappan stone sculptures were found at Harappa itself, whence contacts with Namazga seem to have been closest, the 'dancing girl' was found at Mohenjo-daro, whose external trade was more orientated to the Persian Gulf and Mesopotamia. A better case will need to be made before the Harappans are robbed of their most celebrated representative.

Trade, both within the sprawling Harappan world and without, was clearly essential to the development of its culture. Bronze or tin (for making bronze), silver and certain precious stones like lapis lazuli and soapstone are not found within easy reach of the Indus valley, and must therefore have been imported from elsewhere. Likewise it is clear that the Mesopotamian cultures obtained numerous commodities from the Harappans, including copper, gold, timber, ivory and probably cotton textiles. Harappan sealings and seals have been found in Sumerian sites, and Sumerian documentation makes frequent reference to relations with the distant lands of 'Dilmun', 'Magan' and 'Meluhha'. The first seems to have been in the Persian Gulf, possibly Bahrain, and to have been something of an entrepôt. 'Magan' is usually identified with the coastal regions of Iran and Baluchistan, the modern Makran coast. And 'Meluhha', by a process of deduction from the trade items associated with it, looks to have been the Harappan civilisation. There are objections to this hypothesis. The Mesopotamians claim to have once conquered 'Meluhha', for which there is no archaeological evidence. And a later 'Meluhha' was usually associated with the African coast. Notwithstanding, opinion still favours the idea that in Sumerian references to 'the ships from Meluhha' which King Sargon the Great 'made tie up alongside the quay of Agade' we have a positive identification of the Harappan world.

The importance of Harappan, or 'Meluhhan', trade, and the recent speculation about it, rests heavily on the evidence provided by the Harappan seals. Usually of soapstone, or steatite, the face of each is carved intaglio and in reverse so as to leave a legible impression on soft clay. Most are rectangular and about the size of a postage stamp; and typically they include an average of five characters, or word symbols, in that unintelligible script, plus one or more images. The latter are often of animals and, in the famous examples of a humped bull with pendulous dewlap, the Harappan genius for vivid depiction from life in the minutest and most demanding of mediums has been universally acknowledged.

Several thousand seals and sealings have now been found. The seals appear to have been distributed throughout the Harappan world, not simply in its major population centres, and to have been carried about or worn, each having a boss or hole by which they could be threaded on a string. The distribution of the sealings suggests that seals may have been used to facilitate the exchange of goods over long distances. Thus the stamped image, attached to a consignment of goods, might have identified their owner, provenance, destination or contents, and so have served somewhat the role of a waybill or even a bar-code. Clearly, if this was indeed their purpose, their multiplicity and far-flung distribution argues for a vast and buzzing commercial network. Perhaps, instead of conspicuous expenditure on monuments and memorials, the Harappans pumped their surplus into commodity exchange. It has even been suggested that the Harappans were so dependent on this exchange that its apparent decline in the early second millennium BC was a cause, rather than an effect, of the disintegration of urban life.

Although the script remains indecipherable, interesting conclusions have been drawn from the images which usually accompany it on the seals. These are often single animals, as with the humped bull, the elephant, the tiger and a magnificent rhino. Commonest of all, however, is a stocky creature unknown to zoology with the body of a bull and the head of a zebra, from which head a single horn curls majestically upwards and then forwards. In fact, 'the "unicorn" occurs on 1156 seals and sealings out of a total of 1755 found at Mature Harappan sites, that is on 60 per cent of all seals and sealings.'[9] Shireen Ratnagar, an authority on Harappan trade, also notes that, since the word symbols which accompany these images vary from seal to seal, image and text must have conveyed different information; and that, since the images recur frequently and look like totemic subjects, they may be the identifying symbols of different social groups. Assuming such groups were based on descent, as with the Vedic Aryans, Ratnagar calls them 'lineages' or clans.

> ... we would therefore infer that the 'unicorn' was the symbol of the dominant lineage which had expanded, or was expanding, by assimilation or alliance at the expense of other lineages, and administrative office and lineage affiliation would be closely connected. In other words, we may interpret the unicorn as the religious expression of a system of political control operating through lineage connexions.[10]

How this political control operated, and whether oppressively or consensually, it is impossible to say. Likewise, as noted, we have no clear idea what religious practices the Harappans subscribed to. Here, and in other researches, there is, though, a gradually emerging notion of a Harappan state. Ratnagar conjectures that it began to emerge when numerous ethnic and/or cultural groups were drawn together by alliance, intermarriage and agricultural or industrial specialisation. By the time of the Mature Harappan phase these groups formed not a federation but a single state. In fact 'at this stage of knowledge it appears to me that we are dealing with a veritable Harappan "empire".'

This being the case, the total, albeit gradual, eclipse of Harappan civilisation is all the more mystifying. Sumerian civilisation led on to that of

Babylon, Egypt's Old Kingdom was succeeded by the Middle Kingdom and the New Kingdom, China's dynastic succession scarcely faltered. But in the Indian subcontinent the first great experiment in urban living, in political organisation and in commercial enterprise disappeared without trace beneath the sand and the silt. In the land of reincarnation there was to be no rebirth for the bustling and ingenious world of the Harappans. History would have to begin again with a very different group of people.

Vedic Values

C1700–900 BC

THE MYTHIFIED ARYAN

THE HARAPPANS, winkled out of oblivion by the archaeologist's trowel and scrutinised by scholars from every conceivable discipline, have lately been attracting funds and advancing on all fronts, just like their 'empire'. The Aryans, on the other hand, they of that rich Sanskrit literary heritage whence all knowledge of India's ancient past was traditionally derived, are in retreat. Badly discredited by over-zealous championship in the nineteenth century and then by Teutonic adoption in the 1930s, the mighty Aryans have fallen from academic favour. Questions tantamount to heresy amongst an earlier generation of historians are now routinely raised as to who the *arya* were, where they came from, and even whether they were really a distinct people.

'It is doubtful whether the term *arya* was ever used in an ethnic sense,' writes Romila Thapar, doyenne of ancient India's historians.[1] What she calls the 'Aryan problem', or 'myth', is now to be regarded as 'perhaps the biggest red herring that was dragged across the path of India's historians'.[2] The authenticity of all those Sanskrit literary compositions remains undisputed. So does their seminal importance in India's social, cultural and religious development. But whether those who composed them were anything more than a proud minority self-consciously endeavouring to retain their mainly linguistic identity amongst a diverse, industrious, and probably indifferent local population is questionable.

For Hindus, of course, the traditions of Sanskrit literature are still sacrosanct. Vedic prayers are still said; televised serialisations of the Sanskrit epics can bring the entire Indian nation to a hushed standstill. The compositions of the ancient *arya* are not just history; they are the nearest thing to revelation. The *arya* themselves, though, are not revered and never have been. In no sense are they seen as a divinely 'chosen people'. Individual priests, heroes, sages and deities are cherished but their ethnic affinity is neither emphasised nor invariable. This is unsurprising since in Sanskrit the word *arya* is usually adjectival. Certain people or classes once used it to distinguish themselves from others; it was clearly a good thing to be. But like many words, its meaning changed over the centuries and the original is now hard to pin down. In English it is variously rendered as 'pure', 'respectable', 'moral', 'noble' or 'wealthy'. By the time it had travelled to south India and thence on to what is now Indonesia it had simply become a respectful term of address, like 'Sahib' or 'Mister'.

'Aryans', on the other hand, as the generic title of a distinct race of people to which this *arya* adjective exclusively applied, nowhere feature in Sanskrit literature. They only appeared when Europeans got to work on Sanskrit. And it was not the literature which so inspired Europe's scholars, but the language itself.

That some words in Sanskrit bore a strange similarity to their Greek and Latin equivalents had long been noted. Then in 1785 Sir William Jones, an English polymath and truly 'one of the most enlightened sons of men' (as an admiring Dr Johnson described him), began studying Sanskrit. A year later he announced his preliminary verdict on the language. It was 'of a wonderful structure', he declared, 'more perfect than Greek, more copious than Latin . . .',

> . . . yet bearing to both of them a stronger affinity, both in the roots of verbs and the forms of grammar, than can possibly have been produced by accident; so strong, indeed, that no philologer could examine them all without believing them to have sprung *from some common source*, which perhaps no longer exists.[3]

This being the case, most north Indian languages, which derive from Sanskrit, were related to most of Europe's, which derive from Latin. Jones rightly added that the Germanic and Celtic languages also probably belonged to this linguistic family, and likewise ancient Persian (Avestan). But, personally more enamoured of Sanskrit's literature than its language, he did not pursue the search for that 'common source'. This was left to others who recognised in Jones's insights not only a specific challenge – to discover the 'common source' and chart its distribution – but also the means by which to do so. For Jones had shown that the study of language, or philology, could serve the historian much as does archaeology. Given a reasonable mound of literature, the philologist could delve in the syntax and sift through the syllables so as to record the changing forms of words and grammar. Identifying shared roots, typical word forms, new structures and extraneous influences, he could establish rules about how the language had developed and spread, and so formulate, as it were, a sequence of strata whereby tentative dates could be assigned to any particular text purely on the basis of its language.

Using and developing this new discipline, scholars at first called the elusive 'common source' language (and the family of languages which derived from it) 'Indo-Germanic' or 'Indo-European'. This changed to 'Indo-Aryan', or simply 'Aryan', after it was realised that the ancient Persians had indeed used their *arya* word in an ethnic sense; they called themselves the 'Ariana' (whence derives the modern 'Iran'). Numerous writers continued to warn against the assumption that a shared language necessarily meant a shared ethnicity. Yet the idea of a single race sowing the seeds of civilisation from Bengal to Donegal proved intensely exciting, and ultimately irresistible. To Friedrich Max Muller, the distinguished German Professor of Sanskrit at Oxford in the mid-nineteenth century, it seemed that the Aryans had a 'mission to link all parts of the world together by chains of civilisation, commerce and religion'. They were 'the rulers of history'.[4] Muller, too, warned against drawing any simplistic conclusions about race, but already Aryan descent was popularly seen as the mark, if not yet of a master race, at least of ethnic distinction. Gratified by the discovery of their proud historical pedigree, India's aspiring nationalists embraced the Aryans as readily as did Europe's cultural supremacists.

Given the vast spread of the Indo-Aryan languages, an Aryan homeland was soon being sought somewhere in the middle of the Eurasian landmass. Most scholars favoured the steppes of southern Russia and the Ukraine, or the shores of the Caspian. Nomadic pastoralists, the Aryans needed plenty of room. Thence, in a series of sweeping migrations spread over many centuries, they supposedly took their language, plus their gods, their horses and their herds, to Iran and Syria, Anatolia and Greece, eastern Europe and northern India.

India's Aryans were therefore originally immigrants, and to judge by their exploits as recorded in the Vedas, highly combative ones. Aided and encouraged by deities like the fire-breathing Agni and the thunderbolt-throwing Indra, the Aryan conquistadors were seen as having hurtled down the passes from Afghanistan to career across the plains of the Panjab. Dealing death and destruction from fleets of horse-drawn chariots, they subdued the indigenous peoples and appropriated their herds. As *dasa* or *dasyu*, these indigenes or aborigines were characterised as dark, flat-nosed, uncouth, incomprehensible and generally inferior. The Aryans, on the other hand, were finer-featured, fairer, taller, favoured above others in the excellence of their gods, their horses and their ritual magic, and altogether a very superior people.

Nineteenth-century British colonialists, reflecting on this new and unexpected Aryan dimension to India's history, could draw great comfort. All that was fine and 'classical' in ancient India's history could now be credited to this influx of manly heroes from the west. The Aryans, spreading their superior culture right down the valley of the Ganga and then deep into the peninsula, had conferred on India an unprecedented cultural integrity and an enviably high degree of civilisation. In time, however, the purity of the Aryan race had become hopelessly diluted; manliness, creativity and drive had succumbed to the enervating effects of an intolerable climate and an insidious social system. Hence no serious resistance had been offered either to the thrust of Islam or to the advent of the colonial powers. India had slumped into seemingly irredeemable decadence and degeneracy. Then, in the nick of time, out of the west came the British. No less fair, no less manly and no less confident of their superiority, they were the neo-Aryans, galvanising a naturally lax people into endeavour and industry, showering them with the incomparable benefits of a superior civilisation and a humane religion, and ushering in a new and golden age. Or so some liked to think.

This illusion was rudely shattered in the 1930s. Just when Indian demands for self-government were obliging the British to reconsider their colonial mission, the Aryan thesis became both discredited by Nazi propaganda in Europe and challenged by the archaeological reports coming from Mohenjo-daro and elsewhere in India. Initially, with the chronology even vaguer than now, it was not clear that the Harappans pre-dated the Aryan 'invasions'. Indeed, there are still some scholars who insist that it was the Aryans who preceded the Harappans and, despite ample testimony to the contrary, that the Harappan civilisation was therefore an Aryan achievement. This means pushing the first Aryan 'invasions' back to the fourth or fifth millennium BC, which does not square with that philological stratification, and crediting to cattle-rustling tribesmen a mastery of urban refinement for which there is absolutely no evidence in their copious literature.

Despite the more general belief that the Harappan civilisation came first, the Aryan 'myth' was not immediately dumped, even by Harappanists. Thus another theory, championed by Sir Mortimer Wheeler – 'Mr Indus Valley' himself – was that, if the Aryans could not possibly have created the Harappan cities, they might have been responsible for destroying them. This, of course, assumed that the Harappan cities had succumbed to conquest. Wheeler cited evidence at both Harappa and Mohenjo-daro of 'massacres'. Skeletons of men, women and children, some incomplete, one or two with cranial damage, had been found scattered in the streets, presumably struck down where they still lay. There were other suggestions of a hasty evacuation. And in the Vedas Wheeler found numerous references to cities, or rather '*pur* meaning a "rampart", "fort", or "stronghold"'. Moreover Indra, the bellicose and bloodthirsty Mars of the Aryan pantheon, was specifically referred to as 'the destroyer of forts', or *purandara*, he who 'rends forts as age consumes a garment'. Why, asked Wheeler, would he be so described if there had not been forts to rend? And what were these forts if not the Harappan 'citadels'? Thus the Late Harappans could now be numbered amongst those dark and wretched *dasa* over whom the Aryans habitually lorded it; and the mystery of what fate had overtaken their cities was solved. 'On circumstantial evidence, Indra stands accused,' declared Wheeler in 1947.[5]

Indra stood accused throughout the 1950s, but in 1964 the case against him collapsed. The American George F. Dales took a long, hard look at all those skeletons, and could find only two that might have been massacred where they lay. Most of the others appeared to have been casually interred centuries later, when the ground had risen well above street level. 'There is no destruction level covering the latest period of the city [Mohenjo-daro], no sign of extensive burning, no bodies of warriors clad in armour and surrounded by the weapons of war, [and] the citadel, the only fortified part of the city, yielded no evidence of a final defence.'[6] There was also no proof that *pur* meant either a city or a fort. Current placenames like Kanpur, Nagpur and so on preserve the word in exactly that sense, but in the Rig Veda, the earliest of Sanskrit compositions, it seems to have implied little more than a well-fenced village or settlement. Nor is it clear that Aryan chariots and catapults could have made much impression on Harappan walls thirteen metres thick, according to the archaeologists, and every bit as high.

The possibility of some contact between Aryans and Harappans can never, of course, be totally dismissed. As the dates for the Late Harappan phase have been slowly pushed forward to around 1700 BC, the gap, if there is one, between Harappan and Aryan has closed to perhaps a couple of centuries. Across such a timespan, some web of collective memory could well have spread. At Harappa and elsewhere in the Panjab, where the Aryans initially settled, there is some largely ceramic evidence of comparatively sophisticated post-Harappan cultures. They could represent a revival of Harappan skills under some kind of Aryan patronage or stimulus.

In the Vedas there is even mention of 'Hariyupiya' as a placename. It could be the Harappan site itself, although most scholars take its context to indicate a river, probably west of the Indus. Finally, there is the intriguing possibility that the word 'Meluhha', the name by which the Sumerians apparently designated their Harappan trading partners, eventually resurfaced in Sanskrit as *mleccha*. The latter was a term of contempt used by the *arya* to disparage those whom they regarded as non-*arya*. It thus meant much the same as *dasa* and *dasyu*, words which unfortunately predate its appearance. Philologists, however, insist that *mleccha* cannot possibly be Sanskrit in origin. The reflexive consonants clearly show the word to have been borrowed from some local tongue. Perhaps it was just an onomatopoeic word derived from the uncouth gobbledygook in which, to *arya* ears, the *dasa* spoke. But if it was derived from the term by which the *dasa* peoples described themselves, then coincidence can scarcely deny that the *mleccha* people must have been the Harappans, or rather the 'Meluhhans'.

INVASIONS OR MIGRATIONS?

Other examples of loanwords in the Sanskrit of the Vedas can be equally revealing. The word for 'plough', for instance, is said to be non-Sanskritic. If the *arya*, when they arrived in India, did not have a word for a plough – and so had to borrow someone else's – it is safe to assume that they did not have a plough. The Harappans, however, did. It therefore follows that the *arya* probably learned about ploughs and their use from the indigenous successors of the Harappans. These may have been the despised *dasa* of the Vedic texts, although there are now grounds to suppose that the *dasa* were in fact survivors of an earlier wave of the Indo-European diaspora and were not therefore indigenous. It has also been suggested that *arya–dasa* contact may have taken place in Afghanistan before the *arya* reached India.

Similar conclusions may be drawn about the *arya*'s words for 'furrow' and for 'threshing floor'. They too appear to be non-Sanskritic. Obviously the Aryans were not engaged in arable farming in any big way. Nor, evidently, were they interested in architecture. Whereas it is no surprise that they had to borrow a word for 'peacock', a bird then not much known outside India, or that they had to invent one for 'elephant' (they called it the 'beast with a hand', i.e. a trunk), it is more revealing that they had also to borrow a word for 'mortar'. Archaeology supports the obvious inference; no buildings have yet been found which can certainly be ascribed to the Vedic *arya*.

For 'writing', 'record', 'scribe', or 'letter' the *arya* of the Vedas had no words at all, not even borrowed ones. It is therefore almost certain that they brought no knowledge of writing into India with them and that, by the time they arrived, the literacy skills of the Harappans had been forgotten, at least in areas where the *arya* first settled. When and how later scripts emerged is unknown. The first mention of writing occurs in oral compositions dating from after 500 BC. Inscriptions do not appear until two hundred years later, but they use two comparatively sophisticated scripts which suggest several centuries of prior familiarity. One of these scripts may owe something to the ideograms of the Harappan seals; the other looks to have been derived from the Aramaic script of western Asia.

Illiterate and ignorant of many basic agrarian skills, the *arya* yet knew all, and more, about livestock. While the Harappans used ox-transport and may have found totemic roles for bulls and many other animals, they do not seem to have had a passion for dairy farming or horse-racing; in fact the horse was probably unknown to them, India's lack of native bloodstock being then, as ever after, the Achilles heel of its ambitious empire-builders. The *arya*, though, were veritable cowboys. As well as advertising their prowess in the rustling of cattle and the driving of two-horse chariots, they spattered their verses with metaphors about affectionate cows and fiery steeds. In the Rig Veda storm clouds invariably 'gallop' across the heavens; their thunder is as the neigh of a stallion. Rivers rush from the hills like cattle stampeding towards pasture; and when the Beas river is joined by a tributary, 'one the other licks, like the mother-cow her calf'. Cattle were also currency, value being expressed in so many cows; and *go*, the Sanskrit root for 'cow', also features in the word used to indicate warfare, evidence that strife originally resulted from competition not for land and territory but for cows and wealth.

The *arya* were therefore originally pastoralists and, assuming a migration into India, plus the herdsman's need to be forever seeking new pastures, they must have been semi-nomadic. We may infer that, like pastoralists the world over, they lived an itinerant outdoor life. Much exposed to the elements, they may have been inclined to discover divine powers in the forces of nature and to assume a ready communion with these powers. The names of their gods predate arrival in India, many (e.g. Indra, Agni, Varuna) being almost synonymous with their counterparts in Persian, Greek and Latin mythology; but their attributes and achievements relate to the Indian environment. It would seem, also, that the basic unit of human society was initially the small nomadic group rather than the settlement. The word *grama*, although it soon came to mean a village, was originally indicative of a troupe of wagons and their perhaps three or four related families, plus livestock.

During the monsoon months, when pasture became plentiful and transhumance difficult, the *arya* must have formed their first temporary settlements. No doubt they then also planted their grain crop which, watered by the rains and fertilised by the manure from their cattle pens, would have been harvested during the winter months. The grain was probably barley. Rice, although apparently cultivated by the Harappans, does not feature in the earliest of the Vedas. Nor is the word used to designate it Sanskritic. It, too, was probably acquired from one of India's aboriginal peoples. Later, however, after the *arya* had adopted a settled life, rice receives its first mention, and later still, following their colonisation of the middle Ganga in the early centuries of the first millennium BC, the cultivation of irrigated *padi* would become crucial to their pattern of settlement.

That they initially settled in the Panjab and astride what is now the Indo–Pakistan frontier is clear from references in the Rig Veda to the *Sapta-sindhu*, 'the Land of the Seven Rivers'. Each of these rivers has been identified, and most were tributaries of the Indus. They are mentioned frequently, and must therefore have been familiar to the *arya* (although the most important, the Saraswati, has since dried up). On the other hand, there is only one mention of the mighty Ganga, and that in what is thought to be the latest of Rig Vedic compositions. Subsequent works, like the *Brahmanas* and *Upanisads* (c900–600 BC), confirm a shift in geographical focus to the east and specifically to the Doab, the crescent of land between the Jamuna and the Ganga (immediately east of Delhi). As the setting for the *Mahabharata*, the Doab became *arya-varta*, 'the land of the *arya*'. If one accepts c950 BC as the probable date of the Bharata war, this migration, or colonisation, may therefore have occurred c1100–1000 BC. It would be followed by a further move into the valley of the Ganga itself before the *arya*, much changed in the interim, began founding states, building cities and rediscovering the trail of civilisation which the Harappans had trodden two thousand years earlier.

As to when the *arya* made their initial debut in India there remains grave doubt. Nearly two hundred years ago Mountstuart Elphinstone, one of the most outstanding scholar-administrators in the employ of the English East India Company, headed the first British mission into Afghanistan. He failed to reach Kabul, but from Peshawar in what was then Afghan territory Elphinstone got a look at the Khyber Pass and formed some idea of the harsh lands whence the Aryans supposedly came. Years later, having declined the governor-generalship to concentrate on his studies, he produced a magisterial *History of India*. In it he devoted much attention to Sanskrit tradition, and recalling that dramatic contrast between the arid Afghan hills and the smiling gardens of Peshawar, he for the first time threw serious doubt on the central Asian provenance of the Aryans.

> Neither in the code of Manu [the survivor of the flood, who was later credited with compiling a standard compendium of Hindu law] nor, I believe, in the Vedas, nor in any other book that is certainly older than the code, is there any allusion to a prior residence, or to a knowledge of more than the name of any country out of India. Even mythology goes no farther than the Himalaya chain, in which is fixed the habitation of the gods.[7]

To Elphinstone it was quite incredible that the Aryans could have made the transition from mountain desert to monsoonal paradise and yet failed to record it. He also noted that, throughout the ages, civilisation had more commonly spread from east to west than vice versa. Perhaps, therefore, the Aryans had originated in India.

Although this idea currently derives no credibility from its aggressive repetition in Hindu nationalist publications, and although it is flatly denied by the *arya*'s familiarity with horses (typically central Asian) and their ignorance of elephants (typically Indian), it is certainly curious that the Vedas say nothing of life in central Asia, nor of an epic journey thence through the mountains, nor of arriving in the deliciously different environment of the subcontinent. The usual explanation is that, by the time the Vedas were composed, this migration was so remote that all memory of it had faded; and on this basis a tentative chronology is proposed. Allowing, then, first for a major time-lapse (say two hundred years) between the Late Harappan phase and the Aryan arrival in India, and then for a plausible memory gap (say another two hundred years) between arrival and the composition of the earliest Vedas, it looks as if the *arya* must have entered India some time between 1500 BC and 1300 BC. Most authorities now suppose several waves of migration rather than a single mass movement. These waves probably consisted of different tribes and, on linguistic evidence, may have been spread over centuries. So possibly the entire period was one of Aryan incursion.

As to whether all or any of these incursions constituted invasions rather than migrations it is impossible to say. We may, though, speculate. Considered in the light of later incursions into north-west India by Alexander the Great and a host of other intruders, including those afire with the spirit of Islam, the Aryan coming has traditionally been seen as a full-scale invasion. The indigenous people 'naturally resisted the newcomers, and a fierce and protracted struggle ensued'. In a standard textbook on ancient India, R.C. Majumdar goes on to identify the indigenous resistance as coming from 'Dravidians', the assumption being that the indigenous *dasa* spoke a Dravidian, as opposed to a Sanskritic, language.

> It was not merely a struggle between two nationalities. The Dravidi-
> ans had to fight for their very existence . . . But all in vain . . . The
> Dravidians put up a brave fight, and laid down their lives in
> hundreds and thousands on various battlefields, but ultimately had
> to succumb to the attacks of the invaders. The Aryans destroyed
> their castles and cities, burnt their houses, and reduced a large
> number of them to slaves.[8]

Recent theories of multiple migrations have somewhat softened this picture. Perhaps some of the Aryan clans were invited into India as allies, mercenaries or traders; the indigenous *dasa* may not have been 'Dravidians' but earlier Indo-Aryan arrivals; there is nothing to suggest that they ever constructed 'castles and cities'; and the archaeological evidence, being almost entirely ceramic, gives no hint of the sudden change one would expect from the conquest and suppression of an entire 'nationality'.

There is, though, another explanation. Seen in the context not of later invasions in the north-west, but of later extensions of *arya* influence to the rest of India, a rather different and more intriguing picture emerges. Arguably this process of 'Aryanisation' by which *arya* culture spread to non-*arya* peoples continued throughout the subcontinent's history, indeed is still going on to this day. In little-frequented enclaves of central and north-eastern India tribal communities of *adivasi*, or aboriginal, people may even now be found in various transitional stages of Aryanisation (or 'Sanskritis-ation'). A similar process is said to have been observable amongst distant peoples, like the Fijians, who were affected by the Indian diaspora of colonial times. In both cases, Aryan ideas and influence were initially carried by work-seekers and traders, not warmongers. More significantly, exactly the same process probably accounted for the gradual Aryanisation of penin-sular India plus much of south-east Asia.

An Aryanised society may be defined as one in which primacy is accorded to a particular language (Sanskrit), to an authoritative priesthood (brahmans) and to a hierarchical social structure (caste). To establish these three 'pillars' of Aryanisation in, say, Kerala or Java no sizeable relocation of people would have been necessary. As will be seen, the process appears simply to have been one of gradual acculturation requiring neither mass migration nor enforced concurrence. A small admixture of fortune-seekers, traders or teachers who happened to be in possession of a superior technology and of a persuasive ideology could and did, if prepared to compromise with existing custom, create a convincing and lasting veneer of Aryanisation without apparently antagonising anyone.

Admittedly, indeed on their own admission, the *arya* cattle-rustlers of the Rig Veda did antagonise the *dasa*. But they also compromised with them, adopting *dasa* technology, *dasa* cults and *dasa* vocabulary, and inducting *dasa* clans and leaders into their society. Despite the importance attached to the purity of Sanskrit, there is even a hint of *dasa-arya* bilingualism. With the horse and the chariot by way of a dazzling new technology, and with the subtleties of ritual sacrifice as a mesmerising ideology, the *arya* may have secured recognition of their superiority by a process no more deliberate and menacing than social attraction and cultural osmosis; thus the Aryan invasion and conquest of India could be as much a 'myth' and a 'red herring' as the existence of an Aryan race.

It should, however, be emphasised that in the second millennium BC the familiar traits of Aryanisation, those three pillars of language, priesthood and social hierarchy, were only just beginning to emerge. All are evident in the earliest Vedas, but they are undeveloped. They only assume definition and primacy in the context of contact between the *arya* and the various indigenous peoples. Quite possibly the latter contributed to, or participated in, the formulation of these 'pillars'. *Arya* culture may itself have been a hybrid, and 'Aryanisation' may therefore be a misnomer.

NO BAD HYMNS

Such speculation is justifiable because of the unsatisfactory nature of Vedic literature as historical source material. The Rig Veda, earliest (perhaps c1100 BC) of the Vedic compositions, comprises ten *mandala* or 'cycles' of ritual hymns and liturgical directives. Although generally considered the most informative of the Vedic texts, its clues as to the lifestyle, organisation and aspirations of the *arya* are 'submerged under a stupendous mass of dry and stereotyped hymnology dating back to the Indo-Iranian era [i.e. before the Aryans reached India], and held as a close preserve by a number of priestly families whose sole object in cherishing those hymns was to utilise them in their sacrificial cult'. Dr B.K. Ghosh of Calcutta University then goes on to cite an example from Mandala I. He calls it 'the worst in the

Rig Veda'; even its brahman composer seems to have had a premonition of failure. Yet in terms of content it is not untypical.

No bad hymns am I offering by exerting my intellect
In praise of Bhavya ruling on the Indus
Who assigned to me a thousand sacrifices,
That incomparable king desirous of fame.
A hundred gold pieces from the fame-seeking king,
Together with a hundred horses as a present have I received,
I, Kakshivant, obtained also a hundred cows from my master
Who exalted thereby his fame immortal up to heaven.

'This dismal hymn,' writes Dr Ghosh, 'ends with two verses notable only for their extreme obscenity.'[9] In translation the obscurity is more evident than the obscenity but, by substituting sexual terms for words like 'bliss' and 'creation', it is just possible to grasp the nub of his objection.

O resplendent lord, with brilliant radiance may you be delighted.
May your own bliss be consummated. Your delightful creation,
The holder of your bliss, is as exhilarating as the bliss itself.
For you, the vigour, equally envigorating is the bliss,
O mighty, giver of a thousand pleasures.[10]

Later Vedic collections (*Samaveda*, *Yajurveda* and *Atharvaveda*) reiterate and supplement such verses from the Rig Veda, but they rarely illuminate them. As for the *Brahmanas* and *Upanisads*, the latter explore the mystical and metaphysical meaning of the Vedas and are important for the development of Indian philosophy, but they contain little historical information, while the former, 'an arid desert of puerile speculation on ritual ceremonies', again fail to measure up to Dr Ghosh's exacting standards. Elsewhere he calls them 'filthy', 'repulsive', 'of interest only to students of abnormal psychology' and 'of sickening prolixity'.

There are also, though, especially in the Rig Veda, some hymns of dazzling lyricism. Most often cited are those dedicated to the delectable Ushas, the goddess of dawn who reveals herself each morning, upright and naked, her body 'bright from bathing'; or those to Ratri, the spirit of the night, who from the stars that are her eyes keeps watch when men, like birds to roost, go home to rest. Even in excessively literal translations, these pearls of descriptive verse from poetry's remotest past suggest that there was more to the *arya* than the earthy obsessions of the stockman and the swagger of the charioteering oppressor. The prerequisites of civilisation – economic surplus, social and functional specialisation, political authority, urbanisation – were still lacking, but already the people of the Vedas had acquired a linguistic mastery of their environment and were beginning to deploy that same remarkable language to explore its logic.

Nowhere is this more apparent than in the conduct and elaboration of those sacrificial rites with which the Vedas are directly concerned. If Vedic translations tend to be literal it is because of the obscurity of the allusions and the language. Both were probably just as obscure to those who first committed these hymns to writing in a number of different recensions, none of which is older than c500 BC. In other words, for at least five hundred years the ten thousand verses of the Rig Veda were learned by heart and handed down by word of mouth. This, however, does not mean that they underwent significant change. Quite the contrary. As the recited accompaniment to the performance of sacrifices, their actual wording, even their intonation and their pronunciation, had to be perfect for the sacrifice to be effective. Conversely, a mangled syllable or an improvised coda could be fatal. Like the magician who forgets the magic formula, the supplicant could then find the sacrifice redounding to his disadvantage and condemning him to the very disaster he was trying to avert.

Such, at least, was the theory inculcated by those who made it their responsibility to shoulder this burden of memorised knowledge and so to serve as intermediaries in the communion of men and gods. Probably even they no longer used the elaborate constructions of Vedic Sanskrit in their everyday speech, and were therefore unsure of the meaning of some of their hymns. Obfuscation was, after all, in their interest; like specialists the world over, they found that the jargon and ritual deemed essential to their arcane science were also well calculated to impress the layman. Originally these intermediaries may have been no more than tribal bards, seers (*risis*) and shamans, and were not necessarily of *arya* descent. They became more influential possibly as a result of their pastoralist patrons adopting a more settled way of life, which involved grappling with new techniques of cultivation and discovering their vulnerability to the depredations of climate and pestilence. More elaborate sacrifices were needed, and so was a more specialised band of sacrificiants. Thus eventually, and perhaps with popular encouragement, the bards and shamans of old developed into a hereditary class of priests or *brahmana* (brahmans).

Handling the gods could be even more demanding of *arya* prowess than handling their enemies. Sacrifices and the elaborate rituals which accompanied them were mandatory and reciprocal. The gods depended on them for their strength; and the *arya* depended on the strength of their gods. Without effective intervention by their gods, their leaders would fall, their cattle would die, their enemies would triumph and their crops would fail. It was not just a question of propitiating remote but powerful supernaturals. Gods and men were equally engaged in the ticklish business of maintaining a cosmic equilibrium. Each had a legitimate and vital interest in the other's affairs. A close liaison between the two was essential.

In the Rig Veda brahmans, like the unctuous Kakshivant quoted above, extol the prowess and generosity of their patrons as well as the power and might of their deities. Initially it would seem that it was these patrons, the *rajanya* or clan leaders, who comprised the elite of *arya* society, not the brahmans. This situation may have reflected the leadership's role in warfare and in directing the seasonal migrations. But with the switch to a more settled and secure way of life, the *rajanya*'s role was diminished. Increasingly the clan leader looked to the brahman rather than the battlefield for the legitimation of his authority. The risks and the expenditure inherent in combat were replaced by the risks and expenditure inherent in sacrifice. Both could reveal the extent of divine favour enjoyed by the *raja* and so reinforce his right to rule. The great sacrificial gatherings became exhibitions of conspicuous consumption in which the munificent *raja*, besides indulging his kinsmen with orgies induced by *soma*, a hallucinogenic drink, was expected to donate herds of cattle and of horses, buckets of gold and bevies of slave-girls by way of compelling divine favour and rewarding brahmanical support. The gambling with dice so often referred to in Sanskrit literature formed part of the ritual (as well as of the fun) and symbolised the element of risk implicit in the sacrifice itself, as well as affording a further opportunity for divine favour to reveal itself.

Although the *arya* occasionally practised human sacrifice, the sacrificial offerings mentioned in the Vedas are predominantly of cattle, representing wealth, and of horses, symbolic of power and virility. Both were also associated with fertility. In the *aswamedha*, or horse sacrifice, a somewhat problematic injunction about the sexual coupling of the sacrificial stallion with the *raja*'s bride was meant to symbolise the endowment of his lineage with exceptional strength. The horse, in other words, represented the power of the chief, and would continue to do so in later *aswamedha*. But these later *aswamedha* reveal an important transition in the nature of *arya* authority. As will be seen, their intention became less that of boosting a chief's leadership credentials in respect of his clansmen and more that of legitimising kingship and territorial sovereignty, notions that were both novel and progressive in a semi-nomadic, clan-based society.

Thus in the later *aswamedha*, the horse seems to have been excused romantic duties. Instead it was first set free to roam at will for a year while a band of retainers followed its progress and laid claim in the putative king's name to all territory through which it chanced to pass. Only after this peregrination, and after the successful prosecution of the conflicts to which it inevitably gave rise, was the horse actually sacrificed.

A particularly elaborate version of such an *aswamedha* is commemorated in the heart of Varanasi (Benares), otherwise the City of Lord Shiva and the holiest place of pilgrimage in northern India. Legend has it that Shiva, while temporarily dispossessed of his beloved city, hit on the idea of regaining it by imposing on its incumbent king a quite impossible ritual challenge, namely the performance of ten simultaneous horse-sacrifices. The chances of all ten passing off without mishap could be safely discounted and thus the king, disgraced in the eyes of both gods and men, would be obliged to relinquish the city. So Lord Shiva reasoned and, just to make sure, he also arranged for Lord Brahma, a stickler for the niceties of ceremonial performance, to referee the challenge. Shiva failed, however, to take account of King Divodasa's quite exceptional piety and punctiliousness. All ten *aswamedha* were faultlessly performed. The king thereby gained untold merit and favour; Brahma was so impressed that he decided to stay on in the city; and Shiva slunk away to fume and fret and dream up ever more ambitious schemes to recover his capital. Thus to this day, when approaching the celebrated river-front at Varanasi, pilgrims and tourists alike get their first glimpse of the Ganga and of the steep ghats (terracing) which front it from 'Dashashwamedh' ghat, the place of 'the ten horse-sacrifices'. And the merit of this extraordinary feat, it is said, continues to attend all who here bathe in the sacred river.

This story, though obviously of much later provenance (Shiva was not one of the Vedic gods), well illustrates the importance attached to ritual exactitude. In the Vedas this preoccupation with the precise performance of sacrificial rites extended to minutiae like the orientation of the sacrificial altar and the surgical dissection of the sacrificial victim. Both had scientific repercussions: the positioning of the altar stimulated the study of astronomy and geometry, while dissection encouraged familiarity with anatomy. Similarly that obsession with the 'word perfect' recitation of the liturgy would inspire the codification of language and the study of phonetics and versification for which ancient India is justly famed. To anxieties about the impeccable conduct and the sacred siting of such rituals may also be ascribed early notions about the purity, or polluting effect, of those present. Participants had first to undergo purificatory rites which were more rigorous for those who might, because of their dubious descent or profession, prejudice the occasion. A scheme of graded ritual status thereby arose which, as will be seen, contributed to that hierarchical stratification of society known as caste. Thus to the Vedic rituals may be traced the genesis of some of the most distinctive traits of ancient Indian society, culture and science.

PASTORAL PEOPLES

All this, however, scarcely adds up to a convincing picture of the Vedic world, let alone to any kind of understanding of the historical processes at work within it. Somehow this primitive, or pre-modern, society of tribal herdsmen gradually learned about arable farming, assimilated or repulsed neighbours, discovered new resources, developed better technologies, adopted a settled life, organised itself into functional groups, opened trade links, endorsed frontiers, built cities, and eventually subscribed to the organised structures of authority which we associate with statehood. It all took perhaps a thousand years (1500–500BC), but as to the processes involved and the determining factors, let alone the critical events, the sources are silent. They provide a few cryptic clues but no ready answers; and the historian has first to ask the right questions.

The better to identify these questions, scholars have turned to other disciplines, and particularly to comparative anthropology and the study of pre-modern societies that are less remote from our own experience. Thus tribal structures in Polynesia and South America have provided clues about how kin-based societies may become socially stratified and about how notions of land as property may emerge. From the customs of pastoralist peoples in Africa conclusions have been drawn about the importance of cattle-offerings and gifts as a prestige-generating activity. And from native American customs much has been learned about the economic role of sacrifice. Thus the great Vedic sacrifices have been likened to the potlatch, in which the indigenous inhabitants of north-west America indulged in an extravaganza of consumption designed to burn off any surplus and at the same time enhance the status of the leading kin groups. Indeed the central action of the *Mahabharata* has been likened to one massive potlatch.

All these examples draw on tribal, or lineage, societies united by a shared ethnicity. If the Vedic *arya* are to be regarded as united principally by language rather than ethnicity, a comparison might also be made with the pre-modern society of the Scottish Highlands and Islands. The Vedic *jana* is often translated as the Gaelic 'clan' since, like the Highland clan, each *jana* acknowledged descent from a single ancestor. Thus, just as all

MacDonalds claim descent from a Donald of Isla who was a distant descendant of the Irish king 'Conn of the Hundred Battles', so the Bharatas, the most prominent of the Rig Vedic *jana*, claimed descent from Bharata, a distant descendant of Pururavas, grandson of Manu. The *jana*, like the clan, was further divided into smaller descent groups, or septs, which might break away from the parent clan and adopt the name of their own common ancestor as a patronymic. Real or mythical, these ancestral figures were not, however, necessarily of the same race. Some of the Highland clans were of Norse (Viking) origin and others of Pictish or Irish origin; similarly some of the Vedic *jana*, like the Yadavas, are thought to have been of *dasa* origin. Hence too the clearly -*dasa* names of Su-*dasa*, a Bharata chief who scored a notable victory over ten rival 'kings', and Divo-*dasa* of the ten horse-sacrifices at Varanasi. All, though, whatever their ethnic origin, and whether Indians or Scots, shared a language (Gaelic/Sanskrit), a social system in which precedence was dictated by birth, and a way of life in which both wealth and prestige were computed in cattle.

In Scotland as in India, the rustling of other clans' herds constituted both pastime and ritual, with success being an indicator of leadership credentials as well as of divine favour. As with the Vedic *rajanya*, each Highland chief had his bard whose business it was, like Kakshivant, to extol the might and generosity of his chiefly patron and to harness the forces of magic. His, too, was the job of memorising the clan's genealogy and record-ing its achievements in verses that might be easily handed down by word of mouth. In Vedic society the bard was originally the chief's charioteer. His function was not necessarily hereditary nor exclusively reserved to a particular social group. The author of the Mandala IX of the Rig Veda frankly avows humble origins which would have been anathema in a later caste-ridden society.

> A bard am I, my father a leech,
> And my mother a grinder of corn,
> Diverse in means, but all wishing wealth,
> Alike for cattle we strive.

In north-west Scotland as in north-west India, cattle were currency; but land was a common resource, not subject to individual rights of owner-ship and enjoyed in common by the whole clan and its herds. In Scotland this situation changed only under the pressure of a growing population and after the discovery of the land's greater potential under a different farming regime – namely wool production. Previously, annual migrations to traditional areas of seasonal pasturage had rendered notions of territory and of frontiers fluid and often meaningless. Allegiance focused not on a geographical region nor on a political institution but exclusively on the descent group of the clan chief. This too changed under the new regime, and the chiefs had to find a new role. Perhaps similar pressures confronted the Vedic *jana*, and similar adaptations to a new farming regime – namely crop-growing – demanded of the *rajanya* a more possessive attitude to territory and property.

Such comparisons can, of course, be misleading. Technologies and markets not available to the *arya* in the second millennium BC had ensured a ready demand for Highland beef in the second millennium AD. Hence burning off the year's surplus in an orgy of sacrifice, gift-exchange and gargantuan consumption was not a Scottish tradition. Conversely, climatic and geographical factors which made livestock farming the only surplus-creating occupation available to upland agriculturalists in Scotland made it a less suitable occupation in the tropical flood-plains of northern India. Although pastoralism would continue in areas like the west bank of the Jamuna and along the skirts of the Himalayas, the environment of the Ganga plain invited more intensive farming and a more sedentary lifestyle. Reference to other pre-modern societies merely helps to clarify the norms which may have characterised Vedic society, and perhaps to render it more intelligible than does that 'stupendous mass' of Vedic hymns.

The Epic Age

C900–520 BC

FROM WEST TO EAST

WHILE TOILING in the two-thousand-kilometre patchwork of fields which is the Gangetic plain today, farmers have occasionally unearthed substantial hoards of copper implements and even copper bars. Associated with them at some sites are poorly fired and 'unspeakably crude'[1] bits of ochre-coloured pottery (OCP) which tend to disintegrate at the touch. Unworthy of the Late Harappans and distributed too widely and too far east to be credited to the *arya* of the Vedas, these copper hoards remain a mystery. They are assumed to have been the property of itinerant smiths or traders who, for reasons unknown, stashed away their wares some time before 1000 BC. But the trouble with copper, or indeed iron, which first appears soon after this date, is that one can never be sure that the form in which it survives is that in which it was first cast. The harpoons and axes of this 'copper hoard culture' could have been made from the melted-down pins and arrowheads of an earlier people, while the presence of copper bars strongly suggests that the metal was already being widely traded.

Like metals, myths too get recycled. Reworked and so richly embellished as to be almost unrecognisable, stories which may once have reflected genuine historical events are liable to be re-used by later generations in a totally different context and for purposes quite other than that for which they were originally intended. This is not the case with the corpus of Vedic literature; the form and content of its sacrificial formulae were, as has been noted, too ritually crucial to be tampered with. Less sacred compositions, like the two great Sanskrit epics, were a different matter.

Both the *Mahabharata* and the *Ramayana* survive in several versions, the earliest of which are at least five hundred years later than the Vedas. Yet their core narratives seem to relate to events from a period prior to all but the Rig Veda. As with the Greek epics attributed to Homer, this extraordinary antiquity justifies the attention accorded them in traditional histories. The wildly different dates adduced for the Mahabharata war – or for the Trojan war – scarcely matter if the events themselves can be verified. Sadly, though, in both cases so heavily have these tales been reworked for propaganda purposes, and so crammed and padded have they become with edifying sermons and other extraneous additions, that their original core stories are as hard to isolate as their dates.

Theoretically the *Puranas*, another group of Sanskrit texts, should be able to resolve this problem for the Indian historian. The most important collection of the *Puranas*, or 'ancient legends', is even later, dating only from c500 AD; yet it contains myths and genealogies which purport to go back to Manu (and beyond). Sure enough, here figure the names of protagonists from the epics as well as of Vedic chiefs and *arya* tribes. No doubt these lists were compiled from an ancient oral tradition which originated with the *arya* bards and would have been carefully memorised by their successors. But, like the epics, the Puranic compositions show signs of having been reworked. When finally they were written down, it was not in a spirit of disinterested scholarship but to elevate the pedigree of later dynasts and to enhance the repute of their brahmanical backers.

> In their present form [the *Puranas*] are only religious fables and cant, with whatever historical content the works once possessed heavily encrusted by myth, diluted with semi-religious legends, and effaced during successive redactions copied by innumerable careless scribes; so that one finds great difficulty in restoring as much as the king-lists.[2]

This does not mean that they are worthless. Despite what D.D. Kosambi, himself a brahman, called 'the deplorable brahman habit'[3] of organising and categorising unrelated traditions into a convenient pattern, large chunks of the Puranic genealogies may be as authentic as the central characters and events in the epics. Moreover, just as the copper hoards, whatever their original provenance, reveal something about the uses, smelting techniques and distribution of copper, so these literary hoards can reveal something about the changes at work within north Indian society. The period between the events they describe and their being finally written down, roughly the first millennium BC, is of crucial importance. It is 'the real formative period of Indian civilisation . . . : henceforth we can trace the continuity of civilisation through the succeeding ages.'[4] Thus scholars like Kosambi and Romila Thapar, anxious to understand how, for instance, tribal structures crumbled and states emerged, focus less on the stirring events described in the epics and more on the contexts – geographical, social, environmental and economic – in which they occurred.

Like a self-denying ordinance, this stern approach deprives the historian of many a gallant hero plus whole chapters of rip-roaring narrative. More agreeably, it also diverts attention from that nagging problem of Indian history being so light on dates.

> Because of the difficulty in assigning an exact chronology to the sources [i.e. the epics] it is impossible to be precise or dogmatic as to when particular changes took place ... Consequently the major significance of these sources lies more in their indication of the nature of the trend of change which they delineate rather than in the precise dating of the change.[5]

The historicity of a hero demands that his place and dates be established; no such figure graces Indian history until the Buddha illumines the scene after 500 BC. But 'the nature of a trend of change' can reasonably be assigned to an entire river basin and a timespan of centuries.

The 'trends' which emerge from such studies are numerous and important though seldom explicit. For instance, central to both of the great epics is the question of succession. The Pandava heroes of the *Mahabharata* (Yudhisthira, Bhima, Arjuna, Draupadi, etc.), like their counterparts in the *Ramayana* (Rama, Sita and Lakshmana), are initially denied 'kingdoms' which would seem to be theirs by birthright and are forced into exile. Primogeniture evidently influenced succession and there are hints about the divine sanction of kingship; both of these ideas would become cardinal features of later monarchies. Yet Puranic references can be highly ambiguous about kingship as an institution, although one should not perhaps read too much in its oft-repeated adage: 'As bad as ten slaughter houses is one oil-presser's wheel, as bad as ten oil-pressers' wheels is one inn sign, as bad as ten inn signs is a harlot, and as bad as ten harlots is a king.'[6]

But it is also clear that society at the time, though now settled and familiar with agriculture, was still clan-based. Kingship was subordinate to kinship and probably amounted to no more than chieftainship-among-equals. Succession by primogeniture was thus heavily qualified; much depended on the physical and moral perfection of the candidate, on the approval of his peers, and on his successful avoidance of fortuitous mishaps and curses. Ideas of a kingship which transcended clan affiliation and of automatic succession by right of birth, though obviously important to those who reworked the original stories, would only become the norm towards the middle of the millennium and then only among certain tribes.

As for the retreat into exile, the other central theme in both epics, this is taken to indicate the process by which clan society resolved its conflicts and at the same time encroached ever deeper into the subcontinent. Eventually population pressures on land and other resources would encourage greater social specialisation and the assertion of a central authority, two of the prerequisites of a state. But during the first centuries of the first millennium BC, these same pressures seem merely to have encouraged a traditional solution whereby clans segmented and split away to explore new territories.

Exile meant withdrawing from settled society not into the desert (which even renunciates seem to have shunned) but into the *aranya*, the forest. Here life was challenging though full of possibilities; numerous venerable sages and barely-clad nymphs could even make it idyllic. Something of the later antithesis between the safely settled, caste-based society of the village and the dangerously peripatetic and egalitarian society associated with the forest is already apparent. But for every agreeable sylvan experience there also lurked amongst the trees a monstrous demon or some other species of hostile primitive. These creatures, even if recognisably human, possessed no houses and subsisted as hunter-gatherers. To exiles who prided themselves on being settled agriculturalists, the nomadic ways and uncouth habits of the forest were anathema. The monsters had therefore to be exterminated, while harmless savages, like the snake-worshipping 'Nagas', could be enlisted as allies or tributaries, usually through marriage and through inventing acceptable pedigrees for them. In effect the relationship between the epic heroes and their forest foes mirrored the presumed pattern of Aryan 'colonisation' and settlement.

'The people move from west to east and conquer land,' says the *Satapatha Brahmana*. By the time of the *Mahabharata* they had evidently reached the upper Ganga, for there stood Hastinapura, the story's disputed capital. Forest exile in this geographical context could only mean that, in their eastward spread, the pioneers of Aryanisation were entering the main Gangetic basin. Decidedly different from today's dusty chequerboard where tufts of trees survive only as shade for huddled villages, Uttar Pradesh and Bihar were then a moist green wilderness of forest and swamp, a tropical *taiga* of near-Siberian extent. Here, unlike in the drier Panjab, land clearance posed a formidable challenge. The soils were heavier and the jungle thicker; even fire-breathing Agni's work must have been quickly undone as smoke-blackened stumps burst back into leaf. On the other hand the forest was rich in resources. The exiles invariably used their sojourn in the wilderness to re-arm with a formidable arsenal of new weapons. Though ascribed to divine provenance, these unbreakable swords, bows with un-erring arrows, and devastating missiles may more plausibly have been fashioned from the exotic timbers and minerals only to be found in the *terra incognita* beyond the then confines of the western settlements.

Although copper from Rajasthan had been used by the Harappans, the best-quality deposits lie much further east in what is now southern Bihar. Thence too came iron. Whether its use was first learned from indigenous smiths in peninsular India or whether through trade contacts with west Asia is uncertain. Likewise the revolution it eventually effected. After 500 BC iron axes and probably ploughshares were indeed helping to solve the problem of clearing the land and working heavier soils; but until that time the 'black metal' seems to have been reserved almost exclusively for weapons and knives. Access to the new metallurgy may not, then, have eased the settler's lot, but it could at least have given the exiled Pandavas a military edge – literally – over their enemies. Adopted by the other clans, iron represented a major technological advantage, comparable to the horse-drawn chariots of their *arya* ancestors and perhaps of more utility in the closer confines of the new environment.

Unfortunately, charting the eastward progress of Sanskritic but still tribal intruders was not germane to the purposes of those who retold the epics for the edification of later generations. Indeed surviving versions of the *Mahabharata* would have us believe that the Pandavas and their Kaurava rivals were not only far from primitive but that they already monopolised the resources of the subcontinent. When not in exile, they are described as living in pillared pavilions and marble halls, their interiors opulently furnished and their floors so highly polished that visitors hitched up their robes in the belief that across such glimmering expanses they must needs wade. The Kuru 'kingdom', centred on Hastinapura, is projected as being of vast extent and untold wealth, its armies feared throughout the subconti-nent and its potential allies extending from coast to coast.

Such descriptions served solely to legitimise the grandiose ambitions of later empire-builders. (And if one may judge by the television serialisations of the 1980s, they still serve to underpin conceits about a pan-Indian prehistory of spectacular sophistication.) In reality, though, the core geogra-phy of the *Mahabharata* is limited to a small area of the Ganga-Jamuna Doab which was the maximum extent of Kuru territory. This is self-evident from an early episode in the story when, the territory having been divided, the Pandavas set out to the ends of the 'kingdom' to found a new capital. They choose Indraprastra, just sixty kilometres away and still so named –

indeed still fortified; its crumbling walls, although not those of the Pandavas, served the British designers of New Delhi as a suitable feature with which to terminate the vista from their own marbled halls of Viceroy's House (now Rashtrapati Bhawan).

Further detail on the Indo-Aryan *drang nach osten* may be gleaned from the archaeological evidence for the first half of the first millennium BC. At Hastinapura and other sites that 'unspeakably crude' ochre-coloured pottery which is sometimes found with the copper hoards is succeeded by a very superior painted grey ware. 'PGW' was evidently produced on a wheel, and was confidently decorated with geometric and floral motifs. It is found principally throughout the Ganga-Jamuna Doab and in adjacent areas of the Panjab, Rajasthan and the western Gangetic valley, a distribution which tallies nicely with the geographical context of the *Mahabharata*. Often it occurs in quantities which imply a greater population density than previously, and thus 'it marks an assertive society, richer than its immediate predecessors'.[7] It was also a society which, judging by associated finds, worked the land as well as keeping both cattle and horses. Finally, the dating of this PGW also tallies well with that of the c950 BC date for the great war. If not the pottery from which Vedic chieftains once quaffed their psychedelic *soma*, it may well have been off PGW dishes that Bhima, trencherman *par excellence* amongst the Pandavas, prodigiously fed. In short, the PGW looks to have been the distinctive pottery style of the Kuru and associated clans on the north-west fringes of the Gangetic plain.

Another pottery style known as black and red ware (BRW) seems to have been contemporary with PGW but to have had a wider and patchier distribution which included much of western and central India. This has suggested an association with the Yadava clan, a sept or segment of which is said to have migrated south from its base at Mathura (between Delhi and Agra). In the process it seems to have established an important corridor of Aryanisation to Avanti (later called Malwa), where the city of Ujjain would soon arise, and further still into Gujarat and possibly down the west coast. The Yadava dimension has to be pieced together from scattered references in the *Puranas*, since it lacks the detailed documentation provided for the Kuru by the *Mahabharata*. Nevertheless into the latter epic as the Pandavas' mentor and guardian is worked the legend of Lord Krishna, the scion and hero of the Yadava lineage. Krishna, although used as a mouthpiece for the revered but later *Bhagavad Gita* (and although later still to become the frolicsome toddler and pastoral heart-throb so dear to Indian sentiment), is here an aloof and awesome figure whose no-nonsense approach is partly an indictment of human frailty but also stems from an insistence on the centrality of clan loyalty and *arya* tradition. The Yadavas were evidently a conservative lot. In Gujarat as in Mathura pastoralism and dairy farming would retain their economic importance long after arable farming had become the mainstay of life and the source of surplus in the Gangetic basin. Likewise the western clans would cling to their traditional hierarchies long after their eastern cousins had adopted state formations.

Another salient of black and red ware suggests a south-east movement from Mathura along the edge of the Vindhya hills. These form the southern perimeter of the Gangetic basin whence, in Bihar, the BRW descends again into the plain. It there re-meets the painted grey ware, a parallel arm of which is discernible extending east along the skirts of the Himalayas. The impression gained is therefore that of a pincer movement, possibly dictated by the problems of clearing the dense forest and draining the swamps which blocked progress along the banks of the Ganga itself. Instead the tide of migration and acculturation seems to have worked its way round the edges, and especially round the top edge. Thus the principal chain of *janapada*, or clan territories (literally 'clan-feet'), lay well to the north of the main river, on the banks of the Ganga's tributaries as they flow down from what is now Nepal. In the *Satapatha Brahmana* there is even a detailed description of Agni burning a trail eastwards and eventually leapfrogging what is thought to have been the Gandak river so as to ignite the forest beyond and clear its land for settlement and tillage by the Videha clan.

This northerly route of east–west transit and trade, extending from the Panjab and the upper Indus to Bihar and the lower Ganga, now became as much the main axis of Aryanisation as it would subsequently of Buddhist proselytisation and even Magadhan imperialism. It was known as the *Uttarapatha*, the Northern Route, as distinct from the *Daksinapatha* (whence the term 'Deccan') or Southern Route. The latter, largely the Yadava trail from the Gangetic settlements to Avanti (Malwa) and Gujarat, would also become a much-travelled link giving access to the ports of the west coast and the riches of the as yet un-Aryanised and historically inarticulate peninsula. But it was along the *Uttarapatha* that the Aryanised territories would first begin to assume the trappings of statehood. Initially those at the western end in the Panjab and the Doab tended to look down on those on the eastern frontier in Bihar and Bengal; the latter were *mleccha*, uncouth in their *arya* speech and negligent in their sacrificial observance. By mid-first millennium BC it would be the other way round. As the eastern settlements grew into a network of thriving proto-states, many laid claim to exalted pedigrees and, assuming the mantle of Aryanised orthodoxy, would be happy to disparage their Panjabi cousins as *vratya* or 'degenerate'.

THE *MAHABHARATA* VERSUS THE *RAMAYANA*

The *Ramayana*, second of the great Sanskrit epics, has been subjected to
the same sort of revision processes as the *Mahabharata*. So much so that
attempting to tease India's past from such doubtful material has been
likened to trying to reconstruct the history of ancient Greece from the
fables of Aesop, or that of the Baghdad caliphate from *The Thousand and
One Nights*. The *Ramayana*'s story is, however, simpler than the *Mahabharata*'s and its purpose is clearer. No one under Lord Rama's sway would
swap a king for ten harlots, let alone for a thousand slaughterhouses. For
in the form we now know it, the *Ramayana* may be seen as 'an epic
legitimising the monarchical state'.[8]

When it took this form is uncertain. A condensed version of the story
is told in the *Mahabharata*, but it would appear to be an interpolation. It
is certainly no proof that the characters in the *Ramayana* preceded those
in the *Mahabharata*. The opposite seems more probable, in that Lord
Rama's capital of Ayodhya lay astride the *Uttarapatha* and five hundred
kilometres east of the Kuru/Pandavas' Hastinapura. That, in its final form,
the *Ramayana* is definitely later than the *Mahabharata* is shown by the
prominence given to regions which are unheard of in the latter. Indeed,
while the main wanderings of the exiled Pandavas seem to have been
restricted to the immediate neighbourhood of the Doab, those of Lord
Rama and his associates are made to extend deep into central and southern
India. No doubt much of this was a gloss by later redactors, but it is still
precious evidence of the continuing spread of Aryanisation during the first
millennium BC. If the *Mahabharata* hints at the pattern of settlement in
the north and west, the *Ramayana* continues the story eastwards.

Thus while the *Mahabharata* belongs to the Ganga-Jamuna Doab, the
Ramayana is firmly rooted in the middle Ganga region. Rama's Ayodhya
was the capital of an important *janapada* called Koshala, roughly north-
eastern Uttar Pradesh, which some time in mid-millennium would absorb
its southern neighbour. The latter was Kashi, which is the old name for
Varanasi (Benares). In a popular Buddhist version of the epic, Varanasi
rather than Ayodhya actually becomes the locus of the story. And much
later, in Lord Shiva's city, in a quiet whitewashed house overlooking the
Ganga and well away from the crowds thronging Dashashwamedh Ghat,
the seventeenth-century poet Tulsi Das would pen for the delight of future
generations the definitive Hindi version of the epic. Varanasi would make
the *Ramayana* its own, and to this day slightly further upstream, on rolling
parkland beside the ex-Maharaja of Varanasi's palace, the annual week-long

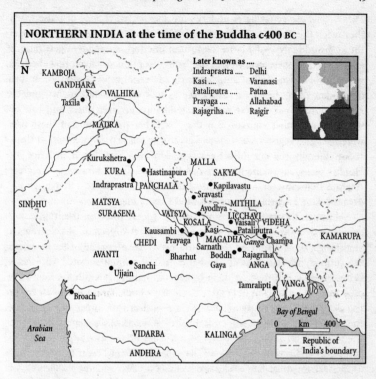

NORTHERN INDIA at the time of the Buddha c400 BC

N

KAMBOJA
GANDHARA
VALHIKA
Taxila
MADRA

Later known as ....
Indraprastra .... Delhi
Kasi .... Varanasi
Pataliputra .... Patna
Prayaga .... Allahabad
Rajagriha .... Rajgir

Kurukshetra
KURA
Hastinapura
MALLA
SAKYA
Indraprastra
PANCHALA
Kapilavastu
Sravasti
SINDHU
MATSYA
SURASENA
VATSYA
Ayodhya
KOSALA
MITHILA
LICCHAVI
Vaisali
VIDEHA
Kausambi
Kasi
Pataliputra
KAMARUPA
CHEDI
Prayaga
MAGADHA
Ganga Champa
AVANTI
Sarnath
Sanchi
Bharhut
Boddh
Gaya
Rajagriha
ANGA
Ujjain

Tamralipti
VANGA
Broach

Arabian Sea

Bay of Bengal

0   km   400

VIDARBA
KALINGA
ANDHRA

Republic of
India's boundary

performance of the *Ram Lila* (a dramatised version of the epic) remains one of the greatest spectacles in India.

This suggests that whereas the *Mahabharata* survives in the popular imagination as a hoard of cherished but disjointed segments, like the scattered skeleton of a fossilised dinosaur, the *Ramayana* is still alive – indeed kicking, if one may judge by the events of the early 1990s. Casting about for an evocative issue around which to rally Hindu opinion, it was to the sanctity of Ayodhya and its supposed defilement by the presence of a mosque that fundamentalist Hindu opinion turned. Loudly invoking Lord Rama, in 1992 saffron-clad activists duly assailed the Ayodhya mosque and so plunged the proud secularism of post-Independence India into its deepest crisis of conscience.

That Ayodhya/Varanasi score higher in the sacral stakes than Hastinapura/Indraprastra may also have something to do with the different cosmic perspectives of the two epics. A clue is provided by the language of the

Puranas, whose genealogies undergo an unexpected change of tense when they reach the Bharata war. From one of Sanskrit's innumerable past tenses the verb suddenly switches to the future; in effect, subsequent generations as recorded in these genealogies are being prophesied. Given that the lists were not written down until centuries later, the succession of future descendants may be just as authentic as that of past antecedents, indeed rather more so since later names extend into historic times and can be verified from other sources. But the point that the authors of these lists were trying to register was that the great war marked a watershed in time. It was literally the end of an era. The *Dvapara Yug*, the 'Third Age' of Hindu cosmology, came to a close as Pandavas slew Kauravas in the great Bharata holocaust at Kurukshetra, 'the field of the Kuru'; thereafter the dreaded *Kali Yug*, the still current 'Black Age', began.

Although the battle does not mark the end of the epic, the impression gained is that the *Mahabharata* is essentially retrospective. It celebrates a vanishing past and may be read as the swansong of an old order in which the primacy of clan kinship, and the martial ethic associated with it, is being slowly laid to rest. In the eighteen-day battle nearly all the Kauravas, plus a whole generation of Pandavas, are wiped out. Yudhisthira, ostensibly the principal victor, surveys the carnage and is overcome with remorse; the rivalry and conflicts endemic in the clan system are repudiated; with the intention of returning to the forest, Yudhisthira asks his followers to accept his abdication. Krishna will have none of it: the ruler must rule just as the warrior must fight; release depends on following one's *dharma*, not indulging one's grief. Reluctantly Yudhisthira concurs, performing the royal sacrifices of *rajasuya* and *aswamedha*. But regrets continue, and when Krishna himself dies, it is as if the last remaining pillar of the old order has been removed. All five Pandavas, plus their shared wife Draupadi, can then gratefully withdraw from public life to wander off into the Himalayas.

By way of contrast, the *Ramayana* may be considered as decidedly forward-looking. It opens new frontiers and it formulates a new ideal. Although nothing is said about a new era or a system of governance specifically designed for it, the implication is clear. When Rama eventually regains his capital, it is not to indulge in remorse or even to reaffirm Vedic values but to usher in a dazzling utopia of order, justice and prosperity under his personal rule. The resultant *Rama-rajya* (or *Ram-raj* in Hindi, 'the rule of Rama') quickly became, and is still, the Indian political ideal, invoked by countless dynasts and pledged by countless politicians, secularist as well as Hindu nationalist. Likewise Ayodhya itself would come to represent the model of a royal capital and as such would feature in many subsequent Aryanised state systems. In this guise it would travel far, making landfalls in Thailand where Ayuthia, the pre-Bangkok capital of the Thai monarchs, supposedly replicated Rama's city, and even in central Java where the most senior sultanate is still that of Jogjakarta, or *Ngajodya-karta*, the first part of which is a Javanese rendering of 'Ayodhya'.

MONARCHIES AND REPUBLICS

Legitimising monarchical rule, in India as in south-east Asia, was the *Ramayana*'s prime function. But in both places its use for this purpose was dictated as much by current challenges as by residual loyalties to a past order. For in north India of the mid-first millennium BC other experiments in the organising of a state were already well underway. Monarchical authority was not, it seems, essential to state-formation. Nor was its absolutism, as heavily promoted by its brahman supporters, congenial to all. Other sources suggest dissent and bear copious testimony to alternative state systems with very different constitutions.

The textual sources concerned are all either Buddhist or Jain. Nataputta, otherwise Mahavira ('Great Hero'), would formulate the Jain code of conduct in the sixth-to-fifth centuries BC, just when Siddhartha Gautama, otherwise the Buddha ('Enlightened One'), was preaching the Middle Way. This was a coincidence of profound moment. It would make the history of the mid-Gangetic plain in the first millennium BC a subject of abiding and even international interest; more immediately, it directs the historian's attention to aspects of contemporary Indian society that would otherwise be ignored. For the lives and teachings of the great founding fathers of Buddhism and Jainism quickly inspired a host of didactic and narrative compositions which supplement and sometimes contradict orthodox sources like the *Puranas*. Moreover, both men were born into distinguished clans which belonged not to kingdoms modelled on Rama's Ayodhya but to one of these alternative, non-monarchical state systems. Jain and Buddhist versions of the *Ramayana* story, or of episodes within it, thus show a rather different emphasis. They also incorporate significant information on places other than Ayodhya and on state systems other than monarchies.

These alternative state systems have been variously interpreted as oligarchical, republican or even democratic. The term now used for them is *gana-sangha*, evidently a compromise reached after some early-twentieth-century scholarly sniping, since we are told that 'in the years 1914–16 a great controversy raged [presumably amongst blissfully bunkered academics] about the term *gana*.[9] A variant of *jana*, basically it means a 'clan' or 'horde' which, qualified by *sangha*, an 'organisation' or 'government', supposedly gives a meaning of 'government by discussion'. Such 'governments by discussion', or more commonly 'republics', could of course take many forms. The extent to which all or only some of their constituents participated in decision-making, the institutions and assemblies through which they did so, and the degree to which they elected or merely endorsed a leadership are not clear. Nevertheless, all these matters are currently the subject of debate, partly because of obvious parallels with the contemporary republics and democracies of ancient Greece, and partly because modern India itself has a republican and democratic constitution whose pedigree occasionally generates some warmth.

That a clan-based society should opt for a constitution which was more egalitarian and less autocratic than monarchy seems perfectly logical. In a sense the republics merely institutionalised traditions of consultation amongst the leading clansmen which go back to Vedic times. These took the form of assemblages which ranged from the open *samiti* to the more restricted and specialised *sabha* and *parisad*. As consultative groups the latter would develop into ministerial councils in the monarchical states, while the former seems to have retained its sovereign status in the republics.

Most of the mid-millennium republics of Bihar and Uttar Pradesh (UP) – those of the Licchavis, Sakyas, Koliyas, Videhas, etc. – came into being as a result of the usual process of segmenting off from a parent clan. In due course the breakaways claimed their own *janapada*, their territory, and perhaps intentionally, perhaps through neglect or penury, they skimped on performing the full programme of Vedic sacrifices and paid scant attention to brahmanical authority. Surplus produce and booty, when they materialised, would not therefore have necessarily been 'burned off' in ritual orgies designed to impress the gods and enhance the sacrificer's prestige. Instead they would have become available for other purposes, like administration, urbanisation, industry and trade.

This, however, is a simplistic explanation for the emergence of states, and would certainly not have encouraged the formation of monarchies. In brahmanic tradition kingship is said to have been pioneered by the gods. Facing defeat by their supernatural enemies, the gods put their heads together and decided to choose a leader; Indra got the job. A *raja*, in other words, should be chosen by his peers, his role was principally military, and his *raj* had the sanction of divine precedent. Other myths reformulated the concept. One, already noticed, promoted kingship as the only insurance against anarchy. In the evil times ushered in by the *Kali Yug*, men found themselves obliged to compete with one another for wealth, women and favour. Society was thus reduced to the free-for-all of *matsya-nyaya* ('the law of the fishes', i.e. of the jungle); and men were accordingly obliged to formulate rules of conduct and to seek a means of enforcing them. The gods, or Lord Vishnu in the shape of that rapidly growing fish, proposed a *raja*; and they selected Manu. He agreed, but only on four nicely judged conditions – that he receive a tenth of his subjects' harvest, one in every fifty of their cows, a quarter of all the merit they earned, and the pick of their choicest maidens. In other words, authority and law-enforcement were the now *raja*'s main responsibilities; he was chosen by the gods rather than men; and under an advantageous reciprocal arrangement he had a right to a substantial contribution of the good things his subjects produced.

Here, then, was a firm ideological basis for kingship. But while the element of contract implicit in the Manu myth was much emphasised by Buddhist sources, brahmanic sources focused on the element of divine sanction. Either way, a monarch was theoretically subject to constraints, human or divine, and should not be regarded as an outright despot. Conversely, all theories of kingship provided ample justification for the administrative and coercive structures which would constitute a state system.

But as with the more spontaneous evolution of the *gana-sanghas* (republics), state-formation was prompted not simply by the appeal or logic of a particular constitution. Just as important were the challenges and opportunities created by new technologies and new social and economic conditions. It seems fairly certain from the abundance of artefacts unearthed by archaeology that, by mid-millennium, population densities had increased, and that migration had slowed as the more easily worked tracts became settled. The population increase owed as much to the incorporation, or Aryanisation, of indigenous peoples as to a soaring birth-rate amongst the immigrants; and both processes would heighten social awareness and caste/class distinctions.

On the other hand, agricultural production seems to have more than kept pace with the growing population. The use of heavy ploughs drawn by eight oxen or more, the widespread adoption of rice and the development of irrigation are all well attested by 500 BC: 'Buddhist texts describe rice and its varieties with as much detail as the Rig Vedic hymns refer to cows.'[10] It has been suggested that the wetter soils of northern Bihar were so unsuitable for barley that only some understanding of wet rice-cultivation would have made them worth settling. The effort of clearing such lands and building embankments for water retention would still have been arduous; yet it paid off. By the sixth-fifth centuries BC the Lichhavi and other republics north of the Ganga would together represent a formidable power well capable of meeting a challenge from their monarchical neighbours, notably the Koshala/Kashi kingdom in the south-west and, south-east across the Ganga, the aggressive new dynasty of Magadha.

More intensive farming regimes also made for new attitudes towards the land. The grazier's seasonal parameters had given way to the fixed dimensions of the ploughman's field. Anchored to a dependable supply of water and labour, the *grama* grew into a village of mud-brick housing which was home both to families of clan descent and to a growing band of socially differentiated dependants and subordinates. From the village there now spread a quilt of carefully supervised plots within a network of ditchings. The common rights of ownership typical of a pastoral society were being edged out by local initiative and the use of subject labour. Quick to claim the fields which they had reclaimed, the *grhpatis*, or heads of households, pressed for title to land, labour and water as the best way to meet their obligation of supplying the livestock and, increasingly, the grain needed for the leadership's ritual sacrifices. Imperceptibly terms like *bali*, which originally meant an offering intended for the clan-chief's sacrificial disposal, came to denote a fixed and regular contribution which, when subject to record and assessment, duly became a tax. Similarly *bhaga*, originally a 'share' of the spoils of war exacted by the chief, came to signify a tax on produce, usually of one sixth.

As cultivable land came to be considered as familial property, so the wider but ill-defined *janapada*, the ancestral territory of a particular clan, assumed fixed boundaries. The Gangetic basin's abundant rivers and riverbeds made convenient frontiers for the newer *janapada* in the east. Buddhist texts list sixteen *maha-janapada*, or major *janapada*, as having been extant in the sixth century BC. They extended from Gandhara and Kamboja in the north-west of what is now Pakistan to Avanti and Chedi in central India and Anga and Kalinga in Bengal and Orissa. Soon to be known as *rashtra*, or 'kingdoms', many still retained their tribal names; Kuru was still the land of the Kuru, and Malla of the Malla. But allegiance was now dictated less by the horizontal bonds of kinship and more by the vertical ties of economic and social dependency. Instead of being focused on tribe or clan, loyalty was increasingly to the territory itself, to the individual or body which had sovereignty over it, and to the town or city where that power resided.

CITY AND CASTE

India's second urbanisation (the first being that of the long-forgotten Harappans) may be attributed partly to this process of state-formation and to
the institutions it engendered, and partly to the surplus generated by the
new agricultural regime pioneered in the east. The post-Vedic texts, of
course, would have us believe that towns and cities had dotted the land
for aeons. But it is only from c600 BC that archaeology lends any weight
to their optimistic imagery. Earthen ramparts of about this period have
been uncovered at Ujjain (in Malwa), Varanasi and Kaushambi (the post-
Hastinapura capital of the Kuru, west of Allahabad). These ramparts have
'civic dimensions and must have enclosed real cities'.[11] Other sites like that
of Sravasti, the post-Ayodhya capital of Koshala, and Rajgir, the Magadha
capital, seem soon to have followed suit. In the west, Taxila and Charsadda
may have preceded them; but that was under a different impetus if not a
different dispensation. In the north-west, with stone plentiful, there is also
evidence of monumental structures.

Nothing comparable is found in the city sites of the Gangetic basin;
even kiln-fired brickwork, the Harappans' speciality, does not reappear
until the last centuries BC. Buildings, including state edifices and royal
residences, were evidently of timber and mud. The first Buddhist stupas
(commemorative mounds, often erected over relics of the Buddha) were
of just such perishable materials, although it was precisely these sacred
structures which would be amongst the earliest to be clad, then gloriously
cloistered, in stone. Of architecture and sculpture, the signposts to so much
of later Indian history, nothing remains.

Although unused, the technology for kiln-fired bricks was familiar
enough, for what distinguishes this period of urbanisation is a new and
invasive ceramic ware. Known as the northern black polished (NBP), it
first appears after 500 BC, rapidly supersedes the earlier styles (PGW, BRW)
in Bihar and UP, and eventually extends west across the Doab and deep
into Panjab, east to Bengal and south to Maharashtra. Were there no other
evidence for urbanisation, the concentrated finds of this high-quality ware
would prompt the idea of city life. Similarly, were there no other evidence
than its widespread distribution, one might yet guess that such standardisation amongst the numerous kingdoms and gana-sanghas of north India
during the last half of the first millennium BC must presage some major
new integrational influence. Sure enough, within two centuries of the NBP
ware's first appearance, all of north India (plus much more besides) would

be conspicuously linked by the first and the most extended of India's home-grown empires.

Trade, of course, also played its part. The first coins are datable to the mid-millennium and are found mostly in an urban context. Of silver or copper, they were punch-marked (rather than minted) with symbols thought to be those of particular professional groups, markets and cities. They 'were therefore a transitional form between traders' tokens as units of value and legal tender issued by royalty'.[12] The cash economy had evidently arrived, and with references to money-lending, banking and commodity speculation becoming commonplace in Buddhist literature it is clear that venture capital was readily available. Items traded included metals, fine textiles, salt, horses and pottery. Roads linked the major cities, although river transport seems to have been favoured for bulky consignments.

All of which presupposes the existence of specialised professions: artisans and cultivators, carters and boatmen, merchants and financiers. It was all a far cry from the clan communities of the Vedas. North Indian society had been undergoing structural changes every bit as radical as those affecting its agricultural base and its political organisation. These changes are usually interpreted in terms of the emerging caste system. They have to be extracted, with some difficulty, from the changing terms used to designate individuals and social groups in the different texts. And it would appear that the process of change was gradual, uneven and complex.

Basically the Vedas and the epics portray the concerns, and celebrate the exploits, of a society consisting almost entirely of well-born clansmen. Known as *ksatriya* and *rajanya*, these warrior families acknowledged a chief with whom they shared a common ancestor. The chief was their *raja*, a term rich in potential for misunderstanding in that it later came to mean a king in the monarchical states and an elector, or a participant in government, in the republics. Thus Vaisali, the capital of the Licchavi *gana-sangha* in northern Bihar,is said to have housed 7707 *rajas*, or in another account 'twice 84,000 *rajas*'. As well as the leadership of their *rajas*, the *ksatriya* also acknowledged the ritual insights and sacerdotal authority of a non-*ksatriya* priesthood, the brahmans. The latter, their profession becoming hereditary and exclusive through emphasis on their descent from certain ancient *risis* or seers, assumed the status of a parallel caste with well advertised rights and taboos derived from their monopoly of sacrificial lore, of religious orthodoxy and of academic jargon.

To these two castes was appended a third, possibly to differentiate clansmen of less distinguished descent who had forsaken their warrior past for agriculture and other wealth-generating pursuits. *Vaisya*, the term used to describe this caste, derives from *vis*, which originally meant the entire tribal community. They were thus considered to be of *arya* descent and, like the brahman and *ksatriya*, were *dvija* or 'twice born' (once physically, a second time through initiation rituals). As the *ksatriya*, literally 'the empowered ones', assumed military, political and administrative powers within the new state structures, the unempowered remainder of the erstwhile *vis*, that is the *vaisya*, continued as *gramini* and *grhpati*, villagers and household heads. Their role was that of creating the wealth on which the *ksatriya* and brahman depended or, as the texts have it, on which *ksatriya* and brahman might 'graze'. In pursuit of this productive ideal many *vaisya* accumulated land holdings while others invested in trade and industry. Much later, just as the *ksatriya* in recognition of their martial status would be equated with 'rajputs', so the *vaisya* would be identified with the essentially mercantile 'bania'.

Beyond the pale of the *arya* were a variety of indigenous peoples like the despised *dasa* of the Vedas. All were, nevertheless, subject to varying degrees of Aryanisation. Some, perhaps in recognition of their numerical superiority in regions newly penetrated by the clans, were actually co-opted into the three *dvija* castes while their cults and deities were accommodated in the growing pantheon of what we now call Hinduism. Others obstinately retained forms of speech and conduct which disqualified them from co-option and, perhaps as a result of conquest, they were relegated to functional roles considered menial and impure. *Dasa* came to denote a household slave or rural helot and *dasi* a female domestic or slave-concubine. Slavery was not, however, practised on a scale comparable to that in Greece or Rome, perhaps because most of these indigenous peoples were in fact assigned an intermediate status as *sudra*. The term is of uncertain origin and seems also to have embraced those born of mixed-caste parentage. Its functional connotation is clear enough, however. Just as the *vaisya* was expected to furnish wealth, the *sudra* was expected to furnish labour.

These then were the four earliest castes, and a much-quoted passage from the latest mandala (X) of the Rig Veda clearly shows their relative status. When, in the course of a gory creation myth, the gods were carving up the sacrificial figure who represented mankind, they chose to chop him into four bits, each of which prefigured a caste. 'The brahman was his mouth, of both arms was the *rajanya* (*ksatriya*) made, his thighs became the *vaisya*, from his feet the *sudra* was produced.'[13] Thus organised into a stratified hierarchy, each caste was theoretically immutable and exclusive; the purity taboos which derived from sacrificial ritual provided barriers to

physical contact, while the lineage obsessions of clan society provided barriers to intermarriage.

The term used for caste in the Vedas is *varna*, 'colour', which, in the
context of the *arya*'s disparaging comments about the 'black' *dasa*, is often
taken to mean that the higher castes also considered themselves the fairer-
skinned. This is now disputed. According to the *Mahabharata* the 'colours'
associated with the four castes were white, red, yellow and black; they
sound more like symbolic shades meted out by those category-conscious
brahmanical minds than skin pigments. Similarly the excessive rigidity of
the caste system should not be taken for granted. Then as now, caste was
not necessarily an indicator of economic worth; even the four-tier hierarchy
was variable, with *ksatriya* more dominant than brahmans in the republics;
and entry into the system – indeed progression within it – was never
impossible. It may be precisely because alien cults, tribes and professions
could in time, if willing to conform, be slotted into its open-ended shelving
that the system proved so pervasive and durable: '*Varna* was a mechanism
for assimilation.'[14] Though undoubtedly a form of systematised oppression,
it should also be seen as an ingenious schema for harnessing the loyalties
of a more numerous and possibly more skilled indigenous population.
Certainly, like the NBP ware, its acceptance from one end of northern
India to the other hinted at a social, cultural and linguistic cohesion which
belied the multiplicity of states and could – indeed imminently would –
transcend them.

In Buddhist texts, and in common parlance even today, the more usual
word for caste is not *varna* but *jati*. *Jati* derives from a verb meaning 'to
be born', the emphasis being less on the degree of ritual purity, as in the
four-tier *varna*, and more on caste determination as a result of being born
into a particular kinship group. If *varna* provided the theoretical framework,
jati came to represent the practical reality. With society assuming a complexity undreamed of in Vedic times, caste formation was veering away
from ritual status to take greater account of the proliferation of localised
and specialised activities. Geographical, tribal, sectarian and, above all,
economic and professional specialisations determined a group's *jati*.

Specialisation plumbed the depths of the social hierarchy, with tasks like
disposing of the dead keeping the lowly *candala* as outcastes, irredeemably
degraded by the nature of their work. It also cleft the pinnacles of the
system, with some brahman groups artfully deploying their expertise as
kingmakers and dynastic-legitimisers, while others had to rest content with
handling ritual requirements at domestic and village level.

In the monarchical states leading associates of the ruling lineage assumed quasi-bureaucratic functions within the royal retinue. As the *rat-nins*, or 'treasures', of ancient ritual, their designations date back to Vedic times and include such functionaries as the charioteer, the huntsman and the bard. Out of their ranks arose the *senapati*, or *senani*, who became commander of the army, and the *purohita*, or high priest. The charioteer seems to have become a treasurer, and the messenger 'an official who looked after the state horses and was responsible for the maintenance of dynastic tradition'.[15] A similar process whereby household officials became officers of state would apply in Europe: in the Norman kingdoms the master of the royal stables (*comes stabuli*) became the 'constable' of the realm, and the keeper of the royal mares (*mareschal*) the 'marshal' of the realm.

But it is in trade and manufacturing that specialisation is most apparent. The carpenter, once one of the royal retinue, or *ratnins*, by reason of his skill in building chariots, was now joined by a host of other craftsmen – ironsmiths and goldsmiths, potters, weavers, herbalists, ivory-carvers. Some were tied to a particular locality or village by their source of raw materials; others were encouraged to settle in designated areas of the new cities and towns by their predominantly royal patrons. Physically segregated and learning their skills by hereditary association, such groups were readily accorded *jati* status which, in the context of their specialisation, bore a close affinity to a professional fraternity or guild. Besides being more numerous and capable of endless proliferation, each *jati* was firmly based on an economic community. They contained an element of mutual support, and they may be seen as extending caste organisation deep into the burgeoning economies of the new states.

Similar changes may have been underway in peninsular India. Since neither Mahavira nor the Buddha ventured south, their followers had little to record of the area and there are no textual sources for it before the end of the first millennium BC. But it is clear that by then proto-states were well established in the extreme south and that they were already engaged in maritime trade. How much they owed to Aryanising influences is debatable. Although the epics were evidently known and brahmans respected, social stratification took a rather un-Aryan form, with different taboos and no place for two of the four *varnas*. In fact to this day indigenous *vaisya* and *ksatriya* castes are practically unknown in peninsular India.

Out of the Myth-Smoke

C520–C320 BC

INDUS AND INDIA

MAPS PRINTED AFTER 1947 sometimes show the republic of India not as 'India' but as 'Bharat'. The word derives from *Bharata-varsha*, 'the land of the Bharatas', these Bharatas being the most prominent and distinguished of the early Vedic clans. By adopting this term the new republic in Delhi could, it was argued, lay claim to a revered *arya* heritage which was geographically vague enough not to provoke regional jealousies, and doctrinally vague enough not to jeopardise the republic's avowed secularism.

In the first flush of independence 'Bharat' would seem preferable, because the word 'India' was too redolent of colonial disparagement. It also lacked a respectable indigenous pedigree. For although British claims to have incubated an 'India consciousness' were bitterly contested, there was no gainsaying the fact that in the whole colossal corpus of Sanskrit literature nowhere called 'India' is ever mentioned; nor does the term occur in Buddhist or Jain texts; nor was it current in any of South Asia's numerous other languages. Worse still, if etymologically 'India' belonged anywhere, it was not to the republic proclaimed in Delhi by Jawaharlal Nehru but to its rival headed by Mohammed Ali Jinnah in Pakistan.

Partition would have a way of dividing the subcontinent's spoils with scant reference to history. Pakistan inherited the majority of the main Harappan sites, so depriving India of the most tangible proof of its vaunted antiquity. Conversely, India inherited most of the subcontinent's finest Islamic architecture, so depriving Muslim Pakistanis of what they regard as their own glorious heritage. No tussle over the word 'India' is reported because Jinnah preferred the newly coined and very Islamic-sounding acronym that is 'Pakistan' (see p. 496). Additionally, he was under the impression that neither state would want to adopt the British title of 'India'. He only discovered his mistake after Lord Mountbatten, the last British viceroy, had already acceded to Nehru's demand that his state remain 'India'. Jinnah, according to Mountbatten, 'was absolutely furious when he found out that they [Nehru and the Congress Party] were going to call themselves India'.[1] The use of the word implied a subcontinental primacy which Pakistan would never accept. It also flew in the face of history, since 'India' originally referred exclusively to territory in the vicinity of the Indus river (with which the word is cognate). Hence it was largely outside the republic of India but largely within Pakistan.

The reservations about the word 'India', which had convinced Jinnah that neither side would use it, stemmed from its historical currency amongst outsiders, especially outsiders who had designs on the place. Something similar could, of course, be said about terms like 'Britain', 'Germany' or 'America'; when first these words were recorded, all were objects of conquest. But in the case of 'India' this demeaning connotation had lasted until modern times. 'Hindustan', 'India' or 'the Indies' (its more generalised derivative) had come, as if by definition, to denote an acquisition rather than a territory. Geographically imprecise, indeed moveable if one took account of all the 'Indians' in the Americas, 'India' was yet conceptually concrete: it was somewhere to be coveted – as an intellectual curiosity, a military pushover and an economic bonanza. To Alexander the Great as to Mahmud of Ghazni, to Timur the Lame as to his Mughal descendants, and to Nadir Shah of Persia as to Robert Clive of Plassey, 'India' was a place worth the taking.

The first occurrence of the word sets the trend. It makes its debut in an inscription found at Persepolis in Iran, which was the capital of the Persian or Achaemenid empire of Darius I, he whose far-flung battles included defeat at Marathon by the Athenians in 490 BC. Before this, Darius had evidently enjoyed greater success on his eastern frontier, for the Persepolis inscription, dated to c518 BC, lists amongst his numerous domains that of 'Hi(n)du'.

The word for a 'river' in Sanskrit is *sindhu*. Hence *sapta-sindhu* meant '[the land of] the seven rivers', which was what the Vedic *arya* called the Panjab. The Indus, to which most of these seven rivers were tributary, was the *sindhu par excellence*; and in the language of ancient Persian, a near relative of Sanskrit, the initial 's' of a Sanskrit word was invariably rendered as an aspirate – 'h'. *Soma*, the mysterious hallucinogen distilled, deified and drunk to excess by the Vedic *arya*, is thus *homa* or *haoma* in old Persian; and *sindhu* is thus *Hind[h]u*. When, from Persian, the word found its way into Greek, the initial aspirate was dropped, and it started to appear as the route 'Ind' (as in 'India', 'Indus', etc.). In this form it reached Latin and most other European languages. However, in Arabic and related languages it retained the initial 'h', giving 'Hindustan' as the name by which Turks and Mughals would know India. That word also passed on to Europe to give 'Hindu' as the name of the country's indigenous people and of what, by Muslims and Christians alike, was regarded as their infidel religion.

On the strength of a slightly earlier Iranian inscription which makes no mention of *Hindu*, it is assumed that the region was added to Darius' Achaemenid empire in or soon after 520 BC. This earlier inscription does, however, refer to 'Gadara', which looks like Gandhara, a *maha-janapada* or 'state' mentioned in both Sanskrit and Buddhist sources and located in an arc reaching from the western Panjab through the north-west frontier to Kabul and perhaps into southern Afghanistan (where 'Kandahar' is the same word). According to Xenophon and Herodotus, Gandhara had been conquered by Cyrus, one of Darius' predecessors. The first Achaemenid or Persian invasion may therefore have taken place as early as the mid-sixth century BC. That it was an invasion, rather than a migration or even perhaps a last belated influx of charioteering *arya*, seems likely from a reference to Cyrus dying of a wound inflicted by the enemy. The enemy were the 'Derbikes'; they enjoyed the support of the *Hindu* people and were supplied by them with war-elephants. In Persian and Greek minds alike, the association of *Hindu* with elephants was thereafter almost as significant as its connection with the mighty Indus. To Alexander of Macedon, following in the Achaemenids' footsteps two centuries later, the river would be a geographical curiosity, but the elephants were a military obsession.

If Gandhara was already under Achaemenid rule, Darius' *Hindu* must have lain beyond it, and so to the south or the east. Later Iranian records refer to *Sindhu*, presumably an adoption of the Sanskrit spelling, whence derives the word 'Sind', now Pakistan's southernmost province. It seems unlikely, though, that *Sindhu* was Sind in the late sixth century BC, since Darius subsequently found it necessary to send a naval expedition to explore the Indus. Flowing through the middle of Sind, the river would surely have been familiar to any suzerain of the region. More probably, then, *Hindu* lay east of Gandhara, perhaps as a wedge of territory between it, the *janapadas* of eastern Panjab, and the deserts of Rajasthan. It thus occupied much of what is now the Panjab province of Pakistan.

Under Xerxes, Darius' successor, troops from what had become the Achaemenids' combined 'satrapy' of Gandhara and *Hindu* reportedly served in the Achaemenid forces. These Indians were mostly archers, although cavalry and chariots are also mentioned; they fought as far afield as eastern Europe; and some were present at the Persians' bloody victory over Leonidas and his Spartans at Thermopylae, and then at the decisive defeat by the Greeks at Plataea. Through these and other less fraught contacts between Greeks and Persians, Greek writers like Herodotus gleaned some idea of 'India'. Compared to the intervening lands of Anatolia and Iran, it appeared a veritable paradise of exotic plenty. Herodotus told of an immense population and of the richest soil imaginable from which kindly ants, smaller than dogs but bigger than foxes, threw up hillocks of pure gold-dust. The ants may have intrigued entomologists, but the gold was what registered in political circles. With rivers to rival the Nile and behemoths from which to give battle, it was clearly a land of fantasy as well as wealth.

Herodotus, of course, knew only of the Indus region, and that by hearsay. Hence he did not report that the land of *Hindu* was of sensational extent, nor did he deny the popular belief that beyond its furthest desert, where in reality the Gangetic plain interminably spreads, lay the great ocean which supposedly encircled the world; *Hindu* or 'India' (but in fact Pakistan) was therefore believed to be the end of *terra firma*, a worthy culmination to any emperor's ambitions as well as a fabulous addition to his portfolio of conquests. In abbreviated form, Herodotus' *History* circulated widely. A hundred years after his death it was still avidly read by northern Greeks in Macedonia, where a teenage Alexander 'knew it well enough to quote and follow its stories'.[2]

The traffic that resulted from the Achaemenid incursion into India was not all one-way. It may well have been from contacts between Indian troops and the enemies of the Achaemenid empire that Sanskrit acquired a name for the Greeks. Long before Alexander's arrival on the scene, they became known in India as *Yona* or *Yavana*, words derived from a Persian spelling of 'Ionian' but which would thereafter serve to designate almost any people belonging to the lands west of the Indus who were alien to India's traditions. Such peoples were also by definition *mleccha* (foreign and unable to speak properly), and hence despicably casteless. But caste being assimilative as well as exclusive, they might, as overlords, aspire to the status of *vratya ksatriya*, or 'degenerate' *ksatriya*. Macedonians, Bactrians, Kushans, Scythians and Arabs would all at some time be called *Yavanas*, and many would eventually be awarded *vratya* caste status.

WHERE WEST MEETS EAST

On the frontier of the Achaemenids' Indian satrapy lay the city of Taxila (Takashila). Some thirty kilometres from what is now Pakistan's capital of Islamabad, it was not agriculturally disadvantaged, although in the absence of major irrigation schemes the Panjab was scarcely the land of wheat, sugarcane and canals which it is today. Indeed, Taxila seems to have owed its early urbanisation more to its economically strategic location. Here, by way of rugged trails like that of the Khyber from Afghanistan, passed all trade – horses, gold, precious stones and luxury textiles – between the Achaemenid world and the emerging Gangetic states. The city prospered as did the satrapy. According to Herodotus, the latter yielded to the Achaemenids a tribute of 'ant-gold' which was nearly five times more than the tribute extracted from Babylon and seven times that from Egypt.

Such wealth attracted to Taxila artisans and scholars as well as merchants. Sir John Marshall, who excavated the site in the 1940s, found three cities, the oldest of which lay beneath the Bhir Mound. There rubble walls indicated several levels of occupation, beginning with one which certainly belonged to the Iron Age and probably to 'the close of the sixth century BC'.

> ... it would follow that this, the earliest settlement on the Bhir Mound, was little, if at all earlier than the invasion of Darius I; and it may even be plausibly conjectured, though there is no tangible evidence to support the conjecture, that Taxila owed its foundation to the Persian conqueror.[3]

Amongst Taxila's imports from the west came the Aramaic script, which may have been the first script to be used in India since that of the Harappans. Whether or not the city was founded by the Achaemenids, it began heavily in debt to its western contacts, and would later become something of a showcase for imported western and even Mediterranean ideas and artefacts.

Yet it was also revered as a citadel of orthodoxy by the *janapadas* in the east. In the *Ramayana* it is claimed that Taxila was founded by one of Lord Rama's nephews; in the *Mahabharata* it is said that it was actually at Taxila that the story of the great Bharata war was first told. Clearly the place was highly regarded throughout northern India. Students went there to learn the purest Sanskrit. Kautilya, whose *Arthasastra* is the classic Indian treatise on statecraft, is said to have been born there in the third century BC. It was also in Taxila that, in the previous century, Panini compiled a grammar more comprehensive and scientific than any dreamed of by Greek grammarians. 'One of the greatest intellectual achievements of any ancient civilisation',[4] it so refined the literary usage of the day that the language became permanently 'frozen' and was ever after known as *Samskrta* ('perfected', hence 'Sanskrit'). Given the defining role of language in *arya* identity, ritual observance and social differentiation, the importance of Panini's work and of Taxila's patronage can scarcely be exaggerated.

From Panini's examples of different grammatical forms some historical information may also be garnered. 'Eastern Bharatas', for instance, is Panini's example of tautology and verbosity; the 'eastern', he implies, is a superfluous qualification since everyone knows that Bharatas live in the east. It follows that by the fourth century BC all clans claiming Bharata descent must long have been located to the east of Taxila – like the Kuru in the Doab. Incidentally, by this chance example Panini also hinted at a definition of *Bharata-varsha* which, as 'Bharat', would nicely serve the purposes of twentieth-century nationalists in a Pakistan-less India.

Legitimacy as conferred by descent from the Bharatas, or one of the other *arya* clans, was yet more critical to emerging dynasties of dubious origin in the late first millennium BC. It accounts for the emphasis on genealogy in the much-revised epics and for the manipulation of descent lines in the *Puranas*; it may also account, along with trade, for the primacy accorded to Taxila located in the heartland of the *arya*'s original 'land of the seven rivers'.

Nowhere was this need for legitimacy more acutely felt than amongst the thrusting new states and cities far away to the east in Bihar and Uttar Pradesh. By way of the *uttarapatha*, the 'Northern Route' along the base of the Himalayas, they maintained close contacts with Taxila and, judging by the punch-marked coins found in the Bhir Mound, were soon financing much of its trade. To them the city owed its prominence quite as much as to Achaemenid enterprise. For while Gandhara and 'India' remained under Achaemenid suzerainty well into the fourth century BC, another would-be imperium, India's first and much its proudest, had begun flexing its muscles in the distant plains of southern Bihar.

Here, in the kingdom of Magadha, between the south bank of the sprawling Ganga and the rolling forests of Chota Nagpur, in a region today of the bleakest rural poverty with cities of almost unendurable squalor, the historian's patience is finally rewarded. From a pre-historic dawn as shrouded in myth as any, the smoke of burnt offerings and ancient obscurities begins at last to lift. A sparsely featured but genuinely historical landscape is briefly revealed.

At the easternmost extremity of the *uttarapatha*, the kingdom of Magadha, with its capital at Rajagriha (Rajgir), occupied the region between today's unlovely cities of Patna and Gaya. Its location coincided with that of the sacred trails trodden by the Buddha and Mahavira; and its rise coincided with their followers' concern for an accurate record of the masters' lives and teachings. In consequence, a succession of authentic historical figures, together with a chain of related events, at last looms dimly from the myth-smoke.

THE MARCH OF MAGADHA

Only the dates remain problematic. Buddhist sources show a healthy respect for chronology, and usually disdain the mathematical symmetries and astronomical exaggerations found in Vedic and Jain texts. Like Christians, they count the years to, and then from, a major event in the life of their founder. Thus, just as Christians measure time from the birth of Christ, so do Buddhists from the death, or *parinirvana* (achievement of *nirvana*), of the Buddha. Neither of these benchmarks can be determined with absolute precision. But because the Christian BC/AD system has become something of an international convention, it matters little that Christ may in fact have been born, not in zero AD, but several years later. On the other hand, it matters much that, depending on the tradition endorsed, the Buddha may have died either 350 to 400, 483 to 486, or even 544 years 'Before Christ'.

Obviously, if the Buddhist chronology had commanded international regard, an agreed date for the *parinirvana* would long since have emerged, and it would then be the uncertainties about when Christ was born in terms of the Buddhist reckoning which would be considered unsettling. Euro-centric, or Christo-centric, assumptions about the measurement of time should be viewed with caution. Like those map projections which give mid-sheet prominence to Europe or the Americas, they carry an inherent distortion.

Nevertheless, the widely divergent dates adduced for the Buddha's *parinirvana* do pose serious problems. That of 544 BC derives from a much later Sri Lankan tradition and is usually discarded. As between the 486 BC of Indian tradition and the 483 BC of a Chinese record, the difference is slight and not too important. Indeed, it was the near congruence of these two dates which led the majority of scholars to accept their validity; one or other was used to deduce a date for the Buddha's birth of c566–3 BC, which thus became 'the earliest certain date in Indian history'. Recently, however, opinion has swung towards a much later dating for the *parinirvana*, in fact 'about eighty to 130 years before Ashoka's coronation [in 268 BC], i.e. not a very long time before Alexander's Indian campaign [327–5BC], i.e. between c400 BC and c350 BC'.[5] This reappraisal of the evidence, mainly by German scholars, shunts the Buddha forward by around a century. Besides promoting the Achaemenid conquest of *Hindu* in c520 BC to the status of India's first (more or less) certain date, it carries potentially devastating consequences for the chronology of just about every development in India of the first millennium BC. The Vedic period may have to be extended into the sixth century, state-formation and urbanisation brought forward to the fifth century, and the chronology of Magadha before the appearance of Ashoka condensed into a hundred years.

Alternatively, it may be taken to suggest a much longer time-lapse between the India of later Vedic texts, like the *Upanisads*, and that of the earliest Buddhist and Jain texts. Even a cursory acquaintance with these sources leaves the reader wondering whether they can possibly refer to the same society. The Sanskrit texts evoke a mostly agrarian way of life in which states play a minor part and status is governed by lineage and ritual observance. Buddhist and Jain texts, on the other hand, portray a network of functioning states, each with an urban nucleus heavily engaged in trade and production. Here wealth as much as lineage confers status. Indeed, the Buddhist concept of 'merit' as something to be earned, accumulated, occasionally transferred and eventually realised seems inconceivable without a close acquaintance with the moneyed economy. By interleaving between these two societies a further century, Buddhism's newly revised or 'short chronology' allows for a more gradual and credible evolution of state and city without unduly taxing the archaeological record.

Similarly, it allows room for the evolution of a tradition of heterodoxy and dissent. Buddhist texts in particular portray a society that was already in religious ferment when the Buddha was born. Rival holy-men swarm across the countryside performing feats of endurance, disputing one another's spiritual credentials and vying with one another for followers and patronage. That this was not simply the impression of partisan hotheads is shown by the dispassionate Kautilya whose compendium on statecraft, the *Arthasastra*, recognises such renunciates as an important constituent of any state; they are to be given legal protection and free passage; special forest areas are to be allotted to them for meditation, and special lodging-houses in the city. Saints or charlatans, they evidently mirrored a society to which the paranormal, the supernatural and the metaphysical had a strong appeal. Many of them went naked or unwashed and they cheerfully flouted the taboos of caste status. Defying social convention, they yet enjoyed society's indulgence. Renunciation had become an accepted way of life in which asceticism was seen as a prerequisite to spiritual enlightenment.

The philosophies on offer from this rag-tag army of reformers ranged from mind-boggling mysticism to defiant nihilism and blank agnosticism, from the outright materialism of the Lokayats to the heavy determinism of the Ajivikas, and from the rationalism of the Buddha to the esotericism of Mahavira. Most, however, agreed in condemning the extravagance of Vedic sacrifice, in sidelining the Vedic pantheon, and in ignoring brahmanical authority. Moreover many, including the Jains, Buddhists and Ajivikas, recognised an assortment of antecedents whose teachings or experiences had in some sense anticipated their own. In other words, Mahavira, the Buddha, and Gosala of the Ajivikas acknowledged well established traditions of heterodoxy; and as one might infer from their own reception, they were able to capitalise on an already existing thirst for spiritual and moral guidance, as well as on an abiding credulity. Clearly the new sources of wealth and authority associated with state-formation and urbanisation had plunged society into a crisis which the rigidities of the *varnasramadharma* (the organisation of society into caste *varnas* and into social vocations based on age) could scarcely accommodate, and to which the ritual oblations of the Vedas seemed irrelevant as well as wildly extravagant.

Adopting, then, not the conventional 486–3 B C for the *parinirvana* but some date between 400 and 350 B C, one may place the birth of Siddhartha Gautama, the 'Buddha', some time in the mid-fifth century. Like his contemporary, Mahavira Nataputta of the Jains, he was a *ksatriya*, the son of Suddhodana, *raja* of the Sakyas. The Sakya state being one of those republican *gana-sanghas*, it had many *rajas*. And since their chief was elected, the 'Prince' Siddhartha of later legend must be considered a fabrication. Moreover, Kapilavastu, the Sakya capital, was not a major political centre. Just within the southern border of present-day Nepal, it may have served as a staging post on the *uttarapatha*. Trade and craftsmanship were more the Buddha's milieu than royal ceremonial. The affluence against which he eventually reacted by renouncing his wife and family to begin an enquiry into the human condition may have been real; equally it may have been the perceived luxury of more celebrated urban centres like Vaisali, capital of the Licchavis, or the Koshalan metropolis of Sravasti, or Rajagriha in Magadha.

In the course of his quest, Siddhartha visited all of these places and studied under a variety of distinguished but ultimately unconvincing teachers. On one occasion, while traversing Magadha, he met its king. His

name was Bimbisara and the date (given the Buddhist 'short chronology')
must have been around 400 BC. Bimbisara's origins are uncertain, but he
is said to have lived for over fifty years. He was now in the middle of his
reign, and had already added to his domain the important kingdom of
Anga.

Anga lay to the east, with its famed capital at Champa in west Bengal.
Thence Magadha gained access by river to the Bay of Bengal, where Tamluk
(Tamralipti, near Calcutta) would become a thriving port for trade with
the peninsula, Burma and Sri Lanka. Having inherited access to the rich
copper and iron deposits of southern Bihar, Bimbisara had thus in effect
laid another of the foundations of Magadhan supremacy. Seemingly a just
and practical ruler, he married much but not always wisely. Dealings with
Koshala, Avanti (Malwa), Taxila and the Licchhavis are recorded and, with
the exception of the last, they were generally amicable. A rudimentary
administrative system is evident and, possessed of a ready source of both
elephants and metals, it has been suggested that Magadha's military establishment was well equipped and professionally organised. Whether Bimbisara worried about manpower being drained off by the ferment of heterodox
sects is not recorded. But he did advise the wandering Siddhartha to return
to his proper *ksatriya* station, and offered to provide him with a suitable
establishment.

The advice was rejected. For the next few years Siddhartha remained
in Magadha but was much on the move. Like those earlier exiles in the epics,
he had forsaken the security of a settled, civilised life for the uncertainties of
the vagrant and the outcaste. Austerities, whether unavoidable or self-
imposed, cowed the appetites, cleared the mind, and let the spirit soar.
After prolonged meditation beneath a tree at the place henceforth called
Buddh Gaya, the now thirty-five-year-old Siddhartha Gautama at last isolated the nature of suffering and transience, formulated a scheme for overcoming it, and so attained Enlightenment. As the Buddha, the 'Enlightened
One', he hastened to Varanasi, and in the Deer Park at nearby Sarnath,
evidently one of those forest areas reserved for ascetics, he propounded his
reasoning to five erstwhile companions in what is known as the First
Sermon.

The imagery of the Buddha's 'Middle Way' (between the extremes of
indulgence and asceticism) with its 'Noble Eightfold Path', as also that of
the 'Wheel of *Dharma*' and of the 'Three Refuges' (the Buddha, the *dharma*
or teaching, and the *sangha* or monastic community), clearly reflected the
itinerant's experience. Buddhism began as a code for the road, a set of
rationalised precepts designed to direct and smooth man's progress along

life's unhappy highway. Suffering came from within, from desire and indulgence. By mastering desire, restraining indulgence and yet eschewing
extreme asceticism, the human condition became bearable, and merit might
be accumulated whereby release (*nirvana*) might eventually be attained.
The notion of continuous rebirths and the challenge of escaping from their
endless cycle were common to both orthodox teachings derived from the
Upanisads and to the Buddha's teaching. Buddhism was not a belief system,
not a rival faith to the post-Vedic cults and practices which prevailed under
brahmanical direction, but more a complementary discipline. About gods,
worship, offerings, prayers, priests and ritual, the Buddha claimed no special
knowledge. He offered merely heightened insight, not divine revelation. It
was his followers in the generations to come who would elevate the Buddha
and other semi-enlightened ones (Boddhisatvas) into deities, thus claiming
for Buddhism the authority and the supernatural paraphernalia of a
religion.

For the remaining forty-four years of his long life the Buddha continued
as a wandering ascetic, criss-crossing the states bordering the middle Ganga.
Teaching and elaborating his ideas to an ever-growing band of followers,
especially merchants and artisans, he also won the support of kings, this
being a prerequisite for the establishment of the communities of followers
and the monastic institutions which would continue his mission after his
parinirvana.

Amongst the kings who patronised the new teaching were Prasenajit,
king of Koshala, and Magadha's Bimbisara. In the Koshalan capital of
Sravasti the Buddha delivered numerous discourses and, since his own
Sakya republic had been overrun by Koshala and remained under its suzerainty, he may have felt some allegiance to Prasenajit. But it was Bimbisara's
patronage that would prove crucial. When the Buddha died (at Kushinara
in the Malla republic), it was Bimbisara's Magadha which made good its
claim to most of his hotly contested relics and, immediately afterwards, it
was in the Magadhan capital of Rajagriha that the first Buddhist council
was convened. Magadha's economic expansion provided a social ambience
particularly favourable to Buddhism. In the wake of Magadha's political
expansion Buddhism would prevail over most of the other heterodox sects
(although not brahmanical orthodoxy) and spread throughout the subcontinent.

Meanwhile, Bimbisara had predeceased the Buddha. His long reign
came to an end when Ajatashatru, one of his sons, either seized the throne
and starved his father to death or was nominated his successor so that the
aged Bimbisara, having renounced the throne, could starve himself to death.

Both practices appear to have been standard. But Ajatashatru's elevation was not uncontested and his conduct not unchallenged. He was soon involved in warfare with both Koshala and a powerful coalition of republics headed by the Licchavis. Magadha was about to take another giant stride towards hegemony in the middle Ganga region.

The trouble with Koshala seems to have arisen over a piece of land in the vicinity of Varanasi. It had passed to Bimbisara as the dowry of his Koshalan bride. When she died of grief over Bimbisara's death, Prasenajit of Koshala, her father, revoked the grant of this land and resumed control of it. Ajatashatru endeavoured to retake it but seems at first to have been defeated. His claim to the disputed enclave was, however, enhanced when the aged Prasenajit, falling prey to the usurpation of his own son, headed for Magadha as a supplicant. Alone but for a devoted servant, the old king reached the walls of Rajagriha and there, while waiting overnight for the gates to open, died of exhaustion and exposure. Despite their past differences, Ajatashatru of Magadha promptly honoured the memory of this Indian Lear and vowed to avenge his treatment by the Koshalans. But he bided his time, first dealing with another major threat to his kingdom and then benefiting from the chance annihilation of the Koshalan army; encamped in the dry bed of the river Rapti, it had been suddenly overwhelmed by a flash flood. Thereafter, although the sources are silent on the details, Ajatashatru seems to have overrun Koshala, which promptly disappears from the record.

This important conquest was made possible by a decisive Magadhan victory in the protracted struggle with its other principal neighbour, namely the Licchavi republic. The Licchavis, with their capital at Vaisali wherein lived those innumerable Licchavi *rajas*, headed a confederation of republics to the north of Magadha. As with the defeated Sakyas, their defiance has been seen as part of a last stand by the 'knights-*raja*' of the republican *gana-sanghas* of the east against the professional armies of the centralised monarchies of the Ganga valley. Here again, though, Magadha's problem seems to have started back in the reign of Bimbisara and to have been greatly complicated by an affair of the heart.

As one might expect in a republic, the beautiful Amrapali (or Ambarapali) was not a princess. In fact she was a courtesan whose physical perfection and outstanding skills had secured her elevation to the status of a national asset. In other republics an elaborate beauty contest was held to select the principal courtesan, and this may also have been the case in Vaisali. But Amrapali, as befitted one of the Buddha's most devoted future followers, was shrewd as well as comely. Though her favours were supposedly reserved exclusively for those 7707 (or 'twice 84,000') Licchavi 'knights-*raja*', she also wielded great political influence and became, in effect, Vaisali's 'first lady'. It was therefore a crushing blow to Licchavi self-esteem when it was discovered that, in the midst of desultory fighting with Magadha, the Magadhan king had entered Vaisali in disguise and, undetected, had there enjoyed a week's dalliance in Amrapali's delectable company. Bimbisara had to be made to pay for his indiscretion, and the Licchavis had duly multiplied their attacks on Magadhan territory.

Admittedly the detail of this story survives only in a later Tibetan source. Better known, it would surely have inspired poignant verse and operatic libretti. But from other Buddhist texts it is clear that Bimbisara did indeed incur the wrath of the Licchavis and that 'something really harmful and injurious'[6] provoked his son Ajatashatru to seek revenge. The subsequent war seems to have lasted on and off for at least twelve years. Initially it was compounded by a succession struggle between Ajatashatru and one of his brothers. The brother, who was domiciled in Anga (presumably as its governor), refused to surrender a priceless necklace. He also withheld an even more priceless elephant which had been trained to act as a shower-hose, sprinkling the ladies of the Magadhan household with a deliciously scented spray when they were bathing. No doubt both necklace and elephant were seen as in the nature of regalia. Ajatashatru's acquisition of them was therefore essential to the legitimacy of his rule. But his brother remained defiant and, fearing attack, eventually fled to Vaisali where he secured the support of the hated Licchavis.

Another account makes the item of dispute a mountain from which oozed a highly prized, because highly scented, unguent; yet another seems to indicate a disputed island in, or port on, the Ganga, which formed the Magadha–Licchavi frontier. We know of such details because Ajatashatru saw fit to consult the Buddha about the impending hostilities and because later Buddhist commentators therefore saw fit to record them, albeit variously. Buddhist sculptors followed suit. In a relief panel from the second-century BC stupa at Bharhut (now in the Calcutta Museum) a demure and most unwarlike Ajatashatru is depicted arriving on elephant-back with a retinue of wives and then making obeisance before the throne of the Buddha. Well preserved in the hard russet sandstone of Bharhut, this eloquent scene may rate as the earliest depiction in Indian art of a genuine historical figure. Buddhist texts also mention that on his last journey north the Buddha, after his meeting with the king but before crossing the Ganga, passed a building site where a new Magadhan fort was being erected. The place was called Pataligrama. To it the Magadhan court would remove under Ajatashatru's successor and, greatly extended and beautified, the city by the Ganga at what is now Patna would become, as Pataliputra, the metropolis of the Magadhan empire under the Mauryas.

In its infancy the fort at Pataligrama failed to overawe the Licchavis. Initially the war seems to have gone badly for Ajatashatru, who may even have been forced to seek terms. Further hostilities, as recorded in Jain sources, produced two epic battles with echoes of the great Bharata war, except that Ajatashatru eventually won both thanks to some precocious mechanisation. A new catapult capable of firing massive rocks was developed, and then a heavily armoured robot equipped with club-wielding arms and powered by some invisible means of propulsion – 'It has been compared to the tanks used in the two great world wars.'[7] Before this veritable *blitzkrieg* the Licchavis withdrew to their capital and prepared for a siege. Evidently even the tank made no impression on Vaisali's fortifications. The siege dragged on, and Ajatashatru was obliged to try psychological warfare. Insinuating into the Licchavi counsels a particularly wily brahman, or suborning the city's tutelary ascetic with an irresistible prostitute, he either reduced his enemies to discord or duped them into surrender. Magadhan forces occupied Vaisali unopposed, the Licchavi republic was finally reduced, and the 7707 *rajas* were dispersed, although not eliminated. When the Second Buddhist Council was convened in Vaisali some time in the latter half of the fourth century BC the city was under Magadhan control.

Thus, in the space of two reigns which conveniently straddled the long life of the Buddha, Magadha had emerged from comparative inconsequence to dominate the lower Ganga with a territorial reach that extended from the Bay of Bengal to the Nepal Himalayas. Further up the Ganga, the kingdom of Vatsya, possibly the successor state to that of the Kuru of Hastinapura, still flourished with its capital at Kaushambi (near Allahabad). So did the kingdom of Avanti, based on Ujjain (near Indore) far to the south on the banks of the Narmada river. Kaushambi and Ujjain were engaged in their own power struggle. Into it Magadha seems occasionally to have been drawn, and from it Ajatashatru's successors were able to profit, although it is unclear when Magadhan supremacy was recognised in these distant regions.

In fact the grave uncertainty which surrounds the history of Magadha immediately after Ajatashatru extends even to the succession. Between Ajatashatru's death some time between c380 BC and c330 BC (according to the 'short chronology') and the accession of Chandragupta Maurya in c320 BC the sources speak mainly of court intrigues and murders. Evidently

the throne changed hands frequently, perhaps with more than one incumbent claiming to occupy it at the same time. Eventually it was secured by
Mahapadma Nanda, the son of a barber and therefore not only a usurper
but also a low-caste *sudra*. According to the orthodox *Puranas*, he invoked
his caste status to conduct a vendetta against all *ksatriyas*. Since most
existing kings were, or claimed to be, *ksatriyas*, this represented a declaration
of war on the entire political order. Remarkable conquests resulted. By 326
BC the Nanda family was ruling over a greatly extended kingdom which
included the whole of the Ganga valley plus Orissa and parts of central
India.

Mahapadma Nanda himself may have been responsible for these conquests. He is the first to be described as a 'one-umbrella sovereign', a
concept closely related to the Buddhist idea of a pan-Indian *cakravartin* or
'world ruler' and implying the association of all existing polities under a
single sovereign. Patriotic Indian historians tend to pounce on this early
evidence of national integration and to hail Mahapadma Nanda as 'the
first great historical emperor of Northern India'. The wealth of the Nandas
also became legendary, and was supposedly buried in a cave in the bed of
the Ganga. Their exactions and unpopularity were remembered too,
although this may have been the result of failing to placate either brahmanical or Buddhist opinion with the munificence expected of royal patrons.

The Nanda family undeniably commanded the most formidable standing army yet seen in India. Military statistics readily lend themselves to
exaggeration, especially when provided by a disappointed adversary. Yet the
Nandas' army of 200,000 infantry, twenty thousand cavalry, two thousand
four-horse chariots and three to six thousand war-elephants would have
represented a formidable force even if decimated by roll-call reality. It was
certainly enough to strike alarm in stout Greek hearts, to awaken in them
fond memories of Thracian wine and olive-rich homesteads beside the
northern Aegean, and to send packing the age's only other contender as a
'one umbrella' world ruler.

THE MACEDONIAN INTRUSION

Alexander the Great's Indian adventure, though a subject of abiding interest
to generations of classically-educated European historians, is not generally
an episode on which historians of Indian nationality bother to dwell. They
rightly note that it 'made no impression historically or politically on India',
and that 'not even a mention of Alexander is to be found in any [of the]

older Indian sources.'[8] 'There was nothing to distinguish his raid in Indian history [except "perfidious massacres" and "wanton cruelty"] . . . and it can hardly be called a great military success as the only military achievements to his credit were the conquest of some petty tribes and states by instalment.'[9]

Alexander's great achievement was not invading India but getting there. A military expedition against the Achaemenid empire, originally planned by his father, became more like a geographical exploration as the men from Macedonia triumphantly probed regions hitherto undreamed of. Anatolia, the modern Turkey, was overrun in 334–3 BC. To protect his southern flank before invading Persia, Alexander then swept down through Phoenicia (Syria and Palestine) to claim Egypt and Libya. That was in 333–2. In 331–0 the last Achaemenid ruler was chased from his homeland and Persepolis was sacked. The twenty-five-year-old Alexander was now master of all that had comprised the largest empire the world had yet seen – all, that is, except for its easternmost provinces, including Gandhara and 'India'.

Although Indian troops still served in the Achaemenid forces, it seems that Gandhara and 'India' had probably slipped from direct Achaemenid rule some time in the mid-fourth century BC. For Alexander it was enough that once upon a time these provinces had indeed been Persian; to excel Darius and Xerxes, he must needs take them. First, though, another long detour was necessary, this time along his northern flank. In 329–8 he pushed north-east into Arachosia (Afghanistan) and then crossed in succession the snows of the Hindu Kush, the swirling Oxus river and the parched scrubland of Sogdia (Uzbekistan). He then laid claim to the Achaemenids' central Asian frontier on the distant Jaxartes (Syr) beyond Samarkand. It was not till late 327 BC that, returned to the vicinity of Kabul, he was ready with a force of fifty thousand to cross India's north-west frontier.

Determined now to upstage not only the empires of Darius and Xerxes but also the mythical conquests of Heracles and Dionysos, Alexander seems increasingly to have seen his progress in terms of a Grail-like quest for the supposedly unattainable. He sought the 'ocean', the ultimate limit of terrestrial empire. Through knowledge of this great 'beyond', he aspired to a kind of enlightenment which, although very different from that of the Buddha, would become a cliché of Western exploration. More crudely, he hankered after sheer bloody immortality. 'His motives need a little imagination,' writes the best of his biographers, who then quotes one of Alexander's companions: 'The truth was that Alexander was always straining after more.'[10]

More was precisely what India offered. Like a tidal wave, news of Alexander's prowess had swept ahead of him, flattening resistance and

sucking him forward. Indian defectors from the Achaemenid forces primed
his interest and paved the way; local malcontents promised support and
provided elephants; judicious potentates sought his friendship. Principal
amongst the latter was a king known to the Greeks as 'Omphis' or 'Taxiles'.
As the latter name implied, he was the ruler of Taxila, reportedly the largest
city between the Indus and the Jhelum; and from a chance mention in an
appendix to Panini's grammar he has since been identified as Ambhi, an
otherwise enigmatic figure in Indian tradition.

'The first recorded instance of an Indian king proving a traitor to his
country'[11] seems an over-harsh judgement on the ambiguous Ambhi of
Taxila. Alexander had divided his forces so that half marched largely unopposed down the Kabul river and across the Khyber Pass, while he himself
led the remainder by a northerly route through the wintry hills to Swat.
There, up among the pine forests of the supposedly impregnable hill fort
of Aornos (Pir-i-Sar), he inflicted one of several vicious and salutary defeats
on the mountain tribes. By the spring of 326 BC, when back in the plains
he crossed the Indus to join up with the rest of his forces, the Macedonian's
reputation stood high.

A city built on trade and scholarship with little in the way of natural
defences stood no chance. Taxila had survived the Achaemenids, indeed
was a part-Achaemenid city. It could manage the Greeks in the same way.
When Alexander descended to the Indus he found thousands of cattle and
sheep, as well as elephants and silver, awaiting him. Ambhi, with nought
to gain by resistance except the annihilation of his illustrious city and the
applause of a very remote posterity, was playing safe. Alexander confirmed
him as his satrap and generously repaid his liberality.

At the time Taxilan territory extended modestly from the Indus to the
Jhelum. Beyond, occupying the next sliver of the Panjab between the Jhelum
and the Chenab, the kingdom of 'Porus' lay across the invaders' line of
march. In Greek as in Indian tradition, Porus is all that Ambhi is not. A
giant of a man, proud, fearless and majestic, he may have owed his name
to Paurava descent, the Pauravas being only slightly less distinguished than
the Bharatas in the pecking order of Vedic clans. Alexander had summoned
him, along with other local rulers, to meet him and render tribute. Porus
welcomed a meeting, adding casually that an appropriate venue would be
the field of battle.

As good as his word, and despite the fact that the monsoon had already
broken, Porus massed his forces on the banks of the Jhelum. Normally the
monsoon brought all campaigning in India to an end. Indian troops were
ill-equipped to fight in the rain, and Porus probably trusted to the flooding

Jhelum to halt the enemy. But Alexander, well used to river crossings, organised boats, duped the enemy as to his crossing place, and between torrential downpours gained the further bank. The battle that followed was anything but a formality. Porus' chariots slithered uncontrollably in the mud and his archers could find no purchase for their massive bows, one end of which had to be planted in the ground. Yet the Indian forces, though outnumbered as more of the enemy crossed the river, fought valiantly. Abristle with spearsmen, the elephant corps trundled across the battlefield like towering bastions on the move. Their repeated charges drove all before them, the Greeks merely peppering them with missiles as they reformed. But Alexander now knew enough of elephants to bide his time. His tactical skills were unmatched, and his cavalry easily outmanoeuvred their rivals. As the battle wore on, the Indians found themselves penned into an ever smaller circumference. Enraged elephants now trampled friend and foe alike. Exhausted, 'they then fell back like ships backing water, and merely kept trumpeting as they retreated with their face to the enemy'. With shields linked, the Macedonian phalanx then pressed in for the kill. 'Upon this, all turned to flight wherever a gap could be found in the cordon of Alexander's cavalry,' according to the account compiled by Arrian.

Porus, wounded but still conspicuously fighting from the largest of the elephants, was captured. 'How did he expect to be treated?' asked Alexander. 'As befits a king,' he famously replied. To the Greeks it sounded, under the circumstances, like an extraordinarily noble and fearless request. Alexander responded magnanimously, reinstating him as king and subsequently augmenting his territories. But Porus' words could as well have been those of Lord Krishna, whose advice to Arjuna in the *Mahabharata* made much the same point. Each must live according to his *dharma*; it was the *dharma* of a *ksatriya* to fight and to embrace the consequences. Probably Porus was not boldly appealing to Alexander's clemency, nor presuming on some brotherhood of sovereignty; he was simply stating his *dharma*.

After exceptionally elaborate celebrations, the Macedonians moved on, continuing east and south across the grain of the Panjab river system. The rains ended and the land blossomed. They crossed the Chenab, then the Ravi. Countless 'cities' capitulated, others, some evidently republican *gana-sanghas*, offered a short-lived resistance. Even to Alexander it was becoming apparent that 'there was no end to the war as long as an enemy remained to be encountered'. Rumours of the vast forces commanded by the Nandas of Magadha (the 'Gangaridae' and 'Prasii' to the Greeks) now began to infiltrate the ranks. 'This information only whetted Alexander's eagerness to advance further,' says Arrian. The Ganga, mightier even than the Indus,

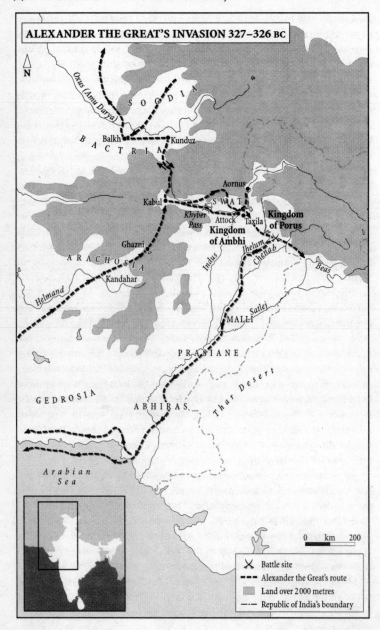

ALEXANDER THE GREAT'S INVASION 327–326 BC

N

Oxus (Amu Darya)

SOGDIA

BACTRIA

Balkh • Kunduz

Aornus

Kabul SWAT

Khyber Pass Attock Taxila **Kingdom of Porus**

Kingdom of Ambhi

Ghazni

ARACHOSIA

Kandahar

Helmand

Indus

Jhelum

Chenab

Beas

Satlej

MALLI

PRASIANE

Thar Desert

GEDROSIA

ABHIRAS

Arabian Sea

0   km   200

✕ Battle site
- - - Alexander the Great's route
▨ Land over 2 000 metres
–·–· Republic of India's boundary

must surely carry them to the ocean at the end of the world. Its plain was reported as exceedingly fertile, its peoples excellent farmers as well as doughty fighters, and its governments civilised and well organised. Alexander sniffed the prospect of an even more glorious dominion.

But his men were unimpressed. They crossed what is now the frontier between Pakistan and India somewhere in the vicinity of Lahore. Then, near Amritsar, they reached the Beas, fourth of the *Panj-ab*, the 'five rivers'. In this weird and interminable land where the clothes were all white and the complexions all black, it was as good a place as any for a showdown with their commander.

Alexander sensed the mood of mutiny. In a lengthy appeal to his commanders he invoked their past loyalty and stressed the consequences of retreat. Extricating themselves would be difficult. Were the tide of conquests now to ebb, they would find the sands sucked from under their feet. New friends would review their allegiance and old enemies would take their chance. Trumpeting an empty defiance, the Greeks would find themselves backing away amidst a shower of missiles just like Porus' exhausted elephants.

But to men who had been on the march for eight years, such arguments had little appeal. They had bathed in the Tigris and the Indus, the Nile and the Euphrates, the Oxus and the Jaxartes. Across desert, mountain, steppe and field they had trudged for over twenty-five thousand kilometres. Of victory, booty, glory and novelty they had had their fill. With respect and real affection, they listened to their leader, moved but unpersuaded.

Alexander withdrew to his tent like his hero Achilles. A three-day sulk made no greater impression on the men's resolve, while a sacrifice for safe passage of the river produced only adverse omens. In the end Alexander had no choice but to announce a withdrawal. The banks of the Beas erupted with cheers of relief; many wept but all rejoiced. As Arrian noted, Alexander was vanquished only once – and that by his own men.

To round off his conquests, complete his explorations, and disguise his failure, Alexander opted to return by sailing down the Jhelum and the Indus to the ocean. Ships were readied and he sailed in late 326 BC. The voyage downriver took six months. Stern opposition came from numerous riverine peoples, some of whom have been tentatively identified, and from sizeable townships which clearly included well established brahman communities. Some of these townships no doubt occupied sites beneath which the Harappan cities had already lain, cocooned in alluvial oblivion, for 1500 years.

In an engagement with the 'Malloi' Alexander himself was seriously wounded. An arrow struck him in the chest and may have punctured his lung. He barely recovered. The wisdom of forgoing a contest with the Nandas' multitudinous cohorts was amply demonstrated; so were the dangers of withdrawal. With few regrets, in September 325 BC the fleet sailed out of the Indus into the Arabian Sea. Meanwhile Alexander led the rest of his men west on what proved to be, for many, a death-march to Babylon along the desert coast of Gedrosia (Makran). There was still some talk of returning to India, of resuming the march with fresh troops, and of consummating the ultimate conquest. But other appetites proved Alexander's undoing. Within two years he died from hepatoma following a massive banquet in Babylon.

With him from India had gone the wherewithal for a vastly enriched Western image of the land beyond the Indus. He had prised open a window on the East through which emissaries would pass, ideas would shine, and prying eyes would covet. With him too went all those Hellenised personae and places – Omphis, Aornos, Porus, the Malloi and countless others – never to be heard of again in India's history. The 'invasion' had amounted to little more than a hasty intrusion, scuffing a corner of the carpet but neither baring its boards nor troubling its political furniture.

With Alexander there had also gone one 'Calanus', a figure worth remembering in that he seems to be the first Indian expatriate to whom a name and a date can confidently be given. One of a group of ascetics encamped near Taxila, Calanus had accepted Alexander's invitation to join him in that city and subsequently accompanied him back to the west. There, in Persia shortly before his patron's death, his own death would cause a sensation.

Calanus' doctrinal persuasion is uncertain. As one of his companions at Taxila had put it, trying to explain one's philosophy through a wall of interpreters was like 'asking pure water to flow through mud'. In that Calanus and his friends went naked, a condition in which no Greek could be persuaded to join them, they may have been *nigrantha* or Jains. Jain nudity was dictated by that sect's meticulous respect for life in all its forms. Clothes were taboo because the wearer might inadvertently crush any insect concealed in them; similarly death had to be so managed that only the dying would actually die. Jains bent on ending their life, therefore, usually starved themselves to death. Yet Calanus, a man of advanced years, chose to immolate himself on his own funeral pyre. Though an extraordinarily stoical sacrifice in Greek eyes, this was a decidedly careless move for one dedicated to avoiding casual insecticide. Evidently the Persian winter had induced a chill, if not pneumonia, and Calanus had decided it was better to die than be an encumbrance. No one, not even Alexander, could dissuade him from his purpose. He strode to his cremation at the head of an enormous procession and reclined upon the pyre with complete indifference. This composure he maintained even as the flames frazzled his flesh.

Visibly shaken by such an exhibition, the Greeks held a festival in his honour and drowned their sorrows in a Bacchanalian debauch. Calanus, though he had made no converts, had won many friends. He also left a profound impression well worthy of India's first cultural emissary. 'Gymnosophists', or 'naked philosophers', henceforth became stock figures in the Western image of India. As 'Pythagoreans', they were also identified with Greek traditions of abstinence and the conjectures of Pythagoras about rebirth and the transmigration of the soul. Lucian, Cicero and Ambrose of Milan all wrote of Calanus and his naked companions. Much later, as the epitome of ascetic puritanism, India's gymnosophists would be revered by, of all people, Cromwellian fundamentalists. And later still, as mystics, gurus and maharishis, they would come again to minister to another spiritually impoverished Western clientele.

Gloria Maurya

C320–200 BC

FLASHES OF INSPIRATION

ALTHOUGH SEVERAL of those who marched east with Alexander wrote of their travels, and although other contemporaries and near-contemporaries compiled lives of Alexander and geographies based on his exploits, none of these survives. Such accounts were, though, still current in Roman times and were used by authors, including Plutarch, the first-century AD biographer, and Arrian, the second-century AD military historian, to compile their own works on Alexander. These do survive. They do not always agree; scraps of information gleaned from other later sources are included indiscriminately; and when describing India, they often dwell on fantastic hearsay. To the gold-digging ants of Herodotus were now added a gallery of gargoyle men with elephant ears in which they wrapped themselves at night, with one foot big enough to serve as an umbrella, or with one eye, with no mouth and so on.

Allowing for less obvious distortions, these accounts yet provide vital clues to the emergence after Alexander's departure of a new north Indian dynasty, indeed of an illustrious empire, one to which the word 'classical' is as readily applied as to those of Greece and Rome – and with good reason, in that it has since served India as an exemplar of political integration and moral regeneration.

In 326 BC, when Alexander was in the Panjab, 'Aggrames' or 'Xandrames' ruled over the Gangetic region according to these Graeco-Roman accounts. His was the prodigious army at which Alexander's men had balked; and his father was the low-born son of a barber and a courtesan who had founded a dynasty with its capital at Pataliputra. 'Andrames' was therefore a Nanda, probably the youngest of Mahapadma Nanda's sons. And since, unusually, these Graeco-Roman accounts agree with the *Puranas* that Nanda rule lasted only two generations, he was the last of his line. Immensely unpopular as well as dismally documented, the second Nanda was about to be overthrown.

According to Plutarch, Alexander had actually met the man who would usurp the Magadhan throne. His name was 'Sandrokottos' ('Sandracottus' in Latin) and in 326 BC he was in Taxila, perhaps studying and already enjoying Taxilan sanctuary as he prepared to rebel against Nanda authority. No such person, however, is known to Indian tradition, the voluminous king-lists in the *Puranas* containing no mention of a 'Sandrokottos' sound-alike. Although from other Greek sources, especially the account of Megasthenes, an ambassador who would visit India in c300 BC, it was evident that someone called Sandrokottos had indeed reigned in the Gang-etic valley, it was still not clear to which if any of the many listed Indian kings he corresponded, nor whether he ruled from Pataliputra, nor whether he could be the same as Plutarch's Sandrokottos. Like Porus and Omphis, it looked as if Sandrokottos was either a minor figure or else someone whose name had been so hopelessly scrambled in its transliteration into Greek that it would never be recognisable in its Sanskritic original.

It was Sir William Jones, the charismatic father of Oriental studies and pioneer of Indo-Aryan linguistics, who in another flash of inspiration res-cued the reputation of Sandrokottos. 'I cannot help mentioning a discovery which accident threw my way,'[1] he told members of the Bengal Asiatic Society in his 1793 annual address. In the course of exploratory forays into Sanskrit literature he had earlier worked out that Sandrokottos' capital could indeed have been the Magadhan city of Pataliputra. He had now come across a mid-first-millennium AD drama, the *Rudra-rakshasa*, which told of intrigues at the court of a King Chandragupta who had usurped the Magadhan throne and received foreign ambassadors there. The flash of inspiration, the 'chance discovery', was that 'Sandrokottos' might be a Greek rendering of 'Chandragupta'. This was later established by the dis-covery of an alternative Greek spelling of the name as 'Sandrakoptos'. The 'Sandrokottos' of Plutarch and of Megasthenes, and the Chandragupta of this play and of occasional mention in the *Puranas*, must be the same person. Crucially and for the first time, a figure well known from Graeco-Roman sources had been identified with one well-attested in Indian tra-dition.

At the time, the late eighteenth century, the excitement generated by this discovery stemmed from its relevance for Indian chronology. Very little was yet known of Chandragupta or the empire he had founded; the latter would only be recognised as an exceptional creation following even more exciting discoveries in the nineteenth century. In Jones's day his breakthrough was applauded solely because it at last made possible some cross-dating between, on the one hand, kings (with their regnal years) as recorded in the *Puranas* and, on the other, ascertainable dates in the history of western Asia. Thus, for instance, if Chandragupta was planning his rebellion against the Nandas when Alexander was in the Panjab, if according to Indian tradition he ruled for twenty-four years, and if Megasthenes, the Greek ambassador to the court of 'Sandrokottos', could not have been sent until after 305 BC, it followed that Chandragupta's revolt must have started soon after 326 BC and have lasted three to four years, so that he then reigned from his many-pillared palace in Pataliputra from approximately 320 to 297 BC. That meant that his successor, Bindusara, ruled from 297 to 272 BC, and that Bindusara's successor, an enigmatic figure who had yet to be clearly identified (let alone accorded universal recognition as 'one of the greatest monarchs the world has ever seen'[2]), must have acceded (after a four-year interregnum) in about 268 BC.

These dates have since been further substantiated by cross-reference with later Buddhist sources. Buddhist and Jain texts have much to say about the dynasty they call 'Maurya' and, along with surviving extracts of the report written by ambassador Megasthenes, plus a truly remarkable series of inscriptions, they constitute important sources for the period. But what would make the early Mauryan empire potentially the best-documented period in the entire history of pre-Muslim India was the discovery of that classic of Indian statecraft, the immensely detailed if almost unreadable text known as the *Arthasastra*. For it would appear that Kautilya, the steely brahman to whom the work is credited, was none other than the instigator, operative, ideologist and chief minister of the self-same Chandragupta. In fact orthodox tradition has it that Kautilya was the kingmaker, and Chandragupta little more than his adopted protégé. Kautilya's great compendium, therefore – with its exhaustive listing of the qualifications and responsibilities required of innumerable state officials, its schema for the conduct of foreign relations and warfare, its enumeration of the fiscal and military resources available to the state, its ruthless suggestions for law enforcement and the detection of dissent, its advocacy of state intervention in all aspects of social and economic activity, and its rules-of-thumb for just about every conceivable political eventuality – such a work should indeed supply uniquely well informed and authoritative insights into the workings of the Mauryan state.

There are, though, grounds for caution. The full text of the *Arthasastra* is comparable in size and excruciating detail to the *Kamasutra* but, though cited 'sometimes eulogistically and sometimes derisively'[3] in other ancient works, it was only discovered in 1904. For Dr R. Shamasastry, the then government of Mysore's chief librarian, as for Sir William Jones, the discovery was accidental. An anonymous pandit simply handed over the priceless collection of palm leaves on which it was written, and then disappeared. Happily, Shamasastry quickly divined the importance of his acquisition; he was also well qualified to undertake its organisation and elucidation. His English translation was published in 1909, since when other editions have appeared and controversy may be said to have raged.

It now seems fairly certain that the work in its present form dates, at the earliest, only from the second century AD, five hundred years after Chandragupta. Moreover, a computer-generated statistical analysis of the frequency with which certain linguistic particles appear in the text would seem to prove that the work was not written by a single author but is an accretion of earlier texts. It may have been compiled by a single person, but it 'has no one creator', writes the American scholar Thomas Trautmann.

> I believe it true to say that the 'author' of the *Arthasastra is* his predecessors, and that his personality as inferred from the work is a composite picture to which three or four different individuals have contributed, one a nose, the other the hair, another the eyes.[4]

Who these individuals were and when they lived is unknown; but Kautilya, though not (as the work implies) its compiler, could well have been one of them. A wily master of intrigue and deception who is elsewhere described as physically deformed, he could have been the eyes. Much of the *Arthasastra* might still be his eye-witness account of the Mauryan state.

But there is another difficulty. Ancient Indian compendia, like the *Kamasutra*, the *Manu-smriti* (the legal Code of Manu) or the *Arthasastra*, none of which was compiled in its present form until the early centuries AD, may not be very reliable guides to actual practice. They were certainly based on observation, but just as it is inconceivable that any swain could have observed all the rules, contrived all the occasions, and mastered all the technical demands of love-making as recorded in the *Kamasutra*, so it seems unlikely that any state can ever have been so minutely organised, so determinedly interventionist, and so uncomfortably vigilant as that in the *Arthasastra*. The latter is, as it says, 'a guide not only for the acquisition of this world but of the next'. Like the Ten Commandments or the Buddha's Noble Eightfold Path, it was a counsel of perfection. Such works should be seen as exercises in comprehending, rationalising and idealising important human activities which, in practice and by implication, may often have been conducted impromptu with inconsistent and unsatisfactory results. Thus if only parts of the *Arthasastra* relate to the Mauryan state, only parts of these parts may be taken to be a statement of how government actually operated under Chandragupta Maurya.

'AN INDIAN JULIUS CAESAR'

Chandragupta Maurya's origins were probably undistinguished; they certainly remain so. Buddhist texts claim that he was related to the Buddha's Sakya clan, others that he was related to the Nandas. Both may be taken as fairly transparent attempts to confer lustre and legitimacy on a new dynasty whose founder was of humble caste, possibly a *vaisya*. If not born in the Panjab, he seems to have spent some time there, as suggested by Plutarch and as confirmed by a legend, found in both Indian and Graeco-Roman sources, associating him with the lion. Tigers were widely distributed throughout India, but the Indian lion, now retaining a clawhold only in a corner of Gujarat, seems never to have roamed further east than Rajasthan and Delhi.

At some point in his youth the self-possessed Chandragupta was adopted as a promising candidate for future glory by Kautilya (otherwise known as Chanakya), a devious and disgruntled brahman who had been slighted at the Nanda court. Kautilya sought his revenge by exploiting the unpopularity of the Nandas; and, disqualified from kingship himself because of deformity (possibly only the loss of his teeth), he championed the ambitions of Chandragupta. An early attempt to overthrow Nanda power in Magadha itself was a failure. Perhaps Kautilya hoped to achieve his ends by a simple *coup d'état* but failed to win sufficient support. The pair resolved to try again, and took their cue from a small boy who was observed to tackle his *chapati* by first nibbling round its circumference. This time, instead of striking at the heart of Nanda power, they would work their way in from its crusty periphery, exploiting dissent and enlisting support amongst its dependent kingdoms before storming the centre.

A good starting place may have been the Panjab, where Alexander's departure had left a potential power vacuum. Settlements founded by the Macedonian seem not to have prospered, and their garrisons to have trailed home or gravitated to older power centres like Taxila. While in western Asia Alexander's successors disputed his inheritance, the Indian satrapies reverted to local control. Ambhi and Porus, designated governors for the region by Alexander, had no love for the Nandas and may, under the circumstances, have felt themselves entitled to endorse Mauryan ambitions. Troops from the *gana-sangha* republics, of which there were still many in the north-west, are also said to have joined Chandragupta, along with other local malcontents. So, more certainly, did a powerful hill chief with whom Kautilya negotiated an offensive alliance.

Overrunning the satellite states and outlying provinces of the Nanda kingdom, the allies eventually converged on Magadha. Pataliputra was probably besieged and, aided no doubt by defectors, the allies triumphed. The last Nanda was sent packing, quite literally: he is supposed to have been spared only his life, plus such of his legendary wealth as he could personally crate and carry away. The hill chief, with whom Kautilya seems previously to have agreed on a partition of the spoils, was then poisoned, probably at Kautilya's instigation, and Chandragupta Maurya ascended the Magadhan throne in, as has been noted, c320 BC.

Of his reign very little is known for certain. There are hints that pockets of Nanda resistance had to be laboriously stamped out, and there is ample information in the *Arthasastra* that could be used, and usually is, to flesh out the policies and methods on which Mauryan dominion was founded. Firm evidence of the extent of this dominion comes mainly from later sources. But since few named conquests can definitely be credited to his successors, it seems likely that Chandragupta, adding the Nandas' vast army to his own, found ample employment for it. He may reasonably be considered the creator as well as the founder of the Mauryan empire, indeed 'an Indian Julius Caesar' as nationalist historians call him (though chronologically speaking Caesar should, of course, be 'a Roman Chandragupta').

The suggestion has also been made that Chandragupta derived the very idea of an empire based on military supremacy from his observation of Alexander's conceit. Yet unlike Alexander, whose campaigns progress from one victorious encounter to the next, he cannot certainly be credited with winning a single battle. The Mauryan empire was probably the most extensive ever forged by an Indian dynasty; even the Mughals rarely achieved a wider hegemony. Yet we have positive knowledge of only one campaign undertaken by a Mauryan ruler – and we know of that only because the man responsible chose publicly to express his remorse. All of which may say more about relative attitudes to the past and about the variable nature of the source materials than about Mauryan imperialism.

In assessing Chandragupta's conquests it would be helpful to know the extent of the empire to which he succeeded when he overthrew the Nandas. We can only presume that, as well as Magadha and Anga, it included most of the erstwhile Gangetic states (Koshala, Vatsya, Licchavi, etc.) and reached south across the Vindhya hills to central India and the Narmada river; beyond that river the Deccan preserves only highly doubtful hints of any Nanda presence.

From a later inscription found in Kalinga, the modern Orissa, it is evident that that region had also formed part of the Nanda empire. It may have been retained by Chandragupta, but must subsequently have slipped from Mauryan control since it would have to be reconquered by his grandson. A thousand miles away, on the other side of India at Girnar in Junagadh (Gujarat), another inscription refers to the repair of a local dam which, it says, had originally been built under the direction of Chandragupta's governor in the region. Nanda power may have reached as far west as Avanti (Malwa), but is unlikely to have reached Gujarat. It is therefore assumed that Chandragupta conducted a successful campaign in western India and probably also reached the Bombay region. The Mauryan empire thus became the first to stretch from sea to sea – from the Bay of Bengal to the Arabian Sea. The object, however, may not have been 'to unite India', an unlikely ambition at a time when geographical, let alone national, horizons were still hazy. More probably its westward extension was intended to engross that lucrative maritime trade, pioneered by the Harappans, in timbers, textiles, spices, gems and precious metals between the ports of India's west coast and those of the Persian Gulf.

In the Panjab and the north-west Chandragupta's successes were no less extensive, as is coyly acknowledged by those Graeco-Roman sources. From these we know that, after a prolonged struggle, Seleucus Nikator, one of Alexander's generals, succeeded to the eastern half of his empire. Much of it had to be reclaimed, and it was not until 305 BC that Seleucus turned his attention to India. There it seems that Chandragupta had already 'liberated' (as one Latin source has it) the Panjab. Seleucus, nevertheless, crossed the Indus, and possibly the Jhelum too, before he came to terms with Chandragupta and retired. It may be inferred that Seleucus, like Alexander, had to fight his way forward and that, like Alexander's men, he soon thought better of the venture. Perhaps he was roundly defeated. The terms on which he withdrew certainly suggest so. Chandragupta presented him with five hundred war-elephants, which would prove decisive in further struggles with his main rivals in the west, although they can scarcely have dented Mauryan resources. In return Seleucus ceded to Chandragupta not only the Panjab but also Gandhara and all of what is now Afghanistan save Bactria (the northern region between the Hindu Kush and the Oxus). The treaty may have been sealed with a matrimonial alliance by which

Chandragupta, or his son, received a daughter of Seleucus as a bride.

To cement their friendship further, Seleucus appointed an ambassador to the Mauryan court at Pataliputra. This was Megasthenes, whose account of 'Sandrokottos' and his empire, as viewed from its capital, survives only in fragments quoted or paraphrased by later authors. As a first-hand description of anywhere in fourth/third-century BC India east of the Panjab, these fragments are nevertheless valuable. Indeed Megasthenes, in his emphasis on the bureaucratic and absolute nature of Mauryan rule and on the structure of its standing army, goes some way towards vindicating the utility of the *Arthasastra* as a possible source material. Back home in Greece, his work was seen as vindicating those who dismissed all descriptions of India as a pack of lies. To the floppy-eared and umbrella-footed monstrosities already on record were added such palpable fantasies as reeds which yielded syrup and trees that grew wool. Rocking, no doubt, with Attic mirth, his readers confidently rubbished such early accounts of sugar-cane and cotton production as more tall stories from the impossible East.

Although Chandragupta certainly left his successor an empire which reached from Bengal to Afghanistan and Gujarat, there is no clear indication of how far south it extended. Jain tradition insists that, when he abdicated in favour of his son, Chandragupta retired to a Jain establishment in Karnataka. At Sravana Belgola, a picturesque little town nestling in the cleavage between two steeply swelling hills west of Bangalore, the emperor is said to have passed his final days in austerity and devotions. The pinnacle of one of the hills comprises a massive nude sculpture of Gomateshwara, an important Jain teacher; mostly free-standing and nearly twenty metres high, it is one of the sights of south India – 'nothing grander or more imposing exists anywhere out of Egypt and even there, no known statue surpasses it in height.'[5] But it is on the other hill, the less sensational Chandragiri, that Chandragupta is supposed to have resided. Inscriptions and reliefs dating back to the fifth century AD record his presence; and a low cave amidst the granite scarps is said to be where, in the ultimate act of Jain self-denial, the emperor finally starved himself to death.

Scholarly doubts, of course, remain, particularly since the imperial lifestyle as recorded by Megasthenes amidst the splendour and luxury of Pataliputra seems the very antithesis of Jain asceticism. But abnegation was not uncommon in Mauryan society and, in the light of subsequent evidence of Mauryan authority in the south, the story 'may be accepted as proof of his acquisition of this part of the peninsula'.[6]

That it probably represented the frontier of his empire is evident from the prologue to the story. The emperor had chosen to abdicate (c297 BC) after receiving information about an imminent famine from the revered Bhadrabahu, who was reputedly the last Jain monk to have actually known the Jain founder Mahavira Nataputta. (Just such a famine is anticipated in two very early inscriptions, engraved on copper plates found in Bengal and UP, which have been dated to Chandragupta's reign; and unless Bhadrabahu was extraordinarily long-lived, his connection with Mahavira, the Buddha's contemporary, may be further evidence in favour of the Buddhist 'short chronology'.) As a result of this prophecy not only Chandragupta but an entire Jain congregation is said to have migrated south. In what, judging by remarks in the *Arthasastra*, was a continuing pattern of settlement in lands newly conquered or on the margins of existing settlement, the Jains journeyed south till they reached Karnataka. There, where a stream slid between the twin hills of Sravana Belgola, they stopped and stayed, nourishing the legends beloved of generations of pilgrims and patrons whose donations would enable them to dig a fine tank, build a dozen neat temples, and whittle their granite surroundings into megalithic images of the starkest abstraction. The Jains have been there ever since; and to this day they tell much the same story of the emperor Chandragupta.

Such continuities are not uncommon in India. Sir William Jones had likened first meeting his brahman informants to discovering an isolated community of Greeks who, two thousand years on, still wore toga and sandals, worshipped Zeus, recited Homer, and stood guard over a written archive reaching back to the Stone Age. Even now historians of India continue to scrutinise their own surroundings and society for clues to the past. In one of the most compelling exercises in modern historical writing D.D. Kosambi, armed with his notebook and a stout stick ('fitted with a chisel ferrule for prying artefacts out of the surface ... it also serves to discourage the more ambitious village dogs'), conducts his reader on a short walk from his home on the outskirts of Pune (Poona). Chance finds, encounters with neighbouring social groups, careful scrutiny of domestic routines and patient enquiries about local images reveal a three-thousand-year panorama of settlement patterns, trade contacts, and Sanskritic acculturation. 'There is no substitute for such work in the field for the restoration of pre-literate history,' writes Kosambi.[7] Most of India's history prior to the arrival of Islam fits his definition of pre-literate; and no society retains a more rewarding consciousness of the past than India's. Legend and oral tradition, when credible, may be quite as reliable as authentic contemporary documentation.

THE MAURYAS Probable Succession

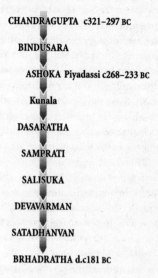

CHANDRAGUPTA c321–297 BC

BINDUSARA

ASHOKA Piyadassi c268–233 BC

Kunala

DASARATHA

SAMPRATI

SALISUKA

DEVAVARMAN

SATADHANVAN

BRHADRATHA d.c181 BC

THE GREATEST OF KINGS

In 1837, following years of conjecture and study by numerous other 'Orientalists', James Prinsep, the assay-master at the British mint in Calcutta, made what remains the single most important discovery in the unravelling of India's ancient history. From inscriptions in an unknown script found on the stone railings of the great Buddhist stupa at Sanchi, he managed to identify two letters of the alphabet. One was 'd', the other 'n'; when added to other letters already tentatively identified, they suggested words which convinced him that the language being used in these inscriptions was Pali. Pali was a Prakrit, one of several derivatives of Sanskrit, that was popular in Magadha in the Buddha's time and was subsequently appropriated as the sacred language of much Buddhist scripture. Armed with his insight into the likely language, plus much of the alphabet, Prinsep proceeded to make the first ever translations from the neat 'pin-man' script now known as Ashoka Brahmi. He translated the short Sanchi inscriptions – they recorded the donation of the stupa's individual stones and the names of their donors – and he began to tackle a series of much longer inscriptions.

Copies of these longer inscriptions had come from puzzled antiquarians as far afield as Orissa, Gujarat, Allahabad and Delhi. 'The memorial in question,' wrote James Tod in 1822 of the Girnar (Gujarat) inscription, 'is a huge hemispherical mass of dark granite which, like a wart upon the body, has protruded through the crust of mother earth, without fissure or inequality, and which, by the aid of the iron pen, has been converted into a book'.[8] Some of the inscriptions were engraved on cliff faces, others on colossal cylindrical pillars; and an odd thing about all of them was that, though found dotted over the length and breadth of the subcontinent, they seemed to contain similar phrasing and even the same message. It was as if, in Europe, chapter-length runes were to be found identically etched, squiggle for squiggle, in the marble of Carrara, the granite of the Grampians, a pillar in the Rhineland and the rock of Gibraltar. Given the obvious antiquity of both script and find-sites, curiosity about their significance was intense. The Harappan civilisation was not as yet even suspected. These looked to be India's earliest monuments and, whatever their message, they must be of enormous historical importance. Some saw parallels with the Egyptian hieroglyphics; others were reminded of the Ten Commandments as found by Moses on Mount Sinai.

Announcing his translation in 1837, an exhausted and dying Prinsep also saw parallels with Moses: 'we might easily cite a more ancient and venerable example of thus fixing the law on tablets of stone.'[9] For, contrary to expectations, these were not obscure Vedic invocations of unfathomable import but hard statements of policy, and so historical documentation of an immediacy as yet unknown in India. Henceforth called Edicts, rather than Commandments, the inscriptions clearly announced themselves as the directives of a single sovereign. 'Thus speaks Devanampiya Piyadassi' was how most began. The formula, echoing that of Persian inscriptions (and later popularised by the Nietzschean 'Thus spake Zarathrustra'), may indeed have been influenced by Achaemenid practice. Some of the pillars carrying the inscriptions still retained fluted, bell-shaped capitals crowned with an animal image, both of which features are anticipated in the monumental sculpture found at Persepolis.

Yet the confident modelling of these animal figures, the incorporation of subsidiary motifs like the Buddhist wheel, and the lustrous finish imparted to the sandstone have no foreign counterparts. Moreover, the restrained use of honorific titles in the Edicts themselves and, when fully comprehended, the extraordinarily humane sentiments expressed in them, could scarcely have been more Indian. 'Devanampiya Piyadassi' unmistakably belonged to the land of the Buddha and Mahavira. A Gandhian ring would be detected in his emphasis on human values, non-violence and moral regeneration; and to Nehru it would be self-evident that the exquisite capital of one of these inscribed pillars should serve as the national emblem of the republic of India. As usual it mattered not that, featuring a four-faced lion rather than a tiger, it bespoke the Mauryas' associations with regions of the subcontinent now largely in Pakistan.

But who was this 'Devanampiya Piyadassi'? Unfortunately for Prinsep no king called anything like that was to be found in the king-lists in the *Puranas*. But from Sri Lanka one of Prinsep's contemporaries, who was working on the Buddhist chronicles preserved in that still Buddhist island, reported that there had been a Sri Lankan king called Piyadassi, and then that the same name had also been that of a famous Indian sovereign. Indeed this Indian king was a figure of gigantic standing and copious legend in Buddhist sources. He had championed Buddhism in India, had sent his own son to convert Sri Lanka, and was otherwise gloriously known as Ashoka.

'Devanampiya', meaning 'The Beloved of the Gods', is now thought to have been an honorific title, like 'His Majesty'. 'Piyadassi' means something like 'gracious of mien' and may have been the name assumed when Ashoka was enthroned in c268 BC. That this man was indeed the third Maurya, the grandson of Chandragupta, who would rule for nearly forty years, became self-evident from his listing as *Asoka* in the *Purana* king-lists.

Information on Ashoka's early life is available neither from the *Puranas* nor from his inscriptions, and must therefore be sought mainly in those Sri Lankan Buddhist chronicles. Of Bindusara, his father (and Chandragupta's son), little is known. Greek sources call him Amitrochates and testify to further exchanges of ambassadors and gifts between Pataliputra and Alexander's successors in Egypt and Syria. The name 'Amitrochates' has been identified with a Sanskrit title meaning 'slayer of enemies'. This could imply that he extended his father's conquests. Additionally he is thought to have patronised the heterodox Ajivika sect in much the same way as his father did the Jains and his son the Buddhists. Clearly considerations of policy, as well as of conscience, may have dictated Mauryan alignment with the new sects; their lay followers were mainly drawn from the rising mercantile and industrial classes and, statecraft being principally about taxation (*Artha-sastra* literally means 'the science of wealth' or 'economics'), their support was to be cultivated.

Bindusara ruled for twenty-five years and was probably at least into his late fifties when he died. Ashoka, evidently one of several sons, therefore had the opportunity to become closely involved in imperial affairs during his father's reign. His first appointment seems to have been to Taxila, where he successfully dealt with a revolt against the local Mauryan administration. Perhaps on the strength of this, he was sent to Ujjain as governor. He stayed there until his father's death. Ujjain nestled beside the Sipra river, a tributary of the Chambal, in the heart of the rolling and well wooded uplands of west central India. Now a major city of pilgrimage, it was then the capital of one of the five main divisions of the Mauryan empire. As the principal power centre in Avanti, or Malwa, it was also well sited to control traffic and trade moving between Broach, the principal west coast port, and either Pataliputra (by way of the Narmada valley) or the upper Gangetic regions (by way of the Chambal and the old *Daksinapatha*).

However, of Ashoka's sojourn there what was thought most worthy of note by Buddhist chroniclers was his love affair with the daughter of a local merchant. The lady in question was Devi or Vidisha-mahadevi, the lovely 'goddess of Vidisha'. She was not apparently married to Ashoka nor destined to accompany him to Pataliputra and become one of his queens. Yet she bore him a son and a daughter. The son, Mahinda, would head the Buddhist mission to Sri Lanka; and it may be that his mother was already a Buddhist, thus raising the possibility that Ashoka was drawn to the Buddha's teachings while still in Avanti. In that Vidisa, about 120 kilometres east of Ujjain and near the modern Bhopal, is where stand the glorious monuments of Sanchi (including the great stupa whose inscriptions so enlightened Prinsep), it was clearly home to an important Buddhist community in Mauryan times. But its earliest *viharas* (monastic halls) and stupas probably date from after 275 BC. It therefore seems just as probable that, instead of Vidisa converting Ashoka, it was Ashoka who converted Vidisa. Mindful of its romantic associations in his youth, he may, in later life as emperor and a lay Buddhist, have retained a soft spot for this peaceful mound in its then sylvan setting near the headwaters of the Betwa river, and by lavish endowment have ensured its religious celebrity.

As with earlier subscribers to the Buddha's teachings like Ajatashatru of Magadha, Buddhist sources tend to represent Ashoka's pre-Buddhist lifestyle as one of indulgence steeped in cruelty. Conversion then became all the more remarkable in that by 'right thinking' even a monster of wickedness could be transformed into a model of compassion. The formula, if such it was, precluded any admission of Ashoka's early fascination with Buddhism and may explain the ruthless conduct attributed to him when Bindusara died. Not only is he said to have killed all rival claimants to the throne, notably ninety-nine of his brothers, but also to have paid a visit to hell so that he could construct on earth something similar, equipped with the very latest in instruments of exquisite torture, for all who incurred his displeasure. This 'Hell-on-Earth' evidently became quite a curiosity: nine hundred years later a Chinese visitor, while touring the locations associated with early Buddhism, records the site, which was then marked with a pillar.

That Ashoka was not his father's chosen successor and that there was indeed a succession struggle is certain. It helps to account for the four-year gap between Bindusara's death and Ashoka's enthronement as also for the fact that only one brother of many (though surely not a hundred) receives further mention; according to one source, the name of this brother was Vitashoka and he became a Buddhist monk, a career move no doubt dictated as much by self-preservation as self-abnegation. If not a monster, Ashoka undoubtedly evinced the Kautilyan ruthlessness essential to gaining the throne and the Kautilyan cunning essential to retaining it.

Eight years after his enthronement, so in c260 BC, there occurred the only campaign that can certainly be attributed to the Mauryas, one which was nevertheless the outstanding event of the reign and the turning point in the life of the emperor. Ashoka conquered, or reconquered, Kalinga (roughly Orissa). The conquest is recorded in the most important of his Edicts, the thirteenth of the fourteen Major Rock Edicts (as opposed to the eight Minor Rock Edicts and Inscriptions, and the seven Major Pillar Edicts). And though the Edict says nothing of the military arrangements, it tells in detail of the human suffering involved – 100,000 slain, 'many times that number perished' (presumably afterwards from wounds and famine) and 150,000 deported. More famously, it also records the emperor's reaction.

> On conquering Kalinga the Beloved of the Gods felt remorse, for, when an independent country is conquered, the slaughter, death and deportation of the people is extremely grievous to the Beloved of the Gods and weighs heavily on his mind ... Even those who are fortunate to have escaped, and whose love is undiminished, suffer from the misfortunes of their friends, acquaintances, colleagues and relatives ... Today if a hundredth or a thousandth part of those people who were killed or died or were deported when Kalinga was annexed were to suffer similarly, it would weigh heavily on the mind of the Beloved of the Gods ...
>
> This inscription of *dhamma* has been engraved so that any sons or great-grandsons that I may have should not think of gaining

new conquests, and in whatever victories they may gain should be
satisfied with patience and light punishment. They should only
consider conquest by *dhamma* to be a true conquest, and delight
in *dhamma* should be their whole delight, for this is of value in
both this world and the next.[10]

'Herein lies the greatness of Ashoka,' writes R.K. Mookerji. 'Even as a
mere pious sentiment this is hard to beat; at least no victorious monarch
in the history of the world is known to have ever given expression to
anything like it.'[11] In just such a 'History of the World' H.G. Wells made
the same point: 'He would have no more of it [the cruelty and horror of
war]. He adopted the peaceful doctrines of Buddhism and declared that
henceforth his conquests would be conquests of religion ... Such was
Ashoka, greatest of kings.'[12]

Renouncing violence, abjuring war, and advocating the elusive but
admirable concept of *dhamma*, Ashoka turned statecraft on its head. Not
the least of those confounded was Kautilya, whose *Arthasastra* makes the
conquest of neighbouring territories one of the sacred duties of a king. It
lists several kinds of war, goes into immense logistical detail on armies and
battle plans, and includes four handy hints on conquering the world. To
a society accustomed to such cynical sentiments, Ashoka's change of heart
must indeed have appeared revolutionary.

Whether it was quite as benign as it seems may, though, be questioned.
One wonders why, for instance, if the emperor was so overcome with
remorse, he did not arrange for the repatriation of all those deportees? Or
why the Edict in question is pointedly omitted from the only rock inscriptions in Kalinga itself, inscriptions which otherwise conform with those in
the rest of the country. In its stead are two separate Edicts ordering imperial
representatives to conciliate the natives with lenient policies and exceptional
diligence so that such wayward people may come to think of Ashoka as
their father. Policy as much as conscience dictated this approach. Whatever
lessons he chose to draw, in reality Ashoka's treatment of the subjugated
Kalingans was exactly as prescribed by the *Arthasastra*: 'having acquired
new territory the conqueror shall substitute his virtues for the enemy's
vices and where the enemy was good, he shall be twice as good. He shall
follow policies that are pleasing and beneficial by acting according to his
dharma and by granting favours and exemptions, giving gifts and bestowing
honours.'[13]

One wonders, too, about those astronomical casualty figures. Megasthenes describes the Mauryan army as a permanent and professional body,

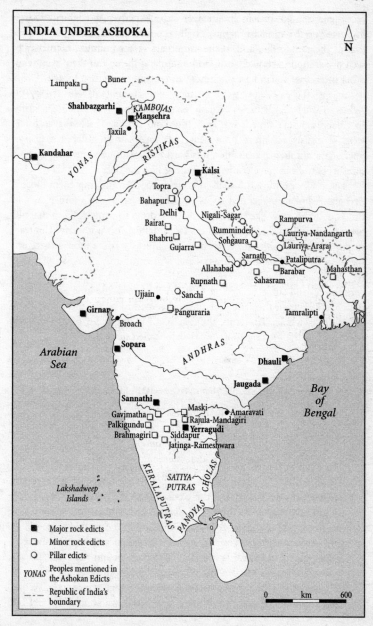

INDIA UNDER ASHOKA

N

Lampaka · Buner

Shahbazgarhi · KAMBOJAS
Mansehra

Taxila

YONAS · Kandahar

RISTIKAS

Kalsi

Topra
Bahapur
Delhi · Nigali-Sagar · Rampurva
Bairat · Rummindei · Lauriya-Nandangarth
Bhabru · Sohgaura · Lauriya-Araraj
Gujarra · Sarnath · Pataliputra · Mahasthan
Allahabad · Barabar
Rupnath · Sahasram
Ujjain · Sanchi
Girnar · Panguraria · Tamralipti
Broach
ANDHRAS
Sopara · Dhauli

Arabian
Sea

Jaugada

Bay
of
Bengal

Sannathi
Maski · Amaravati
Gavimatha · Rajula-Mandagiri
Palkigundu · Yerragudi
Brahmagiri · Siddapur
Jatinga-Rameshwara

KERALAPUTRAS · SATIYA-
PUTRAS

Lakshadweep
Islands

PANDYAS · CHOLAS

■ Major rock edicts
□ Minor rock edicts
○ Pillar edicts
YONAS Peoples mentioned in
       the Ashokan Edicts
- - - Republic of India's
       boundary

0   km   600

recruited, trained and maintained at state expense, and which scarcely impinged on the agricultural masses. 'It therefore not unfrequently happens that at the same time, and in the same part of the country, men may be seen drawn up in array of battle, and fighting at the risk of their lives, while other men close at hand are ploughing and digging in perfect security.'[14] But if this was the case, how were so many non-combatants affected by the Kalingan war? Megasthenes actually gives a figure for the Kalingan army. In Chandragupta's time it was sixty thousand strong. The Mauryan forces were obviously far more numerous but, unless they suffered a disproportionate number of casualties, it is hard to explain how the total of those slain in battle can have come to anything like 100,000.

There was nothing unusual, of course, about conflating enemy losses. Perhaps Ashoka exaggerated so as to make his revulsion more plausible. But equally he may, like most victors, have done so principally to magnify his victory and so discourage others from defying his authority. Contrary to popular opinion, he never specifically abjures warfare, nor is there any mention of his disbanding units of the Mauryan army. This is not to say that his remorse was insincere. The Kalinga war had indeed troubled his conscience, and since, according to the *Arthasastra*, 'the king encapsulates the constituents of the state,' his unease seemed to reflect the wider ills of society as a whole. The cure, though, was not the balm of a disastrous pacifism but the bracing tonic of what he called *dhamma*.

AS LONG AS SUN AND MOON ENDURE

Few rulers have summed up their life's work in a single word, but that was obviously how Ashoka wanted it. Not for conquests, prosperity or majesty did he wish to be remembered, only for *dhamma*. To say the word features prominently in his Edicts is an understatement. Nearly all mention it, some many times, and there are several attempts at defining it:

> Thus speaks the Beloved of the Gods, the king Piyadassi: There is no gift comparable to the gift of *dhamma*, the praise of *dhamma*, the sharing of *dhamma*, fellowship in *dhamma*. And this is: good behaviour towards slaves and servants, obedience to mother and father, generosity towards friends, acquaintances and relatives, and towards *sramanas* and brahmans, and abstention from killing living beings. Father, son, brother, master, friend, acquaintance, relative, and neighbour should say, 'this is good, this we should do.' By

doing so, there is gain in this world, and in the next there is infinite
merit, through the gift of *dhamma*. [Eleventh Major Rock Edict][15]

Elsewhere *dhamma* is equated with 'mercy, charity, truthfulness and
purity'. In English it is variously rendered as 'piety', 'duty', 'good conduct'
or 'decency'. Ashoka clearly thought it anything but anodyne, and practised
it, preached it, and legislated for it with missionary zeal. It was a panacea
not just for India but for the world – this one and the next. The glad
tidings were to be carried beyond his frontiers, even to his fellow rulers in
the west. The mention of some of their names – including an Egyptian
Ptolemy and an Alexander (of Epirus) – provides vital chronological corroboration.

At home, something like a parallel administration was set up to promote
and monitor *dhamma*'s dissemination. The Edicts embodying it were promulgated, proclaimed, and then encapsulated for all time by that laborious
process of gouging them into the very bedrock of India. 'I have done this,'
Ashoka announced when, after twenty-seven years on the throne, he issued
his last Edict, 'so that among my sons and great grandsons, and as long as
the sun and moon shall endure, men may follow *dhamma*' [Seventh Pillar
Edict].[16]

It is the tone as much as the content which sends a shiver down
awe-struck spines. Ashoka is not just India's first defined historical personality but, rarer still for such a remote age, he is an intelligible personality.
Quite probably the Beloved of the Gods did indeed speak just thus. The
language is personal and intimate, not stilted or formalised as is more
usual with official directives, and neither condensed for the purposes of
inscription nor artfully organised for easy memorising. Occasionally repetitive, it slips from third person to first and from direct speech to indirect,
just as one might expect of something dictated and recorded verbatim.

Almost certainly the Edicts first circulated as palm-leaf texts and were
then engraved. Literacy not being a widespread skill in the third century
BC, they were meant to be read out aloud to the people. At Shahbazgarhi
near Peshawar on the edge of the badlands of the north-west frontier, and
at Mansehra in the Himalayan foothills north of Taxila, they were written
in Kharosthi, the local script derived from Aramaic in Achaemenid times.
Further west beyond the Khyber Pass and at Kandahar in the deserts of
southern Afghanistan a shortened Edict is in Aramaic with a translation
into Greek; had it been discovered earlier, it could, like a Rosetta Stone,
have made Prinsep's task redundant. Although the many inscriptions found
deep in the Deccan betray no knowledge of Tamil, elsewhere the adoption

of local scripts and languages shows Ashoka appealing directly not only to his own people but to other peoples beyond his frontiers, and to other generations beyond his times. It is this above all, the directness of his directives, which, transcending the millennia, gives them even now such awesome immediacy.

But if the tone is still arresting, one can hardly say the same for the contents. Why, one wonders, lavish so much love, labour and authority on a set of fairly obvious humanitarian injunctions? Assuming they had no political relevance, many historians have portrayed Ashoka more as a religious reformer, another Buddha or Christ, than as an empire-builder. In religious terms his clear preference, as shown in a number of minor inscriptions, was for the Buddhist community; given 'the rank growth of legend which has clustered round the name of Ashoka' in Buddhist tradition, *dhamma* has often actually been equated with Buddhism. This link appears to be borne out by *dhamma*'s emphasis on non-violence, on preserving life in all its forms, and on 'right conduct' towards one's fellow human beings. The Third Buddhist Council is supposed to have met under Ashoka's patronage at Pataliputra. At least one of his *dhamma* agents, his son Mahinda, was more missionary than emissary. And Ashoka, instead of combining tours of his kingdom with the traditional pastime of a royal hunt, insists that his peregrinations were enlivened only by pilgrimage. Just such a tour, embracing the Buddha's birthplace and the site of his *parinirvana*, is commemorated in a series of pillars erected *in situ* and dated to the twentieth year of his reign, so 248 BC.

However, the tradition that Ashoka actually became a Buddhist monk is now discredited. The inscriptions never mention the Buddha and show no awareness of his 'Noble Eightfold Path' or any other Buddhist schema. Even the idea of 'conversion' is suspect, since codes like those of the Buddhists and Jains were not seen as exclusive. Religion as creed, doctrine as dogma, and faith as truth are equations with little validity in pre-Islamic India. Most subscribed to the inexorable cycle of rebirth and to the notion that there were various ways of effecting eventual escape from it. The propitiation of a particular deity could help, but was more commonly a means of warding off disease and pestilence. Even brahmanical orthodoxy demanded no profession of faith, merely an acceptance of brahman authority and a high degree of caste conformity. There was indeed competition, especially amongst the heterodox sects, for adherents and for patronage. There was also ferocious debate which, on at least one occasion, required Ashoka's intervention. But conversion, in the sense of renouncing one set of doctrines for another, was meaningless.

Instead Megasthenes divided India's 'philosophers' not into like-minded sects but into 'Bramanes and Sarmanes', a distinction also made by Ashoka when referring, as above, to 'Sramanas and brahmans', or elsewhere to 'Sramanas and householders'. 'Sramanas' denoted 'renunciates' and included all those who followed the mendicant and monastic habits of the heterodox sects as well as itinerant devotees of traditional deities. In other words, the crucial distinction was not between different belief systems but between different lifestyles. The individual was defined purely by his relationship to the rest of society. Not doctrine but conduct was what mattered.

Just so for Ashoka. He attempted no philosophical justification of *dhamma*, nor was he much given to rationalising it. It was not a belief system, not a developed ideology, just a set of behavioural exhortations. But because behaviour, conduct, was of such defining importance, any attempt to alter it was indeed revolutionary. Ashoka therefore needed a good reason for introducing his *dhamma*; and it should perhaps be sought in the need to promote a more united and uniform society.

Unprecedented solutions were required for an empire of unprecedented extent. In addition to the vast area roughly defined by the Rock Inscriptions (extending from Orissa to Mysore, Bombay, Junagadh, Kandahar, Peshawar and Dehra Dun), it seems fairly certain that the Kashmir valley was also included, and probably that of Nepal. The terrain varied from jungle to mountain, desert and flood-plain, and the population from nomadic hunter-gatherers to slash-and-burn tribesmen, pastoral herdsmen, fishing communities, arable and dairy farmers, craft villages, urbanised guilds, maritime and overland traders, and the highly sophisticated hierarchical societies of the major cities. Pataliputra itself, according to Megasthenes, lay within a walled and heavily fortified parallelogram of roughly fifteen kilometres by two and a half; its palace rivalled that of the Achaemenids, and even in decay made such an impression on a Chinese traveller that he thought it the work of spirits.

To preserve this empire intact, the Mauryan administration, if one may judge from what Megasthenes says and the *Arthasastra* expands, was one of the most elaborate on record. Government was construed as being largely about collecting taxes and administering justice. In each of these spheres the emperor and his mainly advisory council of ministers headed a hierarchy of officials which reached down through divisional and district officers to the toll-collector, the market overseer and the clerk who recorded the measurement and assessment of fields. The entire apparatus was subject to regular checks by a staff of inspectors who reported direct to the emperor, while a more sinister system of undercover informants provided a further check. All were appointed, directly or indirectly, by the emperor and had instant access to him.

This system was replicated by the four provincial administrations based at Suvarnagiri (near Kurnool in what is now Andhra Pradesh), Ujjain (Avanti/Malwa), Taxila (Panjab) and Tosali (thought to have been near Bhubaneshwar in Orissa). Each was headed by a governor, usually a son or brother of the emperor, although how much autonomy these local administrations enjoyed is questionable. Megasthenes paints a picture of a highly centralised, indeed personalised, administration, but he may have been generalising from conditions in Magadha itself. Centralisation was certainly the intention. The Greek ambassador's enthusiasm for India's roads is more than matched by Ashoka's insistence in one of his Edicts that they be lined with shade trees, clearly marked with milestones, and provided with frequent wells, orchards and rest-houses. Communications were vital for trade; like instant access to the emperor, they were also essential to an effective despotism.

Another declared priority was standardisation. An Ashokan directive on 'uniformity in judicial procedure and punishment' is echoed in the *Arthasastra*, where taxes, duties and pay scales are all represented as standard. More generally, the whole structure of the administration and the use of standard proclamations and inscriptions were intended to knit the empire together. Caste, whether as the four-tier *varna* or the profession-based *jati*, scarcely receives a mention in the Edicts, but sectarian differences were much on the imperial mind. 'The Beloved of the Gods,' according to the twelfth Major Rock Edict, 'honours all sects and both ascetics and laymen with gifts and various forms of recognition.' But these benefits, Ashoka says, are unimportant compared to 'the advancement of the essential doctrine of all sects'. The context here is that of a plea for toleration between the sects. No one is to disparage someone else's teachings – or only mildly and on certain occasions. Concord is the ideal, and this is best realised by developing a recognition of a doctrinal essence that is common to all.

Although not specifically equated with *dhamma*, this supposed doctrinal essence seems to be the genesis of Ashoka's big idea. The word '*dhamma*' is a Prakrit spelling of the more familiar '*dharma*', a concept difficult to translate but imbued with positive and idealised connotations in both orthodox Vedic literature and in the heterodox doctrines of Buddhists, Jains and Ajivikas. Invoking a natural order within which all manner of creation had its place and its role, it was something to which no one, be he brahman or Buddhist, emperor or slave, could reasonably take exception.

Dharma did, nevertheless, have different meanings for different sects, and Ashoka's *dhamma* seems therefore to have sought common ground, borrowing from one what was least objectionable to the others. The emphasis on a respect for life in all its forms and on providing medical facilities for animals as well as men was clearly derived from Jain teachings. It appears that all live sacrifices were forbidden, and even the killing of animals for food was to be discouraged. The emperor was setting an example, in that his kitchen now required only two peacocks and the occasional deer, and 'even these three animals will not be killed in future'. Such injunctions have often been taken to imply a ban on sacrificial extravaganzas and so a provocative swipe at those who derived their prestige and income from conducting them, namely brahmans. But, given a list elsewhere of the prohibited species, it seems that this rule may have applied only to wild creatures, not farm animals. Goats, sheep and cattle, the species most obviously in demand for both ritual and culinary purposes, are protected only when nursing their young. They must otherwise, therefore, have been exempt. Similarly, though adamant that 'it is good not to kill human beings', Ashoka seems to have retained capital punishment just as he retained the option of warfare. *Dhamma* was carefully formulated so that essential interests should not be prejudiced while sectarian concerns were being accommodated.

As well as conciliating the Jains, we know from an inscription in a cave in Orissa that Ashoka continued his father's policy of patronising the Ajivikas. As for his Buddhist sympathies, they have already been mentioned. They found ample expression in *dhamma*, especially in injunctions about right conduct towards relatives, friends and colleagues. He makes, though, a significant addition by adding to the list of such beneficiaries the brahmans. Ashoka had no intention of slighting orthodox society or its deities. 'The Beloved of the Gods' would keep in with the gods, whatever his personal sympathy for the Buddhist *sangha* (monastic community).

> It would appear that Ashoka aimed at creating an attitude of mind among his subjects in which social behaviour had the highest relevance. In the context of conditions during the Mauryan period, this ideology may have been viewed as a focus of loyalty and a point of convergence for the existing diversities of people and activities.[17]

'Yet,' continues Romila Thapar, 'the ideology of *dhamma* died with the death of the emperor [in 231 BC].' Others have conjectured that *dhamma* may even have been the undoing of the empire; perhaps it invited defiance, perhaps it provoked defiance. During his last ten years on the throne Ashoka had no further Edicts inscribed, and his empire may already have been falling apart. Mauryas would continue to rule from Pataliputra for another fifty years but their writ seldom ran beyond Magadha. The provinces, centred on Ujjain, Taxila, Suvarnagiri and Tosali, rapidly broke away as Ashoka's successors proved unworthy of their inheritance and incapable of his vision. If *dhamma* was supposed to hold the empire together, it was an unmitigated failure.

Yet a policy that failed became an intimation that endured. The Ashokan legacy of an empire which stretched from sea to sea and from the mountains to the peninsula was promptly mislaid and would remain so for a couple of millennia. Likewise Ashoka's historicity. But tradition cherished his memory; Indian historians insist that the ideal of a pan-Indian empire was never forgotten; and nor, more certainly, was the spirit of humanity embodied in his Edicts. The innovation which he pioneered of appealing across the barriers of sect, caste and kin to the community of India would be revived by a host of other reformers, not least Guru Nanak of the Sikhs and eventually Mahatma Gandhi.

An Age of Paradox

C200 BC—C300 AD

EBB OF EMPIRE, FLOW OF IDEAS

BETWEEN THE DEATH of Ashoka in 231 BC and the advent of Gupta
power in 320 AD, India's ancient history plummets again to a murky
obscurity. 'Certainties are not many,' bemoans a writer on the period.[1]
Prior to the Mauryas our vision is blurred by the ambiguity of mainly
literary sources whose purpose is suspect and whose dates are vague. After
the Mauryas the source materials are more varied: coins furnish the names
of a host of otherwise forgotten kings; other archaeological finds, plus
inscriptions, provide additional information about guilds and religious
establishments; and texts – Indian, Graeco-Roman and Chinese – hint at
a wider historical context and testify to the importance of trade. Yet the
sum total of these sources remains inadequate and, in respect of the successor states of the Mauryan empire, certainties are indeed 'not many'.
How far the writ of these states ran, whence came their rulers and when
they reigned, even the order in which their dynasties succeeded one another,
are matters of dispute. The *Puranas* continue to prove tantalisingly unreliable; and the greater variety of sources often serves only to introduce
contradictions. A long period of political confusion is deduced and, pre-
modern history necessarily being a reflection of such sources, this confusion
is taken to indicate instability, fragmentation and turbulence. The five
hundred years between the Mauryas and the Guptas become, in fact, 'India's
Dark Age'.[2]

While Rome beamed its civilisation into three continents, handsomely
documenting its conquests in the process, Pataliputra retreated into insignificance and silence. In India no king or dynasty would either scale the
heights of Ashoka's lofty universalism or cast such long imperial shadows
across the subcontinent. Inscriptions claiming otherwise are usually

couched in bombastic phrases which should be treated with caution. Ideals of legitimacy and empire would remain: Ayodhya's utopian *Ram-raj* (the rule of Lord Rama) would continue to exercise a fascination; so would inclusive concepts of a 'one umbrella' sovereignty as claimed by the Nandas and of a world-ruling *Cakravartin* (literally 'wheel-turner') as featured in Buddhist teaching. But the reality was of many jostling umbrellas, of no consensus on legitimacy, and of no universal sovereignty.

Worse still from the viewpoint of latter-day nationalists, many of the dynasties credited with contributing to this turbulence would be of non-Indian origin. In some histories this 'Dark Age' thus also becomes an 'Age of Invasions' characterised by foreign hordes from Bactria, Parthia, and the wilds of Turkestan pouring across the north-west frontier. They would overrun all of what is now Pakistan and strike deep into the Gangetic heartland and central India. To orthodox minds such disasters were no worse than was to be expected of the dreaded *Kali Yug*. Vedic values and brahmanic authority had been undermined by the pushy teachings of the Buddha and his rivals. An earlier spirit of metaphysical enquiry had given way to an unnatural and populist egalitarianism. Fickle sources of royal patronage had been diverted; the neglect of ritual obligations had necessarily prejudiced political legitimacy. A disrespectful age got the discredited history it deserved.

Yet, politics apart, the half-millennium which straddles the birth of Christ was not all petty doom and patriotic gloom. On closer inspection the 'Dark Age' proves to be softly illuminated by the steady glow of cultural integration, especially in peninsular India. There and elsewhere the gloom was also fitfully dispelled by dazzling shafts of artistic, scientific and commercial innovation. Indeed, if an age be judged in terms of art and literature, the tag of 'classical' belongs less to the much-studied decades of the great Mauryas and more to the quickly dismissed centuries of their less distinguished and often non-Indian successors.

The Mauryas, for instance, had done little for India's artistic heritage. If one excludes his pillars and their Achaemenid-style capitals, Ashoka's numerous endowments, principally stupas and *viharas*, seem to have been modest affairs of brick and timber. It was only under his successors that stone became established as the supreme medium of artistic expression. To the first two centuries BC and AD may be attributed the magnificent sculptural reliefs of the Bharhut, Sanchi and Amaravati stupas. Typically crammed with scenes of popular devotion and, judging by their inscriptions, often paid for by commercial and religious benefactors, these were not manifestations of royal prestige nor products of courtly largesse. Ascribing them to a particular dynasty is thus misleading. Rather should they be attributed to a pious merchant class, proud of its skills and increasingly interested in the security and patronage afforded by religious centres in an age of political uncertainty.

Much the same applies to the first of a long succession of 'rock-cut cathedrals', now more prosaically known as 'cave temples', which date from the last century BC onward. They are found principally in western India, inland from Bombay, where sudden folds and gashes at the edge of the Deccan plateau expose long, snaking strata of sheer rock. No doubt here were already natural caves which, affording secluded shelter and yielding readily to the sculptor's chisel, inspired the idea of more elaborate excavations. There followed entire monastic establishments with prayer chambers, deep pillared halls, lofty stupas, finely fretted façades, and airy meditation cells, all connected by galleries and staircases and all cut and carved into the solid rock.

The skills involved appear to have derived from a contemporary tradition of working in the hard timbers of India. In the north, in the first centuries AD, similar skills and similar mainly Buddhist patronage gave birth to two distinctive schools of more portable sculpture. One, deeply indebted to the aesthetic of the Graeco-Roman world, depicts figures from Indian tradition as Apollo Belvederes attended by a 'classical' repertoire of cherubs and acanthus leaves. Fashioned in stucco or carved from a hard grey-black schist, these figures and motifs are particularly associated with Taxila and the north-west frontier region (hence the 'Gandhara school'). The other school is very different. A gloriously voluptuous celebration of nature's mainly female charms, it uses a fleshy pink sandstone flecked with white spots from the region around the city of Mathura where, on the tourist highway from Delhi to Agra, a fine collection of both Gandhara and Mathura figures now languishes largely unseen in the city's museum.

As for literature, in the second century BC Patanjali, a Sanskrit grammarian who wrote a commentary on Panini, compiled the standard text on yoga. Mighty compendia of other important human activities followed, with the *Manusmriti* ('Manu's code' of law), the *Kamasutra* of Vatsyana, and Kautilya's *Arthasastra* all datable in their final form to the second century AD. Meanwhile a Buddhist writer, Asvaghosha of Magadha, may be credited with the first Indian drama; he was a contemporary and protégé of King Kanishka, who would be the age's nearest equivalent to an Ashoka. Subsequently the great tradition of Sanskrit drama got off to a more certain start with Bhasa, whose prolific output of plays probably dates from the third century AD. A debt to his work would be acknowledged by Kalidasa, the Sanskrit Shakespeare, who may have been a near-contemporary although he is usually assigned to the cultural efflorescence that awaited the Guptas after 320. Perhaps the 'dark' centuries on either side of the year zero should be seen more as a sprightly preface to this 'golden age of the Guptas' than as a dire postscript to that of the Mauryas.

The 'Dark Age' looks to have been one of enlightenment and, even more paradoxically, the 'Age of Invasions' looks to have been one of expansion. For every incursion by non-Indians from central Asia, there is good evidence for an excursion by Indians into south-east Asia – or even back into central Asia. Hellenised kingdoms on the upper Indus are matched by Indianised kingdoms on the lower Mekong, Roman trading stations on the Indian coast by Indian trading stations on the Malay peninsula. Just as the archaeology of northern India is being invaded by uncompromising images of Greek adventurers and booted warlords from beyond the Oxus, so that of Sumatra and Sinkiang is invaded by serene Buddhas and handsome stupas. That first Indian drama by Asvaghosa came to light not in some Magadhan archive but in a horde of manuscripts found in the oasis city of Turfan, between the Takla Makan and the Gobi desert on China's silk route. For every inscription in Greek or Sogdian script that is chiselled into India's rocks another in Brahmi or Kharosthi is etched in the cliffs of Afghanistan or echoed in a stele on the coast of Vietnam.

In short, the diaspora of India's culture began just as India itself apparently buckled before a succession of intruders. Both processes would continue, with intermissions, for the next two thousand years. Indeed the great paradox of political vulnerability in the midst of commercial and cultural dynamism may be considered one of Indian history's distinctive features. If for no other reason than to explore the genesis of such a phenomenon, the underrated interlude between the glorious Mauryas and the golden Guptas merits attention.

IN THE DYNASTIC WILDERNESS

Of Ashoka's Mauryan successors in the third to second centuries BC we know practically nothing except that they lost most of their inheritance. There were at least six of them, and they continued to rule, mostly from Pataliputra, for another fifty years. One, Dasaratha, may have been Ashoka's grandson and immediate successor. In the only inscription certainly attributable to the later Mauryas, he dedicated some caves to the Ajivikas. Another, Brhadratha, was by common consent the last of the dynasty; a half-wit, he was murdered by his commander-in-chief. There is nothing to suggest that any of them ever exercised authority in the Deccan or in Orissa, and there is reason to suppose that many other Mauryan provinces, including those in Afghanistan, Gandhara, Kashmir, the Panjab and perhaps Malwa, all broke away at an early stage. Reasons suggested for this rapid decline include the economic crisis implied by an adulteration of the coinage, the reluctance to use force which was supposedly inherent in *dhamma*, and the vulnerability of Ashoka's personalised authority to the presumed failings of his successors.

It is perhaps also worth reflecting on the nature of an empire which could so rapidly disintegrate. For instance, the scatter of Ashokan inscriptions in Karnataka (Mysore) and Andhra Pradesh (Hyderabad) should probably not be interpreted as evidence that Mauryan authority was ever effective throughout the Deccan. Instead, the empire should be seen as consisting of corridors of authority connecting pockets of agricultural, mineral (many of the southern inscriptions are in a gold-mining area), commercial or strategic importance. Beyond this carefully administered root-structure of nodes and conduits lay wild tracts of hill, forest and desert whose peoples produced no surplus of taxable significance. Here the Mauryan policy of containment, if they proved disruptive, or of neglect, if peaceable, may have been an early casualty of retrenchment. For all the evidence of an elaborate fiscal and judicial system under the Mauryas, we know remarkably little about the sanctions which enforced it. Along the highways, as well as rest houses and shade trees, one might expect some mention of garrisons, forts and escorts; but there is none. Mauryan authority, theoretically so extensive and invasive, may, in practice and beyond the confines of Magadha itself, have always been localised and vulnerable.

The last Maurya was murdered and supplanted by his commander-in-chief in about 180 BC. Pushyamitra, the assassin, was a brahman; his family came from Ujjain, where they had once served in the Mauryan administration. An inscription testifies to his performing two horse-sacrifices, and he is portrayed in Buddhist texts as no friend to the *sangha* (the monastic community). Perhaps, after a century of Mauryan patronage of the heterodox sects, Pushyamitra headed an orthodox brahmanical backlash. The dynasty he founded is known as the Shunga and his successors presided over a still disintegrating kingdom for about 110 years. The last Shunga, being reportedly 'overfond of women's company',[3] was assassinated by the daughter of one of his female companions. Vasudeva, his brahman minister, is said to have instigated the crime and it was he who duly founded a new dynasty. This was the Kanva, which lasted barely fifty years and of which almost nothing is known. Thereafter the kingdom of Magadha virtually disappears from the record for three centuries.

The Shungas and the Kanvas, like the later Mauryas, had been challenged on many fronts. An inscription in Orissa tells of the great king Kharavela of Kalinga who, though apparently a devout Jain, led his forces deep into the Deccan as well as invading Magadha and taking Pataliputra. Immense booty was accumulated, Kharavela's horses and elephants were watered in the Ganga, and the king was styled a *cakravartin*, or world-ruler. Perhaps it was by way of a Kalingan revenge for Ashoka's triumph of 260 BC. But Kharavela's dates remain a mystery and his inscription is in 'a rather flowery and pompous style and doubtless much of it was royal panegyric'.[4] The only obvious inference is that Kalinga had long since broken away from Magadhan rule and now held its neighbour in contempt.

Amongst other adversaries over whom Kharavela was supposedly victorious, the inscription mentions the Shatavahana kings of the Deccan and a confederation of Tamil rulers in the extreme south, plus the *Yavanas*, or Greeks. As will be seen, the Deccan and the south begin to feature prominently in Indian history from about the last century BC. Slightly earlier the *Yavanas* had led the procession of intruders who now descended on India from the north-west. They originated in Bactria, or northern Afghanistan, where the Achaemenids had established a Greek colony. Alexander had augmented it, and over it Seleucus had briefly reasserted Macedonian authority before, some time during the reign of Ashoka, one Euthydemus had declared an independent kingdom. His successors, who were not necessarily his descendants, extended Bactrian rule to much of Afghanistan. Then, taking further advantage of the break-up of the Mauryan empire, some of them passed on down the Kabul river to the Indus and the Panjab.

Almost everything that is known of these Bactrian Greeks has been surmised from their splendid coins. Minted and die-cast in imitation of Greek practice, they are mostly circular, of silver, often large, and altogether a great advance on the punch-marked lumps of the Mauryas. Considerable hoards as well as individual examples have been found over a vast area; and coinage design being extraordinarily conservative, they provide somewhat the same information as a modern coin. Thus, we learn of the names of these kings, of their preferred titles, and often of the Greek deity with whom they wished to be associated. From the obverse, or 'heads' side of the coins, we also know what they looked like and what headgear they sported. Such personal insights are rare; knowing nothing of, for instance, Ashoka's mien (other than that it was 'gracious'), we feel personally aquainted with the bull-necked Eucratides and the big-nosed Heliocles. Some wear a curious cap, modelled on an elephant's skull, with the trunk serving as a peak; others favoured the *kausia*, like a shallow upturned bowl, of faintly ecclesiastical look; the chinless Amyntas, whose long nose quests from beneath a sun helmet indistinguishable from the British solar topi, must surely have had knobbly knees and worn knee-length white socks. From such portraits information has been drawn about the likely age of a king when he ascended the throne; and blood relationships, indeed the succession, are sometimes premised on resemblances in their physiognomy and headgear. Lacking much in the way of corroborative sources, scholars have pored over every iota of numismatic detail to ingenious but seldom conclusive effect.

A fundamental problem seems to be that of there being rather too many kings for the, at most, 130 years of their involvement in India. It is as if all these Platos and Stratos, Demetriuses and Diodotuses had got wise to the idea that immortality was theirs provided they could but strike their own coins. Scholars meet this problem by proposing that there was usually more than one king and more than one kingdom. The *Yavanas* had a reputation for quarrelling amongst themselves, and their territories must therefore have frequently been divided and subdivided. As well as rival kings, it seems that sub-kings, joint-kings, expectant-kings and satraps or governors may all have minted their own coins. Where their various territories lay can be vaguely inferred from the find sites of a particular coin-type.

Many clearly never crossed the north-west frontier from Afghanistan, and those who did may not have come as invaders. Perhaps, like other Greeks in Asia, they came bearing gifts. Bactria had grown rich as a corridor of east–west trade and was also an important source of bloodstock. Indians, ever anxious for horses (but blissfully ignorant of the one gifted to Troy), may have welcomed them as both traders and mercenaries. It could be significant that three centuries later, when the Gandhara school of sculpture popularised Greek themes, the Trojan horse seems to have been a favourite.

First of these Indo-Greeks into India was a Demetrius, probably Demetrius II, who seems to have achieved success in the Panjab and to have established himself at Taxila. He may also have continued down the Indus to its mouth. This is thought to have happened some time soon after 180 BC and, from the fact that the legends on his coins are in Prakrit or Kharosthi as well as in Greek, it is clear that he acquired Indian subjects. A successor, Menander, fared even better with mid-century acquisitions to the north in Swat and possibly Kashmir, as well as to the east. How far east is uncertain. He probably extended his territory to the river Ravi, but may have raided much further afield. In Indian sources a *Yavana* force that was probably Menander's is said to have joined the kings of Panchala and Mathura (both in the Ganga-Jamuna Doab) for a raid down the Ganga. Perhaps it was this combination of Greeks and Indians that the all-conquering Kharavela of Kalinga encountered. If so, he failed to stop them since, realising Alexander's dream, they stormed Pataliputra and routed its presumably Shunga incumbent. Then, typically, they quarrelled; maybe Menander, like Alexander, faced a mutiny. 'They came, they saw, but India conquered,' writes one of their biographers.[5]

On his coins Menander does not have the look of a conqueror. His topi-style helmet appears much too big; protruding curls and delicate features suggest effeminacy; and he calls himself '*Basileos*' and '*Soter*', 'King' and 'Saviour', rather then 'Conqueror' or 'Patriot'. With this gentler image his other legacy is more in keeping; for in Buddhist tradition he is remembered as 'Milinda', the great king who in a celebrated question-and-answer session with the philosopher Nagasena became the vehicle for an exposition of Buddhist doctrine; he may even himself have adopted Buddhism. The meeting took place in Menander's capital of Sagala, whose whereabouts are uncertain but which may have been in the boulder-strewn valley of Swat. If this surmise is correct, it must be thanks to Menander that the gentle terraces beside the racing river Swat came to accommodate the pre-eminent centre of Buddhist teaching in the north-west.

Of Menander's successors we know little. One, Antialcidas, is thought to have briefly reunited the Greeks' territories on either side of the Hindu Kush in around 110 BC. He is mentioned in an inscription on a pillar erected by one Heliodorus in a village in central India hundreds of miles away to the south-east but just fields from Vidisha and the stupas of Sanchi. Heliodorus was Antialcidas' emissary to a King Bhagabhadra who is otherwise unknown but who may have been one of the Shungas. Perhaps Antialcidas was seeking some kind of alliance against his ever quarrelsome rivals. The memorial is more revealing about ambassador Heliodorus who, though decidedly a Greek and the son of a certain Dion of Taxila, nevertheless describes himself as a devotee of the god Vasudeva. Accordingly he crowned his pillar with an image of the winged Garuda, Vasudeva's 'vehicle'. Already associated with both the Greek Heracles and the Yadavas' Lord Krishna, the heroic Vasudeva was about to become absorbed into the multiple persona of the great Lord Vishnu. Heliodorus thus provides an early example of the adoption by a non-Indian, not of the generally more accessible and proselytising doctrines of the Buddha, but of an orthodox cult within the so-called 'Great Tradition' of what we now call Hinduism.

Such cross-cultural adoptions, for which the word 'conversion' is still too strong, become commonplace amongst those who in the first century BC supplanted the Bactrian Greeks. On their coins, modelled on those of the Bactrian Greeks, Greek gods are jumbled up with unmistakably Indian deities, amongst whom Lord Shiva and his consort Uma have been identified. Elephants also appear, and kings are often depicted mounted on horseback. The newcomers have unfamiliar names – Maues, Azes, Spalirises; each is typically designated a 'king of kings' and, less proud of their profiles, they eschew the close-up portraits so beloved of the Greeks.

Who these people were, when they reigned and where, is still debated. Most authorities believe that Maues, who first displaced the Greeks in the Taxila region, was a Shaka, others that he was a Pahlava. The Pahlavas, it appears, may or may not be the same as the Parthians of northern Iran, just as the Shakas may or may not be the same as the Scythians of the Caucasus. But if Maues and his immediate successors in the first century BC were Shakas, their immediate successors in the first century AD were probably Parthians.

Of one of these Parthians we know from a source other than his coins and the odd inscription. His name was 'Gondophares', which, as the French scholar M. Reinaud noticed in the 1860s, bears a more than coincidental resemblance to 'Gudnaphar', an Indian king mentioned in an early Christian text. This text was the Acts of St Thomas, wherein the self-same apostle is said to have actually attended the court of King Gudnaphar. Thomas, it seems, had reached the Panjab under protest. After the death of Christ, when the apostles drew lots as to their respective missions, Thomas had drawn India and, ever the 'doubting Thomas', immediately knew that the task was beyond him. 'Whithersoever thou wilt, O Lord, send me,' he prayed, 'only to India I will not go.' But the prayer was of no avail. Thomas, apparently a skilled carpenter, found himself indentured to a passing Indian merchant who took him back to work on Gondophares' new palace. In the Panjab he was eventually rewarded with honours and converts. Later, he would undertake a second mission to peninsular India, where his misgivings would prove tragically well-founded.

Whether this Thomas was really Thomas the apostle, and whether he really reached the Panjab, is suitably open to doubt; likewise the 'converts' he is supposed to have made there. But at least the tradition implies that Gondophares must have ruled after the death of Christ. This may not seem a great point. It deserves, though, to be greeted as something of a milestone in what is otherwise a trackless wilderness of dynastic uncertainty.

Both Shakas and Parthians had originated beyond the Hindu Kush. There, along the desert routes from China and across the steppes of Turkestan, a major upheaval had been taking place. Chinese sources tell of the construction of the Great Wall in the third century BC and the repulse of various marauding tribes. Forced to head west and eventually south, these tribes displaced others in an ethnic knock-on effect which lasted many decades and spread right across central Asia. The Parthians from Iran and the Bactrian Greeks from Bactria had both been dislodged by the Shakas coming down from somewhere near the Aral Sea. But the Shakas had in turn been dislodged by the Yueh-chi who had themselves been driven west to Sinkiang by the Hiung-nu. The last, otherwise the Huns, would happily not reach India for a long time. But the Yueh-chi continued to press on the Shakas and, having forced them out of Bactria, it was sections or clans of these Yueh-chi who next began to move down into India in the second half of the first century AD.

Once again the ready assumption that the Yueh-chi, or Kushana as they are known in Indian history, actually invaded India should be treated with caution. Little is known either of the circumstances which accounted for the movements of these peoples or of the reception they received in India. They may have come as allies or mercenaries, invited by disaffected Indians like Alexander's Ambhi; or they may have come as refugees fleeing invasion just like the Tibetans, Afghans and Bangladeshis of the twentieth century. India's ancient history was first reconstructed largely by British scholars in the nineteenth century who, schooled on the invasions of Aryans, Macedonians and Muslims, readily detected a pattern of incursions. Their own presence conformed to it; indeed this pattern of constant invasion conveniently excused their presence.

The coins and inscriptions of the first few centuries BC/AD certainly testify to alien rulers, but of battles we know nothing, let alone who won them. Marital alliances, economic crises, coups and assassinations have probably triggered more dynastic changes than have successful invasions. Given the crisis of political legitimacy, given too the obscure origins of most indigenous dynasties of the period, plus the absence of anything like a national consciousness, there may have been no fundamental objection to accepting as kings men with strange names, remote origins and unusual headgear.

The Pahlavans/Parthians quickly disappeared from the Indian scene. They would be resurrected only once, and much later, as the doubtful antecedents of the Pallavas of Kanchipuram, a distinguished dynasty but one separated from the Parthians by three centuries and the breadth of the entire subcontinent. The Shakas/Scythians, segmenting into a variety of junior kingdoms, or satrapies, and readily assimilating to Indian society, made a more lasting impression. At one time they penetrated to Mathura and Ujjain but would latterly be penned into Saurashtra (in Gujarat); thence, as the 'Western Satraps', they would resurface briefly in the first and second centuries A D. Only the Yueh-chi or Kushanas, and in particular their great king Kanishka, would establish anything like an Indian empire.

Coins, plus an inscription found at Taxila, bear early testimony to the pretensions of the Kushana. 'Maharajah', 'King of Kings', 'Son of God', 'Saviour', 'Great One', 'Lord of all Lands', 'Caesar' and other such titles are reeled off as if the incumbent wished to lay claim to every source of sovereignty going. 'Son of God' is thought to be a legacy of the Yueh-chi's familiarity with China and its celestial rulers; 'King of Kings' was borrowed from the Shakas, who had imitated the Achaemenids of Iran; 'Saviour' came from the Greeks; 'Caesar' from the Romans. The coins are of the highest quality and show a switch to Roman weight standards; possibly they were actually recast Roman *aurei*. But to accommodate such fanfares of majesty in the limited space available, the name of the king in question was often left out. The succession of the Kushana kings is therefore far from certain. It is thought that there was a Kujula Kadphises and then a Wima Kadphises, evidently another devotee of Lord Shiva, who between them added to their Afghan territories those of Gandhara, the Panjab, and the Ganga-Jamuna Doab at least as far south as Mathura.

After these Kadphiseses came, probably, Kanishka. Inscriptions referring to him (or to the era which supposedly began with his accession) are found over a vast area extending from the Oxus frontier of Afghanistan to Varanasi and Sanchi. Tradition further testifies to his conquest of Magadha and to vast responsibilities in and beyond the western Himalayas, including Kashmir and Khotan in Sinkiang. Buddhist sources, to which we are indebted for much of this information, hail him as another Menander or Ashoka; he showered the *sangha* (the monastic community) with patronage, presided over the fourth Buddhist council and encouraged a new wave of missionary activity. At Purushpura, or Peshawar, his capital still boasts the foundations of a truly colossal stupa. Nearly a hundred metres in diameter and reliably reported to have been two hundred metres high, it must have ranked as one of the then wonders of the world.

Mathura on the Jamuna seems to have served as a subsidiary capital, and nearby have been found suitably massive statues of Wima Kadphises and of Kanishka himself. Unfortunately both have been decapitated. While for the Greeks, thanks to their coins, we have notable heads but few torsos, for the Kushanas we have notable torsos but few heads. Kanishka stands in challenging pose, his outsize feet encased in quilted felt boots and splayed outwards. The full-frontal presentation reveals a belted tunic beneath a stiff ankle-length coat that looks as if it could have been of leather. One hand rests on a grounded sword of skull-splitting potential, the other clutches an elaborate contraption sometimes described as a mace but which could equally be some kind of crossbow. Hopelessly overdressed for the Indian plains and most un-Indian in its angular and uncompromising posture, this statue evokes the harsh landscapes whence the Kushana came and where, while campaigning in Sinkiang, Kanishka is said to have died. Although surely not 'one of the finest works of art produced on Indian soil', his statue is indeed 'unique as the only Indian work of art to show a foreign stylistic influence that has not come from Iran or the Hellenistic or Roman world'.[6]

Kanishka's successors, many with names also ending in '-ishka', continued Kushana rule for another century or more. As with other august dynasties, their territories are assumed to have shrunk as their memorials became fewer and nearer between; in the course of time the Kushanas dwindled to being just one of many petty kingdoms in the north-west. Unfortunately it is impossible to be precise about their chronology since all inscriptions are dated from the accession of Kanishka, itself a subject of yawning complexity which numerous international gatherings on several continents have failed to resolve. Today's Republic of India, as well as having two names for the country (India and Bharat), has two systems of dating, one the familiar Gregorian calendar of BC/AD and the other based on the Shaka era which is reckoned to have begun in 78 AD. Although called 'Shaka' (rather than 'Kushana'), this era is supposed by many to correspond with the Kanishka era. Others have tried to match Kanishka with another Indian era, the Vikrama, which began in 58 BC. This seems much too early. On the other hand the latest scholarship, based on numismatic correlations between Kushana and Roman coins, pushes Kanishka's accession way forward to about 128 AD.

Clearly these variations are significant. Were Kanishka's dates certain, it might be possible to be a little more dogmatic about his achievements, although the same can hardly be said of his elusive successors. If there has to be a blind summit somewhere along north India's chronological highway, the second to third centuries AD would seem as good a place as any. Should, however, the controversy be resolved, it could mean whole-scale revision of our understanding of the preceding centuries; upgrading even chronological highways can have dramatic results.

ACROSS THE ROOF OF THE WORLD

When Pakistani and Chinese engineers began construction of a road link between their two countries in the late 1970s, eyebrows were raised in Delhi and elsewhere. The planned 'Karakoram Highway' was seen as evidence of a menacing alignment between Mao-tse Tung's China and Zulfiqar Ali Bhutto's Pakistan. As well as being politically sinister and strategically unprecedented, it was thought geographically perverse. For if ever there was a frontier decreed by nature it was the Himalayan chain. This, after all, was India's Great Wall; behind it the peoples of the subcontinent had traditionally sheltered from the whirlwinds of migration and conquest which ceaselessly swept the arid pastures beyond. Moreover, nowhere was this wall more formidable than at its western bastion where, in the far north of Pakistan, the Great Himalaya becomes entangled in the pinnacles of the Hindu Kush and the glaciers of the mighty Karakoram. Extremes of temperature, colossal natural erosion, frequent seismic activity and recent glacial acceleration also make this the most unstable region on earth. Breaching the rampart with the viaducts, tunnels and easy gradients of an all-weather, two-lane highway looked to be short-sighted, provocative and exceedingly challenging.

Nevertheless, at fearful cost in lives and plant, the road was built. 'The eighth wonder of the world' was duly hailed, and convoys of battered trucks and buses began occasionally to emerge at its either end after eventful days of motoring across 'the roof of the world'. The benefits have been mixed. At five thousand metres above sea-level, the Sino–Pakistan border on the blizzard-swept Khunjerab Pass has witnessed a modest flow of trade but little other intercourse. The road has been more of a boon to the isolated mountain communities of Pakistan's 'Northern Areas', although the discreet charms of their valleys have been prejudiced in the process. Only to archaeologists and historians has the road opened a wholly welcome perspective.

That from India the teachings of the Buddha had originally spread to China via central Asia had long been known. The Han dynasty had opened trade with the West via the so-called Silk Route in the second century BC; the Route ran north of Tibet, on through Sinkiang and then down the Oxus through Bactria to Bukhara, Iran and the Mediterranean. The Han dynasty had also been in diplomatic contact with the Yueh-chi long before the latter, as Kushanas, entered India. Later, when Kushana dominion spread in a great arc from Sinkiang through Afghanistan and across the Indus into India, an obvious India–China conduit was created. Additionally

Kanishka had clearly revived Ashoka's policy of patronising the Buddhist *sangha* and promoting the spread of Buddhist doctrine. From Chinese sources it was even known that the first Buddhist missionaries to China had set out from India in 65 AD. It was therefore probably under the Parthians or the Kushanas that the monks Dharmaraksa and Kasyapa Matanga had made their way to China, there to found the first monastery and begin their work of preaching and translating the sacred doctrines. In their footsteps would follow the procession of teachers and artists, of icons, texts and relics which over the next three hundred years would nurture the new faith and diffuse new art forms in China and beyond.

Traditionally their route is supposed to have proceeded from Peshawar up the valley of the Kabul river, past Jalalabad, and on to Bamiyan before crossing the Hindu Kush into Bactria.[7] At Bamiyan, a tight valley in the heart of the Afghan Hindu Kush, gigantic statues of the Buddha have been carved high in the vertical cliffs. Beside and around them, the cliff-face is honeycombed with the cells and caves which served the community as places of worship and shelter. Bactria itself boasts further relics of a Buddhist presence, and thence north and east across the Pamirs, round the desert of Takla Makan and across Lop Nor a succession of Buddhist sites marks the trail to China. 'The road is long,' reported a later Chinese pilgrim who had made the return journey to India; looping laboriously right round that mountain bastion of India's 'Great Wall' it is all of three thousand kilometres. There is no doubt that it was indeed an important route for the traffic of both ideas and commodities; but what the road-builders in the 1970s discovered was that there had been a shorter and better signposted route by way of the upper Indus and Hunza rivers along the line of their Karakoram Highway.

As reconstructed by Dr Ahmad Hasan Dani, Pakistan's leading archaeologist, the historical trail begins north of Taxila, where the modern highway strikes off into the hills. Suitably enough the first 'signpost' is a Kharosthi version of Ashoka's Major Rock Edict engraved on two badly weathered boulders at Mansehra. The road runs between them and, in view of the incidence of other Ashokan inscriptions at major route intersections, it seems safe to infer that the Indus route into the mountains was in use in the third century BC and here linked with feeder routes from Taxila, Peshawar and Swat. Thence the new road traverses the switchback hills of Kohistan, where innumerable caves and rock drawings continue the Buddhist theme; one drawing is identified by an inscription as being of 'the monastery of Maharajah Kanishka'. As the roadway wriggles above, and then through, the awesome Indus gorges, more such graffiti on cliffs and rocks – 'beside the tunnel', 'above the petrol station' – record the passage of individual monks and the presence of stupas and *viharas*.

West of Chilas, beneath the snowy massif of Nanga Parbat, the Indus valley opens out into a scorching lunar wasteland, devoid of vegetation but garish with rocks of every hue. Here one of many inscriptions mentions the Kushana king Wima Kadphises. Nearer the windswept little town a scene etched on a boulder by the river clearly identifies the Shaka king Maues; it is 'the first proof of the conquest of this region by the Scythian ruler'[8] who seems to have actually 'invaded' the Panjab by this route. On the other side of Chilas one of many illustrated boulders is known as the Rock of Gondophares; its inscription lauds the Parthian king who was 'doubting Thomas's' patron.

A sculpted Buddha and more stupas lie in the valleys round Gilgit. Thence both highway and Buddhist trail funnel into the Hunza valley for the spectacular climb up to the glaciers. K2 and associated peaks lie to the east with the Khunjerab Pass and the Chinese border dead ahead. The highway terminates at Tashkurgan, an ancient staging post on the main Silk Route. As a final reminder that this vital trail and all the territory through which it passed lay within the Kushana empire, there is a veritable data-bank of ancient kings, cults and passing strangers, including notices of both the first Kadphises and again of *Kusana Devaputra* ['son of God'] *Maharajah Kaniska*, on the so-called Sacred Rock of Hunza.

> The new Karakoram Highway which runs along its southern face
> ... led to the discovery of this monument of world importance
> that had remained hidden for centuries. The Sacred Rock has stood
> adamantly through the ravages of time and maintained the carvings
> and writing of men to tell us about the long-forgotten history of
> the place and of the pathway along which man travelled from
> Gandhara to China.[9]

So the Karakoram Highway, though defying geography, can scarcely be said to have confounded history. In fact it faithfully follows what is now recognised as the preferred route of Buddhist missionaries carrying their teachings to Sinkiang and China.

It is also clear that the teachings in question were increasingly those of Mahayana Buddhism. At the Fourth Buddhist Council held under Kanishka's auspices a long-simmering dispute within the *sangha* had led to schism. Those purists who adhered to the essentially ethical content of the Buddha's teachings became the Hinayana school, while those who would elevate the Buddha and other potentially 'enlightened ones' to the status

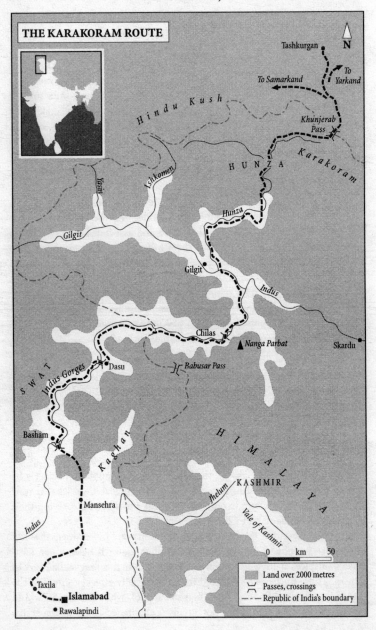

THE KARAKORAM ROUTE

Tashkurgan

N

To Samarkand

To Yarkand

Khunjerab Pass

Hindu Kush

H U N Z A

Karakoram

Hunza

Gilgit

Gilgit

Indus

Chilas

Nanga Parbat

Skardu

Babusar Pass

Dasu

Indus Gorges

S W A T

Basham

Kaghan

H I M A L A Y A

KASHMIR

Mansehra

Jhelum

Vale of Kashmir

Indus

0   km   50

Taxila

■ **Islamabad**

● Rawalpindi

Land over 2000 metres

Passes, crossings

Republic of India's boundary

Left Bronze 'dancing girl' from Mohenjo-daro in Sind province, Pakistan. Although not dancing, this tiny and justly famous figurine is probably Harappan and has been dated to *c.*2000 BC.

Below Mohenjo-daro, the 'Mound of the Dead'. The largest of the excavated Harappan city-sites has typical brickwork, but the foreground 'granary' and the background 'citadel' are conjectural designations.

Sunrise at Dashashwamedh Ghat on the Ganga (Ganges) at Varanasi (Benares). The name of the *ghat* recalls the tenfold *aswamedha* (horse-sacrifice) of the saintly King Divodasa which so discomfited Lord Shiva.

A scene from the *Ramayana* by an early-nineteenth-century artist. The Sanskrit epic shows a growing familiarity with peninsular India, as here in 'The Battle of [Sri] Lanka' between Lord Rama and the demon-king Ravana.

Above The Ashoka column atop Feroz Shah Khalji's fort in Delhi. Inscribed in the third century BC, it was transported to Delhi by a fleet of barges in the fourteenth century. The famous inscription remained undeciphered until the 1830s.

Above right The Lion capital from Sarnath (near Varanasi). Now the national emblem of the Republic of India, it originally capped an Ashoka column erected at the site of the Buddha's first sermon.

Below The rock at Shahbazgarhi (Panjab province, Pakistan) bearing Ashoka's Edicts. One of the Maurya emperor's many rock-cut inscriptions, this one flanks the Karakoram route by which Buddhism spread to China.

Opposite Bactrian coins of a Bactrian Greek king of the second century BC, and of Kanishka, the great Kushan king of uncertain date. The history of the north-west from the third century BC to the third century AD has been largely reconstructed on the basis of such coins.

Above Bracket carved as a *yakshi* on one of the Sanchi gateways. The incorporation of fertility spirits, like the voluptuous tree-entwining *yakshi*, broadened Buddhism's appeal.

Left Relief panel from one of the gateways to the Great Stupa at Sanchi, first century BC. As with most stupa iconography, this eloquent processional scene is drawn from the life of the Buddha.

Left Seated Buddha of the Gandhara school, second century AD. The treatment of costume and countenance betrays the Graeco-Roman contacts of Gandhara and other kingdoms in the north-west.

Below Seated Buddha from Sarnath, fifth century AD. Such Buddhas of the Gupta period rank supreme. Found as far away as Borneo and Vietnam, they testify to the early diffusion of Indic culture.

Opposite Fresco of a Bodhisattva in Cave 1 at Ajanta, Maharashtra, fifth century AD. A religio-commercial centre under the Shatavahanas, Ajanta was extended and embellished with its world-famous frescoes under the Vakataka kings, allies of the 'golden' Guptas.

The early-eighth-century Shore Temple at Mamallapuram near Madras. One of the first structural temples in the south, it was built by Narasimha-varman II in what was then the main port of his Pallava kingdom.

The eighth-century Kailasa temple at Ellora in Maharashtra. Cut from solid rock for the Rashtrakuta king Krishna I, it is not architecture but the world's most monumental sculpture. 'Oh, how was it that I created this?' exclaimed its designer.

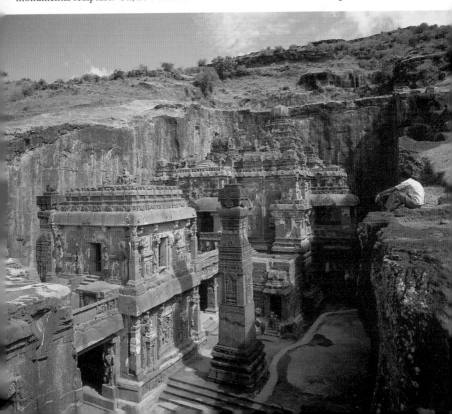

of deities deserving of worship, and so make of his teachings a conventional religion, became the Mahayana. The former persisted in not representing the Buddha as a human figure; in Hinayana art his presence is traditionally indicated merely by a footprint, a throne, a tree, an umbrella. But the Mahayana introduced the Buddha as icon, depicting the 'enlightened one' and a host of other Boddhisatvas, together with their female counterparts, in human form. The idea may have come from the imagery of Graeco-Roman gods introduced by the Bactrian Greeks and from the mainly Roman statuary which was evidently much treasured and traded thereafter. Certainly from this coincidence of Mahayanist demand and Mediterranean supply arose the distinctive style and motifs of Gandhara art.

The Kushana, controlling east–west trade in Bactria as well as vast territories in India, had wealth to lavish on both the new faith and the new art; they may even, like Gondophares, have imported western craftsmen like St Thomas. The style developed rapidly, influencing architecture and painting, and inspiring a narrative art based on Buddhist legend but using Graeco-Roman compositions and mannerisms. Exceptionally, the figure of the Buddha himself proved less susceptible to this 'forum' decorum; though draped in classical folds and endowed with a serene Grecian countenance, his posture, gestures and physical features conformed strictly to Indo-Buddhist iconography. Such was the Gandhara tradition, a curious synthesis of Kushana patronage, Graeco-Roman forms and Indian inspiration. In sculpture, stucco, engraving and painting, it was this synthesis which passed on up the Karakoram route, or round via Bamiyan and Bactria, to fill the monasteries along the Silk Route and provide the inspiration for later Buddhist art in China and beyond.

The Karakoram trail would be little trodden after the fourth century, when Buddhism in north-west India would be eclipsed by more intruders from central Asia, this time the Huns. Despite those ravages of time and nature, the Karakoram records have therefore remained comparatively undisturbed. Significantly, they reveal little about the route being used for trade. Chinese silks, in particular, were imported into India for re-export from India's west coast ports to Egypt and Rome. If such caravans avoided the Karakoram route it was presumably because they found the gradients and the grazing of the Bactrian route more agreeable than the cliff-face ladders of Hunza and the landsliding slopes of the Indus gorges. Lacking commercial potential, the Karakoram route was quietly abandoned.

LOOKING OUTWARDS TO THE SEA

Elsewhere the exchange of ideas matched that of commodities stride for stride, stage for stage. In peninsular India – the region south of the Narmada river comprising the Deccan and the extreme south – the last centuries BC and the first AD witnessed those processes of urbanisation and state-formation which had taken place three centuries earlier in the Gangetic region. But here it was trade which stimulated the transition and trade routes which defined it, especially in the western Deccan (Maharashtra and adjacent regions) and in the extreme south (Tamil Nadu and Kerala). Something of that slow metamorphosis from pastoralism and subsistence agriculture to wet rice-cultivation and an agricultural surplus is also discernible. The construction of irrigation works in the south goes back to the second century BC and was accompanied by a demographic shift from upland settlements to the alluvial and easily watered soils of the deltas. 'In the Chola country, watered by the Kaveri, it was said that the space in which an elephant could lie down produced enough rice to feed seven' (people, presumably, rather than elephants).[10] But here a surplus laboriously realised from agriculture, and then partially squandered on oblations designed to ensure its repetition, was second-best to the surplus on offer from the export of marine and forest produce (especially pearls and pepper) and the re-export of luxury items from further afield. Such options, not open to the Gangetic states, propelled the peninsula from Stone Age to statehood in record time.

Before the first century BC the southern extremity of the subcontinent scarcely features in India's history. Today's southern states – Karnataka, Andhra Pradesh, Tamil Nadu and Kerala – correspond to the languages spoken in each, respectively Kannada, Telugu, Tamil and Malayalam. All belong to the Dravidian family, which is quite distinct from the Indo-Aryan whence Sanskrit and most of north India's contemporary languages derive.

Dravidian-speakers are thought to have preceded Indo-Aryan-speakers in the subcontinent. It has yet to be proved that the Harappans' language was some form of Dravidian, but the survival of a pocket of proto-Dravidian-speakers in Baluchistan, the Pakistan province which borders with Iran, does suggest that the language emanated from somewhere west of the Indus. There is further evidence that this proto-Dravidian once enjoyed a wide currency in Gujarat and Maharashtra, whence it spread to the south. There its advent may have been delayed until the mid-first millennium BC and its adoption may be attributable, as with the Sanskritic *arya* in the Gangetic plain, to the supremacy achieved by a Dravidian-speaking culture possessed of horses and iron weaponry. The same culture may also be responsible for the megalithic sites found in Karnataka and other upland regions of the peninsular interior.

The four Dravidian languages must have developed from proto-Dravidian at an early stage since they were already distinct from one another in prehistoric times. Each, too, was already confined to the region represented by today's states. In fact the continuity of such geo-linguistic entities is the outstanding feature of south Indian history. Here, unusually, definable linguistic units seem to predate the states into which they would become integrated.

Megasthenes in around 300 BC knew of the Pandya kingdom; then, as subsequently, it occupied 'the portion of India which lies southward and extends to the sea'; and it had 365 villages, a not incidental number in that each was expected to supply the needs of the royal household for one day in the year. Ashoka was even better informed. In the Major Rock Edicts he lists his southern neighbours as the Cholas and Pandyas (respectively the northern and southern Tamil-speaking peoples), the Satiyaputras (whose identity is disputed), the Keralaputras (or the Malayalam-speakers of Kerala), and the people of Sri Lanka. Although none formed part of the Mauryan empire, all, according to the Beloved of the Gods, acknowledged the superiority of *dhamma* and had imitated the Ashokan provision of roadside shade trees and of medical care for men and animals.

Later the all-conquering Kharavela, king of Kalinga (Orissa), also noticed the southern kingdoms. In his one extant inscription he typically pretends to have defeated a confederacy of Tamil states and to have acquired a large quantity of pearls from the Pandyas. Pearls and shells, along with the fine cottons of Madurai, the Pandya capital, are also mentioned in the *Arthasastra*. There, in a discussion on how to maximise the state's revenue, Kautilya's mentor rashly suggests that north India's most valuable trade is that with central Asia. The know-all brahman puts him right in no uncertain terms: the trade via the *Daksinapatha* (the 'Southern Route') is the more valuable and, besides, the route is very much safer. Thus trade with the south, albeit in prestige goods, was well-established in Mauryan times; and by way of the secure – and, no doubt, well-shaded – *Daksinapatha* prestigious ideas also travelled down the peninsula.

Of these and much else about the south we know from anthologies of Tamil poetry and from an early Tamil grammar. The poems, of which the oldest date from about the time of Christ, were composed and first recited at marathon arts festivals, or assemblages (*sangam*), organised by the Pandyan court. They were collected into the 'Sangam' anthologies and committed to writing only very much later. Like the Sanskrit classics, they may therefore contain additions and revisions. On the other hand, unlike the Sanskrit classics, they were not the property of a particular caste and served no obvious ritual purpose. Moreover, they provide much reliable detail about social conditions. 'It would be difficult to make too much of this fact,' writes an American authority on Sangam literature. 'Not only does ancient Tamil literature furnish an accurate picture of widely disparate classes; it also describes the social conditions of Tamil Nadu much as it was before the Aryans arrived in the south.'[11]

This verdict suggests some future Aryan mass-migration, for which the evidence is scant. Besides, Sangam literature was already aware of Aryan and Sanskritic ideals. The Tamil poets – and poetesses – knew the epics well and were keen to associate their patrons with the heroes of the *Mahabharata*. Place-names like Madurai, a variant of 'Mathura', reflect the early adoption of the sacred geography of the epics; and just as 'Ayodhya' travelled on to Thailand and central Java, so 'Mathura/Madurai' would make a further landfall in the crowded island of Madura off eastern Java. The Sangam poets also knew of the fabled wealth of the Nandas and of the one-time presence of the Mauryas in Karnataka. Brahmans were already well-established in the south and were the recipients of land grants; Buddhism and Jainism were also familiar; and the script used in the Tamil dedications of their caves was a form of north Indian Brahmi.

Caste distinctions were also observed in the south, but may well predate contact with the Sanskritic north. Certainly they did not conform to the hierarchical four-tier *varna* system; native *ksatriya* and *vaisya* are practically unknown in the south to this day. In caste functions, in hero-worship of the dead, and in the taboos and importance attached to relations between the sexes, there is indeed much that is non-Aryan. Equally unprecedented is the Sangam's spirit of joyous celebration, which pervades both the endless wars between Cheras (Keralans), Pandyas and Cholas as well as the scenes of peaceful plenty and royal munificence which intervene. The impression given by these poems is not that of a society defying the rigid orthodoxies of inevitable Aryanisation, more of one voluntarily adjusting to prestigious new values and selectively adopting from them.

Patterns of Aryanisation were typically spontaneous and here, as outside India, Sanskritic innovations did not necessarily spread through direct contact with the Gangetic heartland. Thus it seems that the southern kingdoms derived as much from their seaward contacts as from landward intercourse. Literacy, for instance, 'and indeed incipient civilisation in general'[12] look to have originally spread not southward from the Gangetic valley but northward, from Sri Lanka. Heavily indebted to Ashoka's missionising, Sri Lanka had stolen a march on the mainland. Its Buddhist chronicles provide the only cross-dating yet established for any of the kings mentioned in the Sangam poems. And from Sri Lanka the Brahmi script is thought to have crossed the straits to neighbouring parts of the Pandya country and thence on to Kerala and the Chola country. By this roundabout route other Aryanising traits may have followed.

The maritime dimension would continue to be crucial; in fact it is from their detailed descriptions of commercial life and foreign trade that the Sangam poems derive much of their authenticity. For in references to busy markets, bulging warehouses, ships from many lands, elaborate import/export procedures, and the *Yavanas* (not only the Bactrian Greeks, but foreigners in general) 'whose prosperity never wanes', there is an impressive convergence of Tamil testimony with what we know of south India in the first century AD from other sources, principally archaeology and copious references in the literature of the Roman empire.

This was the age of Rome's commercial expansion. The new empire's demand for exotica was insatiable, and the acquisition of Egypt in 30 BC had opened the maritime route to the East to Roman investors. A text written by a Greek of the first century AD, the *Periplus of the Erythraean Sea*, contains detailed navigational, commercial and even political information on the ports of the Indian Ocean, many of which have been reliably identified with maritime outlets on India's coast. Ptolemy's second-century 'Geography' adds further details; and the Elder Pliny was already rehearsing an argument, which would become something of a European refrain in the seventeenth century, about Roman bullion being drained away by the purchase of frivolous luxuries from the East. The emperor Augustus claims to have received 'frequent' Indian embassies which look to have come from as far afield as Gandhara and the Pandya kingdom; and it was during his reign (31 BC–14 AD) that Europe's first concerted bid for the exotic produce of the East saw fleets making annual sailings from the Red Sea. Crewed by Greeks and Egyptians, they were familiar with the monsoon trade winds and headed straight for the steamy ports of India's Konkan and Malabar coasts.

There numerous examples of Roman pottery, including wine-impregnated amphorae, have been found in both the south and along the west coast; and hoards of Roman coins have been unearthed in Tamil Nadu, Kerala and elsewhere. On the east coast near Pondicherry (south of Madras) what has been described as 'one of a series of Indo-Roman trading stations' has been excavated at Arikamedu. 'To Arikamedu suddenly, from

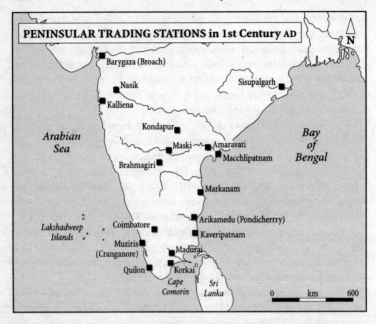

PENINSULAR TRADING STATIONS in 1st Century AD

N

Barygaza (Broach)

Nasik

Sisupalgarh

Kalliena

Kondapur

*Arabian
Sea*

Maski — Amaravati
Macchlipatnam

Brahmagiri

*Bay
of
Bengal*

Markanam

*Lakshadweep
Islands*

Coimbatore

Arikamedu (Pondicherrry)

Kaveripatnam

Muziris
(Cranganore)

Madurai

Quilon — Korkai

*Cape
Comorin*

*Sri
Lanka*

0   km   600

unthought-of lands five thousand miles away, came strange wines, table-wares far beyond the local skill, lamps of a strange sort, glass, cut gems.'[13]

To a neighbouring port at about the same time, there also came the still 'doubting' Thomas. Traditionally on this, his second Indian mission, Thomas made more converts but ultimately paid the price of martyrdom. He was killed in Mylapore, now a suburb of Madras where the cave in which he lived, the hill on which he died, and the grave in which he was laid are named after him and still venerated.

Thomas had landed at one of the palm-fringed ports of Kerala's coconut coast. From converts made there, some sections of Kerala's still thriving Syrian Christian community claim descent. Thence the apostle had proceeded overland to the east coast. A trail of Roman finds extends across the peninsula from Cranganore, otherwise the Roman port of 'Musiris' (near Cochin), to Arikamedu and the mouth of the Kaveri. It would seem, therefore, that Roman shipping did not usually round Cape Comorin. Kerala's pepper and malabathrum (a kind of cinnamon) were the principal Roman imports, and for these it was unnecessary to risk the contrary winds of the Cape. But clearly some of those amphorae of Tuscan wine, some of

that glass and tableware and some *Yavana* traders must have trundled in
oxcarts through the Coimbatore gap (in the Western Ghats) and down the
Kaveri. At Arikamedu and elsewhere on the east coast they were needed
to sustain a no less important trade – that in the cloves and nutmeg of the
Moluccan spice islands and in the gems and resins of Malaya, Burma and
the eastern Himalayas.

TRAFFIC AND SETTLEMENTS

A pattern of east–west trade thus emerges. It is one in which the Indian
ports served as entrepôts as well as termini and in which the voyage across
the Arabian Sea was only one sector of a much more extensive network.
Further information on this first global exchange, and on the vital role
played in it by Indian shipping and Indian merchants, emerges from two
very different sources: inscriptions in the great cave temples of the western
Deccan, and scattered archaeological finds in south-east Asia.

Unfortunately neither is as geographically explicit as the data available
for the Bactrian and Karakoram routes to China. The archaeological finds
in south-east Asia are particularly unimpressive when compared with the
region's later heritage of Indic monuments. In central Burma a town with
palace and stupas based on Indian Buddhist models has been excavated
and dated to the first centuries A D. In Thailand and Vietnam the odd
Roman coin has been found as well as beads, gems, pottery, intaglios and
metalwork of Indian provenance. Shards of Indo-Roman ceramics similar
to those found at Arikamedu have also turned up in Javanese burial sites.
More emphatically, bronze vessels and a carnelian lion found at Don Ta
Phet in west-central Thailand are said to be Buddhist and to 'strongly
suggest that Buddhist missionaries were already active, indeed were established, in south-east Asia before the Christian era'. If account also be
taken of Indian references to ocean-going ships and missionary and trading
ventures to 'Suvarnabhumi', and of Roman notices of 'Chryse' and 'Cher-
sonese' (all three words meaning 'the land of gold' and variously identified
with Burma, Sumatra, or the Malay peninsula), then 'enough evidence is
now at hand ... to show that south-east Asia was already part of a world
trading system linking the civilisations of the Mediterranean Basin and Han
China.'[14]

Thanks to this trade and missionary activity, there are also the first
signs of Indianised cultures in south-east Asia. Early Chinese texts have

been taken to indicate the existence on the Malay peninsula of 'petty Indian states from the second century AD'.[15] One such, called Tun-Sun by the Chinese, had five hundred families from India plus a thousand brahmans to whom the native population gave their daughters in marriage. 'Consequently many of the brahmans do not go away. They do nothing but study the sacred canon, bathe themselves with scents and flowers, and practise piety ceaselessly by day and by night.'[16]

It seems that traders, rather than head down to the Malacca Strait, took a short-cut across the Malay peninsula, just as they did the Indian peninsula. Indian settlements in Malaya were presumably engaged in this transshipment activity, and it may well have been from one of these communities that Kaundinya, a brahman, continued east across the Gulf of Thailand to the mouth of the Mekong. There, again according to Chinese sources, he is said to have encountered hostility. The local queen, Liu-ye ('Willow-Leaf'), wanted to seize his ship. But when Kaundinya fired an arrow which holed her own ship, Willow Leaf changed her mind.

> Frightened, she gave herself up, and Kaundinya took her for his wife. But, unhappy to see her naked, he folded a piece of material to make a garment through which he had her pass her head. Then he governed the country and passed power on to his descendants.[17]

Thus, according to the Chinese, was founded in about 100 AD the Indic kingdom known as Funan. It would survive for five centuries, providing the impetus for other Hindu-Buddhist trading kingdoms on the Vietnamese coast (Champa, Lin-i), before becoming incorporated into the more famously 'Hinduised' kingdom of the Khmers of Angkor.

For the period prior to 300 AD Funan has left few relics. A port-city excavated at Oc-eo in Long-xuyen province in the Mekong delta may date back to the second century AD and has yielded a stone statuette of Vishnu and other Hindu cult objects as well as what may have been a temple. Up the coast at Vo-canh in the Nha Trang region a stele bearing an inscription in Sanskrit may be of the third century. It refers to a ruler who has not been certainly identified; more importantly, it strongly supports the idea that writing was introduced into south-east Asia from India. These are, however, no more than clues to an Aryanising process which, though begun in the first centuries AD, would only assume the character of a cultural diaspora after India's culture had itself become more clearly defined under the 'golden' Guptas.

As for the information to be gleaned from the cave temples of the western Deccan, it not only corroborates *Yavana* (principally Roman) trading activities but also suggests an important link between religious foundations and commercial pioneering. Excavated and sculpted between about 100 BC and 170 AD, the earliest caves in the western Deccan number nearly a thousand. They include those of Bhaja, Karle, Nasik and some of the Ajanta and Ellora caves. Many incorporate the pillars, stupas, *chaitya* arches and magnificent façades which triumphantly belie their designation as 'caves'; and most are Buddhist.

From their numerous inscriptions, plus coins, we learn of Maharashtra's first dynasty and, by correlation with the listings in the *Puranas*, a rough order of succession has been constructed for its kings. These were the Shatavahanas, or Andhras. They are said to have deprived Magadha's Kanva dynasty of its residual authority; and more certainly, they established an extensive if loosely-knit hegemony throughout central India and the Deccan. Its prosperity may be judged not only by the cave temples but also by the magnificent Amaravati stupa, structurally and sculpturally the most elaborate in India. Commissioned mainly by mercantile interests living under the Shatavahana dispensation, it was originally located in Andhra Pradesh but was dismantled in the nineteenth century and is now divided between several museums, including the British where it rightly ranks with the Rosetta Stone and the Elgin Marbles as a most cherished possession.

Like the reliefs on the Sanchi and Bharhut stupas, those of Amaravati depict incidents drawn from the mythology which had grown up around the life of the Buddha. Incidentally all these reliefs also provide insights into the busy social life of the period. In scenes crammed with vitality, turbaned crowds fill every panel. Musicians crouch intently over their instruments and wasp-waisted dancers sway provocatively. Above them ladies ajangle with necklaces and bangles lean from a first-floor balcony beneath the fanciful gable of a barrel-vaulted roof. Horses prance in the street, bullocks patiently haul an elaborately decorated carriage, and an elephant goes berserk. One can almost hear the hubbub, smell the dust. Laden ox-carts, and ships with sails and oars, attest the importance of trade. Masons and labourers are seen constructing the very stupa on which their work is depicted. Indeed the ubiquitous standards and fly whisks carried by those who attend on the Buddha may well belong to particular trade and craft guilds (*sreni*). From literary sources we know of the social, financial and even political weight exercised by guild organisations. We also know that each had its own banner and, from the inscriptions, that these guilds were major patrons of Buddhist institutions.

Similar organisations operated throughout the Shatavahana kingdom

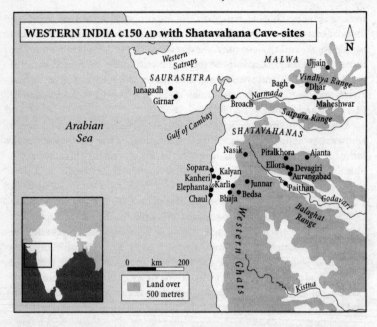

WESTERN INDIA c150 AD with Shatavahana Cave-sites

and it is no coincidence that Shatavahana ascendancy coincided with the boom in overseas trade with both south-east Asia and the Roman empire. The anonymous author of the *Periplus* actually mentions some of the Shatavahana kings, and clearly knew their port-cities well: Broach (Bharu-kaccha, 'Barygaza'), he reports, had a system of pilot boats to escort ocean-going vessels into its tricky anchorage at the mouth of the Narmada, 'where nothing can be observed with certainty'; Sopara and Kalyan (Kalliena), both near Bombay, were also major ports although the latter had lately been grabbed by the Shatavahanas' rivals, the Shaka satraps of Gujarat; its trade was therefore 'much hindered'. After 170 AD recession throughout the Roman world much hindered the entire Indian Ocean trade, and once again this development was faithfully reflected in the western Deccan; the excavation of cave temples abruptly ceased, not to be resumed for another two hundred years, as the Shatavahanas withdrew to the east.

Moreover, the link between trade and dominion was not just one of timing. 'The prosperity ushered in by trade and the need to control the trade routes is apparent in the sites chosen by the Shatavahanas for their earliest inscriptions.'[18] Inland trade routes converged on the Shatavahanas' west coast ports from Ujjain and the Gangetic states as well as from the Shatavahanas' capital at Paithan in the Deccan. In both cases they had to thread their way down the rocky defiles of the Western Ghats. The Shatavahanas' earliest inscriptions are at cave sites clearly related to these passes and defiles. Not without reason did one of the earliest Shatavahana kings describe himself as *daksinapatha-pati*, 'the lord of the *daksinapatha* (the "southern route")'.

The *Periplus* describes vast wagon trains heading down from Ujjain with the exotic produce of the Kushana domains and beyond – spikenard, saffron and costus (a medicinal root) from the Himalayas, ivory and bdellium (a resin), muslins and silks, agate and carnelian, ebony and teak. The trade may go back to Mauryan times since a fragment of an Ashokan Rock Edict has been found at the port of Sopara. But it was the Shatavahanas who were responsible for developing it. They not only controlled the trade routes but also encouraged the settlement of lands which would supply both the ports and the staging posts. It was to further this programme of settlement and strategic control that the Shatavahana dynasty, though orthodox in its adherence to Vedic sacrifice and deities, patronised and encouraged Buddhist establishments as well as making land grants to brahmans.

Buddhism, as noted, had become identified with commerce and manufacturing. Not only did Buddhist doctrine encourage the investment of resources which would otherwise be wasted on sacrifices; it also denied caste taboos on food and travel which made trade so hazardous for the orthodox. Monastic establishments thus became foci of inland trade. Beside and below the extant cave temples it is thought that there stretched bazaars and lodging houses, stables, holding pens and joinery shops, all of course built in long-since-perished timber. The monasteries thus served the functions of caravanserais. And, though initially recipients of royal grants, they soon attracted private donations and mercantile endowments. As guild-members or as individuals, weavers, grain merchants, basket makers, leather workers, shipping agents, ivory carvers, smiths, salt merchants and a host of other craftsmen and dealers are recorded as donors in the cave temple inscriptions. Many hailed from distant parts of India; some even described themselves as *Yavanas*; all clearly had a vested interest in the booming commerce and so in the religious establishments which made it possible.

The nature of Aryanisation within the subcontinent is still debated; so is that of India's growing influence outside the subcontinent. Were Funan and all the later Indianised states in south-east Asia the result of trading links, of missionary activities, of migration, or of conquest? Should they be called 'colonies'? Or were their Indian credentials simply the result of local elites espousing imported ideas of kingship, cultural sophistication and social differentiation? Conquests like Rome's contemporary triumphs in Gaul and Britain can be discounted. It is much more likely that the processes responsible for the diaspora of Indian ideas in south-east Asia mirrored those at work in the western Deccan where trade, religious institutions and royal authority operated in consort to promote security, extend agrarian settlement and stimulate state-formation.

Gupta Gold

C300–500 AD

REDEEMED BY RUDRADAMAN

JUST OUTSIDE the town of Junagadh in the Saurashtra peninsula of Gujarat an isolated massif rears abruptly from low-lying fields and pastures. This is Girnar, or 'Giri-nagar' ('city-on-the-hill'), one of the most remarkable mountains in India,[1] whose several peaks, some over a thousand metres high, are strung about with a garland of the precariously situated temples so beloved of the Jains. Throughout the year a trickle of Jain pilgrims from all over Gujarat and Rajasthan converges on Junagadh to climb the mountain and make a *parikrama* (meritorious circuit) of its craggy shrines.

Their route begins along a trail of deceptive ease which, issuing from the west gate of the town, quickly leads to a bridge. Thence, by the shortest of detours, the curious may inspect Girnar's least-visited attraction. Roughly seven metres by ten, the hump-backed mass of granite that bears Ashoka's Major Rock Edict can hardly compare with the beetling cliffs and the airy vistas that lie ahead. Wayfaring Jains usually give it a miss. Whether bent to their staves or dangling from doolies (seats for one, suspended from a pole borne by two), they press on to the ethereal heights of their local Olympus.

Isolated and ignored in this remote extremity of the subcontinent, the Ashoka rock, 'converted by the aid of the iron pen ... into a book' (as James Tod put it), yet retains the capacity to stir an indologist's dusty emotions. Its improbable location speaks volumes for the extent of ancient India's empires, and it is vastly more impressive than the much-reduced replica which slumps, equally ignored, outside the main entrance of New Delhi's National Museum. It is also rather more informative. On close inspection, the rain-blackened rock is found to be neatly etched not only with the 'pin men' script of the Ashoka Brahmi inscription but also with two much later records. Both relate to repairs carried out on an irrigation system in the vicinity of Junagadh which has long since disappeared. One is of the reign of Skanda-Gupta, last of the five great Gupta emperors, and so dates from the mid-fifth century A D; an important and colourful piece of verse, it will be noticed later. The other is earlier (150 A D) and even more informative. It tells of the history of the dam, how it was constructed by Chandragupta Maurya's governor (hence, as noted, providing the only evidence for the first Maurya's conquests in Gujarat), and how subsequently Ashoka's provincial governor, evidently a *Yavana*, added new conduits or canals. Thanks to such improvements, more land was no doubt cleared and more settlers flocked to Junagadh, whose fine soil must have rewarded the engineers' skills with double cropping and handsome yields.

Sadly, though, according to this second inscription the whole irrigation system had since suffered severe storm damage. In fact it was thought to be beyond repair. Then 'Maha-kshtrapa ('Great Satrap') Rudradaman' decreed otherwise. Under the direction of his minister Suvisakha, a Pahlava (Parthian), the necessary rebuilding had been put in hand and the system was now, in 150 A D, again in operation. According to the inscription, the Great Satrap Rudradaman had done all this 'without oppressing the people of the town or the province by exacting taxes, forced labour, donations or the like'. It had been paid for entirely out of his own treasury. Not unreasonably he claimed to be the most undemanding of rulers.

This episode, although presented as testimony of Rudradaman's indomitable character, may also be taken as symptomatic of his redemptive reign, both of which the inscription describes in fulsome detail. For Rudradaman had inherited a kingdom which was every bit as badly in need of repair as the Junagadh dam. He was in fact one of those, probably Scythian, 'Western Satraps' who were offshoots of the Shaka kingdom established by Maues, Azes and Spalirises in Gandhara and the Panjab and which succeeded that of the Bactrian Greeks. In the Panjab the Shakas had subsequently been eased out by the Kushana, but in Gujarat their Western Satraps had soldiered on. Throughout the late first century A D they ruled, initially as *kshtrapas* (satraps) of Kushana overlords like Kanishka, then as increasingly independent *maha-kshtrapas* (great satraps) of Kanishka's less illustrious successors. To their domains in Gujarat were added parts of what is now Rajasthan, while a satellite satrapy was established north of the Narmada in Malwa (now in Madhya Pradesh). Thence, from Ujjain, Malwa's ancient capital, the Satraps had become embroiled with their richly trading Shatavahana neighbours in the western Deccan. The *Periplus* records the Satraps' occupation of Broach and their blockading of Kalyan under a leader called Nahapana, while, inland, inscriptions in the cave temples of Nasik and Junnar further attest the Shaka presence in Shatavahana territory.

It seems, however, that the Shatavahanas did not long suffer this indignity. Under the great Gautamiputra Satakarni they successfully repelled the Satraps and completely 'uprooted' Shaka rule in Malwa. A large hoard of Shaka coins found near Nasik, most of which had been restruck by the Shatavahana king, would seem to confirm this victory. The Satraps were forced back into Gujarat and immediately began planning their revenge. A certain Chashtana, from his coins a wily-looking strategist, was chosen to lead the Shaka forces, and duly established his own satrapal dynasty. The task of restoring the power of the Western Satraps then started in earnest and, according to the Junagadh inscription, had now, in 150 AD, been successfully completed by Chashtana's grandson, the Great Satrap Rudradaman.

Rudradaman had actually done rather better than that. As well as twice defeating the Shatavahanas and reconquering the whole of Malwa, he claimed to have made extensive acquisitions in Rajasthan and Sind and to have routed the Yaudheyas. The latter were *ksatriyas* who still followed their hereditary calling as professional warriors and who retained a republican form of government in their territory to the west of Delhi. Presumably Rudradaman encountered them somewhere further south, perhaps in Rajasthan; certainly he did not occupy their homeland. Whereas the claimed conquests of, say, Kharavela of Kalinga positively invite suspicion, Rudradaman's are generally plausible. He avoids the usual clichés about an empire reaching from the ocean to the Himalayas; not one of his elephants had ever been watered in the Ganga. His coins, mostly silver, describe him simply as 'Mahakshtrapa'; their royal busts, if we may assume that they are portraits, have been taken to 'show a man of vivacious and cheerful disposition'.[2]

The Junagadh inscription, while failing to elaborate on this cheerful disposition, does add much personal detail. Rudradaman staunchly upheld *dharma*, possibly in imitation of Ashoka, with whose Edicts he was so happy to share rock-space. He was also a fine swordsman and boxer, an excellent horseman, charioteer and elephant-rider, universally praised for his generosity and bounty, and far-famed for his knowledge of grammar, music, logic and 'other great sciences'. Clearly he aspired to what he took to be an essentially Indian ideal of kingship; and he succeeded so well that thereafter his name (which unlike 'Maues' and 'Azes' was a decidedly Indian one) was 'repeated by the venerable . . . as if it was another Veda demanding assiduous study and devout veneration and yielding the most precious fruit'.[3] He also, his inscription claims, wrote both prose and verse which were 'clear, agreeable, sweet, charming, beautiful, excelling in the proper use of words, and adorned'. Moreover, as if to prove his point, he had taken the novel and perhaps presumptuous decision to have his memorial written in classical Sanskrit. Rudradaman's Junagadh inscription is in fact 'the earliest known classical Sanskrit inscription of any extent'.[4]

The records of Ashoka, Kharavela and Kanishka and all those Shatavahana cave inscriptions are in some form of Prakrit, usually Magadhi or Pali. These were the languages of everyday use which, since their adoption by early Buddhist and Jain commentators, had become the normal medium of record. Much-simplified derivatives of classical Sanskrit, the Prakrit languages have sometimes been unfairly likened to pidgin; after a further stage of adaptation, they would spawn the Indo-Aryan regional languages of today – Hindi, Marathi, Gujarati, Panjabi, etc. Sanskrit, on the other hand, remained a prestige language, imbued with sacral powers, reserved mainly for religious and literary purposes, and jealously guarded as well as principally understood by brahmans. Its unexpected emergence as a language of contemporary record in the second century A D, and its subsequent acceptance as the medium of courtly and intellectual discourse throughout India, may be taken as a sure sign of a brahmanical renaissance.

Such would indeed prove to be the case under the Guptas. The great era of all that is deemed classical in Indian literature, art and science was now dawning. It was this crescendo of creativity and scholarship, as much as the unevenly documented political achievements of the Guptas, which would make their age so golden; and it was to the wider use of Sanskrit and the exploration of its myriad subtleties that this awakening owed most.

In the development of languages the classical phase usually precedes the proliferation of vernacular derivatives; thus the Latin of Cicero, Virgil and Horace precedes the vulgarised vernacular from which the Romance languages developed. Sanskrit somehow reversed the process; it was making its great comeback when it should have been dying. Why this happened remains a puzzle. 'The answer cannot be given in purely cultural terms,' wrote D.D. Kosambi. A Marxist as well as a brahman, Kosambi sought an explanation in 'the development of India's productive systems' and 'the emergence of a special position for the brahman caste'.[5] Behind the glittering façade of Gupta culture, society was about to undergo the profound changes associated with the Indian version of feudalism. A gradual process of unsensational devolution, it would give a new impetus to the Aryanising primacy of both the brahmans and their language.

One other linguistic question remains. How was it that Rudradaman and his minister anticipated such a quintessentially classical trend as the triumph of Sanskrit by a couple of centuries, and in an inscription so remotely located that it can have been seen only by a literate few? The suggestion has been made that the Satrap's use of Sanskrit was 'a method followed to endear a ruler of foreign descent to the indigenous ruling class'; thus, in the case of Rudradaman, a Shaka, and his deputy Suvisakha, a Parthian, the adoption of Sanskrit and the patronage of those who held it dear was designed to reconcile brahman opinion to a foreign ruler – or as Kosambi puts it 'to mitigate the lamentable choice of parents on the part of both Satrap and governor'.[6] This seems plausible and is generally accepted in respect of the Sanskrit inscriptions soon to be composed by, or for, Indophil rulers in Sumatra, Java, Indo-China and other parts of Indianised south-east Asia. The employment of a prestige language lent distinction and authority even to non-Indic dynasties. One wonders why, though, if Sanskrit offered such ready legitimacy it was not also adopted by the earlier Shakas or the contemporary Kushanas.

However objectionable to north Indian pride, the possibility must remain that in a little-regarded region of the subcontinent long-Indianised dynasts, albeit originally of foreign extraction, could actually have pioneered and popularised such a cardinal feature of the classical Indian tradition. Aryanisation was, as will appear, a two-way process; and many other cultural achievements associated with the Gupta age cannot readily be ascribed to Gupta rule. To the emerging 'Great Tradition' of Hinduism, borrowing from the subcontinent's far-flung store of local custom and innovation was quite as natural as banking on the Indo-Aryan orthodoxies of the Gangetic heartland.

But the history of India's so-called 'regions' (Gujarat, Bengal, Tamil Nadu and so on) is still today in its infancy. Habitually disparaged as divisive, 'regional' history has few champions in the Senior Common Rooms of power. Untypical and brave are the scholars who insist that Rudradaman of Gujarat did himself write such 'clear, agreeable, sweet, charming, beautiful' and altogether excellent Sanskrit; or that under the Satraps' patronage classical Sanskrit was actively promoted (as is further suggested by its appearance in the donative inscription of a Shatavahana queen who was of Satrapal birth); or that 'the Shakas had shown the way by using Sanskrit in their inscriptions . . . [and] the Guptas only perpetuated the tradition when they came to power.'[7]

THE ARM OF THE GUPTAS

History, whatever its parameters, is said to repeat itself. Seldom, though, does it oblige so readily as with the creators of ancient India's two greatest dynasties. A Chandragupta had founded the Mauryan empire in c320; just so did a Chandragupta found the Gupta dynasty in c320. It could be confusing. But the first date was, of course, BC, the second AD; and to clarify matters further, the Gupta Chandragupta is often phonetically dismembered as 'Chandra-Gupta' or 'Chandra Gupta'. Unfortunately there would be another Gupta Chandra-Gupta. The founder of the Gupta dynasty is therefore designated as Chandra-Gupta I – which naturally brings to mind the Mauryan Chandragupta. (Here the Gupta founder will be called Chandra-Gupta I and his Mauryan counterpart Chandragupta Maurya.) Coincidence, however, continues. As well as a name, the Gupta founder shares with his Mauryan predecessor a shadowy profile, a reputation for important but doubtful conquests, and the misfortune of being hopelessly upstaged by a more illustrious successor – Ashoka in the case of Chandragupta Maurya, Samudra-Gupta in the case of Chandra-Gupta I.

Of earlier Guptas before Chandra-Gupta I, a Sri Gupta and a Ghatot-kacha Gupta are listed in inscriptions. The former would be remembered solely for having endowed a place of worship in Bihar for Chinese Buddhists. By the third century AD the first Chinese monks had begun trickling back along the Karakoram route to tour the sites associated with the Buddha's life. For these foreign pilgrims to the Buddhist 'Holy Land' Sri Gupta built a temple; when first noticed in the fifth century, it was already in ruins. Sri Gupta was probably not a Buddhist but was raja of some minor polity near or within erstwhile Magadha. He was succeeded by his son Ghatotkacha. Their origins are unknown; their caste may have been *vaisya*.

Chandra-Gupta I was Ghatotkacha's son. He is regarded as founder of the dynasty partly because he assumed a new title, partly because later Gupta chronology is calculated from what is taken to be the date of his accession (320 or 321 AD), and partly because by marriage or conquest he acquired more territory and authority than he inherited. The new title was *Maharajadhiraja*, 'great raja of rajas', an Indian adaptation of the Persian 'king of kings' as previously adopted by the Kushanas. Its assumption seems premature, but lofty titles and epithets would be important to the Guptas. They would soon up the stakes to *paramaharajadhiraja* and even *raja-rajadhiraja*, 'king of kings-of-kings'.

Presumably the title reflected growing ambitions. Chandra-Gupta I was

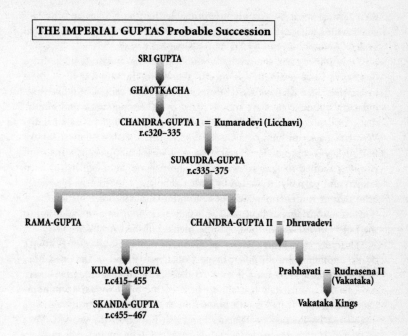

THE IMPERIAL GUPTAS Probable Succession

SRI GUPTA

GHAOTKACHA

CHANDRA-GUPTA I = Kumaradevi (Licchavi)
r.c320–335

SUMUDRA-GUPTA
r.c335–375

RAMA-GUPTA

CHANDRA-GUPTA II = Dhruvadevi

KUMARA-GUPTA
r.c415–455

SKANDA-GUPTA
r.c455–467

Prabhavati = Rudrasena II
(Vakataka)

Vakataka Kings

the first of his line to feature on coins. According to the *Puranas*, his territory stretched along the Ganga from Magadha (southern Bihar) to Prayaga (the later Allahabad in Uttar Pradesh). Whether he conquered this rich swathe of the Gangetic heartland and, if so, from whom, is not known. Magadha, for instance, or part of it, may have come to him as a marriage settlement. Kumaradevi, his chief queen, was a Licchavi and so a descendant of one of those 7707 Licchavi knights-raja who had been defeated by Ajatashatru seven hundred years previously. The Licchavis had a distinguished pedigree which was doubtless highly desirable to unknowns like the Guptas. But the importance the Guptas attached to this union was of an altogether higher order. Chandra-Gupta I's successor would style himself not 'son of a Gupta father' but 'son of a Licchavi daughter'. There are even coins showing king and queen together, an unprecedented development; they bear, as well as the king's name, that of 'Kumaradevi Licchavayah'. It is known that the Licchavis had acquired territory in Nepal and it may be that 'they had taken possession of Pataliputra, the city which had been built and fortified many centuries earlier for the express purpose of curbing their restless spirit.'[8] Certainly it is probable that the Guptas and the Licchavis ruled adjacent territories 'and that the two kingdoms were united under Chandra-Gupta I by his marriage with Kumaradevi'.[9]

Only under their son Samudra-Gupta does the dynasty emerge from obscurity. Once again this is mostly thanks to the survival of a single inscription. Like Kharavela's, it advances extravagant claims, but, like Rudradaman's, these claims are substantiated by other epigraphic and numismatic evidence. The inscription is probably the most famous in all India. Written in a script known as Gupta Brahmi (more elaborate than Ashoka Brahmi), and composed in classical Sanskrit verse and prose, its translation is often credited to James Prinsep of Ashoka fame, although it had been known and partially translated by earlier scholars. Its idiom and language echo that of Rudradaman. So does Samudra-Gupta's choice of site; for as if aspiring to Mauryan hegemony, his panegyric appears as an addition to the Edicts of Ashoka on one of those highly polished Ashokan pillars.

The pillar stands in the city of Allahabad where, soon after Prinsep's death, another Ashokan pillar, or part of it, was found in the possession of a contractor who used it as a road-roller. British antiquarians were mortified. A similar fate had almost befallen the pillar with the Samudra-Gupta epigraph. It had been uprooted in the eighteenth century and was discovered by Prinsep's colleagues lying half-buried in the ground. They re-erected it on a new pedestal and designed an Achaemenid-style replacement for its missing capital. Supposedly a lion, the capital 'resembles nothing so much as a stuffed poodle on top of an inverted flower pot', wrote Alexander Cunningham, the father of Indian archaeology in the nineteenth century.

Cunningham also deduced that the Allahabad column had been shifted once before. Evidently later Muslim rulers had come to see these spectacular monoliths as a challenge to the excellence both of their sovereignty and their transport. They had therefore attempted to relocate them as totemic embellishments to their palatial courts. The truncated pillar which now tops Feroz Shah's palace in Delhi originally stood near Khizrabad higher up the Jamuna. A contemporary (thirteenth-century) account describes how it was toppled onto a capacious pillow, then manoeuvred onto a forty-two-wheeler cart and hauled to the river by 8400 men. Lashed to a fleet of river transports, it was finally brought to Delhi in triumph.

Just so, the Allahabad pillar had apparently been shifted downriver from its original site in Kaushambi. It was meant to enhance the pretensions of the Allahabad fort as rebuilt by the Mughal emperor Akbar in the late sixteenth century. Akbar's son Jahangir would add his own inscription to those of Ashoka and Samudra-Gupta; and thus it is that scions of each of north India's three greatest dynasties – Maurya, Gupta and Mughal – share adjacent column inches in the heart of Allahabad, a city whose further claim to fame is as the home of a fourth great dynasty, that of the Nehru-Gandhis.

Miraculously, all that shunting around of the Allahabad pillar little damaged its inscriptions. That of Samudra-Gupta, if not posthumous, dates from near the end of his reign, which was a long one. He is thought to have succeeded as *maharajadhiraja*, or been so nominated by his father, in c335, and to have died in c380. The inscription may therefore be of about 375 and, with forty years' achievements to cover, it has much to tell. The most important sections consist of long lists of kings and regions subdued by 'the prowess of his arm in battle', otherwise 'the arm that rose up so as to pass all bounds'; indeed the pillar itself 'is, as it were, an arm of the earth' extended in a gesture of command.[10] Some historians take these strong-arm conquests to be arranged in chronological order and, on that basis, have divided them into separate 'campaigns'. Thus the first campaign seems to have taken Samudra-Gupta west where, with the strength of his arm, he 'uprooted' kingdoms in the Bareilly and Mathura regions of what is now Uttar Pradesh and in neighbouring Rajasthan. These were incorporated into the Gupta kingdom.

Next he headed south down the eastern seaboard and, perhaps in the course of several campaigns, elbowed aside a dozen more rivals. He turned back only after capturing Vishnugopa, the Pallava king of Kanchipuram (near Madras). Further campaigns in the north saw Gupta forces overrunning most of Bengal, 'exterminating' independent republics like that of the Yaudheyas west of Delhi, and establishing Gupta rule throughout the ancient *arya-varta* (the Aryan homeland – roughly the modern states of West Bengal, Bihar, UP, Madhya Pradesh and the eastern parts of Rajastan and the Panjab). This became the core region of Gupta rule, within which numerous tribal peoples were also deprived of their autonomy and where most extant inscriptions of the early Guptas have been found. Further afield the Kushanas in Gandhara, Great Satrap Rudradaman's descendants in Gujarat and Malwa, various rulers in Assam and Nepal, and the kings of Sri Lanka and 'other islands' (which could mean the Indianised kingdoms of south-east Asia) are all said to have acknowledged Samudra-Gupta's sovereignty and to have solicited his favour with deferential missions, handsome gifts and desirable maidens.

Now indisputably 'the unconquered conqueror of unconquered kings', Samudra-Gupta stood on the threshold of a pan-Indian empire. Other favourite epithets describe him as 'conqueror of the four quarters of the

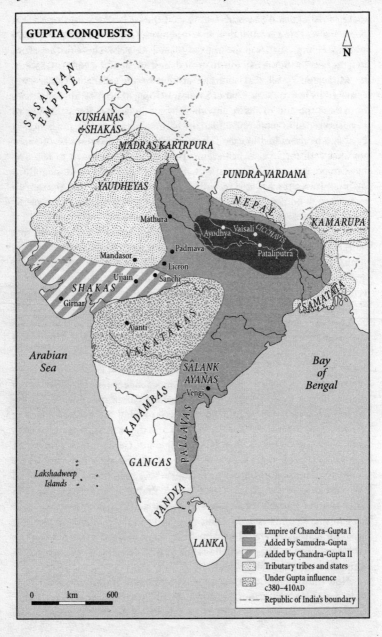

GUPTA CONQUESTS

N

SASANIAN EMPIRE

KUSHANAS & SHAKAS

MADRAS KARTRPURA

PUNDRA-VARDANA

YAUDHEYAS

NEPAL

KAMARUPA

Mathura

Ayodhya   Vaisali   LICHHAVIS

Padmava   Pataliputra

Mandasor

SHAKAS   Ujjain   Licron   Sanchi

SAMATATA

Girnar

Ajanti   VAKATAKAS

Arabian Sea

SALANK AYANAS

Bay of Bengal

Vengi

KADAMBAS   PALLAVAS

GANGAS

Lakshadweep Islands

PANDYA

LANKA

	Empire of Chandra-Gupta I
	Added by Samudra-Gupta
	Added by Chandra-Gupta II
	Tributary tribes and states
	Under Gupta influence c380–410AD
	Republic of India's boundary

0   km   600

earth' and 'a god dwelling on earth'. He performed the horse-sacrifice; 100,000 cows were distributed as gifts, presumably to his brahman supporters. His coins reveal Vaishnavite leanings but, as a world conqueror, he was seen not just as a devotee of Vishnu but as an emanation or incarnation of that deity. Universal dominion was his. Besides the Garuda symbol of Vishnu, some of his coins feature the one-umbrella of a *samrat*. Its welcome shade was seen to engulf the political landscape as he turned the *cakravartin*'s wheel of world-rule.

But what kind of empire was this? Not, it seems, a continually intrusive one. Gupta rhetoric had perhaps outstripped reality; alternatively its richly allusive phrasing may simply have been misinterpreted. For a close scrutiny of Samudra-Gupta's rule reveals little of the bureaucratic interventionism associated with Mauryan empire; and despite the best efforts of patriotic scholarship, the claims advanced by zealous nationalists about his 'unifying India' and arousing a nation are hard to sustain. He may indeed have been 'a man of genius who may fairly claim the title of the Indian Napoleon';[11] the Allahabad inscription certainly refutes the idea that only foreigners have conquered India. But it was a conquest to little lasting political purpose other than dynastic gratification. Just as the celebrity of the Guptas was only perceived after the translation of the Allahabad inscription in the nineteenth century, so a deeper design for their empire was only discovered in the twentieth century. 'Far from the Guptas reviving nationalism it was nationalism that revived the Guptas,' writes Kosambi.[12]

In such championship, Indian nationalism reveals as much about its own ambiguities as about those of the Guptas. Thus we learn that Samudra-Gupta 'was not moved by a lust for conquest for its own sake. He worked for an international system of brotherhood and peace replacing that of violence, war and aggression.'[13] A less likely candidate for the Gandhian mantle of non-aggressive *satyagrahi* it would be hard to find. Nor is this a very convincing explanation for Samudra-Gupta's failure to consolidate his conquests. In the Deccan and elsewhere beyond the frontiers of his Gangetic *arya-varta*, he had made no attempt at annexation. 'Uprooted' kings were reinstated, their territories restored, and the Gupta forces withdrawn. A one-off tribute was exacted and on this the Gupta court waxed wealthy, with conspicuous patronage of the arts and a prolific output of the beautifully minted gold coins to which the Guptas first owed their 'golden' reputation. But unlike the directly administered empire of the Mauryas, this was at best a web of feudatory arrangements and one which, lacking an obvious bureaucratic structure, left the sovereignty of the feudatories largely intact.

In the fourth century BC the Mauryas had been able to extend their rule into politically virgin territories where state-formation, if it existed at all, had been in its infancy. Ashoka had carefully noted several foreign kings in his inscriptions but within India he found not one sovereign worthy of being so named; the 'Cholas' and 'Keralaputras' were families or clans; even Kalinga was just a place and a people. In such a vacuum, Mauryan empire had a pioneering quality and was necessarily one of agricultural settlement, administrative decree and fiscal organisation.

Six hundred years later the Guptas may have found a similar situation in Bengal and have pursued similar policies there. Elsewhere they faced more advanced opponents who were already administering their own states and taxing their own subjects. The submission of all these now carefully named and previously unconquered kings was, of course, most gratifying; 'the Beloved of the Gods' had been merely a *raja*, a 'king'; the Guptas were *maharajadhirajas*, 'kings of kings'. On the other hand they also recognised the difficulty of trying permanently to engross such distant and confident kingdoms. It was more expedient to content themselves with the rich pickings of conquest and to retain the option of perhaps repeating this feat when more such pickings had accumulated.

It also seems that the criteria associated with the status of *cakravartin* did not include sustained government or direct control. In the case of distant rulers a nominal submission looks to have been sufficient, while of those nearer at hand regular attendance on the *cakravartin* was also required. As will emerge, a world-ruler did not actually have to rule the world; it was enough that the world should acknowledge him as such; in fact his status as a *maharajadhiraja* was dependent on the survival of *rajas*, both within and beyond his *arya-varta*, who were powerful enough to justify the title. 'The point here was not to do away with other kings as such and produce a single, absolute kingship, blessed by a monotheist deity, for all India.' Tributary *rajas*, or kings, were essential as validating and magnifying agents. In the same way as local cults and lesser deities were harnessed to the personae of Lords Vishnu or Shiva, so lesser rulers were inducted into an enhancing relationship with the 'world-ruler'. Precedence and paramountcy were what mattered, not governance or integration. 'What distinguished an *imperial* court politically, and especially one whose king claimed to be the universal king of India, was that it was primarily a society of *kings*.'[14]

Samudra-Gupta's immediate successors maintained his elevated status and continued his policies. No inscription as detailed as the Allahabad testimonial is available for any of them, but from minor inscriptions, coins and literary sources it is clear that the Gupta 'empire' now climbed to its ambiguous zenith. There were, however, setbacks and compromises. A sixth-century drama tells of a Rama-Gupta who is thought to have briefly succeeded Samudra-Gupta and who attempted to 'uproot' the Western Satraps in Malwa.[15] The attempt went badly wrong. Rama-Gupta was defeated and, when he tried to disengage, he was informed that the price of escape would be the surrender of his queen. According to a much later biography, the Shaka Satrap sorely coveted the lovely Queen Dhruvadevi. No doubt she had been represented to him as lotus-eyed, with thighs like banana stems, and all the other ripe attributes of desirable womanhood as detailed in textual tradition and epitomised in the *yaksi* temptresses of Mathura and Sanchi sculpture. Aflame with desire, 'the lustful Shaka king' was adamant; Rama-Gupta, hopelessly unworthy of such a desirable consort, conceded defeat and agreed to hand her over.

But the ignominy was too much for Rama-Gupta's younger brother. The latter somehow disguised himself as the shapely Dhruvadevi, was duly given entry to the enemy camp, and promptly slew the Satrap. He must also have made his escape for, Rama-Gupta having been irrevocably disgraced by this affair, it was the righteous brother who now took over the reins of empire as Chandra-Gupta II. He may have had to kill Rama-Gupta in the process; more certainly it was he who eventually claimed the hand of Dhruvadevi.

Not surprisingly Chandra-Gupta II's main offensive was a continuation of this struggle against the Shaka Satraps. Judging by inscriptions in and around Sanchi he seems to have been in eastern Malwa for some years, presumably while he conducted the necessary campaigns. Patience was eventually rewarded. By the year 409 Chandra-Gupta II was issuing silver coins to replace those of the Satraps. The Shaka territories in western India had been annexed to those of the Guptas, and of the Western Satraps no more is heard.

The Guptas thus secured their western frontier and inherited whatever remained of the cultural traditions established by the Sanskrit-loving Rudra-daman and his successors. On the evidence of a Buddhist site in northern Gujarat (Devnimori) which may date to about 375, it has been suggested that Gupta sculpture and architecture owed several motifs and design features to western India. It may also be significant that the cultural achievements usually associated with the Guptas are little in evidence in the fourth century and only become established after Chandra-Gupta II's conquest of the Satraps.

Success against the Satraps also gave the Guptas access to the ports of Gujarat and to the profits of its international maritime trade. There and throughout central India, just as the Satraps had once become embroiled with their Shatavahana trading neighbours, so the Guptas became involved with the Vakatakas, the dynasty which had succeeded the Shatavahanas as the dominant power in the Deccan.

For once, war was not the outcome; perhaps the campaigns against the Satraps were taking their toll. Instead, the Guptas opted for a dynastic alliance whereby Chandra-Gupta II's daughter was married to Rudrasena II, the Vakataka king. The latter soon died and during the ensuing regency (c390–410) it was Prabhavati, this Gupta queen, who as regent controlled the Vakataka state in accordance with Gupta policy. Thereafter the Vakatakas continued as allies and associates of the imperial Guptas.

Other dynastic pairings suggest that the Guptas often made intelligent use of the prestige which attached to the *maharajadhiraja*'s bed-chamber. Prabhavati was Chandra-Gupta II's daughter not by the coveted Dhruvadevi but by a princess of the Naga dynasty. This was an ancient lineage which seems to have re-established itself in Mathura and other parts to the west and south of the Jamuna in the wake of Kushana retraction. Since Samudra-Gupta had earlier 'violently exterminated' the Naga king, it would seem that marriage was used to consolidate existing acquisitions as well as to neutralise external rivals.

Chandra-Gupta II, like his predecessor Samudra-Gupta and his successor Kumara-Gupta, reigned for about forty years. Such longevity over three generations is exceptional and must have been another important factor in the stability of Gupta rule. Of further Gupta feats there is little evidence, the only notable exceptions being a doubtful record of far-flung campaigns by Chandra-Gupta II and an important defensive role undertaken during the reign of Kumara-Gupta.

The former, the campaigns sometimes attributed to Chandra-Gupta II, are recorded in a short inscription engraved on a pillar located at Mehrauli, once a village on the outskirts of Delhi. The pillar, unlike the stone pillars, or *lats*, of Ashoka, is made of iron, and the village is better known as the site where Delhi's twelfth-century sultans would build the renowned Qutb minar and mosque. It is in fact the famously rust-resistant 'Iron Pillar' which now stands in the main courtyard of the mosque and attracts hordes of visitors, many of them convinced that wish-fulfilment awaits those whose arms are long enough to embrace its trunk. Fortunately out of reach, as it might otherwise have been erased by this activity, the inscription commemorates the erection of the pillar as 'a lofty standard of the divine Vishnu'. Its donor was one 'Chandra', supreme world conqueror 'on whose arm fame was inscribed by the sword when in battle in the Vanga countries' and who, having 'crossed in warfare the seven mouths of the [river] Sindhu' defeated the 'Vahlikas'. He also perfumed the breezes of the southern ocean with his prowess. Unfortunately no date is mentioned and, worse still, there is no sign of the word 'Gupta'. 'Chandra' could therefore as well have been a Chandra-sena or a Chandra-varman, both attested kings of the period. And if a Chandra-Gupta, which one? Straining for clarification, scholars, even long-armed epigraphists, find their wishes unfulfilled. The identity of this fragrant 'Chandra' remains a mystery, as does the technology which enabled Guptan smelters to cast an iron obelisk of such rust-resistant purity that sixteen hundred monsoons have scarcely pitted its surface or defaced its inscription.

There is also doubt about this Chandra's listed conquests. 'Vanga', like Anga, was an ancient *janapada* in west Bengal; the 'Sindhu' is usually the Indus; and the 'Vahlikas' have been taken to be the Bactrians. But military successes at such distant poles of the subcontinent strain credulity. In the west no corroborative evidence of Gupta intervention beyond the Indus, let alone beyond the Hindu Kush, is available. However, most of Bengal definitely was within the Gupta ambit. In fact the Guptas were the first north Indian dynasty to extend their rule into and across the heavily forested maze of swamps and waterways that was the Ganga-Brahmaputra delta. Hitherto little exposed to Aryanising influences except along its western seaboard, nearly all of Bengal was now claimed by the Guptas, and it seems reasonable to suppose an accelerated process of drainage, clearance and settlement. From the ruins of the Gupta empire would emerge east and central Bengal's first historical states, amongst which Vanga would be eminent.

Kumara-Gupta, who ruled from c415 to c455, faced a different challenge. In his reign there seems to have been a major uprising in Malwa by one Pushyamitra. Briefly, in the words of the only inscription which refers to it, it 'ruined the fortunes of the Gupta family'. Soon after there first appeared on the Indian scene the *Hunas*, otherwise described as a new breed of *mlecchas* (incomprehensible foreigners). These newcomers were a branch of the Hiung-nu of Chinese history and the Huns of European history. In a new wave of central Asian displacement, an offshoot of this horde, the Ephthalites or White Huns, had established themselves in Bactria in the late fourth century (thus making a Gupta conquest there unlikely). In the mid-fifth they followed their Yueh-chi/Kushana predecessors across the Hindu Kush and into Gandhara, and thence they pushed east against the Guptas.

Fortunately the Guptas produced a champion worthy of the occasion.

In one inscription Skanda-Gupta, a son of Kumara-Gupta, is described as 'subsisting like a bee on the wide-spreading water-lilies which were the feet of his father'. The bee, though, had a sting. It was Skanda-Gupta who took the field successfully against the upstart Pushyamitra. He then made good a doubtful claim to succeed his father. And finally, if only temporarily, he repulsed the Huns.

· It was also during the reign of Skanda-Gupta, he who 'made subject the whole earth bounded by the waters of the four oceans and full of thriving countries round the borders of it', that the last major addition was made to the great rock outside Junagadh in the Saurashtra peninsula. Following the inscriptions of Ashoka and Rudradaman, this third inscription tells of Skanda-Gupta's governor in Gujarat and of his son. Both paragons of virtue, they built a massive embankment when Rudradaman's reservoir was in its turn overwhelmed by floodwaters, and they also added a temple.

But if the temple was meant to guarantee the dam's future security, it failed. Not even a trace of the irrigation system which prompted this unique series of inscriptions beneath the crags of Girnar remains. The rulers of Saurashtra soon deserted Junagadh, perhaps after another disastrous flood, and by 500 a new capital had been established at Vallabhi in the east of the peninsula. Only the hump-backed rock, converted into a book 'by the aid of the iron pen', still mutely protests the majesty of Junagadh's distinguished benefactors.

A similar fate, redeemed only by the tenacity of tradition, now overtook the Gupta empire. After the death of Skanda-Gupta in c467, his nephew Budha-Gupta, then another nephew, his son and then his grandson continued to claim world dominion well into the sixth century. But their reigns were mostly brief and it is clear that by 510 other Guptas, who may or may not have been related to them, operated as independent rulers within the core area of the erstwhile empire. In that year the Huns, led by a formidable leader called Toramana, were again on the move. They overran Kashmir and the Panjab and defeated a Gupta army near Gwalior, thus extending their rule to Malwa. In the face of such disarray, even the fiction of the Guptas' universal sovereignty was unsustainable. Their golden reputation fades from history as the famous gold coinage, debased under Skanda-Gupta, becomes crudely cast, increasingly stereotyped, of rare occurrence, and then non-existent.

THE GUPTA UTOPIA

'Perfection has been attained,' declares the last of the three Junagadh inscriptions. 'While he [Skanda-Gupta] is reigning, verily no man among his subjects falls away from *dharma*; there is no one who is distressed, in poverty, in misery, avaricious, or who, worthy of punishment, is over-much put to torture.' Such a glowing depiction of Gupta society is to be expected from a royal panegyric. It is, however, corroborated by an alien and presumably impartial eye-witness.

> The people are very well off, without poll tax or official restrictions ... The kings govern without corporal punishment; criminals are fined according to circumstance, lightly or heavily. Even in cases of repeated rebellion they only cut off the right hand. The king's personal attendants, who guard him on the right and the left, have fixed salaries. Throughout the country the people kill no living thing nor drink wine, nor do they eat garlic or onions, with the exception of the Chandalas only.[16]

To Fa Hian (Fa-hsien, Faxian, etc.), a Buddhist pilgrim from China who visited India in c400–410, Chandra-Gupta II's realm was indeed something of a utopia. Descending to India by the Karakoram trail, Fa Hian travelled the length of the Gangetic basin in perfect safety as he visited everywhere of note associated with the Buddha's life. Only the lot of the Chandalas he found unenviable; outcastes by reason of their degrading work as disposers of the dead, they were universally shunned and had to give warning of their approach so that fastidious caste-members could take cover. But no other sections of the population were notably disadvantaged, no other caste distinctions attracted comment from the Chinese pilgrim, and no oppressive caste 'system' drew forth his surprised censure. Peace and order prevailed. And if the peace was the peace of past conquests and the order the rigid social hierarchy of *varna* and the professional exclusivity of *jati*, no one was complaining.

From other sources we glimpse a society industrious as well as contented. Those highly influential guilds (*sreni*) regulated elaborate systems of quality control, pricing, distribution and training for every craft and calling. They also acted as bankers, even to the royal court; and their *sresthin*, or aldermen, met regularly in a joint council that has been likened to a chamber of commerce. Trade continued to flourish, both within India and overseas. When Fa Hian returned to China he did so not by the long overland route but aboard an Indian vessel sailing from Tamralipti in

Bengal. After a near-shipwreck off the Burma coast he reached 'Ye-po-ti', which could be Java, Sumatra or Malaya. There, as also in Indo-China, he reported that 'Brahmans flourish although the law of the Buddha is not much known.' After more nautical mishaps, he regained China, again in the company of brahmans and so probably aboard an Indian ship.

In Fa Hian's account of India, Magadha is made to sound especially impressive. Its towns were the largest and its people the richest and most prosperous as well as the most virtuous. True, some Buddhist sites already partook of the archaeological. Kapilavastu, the Sakyas' ancient capital and the Enlightened One's birthplace, was 'like a great desert' with 'neither king nor people'; and of Ashoka's palace in Pataliputra only the ruins remained. But for a Buddhist there was also much to celebrate. Stupas in their thousands, some many-tiered and of gigantic proportions, dotted the landscape – much as they still do today at centres outside India like Pagan in Burma. But then, unlike now, Buddhism still enjoyed the support of large sections of Indian opinion. The monasteries were well-endowed; their monks could be numbered in thousands. Eight centuries after the Buddha, only Sri Lanka was more Buddhist. For Samudra-Gupta it had been particularly gratifying to receive a Sri Lankan embassy whose gifts, coupled with a request for permission to build a monastery on the site of the Buddha's enlightenment at Buddh Gaya, he took to represent a form of tribute.

Not much concerned with political affairs, Fa Hian says nothing of the Gupta court nor of Chandra-Gupta II, its then *maharajadhiraja*. Perhaps, as was normal during the dry season, the court was on the move, receiving the obeisances and consuming the produce of its subject kings or conducting hostilities with the Satraps. In Pataliputra, which along with Ujjain seems to have served as the Gupta capital, the Chinese visitor was more impressed by an annual festival. It was marked by a magnificent procession of some twenty wheeled stupas whose bristling towers accommodated images of the gods decorated with gold and silver as well as sitting figures of the Buddha attended by standing Boddhisatvas. As the procession approached the city Fa Hian watched 'the *brahmacharis* come forth to offer their invitations; the Buddhas then, one after another, enter the city'.[17]

As between the orthodox and the heterodox sects ecumenism was still the norm. The Guptas, although identifying themselves with Lord Vishnu and performing Vedic sacrifices, encouraged endowments to both Buddhist and brahman establishments with even-handed munificence. Yet the physical separation of the two communities, as implied in Fa Hian's account, may be significant. Buddhist monasteries were usually located outside the main centres of population and influence, near enough for collecting alms and instructing the laity but far enough for tranquillity and seclusion. The '*brahmacharis*', on the other hand, technically brahman students but here implying the whole brahman educational establishment, were now located within the city and close to the court.

Hinduism as a religion with specific doctrines and practices was still unrecognisable. Arguably it still is. The criteria of orthodoxy lay – and lie – in conduct rather than belief. Deference and support to brahmans, acceptance of one's caste, public participation in traditional rituals, festivals and pilgrimages, and the propitiation of familial or local deities remained of the essence. As already noted, concepts like those of *dharma*, *karma* and the transmigration of souls, though originally aired in the *Upanisads* and nowadays considered quintessentially Hindu, had hitherto been more zealously championed by the Buddhists. To the Buddhist practice of erecting and adorning stupas of dressed stone have also been traced the first experiments in stone architecture and in the devotional use of sculptural iconography. Only after achieving remarkable expertise in the portrayal of the Buddha figure and of animal and human, mainly female, figures did the stonemasons of Mathura and elsewhere turn to producing images of the deities of the orthodox 'Hindu' pantheon.

How the personae of these deities, especially Vishnu, Shiva and various forms of the mother-goddess, emerged – or converged (for all were composites) – and how they eventually displaced most of the earlier Vedic deities is not well-documented. Vedic sacrifices like the *aswamedha* remained essential to kingship during and long after the Gupta age, but from about this time onwards 'we do not come across the case of a single individual ascribing his greatness or luck to a Vedic deity'.[18] Personal seals found in Bihar and UP usually bear the emblems of either Shiva or Vishnu, and the inscriptions of nearly all the dynasties of the age protest their devotion to some form of these same two deities. Indeed the convergence of the various Shaiva and Vaishnava personae, as well as their growing popularity, may have been partly the outcome of dominant dynasties like the Guptas co-opting the resources, divine and supernatural as well as political and economic, of their conquered feudatories.

This certainly seems to have been the case with many of the legends, incarnations, consorts and relatives associated with Vishnu, including his identification with Krishna (the Yadava deity) and with Vasudeva and Narayana, all cults which seem to have originated in the Mathura region and western India. In Malwa and central India a more popular Vaishnava cult of the period was that of Vishnu in his *Varaha* incarnation as a colossal

wild boar who, not unlike King Kong, hoists to safety a small and naked
nymph representing the earth. The famous fifth-century sculptural representations of this myth at Eran, Udayagiri and elsewhere in eastern Malwa
may well celebrate the incorporation of a local boar cult into the Vishnu
persona as a result of Chandra-Gupta II's long sojourn in the region while
he fought the Satraps.

Whatever their genesis, sanction for this accretion and fusion of cults
was provided by the *Puranas* and the epics as they were recast, expanded
and written down during and after the Guptas. Brahmanic authority was
thus gradually accorded to the new composite deities, and the sculptor
responded by giving them concrete form. Awesome figures of legend,
obscure local deities, and various fertility and tutelary spirits were duly
transformed into worshippable images. Their identity with the gods and
goddesses of orthodox scripture conferred prestige on them; at the same
time it brought them within the brahmanic mainstream of what is now
called the 'Great Tradition' of Hinduism.

It remained only to refine the nature of man's relationship to the new
generation of deities and to develop forms of worship suitable to it. This
process may also have been influenced by Buddhist precedent in that the
new relationship assumed a degree of divine proximity and compassion
which is not often evident in the Vedas but is fundamental to legends
concerning the Buddhist Boddhisatvas. The supplicant's more personalised
response, with its emphasis on devotion rather than propitiation, is evident
in the famous *Bhagavad Gita* whose interpolation into the *Mahabharata*
probably dates from the third to fourth centuries A D. But it was the much
later *Bhakti* movement, drawing its inspiration and fervour from devotional
practices in the south of India and Bengal, which would eventually endow
Hinduism with its public fervour and its private intimacy of communion.
Though seemingly at odds both with the dangerous business of Vedic ritual
and the mind-boggling subtleties of Upanishadic metaphysics, this new
devotional emphasis would become the most distinctive and endearing
characteristic of what we now call Hinduism.

Instead of 'Hinduism', scholars sometimes use the term 'brahmanism'
to distinguish the pre-*Bhakti* orthodoxies of the post-Vedic era from the
teachings of the heterodox sects like the Buddhists and Jains. 'Brahmanism'
would have been as meaningless to its supposed adherents as 'Hinduism',
but the term does have the advantage of accommodating a variety of
orthodox traits, including the authority accorded to the brahman caste, the
innumerable cults to which brahmanical acceptance was extended, and the
complex philosophical notion of *brahman* as an impersonal monotheistic

entity which, like the Word in Christianity, subsumed all deities, the human soul as well as the divine, and indeed all creation.

In the Vedas *brahma(n)* denotes hymn, prayer, sacred word, for-mulation of truth, substratum etc., ideas that developed later to signify, on the practical level, the title brahman for the person who possessed the qualities conveyed by such ideas, and, on the conceptual level, their abstract summation as the immutable uni-versal principle.[19]

Thus we learn that 'the *brahmanas* attributed *brahma* power to the brahmans', an unassailable observation but one of such elliptical import that it deters further enquiry by anyone ignorant of Sanskrit – a category which then as now included most Indians as well as nearly all non-Indians. For as will already be apparent, abstract terms like *brahman* pose insur-mountable problems of translation. Their connotations change over the centuries and their associations, ramifying through the literary canopy like lianas, defy the lexicographer's search for equivalent words in other languages. *Dharma* ('religion', 'duty', 'order'), *artha* ('wealth', 'politics', 'motive'), *danda* ('authority', 'coercion', 'government') and many other such concepts of crucial importance prove no less elusive. Conversely, English words like 'divinity', 'sovereignty', or 'power' have no exact Sanskrit equivalents. Torchless, the cultural explorer feels his way as through an unlit cave whose sculpted figures, traced with the fingertips and not unfamiliar, yet remain unrecognisable.

THEORIES AND DREAMS

'Here is a lovely face – a madonna face. What eyes! . . . I wish I could make out this story; there is certainly a story. What can this all be?'

'The fewer theories you form, the fewer blunders and dreams you will make.'

'But we must form theories – we cannot remain awake and not do so.'[20]

In 1836 two English sportsman, an excited Captain Gresley and a cau-tious Mr Ralph, bivouacked in a gallery of caves above the Vagha river, a headwater of the Godavari river in Berar, anciently Vidarba, in the northern Deccan. To the sculpted façades, the chaitya halls and the pillared viharas of Ajanta's now-famous cave temples the Englishmen were comparatively indifferent. Such wonders were familiar to Europeans from sites like Karli and Kanheri near Bombay. What sent Captain Gresley into such rhapsodies of delight (which he later related in the unusual form of a verbatim transcript), and what stirred even Ralph's critical reserve, were the paintings. Already sadly vandalised, they covered great areas of wall and ceiling and, displaying an incredible brilliance of colour and form, preserved courtly scenes of opulence and sophistication far more convincing than anything conjectured by Sanskrit scholars or culled by archaeological research. At Ajanta more than anywhere the golden age of the Guptas is made manifest. Theories and dreams, like epigraphic uncertainties and semantic niceties, crumble into dry-as-dust irrelevance beside such spectacular evidence of an age of artistic eloquence. The confidence of the draughtsmanship and portraiture, the vitality and intricacy of the compositions, and the skilful use of the palette combine in scenes martial, devotional and sublimely sensual to convey irrefutable proof of a remarkable age.

Ajanta lay in Vakataka territory and, so far as is known, owed nothing to Gupta patronage. The pictorial themes are exclusively Buddhist, their narratives deriving from the *Jatakas* like those of the earlier stupa reliefs of Sanchi and Amaravati or the later ones of Borobudur in Java. Yet frescoes similar to Ajanta's are well attested in domestic and public contexts; and from literary sources we know that Gupta society regarded painting as both a respected profession and a desirable social accomplishment. The art of Ajanta was not exceptional. Nor was its clarity and classicism unique. In terracotta and stone, as well as in language and literature, artists of the Gupta age excelled in conveying just such ordered and appealing visions – visions which, like Gupta imperialism itself as proclaimed in the Allahabad inscription, confidently balanced respect for a credible reality with reverence for an idealised abstraction.

Gupta sculptures have been distinguished as strongly intellectual in flavour and 'composed deliberately as aesthetic objects'.[21] The smooth serenity of the famous Buddha countenances is heightened by framing them within a hairstyle of tight knobbly curls and a large and intricately carved halo; grace of pose is accentuated by the hard outline of an evanescent robe or the ridged symmetry of its folds; the contours of the body are made flesh by the tightness of a waistband or the introduction of metallic accoutrements. Virtuosity is restrained; understatement is preferred. The sculptor of the Gupta age matched mastery of his art with an astonishing maturity of vision to create 'some of the greatest sculptures ever produced anywhere in the world'.[22] Emanating from the workshops of Mathura, inspiring the great school of Sarnath, and influencing a host of lesser centres throughout the Guptan *arya-varta*, this aesthetic set a standard of excellence, and established a canon of iconographic conventions which, as with Hellenic art, would last long and travel far. It may, in short and with complete confidence, be called 'classical'.

As the carvings of Mathura and Sarnath are to Indian sculpture, and as the frescoes of Ajanta are to Indian painting, so are the compositions of Kalidasa to Sanskrit literature. Other dramatists of the Gupta age are highly regarded, most notably Sudraka, whose 'Little Clay Cart', a risqué and action-packed charivari, has obvious appeal and has been much revived. Likewise other poets wrote courtly *kavya* (verses) in an impeccable and even more ingenious Sanskrit: Samudra-Gupta's Allahabad inscription as composed by Harisena, one of his principal ministers, contains passages of great dramatic elegance; and the emperor himself, like Rudradaman, is said to have been a master of the style. But only Kalidasa wrote both plays and poetry, and he did so with an excellence which, by unanimous consent, justifies the inevitable comparisons with Shakespeare. It was Sir William Jones's English version of Kalidasa's famous *Sakuntala* which first roused the West to the merits of Sanskrit drama, and it was adaptations of *Megha-duta* ('The Cloud Messenger') which found their way into nineteenth-century anthologies and won for Sanskrit verse a reputation for superb evocations of nature.

Unfortunately all Sanskrit literature is so rich in metaphors, synonyms, allusions, double meanings and all manner of grammatical and phonetic pyrotechnics that satisfactory translation is impossible. To the uninitiated the word-play, the conventions of metre and the variants of meaning smack of the smug mystique of the cryptic crossword. But ignorance may be compounded by our own conventions. Translations, according to A.L. Basham, merely 'tarnish' the beauty of the original; still more sadly, they have a habit of shying away from the erotic and explicit. Thus renderings of Kalidasa's *Kumarasambhava*, a long poem which deals with the courtship of Lord Shiva and his consort, often omit as 'abhorrent to Western taste' the climactic canto in which this divine union is consummated – a subject of exquisite and eminently communicable interest which later probably inspired the famed sculpture of the Khajuraho temples and to which Kalidasa is said to have done glorious justice. Indeed, to witness the delight with which a Sanskritist savours the lines of Kalidasa is to be convinced that the considerable effort of learning a long-dead Indian language would not be wasted. 'Few who can read [Kalidasa] in the original would doubt that, both as poet and as dramatist, he was one of the great men of the world.'[23]

When and where Kalidasa lived remains a mystery. He acknowledges
no links with the Guptas; he may not even have coincided with them.
Familiarity with Ujjain and telling descriptions of the lush Narmada valley
suggest that he belonged to Malwa rather than Magadha. Tradition insists
that he adorned the court of a shadowy King Vikramaditya whom chronology assigns to the first century BC. On internal evidence, however, he
seems unlikely to have preceded the Guptas; and it may be significant that
Vikramaditya was also one of the many epithets used by Samudra-Gupta.
In another long poem, the *Raghuvamsa*, Kalidasa traces the lineage of King
Rama of Ayodhya with particular emphasis on the empire-building exploits
of Raghu, Rama's grandfather. Raghu led his forces north, south, east and
west. He conquered Bengal, erected victory pillars along the Ganga, overran
Kalinga, crossed the Kaveri and exacted a tribute of pearls from the Pandyas;
the dust clouds raised by his cohorts soiled the hair of the ladies of Kerala;
his horses rolled in the sands of the Indus; hill-peoples quailed before his
onslaught; and the winds of the Himalayas, soughing through the reeds,
sang of his victories. In this poem it was as if Kalidasa, while celebrating
India's immensity, was consciously expanding on Samudra-Gupta's Allahabad pillar inscription. 'In this spirited and martial narrative we may justly
see the reflex in the poet's mind of Samudra-Gupta's great conquests.'[24]

Not just the conquests but the poet's vivid awareness of the terrain of
the entire subcontinent argues strongly for a Guptan provenance. Though
politically the empire of the Guptas was fragmentary, its culture was pervasive. Kalidasa may have been a great traveller; more probably he was a
beneficiary of the traffic and trade which under Gupta rule enabled a
stranger like Fa Hian to pass unmolested from one end of India to the
other – and which tempted him to explore the south as well. The ideals
of the Guptan age transcended frontiers and spanned seas. Gupta-style
Buddhas have been found in Malaya, Java and even Borneo. There and in
Indo-China the Sanskrit inscriptions which begin to appear during the
third and fourth centuries mark the beginnings of literacy, nearly all the
pre-Islamic scripts of south-east Asia being derivatives of Gupta Brahmi.
In all these places as throughout India itself, Sanskrit now triumphed as
the language of scholarship, record and courtly discourse. Moreover the
reworking and recording of the *Puranas*, one of the most important achievements of the Gupta age, plus the raiding of the epics for suitable literary
themes, ensured that Sanskritisation meant a universal currency not just
for the language but for the influence and ideals of the brahman caste
which these works inculcated.

On the conformity of these Sanskrit-borne religious, cultural, social and political ideals rests the case for India's national integrity in pre-Islamic times. Many would argue that it was no more than an elitist veneer. Sanskrit was understood only by that minute percentage of the population whose sophisticated tastes and opulent lifestyle are so vividly portrayed in the Ajanta frescoes. It was for this leisured and aristocratic society that Kalidasa composed, a fact borne out by the convention that servants, members of the lower castes and all the female characters in his dramas speak and understand only Prakrit; Sanskrit is reserved for the 'twice-born' principals.

To this same courtly society the increasingly recherché exercises in Sanskritic obfuscation provided a delicious diversion. It was partly the fault of the language itself. As Patanjali, the second-century writer, had put it, one may order a particular design of pot from a potter but no one goes to a grammarian and says 'Make me such and such a word.' The vocabulary was constant, the grammar frozen. 'Perfected' by Panini, elevated by all, yet spoken by few, Sanskrit was the victim of its own prestige. Borrowings, once significant, became few. Ingenuity replaced innovation as writers strove to achieve succinctness by ever greater compression, and to extract additional meaning by repetition and juxtaposition. Sentences got longer and longer, sometimes running to several pages, while compound words ran to several lines. A word of twenty components with a total of fifty-four syllables is used in the Allahabad inscription to describe the nature of Samudra-Gupta's feudatory sway. No doubt it is an elegant construction, but historians would willingly trade it for a single clear statement of policy.

> There were astounding mnemonic developments, but they too contributed to the same end by over-specialisation and [the creation of] particular jargons for every discipline. There still exist *sastris* who can recite the whole of one veda in any order (literally backwards or forwards) without making a mistake in a single letter or accent. Others know the whole of Panini's grammar and the *Amarakosa* dictionary without exciting special comment. Yet there is no individual who really knows the Sanskrit language as a whole.[25]

Important works on astronomy and, to a lesser extent, medicine indicate that science was not neglected under the Guptas. The length of the solar year was calculated with a precision which even the Greeks had not achieved, and Indian mathematics was probably the most advanced in the world. 'At the lower level of achievement was the perfection of the decimal system and at the higher the solution of certain indeterminate equations'; pi was correctly calculated to four decimal places, and it was also at about this time that the concept of zero made its epigraphic debut, usually in the form of a dot.

Yet the works which embodied these findings were framed with such Sanskritic refinement as to make them incomprehensible to all but the initiated. The craftsman remained ignorant of them, and the mathematician remained jealous of them. Later works on iconography, architecture and painting are often cited as examples of Sanskrit's contribution to applied science. Yet according to Kosambi, himself a scientist as well as a historian, their dicta 'do not tally with the measurements of [actual] statuary and buildings or the chemical analysis of pigments'. Clearly 'the artists and masons went their own way'. Likewise whoever cast the 'Iron Pillar' of Mehrauli was indisputably a master metallurgist; yet there is no known treatise on metallurgy.

Sanskrit's monopoly of scholarship was not, then, fatal to creativity or the development of productive skills. Enormous achievements, especially in architecture, which are barely hinted at in the Gupta era, would soon follow. Nor was the exclusivity of Sanskrit any kind of deterrent to the propagation of its mythology and precepts. During and after the Gupta age the gods and heroes of Sanskrit literature, its endless canons and codes, and its impossible concepts and ideals continued to trickle down through society; they even seeped out into the hills and forests where tribal peoples continued to be absorbed into the caste hierarchy and tribal chiefs into that 'society of kings'.

Although as much by default and exception as by observance and conformity, a degree of integrity was achieved. It was more than an upper-caste veneer. Awareness of India as a territorial entity with a distinctive and shared religio-cultural heritage is clearly evident. Yet it fell far short of anything remotely resembling a national consciousness. The obvious comparison would be with contemporary Europe's awareness of something called Christendom. Briefly a Charlemagne, like a Samudra-Gupta, might impose some semblance of political unity; more typically both these great cultural worlds were riven with rivalries as kings and princelings vied for hegemony and as dynasties rose and fell with bewildering rapidity.

Lords of the Universe

c500–700

COPPER-PLATE FLOURISHES

GIVEN THE TASK of elucidating sixth-century politics for a volume of the monumental *History and Culture of the Indian People*, D.C. Sircar, an outstanding epigraphist and historian, writes at length on each of seventeen major dynasties. Numerous lesser dynasties also claim his attention; and the chapter in question covers only the Deccan. With the addition of western India, the Panjab, the north-west, Kashmir, Bengal, the south and the vast Gangetic *arya-varta*, the sixth century's dynastic count could easily be doubled. All of which makes 'happy hunting for professional historians'.[1] The prospect of tracking three dozen royal houses at once may, however, discourage the non-specialist, who will not be reassured to learn that during the next five centuries the situation gets, if anything, worse. Dynasties multiply, territories (insofar as they can be determined) diminish, authority erodes. Hemachandra Ray's *Dynastic History of Northern India* charts the rise and fall of a further thirty dynasties between 900 and 1100 – and that excludes those of the Deccan, south, and western India. In the history of what used to be called 'medieval' India, the key words are 'fragmentation' and 'regionalisation'.

Whether or not this represented a new state of affairs is debatable, but that it becomes progressively evident is because of the proliferation of a new kind of evidence. So far the reconstruction of India's past has depended on very grudging materials: some enigmatic archaeology, long mostly religious texts of uncertain antiquity, snippets of surviving tradition, the patchy accounts of European and Chinese visitors, coins, and a few mostly stone-engraved inscriptions. All these continue to be relevant, but to them must now be added a more generous corpus of official records, or charters, plus the occasional piece of biographical literature.

The former, the charters, are the more informative. They have been found all over India, and along with royal panegyrics like the Allahabad inscription they are largely responsible for the dynastic log-jam. Indeed many royal lineages, as also the kingdoms over which they ruled, are known only because one or more of their charters happens to have survived. These charters (*sasanas*) usually record grants of land. They were originally written on palm leaves, but as title-deeds they were of sufficient value subsequently to be engraved, sometimes on a cave wall or a temple but more usually on plates of copper which were then kept in a safe place or hidden somewhere. 'A large number of copper plates have been found immured in walls or foundations of houses belonging to families of the donees, or hidden in small caches made of bricks or stone in the fields to which the grant refers.'[2] Some of these plates were used more than once, a cancelled charter being over-struck with a new one; all originally included a royal seal, often of brass; yet forgeries were not uncommon; and many charters were long enough to run to several plates which were then held together, like a heavy set of keys, with a stout copper ring.

It seems likely that such records had been in use since the beginning of the Christian era. The earliest authentic plates to have survived come from south India and were issued by kings of the Pallava dynasty of Kanchi-puram in the fourth century A D. Some of these charters seem to date from before Samudra-Gupta's uprooting of his Pallava contemporary and are in Prakrit. Thereafter they switch to Sanskrit and provide limited information on no less than sixteen early Pallava kings between 350 and 375. The Pallavas, whose origins are uncertain, had established themselves in the region known as Tondaimandalam, west of the later city of Madras. They had already elevated Kanchipuram into an important religious and intellectual centre but, on the evidence of these plates, they were having severe difficulties holding their own. Only after 375 would the Pallavas emerge as the first great south Indian dynasty, and not till the seventh to eighth centuries would they endow Kanchi and Mamallapuram (Mahabalipuram) with the reliefs and temples now associated with their greatness.

In north India similar, but not always helpful, glimpses of dynastic activity are provided by rare copper plates of the Gupta period. Thereafter such plates become more numerous and remain a prime source for many centuries to come. Muslim chroniclers would notice them and they were still in use in the eighteenth century when newcomers, like the European trading companies, sometimes relied on them as title-deeds to their coastal settlements. At the same time the more historically-minded of the companies' employees began to collect them for scholarly study.

Legal documents not being renowned for originality or innovative phrasing, the charters, although written in numerous regional languages as well as Sanskrit, all follow much the same formula. After an invocatory word or passage, the text identifies the royal donor with a string of those compound Sanskritic titles and a long panegyric on his forebears, his exploits and his personal qualities. There then follow details of the grant itself, its recipient(s), the occasion for it, and a stern command that posterity respect it. Hefty, if wishful, penalties are detailed for any transgressor of this last provision: the crime of overruling a *sasana* was commonly equated with that of killing ten thousand Varanasi cows – a sacrilege of unthinkable enormity in a city of unassailable sanctity for which the penalty was that of being reborn as a dung-worm with a lifespan of eighty-four thousand years.

Of all these standard components of a charter, that applauding the donor and his lineage has generally been found the most useful. As noted, entire dynasties and their histories have been reconstructed from the chance survival of a single such charter. Yet their extravagant language should in itself provide a warning. Whether on copper or stone, inscriptions can be misleading.

According to a neat two-plate charter issued in 571 at Vallabhi, which place had succeeded Rudradaman's Junagadh as the capital of Saurashtra, the incumbent king was the son of a maharaja of truly spectacular memory. Maharaja Guhasena had 'cleft the temples of the rutting elephants of his foes'; the toenails of his left foot emitted rays as dazzling as those of the jewels in the head-dresses of his enemies as they lay prostrate before him; in beauty he surpassed the God of Love, in lustre the Moon, in constancy the Lord of the Mountains, in profundity the Ocean, in wisdom the Protector of the Gods and in riches the Lord of Wealth. Carelessly showering his supporters with gifts, 'he was, as it were, the personified happiness of the circumference of the whole earth'.[3]

The rulers of Vallabhi were indeed destined for some distinction, and their capital, misheard as 'Balhara', would be amongst the first to be noticed by Muslim chroniclers. But the ruler of all India whom these same chroniclers called 'The Balhara' was not the Maitraka king of Vallabhi but the '*Valabha-raja*', a title used by the later and much more significant Rashtrakuta dynasty. Moreover in 571 the Maitrakas had barely established themselves at Vallabhi; descendants of a Gupta general, they had only just ceased to acknowledge Gupta suzerainty. Although typical of many other successor dynasties within the region of direct Gupta rule, they had scarcely begun the mysterious business of cleaving rutting elephants' temples and were not politically significant in India as a whole.

The year in question was more notable for an event outside India. Also in 571, but across the Arabian Sea and in obscure circumstances, the wife of an impoverished merchant of the Quraysh tribe gave birth to a son of less suspect lustre. To him, forty years later and now known as Muhammad, the divine word would be revealed; and by him the world would be irrevocably and very rapidly changed. But it would be over a century before the Prophet's followers made any impact on India. And by then most of those sixth-century dynasts, although not the Maitrakas, had long since ceased to outshine the moon and personify all earthly happiness.

No excuse, therefore, is offered for ignoring most of the dynasties which are known to have succeeded the Guptas and which, from their charters, may appear even to have outdone the Guptas. Some will be noted later. Here it is sufficient to mention that several claim to have turned the tide of Hun incursion. It will be recalled that from Gandhara the Huns had been rampaging across the Panjab and as far as Malwa since c500. In the north-west the great Buddhist establishments at Taxila, Peshawar and Swat suffered severely from their iconoclasm. Where Fa Hian in the fifth century had found packed viharas and towering stupas, Hsuan Tsang, another Chinese visitor but in the mid-seventh century, found only devastation. Taxila's monasteries were 'ruinous and deserted, and there are very few priests; the royal family being extinct, the nobles contend for power by force'. In Swat some fourteen hundred Buddhist establishments were 'now generally waste and desolate', their eighteen thousand monks having dwindled to a handful.[4] Buddhism in the Indus basin would never recover from this blow; nor, until the advent of Islam, would the overland trade with China and the west. Although Hsuan Tsang found some commercial activity in Kabul, his omission of any mention of markets or trade in connection with Taxila and Peshawar is significant. The lifeblood of the region had dried up, and with it the all-important supply of equine bloodstock from central Asia to India. Henceforth horses reached India mainly by sea from Arabia, in a trade which would rapidly become a Muslim monopoly. Other frontier trails, like the pilgrim's calvary that had been the Karakoram route, fell into disuse as Buddhist traffic shifted east to the Tibetan tableland.

The rest of India was spared from the Hun perhaps thanks to one Yasodharman of Malwa. Evidently a very successful adventurer if not a noted dynast, Yasodharman claims to have inflicted a defeat on the Huns in c530. Under their leader Mihirakula, the son of Toramana, the Huns then retired to Kashmir, there in a land of sad but incomparable beauty to burnish their reputation for persecution, vandalism and unspeakable atrocities for another generation.

Victories over the Huns are also claimed by Baladitya, a later Gupta, and by the Maukharis and the Vardhanas. The Maukharis, comprising one or more dynasties, had established themselves in central Uttar Pradesh with their capital at Kanauj on the upper Ganga (near Kanpur). Thereby dominating an important slice of the Guptas' erstwhile *arya-varta*, they would provide a thread of legitimacy for the next and arguably the last north Indian *cakravartin*. This was the great Harsha of the Vardhana family from Thanesar near Delhi. The Vardhanas and the Maukharis were already closely allied and may have repelled the Huns in unison. Their territories, too, marched with one another; conjoined, they would soon form the nucleus of Harsha's great empire.

But before returning to the dynastic fray, and lest the charters of the sixth century be dismissed simply as copper-red herrings, it is worth considering the information they provide not only about their royal donors but also about their beneficiaries and about the nature of the grants themselves. To the economic, as opposed to the dynastic, historian these are of great significance since they foreshadow a fragmentation and dispersal of resources far more ominous than what Kosambi calls the 'nice but meaningless' litany of dynasties.

Munificence was incumbent on any ruler and was an essential attribute of kingship; indeed a particularly generous sovereign is described as one who makes so many grants as to exhaust the supply of copper. Distributing land was a way of rewarding supporters and of gaining merit; it also had important economic connotations. In the Vallabhi charter of 571 already cited the beneficiary was a brahman called Rudrabhuti. Nearly all charters of the period are in favour of brahmans or religious establishments – notably temples, Jain communities and, now more rarely, Buddhist monasteries. In this case Rudrabhuti was granted the revenue and other rights in respect of certain lands, such proceeds to be used to finance in perpetuity various important sacrificial rituals. Where once the brahmans' support and performance of rites might have been rewarded with a few hundred head of cattle, it was now prepaid with revenue.

Both the rights and the lands thus granted are specified in detail. Although the meaning of several technical terms is disputed,[5] it seems that in this case the extensive lands were pastures belonging to certain named individuals. Rudrabhuti was to receive their yield in various dues and taxes, plus their mineral and other rights. He was exempted from royal exactions (as, for instance, for the support of the military establishment), and finally he was awarded rights to the forced labour of the incumbents. The lands themselves were not transferred; on the other hand their entire yield was irrevocably alienated so far as the royal exchequer was concerned.

Other grants often include the proceeds from fines for various crimes and the right to exclude royal troops and law-enforcers; even the administration of justice was being devolved. Rudrabhuti and his like were in effect becoming fief-holders. Although as yet grants were made largely to brahmans and for religious purposes, and although as yet they included no provision for the reciprocal military service associated with European feudalism, the basis of a quasi-feudal relationship was being laid. Soon state officials, who according to Fa Hian had been salaried even under the Guptas, were being remunerated with similar grants of lands, villages and even districts. Evidence of commendation (whereby villagers themselves sought the security and protection of a royally approved superior) and of sub-infeudation (when such a superior sub-leased parts of his feu to agents and supporters) would follow.

This 'feudalism from below' is sometimes contrasted with that 'from above', the latter being epitomised in the royal hierarchy of a *maharajadhi-raja* surrounded by his proliferating feudatories or *maha-samantas* (literally 'great neighbours' but now signifying dependent dynasties and vassals). Both contributed to the process of fragmentation, 'feudalism from above' by regionalising authority even as the kings who exercised it shrilly proclaimed their universal sovereignty, and 'feudalism from below' by a more insidious erosion of the loyalties and resources on which all authority depended.

HARSHA-VARDHANA

As if to contradict such theorising, a new 'king-of-kings' was nevertheless about to shine forth in fleeting brilliance. A new chronological era, always a significant pointer, would be inaugurated; and another 'victorious circuit of the four quarters of the earth' (*digvijaya*) would be celebrated. In the early seventh century the rival dynasties, which like close-packed clouds had clustered over *arya-varta* ever since the great Guptas, began to thin. The monsoon, it seemed, had been delayed; northern India was about to experience a last searing glimpse of pre-Islamic empire.

Of the no doubt many *sasana* issued by Harsha-Vardhana of Thanesar (and later Kanauj) few survive. A single seal, once presumably attached to a copper plate, does however list Harsha's immediate antecedents. Apparently he belonged to the fourth Vardhana generation; his father had been the first to assume the title *maharajadhiraja* and his brother the first to call himself a follower of the Buddha. Harsha seems to have adopted both styles, although his Buddhist sympathies would preclude neither aggressive designs nor the worship of orthodox deities. Sadly the seal in question has no room for further information, and were it, and his coins, the only evidence of Harsha, he would be but another shadowy dynast.

Mercifully, though, the somewhat sterile evidence provided by *sasana* is supplemented by two much more informative witnesses. One was Hsuan Tsang (Hiuen Tsiang, Hsuien-tsang, Yuan Chwang, Xuan Zang, etc. etc.), a Chinese monk and scholar who, inspired by Fa Hian's pilgrimage to the Buddhist Holy Land two hundred years earlier, himself spent the years 630–44 visiting India. He returned to China with enough Buddhist relics, statuary and texts to load twenty horses, and subsequently wrote a long account of India which, except in the case of the extreme south, seems to have been based on personal observation.

The other and the more endearing witness was Bana, an outstanding writer and also, incidentally, a rakish brahman whose ill-spent youth and varied circle of friends 'shows how lightly the rules of caste weighed on the educated man'.[6] Of Bana's two surviving works the most important is the *Harsa-carita*, a prose account of Harsha's rise to power. Though more descriptive than explanatory, and though loaded with linguistic fancies and adjectival compounds of inordinate length, it rates as Sanskrit's first historical biography as well as a masterpiece of literature. In it the hectic excitement of camp and court is conveyed with all the vivid incident of a crowded Mughal miniature. Forest and roadside teem with life as Bana minutely observes every detail of rural industry and identifies every species in the natural environment. No Kipling, no Rushdie better evokes India's heaving vitality or the lifelong industry of its people.

Inevitably both Hsuan Tsang and Bana were interested parties. The former depended on Harsha's protection and the latter on his patronage. In no sense is either of their works a critical appraisal. Hsuan Tsang was blinded by a Buddhist bigotry which he would fain hoist on Harsha, while Bana saw Harsha and history as combining to provide the material for a historical romance. Yet in a way each author complements the other, the Chinese monk providing the outline and the Indian author the detail, the Buddhist the libretto and the brahman the music.

They also complement one another chronologically. Hsuan Tsang would coincide with the climax of Harsha's career while Bana records only his early years, from his birth in c590 to his accession in c606 and his first campaign soon after. This period is of particular interest since Harsha, as a second son, was not the obvious successor. His father, *Maharajadhiraja*

Prabhakara-Vardhana, died when Harsha and his elder brother were away, the latter fighting the Huns while the teenage Harsha enjoyed a spot of hunting. Harsha got home first and alone saw the dying king, at which meeting, according to Bana, he named him as his heir. The brother then returned victorious from the battlefield with his troops. Harsha said nothing of their father's last wish and the brother therefore remained heir presumptive.

At this point Bana introduces yet another reason for Harsha's succession. Apparently Rajya-Vardhana, the brother, was so overcome with grief over their father's death that he declined the throne and opted to retire to a hermitage. Improbably he too, therefore, insisted that Harsha succeed their father. Yet from other sources, including Hsuan Tsang, it is known that in fact it was Rajya-Vardhana who succeeded. Bana, in short, protests too much. Perhaps he simply wanted to bolster Harsha's legitimacy by suggesting that he was the direct heir. Or perhaps he had a less creditable motive. As a recent biographer delicately puts it, 'it is hard to escape the conclusion that the unusual twists in the story . . . were rendered inevitable because of some episode uncomplimentary to the author's hero.'[7] More specifically it may be that Bana was trying to lull suspicions, still current at the time he was writing, that Harsha had had a motive, if not a hand, in Rajya-Vardhana's imminent removal.

This came about as a result of more 'unusual twists'. Rajya-Sri, the princes' sister, had been married to their neighbour and ally, the Maukhari king of Kanauj. In the midst of the succession crisis in Thanesar, this Maukhari king was suddenly attacked by the king of 'Malava' (presumably Malwa). The Maukhari king died in battle; Rajya-Sri was taken hostage; and the victorious 'Malava' now moved to attack Thanesar. In this desperate situation it was not Harsha but again his brother who took the initiative. Suddenly abandoning his idea of a quiet life of grief, he now insisted on his right to revenge. Harsha's wish to accompany him was swept aside and, taking ten thousand cavalry, the righteous Rajya-Vardhana raced off to give battle.

Clearly an awesome campaigner, Rajya-Vardhana duly routed the men from Malwa. But then the real villain of the piece emerged. Sasanka, king of Gauda in Bengal, had been assisting the Malwa forces. The victorious Rajya-Vardhana met Sasanka under a safe-conduct, presumably to arrange a truce, and was treacherously murdered. At last the stage was clear for the young and hitherto somewhat subdued Harsha to explode upon it.

Instantly on hearing this [the news of his brother's murder] his
fiery spirit blazed forth in a storm of sorrow augmented by flaming
flashes of furious wrath. His aspect became terrible in the extreme.
As he fiercely shook his head, the loosened jewels from his crest
looked like live coals of the angry fire which he vomited forth.
Quivering without cessation, his wrathful curling lip seemed to
drink the lives of all kings. His reddening eyes with their rolling
gleam put forth, at it were, conflagrations in the heavenly spaces.
Even the fire of anger, as though itself burned by the scorching
power of his inborn valour's unbearable heat, spread over him a
rainy shower of sweat. His very limbs trembled as if in fright at
such unexampled fury...

He represented the first revelation of valour, the frenzy of
insolence, the delirium of pride, the youthful avatar of fury, the
supreme effort of hauteur, the new age of manhood's fire, the
regal consecration of warlike passion, the camp-lustration day of
reckoning.[8]

Understandably his supporters were impressed. Ably, and of course
volubly, encouraged by his commander-in-chief and then by the comman-
dant of his elephant corps, Harsha mobilised 'for a world-wide conquest'.
Meanwhile his enemies were beset by all manner of ill omens: jackals,
swarming bees and swooping vultures terrorised their cities; their soldiers
fell out with their mistresses while some, looking in the mirror, saw themselves headless; a naked woman wandered through the parks 'shaking her
forefinger as if to count the dead'.

Sasanka, 'vilest of Gaudas', would be Harsha's main objective but,
Gauda being thousands of kilometres to the east of Thanesar, many other
kings would have to submit first. One, evidently a hereditary rival of the
Gauda kings, quickly entered into a treaty of friendship and subordinate
alliance with Harsha. This was Bhaskara-varman, king of Kumara-rupa
(Assam) on Gauda's northern border. Sasanka would therefore have to
fight on two fronts. Additionally Harsha could count on the forces of the
Maukharis and on the defeated Malwa army which was now put at his
disposal by his late brother's commander.

The latter also brought news of the escape from her confinement in
Kanauj of Rajya-Sri (Harsha's sister and the queen of the Maukharis).
Unfortunately she had fled into hiding in the Vindhya hills where, as a
widow, she was thought to be about to commit *sati*. Harsha had other
plans. He saw both merit and, though unmentioned by Bana, advantage

in rescuing her. Dousing his rage, therefore, he led a search party into the wild tracts of central India. A community of pioneers who were busily engaged in harvesting forest produce and clearing trees knew nothing of her whereabouts. But at another settlement, this time of assorted Buddhists, brahmans and other renunciates who were pooling their insights in an admirable spirit of ecumenism, he heard tell of a party of grief-stricken ladies hiding nearby. Rajya-Sri, horribly scratched and reduced to rags by her forest odyssey, was amongst them. In the nick of time she was duly plucked from her funeral pyre and reunited with her brother.

Rajya-Sri's only wish now was to become a Buddhist nun. Harsha would not hear of it. He needed her active support and insisted on her accompanying him. As the Maukhari queen, she was vital to his plans since, through her, he in effect controlled the Maukhari kingdom. As a result of this identity of interest he would subsequently move his capital from Thanesar to the more central and significant city of Kanauj. Kanauj now became the rival of Pataliputra as the imperial capital of northern India and, through many vicissitudes and changes of ownership, would remain so until the twelfth century.

Meanwhile the campaign could be renewed. Accompanied by Rajya-Sri and a Buddhist sage who was to act as her confessor, Harsha hastened back to rejoin his army encamped by the Ganga. There, as he related the story of his successful rescue mission, the shadows lengthened and the sun went down in a blaze of gory omens, each of which presaged an imminent victory. The evening, says Bana, advanced as if 'leaning on the clouds' which were flecked and bright with the setting sun, like an ocean sunset. Then, with darkness closing in, the Spirit of Night respectfully presented Harsha with the moon; it was 'as if the moon were a cup to slake his boundless thirst for fame', says Bana, or even 'a *sasana* of silver issued by king Manu himself entitling Harsha to conquer the seven heavens and restore the golden age'. And so, somewhat unexpectedly, amidst a welter of page-long adjectival compounds and with a well-flagged trail of conquest stretching into the distant future, Bana's tale abruptly ends.

If there was more, it has not survived. Instead there is only the odd inscription plus the testimony of Hsuan Tsang, by the time of whose visit Harsha the teenage Galahad had become Harsha the middle-aged Arthur and his little kingdom on the Jamuna a universal dominion over the 'Five Indies'. What this term actually comprehended is not clear. 'He went from east to west,' says Hsuan Tsang, 'subduing all who were not obedient; the elephants were not unharnessed, nor the soldiers unbelted. After six years he had subdued the Five Indies.'[9] The division of India into five parts –

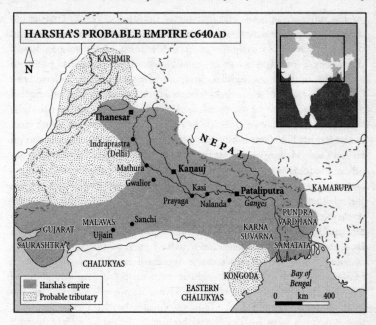

HARSHA'S PROBABLE EMPIRE c640AD

north (*uttarapatha*), south (*daksinapatha*), east, west and centre (*madhya-desa* or *arya-varta*) – was fairly standard; but if this was what Hsuan Tsang meant by the 'Five Indies', he was grossly exaggerating. Harsha had indeed triumphed throughout much of north India, but his conquests were often tenuous and short-lived; they would take much longer than six years; and they certainly never included the Deccan or the south.

From his camp beside the Ganga, where Bana had left him basking in the prospect of bloody victories to come, Harsha seems to have continued east. Prayaga (Allahabad), Ayodhya, Sravasti, Magadha and a host of minor kingdoms in UP and Bihar, many of them previously under Sasanka's sway, must have submitted before he sighted his quarry. According to a much later source, the great encounter with Sasanka of Gauda took place at Pundra in northern Bengal. Sasanka was apparently defeated, but not so decisively as to forfeit his kingdom, for he continued to rule Gauda itself and seems even to have reclaimed parts of Orissa and Magadha. Only after Sasanka's death in c620–30 did Harsha successfully claim these kingdoms and apparently share them with his Assamese ally.

His other 'campaigns' and 'conquests' are no less vague. That he did indeed overrun all of north India from Kashmir to the Arabian Sea and the Bay of Bengal is well-attested. The Maitrakas of Vallabhi in far-off Gujarat were forced to flee their capital, Kashmir was obliged to part with a cherished relic of the Buddha, Sindh and Orissa look also to have been invaded. To reach these places, kingdoms which intervened or were adjacent to the probable line of march must also have submitted. Likewise those kingdoms which were subordinate to Harsha's new vassals, including most of the Panjab hill states in the case of Kashmir. On this evidence, and on Hsuan Tsang's failure to indicate that they were fully independent, numerous other kingdoms and tribes stretching from the eastern Panjab to Rajasthan and Madhya Pradesh are presumed to have formed part of Harsha's empire. But whether he held all of them simultaneously, for how long, and on what terms is very uncertain. The Maitrakas of Saurashtra, for instance, soon returned to their capital of Vallabhi and, despite being united with Harsha's family by a matrimonial alliance, seem to have pursued independent policies.

But perhaps the most persuasive argument for the ephemeral nature of Harsha's empire rests on its sudden and total eclipse. An intimation of troubles ahead had been provided by Hsuan Tsang when he was witness to an attempt on Harsha's life. Those responsible he identified as 'heretics', the Buddhist's term for disaffected brahmans. Evidently by the seventh century not all religious rivalries were being resolved in friendly debate. Sasanka's 'vileness' seems to have had a lot to do with his having allegedly harassed Buddhists and cut down the sacred Boddhi tree under which the Buddha received enlightenment. Elsewhere in *arya-varta* it was the other way round, with orthodox opinion being antagonised by Harsha's growing preference for, and generosity to, the Buddhist *sangha*.

At a lavish ceremony organised by Harsha to celebrate his meeting with the king of Kamarupa, these dissidents attempted sabotage by setting fire to the tower in which the Buddha image was placed. Harsha, according to Hsuan Tsang, put out the flames not by blowing but, no less miraculously, by rushing headlong into them. Frustrated, the 'heretic' fanatics then persuaded one of their followers to make an attempt on Harsha's life. The assassin lunged, knife in hand, but Harsha, still nimble on his feet despite advancing years, dodged the blow and then seized and disarmed his assailant. Hsuan Tsang makes much of the clemency later shown to those responsible. Only their leader was 'punished', which probably means that he was executed; the rest were pardoned. Nevertheless five hundred brahmans had to be packed off into exile. Obviously, if not a rebellion, this was much more than an intrigue.

How Harsha eventually died is not known. But when in 647 his long reign finally ended, so did his empire; it simply fell apart. No Chandra-Gupta II stepped forward to round off his conquests and no Ashoka arose to consolidate his dominions. Confederate kingdoms simply allowed their allegiance to lapse; subject dynasties simply resumed their old rivalries.

The throne itself was usurped by one of Harsha's brahman ministers, who was then badly discredited by the mismanagement of a Chinese embassy. Harsha had cultivated good relations with the new T'ang empire and, thanks to his Buddhist sympathies and his generous treatment of visitors like Hsuan Tsang, several diplomatic missions had been exchanged. But, according to Chinese sources, a T'ang embassy which arrived immediately after his death found India in confusion. In what looks like an incident born more of sectarian than political rivalry, the Chinese were robbed and taken captive while the Celestial Emperor's emissary barely escaped to Tibet with his life. Thence he organised reprisals which apparently culminated in a resounding Chinese victory, 'whereupon India was overawed'.

Although there is no mention in Indian sources of this first trans-Himalayan incursion, and although it was probably no more than a raid into northern Bengal, it was indicative of the vacuum left by Harsha. Thanks to Bana, his personal fame would indeed last, and in that he also sponsored religious debate, championed scholarship, and himself wrote plays, he has often been compared with Akbar, greatest of the Mughals. But there would be no 'House of Harsha' to bestride India during succeeding generations, no 'Vardhana Age' to foster the memory of northern India's last *cakravartin*, and no 'Kanauj School' to continue his patronage of Buddhist 'universities' like Nalanda (Bihar) and of scholars like Bana. The red-hot coals vomited so freely by the fiery Harsha were extinguished in a hiss of steam as the political monsoon finally broke over the *arya-varta* heartland of northern India.

ROUND AND ROUND THE *MANDALA*

It was not so elsewhere. Indeed there is ample evidence that the ideal of a universal, or pan-Indian, sovereignty simply shifted ground. With Harsha the hegemony so long assumed by northern India came to an end. Sixty years after his death, Arabs would establish a Muslim bridgehead in Sind, their task eased by his own incursions into that region. The north-west, or in other words most of what now comprises the rest of Pakistan, had been irrevocably humbled by the Huns and was now politically irrelevant. Into the Gangetic heartland itself, adventurous dynasts from Kashmir, Bengal and the Deccan were about to raid, indeed briefly rule, with impunity. And where Harsha had signally failed to make of the Gupta tradition of paramountcy any more than a fragile and fleeting confederacy, other great dynasties, especially those of the Deccan and the south, would so refine and substantiate the concept as to make it their own.

In the course of his wanderings round India, Hsuan Tsang traversed an area of the western Deccan which he calls 'Mo-ho-la-ch'a'. The translation of proper names from Chinese back into Sanskrit often stretches credulity, but in this case there is little room for doubt: by 'Mo-ho-la-ch'a' Hsuan Tsang meant Maharashtra. This was the land either side of the Western Ghats, once the patrimony of the trading Shatavahanas whose cave temples pocked its rocky outcrops, then of the Vakatakas who so loyally served the Guptas, and nowadays more or less the modern state of Maharashtra centred on Bombay. Hsuan Tsang found the soil rich and fertile, which in parts it is; the people were honest but implacable, and they included 'a band of champions' who, when both they and their elephants were fired up on alcohol, proved irresistible in battle. 'No enemy can stand before them,' wrote the visitor, wherefore their king was able to 'treat his neighbours with contempt'.[10]

The name of this contemptuous sovereign was given as 'Pu-lo-ki-she', otherwise Pulakesin II, and according to Hsuan Tsang his ambitions were extensive. At the time in question, c630, he was confidently defying even Harsha who, despite summoning all his troops plus the ablest commanders from his 'five Indies', and despite himself leading this horde in battle, had failed to impress Pulakesin II's gladiators or to dent his roving ambitions.

Hsuan Tsang, and no doubt Harsha, saw this impasse as a stalemate; Pulakesin not unreasonably celebrated it as a victory. He belonged to a dynasty, the Chalukya, which because of its long-lasting consequence and numerous offshoots (whence it is often distinguished as the 'Western Chalukya') deserves special attention. The Chalukyas hailed from Karnataka to the south, and in the course of a couple of generations had soared to prominence at the expense of various neighbours, including the Kadambas, their erstwhile suzerains. Their capital, fortified by Pulakesin I, founder of the dynasty and the first to perform the horse-sacrifice (and also Pulakesin II's grandfather), was situated at Vatapi, now Badami, a small town scrabbling up both sides of a cliff-stepped ravine in northern Karnataka.

There or thereabouts the Chalukyas would continue to celebrate their successes with a remarkable series of temples, at first cut into the rock but by the time of Pulakesin II already free-standing buildings. They were not the first structural temples, timber and brick having been used for such constructions since long before the time of Christ. Nor were they the first stone-built temples: at Sanchi, Nalanda, Buddh Gaya and several other sites in eastern Madhya Pradesh, UP and Bihar a dozen scattered temples from the Gupta period survive in various degrees of dilapidation or over-zealous restoration. But at Badami and its neighbouring sites (Aihole, Mahakuta and Pattadakal) the feast of architecture and sculpture heralds a new identity between dynasty and endowment in which temple-building becomes an expression and paradigm of a sovereign's authority.

On one of these temples, a rather plain construction dedicated to a Jain saint at Aihole, the poet Ravikirti recorded Pulakesin II's successes. Reminiscent of Samudra-Gupta's great Allahabad inscription, this record has the bonus of a date, equivalent to 636 in the Christian calendar. It makes the shrine 'one of the earliest dated temples in India'[11] and, as noted earlier, has provided a benchmark for chronological calculations reaching back even to Manu and the Flood. Here too, in presumptuously comparing his literary talents with those of Kalidasa, Ravikirti provides the earliest dated reference to 'Sanskrit's Shakespeare'; whenever Kalidasa lived, he must have been well dead by 636.

Of more relevance to the Chalukyas is the detailed listing of Pulakesin II's extensive conquests. Since he succeeded to the throne after a period of internal strife, he had first to consolidate his hold on the Badami region, his base, by again subduing the Kadambas, Gangas and other rival kings in Karnataka. It was probably after this feat that he assumed the titles of *maharajadhiraja* and *paramesvara* ('lord of the others'). The west coast (Konkan) from Goa up to and beyond where Bombay now stands was also subjugated while several of its islands, probably including that of Elephanta, were assaulted by the Chalukyan navy. Further north the Malavas of Malwa and the Gurjaras of southern Rajasthan submitted; and a Chalukyan vice-royalty was established in Gujarat. Clearly Chalukyan forces had crossed both the Tapti and Narmada rivers and were therefore threatening Harsha and his confederates.

Next in the Aihole listing comes Harsha himself. His stature is acknowledged in a well-worn cliché about his lotus feet gleaming with the jewels of those who bowed to his sway. But in identifying this formidable challenger the poet also introduces a neat pun on the word *harsa* ('harsha'). *Harsa* as a noun means 'joy', and thus Pulakesin's victory is signified by a phrase about how 'the *harsa* [of his enemy] was melted away by fear'. Another source has it simply that the lord of the *Daksinapatha* (the 'South') routed the Lord of the *Uttarapatha* (the 'North').

Pulakesin's circuit of conquest then continued east, flattening more rivals and reaching the Bay of Bengal in Orissa. Most of the rich lands comprising the Kistna and Godavari deltas in what is now Andhra Pradesh were placed in the care of his younger brother, whose descendants would constitute the 'Eastern Chalukyas', a dynasty which would survive until the eleventh century when it merged with its Chola allies of Tamil Nadu. From Vengi, as the Eastern Chalukya kingdom would be called, Pulakesin II resumed his victorious progress down the east coast into Pallava territory. Again his champions and their punch-drunk elephants triumphed as the Pallava king was forced to seek safety within the walls of Kanchipuram. There, unwisely in view of the sequel, Pulakesin left the Pallava and continued south. He crossed the Kaveri and completed his circuit by accepting overtures of friendship from the ancient kingdoms of the extreme south – the Cholas of the Kaveri delta, the Pandyas of Madurai and the Cheras of the Kerala coast.

Now 'lord of both the eastern and the western seas' and indisputably master of all India south of the Vindhya hills, Pulakesin II returned to Badami. Hsuan Tsang calls him a *ksatriya* yet credits him with magnanimity and foresight, qualities rarely accorded to a 'heretic' by the devout Buddhist, let alone to an enemy of his beloved Harsha. He is not mentioned in any other Chinese sources but some authorities insist that an Indian mission received by Khusru II of Persia in 625 must have been from the Chalukyan king.

However far-flung his fame, Pulakesin II's manoeuvres as listed in the Aihole inscription are of great interest as an illustration of the theory of Indian paramountcy. The assumption is usually made that his triumphs, like those of Samudra-Gupta as recorded on the Allahabad pillar, are organised in chronological sequence. It cannot be proved; but what here is self-evident is that, whether chronological or not, they were certainly logical. Pulakesin was doing the rounds of his neighbours. South, west, north, east, and back to the south, the Chalukyan was circling – or was seen to be circling – a universe of territory, riding its bounds as it were just like Raghu in Kalidasa's *Raghu-vamsa*. Both kings were, in Indian terms, defining a *raja-mandala*, the diagram of concentric 'circles of kings' which is discussed at length in Kautilya's *Arthasastra* and other works on political theory.

In Indian cosmology the *mandala* design commonly serves as a map. At the centre is the sacred Mount Meru, the axis of the world, outside which the innermost circle is divided into four lands (*dvipa*); one of these four, *jambu-dvipa* ('the land of the rose-apple'), is the earth. Outside this, the next circle is the sea, the next more land, then more sea and so on. The seas are filled with, or named after, familiar liquids – obviously salt-water in the case of the first, then treacle, wine, butter and other kitchen ingredients. To literal minds, like that of Thomas Babington Macaulay, minds which had been schooled on the scientific certainties and rational arguments of the European Enlightenment, these 'seas of treacle and butter' would seem contemptible absurdities; India's only hope of advancement lay in forsaking such nonsense, and to this end Macaulay, in a famous minute on Indian education in the 1830s, would issue a damning and still resented indictment of Indian culture as he insisted that India's schools forsake Sanskrit and adopt a Western-style curriculum.

A no less exasperated attitude is detectable in many nineteenth-century attempts to reconstruct India's history. From inscriptions and *sasana* the flowery epithets about lotus-footed ancestors and star-bright toenails were ruthlessly discarded in an effort to extract some credible nugget of political or genealogical import. The *raja-mandala* as a useful symbol of political relations suffered the same fate. Crudely, it represented the idea that just as cosmic harmony depended on the hierarchy of gods and men actively participating in the triumph of *dharma*, so political harmony depended on the triumph of *dharma* through an ordered hierarchy of kings. But because this earthly hierarchy was constantly under threat from the *matsya-nyaya* (the 'big fish eats little fish' syndrome), it required frequent adjustments.

The *raja-mandala*, in which the *maharajadhiraja* took the place of Mount Meru at the centre or axis, demonstrated the basic principle of these adjustments. Thus the immediate neighbours of the axial 'king of kings', those therefore within the first circle, are to be regarded as his natural enemies; those beyond them in the next circle are his potential allies; those in the third circle are his enemies' potential allies, those in the fourth his allies' natural allies, and so on. According to Kautilya, this was the basis of all external relations and of any world order.

Additionally the *raja-mandala*, when represented as a diagram, was divided by vertical and horizontal radials into four quadrants or quarters. These were seen to correspond to the four *dwipa*, or lands, of a *mandala* map. Harsha's *digvijaya*, or 'conquest of the four quarters', was therefore a bid for universal dominion. In the same way the *maharajadhiraja* who would be a *cakravartin*, a 'wheel-turning' world-ruler, must as it were weld the rims to the hub by spokes of conquest and alliance and so oblige the kings within each circle of the *mandala-raja* to acquiesce in and harmonise with his new and, of course, self-centring world order.

This geography, indeed geometry, of empire was crucial. It presupposed that 'society of kings' already mentioned and it necessitated frequent or, in the case of Harsha and Pulakesin, almost continual perambulation of one's domains. But it also made conflict a largely dynastic affair which, though of great frequency, may have been of low intensity. The troops involved seem to have been professional warriors who, while dependent on local supplies and transport, otherwise left the agricultural classes alone, as in Megasthenes' day. Acts symbolic of submission were highly prized; so was the acquisition of accumulated wealth, war elephants, musical instruments, jewels and other symbols of sovereignty. On the other hand the heavy casualties and widespread devastation implied by boasts of 'annihilation' cannot be substantiated, nor is there evidence of any consequent economic collapse. On the contrary, the ease with which 'uprooted' kings again took root suggests an almost ritualised form of warfare not unlike that which survived, even into the twentieth century, amongst another society of Hindu kings – namely that on the Indonesian island of Bali.

Back in the south India of the seventh century, while Pulakesin II was still celebrating his success in overrunning the rich Pallava country in Tamil Nadu, the Pallava king was ready to take the field again. At Polilur, a place near Kanchipuram where the British would suffer one of their worst defeats in India, the Pallava king claims to have 'annihilated his enemies', presumably the Chalukyas, and by 642 he was marching on their capital at Badami. Pallava records claim that Badami was then destroyed and that the Pallava king, Narasimha-varman I, made such a habit of defeating the great Pulakesin II that he fancied he could read the word 'victory' engraved on his adversary's backside as he again took to flight. More certainly Narasimha-varman engraved a record of his success on a rock at Badami and thereafter assumed the title of *Vatapi-konda*, 'conqueror of Vatapi [i.e. Badami]'.

The Chalukyas would return the compliment. Pulakesin seems to have died in the midst of these reverses and the Chalukyan kingdom to have remained in relapse during a succession crisis. But in 655 one of Pulakesin's sons, Vikramaditya I, claimed the throne, quickly reasserted Chalukyan sovereignty, and was soon hammering again at the Pallavas. This time Kanchi was surrendered. Then once again the Pallavas struck back. With intermissions while the Pallavas dealt with the Pandyas of Madurai to the south or went to the aid of their allies in Sri Lanka, and while the Chalukyas saw off their own rivals, including the first Arab incursion into Gujarat, the ding-dong struggle between the paramount powers of the arid Deccan and lush Tamil coast continued for over a century. Not infrequently it well demonstrated the Kautilyan *raja-mandala*. The Pandyas, the southern

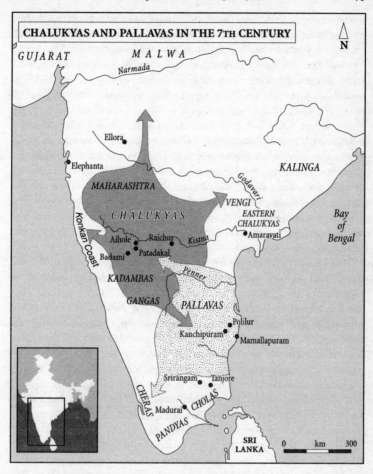

CHALUKYAS AND PALLAVAS IN THE 7TH CENTURY

neighbours and so natural enemies of the Pallavas, assisted the Chalukyas, while the Pandyas' neighbours and natural enemies, the Cheras of Kerala and the kings of Sri Lanka, rendered support to the Pallavas.

In c740 Vikramaditya II, a Chalukya, again captured Kanchi and this time took the opportunity to leave a record of his success. His inscription in the soft sandstone of one of the pillars of the Pallavas' just-built Kailasanatha temple is still legible and boasts not only of his conquest but also of his generosity to the city, which he spared, and to the temple, to which he returned the gold that belonged to it. Significantly, as with the Pallava inscription at Badami, no attempt seems to have been made to erase this patronising record when the Pallavas duly recovered their capital.

Nor does this almost constant warfare with its frequent 'annihilations' seem to have inhibited either dynasty in the practice of kingship. The *sasanas*, from which our knowledge of their struggles is largely derived, continued to be issued; and the great temples, for which both dynasties are now best remembered, continued to be built. Narasimha-varman I, Pulakesin II's eventual conqueror, was also known as Mahamalla or Mamalla ('great wrestler'), and after him the Pallavas' main port at Mamallapuram (Mahabalipuram) was named. There the famous stone-cut temples, or *raths*, each hewn from a single giant stone, were probably the work of Narasimha-varman II (also known as Rajasimha), who 'assumed titles galore – about 250 of them'[12] – and reigned from c695-c728. He also built the so-called Shore temple at Mamallapuram, and began the Kailasanatha at Kanchi.

His Chalukya contemporary was Vijayaditya, the grandson of Vikramaditya I and another man of many titles and many temples; most of the structures at Aihole belong to his reign. He also began, but never completed, the first temple at Pattadakal. A level site lying between the twin towns of Badami and Aihole, Pattadakal would under his successors usurp the ceremonial role of both places as the commemorative capital of the Chalukyas. Here during the first half of the eighth century the Chalukyan temples assumed a size and magnificence of ornamentation unsurpassed by anything in contemporary India and rivalled only by the temples of Kanchi. But whereas today the latter are scattered about a large city richly endowed with later architecture, at Pattadakal, always a site rather than a city, the temples now rear up amongst soggy fields of sugarcane where a mud village and a milky cup of tea is the height of modern magnificence.

Two of these temples, parked side by side like vehicles from another planet, were commissioned by two sisters who were the successive wives of Vikramaditya II, he who left his mark on Kanchi's Kailasanatha temple. Celebrating this victory, the sisters' twin temples closely resemble the Kailasanatha and so are indisputably of the so-called Dravida style (which climaxes with the great eleventh-century Chola temple of Tanjore). Others, however, both here and at Aihole, show features like the curvilinear *sikhara* (tower) which are distinctive of what used to be called the Nagara or northern style of temple (as famously represented by the later Khajuraho temples). There are also examples of the straight-sided pyramidal style of tower later associated with the Orissan temples, especially of Bhuvaneshwar.

THE CHALUKYAS AND THE PALLAVAS The Rival Successions

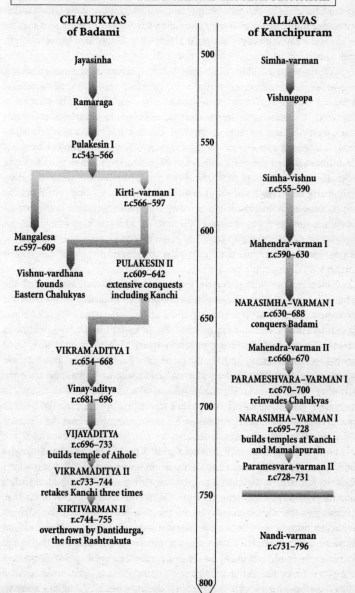

**CHALUKYAS
of Badami**

Jayasinha

Ramaraga

Pulakesin I
r.c543–566

Kirti–varman I
r.c566–597

Mangalesa
r.c597–609

Vishnu-vardhana
founds
Eastern Chalukyas

PULAKESIN II
r.c609–642
extensive conquests
including Kanchi

VIKRAM ADITYA I
r.c654–668

Vinay-aditya
r.c681–696

VIJAYADITYA
r.c696–733
builds temple of Aihole

VIKRAMADITYA II
r.c733–744
retakes Kanchi three times

KIRTIVARMAN II
r.c744–755
overthrown by Dantidurga,
the first Rashtrakuta

**PALLAVAS
of Kanchipuram**

Simha-varman

Vishnugopa

Simha-vishnu
r.c555–590

Mahendra-varman I
r.c590–630

NARASIMHA–VARMAN I
r.c630–688
conquers Badami

Mahendra-varman II
r.c660–670

PARAMESHVARA–VARMAN I
r.c670–700
reinvades Chalukyas

NARASIMHA–VARMAN I
r.c695–728
builds temples at Kanchi
and Mamalapuram

Paramesvara-varman II
r.c728–731

Nandi-varman
r.c731–796

500

550

600

650

700

750

800

It seems unlikely that, as once thought, all these variations were developed by the Chalukyas' architects. Sculpture and iconography show Gupta influences and imply rather that the far-ranging Chalukyas, in their architecture as in their empire, made of the great Deccan divide a bridge between north and south.

Culturally their Pallava rivals look to have performed the same bridging role between the Indian subcontinent and the Indic kingdoms of south-east Asia. No region or dynasty of India had a monopoly of south-east Asian contacts. We know that Bengal had regular contacts with both mainland south-east Asia and its archipelago; Fa Hian sailed for Indonesia or Malaya from the Bengali port of Tamralipti, and many Chinese and south-east Asian Buddhists reached the great university of Nalanda in Bihar via the same port. Orissan influences have also been traced in Burma and the Indies; failing any better explanation, it is quite possible that 'Kling', the name by which people of Indian origin are still known in Sumatra and parts of Malaysia, derives from 'Kalinga', the ancient Orissan kingdom. Likewise Kerala and Gujarat seem to have had regular contacts with south-east Asia, which with the entry of the Arabs into the carrying trade of the Indian Ocean would be greatly increased.

However, the most pervasive influence in south-east Asia during the fifth to seventh centuries seems to have been that exercised by the Pallavas of Kanchi. In mainland south-east Asia an important new kingdom had begun to emerge in the sixth century. Based in Cambodia, it would soon absorb Funan, the Indic kingdom on the lower Mekong from which it had probably broken away, and would eventually emerge as the great Khmer kingdom of Angkor. Its kings, like many of those of Funan and Champa (another Indic state in Vietnam), almost always bore names ending in '-varman', just like the Pallavas. More significantly, they claimed descent from the union of a local princess with a certain Kambu whose descendants were known as 'Kambujas'.

From this word came 'Cambodia' and 'Khmer'. But the Kambujas, as both a people and a place, first occur in the epics and the *Puranas* where they are located in the extreme north-west of the Indian subcontinent, a good three thousand kilometres from Cambodia. It has already been suggested that the sacred geography of the Sanskrit classics tended to get replicated as new regions became Sanskritised (e.g. Mathura, Madurai, and Madura in Indonesia). Kambuja's improbable removal from the upper Indus to the middle Mekong looks to be another case in point. Moreover the adoption of Kambu as a common ancestor would seem to show how such transpositions might have come about, with kings as far away as

Indo-China laying claim to the legitimacy provided by an adopted Sanskritic forebear. But what is also significant is that this particular myth seems to have been a revision of the story of the brahman Kaundinya and 'Willow-Leaf', his ill-clad local queen. And that in its turn 'shows a certain kinship with the genealogical myth of the Pallavas of Kanchi',[13] indeed 'is strikingly similar' to it.[14]

Indo-China apart, the Pallavas are known to have become involved in dynastic struggles in Sri Lanka, to have developed Mamallapuram as a long-distance trading station, and to have had diplomatic relations with China. No doubt commercial, religious and political factors all played their part in promoting a more direct, if still conjectural, Pallavan influence in the south-east Asian archipelago. An inscription found in Java uses the Pallava script and that island's earliest surviving Hindu temples, small stone-built shrines scattered across the misty highlands of Dieng and Gedong Songo, show clear affinities with the architecture of Mamallapuram.

In Indonesia as in Indo-China important political developments were under way. The eighth century saw the emergence from obscurity of Srivijaya, a maritime power and possibly a dynasty, which would control a seaborne empire stretching from Sumatra to Malaya, Thailand, Cambodia and Vietnam. In terms of national psyche the watery imperium of Srivijaya is as important to modern Indonesia, itself 'a pelagic state', as is the continental empire of the Mauryas to Indian centralists. Like Cham-pa and Cambodia, Srivijaya was nevertheless a decidedly Indianised polity, although apparently more Buddhist than brahmanical. Its capital, near Palembang in south-eastern Sumatra, looks to have been the place where in the late seventh century I-tsing (I-ching), another Chinese scholar, found a thriving monastic community. From its monks he received preliminary instruction before proceeding on to Bengal and Nalanda. Returning, he lived with the Srivijayan Buddhists for several years as he worked on the translation of texts acquired in India.

Also in the seventh and eighth centuries there arose in central Java the rival, but eventually joint, kingdoms of the Sailendra and Sanjaya. The origins of these dynasties and their relationship with Srivijaya, let alone India, are subjects of much debate; but to one or both of them must be ascribed the first glorious phase of Javanese temple-building which began c780. As in the Deccan and south India, the temples are all clustered within a small compass, here centred on the city of Jogjakarta. Moreover many conform in all but detail to the norms of layout and elevation found at the Pallavan and Chalukyan sites.

The one glowering exception is the sculptural colossus of Borobudur,

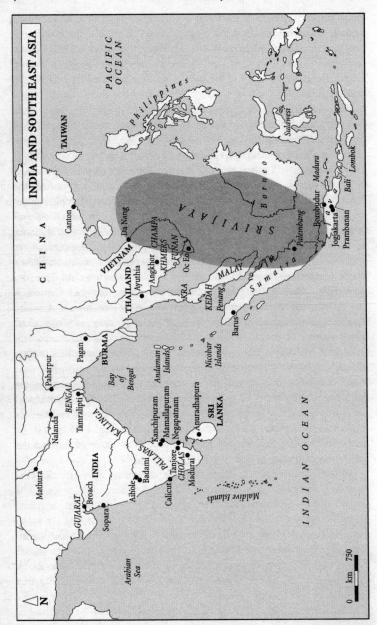

INDIA AND SOUTH EAST ASIA

PACIFIC OCEAN

CHINA

TAIWAN

Canton

Philippines

Sulawesi

Borneo

SRIVIJAYA

Palembang

Borobudur *Madura*

Jogjakarta *Bali Lombok*

Prambanan

Java

Da Nang

CHAMPA

VIETNAM

Angkhor

KHMERS

Oc Eo

FUNAN

MALAY

Sumatra

Ayuthia

THAILAND

KRA

KEDAH

Penang

Barus

Pagan

BURMA

Bay of Bengal

Paharpur

Nalanda

Tamralipti

BENGAL

KALINGA

Andaman Islands

Nicobar Islands

Kanchipuram

Mamallapuram

Negapatnam

Anuradhapura

SRI LANKA

PALLAVAS

Badami

Tanjore

CHOLAS

Calicut

Madurai

Maldive Islands

INDIAN OCEAN

Mathura

GUJARAT

Broach

Aihole

Sopara

Arabian Sea

0   km   750

N

much the most outstanding if enigmatic example of Indian cultural transference in south-east Asia. As a stepped stupa of unprecedented proportions, possible prototypes for it have been inferred from the descriptions
offered by Hsuan Tsang of now vanished north Indian stupas and from
archaeological evidence of massive ruins and plinths at sites like
Nandangarh and Paharpur in Bengal. On the other hand, if the stupa was
originally a hill which was then cut into terraces and clad with stone, local
parallels with the elaborately terraced landscape of Java and its pre-Indic
mountain deities may be more relevant.

The archaeology of the building does nothing to resolve these contradictions. Apparently begun about 775, it only assumed its final shape in 840,
by which time it had been frequently redesigned and even reinterpreted.
'The monument was built in at least four different stages . . . it was probably
begun as a Hindu temple, and was transformed into a Buddhist place of
worship after its second stage.'[15] However this may be, there is universal
consensus that the ground-plan of Borobudur, both as originally conceived
and as finally realised, represents a classic *mandala*. Its four sides, each
about as long as the touchline of a football pitch, are progressively indented
so as to round, as it were, the corners, and render the four-square outline
as near circular as rectangular masonry will allow. Succeeding tiers, the
inner circles on the ground plan, follow the same pattern until the three
topmost, or innermost, are in fact circular. Moreover each tier is accessible
only by flights of steps located in the middle of each side and which,
connecting, divide the monument into four quadrants.

A similar design can be detected in the base-plan of contemporary
temples, as opposed to stupas, in both Java and India. Elevations add a
further important dimension to this symbolism, as will appear from the
soaring ambitions of the Chalukyas' successors in the Deccan. Here it will
suffice to note that building temples had now become a royal prerogative.
All, except subsidiary shrines, were in part intended as expressions of royal
paramountcy designed to impress subjects, remind vassals, and challenge
rivals.

Hence 'the construction of a temple, Buddhist or Hindu, was an important political act,'[16] indeed 'as much an act of war as it was an act of
peace'.[17] It could, though, be misconstrued. As new Islamic challengers
ventured across the deserts of Sind and over the Hindu Kush, India's
dynasties appeared to be woefully indifferent as they lavished all available
resources not on forts and horsemen but on flights of architectural fantasy.
In fact they were meeting the new threat by a gloriously defiant assertion
of self-belief in their superior sovereignty.

Dharma and Defiance

c700–c900

THE DAWN MUEZZIN

THE URGENCY WITH WHICH the followers of the Prophet carried his teachings out of Arabia resulted in one of the campaigning wonders of world history. Within twenty years of his death in 632, Arab forces, although lacking in military pedigree and with no prior knowledge of siegecraft, had overrun much of the Byzantine empire in Syria and Egypt and all of the Sassanid empire in Iraq and Iran. Forty years later, with the addition of North Africa, Spain, most of Afghanistan, and vast areas of central Asia, the Arab domains spanned three continents in a broad swathe of conquest which stretched from the Atlantic to the Indus and from the upper Nile to the Aral Sea. Alexander had been upstaged, Caesar overshadowed. If Muslim authors celebrated this success with the chronicles, geographies and travelogues which now constitute important source materials for the period, it was hardly surprising; evidence of Islam's triumph was proof of Islam's truth. By 700 China and India shared uncertain borderlands with Islamic neighbours just as did the Frankish kingdom in western Europe and what remained of Byzantium's empire in Anatolia.

This phenomenal rate of expansion could not be sustained. External resistance hardened, internal stresses led to the breakaway of peripheral provinces. When in 750 the Umayyad caliphate of Damascus was succeeded by the Abbasid caliphate of Baghdad a long period of consolidation and cultural distinction set in. In the east the Arabs had reached the Indus a hundred years earlier, yet only rarely had they ventured beyond it. Their Turkish successors in Afghanistan, reluctant rulers if less reticent raiders, would also for long be content merely to ravage India's northern cities.

Islam's Indian frontier would therefore come to assume a near permanence. Running roughly up the Indus from Sind in what is now Pakistan to Kabul in Afghanistan, it would scarcely advance for three centuries. Kanauj and India's other front-line kingdoms had, like Constantinople, ample time to become acquainted with their new neighbours, with the faith they held so dear and with the tactics they used so well. None would seem invincible. Moreover, a catastrophe that takes centuries to materialise loses some of its menace. Illusions of successful resistance were nursed; prospects for co-existence were explored. The India which finally succumbed to Muslim dominion in the thirteenth century, though politically more divided than ever, would be both more resilient and more receptive than the brittle dynastic structures of the eighth century. Similarly the Islamic conquerors who would eventually hoist their standards over Delhi, though no more tolerant of idolatry than their Arab predecessors, had few illusions about the mass conversion of India's multitudes, but real expectations of a fruitful and lasting Indian dominion.

Arab forces, possibly including a few grey-bearded disciples who had prayed with the Prophet himself, had first ventured onto Indian soil by crossing the Bolan pass (near Quetta in the Baluchistan province of Pakistan) in c663. The pass provides comparatively easy access from southern Afghanistan into valleys which thread their way down to the Indus in upper Sind. Much further south, on the coast of lower Sind, desultory naval raids had preceded this assault. Maritime objectives would remain important. In fact twenty years earlier the first Muslims to reach India had been newly converted Arab merchants trading across the Arabian Sea to India's west coast. Their destinations included the port-cities of the Maitrakas in Saurashtra, of the Chalukyas in Maharashtra, the Cheras in Kerala, and even the kings of Sri Lanka. By the mid-seventh century there were sizeable communities of Muslims in most of these ports. Without provoking undue hostility amongst already cosmopolitan populations, the newcomers rapidly engrossed the valuable carrying trade in Arabian horses to India and in Indian and south-east Asian spices to Arabia. The protection of this route and those who sailed it was thus an early Arab priority; and it called for particular attention to the coastal regions of Sind, whose estuarine inlets provided a muddy sanctuary amidst the mangroves for scavenging sea tribes and hereditary pirates.

Whether it was also the Arabs' intention to use Sind as a springboard for the invasion of India is less certain. The idea would surface in the eighth century, but in the seventh the more usual route to India via Kabul and the Khyber Pass seems to have been preferred and had already resulted in a succession of abortive Arab raids directed at the Kabul valley. Sind, on the other hand, was something of a dead-end as well as a backwater.

This was because any eastward progress was largely barred by the Thar, otherwise the Great Indian Desert, where now runs the Indo–Pakistan border. Even history, as if aware that the lower Indus would have more than its fair share of exposure after the Harappan discoveries, has little to report of the region during the thousand years since Alexander and his men had come sailing downriver. That it was then already Aryanised is clear from the ferocious opposition which the Macedonians encountered even from brahman communities.

Subsequently Buddhism had also claimed many followers in Sind and seems to have become the predominant creed. Hsuan Tsang, writing only twenty years before the first Arab incursion, found innumerable stupas, amongst them perhaps those in the vicinity of Mohenjo-daro which thirteen centuries later would attract the first glimmer of archaeological interest in Harappan prehistory. He also reported on Sind's 'several hundred *sangha-ramas* occupied by about ten thousand monks'. Admittedly the monks, being of the Hinayana school of which the Chinese Mahayanist heartily disapproved, seemed somewhat 'indolent and given to indulgence and debauchery'. But the people as a whole were 'hardy and impulsive' and their kingdom, then one of Harsha's confederate states, was famed for its cereal production, its livestock and its export of salt.[1]

Unfortunately Hsuan Tsang's generally reliable, if partisan, account says nothing about the political situation, only that Sind's unnamed king was of *sudra* caste. He was also 'an honest and sincere fellow' who, not unexpectedly after such a character reference, 'reverenced the law of the Buddha'. Presumably he was of the Rai dynasty, and probably the last of that dynasty for, according to Muslim sources, in c640 the throne of the Rais was usurped by a brahman named Chach. For an infidel, Chach would be rated highly by Muslim writers. In the *Chach-nama*, an Islamic history of Sind compiled in the thirteenth century but supposedly based on contemporary accounts, he is said to have immediately set out 'to define the frontiers of his kingdom'.[2]

No charters of his reign survive, but it may be supposed that what Muslim historians saw as an exercise in border demarcation Chach intended as a traditional *digvijaya*. Nor, as 'conquests of the four quarters' go, was it inconsiderable. In the north, we learn, he reached 'Kashmir'. Even if this meant not the Kashmir valley but Kashmir territory, which then extended down to the plains of the Panjab, he must at least have entered the Himalayan foothills, for he marked his frontier by planting a chenar, or plane tree, and a deodar, or Himalayan cedar; both are native to the hills. Heading west he laid claim to Makran, the coastal region of Baluchistan where he planted date palms, and heading south he reached the mouth of the Indus. Chach's kingdom lacked only the erstwhile Gandhara in the north-west to qualify as a proto-Pakistan. Similarly, as a *digvijaya*, his conquests were incomplete only in respect of the *mandala*'s eastern quadrant where lay the fearful sands of Thar.

As if to make up for this omission, it was Chach, or his governor in upper Sind, who successfully saw off the Arab attack of 663 via the Bolan pass. No further assaults materialised, and in c674, after what was undoubtedly a glorious reign, Chach 'died and went to hell', this being the invariable fate of even the noblest infidel in Muslim histories. It was therefore his son, Dahar (Dahir), who in c708 faced the next and more determined Arab invasion.

This time the trouble is specifically attributed to a flagrant act of piracy. A ship from Sri Lanka, whose Basra-bound passengers included a bevy of maidens, had been waylaid off the port-city of Debal (in the vicinity of modern Karachi) by the dreaded Meds. The Meds were pirates while the maidens, all daughters of deceased Muslim merchants, had been intended as a courtesy from the king of Sri Lanka to al-Hajjaj ibn Yusuf, the Caliph's governor of Iraq and viceroy for the eastern empire. In what reads like an early-eighth-century version of quarrels which would recur in the late eighteenth century over the policing of the Arabian Sea, al-Hajjaj demanded that King Dahar of Sind secure the release of the maidens. But Dahar, even if willing, was unable to oblige. As he explained, 'They are pirates who have captured these women, and over them I have no authority.'[3] Unsatisfied with this reply, al-Hajjaj despatched a naval force to Debal. It was defeated and its commander killed. Another armada met a similar fate. Whether or not Dahar took an active part in these skirmishes, he was clearly doing nothing to restrain his coastal subjects. Al-Hajjaj therefore continued to hold him responsible and resolved on the all-out amphibious offensive of c708.

Command of the caliph's forces was given to Muhammad ibn Qasim, al-Hajjaj's cousin and an able leader, who was to be supplied with siege engines by sea and with six thousand crack Syrian troops for the march through Makran. Nothing was left to chance; according to al-Biladuri, one of the earliest Muslim chroniclers, ibn Qasim 'was provided with all he could require, without omitting even thread and needles'. Although apparently just a figure of speech, this reference to needlecraft would be of some significance for Muhammad ibn Qasim.

More immediately the siege engines came into their own. The land forces had effected a rendezvous with the seaborne reinforcements outside

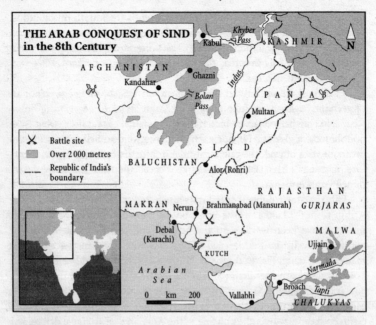

THE ARAB CONQUEST OF SIND in the 8th Century

Debal, but they were unable to force entry to the city. Even the *manjanik*, a gigantic martinet, or calibrated catapult, which required five hundred men to operate it, was ineffective against Debal's stout walls. But by shortening its chassis so that it aimed high, the *manjanik* was trained on a flagstaff whose bright red flag fluttered defiantly from the top of Debal's temple tower. After no doubt several misses, the *manjanik*-master struck lucky and the flagstaff was shattered, 'at which the idolaters were sore afflicted'. In fact, they threw caution to the wind and, issuing forth to avenge this sacrilege, were easily routed. 'The town was thus taken by assault and the carnage endured for three days,' says al-Biladuri. The temple was partly demolished, its 'priests' (who may have been Buddhists or brahmans) were massacred, and a mosque was laid out for the four-thousand-man garrison which was to remain in Debal.

Meanwhile ibn Qasim moved inland, then up the west bank of the Indus. Some 'Samanis' (presumably *sramanas*, or Buddhist monks) of 'Nerun' (perhaps the Pakistani Hyderabad) were reminded of their vows of non-violence and came to terms with the invader. Thanks to these

'Buddhist fifth-columnists',[4] as an eminent Indian historian mischievously calls them, Nerun capitulated. On the opposite bank of the river, a despondent Dahar was apparently safe since ibn Qasim seemed unable or unwilling to cross the flood. Eventually orders came from Governor al-Hajjaj in Baghdad to do just that. A bridge of roped boats was assembled on the west bank. With one end released into the current, it swung into place and the Arabs began crossing immediately.

'The dreadful conflict which followed was such as had never been heard of,' reports al-Biladuri. It does, though, bring to mind Alexander's titanic struggle with Poros; for again the Indian forces displayed exceptional bravery and again the outcome hung in the balance until decided by the ungovernable behaviour of panic-stricken elephants. The beast ridden by Dahar himself, a rather conspicuous albino, was hit by a fire-arrow and plunged into the river. There Dahar made an easy target. He fought on with an arrow in his chest but, dismounting, was eventually struck by a skull-splitting sword blow. It was towards evening, according to al-Biladuri, and when Dahar 'died and went to hell', 'the idolaters fled and the Mussulmans glutted themselves with massacre'.

Muhammad ibn Qasim then resumed his march upriver. Brahmanabad (the later Mansurah), then Alor (Rohri) and finally Multan, the three principal cities of Sind, were either captured or surrendered, probably during the years 710–13. Astronomical casualty figures are given, yet both al-Biladuri and the *Chach-nama* agree that ibn Qasim was a man of his word. When he offered, in return for a peaceful surrender, to spare lives and guarantee the safety of temples he was as good as his promise. Hindu and Buddhist establishments were respected 'as if they were the churches of the Christians, the synagogues of the Jews or the fire temples of the Magians [Zoroastrians]'. The *jizya*, the standard poll-tax on all infidels, was imposed; yet brahmans and Buddhist monks were allowed to collect alms, and temples to receive donations. Ibn Qasim was no mindless butcher. When he was disgraced and removed following the death of his patron al-Hajjaj, it may well be that 'the people of Hind wept'.

Al-Biladuri merely explains that Muhammad ibn Qasim was sent back to Iraq as a prisoner and there tortured to death because of a family feud with the new governor. The *Chach-nama* gives a different story and much more detail. Apparently ibn Qasim had previously captured two of Dahar's virgin daughters and sent them to Baghdad as an adornment to Caliph Walid's seraglio. There one of the young princesses, Suryadevi, caught the caliph's eye; but when he deigned to draw her near, 'she abruptly stood up'. As she very respectfully explained, she felt unworthy of the royal couch since both she and her sister had been similarly favoured in Sind during their detention by Muhammad ibn Qasim. The caliph was not pleased. 'Overwhelmed with love and letting slip the reins of patience', he immediately dictated a missive ordering the perpetrator to 'suffer himself to be sewed up in a hide and sent to the capital'.

The order was obeyed to the letter; the needles and the thread were at last put to good use and ibn Qasim, trussed and labelled, was despatched to Baghdad. Two days into this long and excruciating journey 'he delivered his soul to God and went to the eternal world'. When finally the unsavoury package was delivered to Walid, the princesses were invited to bear witness to the caliph's awesomely impartial justice. Not without glee they surveyed the grisly cadaver and then bravely, if unwisely, revealed that Muhammad ibn Qasim had in fact behaved with perfect propriety.

> But he had killed the king of Hind and Sind, destroyed the dominion
> of our forefathers, and degraded us from the dignity of royalty to
> a state of slavery. Therefore, to retaliate and revenge these injuries,
> we uttered a falsehood and our object has been fulfilled.

So Muhammad ibn Qasim had been stitched up in more ways than one. Again the Caliph was mightily displeased, 'and from excess of regret he bit the back of his hand'. Then he consigned the princesses to lifelong incarceration.[5]

Like most good stories, this one has not always been endorsed by professional historians, although why a Muslim should have fabricated a tale so creditable to the infidel is not explained. It does, moreover, offer a plausible reason for the downfall of Sind's respected and highly successful conqueror. His like would be hard to find. The next Arab governor of the province died on arrival, and his successor seems to have made little impact on a situation which had already declined, with Brahmanabad back under the control of Dahar's son. The latter, in c720, accepted Baghdad's offer of an amnesty whereby in return for adopting Islam he was granted immunity and the chance to participate in government. But this looks to have been a tactical move for, as a succession crisis engulfed the Umayyad caliphate, the Sindis happily discarded both their allegiance and their new faith.

Dahar's son was eventually captured and killed by Junaid ibn Abdur Rahman al-Marri, who in the mid-720s seems to have recovered much of the province – and more besides. His successors fared less well, and there is evidence of the caliph's governors being penned within fortified enclaves before again 'seizing whatever came into their hands and subduing the neighbourhood whose inhabitants had rebelled'.[6] This pattern continued to repeat itself during the early years of the Abbasid caliphate. Baghdad's control of the entire province remained a rare phenomenon until, c870, the local governors, or amirs, gradually threw off their allegiance to the caliph and managed matters for themselves.

By the tenth century the province was divided between two Arab families, one ruling from Mansurah in the south and the other from Multan in the north. In Multan the resentment of the still largely non-Muslim population was curbed only by their Muslim masters threatening to vandalise the city's most revered temple whenever trouble stirred or invasion threatened. If conquest had been difficult, conversion was proving even more so. Yet the obstinacy of the idolaters, if indulged, could be put to some advantage, and if condemned, always afforded an excellent justification for pillage and plunder. So it was in Sind and so it would be in Hind (i.e. India). In fact Sind's governors had already had a foretaste of what lay ahead. Muhammad ibn Qasim may have pushed east towards Kanauj, Junaid certainly tried his luck in western India, and later governors may have followed suit.

Their experiences, in so far as they can be inferred from the scanty evidence, would not be encouraging. Al-Biladuri claims conquests for Junaid which extended to Broach in Gujarat and to Ujjain in Malwa. From a copper plate found at Nausari, south of Broach, it would appear that the Arabs had crossed Saurashtra and so must have squeezed through, or round, the Rann of Kutch. This was the incursion which put paid to the Maitrakas of Vallabhi, they of the dazzling toenails whose enemies' rutting elephants had had their temples cleft. It was also the incursion which was finally halted by, amongst others, a vassal branch of the Chalukya dynasty. The date is thought to have been c736.

Ujjain and Malwa look to have been the target of a separate and probably subsequent offensive by way of Rajasthan.[7] It too was defeated, in this instance by a rising clan of considerable later importance known as the Gurjaras. Clearly, when the subcontinent first faced the challenge of Islam, it was neither so irredeemably supine nor so hopelessly divided as British historians in the nineteenth century would suppose.

THE RISE OF THE RASHTRAKUTAS

In contemporary Indian sources these first marauding disciples of Islam are occasionally identified as *Yavanas* (Greeks), *Turuskas* (Turks) or *Tajikas* (Tajiks or Persians), but more usually as *mlecchas*. The latter term meant what it always had: foreigners who could not talk properly, outcastes with no place in Indian society and, above all, inferiors with no respect for *dharma*. Like all *mlecchas* the Muslims were seen as essentially marginal, negative and destructive, just like the Huns. There is no evidence of an Indian appreciation of the global threat which they represented; and the peculiar nature of their mission – to impose a new monotheist orthodoxy by military conquest and political dominion – was so alien to Indian tradition that it went uncomprehended.

No doubt a certain complacency contributed to this indifference. As al-Biruni (Alberuni), the great Islamic scholar of the eleventh century, would put it, 'the Hindus believe that there is no country but theirs, no nation like theirs, no king like theirs, no religion like theirs, no science like theirs.' He thought they should travel more and mix with other nations; 'their antecedents were not as narrow-minded as the present generation,' he added.[8] While clearly disparaging eleventh-century attitudes, al-Biruni thus appears to confirm the impression given by earlier Muslim writers that in the eighth and ninth centuries India was considered anything but backward. Its scientific and mathematical discoveries, though buried amidst semantic dross and seldom released for practical application, were readily appreciated by Muslim scientists and then rapidly appropriated by them. Al-Biruni was a case in point: his scientific celebrity in the Arab world would owe much to his mastery of Sanskrit and access to Indian scholarship.

Aspects of eleventh-century India which al-Biruni omitted from his catalogue of criticism were its size and its wealth. Unlike Alexander's Greeks, Muslim invaders were well aware of India's immensity, and mightily excited by its resources. As well as exotic produce like spices, peacocks, pearls, diamonds, ivory and ebony, the 'Hindu country' was renowned for its skilled manufactures and its bustling commerce. India's economy was probably one of the most sophisticated in the world. Guilds regulated production and provided credit; the roads were safe, ports and markets carefully supervised, and tariffs low. Moreover capital was both plentiful and conspicuous. Since at least Roman times the subcontinent seems to have enjoyed a favourable balance of payments. Gold and silver had been accumulating long before the 'golden Guptas', and they continued to do so. Figures in the Mamallapuram sculptures and the Ajanta frescoes are as strung about with jewellery as those in the Sanchi and Amaravati reliefs. Divine images of solid gold are well attested and royal temples were rapidly becoming royal treasuries as successful dynasts endowed them with the fruits of their conquests. The devout Muslim, although ostensibly bent on converting the infidel, would find his zeal handsomely rewarded.

Thanks to the peculiarities of the caste system, Indian society also seemed admirably stable, if excessively stratified. But although in theory the ritual-and-pollution-based *varna*, and in practice the profession-based *jati*, precluded social mobility, Muslim writers seldom correctly identified the four *varnas* or divined the variety of the innumerable *jatis*. It would seem, then, that the 'system' was not obviously systematic. Kings of *sudra* or brahman origin, like those of Sind, were as common as those whose forebears were, or pretended to be, of the supposedly royal and martial *ksatriya varna*.

Nor was caste wholly prohibitive and repressive. Indeed it has been argued that caste membership conferred important rights of participation in the economic and political processes as well as obligations of social conformity. In other words, it was as much about being a citizen as being a subject. Through various rural and, more obviously, urban assemblies like caste and guild councils, endorsement of a particular leadership was demonstrated by attendance in the myriad rituals of state. 'Rather than being excluded from the life of Indian polities, [castes] actively participated in it. Indeed, by doing so, they partly constituted it.'[9] Such participation in, for instance, the elaborate ceremonies involved in installing a new king or launching a *digvijaya* signified assent to the traditional fiscal and military expedients available to such a leader. But by caste councils, as by reluctant feudatories and vassals, such connivance in the political order might always be subtly withheld or transferred.

A further argument has it that caste assumed its passive and static connotations only after the Muslim conquest, when religious discrimination and oppressive taxation conspired to remove opportunities for political participation and economic advancement. Caste membership, shorn of its influence, then became primarily a distinguishing characteristic of orthodox Indian-ness, or 'Hinduism'. The notion of *karma* – whereby one's status was determined by one's conduct in past lives and could in subsequent lives be improved by one's conduct in this – provided a rational explanation for the system as well as a welcome solace for those most disadvantaged by it; their prospects now depended not on the exercise of caste rights but on resignation to caste obligations. The doctrine of *karma*, first scouted in the *Upanisads*, then elaborated in Buddhist teaching, thus came, like caste, to be perceived as fundamental to Hindu orthodoxy.

Politically, according to Muslim observers, India comprised many kingdoms, each with a formidable army that included elephants and cavalry as well as infantry. According to a Baghdad adage quoted by al-Biruni, the Turks were famous for their horses, Kandahar (for some reason) for its elephants, and India for its armies. One of India's rulers, 'the Balhara', was reckoned as being amongst 'the four great or principal kings of the world' according to the much-travelled merchant known to us simply as Suleiman (the other great rulers were the kings of Baghdad, of Byzantium-Constantinople, and of China). Admittedly 'the Balhara's' claim to be India's king of kings was constantly under threat; but in the opinion of Suleiman, who made several trips to India during the first half of the ninth century, this did not necessarily occasion great upheaval. India had learned to contain conflict and to minimise its effects.

> The Indians sometimes go to war for conquest, but the occasions are rare. I have never seen the people of one country submit to the authority of another, except in the case of that country which comes next to the country of pepper [i.e. the Malabar coast]. When a king subdues a neighbouring state, he places over it a man belonging to the family of the fallen prince who carries on the government in the name of the conqueror. The inhabitants would not suffer it to be otherwise.[10]

Once again one is reminded of Megasthenes' description of agricultural-ists 'ploughing in perfect security' while armies did battle in the next field. Although the ploughmen may have had a stake in the outcome of the battle or may have contributed to the equipage of one of the protagonists, they were not expected to get involved. Warriors fought with warriors; the ploughman's *dharma* was to plough.

Bearing this peculiarity in mind – and not without a deep breath – one may return to the dynastic fray as it intensified during the eighth to eleventh centuries. In the Deccan the century and a half of glorious domination by the Chalukyas of Badami came to an end around 760. Distracted if not exhausted by their endless wars in the south with the Pallavas of Kanchi, the Chalukyas had allowed one of their northern officials to accumulate considerable territory on the upper Godavari river in Berar, a region as near the dead centre of India as anywhere and now dominated by the city of Nagpur. From c735–56 the senior member of this rising family was Dantidurga and, since his function within the Chalukyas' empire was that of *rastrakuta* or 'head of a region', the dynasty he founded is known as that of the Rashtrakutas.

After loyally serving the Chalukya Vikramaditya II in his Pallava wars and possibly also against the Arabs of Sind, Dantidurga took the opportu-nity of Vikramaditya's death in 747 to enlarge his territories. In a modest *digvijaya* which carefully avoided the Chalukyan heartland of Karnataka, he expanded his authority to include much of Madhya Pradesh and parts of southern Gujarat and northern Maharashtra. Additionally, according to a set of copper plates from Ellora (which place he seems to have adopted as his ceremonial capital), he assumed the title of *prithvi-vallabha. Vallabha* means 'husband' or 'lover', while *prithvi* means 'the earth' and is also the name of the earth goddess who was one of Lord Vishnu's consorts. Dantidurga and his successors were therefore advancing an ambitious claim to be acknowledged as Lords of the Earth and emanations of Vishnu. Incidentally, it was also this title, abbreviated to *vallabha*, which registered with Muslim observers and reappeared in their writings as 'the Balhara'.

Compared to the Byzantine emperors or any of the other 'four great or principal kings of the world', the Balhara's rise to fame was rapid and comparatively painless. Dantidurga completed his *digvijaya* by belatedly confronting the Chalukyan king who, also belatedly, had just awoken to the danger of this rival on his northern frontier. Again it was the Rashtrakuta who triumphed, although in mysterious circumstances: 'success seems to have been due to a stratagem, for his court poet tells us that he overthrew the Karnataka army by a mere frown of his brow, without any effort being made and without any weapons being raised or used.' The fruits of this victory, if such it was, were proportionately modest. The Chalukyas were soon back in the field and Dantidurga would frown no more. He died prematurely in c756 'probably owing to the pressing requests [for his company] of the heavenly damsels', suggests one record.[11]

Being childless, he was succeeded on the Rashtrakuta throne by his uncle Krishna I. Krishna it was who concluded matters with the Chalukyas. In what looks to have been a rather violent battle – and which could be that to which the merchant Suleiman would refer as involving 'the country which comes next to the country of pepper' – Krishna decisively disposed of his family's erstwhile suzerains; 'the ocean of the Chalukya army' was well and truly 'churned', we are told, and from its waves arose the 'Goddess of Royal Glory'. Badami fell and all Karnataka was added to the Rashtrakutas' territories, while subsequent campaigns secured the submission of the Konkan coast and of the eternally hard-pressed Ganga dynasty (of the Mysore area). Additionally, in the east, one of Krishna's sons triumphed over the Chalukyas of Vengi who were a satellite branch of the Badami family. These 'Eastern Chalukyas' were now wedded to the Rashtrakuta cause by a matrimonial alliance.

When Krishna I died in c773 the Rashtrakutas were undisputed masters of the entire Deccan. Further conquests could only be made at the expense of the kingdoms of the extreme south or by crossing the Vindhya hills into the Gangetic plains. No Deccan-based dynasty had yet tried its luck in the hallowed and hotly contested *arya-varta* but under Dhruva, who in c780 ended a short and chaotic reign by his brother, the Rashtrakutas did just that. Dhruva first secured his southern flank by again rubbishing the Gangas and rattling the Pallavas. Then in c786 he forded the Narmada, a veritable Rubicon, and led his best troops north. Malwa quickly submitted. Following the Chambal river along the well-worn trail once known as the *Daksinapatha*, Dhruva crossed into the Gangetic basin and headed for Kanauj.

THE KANAUJ TRIANGLE

Centrally sited and beside the holy Ganga, Kanauj had been acknowledged as the seat of northern empire ever since Harsha's day. By the ninth century, though, it was a capital without much of a kingdom, its ruler being generally a puppet of one or other of the two great powers that were contesting the hegemony of the north. These were the Palas from eastern India and the Gurjara-Pratiharas from western India. With the eruption onto the scene in c786 of the Rashtrakutas from the Deccan this became a three-sided contest. It would last for two centuries and, though its details are anything but clear, the evidence suggests glorious interludes during which one or other of the contestants successfully performed a *digvijaya*, laid claim to Kanauj, and grandiloquently advertised his universal paramountcy. Hence the period is sometimes called the 'Imperial Age of Kanauj'. But the chronology is too confused for anything but a conjectural narrative, and of the temples and fortifications of Kanauj itself too little remains to inspire even a hopeful reconstruction.

More interesting than the power struggle is the very different provenance of the participants. All three are noticed by Muslim writers who understandably have least to say about the remotest, namely 'Rahma', 'Rahmi' or 'Ruhmi'. The word may derive from Dharmapala who ruled c775–810, and certainly it seems to refer to his dynasty, that of the Palas of Bengal. The Pala country, we learn, was on the coast but stretched well inland; it produced very fine cottons and aloe wood, and the king possessed fifty thousand elephants and more troops than either of his rivals. Dharmapala was the son of Gopala, who looks to have founded the dynasty in c750. Unusually, but not uniquely since similar claims are made for one of the Pallavas and for a king of Kashmir, Gopala's elevation is said to have been the result of a selection, if not an election, process. Perhaps already a minor king of northern Bengal, he was invited to assume sovereignty over the whole of Vanga, or eastern Bengal, and then rapidly consolidated his rule throughout Bengal and Bihar.

Dharmapala continued his father's expansionist policies. Excepting for Sasanka's brief and uncertain challenge in Harsha's day, this was the first Bengali bid for control of *arya-varta*, and it began badly. But eventually, taking full advantage of the disruption caused by the first Rashtrakuta incursion, Dharmapala reached Kanauj and there held a great ceremony at which his chosen candidate was installed as a tributary king. The loan of Dharmapala's own golden pitcher for the sacred ablutions essential to this induction neatly demonstrated his primacy. Kings from all over north India, including an unexplained 'Yavana' (possibly a Muslim from Sind), witnessed the event and 'paid homage with the bending down of their quavering diadems'.[12]

Through as many setbacks as triumphs, the Palas clung to their supremacist claims for the best part of a century. As with the Guptas, this was partly thanks to their longevity. Dharmapala reigned for forty years and Devapala, his son, seems to have lasted quite as long (c810–50). To their collection of 'quavering diadems' were briefly added those of the kings of Kamarupa (Assam), Utkala (an Orissan kingdom) and possibly other kings from lands as far-flung as the deep south and the extreme north-west. This, however, temporarily exhausted the Palas' taste for earthly dominion. Although there would be a brief revival in the eleventh century, in the tenth their role was simply as a whipping boy for their rivals. 'The Pala empire, shorn of its plume, lay tottered,' writes an Indian historian.[13] Seemingly it disintegrated under a succession of rulers of a 'pacific and religious disposition'.[14] One renounced the throne to become an ascetic, others attended to their spiritual advisers and to the welfare of the monastic establishments which still flourished in the Pala heartland of Bihar and Bengal.

For the Palas were Buddhists, indeed the last major Indian dynasty to espouse Buddhism. Their lavish endowments included the revival of Nalanda's university and a colossal building programme at Somapura, now Paharpur in Bangladesh, where sprawling ruins and foundations, all of brick, attest 'the largest Buddhist buildings south of the Himalayas'.[15] They also founded an important new centre of learning at Vikramashila, which was somewhere on the Ganga in Bihar. The fame of all these places travelled widely and suggests that Pala patronage was crucial to the future of Buddhism as a world religion. To the Pala kingdom came students from Sind, Kashmir, Nepal, Tibet, China, Burma, Cambodia, Sri Lanka and Indonesia. Pala architecture probably influenced the final remodelling of Borobudur and would be echoed in the stupas and temples of Pagan (Burma) and Prambanam (Java). Pala images, often in highly polished stone and bronze, anticipated and inspired the distinctive iconography of Tibet and Nepal. And the Mahayanist Buddhism of both these countries developed its peculiar traits and doctrines under Pala patronage.

It was a Buddhism far removed from that preached by the Enlightened One, indeed as remote from it in both time and spirit as was medieval Christianity from the New Testament. Although originally a rationalisation of the human condition and a code of ethics, both of which largely ignored the deities and rituals associated with conventional religion, Buddhism had been steadily assuming the trappings of orthodox religious practice ever since the Buddha's death. In the Boddhisattvas it had long since acquired a pantheon whose myths and attributes rivalled those of Shiva and Vishnu; now, in their numerous Taras, or spouses, it acquired glamorous female counterparts of Parvati and Lakshmi. Indeed Buddhist icons of the Pala period are so anatomically exaggerated and so generously provided with extra heads and arms that only a trained eye would identify them as Buddhist.

In eastern India the demarcation between Buddhists and non-Buddhists was further blurred by both countenancing the efficacy of *mantras* (repetitious formulae), *yantras* (mystical designs), *mudras* (finger postures) and the numerous other practices associated with Tantricism. *Tantras* were esoteric texts of uncertain origin and profoundly difficult import which offered initiates the chance of communing with the divinity and assuming supernatural powers and states. The rituals and disciplines involved were complex and secret. Some mimicked the sexual imagery of myths involving the union of the deity and his *shakti*, or female counterpart. Breaking the taboos of caste, diet, dress and sexual fidelity, practitioners might enjoy both a liberating debauch and an enhanced reputation, even if magical powers eluded them.

But it goes without saying that these mystic whisperings, obscurantist doctrines and orgiastic covens were far removed from the Buddha's 'Middle Way'. Worse still, compromise was proving counter-productive for Buddhism. In bidding for popular support and competing with other cults as a parallel religion, the *sangha* had been losing ground throughout India since the time of the Guptas. Populist devotional cults emanating from south India (the so-called *bhakti* movement) were pre-empting Buddhism's traditional appeal as a refuge from brahman authority and caste prejudice. At the same time a reform movement started by Sankara (788–820), a brahman from Kerala, was reclaiming for a distilled essence of Vedic philosophy (*vedanta*) the high moral and doctrinal ground previously enjoyed by the Noble Eightfold Path. As a result Buddhism was already largely confined to the peripheral regions of Sind, Kashmir, Nepal, and of course the Pala heartland in eastern India.

Whether the Pala empire was in any sense a Buddhist state it is hard to say. But in that reference to the 'election' of Gopala, its founder, there could be an echo of the more contractual ideas underlying early Buddhist notions of kingship. His successors, while adopting conventional titles like *maharajadhiraja* and *paramesvara*, seem to have paid particular heed to their religious advisers, and it may not be fanciful to imagine the Palas reviving the mythology of their illustrious predecessors in Magadha – Ajata-shatru, Bimbisara and Ashoka. Certainly Pala patronage of Buddhist institutions afforded to India's greatest religio-cultural export a last climax under Dharmapala and Devapala and then a last refuge under their successors.

It is, however, their mortal rivals for supremacy in northern India who have attracted the closest scrutiny by Indian historians. Based in western India at the opposite extremity of *arya-varta*, the Gurjara-Pratiharas have been awarded an imperial sway greater even than Harsha's and a national resolve worthy of the Congress Party. 'They were of the people and did not stand away from their hopes, aspirations and traditions.'[16] 'The spearhead of a religio-cultural upsurge', the Gurjara-Pratiharas were 'bulwarks of defence against the vanguards of Islam'[17] and 'protectors of *dharma*'. Yet despite such confident statements, despite comparatively frequent references by Islamic writers, and despite a succession of well attested rulers, the Gurjara-Pratiharas remain as much an enigma as their composite title suggests.

'The king of Jurz maintains numerous forces and no other Indian prince has so fine a cavalry,' reported merchant Suleiman in the ninth century. There was also 'no greater foe of the Muhammadan faith'. Moreover Jurz territory comprised 'a tongue of land', presumably Saurashtra in Gujarat, which if correct provides a clue to the identity of its king. For Jurz, sometimes spelled 'Juzr', is taken to be a variant of 'Gurzara' or 'Gurjara', a place or people visited by Hsuan Tsang and mentioned in several inscriptions, including that of the great Chalukya, Pulakesin II, at Aihole. The same word is today found in 'Gujarat', 'Gujranwala' and numerous other place-names as well as in 'Gujars', a ubiquitous community of pastoralists frequenting many parts of the Panjab from the north-west frontier to Uttar Pradesh. This trail of 'Guj-' words suggests that the Gurjaras, or Jurz people, had been on the move. Some suppose that they originated beyond the north-west frontier and moved into the Panjab and then western India in the wake of the Hun invasions. Others suppose that any such migration was more probably in reverse, that they originated in western India and then moved north.

Al-Masudi, writing in the early tenth century, has little to say of Jurz but makes much of 'the Bauura, king of Kanauj'. His forces were reckoned at an incredible three million, and were divided into four armies, one to engage the Arabs of Multan, another to deal with the Balhara (i.e. the Rashtrakutas) and the other two 'to meet enemies in any direction'. Such a description could only apply to the Pratiharas, a late-eighth- to tenth-century dynasty known to have wrested Kanauj from the Palas and to have been occasionally humbled by the Rashtrakutas. And since the Pratiharas are known to have originated in Rajasthan, whence one branch of the family had first set up in a kingdom in Gujarat, it is now generally accepted that Jurz and the Gurjaras refer to kingdoms and rulers closely related to the Bauura and the Pratiharas. In fact the Pratiharas are taken to be one of several Gurjara clans and are hence known as the 'Gurjara-Pratiharas'.

The subject is of more than passing interest because the Pratiharas and their descendants are often numbered amongst those more famous clans known as rajputs. In the centuries immediately preceding and following the Muslim conquest of India, the rajputs were destined to play an often heroic and always pivotal role. Their territories would stretch way beyond Rajputana, or Rajasthan, and would eventually constitute the most numerous of the 'princely states' under British rule. In fact to the British the rajputs would come to represent the quintessence of all that was admirable in India's martial traditions. 'In a Rajpoot,' wrote Colonel James Tod, their annalist and champion, 'I always recognise a friend.'

Tod spent ten years amongst the still-independent rajputs as a political agent in the early nineteenth century. In his subsequent *Annals and Antiquities of Rajasthan*, one of the most substantial and sonorous works of British Indian scholarship, he would claim to have established 'the common origin of the tribes of Rajasthan and those of ancient Europe'. Invoking 'the Scythic tribes' as the common link, this was simply a variation, albeit less remote, of the Indo-Aryan hypothesis advanced by philologists like Jones. Tod also delved deeply into the Puranic pedigrees whereby the various rajput houses claimed descent from heroes of the epics and Vedas. And he valiantly tried to trace each clan to its original homeland. But he failed to explain the greatest mystery of all: why the rajputs, so prominent in Indian history throughout the second millennium A D, had figured in it not once during the first millennium. Where, in short, had the rajputs sprung from?

The mystery is still unresolved. Even if rajput clans like the Pratiharas were really Gurjaras, they can still only be traced back to c500; and there remains the problem of where the Gurjaras sprang from. Legends common to some families of both Gurjaras and rajputs associate them with the region around Mount Abu. Upon the dewy downs of this vast upthrusted plateau in southern Rajasthan a great fire-sacrifice was reputedly held at which the progenitors of these clans were accorded *ksatriya* status and incorporated into royal lineages going back to Lords Rama and Krishna, themselves scions of descent groups from the Sun and the Moon. Clearly in the not too remote past the fortunes of these clans had improved substantially as a result of some dramatic transformation. But whether they were previously indigenous desert tribes who, like those of Arabia, were abruptly inspired to undertake martial exploits in more favoured lands, or whether they should be seen in the context of those republican and tribal entities, like the Yaudheyas, who from roughly the same regions of western India had once offered a stout resistance to Rudradaman of the Junagadh inscription and to Samudra-Gupta of the Allahabad inscription, and whether earlier still they had migrated from somewhere outside India – all such mysteries remain.

What is certain is that the Gurjara-Pratiharas represented a social and political grouping very different from those of their Pala and Rashtrakuta rivals for the imperial patrimony of Kanauj. When they first emerged it was as the most successful amongst several related Gurjara royal families; their extensive conquests were often made and subsequently controlled by feudatories who were often relations; and when their 'empire' disintegrated, it did so into powerful local kingdoms ruled by families who claim a similar *ksatriya* status and a similar Gurjara-rajput provenance. This prevalence of loose, kin-based relationships suggests that tribe and clan were important to the Gurjara-Pratiharas. Unlike the Buddhist Palas, their religious allegiance was variable: some were devotees of Vishnu, others of Shiva, Bhagavati or the Sun-God. And unlike the Rashtrakutas, who were veritable sticklers for ritual refinement, they seem not to have gloried in the elaborate ceremonies of paramountcy. Theirs was a more informal, less rigid and perhaps more effective power structure which, breaking from the *mandala* conventions of the past, anticipated the more flexible relationships demanded by the dire centuries ahead.

Nevertheless, the Gurjara-Pratiharas observed the conventions and assumed the traditional epithets of paramountcy. Vatsaraja, who from Ujjain appears to have ruled over Malwa and much of Rajasthan in the 780s, had been the first to assume the titles of *maharajadhiraja* and *paramesvara*. Despite defeat by Dhruva, the Rashtrakuta king who first threatened Kanauj,

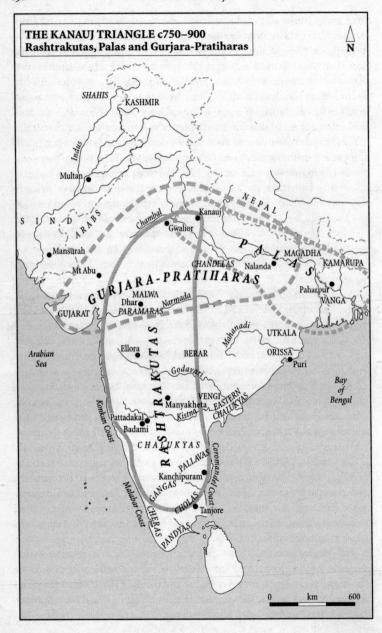

THE KANAUJ TRIANGLE c750–900
Rashtrakutas, Palas and Gurjara-Pratiharas

N

SHAHIS
KASHMIR

Indus

Multan

S I N D

A R A B S

Chambal

Mansurah

Mt Abu

GUJARAT

Arabian Sea

Ellora

Konkan Coast

Pattadakal
Badami

CHALUKYAS

Malabar Coast

CHERAS

PANDYAS

Kanauj

Gwalior

CHANDELAS   Nalanda

GURJARA-PRATIHARAS

NEPAL

P A L A S   MAGADHA

KAMARUPA

Paharpur
VANGA

MALWA
Dhar
PARAMARAS   *Narmada*

RASHTRAKUTAS

BERAR

Godavari

Manyakheta
Kistna

VENGI
EASTERN
CHALUKYAS

Mahanadi

UTKALA

ORISSA
Puri

Bay of Bengal

PALLAVAS

GANGAS
Kanchipuram

CHOLAS
Tanjore

Coromandel Coast

0   km   600

Vatsaraja's son would continue to use and to add to these titles. The son, Naghabhata II, was also the first of his line to seize Kanauj from its Pala puppet and to lay claim to extensive conquests in *arya-varta*. His success was short-lived, but Bhoja, his grandson, more than made amends. Ruling for at least fifty years (c836–886), Bhoja (and then his son Mahendrapala) accumulated by conquest and alliance more feudatory territories than any contemporary. As the Pala empire retracted under Devapala's successors and as the Rashtrakutas entered a period of uncharacteristic quiescence, Bhoja looks to have commanded kings and kingdoms which stretched in a great arc from Saurashtra in Gujarat to Magadha and Bengal.

If Kanauj was Bhoja's capital, Gwalior, a natural fortress of immense strategic value astride the *Daksinapatha* south of Agra, may have served as the fulcrum of his empire. Thereabouts was found the most important of the Pratihara inscriptions, and henceforth Gwalior's bluff and increasingly fortified cliffs would loom large in the affairs of north India and provide something of a barometer of current dominion. Its loss in c950 to the Chandelas of Bundelkhand, soon to win immortality as the builders of Khajuraho, signalled the disintegration of Pratihara dominion. Thence Gwalior quickly passed to the Kacchwahas, later of Jaipur, and eventually to the Tomars, later of Delhi. It was one of the Tomars who would build atop Gwalior's sun-drenched cliffs the unsurpassed Man Singh palace. Significantly all these dynasties, representing a veritable roll-call of rajput prowess, first emerge as feudatories and associates of the Pratiharas.

Only against the Rashtrakutas had Bhoja made little headway. Under Dhruva (c780–93), then Govinda III (c793–814) and much later Indra III (c914–28) the Rashtrakutas repeatedly intervened in the north. Not to be outdone by the parallels between Bhoja and Julius Caesar drawn by latter-day champions of the Gurjara-Pratiharas, Govinda III's generalship has been likened to that of Alexander or Arjuna.[18] After victories in the south, he conducted a dazzling *digvijaya* in the north, defeating the Gurjara-Pratiharas under Nagabhata II somewhere near Gwalior and securing the submission of both Kanauj and the Pala ruler. As was normal the kingdoms of the south took advantage of his absence, but they too were soon favoured with a return visit. By 805 Govinda had brought the Gangas, Cheras and Pandyas to heel and had stormed and occupied Kanchipuram. The drums of the Deccan were heard, we are told, from the Himalaya's caves to the shores of Malabar, and truly Govinda appeared invincible. Yet neither he nor his successors showed much interest in developing their empire. Retaining anything more than the nominal allegiance of distant dynasties was not the Rashtrakuta way.

The Rashtrakuta objective, it has been argued, was much more subtle. Instead of dominating *arya-varta*, their ambition was to appropriate and relocate it; not content with making history, the Rashtrakutas were about to make geography by transposing the sacred Aryan heartland to the Deccan. Their capital was eventually settled at Manyakheta (Malkhed), a place where the frontiers of Maharashtra, Karnataka and Andhra Pradesh now meet. To the Rashtrakutas its significance seems to have lain in its being between the Godavari and the Kistna, the two great rivers of the Deccan. A counterpart to the land between the Jamuna and the Ganga where Kurus and Pandavas had once fought their *Mahabharata* war, this was to be the new *aryavarta*, the Doab of the Deccan. Likewise Manyakheta was to be the new Hastinapura, or a Kanauj of the Deccan. There, in an enormous hall, the Rashtrakutas would enact before a larger-than-life image of the deity, itself cast in gold, the bejewelled ceremonials of a universal dominion by which the world-ruler asserted the triumph of *dharma*.

Before adopting Manyakheta, the Rashtrakutas had patronised today's much better known site at Ellora, above a tributary of the Godavari in northern Maharashtra. Here, where an exposed rock-face, two kilometres long, had already been perforated with the most ambitious of India's cave temples, they took over and rededicated a just-completed Buddhist foundation. This was the vast and airy 'Do Thal' vihara, three storeys high and with halls and courtyards of suitably palatial proportions. An inscription also credits Dantidurga with patronage of the nearby Dasavatara cave. Both were evidently stopgaps, for further along the 'street of rock' a new and more conventional-looking temple was begun by Krishna I. Although architecturally very similar to the Chalukyas' later temples at Pattadakal, this was not, however, architecture; it was sculpture. For the Krishnesvara, or Kailasa as it was also called, is a free-standing excavation, a temple of cathedral proportions complete with precinct, cells, shrines, gateway and pillars all hewn from the same rock stratum. Seeing it, according to a contemporary copper plate, even the gods were moved to favourable comment, and marvelled that human art could produce such beauty. Its creator was no less amazed. 'Oh, how was it that I created this,' he rather touchingly exclaimed.

Indisputably the most elaborate and imposing rock-cut monument in the world, the Kailasa still triumphantly confirms the Balhara's status as 'one of the four great or principal kings of the world'. It also provides a further illustration of the Rashtrakutas' attempt to appropriate the sacred geography of *arya-varta*. Mount Kailasa in the Himalayas is the earthly abode of Lord Shiva. The new Kailasa temple at Ellora, also wrought of rock and also dedicated to Shiva, was designed to reposition Mount Kailasa in the Deccan and so, by implication, to make of the gentle Vindhya hills a Himalayas-in-the-Deccan which would be the northern frontier of the new *arya-varta*. Similarly and symbolically, to the new Kailasa was added a shrine with images of Ganga, Jamuna and Saraswati, the three river deities of *arya-varta*. King Dhruva, we learn, on his invasion of the north had 'taken from his enemies their rivers', a reference which could apply to the deities but seems more probably to mean that the Rashtrakutas actually 'brought the waters of these streams back with them in large jars'. 'So it seems clear that the Rashtrakutas, who had made Mount Kailasa appear in the mountain range north of their domains, also caused the rivers which had originated there, the rivers which defined the middle region of India, to appear in their empire in the Deccan.'[19]

All empires, even those which would refashion the earth as well as rule it, must pass. Assailed in the south by the rising power of the Cholas and in the north by the Paramaras, erstwhile feudatories of the Gurjara-Pratiharas, the Rashtrakutas dwindled into insignificance in the late tenth century. The dream of a Deccan *aryavarta* died with them, although much further south something similar would imminently be attempted by the Cholas of Tanjore. They too would reach the Ganga, and they too would then laboriously haul its waters home to their own *arya-varta* at the mouth of the Kaveri river.

But in the interim northern India had been ravaged by the first Muslim incursions. Any attempt to transpose its sacred geography now looked less like sincere imitation and more like a desperate act of preservation. The real *arya-varta* had been violated, and the Cholas' boast to have watered their horses in the mighty Ganga would merely echo that of a more formidable foe who cared nothing for the gilded fantasies and rock-cut conventions of early India's imperial formations.

Natraj, the Rule of the Dance

c950–1180

APART FROM the Arabs' conquest of Sind and their raids into Gujarat and Rajasthan, all in the early eighth century, no major confrontation with Islamic intruders is known to have taken place before the late tenth century. Indeed Hindu–Muslim relations may often have been amicable. The Rashtrakuta king is said to have afforded generous protection to Muslim merchants. As one of them put it, 'none is to be found who is so partial to the Arabs as the Balhara; and his subjects,' he added, 'follow his example.'[1] Literal application of the *mandala* principle meant that the Rashtrakutas saw the Gurjara-Pratiharas, their immediate neighbours in western India, as their obvious enemy; the immediate neighbours of this enemy, the Arabs of Sind, were therefore their natural allies. If no formal alliance is in fact recorded, it was probably not because the amirs of Mansurah and Multan were Muslims but because they were rarely in a position to render any worthwhile aid to India's 'king of kings'.

Similarly the Gurjara-Pratiharas, though undoubtedly considered hostile by the Arabs, cannot certainly be credited with any campaigns designed either to evict or contain them. As a title, *pratihara* does indeed mean a 'door-keeper' or 'gate-keeper'. But by the dynasty so named it was said to signify their impeccable descent from the *pratihara* of Lord Rama's city of Ayodhya. By the Rashtrakuta king, on the other hand, it was taken to mean that they were fit only to man the gates of his own relocated *arya-varta*.

Those to be kept out, it seems, were not just the Muslim rulers of Sind, but any other marauding neighbours, including Hindus like the kings of Kashmir. Around the year 900 a Gurjara feudatory in the Panjab was obliged to relinquish to Kashmir a sliver of territory in the vicinity of the Chenab river. Previously acquired by the empire-building King Bhoja, it was apparently surrendered to preserve the rest of the Gurjara-Pratihara empire, an action which was likened by Kalhana, the author of an important chronicle of Kashmir, to that of severing a finger to save the rest of the body. East of the Panjab, no Muslim power was as yet even a remote contender for primacy in *arya-varta*, while westward, the thrust of Baghdad's global ambitions had been redirected into Afghanistan and Turkestan. India's so-called 'bulwark of defence against the vanguards of Islam', if there was such a thing, must be sought not in Kanauj beside the Ganga but in Kabul beyond the Indus.

There, in a kingdom reminiscent of the Kushanas' Gandhara which straddled the north-west frontier and extended deep into Afghanistan, an Indian dynasty known to history as the Shahis had risen to prominence in the mid-ninth century. The name 'Shahi' clearly derives from the 'king-of-kings' title (*shah-in-shahi*) adopted by the Kushana in imitation of Achaemenid practice. Al-Biruni actually links the Shahis with the great Kushana emperor Kanishka, and this may not be totally fanciful since Hsuan Tsang in the seventh century had found the kings of the Kabul region to be still devout Buddhists. Latterly a palace revolution not unlike that engineered by Chach in Sind had brought about the downfall of the last Buddhist king and the succession of his brahman minister, Lalliya. It is the latter and his successors who comprise the Hindu Shahis, and in the late ninth century great was the fame of these far-flung Indian dynasts.

According to Kalhana 'their mighty glory outshone the kings in the north just as the sun outshines the stars.' He likened their capital to *arya-varta* in that it was hemmed about not by the Himalayas and the Vindhyas but by the *Turuskas* (Turks) and other equally formidable barbarians; within its borders, however, kings and brahmans found sanctuary. In the Panjab the Shahis jostled with Gurjara, Kashmiri and Sindi rivals, sometimes as allies, sometimes as enemies; while in Afghanistan their feudatories clung to considerable territories to the south and east of Kabul. These latter were the first to go, and in 870 Kabul itself was captured. In Afghanistan the Shahis retained only Lamghan or Lughman, which was that part of the Kabul river valley west of Jalalabad. But in the Panjab they consolidated their kingdom and established a new capital first at Hund or Ohind near Attock on the Indus and later, seemingly, at Lahore.

Meanwhile in Afghanistan those territories seized from the Shahis in the name of Islam invited the interest of would-be adventurers from further afield. Muslim conquests in eastern Iran and Turkestan had brought a host of Turkic peoples into the Islamic fold. Arab influence there was already on the wane, and in central Asia Baghdad's authority had been eclipsed by

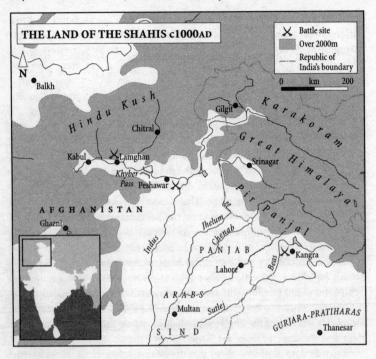

THE LAND OF THE SHAHIS c1000AD

Battle site
Over 2000m
Republic of
India's boundary

0   km   200

N

Balkh

Hindu Kush

Chitral

Gilgit

Karakoram

Great Himalaya

Kabul   Lamghan

Srinagar

Khyber Pass   Peshawar

Pir Panjal

AFGHANISTAN

Ghazni

Jhelum

Chenab

PANJAB

Kangra

Indus

Lahore

Beas

A R A B S

Multan   Sutlej

S I N D

GURJARA-PRATIHARAS

Thanesar

that of Bukhara, whose Safarid and Samanid dynasties zealously carved out Islamic empires north of the Hindu Kush. In 963 Alptigin, an ambitious but out-of-favour Samanid general, crossed the Hindu Kush from Balkh and seized Ghazni, a strategic town on the Kabul–Kandahar road. Himself once a Turkic slave, Alptigin was succeeded in 977 by Sabuktigin, also an ex-slave and also a Turkic general whose elevation owed nothing to scruple. Sabuktigin's kingdom-building ambitions brought him into conflict with the Shahis. In c986, 'girding up his loins for a war of religion', says the Muslim historian Ferishta, 'Sabuktigin ravaged the provinces of Kabul and Panjab'.

Jayapala (Jaipal), the Shahi king, responded with the utmost reluctance. 'Observing the immeasurable fractures and losses every moment caused in his states ... and becoming disturbed and inconsolable, he saw no remedy except in beginning to act and to take up arms.' This he did with some success, mustering a vast army and conducting it across the north-west frontier to confront Sabuktigin from a fortified position amongst the crags of Lughman. Hindu and Muslim then joined in battle.

> They came together upon the frontiers of each state. Each army mutually attacked the other, and they fought and resisted in every way until the face of the earth was stained red with the blood of the slain, and the lions and warriors of both armies were worn out and reduced to despair.[2]

The battle, in other words, ground to an indecisive standstill. Foremost amongst the lions of Ghazni was Mahmud, the eldest son of Sabuktigin and a man with an awesome reputation in the making. Yet even he, the future conqueror of a thousand forts, could see no way of overcoming Jayapala's position. Then, supposedly thanks to a bit of Islamic sorcery, the weather intervened; seemingly it was the beginning of the Afghan winter. A contemporary chronicler says it was more like the end of the world: 'fire fell from heaven on the infidels, and hailstones accompanied by loud claps of thunder; and a blast calculated to shake trees from their roots blew upon them, and thick black vapours formed around them.'[3] Jayapala thought his hour had come. He immediately sued for peace while his troops, unaccustomed to the cold and ill-equipped to bear it, embraced the prospect of a quick withdrawal. Sabuktigin, pleasantly surprised by this development, settled for an indemnity of cash-plus-elephants and a few choice fortresses. Finally, in a scene rich in instruction for nineteenth-century imperialists and twentieth-century superpowers, the benumbed and humiliated infidels trailed through the fearful gorges of the Kabul river back down to India as Sabuktigin's jubilant *mujahideen* watched from their crags.

Jayapala did not apparently regard this as a defeat. His troops had given a good account of themselves and for once it was the elements, rather than the elephants, which had deprived them of victory. When safely back in the Panjab, he therefore treated Sabuktigin's envoys as hostages. The Ghaznavid responded by again 'sharpening the sword of intention' and swooping on the luckless and now undefended people of Lughman. In a taste of things to come, the Muslim forces butchered the idolaters, fired their temples and plundered their shrines; such was the booty, it was said, that hands risked frostbite counting it.

To avenge this savage attack, Jayapala again felt obliged to take up arms. Al-Utbi, young Mahmud's secretary, says that the Shahi king assembled an army of 100,000, but we have only the much later testimony of the historian Ferishta that it included detachments from Kanauj, Ajmer, Delhi and

Kalinjar. If so, it represented a notable mobilisation of those erstwhile feudatories of the Gurjara-Pratiharas who would claim rajput descent. Kanauj seems to have been still in Pratihara hands; Ajmer (in Rajasthan) was in territory ruled by the Chahamana rajputs; Delhi, founded in 736 but still a place of little consequence, belonged to the Tomara rajputs of Haryana; and Kalinjar (west of Khajuraho in Madhya Pradesh) was the stronghold of the rising Chandela rajputs. Additionally Jayapala himself may have been a rajput of the Bhatti clan, since his name and those of his successors, all ending in '-pala', have been taken to indicate a break with the earlier Shahis who were brahmans.

Sabuktigin, surveying this host from a hilltop, was not impressed. 'He felt like a wolf about to attack a flock of sheep,' says al-Utbi. The Ghaznavid horse were divided into packs, each five hundred strong, which circled and swooped on the enemy in succession. Evidently the battle was this time being fought in the open, probably somewhere in Lughman, and under a merciless sky. The Indian forces, 'being worse mounted than the cavalry of Subuktigin, could effect nothing against them', claims Ferishta. Close-packed and confused by the barrage of assaults, they were also suffering from 'the heat which arose from their iron oven', says al-Utbi. When satisfied that the enemy were well kneaded and baked, Sabuktigin's forces massed for a concerted attack. So thick was the dust that 'swords could not be distinguished from spears, nor men from elephants, nor heroes from cowards'. When it settled, the outcome was clear enough. The Shahi forces had been routed and those not dead on the field of battle were being butchered in the forest or drowned in a river. No mercy was to be shown: God had ordained that infidels be killed, 'and the order of God is not changed'.

As well as two hundred elephants, 'immense booty', and many new Afghan recruits eager for a share of India's spoils, Sabuktigin acquired by this victory the region west of Peshawar including the Khyber Pass. A foothold on Indian soil, this corner of the subcontinent would serve well as a springboard for more ambitious raids. These, however, were delayed. Sabuktigin next led his troops north across the Hindu Kush and, after a series of victorious campaigns in the Herat region, was recognised by the Baghdad caliph as governor of vast territories embracing all northern Afghanistan plus Khorasan in eastern Iran. He died in Balkh in 997 and was succeeded by his son Mahmud, who quickly secured his father's conquests in central Asia.

Mahmud, though a military genius, has few admirers in India. If the Hindu pantheon included a Satan, he would undoubtedly be that gentleman's avatar (incarnation). 'Defective in external appearance', he even looked the part. While gazing in the mirror he once complained that 'the sight of a king should brighten the eyes of his beholders, but nature has been so capricious to me that my aspect seems the picture of misfortune.'[4] His empire, now stretching from the Caspian to the Indus, afforded a more encouraging prospect; there misfortunes could be discounted provided he could somehow consolidate it. While continuing the God-given duty of every Muslim to root out idolatry, he needed to maintain and reward his large standing army and to make of Ghazni a worthy capital, focus of loyalty and citadel of Islamic orthodoxy. These ambitions, he decided, could best be realised by trouncing his infidel neighbours and appropriating their fabled wealth. He therefore resolved on a pattern of yearly incursions designed to serve both God and Ghazni. Intent, we are told, on 'exalting the standard of religion, widening the plain of right, illuminating the words of truth, and strengthening the power of justice', he 'turned his face to India'. The frontier was crossed, on what would be the first of perhaps sixteen blood-and-plunder raids, some time during the post-monsoon months of the year 1000.

Thanks to secretary al-Utbi's contemporary account, and additional details provided by the likes of Ferishta, more is known about the Ghaznavid invasions than any other military campaign since Alexander's. We even have a few dates. If for no other reason than that 'it happened on Thursday the 8th of Muharram, 392 AH' (i.e. 27 November 1001), Mahmud's next crushing defeat of the ever-obliging Jayapala is something of a milestone; a date so precise carries conviction. The encounter took place near Peshawar in the course of Mahmud's second invasion; and this time 'the enemy of God', otherwise Jayapala 'the villainous infidel', 'polluted idolater', etc., commanded a much smaller force. He still lost an unlikely fifteen thousand men and was himself taken prisoner along with many of his household. Although freed for a fifty-elephant indemnity, Jayapala acknowledged the loss of caste implicit in capture and did the noble thing. He abdicated in favour of his son Anandapala; then, like Calanus, he climbed onto his own funeral pyre.

In 1004 Mahmud was back in India. This time he crossed the Indus and, after another hotly contested battle, took the city of Bhatia (possibly on the Jhelum). He then lost most of its wealth along with his baggage when overtaken by early monsoon rains and belated enemy raids. The following year he determined to attack Multan, whose amir, though a Muslim, was now a heretical Ismaili Shi'ah. Anandapala refused Mahmud safe passage through his domains and duly felt 'the hand of slaughter, imprisonment, pillage, depopulation and fire' once again. Then Multan fell, 'heresy, rebellion and enmity were suppressed', and Mahmud's fame occasioned comment as far away as Egypt. In fact, al-Utbi boasted that it now 'exceeded that of Alexander'.

The raids continued. In 1008 Anandapala suffered the Shahis' most crushing defeat as Mahmud overran the whole of the Panjab and then took the great citadel and temple of Kangra (in Himachal Pradesh), in whose vaults had been stored the Shahis' accumulated wealth. Here the gold ingots hauled away by Mahmud weighed 180 kilos and the silver bullion two tonnes, while the coins came to seventy million royal *dirhams*. Also included was a house, in kit form and fashioned entirely from white silver. The Ghaznavid's appetite for dead Indians, desirable slaves and portable wealth was whetted, but not satisfied. In 1012 it carried him to Thanesar, Harsha's original capital due north of Delhi. Anandapala, whose kingdom was now reduced to a small corner of the eastern Panjab and whose status was little better than that of a Ghaznavid feudatory, tried to intercede. He offered to buy off Mahmud with elephants, jewels and a fixed annual tribute. The offer was refused, Thanesar duly fell, and 'the Sultan returned home with plunder that it is impossible to recount'. 'Praise be to God, the protector of the world for the honour he bestows upon Islam and Musulmans,' wrote al-Utbi.

In 1018 it was the turn of Mathura, a well-endowed place of pilgrimage beside the Jamuna which was sacred to Lord Krishna as well as the source of so much Gupta sculpture. Here the main temple, a colossally intricate stone structure, impressed even Mahmud. Already busy endowing Ghazni with stately mosques and madrassehs, he reckoned that to build the like of the Mathura temple would take at least two hundred years and cost a hundred million *dirhams*. According to al-Utbi, the building was simply 'beyond description' – though not desecration. After tonnes of gold, silver and precious stones had been prised from its images, it shared the fate of the city's countless other shrines, being 'burned with naptha and fire and levelled with the ground'.

Kanauj itself was then sacked as Mahmud at last reached the Ganga. The Pratihara ruler seems to have left his capital, with its 'seven forts and ten thousand temples', almost undefended. Evidently the reputation of the uncompromising Ghaznavid and his bloodthirsty zealots now preceded them. Al-Utbi quotes a letter written by 'Bhimpal', possibly the son of the Pratihara leader, to one of his father's less defeatist feudatories which sums up Indian consternation at this new form of total warfare. It also betrays Bhimpal's ambivalence about offering resistance.

Sultan Mahmud is not like the rulers of Hind ... it is obviously advisable to seek safety from such a person for armies flee from the very name of him and his father. I regard his bridle as much stronger than yours for he never contents himself with one blow of the sword, nor does his army content itself with one hill out of a whole range. If therefore you design to contend with him, you will suffer; but do as you like – you know best.[5]

From this campaign Mahmud returned with booty valued at twenty million *dirhams*, fifty-three thousand slaves and 350 elephants. There followed expeditions even further afield into what is now Madhya Pradesh to chastise the Chandela rajputs. These look to have been less rewarding, but in 1025 he targeted Somnath, another temple-city and place of pilgrimage. To reach this sacred site on the shore of the Saurashtra peninsula meant crossing the 'empty quarter' of Rajasthan from Multan to Jaisalmer and then penetrating deep into Gujarat. It was new territory, and this was his most ambitious raid. But, taking only cavalry and camels, Mahmud swept across the desert, thereby taking his would-be enemies by surprise, and reached the Saurashtra coast with scarcely a victory to record.

Somnath's fort looked more formidable. It seems, though, to have been defended not by troops but by its enormous complement of brahmans and hordes of devotees. Ill-armed, they placed their trust in blind aggression and the intercession of the temple's celebrated *lingam* (the phallic icon of Lord Shiva). With ladders and ropes Mahmud's disciplined professionals scaled the walls and went about their business. Such was the resultant carnage that even the Muslim chroniclers betray a hint of unease. What one of them calls 'the dreadful slaughter' outside the temple was yet worse.

Band after band of the defenders entered the temple of Somnath, and with their hands clasped round their necks, wept and passionately entreated him [the Shiva *lingam*]. Then again they issued forth until they were slain and but few were left alive ... The number of the dead exceeded fifty thousand.[6]

Additionally twenty million *dirhams*-worth of gold, silver and gems was looted from the temple. But what rankled even more than the loot and the appalling death-toll was the satisfaction which Mahmud took in destroying the great gilded *lingam*. After stripping it of its gold, he personally laid into it with his 'sword' – which must have been more like a sledgehammer. The bits were then sent back to Ghazni and incor-

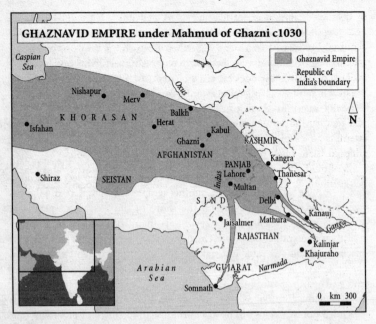

GHAZNAVID EMPIRE under Mahmud of Ghazni c1030

porated into the steps of its new Jami Masjid (Friday Mosque), there to be humiliatingly trampled and perpetually defiled by the feet of the Muslim faithful.

With this supreme gesture of devotion – or sacrilege – Mahmud's career soared to its zenith. He made one more Indian expedition, an amphibious assault into southern Sind, but died in 1030. He would not be forgotten. 'Mahmud was a king who conferred happiness upon the world and reflected glory on the Mohammedan religion,' declaims Ferishta. The historian goes on to admit that he was sometimes accused of 'the sordid vice of avarice', but concludes that this was all in a noble cause; for 'no king ever had more learned men at his court, kept a finer army, or displayed more magnificence.'[7] The great scholar al-Biruni enjoyed his patronage; so did Firdausi, the poet, although he found it niggardly; and the Ghazni they adorned was indeed transformed into a worthy capital. Yet for Hindus, this paragon of valour and piety would ever be nothing but a monster of cruelty and iconoclasm.

Either way, the trouble with such a well-documented career is that the richness of detail may obscure the results; certainly the partisan enthusiasm of the chroniclers leads them to gloss over setbacks. Mahmud terrorised and plundered to sensational effect, but despite all those campaigns he acquired little territory. Only the Shahi lands in the Panjab were actually retained under Ghaznavid rule. Elsewhere, and notably in Kashmir, central India and Gujarat, he made no attempt to secure his conquests or even to organise future tribute. In fact he seems often to have had considerable difficulty just in extricating himself. The great rajput fortresses of Gwalior and Kalinjar did not fall into his hands, although both were attacked. And attempts to employ as feudatories Indian princes who had supposedly adopted Islam often proved as short-lived as their conversions.

Mahmud's forces, better led than those of his adversaries, and much better mounted thanks to their access to central Asian bloodstock, enjoyed a definite tactical superiority. They were also powerfully motivated by religious zeal, plus the prospect of booty and women in this world or something equally agreeable in the next. The Indian forces, on the other hand, betrayed an understandable reluctance to engage. The most they could expect from battles with these rough-riding ghazis from the wilds of central Asia was perhaps a fleeter horse and a slim chance of survival. Victory, were it ever attained, promised only reprisals; and for Hindus no particular merit attached to the massacre of *mlecchas*. In fact there is good evidence that the superior prospects on offer to the champions of Islam induced some Hindus from the north-west frontier to switch both religion and allegiance and to fight for the Ghaznavids.

One can hardly blame them. The exemplary resolve displayed by the Shahis was conspicuously absent amongst most of their fellow kings. Kalhana, whose *Rajatarangini* provides the only non-Muslim references to the period, gives an interesting illustration. In 1013 Trilochanapala, the son of Anandapala and the last of the Shahis to offer any serious resistance to Mahmud, was forced to seek safety in Kashmir territory. Hotly pursued, he took up a strong position high above a precipitous valley in the Pir Panjal, the outermost of the Himalayan ranges, whence he urged King Samgramaraja of Kashmir to come to his aid. Instead the king sent Tunga, his commander-in-chief. Originally a goatherd to whom a queen of Kashmir had taken a fancy, Tunga was an experienced warrior who thought nothing of seeing off the Ghaznavids. In fact he was so confident that he scorned the Shahi's prudence and declined to take even elementary precautions like sending out scouts or setting night watches. Trilochanapala tried to cool his ardour. 'Until you have become acquainted with the *Turuska* warfare,' he told him, 'you should post yourself on the scarp of this hill and restrain your enthusiasm with patience.' But Tunga would have none of it. He even crossed the river to give battle to a small Ghaznavid reconnaissance party. Then came Mahmud himself, the master tactician, ablaze with rage and in full battle array. Tunga took one look at his massed ranks and fled, his troops dispersing into the hills.

'The Shahi, however,' we are told, 'was seen for some time moving about in battle.' In what seems to have been the Shahis' last stand, Trilochanapala was eventually dislodged and became a refugee in Kashmir. But while he dallied there, Mahmud would leave the valley alone. Samgramaraja retained his independence and, under the Lohara dynasty which he founded, Kashmir enjoyed another three centuries of Hindu rule. 'Who would describe the greatness of Trilochanapala whom numberless enemies even could not defeat in battle?' asks the patriotic Kalhana. Amazingly it was a Muslim, indeed one of Mahmud's protégés, who provided the answer. To al-Biruni, the greatest scholar of his age, the Shahis owe their epitaph.

> The dynasty of the Hindu Shahis is now extinct, and of the whole house there is no longer the slightest remnant in existence. We must say that, in all their grandeur, they never slackened in the ardent desire of doing that which is good and right, and that they were men of noble sentiment and bearing.[8]

THE TIGERS OF TANJORE

In the Hindu cycle of rebirth, death is but the prelude to life. Acts of destruction become acts of creation, as in Lord Shiva's manifestation as *Nataraja*, 'the Lord of the Dance', he who whirls the world to perdition and so to regeneration. The now clichéd image of the deity pirouetting in a tangle of arms, legs and dreadlocks within a halo of flames first appears, as if on cue, in bronze figures from the Tamil country of the tenth century. Troubled times, one might suppose, heightened the popularity of both the idea and the image. Yet in the Tamil south this was not an inordinately turbulent age, more in fact of a golden age. And if one may judge by the officially inscribed panegyrics of practically any ruler since the time of Ashoka, cycles of order and disorder, of construction and destruction, expansion and retraction were constants of the Indian scene.

Dynasties died only to make way for yet more dynasties; deities were subsumed only to make room for yet more deities; and Mahmud, seemingly, ravaged only to revive. Even as he was demolishing some of the north's greatest temples, others were being built; even as he carted away their

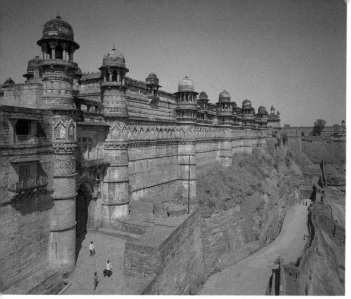

Man Singh palace in Gwalior fort, Madhya Pradesh, 1486–1516. Northern India's most commanding fortress changed hands repeatedly. Occupants included numerous rajput clans, Delhi sultans, Mughals, Marathas, British and, in 1858, Lakshmi Bai of Jhansi.

Qutb Minar, Delhi. Celebrating the triumph of Islam, the world's most massive minaret was begun beside Delhi's first mosque by Qutb-ud-din Aybak, continued by Iltumish, and completed by Feroz Shah Tughluq.

Lingaraja temple, Bhuvaneshwar, Orissa, *c*.1100. Spectacular temple-building at Bhuvaneshwar, Khajuraho and elsewhere coincided with the triumph of Islam and may have been a response to it.

Interior dome of Adinatha (Vimal Vasahi) temple, Mount Abu, Rajasthan, eleventh–twelfth century. The Jain temples of Mount Abu, exquisitely fretted in white marble, belie the notion that Islamic conquerors habitually destroyed all temples.

Tughluqabad Fort, Delhi, 1321–5. Ghiyas-ud-din Tughluq massively fortified his new Delhi but was forestalled in its enjoyment by his maligned son Muhammad bin Tughluq, 'the Bloody Sultan'.

Daulatabad (Devagiri, Deogir) Fort, Maharashtra. A stronghold of the Seuna kings, Daulatabad became the springboard for Islamic raids into peninsular India and was briefly adopted by Muhammad bin Tughluq as his capital.

Above Hoysaleshwara temple at Dorasamudra (Halebid), Karnataka, mid-twelfth century. The Hoysala capital, first occupied by Muslim forces under Malik Kafur in 1310, was supposedly destroyed in 1326.

Left Babur and his son Humayun, sixteenth-century miniature. The Indian empire won by Babur, first of the six Great Mughals, was lost but eventually reclaimed by Humayun, the second Great Mughal.

Above left Akbar hunting tigers, from the *Akbar-nama,* *c.*1590. Akbar, the third Great Mughal and the most fearless campaigner and sportsman, could neither read nor write. He was probably dyslexic.

Above Akbar giving an audience, from the *Akbar-nama.* The supplicant (below throne, left) presents the emperor with customary gifts including a bolt of cloth (below throne, right).

Left Rejoicing over the birth of Salim (Jahangir) at Fatehpur Sikri, from the *Akbar-nama.* Akbar's gratitude for the birth of an heir resulted in the selection of Sikri as the site of his new Fatehpur ('City of Victory').

Left Taj Mahal, Agra, from across the Jamuna river, 1630–52. Dynastic pride and Islamic symbolism, not romantic heartbreak, inspired Shah Jahan's tomb for Mumtaz Mahal who had died giving birth to their fourteenth child.

Below left Equestrian portrait of Shah Jahan, seventeenth century. The exaltation of the Mughal sovereignty by Shah Jahan included the creation of dazzling architectural settings and the adoption of quasi-divine symbols, like the Christian halo.

Below Ali Adil Shah II of Bijapur, Deccani miniature of *c.*1660. In architecture as in portraiture, the Deccan sultanates of Bijapur and Golconda vied with the Great Mughals. Ali Adil Shah's riposte to the Taj was the Gol Gumbaz.

Overleaf The Golden Temple (Hari Mandir) at Amritsar, eighteenth century and later. The holiest shrine of the Sikh faith houses the original Granth Sahib. Much restoration has been undertaken since the temple was stormed in 1984.

Above St Mary's Anglican church, Fort St George, Madras, 1679. The English East India Company's fort at Madras dates from 1640 and is contemporary with the Taj, but not till the 1740s did the Company espouse territorial ambitions.

Right Sir Henry Havelock relieving the British besieged in Lucknow in 1857, from an illustration by Howard Davie of *c*.1910. Lucknow and Awadh evidenced the popular appeal of the Great Rebellion while steeling British resistance to the 'Indian Mutiny'.

wealth, more was accumulating elsewhere. It was as if his labours in casting down one idol merely caused a couple more to rise up. Heracles would have sympathised. For every fifty thousand idolaters that were massacred, fifty thousand equally unregenerated devotees swarmed to some other place of pilgrimage or centre of politico-religious significance. The levelling of Mathura and Kanauj coincided precisely with the rise to architectural glory of other dynastic temple complexes. All this flatly contradicts the once popular notion that the Islamic invasions found India atrophied and supine. In fact 'dynamic' would seem better to describe a society so productive of soaring monuments, ambitious dynasties, dazzling wealth and buzzing devotion.

India's largest concentration of temples, at what is now the Orissan capital of Bhuvaneshwar, were constructed over many centuries and by a succession of dynasties. Although they display a remarkably consistent style – pineapple-shaped *sikharas* with strongly horizontal vaning being particularly distinctive – some date from as early as the seventh century and others from as late as the thirteenth. But the most celebrated, amongst them the exquisite Mukteshwara, the chaste Rajarani and the colossal Linga-raja, all belong to the late tenth to late eleventh centuries. While, in the west, the temples of Mathura and Somnath were being levelled, in the east structures equally 'beyond description' were being gloriously erected.

In between, at Khajuraho, the ceremonial capital of the Chandelas in central India, the chronological clustering is even more notable. Of the twenty more-or-less intact temples, none is earlier than the beginning of the tenth century or later than the early twelfth. Indeed the Vishvanatha temple with its much-loved Nandi (Lord Shiva's bull) carries an inscription of the reign of King Dhanga, who was ruling when Mahmud first invaded India. Nearby the Khandariya Mahadeva, the largest and most sculpturally elaborate of this justly famous complex, seems to have been constructed within a decade or so of the Ghaznavid assault on the Chandelas' stronghold of Kalinjar. If temple-building was indeed 'a political act', there could be no more eloquent testimony to the Chandelas' defiance of both their erstwhile Pratihara suzerains and the Muslim invader.

Later waves of iconoclasm under Muhammad of Ghor and the Delhi sultans will account for the disappearance of many other north Indian temple complexes of the tenth to twelfth centuries. Bhuvaneshwar and the other Orissan sites (Puri and Konarak) were spared only because they were sufficiently remote not to attract early Muslim attention. Khajuraho, on the other hand, looks to have survived thanks to its timely desertion by the Chandelas when the axis of their dwindling authority shifted eastwards.

Five hundred years later, when a British antiquarian, Captain Burt, stumbled upon 'the finest aggregate number of temples congregated in one place to be met with in all India', he found the site choked with trees and its elaborate system of lakes and watercourses overgrown and already beyond reclaim. Like Cambodia's slightly later Angkor Wat when it was 'discovered' by a wide-eyed French expedition, the place had been deserted for centuries and the sacred symbolism of its elaborate topography greedily obliterated by jungle. Nor was there any local recollection of either site having ever been otherwise. Henri Mouhot at Angkor would echo, almost word for word, the surprise of Burt who, noting the then scant population of villagers who frequented Khajuraho, 'could not help expressing a feeling of wonder at these splendid monuments of antiquity having been erected by a people who have continued to live in such a state of barbarous ignorance'.[9]

The inscriptions of the Chandelas have since revealed something of that dynasty's distinguished history, while the study of Khajuraho's deliciously uninhibited iconography has established the importance of the site as a centre of Shaivite worship.[10] 'Barbarous ignorance' may now be emphatically discounted. But of the rituals which Khajuraho witnessed, of its construction and maintenance, and of its economic and dynastic function, an idea can best be formed by looking at sites more comprehensively documented and less sensationally neglected. Such are to be found on or beyond the tidemark of Muslim encroachment, and most notably in the Tamil south.

By chance Mahmud's raids into the Ganga-Jamuna Doab at the western extremity of the ancient *arya-varta* had coincided with another unexpected incursion at the eastern end of *arya-varta*. No less adventurous, this surprise attack had originated in the extreme south of the peninsula. Far from the interminable plains of northern India and the wooded Vindhya hills where Harsha had once sought his widowed sister, beyond the Narmada river whence the Rashtrakutas had launched their challenge for 'Imperial' Kanauj and the bald Deccan plateau whence the Chalukyas had interminably challenged the Pallavas, below the teak forests and hill pastures of the Eastern Ghats, in a land without winter where the Kaveri river fans out into the lushest of rice-rich deltas – there, in the extreme south of Tamil Nadu, this spectacularly traditional retort to Mahmud's iconoclasm had been mounted by the Chola king Rajendra I.

The date seems to have been about 1021, so just before Mahmud turned his attention to Somnath. Upstaging even the Rashtrakutas of the Deccan, and reversing the trend of conquest set by the Mauryas and Guptas, the Cholas were the first south Indian dynasty to intervene in the north. Nor was this by any means the most ambitious of their foreign adventures. Turning the supposed hegemony of north India on its head, the Cholas were in fact the most successful dynasty since the Guptas. In terms of literature, architecture, sculpture and painting, theirs is an equally distinguished tradition; and thanks to it, and to their prolific output of inscriptions and copper plates, recent scholarship has constructed a uniquely detailed picture of the Chola state. It may not be entirely representative of other contemporary kingdoms; and as so often, the benefit of more evidence has generated the bane of more controversy. But here at least there are clues as to the dynamics of dynastic expansion as well as to its extent.

The Cholas, a Dravidian people first mentioned in Ashoka's inscriptions, seem to have occupied the region of the Kaveri delta since prehistoric times. During the long Pallava supremacy over the Tamil south from the sixth to ninth centuries they figure as a tributary lineage of their more assertive northern neighbours. But as the Pallavas vainly pursued their vendettas with Chalukyan and then Rashtrakutan rivals in Karnataka and with the Pandyan kingdom of Madurai, Chola ambitions revived. A decisive battle seems to have taken place in c897 when the Chola king Aditya, having withstood a Pandyan invasion, intervened in a Pallavan succession crisis. This brought outstanding results, with the overthrow of the mighty Pallavas and the acquisition of Tondaimandalam, the Pallava heartland (around Madras) which included Kanchipuram and Mamallapuram. A subsequent victory over the Pandyas encouraged Aditya to call himself *Madurai-konda*, 'Conqueror of Madurai', and he is said to have lined the banks of the Kaveri with stone temples. Initially his son Parantaka improved on this *digvijaya*; but in 949 he suffered a crushing defeat at the hands of Krishna III, the last of the great Rashtrakutas. Now it was the Rashtrakuta who termed himself 'Conqueror of Kanchipuram' and even 'of Tanjore', the Chola capital. For the next forty years Chola endeavours were directed towards recovering lost ground.

The classic expansion of Chola power began anew with the accession of Rajaraja I in 985. Campaigns in the south brought renewed success against the Pandyas and their 'haughty' Chera allies in Kerala, both of which kingdoms were now claimed as Chola feudatories. These triumphs were followed, or accompanied, by a successful invasion of Buddhist Sri Lanka in which Anuradhapura, the ancient capital, was sacked and its stupas plundered with a rapacity worthy of the great Mahmud. Later still Rajaraja is said to have conquered 'twelve thousand old islands', a phrase which could mean anything but is supposed to indicate the Maldives.

In the north the Cholas ran up against stiffer resistance in the shape of a dynasty which had just overthrown the Rashtrakutas. Claiming descent from the Rashtrakutas' original suzerains, these new overlords of the Deccan considered themselves another branch of the ubiquitous Chalukyas, once of Badami and Aihole. Usually known as the Later Western Chalukyas (of Kalyana in Karnataka), they may still be confused with that other branch, the earlier Eastern Chalukyas (of Vengi in Andhra Pradesh). But the Eastern Chalukyas now looked to the Cholas as allies and patrons; and it was while championing them, the old Eastern Chalukyas, against the new Western Chalukyas, that the Cholas became embroiled in the affairs of both Vengi and the Deccan.

In the course of perhaps several campaigns, more triumphs were recorded by the Cholas, more treasure was amassed, and more Mahmudian atrocities are imputed. According to a Western Chalukyan inscription, in the Bijapur district the Chola army behaved with exceptional brutality, slaughtering women, children and brahmans and raping girls of decent caste. Manyakheta, the old Rashtrakutan capital, was also plundered and sacked. But the Cholas did not have it all their own way, and their efforts served to make of the Western Chalukyas not obedient feudatories but inveterate enemies. The ancient rivalry between upland Karnataka and lowland Tamil Nadu, once epitomised in the struggle between the Chalukyas of Badami and the Pallavas of Kanchi, was revived as between the Cholas and the new Western Chalukyas. The old Eastern Chalukyas, on the other hand, became faithful subordinates with whom the Cholas inter-married.

These northern campaigns of the Cholas look to have been masterminded, if not conducted, by the son of Rajaraja I who would succeed as Rajendra I in 1014. As Rajaraja's reign drew to an end he not only secured the succession but set about memorialising his remarkable achievements. This he did by constructing in Tanjore a temple. Conceived as a single entity, built within about fifteen years and little altered since, it remains the most impressive, and allegedly 'the largest and the tallest',[11] in all India. To many, it is also the loveliest. Additionally it hosts a veritable Domesday Book of contemporary inscriptions and a small gallery of partially obscured Chola paintings. A monumental *lingam* in the main shrine beneath the sixty-five-metre *sikhara* proclaims it as sacred to Lord Shiva, a dedication which is confirmed by its current designation of 'Brihadesvara' and its original title of 'Rajarajesvara', or 'Rajaraja's Lord [Shiva]' temple. The latter name, however, makes the more important point: Tanjore's great temple is as much about the king as his god.

Muslim writers who chronicled the successes of Mahmud were often

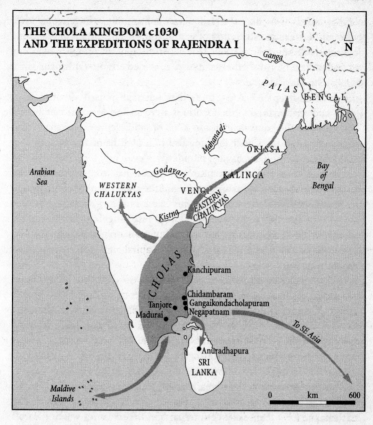

scandalised by the hordes of celebrants, musicians, dancing-girls and ser-vants who were attached to Indian places of worship. The five hundred brahmans and as many dancers reported at Mathura or Somnath might be taken for an exaggeration were it not clear that the Rajarajesvara in Tanjore supported a complement even larger. As well as contributing to its construction and embellishment, king, court and a variety of other military and religious donees deluged the temple with grants of land, pro-duce, and treasure to provide for the maintenance of this retinue and for the performance of a calendar of impressive rituals. The yields of villages dotted throughout the Chola kingdom and as far away as Sri Lanka were in this way attached to the temple, which reciprocated by reinvesting some of its accumulated wealth as loans to such far-flung settlements. The temple, in other words, was like a metropolitan community which served as a centre for both the redistribution of wealth and the integration of the Chola kingdom. No less important, since the supervision of the temple's economy was undertaken by royal officials, it also 'provided a foothold for the kings to intervene in local affairs'.[12]

It is clear from the inscriptions that Rajaraja himself was the main donor, and that many of his donations were in the form of war booty. They included the equivalent of 230 kilos of gold, yet more of silver, and jewels by the sackful. Other temples also benefited from this largesse. To the Cholas as to the Ghaznavids, plunder was evidently a necessity and so a prime motive in military adventures. Indeed it has been argued that the prestige of conducting rewarding raids, and the subsequent liberality which they made possible, were what held the Chola kingdom together. Its sensational expansion through 'quixotic' forays into neighbouring kingdoms, and still further afield, was therefore prompted by domestic necessity, and could even be taken as a measure of royal vulnerability rather than of an autocratic supremacy.

The comparison sometimes made is with the Frankish kingdom of early medieval Europe. 'As for these kings,' writes the distinguished French historian Georges Duby, 'their prestige was a reflection of their liberality; they would plunder with seemingly insatiable greed only to give more generously.'[13] Thus every royal occasion became the pinnacle of 'a regular system of free exchange, permeating the whole social fabric and making kingship the real regulator of the economy'. Commenting on these observations, an American authority on early south India draws the obvious parallel. 'The treasures allocated to pious causes by Charles Martel and Charlemagne have their exact counterparts in the treasures which Rajaraja I looted from the Cheras and Pandyas and then donated to his great temple of Tanjavur [Tanjore].'[14]

This notion of 'the politics of plunder and gift-giving' assumes that the Cholas inherited a 'peasant' or 'segmentary' state whose rural units enjoyed a high degree of autonomy and communal ownership which, in the absence of an effective central bureaucracy, made tax-collection difficult. Such a situation may have existed in Pallava times and earlier, but the evidence for the high Chola period is more ambiguous. The inscriptions reveal a host of what look like bureaucratic titles, and there are other pointers to the creation of a more integrated, amenable and taxable society.

For instance, the practice, well attested in the Tanjore inscriptions, of making land grants to brahmans (*brahmadeya*) may have been more than a royal expedient for rewarding brahman support and ensuring its continuance. Established by royal order and flourishing under royal protection, these grants also gave brahman recipients domination and direction of the non-brahman population. *Brahmadeyas* thus became a way of furthering political integration and, since brahmans were knowledgeable about subjects like irrigation, also of promoting productivity. The Cholas seem to have exploited such grants quite systematically so that two or three such brahman settlements became implanted in every district in their kingdom. In effect *brahmadeyas* became 'the local nuclei of the Chola power structure, their function being to integrate and control the surrounding non-*brahmadeya* villages'.[15]

Likewise the Cholas successfully harnessed and institutionalised the various cults associated with the popular *bhakti* ('devotional') movement in southern India. In the dark vestibule between the main shrine and the outer walls of the Tanjore temple, paintings depict not only Lord Shiva in his *nataraja* and *tripurantaka* ('demon-destroying') aspects but also delightful narrative scenes from the legends of Sundramurti and his associate Ceraman Perumal. Both were Nayanars, Tamil saints associated with the worship of Lord Shiva. There were also Alvars, who were Vaishnavite saints. The number of these local Tamil and Keralan intermediaries was considerable. Some were women, some *paraiyar* outcastes, and many were non-brahmans. If one may judge by occasional demands for equal access to temples, the *bhakti* movement had originally contained an element of protest against brahman exclusivity. As such it had competed with Jainism and Buddhism for followers and patrons and had occasioned some sectarian persecution, especially of Jains. More typically it sidetracked brahmanic ritual by its emphasis on a direct personal relationship of love and impassioned subservience between the devotee and the deity.

In this manifestation as a popular (and cheaper) form of worship, *bhakti* revivalism had been sweeping the entire subcontinent, stirring up, for instance, the fervent devotion shown for Lord Krishna at Mathura or for Lord Jagganath at Puri, and encouraging traditions of pilgrimage and temple festivals. But the phenomenon of *bhakti* saints had been strongest in, if not peculiar to, the south, where it drew heavily on regional literary traditions dating back to the *Sangam* age. Cutting across political, caste and professional divisions, 'it promoted a new Tamil consciousness which has significantly contributed to the Tamil heritage'.[16] By the tenth century, though the movement retained its mass appeal, it centred on the celebration in hymns, verses and local tradition of the often miraculous exploits, and the always ecstatic devotion, of the saints themselves. The Cholas seem consciously, as in their Tanjore paintings, to have cultivated this tradition. 'They adopted, elaborated, and zealously practised [its] ideology through various measures like the collection of the *bhakti* hymns, their popularisation through temple rituals and grants for such rituals, and the construction of temples in all the centres associated with the *bhakti* hymns.'[17]

Whatever the truth, then, about the existence of a Chola administrative bureaucracy, it is clear that for Rajaraja, and probably for other contemporary dynasts, there were alternative means of asserting royal authority and integrating a vast kingdom. The conspicuous generosity which such patronage demanded did, however, necessitate access to substantial revenue; and although taxation undoubtedly provided some of it, the rich pickings of predatory warfare were essential. For economic as well as ideological reasons, a successful *digvijaya* was a requisite for any new king. When, therefore, Rajendra I succeeded Rajaraja and assumed the reins of power in 1014, his priority was obvious. Sri Lanka was promptly reinvaded and more treasures and priceless regalia seized; prising open even relic chambers, says a Sri Lankan chronicle, 'like blood-sucking *yakkhas* they took all the treasures of Lanka for themselves'. Next the Chera and Pandya kingdoms witnessed another triumphal progress; then the born-again Western Chalukyas were re-engaged following their unwelcome intervention in the affairs of their Eastern namesakes.

In c1020, while completing this campaign in Vengi (Andhra), Rajendra's general is thought to have pushed north into Kalinga (Orissa) against the Eastern Ganga dynasty of Bhuvaneshwar, who may have been helping the enemy. There he received instructions to continue north, allegedly to obtain water from the Ganga river with which to sanctify the Chola land. Thus, somewhat incidentally, was launched Rajendra's great northern escapade. The name of the general is not known, nor is his route very clear, although it seems to have followed the east coast. He certainly crossed a lot of rivers, his elephants being lined up to breast their currents and so form bridges for his infantry to march over. Some of the peoples he defeated have been tentatively identified. 'Strong Mahipala', whom he put to flight in a hotly contested battle by sounding his deep-sea conch, was almost certainly Mahipala I, who briefly revived the fortunes of the Buddhist Pala dynasty in Bengal during the early decades of the eleventh century. 'Odda-Visaya defended by thick forests' must be Orissa, and 'Vangala-desa where the rain water never stopped' sounds like a fair description of Bengal in the monsoon. From the Pala king he obtained 'elephants of rare strength, women and treasure'. No doubt there was other booty. There was certainly no question of retaining any territory. It was as short and risky a venture as any undertaken by Mahmud, and one in which any reverses were patently 'glozed over', as Professor Nilakantha Sastri, the champion of the Cholas, nicely puts it.

But the main trophy, according to the inscriptions, was the water of the sacred Ganga, 'whose flow, strewn with fragrant flowers, had splashed against the places of pilgrimage'. Brought back, presumably, in jars, it was presented to Rajendra as he waited for the return of his expedition on the banks of the Godavari river. Thence he carried it home with triumphal purpose. For, like his father, Rajendra had conceived the idea of building a royal temple and, if it would not be quite as tall as the Tanjore Rajarajes-wara, he intended it to be even richer in imperial symbolism, and the focus of a new Chola capital. The water was for the ceremonial tank, a vast sheet of water five kilometres long which was duly known as the 'Chola-ganga'. Similarly the city itself was wordily named in honour of this same great exploit as 'Gangai-konda-chola-puram', 'the city of the Chola who con-quered the Ganga'. Whether Rajendra was aware of the earlier Rashtrakuta ploy to relocate *arya-varta* in the Deccan is not known, but clearly this was another attempt to appropriate the sacred geography of the *Puranas* and to centre it anew around the all-conquering Cholas.

'Well worth a visit,' says Murray's *Handbook* of Gangaikondacholapu-ram. But few pay heed, and the site of the Cholas' most ambitious creation remains a forlorn reminder of the monumental lengths to which a king might go to validate his rule and integrate his kingdom. The city, if it was ever built, has vanished, the Cholas' Ganga has been drained by recent irrigation canals, and the magnificent temple stands incongruously amidst straggling acacia and fields of *padi*, as if embarrassed by its own distinction.

An air of improbability haunts the exploits of the Cholas, not so much discrediting their authenticity as imputing their wisdom. For while, to the intense annoyance of generations of historians, other dynasties were content to let their eulogists award them impossible conquests, the Cholas, with a rare regard for the literal truth, seem to have determined on fulfilling such claims to the letter.

In the same spirit, and probably in search of more plunder, possibly in support of Chola trade, Rajendra lit upon his most 'quixotic' exploit, a naval expedition to south-east Asia. Whether the Cholas actually had a navy has been disputed. But since such a unit's function was simply troop-carrying, any shipping would have served; and there is no doubt that Indian ships were still maintaining regular commercial contacts with the Indianised kingdoms of the East and even with China, where several Chola missions are recorded. The partial conquest of Sri Lanka had demonstrated a Chola naval capacity, and no logistical barrier prevented its deployment still further overseas. What was novel about Rajendra's expedition was his willingness to champion such an exploit, and its obviously warlike intent in a theatre where the use of Indian troops had not previously been recorded. It is, in fact, another of those rare examples of Indian aggression beyond the frontiers of the subcontinent.

The evidence for the expedition comes almost entirely from an inscription on the west wall of Rajaraja's Tanjore temple. Presumably it was recorded there because Rajendra's new temple at Gangaikondacholapuram was not ready for inscriptions. The precise date is disputed: it may have been before the Ganga expedition, but was probably in c1025; alternatively there may have been more than one expedition. The inscription consists mainly of a longish list of 'taken' places, and on their identification great theories about south-east Asian polities have been constructed. 'Six [of the places tentatively identified] are located on the Malay peninsula or in Tenasserim while four are located on Sumatra, and "Nakkavaram" certainly represents the Nicobar islands.'[18] But the first listed, and seemingly the most important, was 'Kadaram', or Kedah, the once Thai, then Malay and now Malaysian state north of Penang; and the second, the name on which historians invariably pounce, was 'Srivijaya', the maritime power which supposedly controlled the Malacca Straits and had been well known to the Chinese since Buddhist pilgrims en route to India had received instruction there in the seventh century.

One theory has it that the Cholas were endeavouring to break Srivijaya's control of the straits. This is disputed, but commercial considerations may well have played their part. In the wake of the Cholas' conquests in India and Sri Lanka, there had spread and prospered an organisation usually known in inscriptions as the 'Five Hundred Swamis of Ayyavole'. More a robust trading league than a simple guild, the 'Ayyavole Five Hundred', or 'Aihole Five Hundred' (from which place it had originated), seems to have specialised in the organisation and protection of long-distance transport and exchange. It managed fortified trading depots and employed its own troops. There is no reason to suppose that, like the Hanseatic League, it pursued its own policies. Yet, as a substantial contributor to the welfare and defence of the realm, it was clearly influential. It would therefore be interesting to know more of the part it played in Rajendra's south-east Asian exploit, particularly since later in the century the Ayyavole swamis are found to have had an outpost at Barus on the west coast of Sumatra.

Religion may also have figured. Rajaraja is known to have provided for a Buddhist vihara to be built by the ruler of 'Kadaram' at Tanjore's port of Negapatnam. Presumably it was for the convenience of Kadaram Buddhists visiting India. But it seems reasonable to suppose that subsequent relations with the Buddhists of Kadaram may well have been soured by Rajendra's 'blood-sucking' of Sri Lanka's monasteries and his worsting of the Buddhist Palas in Bengal. With both of these kingdoms the Srivijayan world was in close contact. Retaliatory measures against Chola traders at the Srivijayan ports could well have followed, and so have provoked Rajendra's raid.

Yet if one returns to the Tanjore inscription, there is mention of neither pious nor commercial gains, only of military matters, of formidable defences overcome and of desirable booty secured. The 'jewelled gates' of Srivijaya and the 'heaped treasures' of Kadaram were what mattered. Plunder once again proves to be the constant factor behind Chola expansion.

Rajendra's reign lasted thirty-three years, during which time, we are told, he 'raised the Chola empire to the position of the most extensive and most respected Hindu state of his time'.[19] The fact that his most ambitious conquests were hurried forays in search of booty and prestige, that he failed to subdue his immediate neighbours in the Deccan, and that even Sri Lanka would have to be evacuated by his successors in no way discredits this statement. On such doubtful foundations lay most other claims to extensive empire and dynastic regard in pre-Islamic India.

FISH-RICH WATERS

The Cholas' supremacy in the south would last until the early thirteenth century. Territorially their sway was much reduced with the loss of Sri Lanka in c1070, the gradual reassertion of Pandyan sovereignty from about the same time, and the ebb and flow of fortune in the almost continuous hostilities with the Later Western Chalukyas and other Deccan powers. But the Cholas' international prestige remained intact. A seventy-two-man Chola mission reached China in 1077. In 1090 the Chola king received another deputation from Kadaram in connection with the affairs of the Buddhist establishment at Negapatnam, and in subsequent years diplomatic exchanges are recorded with both of south-east Asia's master-building dynasties, the Khmers of Angkor and the Burmans of Pagan.

The Cholas themselves continued to build, although the sites were fewer and the pace slackened as resources diminished. The classic example is the Nataraja temple of Chidambaram. Nothing if not transitional, its construction spanned several reigns from c1150 to 1250. Its profile marries 'a

THE RISE AND FALL OF THE CHOLAS OF TANJORE

Vijayalaya
r.c846–871. Seized Tanjore

ADITIYA I
r.c871–907. 'Conqueror of Madurai'

PARANTAKA I
r.c907–953. Defeated by Krishna III, Rashtrakuta

Arinjaya
d.c957

Gandaraditya
d.c957

Parantaka II
r.c957–973

Uttama
r.c973–985

Aditya
d.c969

RAJARAJA I
r.c985–1014. Re-establishes Chola power,
invades Sri Lanka, builds Tanjore temple

RAJENDRA I
r.c1014–1044. Expeditions to Ganga and
SE Asia, builds Gangaikondacholapuram

Rajaraja = Ammangadevi
(East Chalukyan)

Rajadhiraja I
r.c1044–1054. Takes Kalyani
Chalukyan capital

Rajendra II
r.c1054–1063

Virarajendra
r.c1063–1069. Second
expedition to SE Asia

Rajendra III (Kulottunga I)
r.c1070–1122. Cholas expelled from
Sri Lanka, mission to China c1077

Vikrama Chola
d.c1135

Kulottunga II
d.c1150

daughter

Rajaraja II
d.c1173

Rajadhiraja II
d.c1178

Kulottunga III
r.c1178–1216. Defeats, and is
then defeated by Pandyas.
Chola Empire in decline

compendium of the entire Chola style' with cardinal features of later south Indian architecture, most obviously the colossal *gopuras* or gateways. In that the Chidambaram temple seems to have replaced those of Tanjore and Gangaikondacholapuram as the dynasty's symbolic focus, its varied iconography and extremely confused layout ('it is still impossible, for example, to determine its original orientation'[20]) may be taken as an apt commentary on the uncertain aspirations of the later Cholas.

But they did at least survive; and any continuity in a period of such dismal confusion is welcome. The historian who looks for a classic example of *matsya-nyaya*, that 'big-fish-eats-little-fish' state of anarchy so dreaded in the *Puranas*, need look no further than India in the eleventh to twelfth centuries. *Dharma*'s cosmic order appeared utterly confounded and the geometry of the *mandala* hopelessly subverted. Lesser feudatories nibbled at greater feudatories, kingdoms swallowed kingdoms, and dynasties devoured dynasties, all with a voracious abandon that woefully disregarded the shark-like presence lurking in the Panjab.

Even there the Muslim descendants of Mahmud, though they clung to their patrimony with a rare constancy, seemed to be succumbing to the spirit of a senseless age. Seldom did a Sultan succeed without a major succession crisis and a horrific bloodbath. Since two of Mahmud's sons had been born on the same day but of separate mothers, this was initially understandable. But thereafter it became a habit, and the Ghaznavids' Panjab kingdom was rent with internal dissension. Externally, sporadic raids into neighbouring Indian territories produced more treasure but few political gains. The reign of Masud, Mahmud's immediate successor, is said to 'mark a phase of total strategic confusion, as far as his relations with India go'.[21] They went not far, nor for long; Masud was overthrown and killed in a palace revolution. Meanwhile, beyond the Hindu Kush, the Ghaznavids' once-extensive territories were subject to steady encroachment by the Seljuq Turks and others. The loss of Khorasan in c1040 had the effect of shifting the focus of the shrinking empire from Afghanistan to India. Lahore virtually replaced Ghazni as the capital, which latter city, once the pride of the dynasty, was now held on sufferance and, after several devastating raids, irrevocably lost in c1157. A few years later it changed hands yet again. No longer an epicentre of empire, its principal charm was now as a strategic gateway to the Muslim kingdoms in Sind and the Panjab.

The new lords of this much-diminished Ghazni were complete outsiders from the remote region of Ghor in central Afghanistan. Warlords of possibly Persian extraction, they would nevertheless continue their presumptuous encroachment. After several incursions across the north-west frontier, in 1186 they would overthrow the last of Mahmud's successors. Lahore thus fell to the Ghorids; and their leader Muizzudin Muhammad bin Sam saw no reason to stop there. Determined to succeed where both Alexander and Mahmud had failed, this 'Muhammad of Ghor' would press on, east and south, to cruise with devastating effect in the fish-rich waters of the Indian *matsya-nyaya*.

It was not just a case of India being hopelessly fragmented. A discouraging prospect for the political historian, the eleventh to twelfth centuries have won yet more disgusted comment from social and economic historians.

> Never before was land donated to secular and religious beneficiaries
> on such a large scale; never before were agrarian and communal
> rights undermined by land grants so widely; never before was the
> peasantry subjected to so many taxes and so much sub-infeudation;
> never before were services, high and low, rewarded by land grants
> in such numbers as now; and finally never before were revenues
> from trade and industry converted into so many grants.[22]

It reads like a prescription, if not for revolution, then certainly for a reformation. According to this diagnosis, economic collapse, social oppression and caste discrimination went hand in hand with political fragmentation. India was bracing itself for a renewal of the Islamic challenge by squandering the resources, oppressing the people and pulverising the authority on which any effective resistance must depend. Indeed the triumph of an alternative dispensation which, like that of Islam, promised social justice, the equality of the individual and firm government would seem to be assured. Instead of warring for centuries to win minority acceptance, Islam should have won spontaneous adoption.

That it did not suggests that the situation was not that dire. Economic activity may have declined, but evidence of social protest is lacking. Instead there are many examples of contemporary rulers who enjoyed great repute in their lifetimes and have been the subjects of popular romance ever since. Even from the murky mêlée of competing dynasts in north and central India a few figures of striking stature emerge, none more revered than the great 'philosopher-king' Bhoj of Dhar.

Not to be confused with the ninth-century Pratihara King Bhoj (or Bhoja) of Kanauj, this eleventh-century Bhoj belonged to a clan of the Paramaras who had once been feudatories of the Rashtrakutas in Gujarat. Claiming *ksatriya* (or rajput) status like so many of their contemporaries, the Paramaras had asserted their independent rule in Malwa in the mid-tenth century when both the Rashtrakutas and the Pratiharas were slipping into terminal decline.

As their capital they chose Dhar, now a small town between Ujjain and Mandu in Madhya Pradesh. Ujjain, beside the Sipra river, was the ancient centre of Malwa where Ashoka had allegedly misspent much of his youth, while Mandu, now a heavily fortified but eerily deserted headland high above the Narmada, would become the redoubt of Malwa's next rulers. Such a scatter of regional centres within a small radius is not unusual. In the progression from hallowed but indefensible Ujjain to upland Dhar to near impregnable Mandu one may detect a response to changing times.

Bhoj succeeded to the throne of Dhar in or about the year 1010 and seems to have reigned for nearly fifty years. He was therefore an exact contemporary of the Chola, Rajendra I. From his uncle and his father, both bellicose *digvijayins*, he inherited suzerain claims over a host of rival kings and sub-kings scattered throughout Rajasthan, central India and the Deccan. They certainly did not include the 'Keralas and the Cholas', whose bejewelled diadems are nevertheless said, in a by-now threadbare cliché, to have coloured his uncle's lotus feet. But amongst the many to whom these claims were unacceptable were just about every other contemporary dynasty including the Chandelas of Khajuraho, their formidable Chedi and Kala-churi neighbours, the reborn Western Chalukyas of the Deccan, the Solankis of Gujarat, and numerous other incipient rajput kingdoms plus assorted minor potentates in Maharashtra and on the Konkan coast.

Lumbered with such a contentious inheritance, the youthful Bhoj felt obliged to take the field on his own *digvijaya*. The results were mixed, his successes being much contradicted and his failures quickly reversed. Generally speaking, in Gujarat and Rajasthan he seems to have held his own but in the Deccan he made little progress. This was despite an anti-Chalukyan alliance with the Cholas and a legacy of exceptional bitterness left by his uncle, who had been captured, caged and executed by the Chalukyas. 'His head was then fixed on a stake in the courtyard of the royal palace and, by keeping it continually covered with thick sour cream, [the Chalukya] gratified his anger.'[23] Such an outrage rankled deeply with the Paramaras, and may explain Bhoj's obsession with chastising the Chalukyas.

In this he not only failed but, at one point, was surprised by a Chalukyan raid and had to flee from his beloved Dhar. The capital, though said to have been devastated, must have been speedily regained and then restored, for it is as 'Dharesvara', the intellectual magnate and 'lord of Dhar', that Bhoj is principally remembered. Compared to the Cholas or the Pratiharas,

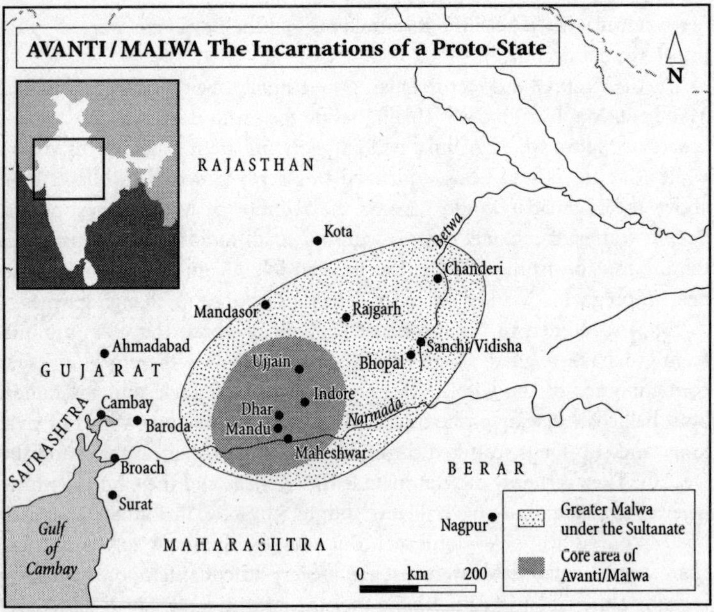
AVANTI / MALWA The Incarnations of a Proto-State
N
RAJASTHAN
Kota
Betwa
Chanderi
Mandasor
Rajgarh
Ahmadabad
Sanchi/Vidisha
GUJARAT
Ujjain
Bhopal
Indore
Cambay
Dhar
Narmada
SAURASHTRA
Baroda
Mandu
Maheshwar
Broach
BERAR
Surat
Greater Malwa under the Sultanate
Nagpur
Gulf of Cambay
MAHARASHTRA
Core area of Avanti/Malwa
0 km 200

claims as to his military prowess ring somewhat hollow. But if military success was an essential attribute of kingship, so too was scholastic attainment and patronage. In this respect Bhoj outshines even Harsha's intellectual genius as portrayed in Bana's *Harsa-carita*; for whilst to Harsha have been attributed works which he certainly did not write, 'we have no real knowledge to disprove Bhoj's claim to polymathy exhibited in a large variety of works.'[24]

These range over subjects as various as philosophy, poetics, veterinary science, phonetics, archery, yoga and medicine. 'To study Bhoj is to study the entire culture of the period.' Dhar seems to have been transformed into a veritable Oxford, with its palaces serving as common rooms of intellectual discourse and its temples as colleges of higher education. Other kings, contemporary and subsequent, could hardly contain their admiration. 'Bhoj was such a versatile personality and left such a deep impression . . . that even the pro-Chalukya chronicle, the *Prabandhacintamani*, felt constrained to conclude its account of Bhoj with the words: "Among poets, gallant lovers, enjoyers of life, generous donors, benefactors of the virtuous,

AVANTI / MALWA The Incarnations of a Proto-State

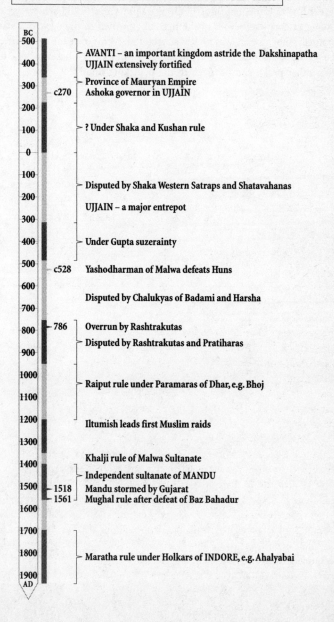

BC		
500		
400		AVANTI – an important kingdom astride the Dakshinapatha UJJAIN extensively fortified
300	c270	Province of Mauryan Empire / Ashoka governor in UJJAIN
200		
100		? Under Shaka and Kushan rule
0		
100		
200		Disputed by Shaka Western Satraps and Shatavahanas
300		UJJAIN – a major entrepot
400		Under Gupta suzerainty
500	c528	Yashodharman of Malwa defeats Huns
600		Disputed by Chalukyas of Badami and Harsha
700		
800	786	Overrun by Rashtrakutas / Disputed by Rashtrakutas and Pratiharas
900		
1000		Raiput rule under Paramaras of Dhar, e.g. Bhoj
1100		
1200		Iltumish leads first Muslim raids
1300		
1400		Khalji rule of Malwa Sultanate
1500	1518	Independent sultanate of MANDU / Mandu stormed by Gujarat
1600	1561	Mughal rule after defeat of Baz Bahadur
1700		
1800		Maratha rule under Holkars of INDORE, e.g. Ahalyabai
1900 AD		

archers, and those who regard *dharma* as their wealth, there is none on the earth who can equal Bhoj." ' Other rajput kings would achieve greater popular celebrity as heroes of the martial ethos which their *ksatriya* status enjoined. Bhoj's legacy was no less substantial. As his own eulogy succinctly puts it, 'he accomplished, constructed, gave, and knew what none else did. What other praise can be given to the poet-king Bhoj?'[25]

The Triumph of the Sultans

c1180–1320

FRIENDS, RAJPUTS AND CONQUERORS

THE WORD 'RAJPUT' (*raja-putera*) simply means 'son of a raja'. Although it therefore implied *ksatriya* status and eventually came to mean just that, someone of *ksatriya* caste, it originally had no particular ethnic or regional connotations. To those ex-feudatories of the Gurjara-Pratihara kings of Kanauj to whom the term is so freely applied, and to other Indian opponents of Islam to whom it was occasionally extended, it was probably meaningless other than as one of many hackneyed, and usually much more grandiloquent, honorifics. Not until the Mughal period did the word come to be used of a particular class or tribe and, given the prejudices of Aurangzeb's reign, its connotation soon became decidedly pejorative: 'Rashboots', as they sometimes appeared in English translation, were freebooters and trouble-makers, 'a sort of Highway men, or Tories' according to a seventeenth-century travelogue by the German Albert de Mandelso.[1] Always 'gentiles' (the contemporary designation for Hindus), they were encountered mainly in Gujarat and Rajasthan and were usually under arms, soldiering being their hereditary profession.

Colonel James Tod, who as the first British official to visit Rajasthan spent most of the 1820s exploring its political potential, formed a very different idea of the 'Rashboots'. Not only was it his boast that 'in a Rajpoot I always recognise a friend,' but seemingly in a friend he always recognised a rajput. Their hospitality to one who was offering acknowledgement of their sovereignty plus protection from the then devastating attentions of the Marathas was overwhelming. Tod found rajputs all over Rajasthan; and the whole region thenceforth became, for the British, 'Rajputana'. The word even achieved a retrospective authenticity when, in an 1829 translation of Ferishta's history of early Islamic India, John Briggs discarded the phrase

'Indian princes', as rendered in Dow's earlier version, and substituted 'Rajpoot princes'. As Briggs freely admitted, he was 'much indebted for the unreserved communications on all points connected with the history of Rajpootana ... to my good friend Colonel Tod'.[2]

Nor, according to Tod, were these ubiquitous 'Rajpoots' outlaws – or even Tories. They were sovereign chiefs and princes, scions of a noble race amongst whom, opined Tod, 'we may search for the germs of the constitutions of European states'. Although perjured and persecuted during centuries of Islamic supremacy, they were in fact the native aristocracy of India, an indomitable people whose ethnic origins could be traced back to a common ancestry with the earliest tribes of Europe and whose genealogies as recorded in the *Puranas* reached back to the epics and the Vedas.

Thanks to the rajputs' naturally generous disposition and to the assistance of their royal archivists and bards, Tod had been privileged to attempt a reconstruction of their history; and what a glorious tale it was. In his majestic *Annals and Antiquities of Rajast'han*, published in 1829, he regaled his readers with examples of a chivalry to shame Camelot and of a resolve worthy of Canute. Frequent references to the rajputs' clan organisation and aristocratic sense of *noblesse oblige* went down especially well with an audience steeped in British history; and in the feudal structure of rajput society Tod thought he saw an exact equivalent of that which had pertained nearer to home in Anglo-Norman times. For 'the martial system peculiar to these Rajpoot states' invariably and specifically made vassalage and land grants contingent on military service and the provision of fighting men.

Admittedly, for the rajput knights themselves feudalism seemed less about tenurial feus and more about the interminable feuds to which they often gave rise. Rivalry between the various rajput houses was intense and disastrous.

> The closest attention to their history proves beyond contradiction that they were never capable of uniting, even for their own preservation: a breath, a scurrilous stanza of a bard, has severed their closest confederacies. No national head exists amongst them ... and each chief being master of his own house and followers, they are individually too weak to cause us [i.e. the British] any alarm.[3]

They had, nevertheless, shown a bold front in the face of Muslim aggression. And for whatever that defiance had lacked in the way of coherence, they had amply compensated with a stalwart perseverance unequalled in the annals of mankind.

In support of this contention Tod adduced a litany of patriotic heroes and tales of martial romance from the twelfth to eighteenth centuries. The earliest was 'the heroic history of Pirthi-raj by Chund', a particularly instructive saga to which he devoted considerable space. For 'Pirthi-raj' was otherwise Prithviraj III of the Chahamana (Chauhan) dynasty, who ruled an extensive kingdom in northern Rajasthan and the eastern Panjab from c1177. It was he therefore whose territory marched with that of the Ghaznavids at Lahore and, when that city fell to Muhammad of Ghor in 1186, it was he who stood between the Ghorid kingdom and the rest of India. Tod was wrong in imagining that the bard 'Chund' was a contemporary eye-witness, let alone 'his [i.e. Prithviraj's] friend, his herald, his ambassador'. He was therefore mistaken in taking Chand's 'poetical histories' as reliable evidence. But in rehabilitating Prithviraj, as also the *ksatriya* dynasties of Rajasthan whom he had so determinedly designated as 'Rajpoots', Tod did both history and Indian nationalism a useful service.

The Chahamanas, like the Pratiharas and Bhoj's Paramaras, claimed (or would eventually claim) to have acquired their *ksatriya* status from the great fire-sacrifice once held on Mount Abu. More prosaically they look to have been a desert tribe from the region around lake Sambhar, west of modern Jaipur, who over the centuries, like countless other peoples in out-of-the-way places, had undergone a long process of 'Aryanisation'. Hemachandra Ray's *Dynastic History of Northern India* lists no fewer than eight Chahamana families of princely standing, one of which, the Sakambhari (i.e. Sambhar) branch, remained on home ground in the vicinity of lakes Sambhar and Pushkar. Inducted into the Gurjara-Pratihara empire by marriage, they had eventually broken away and, early in the twelfth century, one King Ajaya-raja established a new capital. He called it 'Ajaya-meru', or Ajmer.

In the mid-twelfth century Vigraha-raja, one of Ajaya-raja's successors, greatly extended the dynasty's sway by pushing northwards into what is now Haryana and what remained outside Ghaznavid rule of the eastern Panjab. Delhi, too, fell to Vigraha-raja, and to record this brilliant campaign he added his own inscriptions to those of Ashoka on one of the latter's still-standing pillars. By a strange coincidence the pillar he chose was the one, then located higher up the Jamuna, which two centuries later would be so laboriously shipped downriver for re-erection in Delhi. There, fortuitously relocated in the heart of the city to which he had laid claim, it records Vigraha-raja's conquest of the whole region up to the Himalayas and also mentions frequent exterminations of the *mlechhas*, presumably a reference to conflicts with the declining Ghaznavids. Another inscription speaks of his having thereby made *arya-varta* 'once more the abode of the *arya*'.

Vigraha-raja died c1165. The Chahamana succession then became convoluted until Prithviraj III ascended the throne of Ajmer twelve years later. Evidently a minor at the time, he seems to have celebrated his coming of age by eloping with the daughter of the king of Kanauj. This much-loved romance is told in some detail by the unreliable Chand. On the other hand the young Lochinvar's ambitious *digvijaya* of c1182 is shrouded in uncertainty. It seems to have brought him into conflict with, amongst others, the Chandelas and their allies and also the Solanki rajputs of Gujarat. In all such encounters he is said to have fared well and, according to another popular narrative of the period, he waxed strong enough to vow next to extirpate his *mlechha* neighbours in the Panjab.

In this he was emboldened by the decline of the Ghaznavids and the rather unimpressive showing so far made by Muhammad of Ghor. From Ghazni the Ghorid had first turned his attentions to Sind, routing the restored Ismaili ruler of Multan and eventually pushing down the Indus to Mansurah and Debal. He had thence attempted to attack the Solankis of Gujarat by crossing the Thar desert in imitation of Mahmud's raid on Somnath. He even invited the young Prithviraj to support him in this venture. Prithviraj declined and briefly considered joining his Solanki rival to eject the *Turuskas*. But in the event this proved unnecessary, for the Ghorids were roundly defeated in Gujarat. Muhammad thereupon abandoned the idea of a trans-Thar invasion and directed his attention northeast to Lahore. Having secured that place in 1186–7, he was ready to meet Prithviraj's challenge. Along a Panjabi frontier not dissimilar to today's Indo–Pakistan border, 'the Ghorid and the Chahamana now stood face to face. The Muslim knew that the wealth of the rich cities and temples in the Jamuna-Ganga valley and beyond could only be secured by the destruction of the Hindu power which held the key to the Delhi gate.'[4]

Twentieth-century parallels with a situation in which Sind and Gujarat lay divided from one another by religion, and the Panjab in effect partitioned between Muslim and Hindu rulers, are hard to overlook. Pakistanis may take comfort from the fact that this division had already subsisted for nearly two hundred years in the case of the Panjab and for over four hundred in the case of Sind/Gujarat. Indians, on the other hand, take little note of the chronology and more of the outcome.

It should, though, be emphasised that during this long political stand-off there were contacts of an informal nature. Apart from commercial links, which continued much as under the Balhara's even-handed patronage, Muslim immigrants and missionaries seem to have enjoyed the freedom of north India much as Hindus did that of Sind and the Panjab. Writing of the Varanasi region, Ibn Asir, a contemporary scholar, insists that 'there were Mussalmans in that country since the days of Mahmud bin Sabuktigin [i.e. Mahmud of Ghazni], who continued faithful to the law of Islam, and constant in prayer and good work.'[5] Numerous other examples of pre-Ghorid Muslim communities in India have been noticed;[6] and so has the existence of a *Turuska* tax. This could have been a levy to meet tribute demands from the Ghaznavids, but seems more probably to have been a poll-tax on Muslims resident in India and so a Hindu equivalent of the Muslim *jizya*. But perhaps the most striking evidence of pre-Ghorid Muslim communities comes from Ajmer itself. There, if later tradition is to be believed, Shaikh Muin-ud-din Chishti founded the most famous of India's Sufi movements in the months immediately preceding Muhammad of Ghor's assault, and so under the very nose of Prithviraj III.

To what extent religion was uppermost in the mind of either Prithviraj or Muhammad of Ghor when first they met is therefore debatable. In 1191 Muhammad took the offensive by storming a fort in the Panjab which is thought to have been either that of Sirhind near Patiala or of Bhatinda near the current Indo–Pakistan frontier. The fort was taken; but Prithviraj hastened to its rescue and, at a place called Tarain near Thanesar (about 150 kilometres north of Delhi), he was intercepted by the main Ghorid army.

The ensuing battle is described as having been decided by a personal contest between Muhammad of Ghor and Govinda-raja of Delhi, who was Prithviraj's vassal. Govinda lost his front teeth to the Ghorid's lance but then took fearful revenge with a spear that struck the latter's upper arm. Barely able to keep his seat, Muhammad was saved by 'a lion-hearted warrior, a Khalji stripling' who leapt up behind him in the saddle and piloted him from the battlefield. Seeing this, many of Muhammad's troops feared the worst; they believed their leader to be dead and so broke off the encounter. Had the Chahamana forces taken advantage of the situation, it might have become a rout. But Prithviraj, fresh from the ritualistic manoeuvres of a conventional *digvijaya*, mistook retreat for an admission of defeat. Ignorant of the advice once given by 'Bhimpal', it was as though he rejoiced over the capture of a hill and bothered not with the rest of the range. The Muslim forces were allowed to withdraw in good order. Prithviraj then ordered his army forward to a laborious siege of the Sirhind/ Bhatinda fort.

Muhammad withdrew to Ghazni to convalesce and assemble more troops. The Ghorid forces included Afghans, Persians and Arabs, but the most numerous and effective contingents were of Turkic stock. Meanwhile

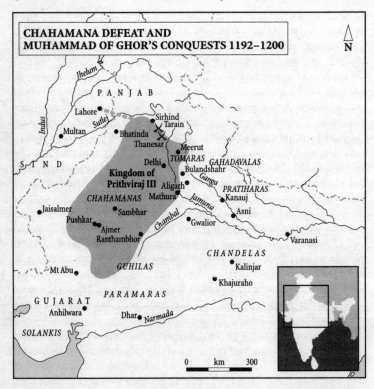

CHAHAMANA DEFEAT AND
MUHAMMAD OF GHOR'S CONQUESTS 1192–1200

N

Kingdom of
Prithviraj III

those who had fled the field at Tarain were obliged to don their horses'
nosebags and tread the thoroughfares of Ghazni munching on grain. By
mid-1192 Muhammad was back in the Panjab at the head of 120,000 horse
and with an uncompromising ultimatum for the king of Ajmer: apostasise
or fight. Prithviraj returned 'a haughty answer': he would not capitulate nor
would he embrace Islam but, if Muhammad was having second thoughts, he
was willing to consider a truce.

Endearingly susceptible to the perquisites of power, Prithviraj is said
to have been enjoying himself since his earlier victory. He was still in his
mid-twenties and, returning now to the fortunate field of Tarain at the
head of an army said to have comprised 300,000 horse, he was in an even
better position to dispose of the Ghorid challenge. If Ferishta was right
about his 150 royal vassals – and translator Briggs about their being 'Rajpoot

princes' – he headed the most formidable rajput confederacy on record. Tod, despite his insistence on the rajputs' chronic disunity, seems to agree: 'Pirthi-raj' was now 'the ruler of Rajasthan'; and amongst those 'Rajpoot princes' who supposedly flocked to his standard was Tod's particular hero, the Guhila ruler of distant Mewar (later capital Udaipur) in southern Rajasthan.

From Ferishta's much later and, it must be said, suspiciously detailed account there also comes evidence of trickery. Muhammad allegedly responded to Prithviraj's suggestion of a truce with a letter couched in terms sufficiently ambiguous to give the Indians cause for celebration. 'The letter produced the intended effect; for the enemy, conceiving that Muhammad was intimidated, spent the night in riot and revelry, while he was preparing to surprise them.' When they awoke, late and in urgent need of ablutions, they found the Ghorid forces already entering their lines. The battle thus began amidst some confusion. Only Muhammad had a plan: like the great Mahmud he would launch wave after wave of mounted archers, but not try to force the Indian position, and in fact withdraw as the Indians' elephant-phalanx advanced. Prithviraj, happy with this apparent success, duly advanced. But the buffeting assaults of the Turkish horse took their toll of the all-night revellers; sore rajput heads began to droop, and the scent of morning victory soured as the day wore on. By sunset Muhammad was ready to strike back.

> Thinking he had sufficiently worn out the enemy and deluded them with a hope of victory, he put himself at the head of twelve thousand of his best horse, whose riders were covered with steel armour, and making one desperate charge, carried death and destruction through the Hindu ranks. The disorder increased everywhere until at length the panic became general. The Muslims, as if they only now began to be in earnest, committed such havoc that this [Prithviraj's] prodigious army, once shaken, like a great building tottered to its fall and was lost in its ruins.[7]

Govinda-raja of Delhi, the hero of the first battle at Tarain, was slain; his body was recognised by its missing teeth. Slain too was the Guhila king Samatasimha, Tod's 'Ulysses of the Rajpoot host'. In all 100,000 are said to have been sent to their death. Prithviraj was taken prisoner and would soon join them.

The 1192 rout of the rajputs at Tarain is arguably the most decisive battle in the history of India. Prithviraj had succeeded in uniting at least some of the rajput princes and in cordoning off the Islamised Panjab. The blood-and-plunder raids had been stopped. But this interdiction had served only to increase the pressure for a more decisive encounter. The Ghorids rose to the challenge because for them, as for their Indian contemporaries, plunder was a necessity.

Prithviraj had upped the stakes, and he paid the price. When the Chahamana army succumbed, it became painfully clear that his earlier successes had only made his eventual failure all the more catastrophic. The 'key to the Delhi gate', indeed to the whole of *arya-varta*, now belonged to Muhammad of Ghor and his victorious Turks.

> Scenes of devastation, plunder, and massacre commenced, which lasted through the ages; during which nearly all that was sacred in religion or celebrated in art was destroyed by these ruthless and barbarous invaders.

Colonel Tod could have been writing of the fall of the Roman empire. Fresh from the study of Edward Gibbon's epic, he relished another apocalypse and saw the decline and fall of Hindu empire as a history which was there for the telling. Not beset by niggling scruples about impartiality, he conjured up the heroes of his choice in a language rich in the exaggeration typical of their bardic traditions. His verdict on the years that followed, like his estimate of the 'Rajpoots' themselves, would enjoy a long if controversial currency.

> The noble Rajpoot, with a spirit of constancy and enduring courage, seized every opportunity to turn upon his oppressor. By his perseverance and valour he wore out entire dynasties of foes, alternately yielding to his fate or restricting the circle of conquest. Every road in Rajast'han was moistened with torrents of blood of the spoiled and the spoiler. But all to no avail; fresh supplies were ever pouring in, and dynasty succeeded dynasty, heir to the same remorseless feeling which sanctified murder, legalised spoliation, and deified destruction. In these desperate conflicts entire tribes were swept away, whose names are the only memento of their former existence and celebrity. What nation on earth could have maintained the semblance of civilisation, the spirit or the customs of their forefathers, during so many centuries of overwhelming oppression, but one of such singular character as the Rajpoot?[8]

THE SLAVE KINGS

Within a year of the victory at Tarain, Muhammad of Ghor's forces had taken Delhi, plus Meerut, Kol (Aligarh) and Baran (Bulandshahr), commanding the upper Ganga-Jamuna Doab. Ajmer was also under Ghorid control, and within another three years much of *arya-varta* shared its fate. Of the three great natural fortresses screening Rajasthan and the routes south, Ranthambhor had been won, Gwalior assailed and Narwar targeted. To the east, after another decisive battle, Kanauj, Asni and Varanasi on the Ganga had also been overrun; and in the south-west, following victory at Mount Abu over a western rajput combination, the Gujarati capital of Anhilwara (Patan) had been sacked. The thirteenth century opened with even more sensational conquests as Muslim forces pushed further east into Bihar, Bengal and Assam; others moved into the Chandela country south of the Ganga and captured, amongst many, the stronghold of Kalinjar. On paper the Ghorid empire in India already exceeded that of Harsha.

Given, however, their predatory imperative, many of these conquests were temporary. Ajmer and Ranthambhor, for instance, changed hands several times; Gwalior and Kalinjar were lost shortly after they were won; Anhilwara was evacuated as soon as it was sacked. In some cases existing rulers were reinstated but then renounced their submission once the *Turuskas* had departed or further support had been recruited. In other instances, most notably in Bengal, the victorious *Turuska* generals would soon themselves renounce their allegiance to Delhi. It would be a characteristic of the Muslim advance that most major cities and forts were taken and then retaken, sometimes four or five times, before their fate was finally decided.

Nor can many of these early successes be attributed to Muhammad of Ghor himself. Soon after the second battle of Tarain he returned to Ghazni and, although he paid subsequent visits to India, it was the more pressing affairs of central Asia which commanded his attention. There, at the instigation of the Baghdad caliph, the Ghorids had by 1201 won another empire. Like that of the Ghaznavids it reached west to the Caspian, and as before, the wide-open spaces of Khorasan were soon proving harder to hold than to win. Within a matter of months the Ghorids had been ejected by the Turkic rulers of Khwarasm, or Khiva (on the lower Oxus), who were themselves soon to be ejected by an even more formidable horde, alien and infidel to boot, under Ghenghiz Khan.

Reeling from the heftiest of defeats in north-west Afghanistan, Muhammad found Ghor itself in danger and his lines of communication from

Ghazni to Lahore under threat from a Panjabi hill-tribe known as the Ghakkars. By 1206 he had suppressed this revolt, but during a dark and sultry night a party of vengeful Ghakkars somehow penetrated his camp on the banks of the Jhelum and 'sheathed their daggers in the King's body'. 'Thus fell Sultan Moyiz-ood-Deen Muhammad Ghori after a reign of thirty-two years,' notes Ferishta.

Rarely the work of Muhammad himself, his conquests in India had been principally achieved by his Turkish commanders, amongst whom the most successful was Qutb-ud-din Aybak (Aibak, Eibek). Aybak was also the most trusted and, since Muhammad had no sons, he looked to be his likeliest successor. Not without the bloody elimination of rivals which accompanied almost every succession of a Delhi sultan, Aybak eventually secured his position in India and would no doubt have made as great a sovereign as he had a viceroy. But in 1210, after just four years on the throne, he fell while playing polo, and his pony fell on top of him 'so that the pommel of the saddle entered his chest and killed him'. He is remembered as the founder of what is sometimes called the 'Slave Dynasty' of Delhi, and as the creator of that city's earliest surviving Islamic monuments, the so-called Qutb mosque and minar.

Like the nearly contemporary slave, or Mameluke, rulers of Egypt, the 'Slave Kings' of Delhi were anything but servile. The term simply indicates that, as one-time captives, they had once been slaves. In fact they may even have found this station to their advantage. In a court awash with intrigue and opportunity, India's Turkish conquistadors regarded a slave's loyalty as more dependable than that of their own kin. Purchased, rapidly promoted, eventually freed, and still highly trusted, the erstwhile slave of a royal patron was ideally placed to act as either power-broker or pretender. Aybak would be succeeded, after a brief interlude of confusion, by Shams-ud-din Iltumish, another ex-slave of Turkic extraction. That no stigma attached to either of them is clear from Aybak's recognition as sultan by his titular superior in Ghazni, and from Iltumish's yet grander recognition by the caliph himself.

Their elevated status is equally proclaimed by their monuments. The Qutb mosque in Delhi boasts a tower of victory which doubles as India's, and perhaps Islam's, most massive minar(et). Five balconied tiers tall, many of them fluted and the whole thing heavily tapered, it rears above the now outrageously-priced housing of south Delhi, its red sandstone reminding irreverent neighbours of a brick-built smokestack awaiting demolition. No doubt it made a braver showing until its topmost cupola was toppled by an earthquake in 1803. Down below, the mosque is properly that of Quwwattu'l Islam, the 'Might of Islam'. Such triumphalism is well substantiated by its construction from the reassembled components – pillars, capitals, lintels – of what had previously been twenty-seven Hindu and Jain temples. Evidently the first sultans were more anxious to see their mosque open for worship than to gratify architectural purists. It stands, where the temples probably had, in what was Rai Pithaura, the Chahamana citadel named after Prithviraj. Renamed Lalkot, this 'red fort' area (not to be confused with the Shah Jahan's 'Red Fort' in the Mughal city now known as Old Delhi) was also graced with a 'white palace' whence Iltumish and his successors reigned. The palace has gone, but the ruins of Iltumish's tomb (Aybak was buried in Lahore) stand beside the Qutb mosque, the first in a long and sublime succession of Indo-Islamic mausolea. As if by way of a nod to the later glories of Humayun's tomb and the Taj Mahal, white marble makes its Delhi debut in the interior of Iltumish's resting place.

At Varanasi, according to Ferishta, Muhammad of Ghor and Qutb-ud-din Aybak demolished the idols in a thousand temples and then rededicated these shrines 'to the worship of the true God'. They also carted away treasure by the camel-load – fourteen hundred camel-loads according to one estimate. Then, as indeed now, most of the Varanasi temples may have been small and airless cells unsuited to the Muslim ideal of the whole community worshipping in unison. Temples were designed for a more intimate kind of communion and did not readily lend themselves to congregational assemblies. If piety and plunder necessitated the destruction of idols, temples may more commonly have been dismantled for their already dressed stones. At Ajmer, where Qutb-ud-din Aybak caused another great mosque to be built, the requisite height for the prayer chamber was obtained by sticking as many as three squat temple pillars on top of one another.

The iconoclasm of the early sultans was not always so thorough. In the south-west, despite victory at Mount Abu and the destruction of nearby Anhilwara, the Muslim forces left untouched the magnificently decorated Jain temple of Adinatha at Dilwara on Mount Abu itself. Here white marble, and little else, has been fretted into a lacy membrane of intricate sculpture which, womb-like, lines the entire interior. The temple dates from 1032 and so belongs to that defiant period of construction immediately after Mahmud of Ghazni's raids. It was commissioned by a minister of the Solanki rajput dynasty of Gujarat but is so unobtrusively sited and of such inconspicuous profile that it may simply have been overlooked by the invaders.

Just how disastrous the Muslim conquest was for India's heritage, how heavily Muslim rule bore on the Hindu population, and how determinedly it was resisted are contentious subjects. 'An analysis of the military operations of the period reveals the fact that never once were the Turkish armies called upon to deal with a hostile population,' insists an eminent Muslim historian; 'we do not come across a single revolt of the Hindu *masses* as such.'[9] Yet, following Tod's lead, a no less eminent Hindu authority writes of 'ceaseless resistance offered with relentless heroism' as warriors, 'boys in their teens', 'men with one foot in the grave' and 'women in thousands' fought and died 'to break the volume and momentum of the onrushing tide of invasion'.[10] Curiously neither makes mention of what sounds like a devastating revolt in Awadh (or 'Oudh' in Uttar Pradesh) of c1220 during which, according to a contemporary, '120,000 Muslims received martyrdom at the hands and sword of the accursed Bartuh'.[11] It is clear that 'Bartuh' was a Hindu but his identity is otherwise uncertain. As with other mysterious 'heroes of the resistance', like the Ghakkars of the Panjab or the Mhers and Mewatis of Rajasthan, it would seem that some of the most determined opposition came from tribal, or at least non-rajput, peoples, about whose existence the Hindu dynastic records, and Tod, are silent.

Given that the Muslim conquest of India took several centuries, all generalisations must be suspect. The well-authenticated oppression of Muhammad bin Tughluq in the mid-fourteenth century cannot simply be presumed of his predecessors or his successors. Similarly a Hindu inscription of c1280 which lauds the security and bounty enjoyed under the rule of Sultan Balban should not be taken as a blanket endorsement of firm Islamic government. Not all temples were destroyed, although many were. The *jizya* tax on non-Muslims was not levied on brahmans until the reign of Feroz Shah Tughluq (1351–88),[12] and may never have been very effectively collected. Idolatry was condemned yet Hindus were not prevented from practising their religion. And since the records often make no clear distinction between military and civilian casualties, it is hard to assess the extent of gratuitous violence.

Many would argue that the sultans, like other Indian dynasts, were more interested in power and plunder than in religion. Muslim chroniclers chose to portray the occupation of northern India as a religious offensive and to paint its principals as religious heroes; 'but such a view cannot stand the test of historical scrutiny'.[13] The more informative chroniclers in fact say surprisingly little about Muslim–Hindu relations. They are much more revealing about the power struggles amongst the conquistadors themselves; indeed these feuds, together with the chaos induced by the Mongol invasions, look to have slowed the pace of conquest quite as much as any resurgence of Hindu resistance. According to one authority the entire his-

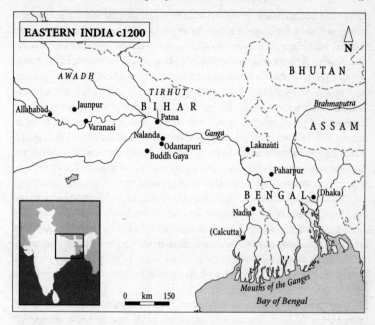

EASTERN INDIA c1200

tory of the ruling Turkish elite 'can be summed up in these words; *they united to destroy their enemies and disunited to destroy themselves*'.[14]

During the twenty-six years of his reign Iltumish was almost continuously in the field, yet beyond raids into Malwa he brought little new territory within the Muslim ambit and was as often engaged against fellow Muslims as against Indian 'idolaters'. In the west, Sind and the Panjab were in constant turmoil as Ghenghiz Khan neared and then crossed the Indus in 1222. The turmoil was caused not just by the Mongols themselves but by the tide of armies, princes, scholars and artisans from all over Turkestan, Khorasan and Afghanistan whom the Mongol invaders rolled before them. Figures are not available but it seems probable that far more Muslims entered India as refugees from the Mongol invasions than as warriors in the Ghaznavid and Ghorid armies combined.

East of Delhi Iltumish had to reconquer much of what is now Uttar Pradesh and then face Muslim rivals in Bihar and Bengal. These were the Khaljis or Khiljis, originally tribal neighbours of the Ghorids in central Afghanistan, who had followed Muhammad of Ghor to India. Muhammad Bakhtiyar, the founder of Khalji rule, had been denied lucrative office in both Ghazni and Delhi before eventually securing what was then a frontier fief (*iqta*) near Varanasi. Thence he organised freelance raids into Bihar, one of which was rewarded with the unexpectedly easy capture of what the Khaljis thought was a fortified city. Here the inhabitants, all of whom seemed to have shaven heads, were indeed put to death and great plunder was made. Amongst the spoils were whole libraries of books but, since all the people had been killed, no one could tell what the books were about. Further investigation, however, clarified the situation. According to Min-haju-s Siraj, a distinguished scholar who after being flushed out of Afghani-stan by the Mongols spent two years with the Khaljis, 'it was then discovered that the whole fort and city was a place of study';[15] it was in fact the famous Buddhist monastery-cum-university of Odantapuri.

Such fearless feats of arms won the applause of Qutb-ud-din Aybak and brought followers flocking to the Khalji standard. Bakhtiyar had then ventured through south Bihar and, in another daring escapade, captured Nadia, the capital of the Senas, which dynasty had succeeded that of the Buddhist Palas as the most important in Bengal. With just eighteen fol-lowers Bakhtiyar is supposed to have gained entrance to the Sena palace and surprised King Lakshmanasena in the middle of lunch. The Senas' other capital of Lakhnauti, otherwise Gaur on what is now the Indo–Bangladesh frontier, was also taken. With Lakhnauti as his headquarters, Bakhtiyar continued east into Assam and then 'Tibet' – which was probably not the country now so designated but perhaps Bhutan. How-soever, the Himalayas were certainly too physically challenging for the Khalji forces, most of whom perished in a swollen river. Bakhtiyar made it back to the plains but, a broken man, he either died or was killed soon after.

This was in 1205, and from then onwards the governorship of Bengal and Bihar had been bitterly contested by various Khaljis who acknowledged Delhi's supremacy only on the rare occasions when the sultan's support was deemed personally advantageous. Iltumish endeavoured to rectify the situation by invading Bengal in 1225. Its incumbent Khalji was obliged 'to place the yoke of servitude on the neck of submission' and yield a hefty tribute; then he reverted to his bad old ways. A year later the sultan sent his son Nasir-ud-din to repeat the treatment. This time the Khaljis were routed, their ruler killed and their capital occupied; the problem looked to be solved. But such calculations took no account of Bengal's notorious climate. Nasir-ud-din suddenly sickened and died. Again Bengal, that 'hell full of good things' as the Mughals would call it, slipped the leash and again (in 1229) Iltumish had to invade. His settlement barely lasted until his death, whereupon Bengal, Bihar and sometimes Awadh became again effectively independent. Although over the succeeding century this situation was occasionally threatened and briefly reversed, 'between 1338 and 1538, for long two hundred years, Bengal remained independent without interruption.'[16]

Delhi's chances of reasserting its authority there or anywhere else declined sharply after Iltumish. Before dying of natural causes, a feat which even contemporary writers found worthy of special note, Iltumish had wavered between nominating as his successor a remaining but ineffectual son and an inspirational but gender-handicapped daughter. The son, though liked, had his own handicaps, including a vindictive and detested mother and a predilection to 'licentiousness and debauchery'. Mother and son duly indulged their respective passions during a seven-month period. It barely qualified as a reign, and they were both then toppled by the daughter, the redoubtable Raziya.

> Sultan Raziya was a great monarch. She was wise, just and generous, a benefactor to her kingdom, a dispenser of justice, the protector of her subjects, and the leader of her armies. She was endowed with all the qualities befitting a king, but she was not born of the right sex, and so in the estimation of men all these virtues were worthless. (May God have mercy on her!)[17]

Nevertheless, continued Minhaju-s Siraj, 'the country under Sultan Raziya enjoyed peace and the power of the state was manifest'; even Bengal made a grudging submission. This was short-lived, and the calm merely presaged a storm. Raziya's reign lasted barely four years (1236–40). Perhaps her decision to dispense with the veil and, in mannish garb of coat and cap, to 'show herself amongst the people' was unnecessarily provocative to Muslim sensitivities. So too may have been the appointment as 'personal attendant to her majesty' of Jamal-ud-din Yakut, an 'Abyssinian' who was probably once a slave and very definitely an African. A liaison so conspicuous duly brought unfavourable comment from the historian Isami. Declaring that a woman's place was 'at her spinning wheel [*charkha*]' and that high office would only derange her, he insisted that Raziya should have made 'cotton her companion and grief her wine-cup'.

These lines, written in 1350, are of additional interest in that, according to Irfan Habib, India's most distinguished economic historian, they contain 'the earliest reference to the spinning wheel so far traced in India'. Since the device is known in Iran from a prior period, 'the inference is almost inescapable that the spinning wheel came to India with the Muslims'.[18] So

THE DELHI SULTANATES (1) The 'Slave Dynasty' 1206–90

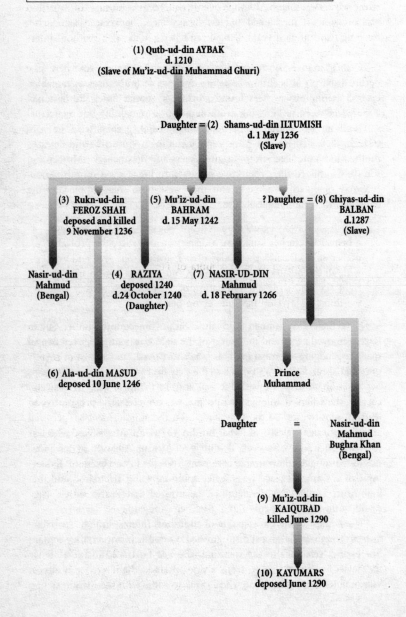

(1) Qutb-ud-din AYBAK
d. 1210
(Slave of Mu'iz-ud-din Muhammad Ghuri)

Daughter = **(2) Shams-ud-din ILTUMISH**
d. 1 May 1236
(Slave)

(3) Rukn-ud-din FEROZ SHAH
deposed and killed
9 November 1236

(5) Mu'iz-ud-din BAHRAM
d. 15 May 1242

? Daughter = **(8) Ghiyas-ud-din BALBAN**
d. 1287
(Slave)

Nasir-ud-din
Mahmud
(Bengal)

(4) RAZIYA
deposed 1240
d. 24 October 1240
(Daughter)

(7) NASIR-UD-DIN
Mahmud
d. 18 February 1266

(6) Ala-ud-din MASUD
deposed 10 June 1246

Prince
Muhammad

Daughter = Nasir-ud-din
Mahmud
Bughra Khan
(Bengal)

(9) Mu'iz-ud-din KAIQUBAD
killed June 1290

(10) KAYUMARS
deposed June 1290

did the paper on which Isami penned his patronising lines, palm leaves having previously served as a somewhat friable writing surface. Both introductions were of incalculable value. Governance and taxation would be expedited, and literature, scholarship and the graphic arts revolutionised by the availability of a uniform writing material which could be readily filed and bound. In fact it became so common that by the mid-fifteenth century Delhi's confectioners were already wrapping their sticky *halwa* in recycled writing paper, a practice which would continue until the triumph of the polythene bag in the late twentieth century.

Likewise, the *charkha* greatly boosted the production of yarn and no doubt provided employment for many more weavers. High-quality cotton textiles had long been an important export; but thanks to the spinning wheel and other innovations, India's cottage-based cotton industry would in time become a barometer of national self-esteem. In adopting the *charkha* as the symbol of Indian independence, Mahatma Gandhi and the Congress Party were not, however, courting Muslim votes. The irony of predominantly Hindu India sporting a national icon of Islamic provenance went unnoticed.

Raziya was elbowed aside by a junta of Turkish, and of course male, chauvinists. While bravely dashing across the Panjab in high summer to douse a revolt at Bhatinda, she was isolated by the conspirators, her Abyssinian friend was killed, and she ended a prisoner in the fort she had come to redeem. There she managed to win the backing and affection of one of the conspirators. They were married and, gathering further support, marched on Delhi. Perhaps if the conduct of their forces had been left to the experienced Raziya, they might have prevailed. But, as a wife, she deferred to her husband and they were heavily defeated. Next day, while fleeing the battlefield, the newlyweds 'fell into the hands of Hindus and were killed'.

Known as 'The Forty' or 'The Family of Forty', the Turkish military oligarchs who now dominated Delhi affairs intrigued both against one another and against a more amorphous grouping composed of Indian converts to Islam and eminent refugees from Afghanistan and beyond. At the whim of these cut-throat godfathers young and ineffectual sultans were casually summoned and quickly despatched, usually to the hereafter.

Raziya's demise had been followed almost immediately by another Mongol eruption. In 1241 the invaders sacked Lahore, whose ruins were then picked over by the predatory Ghakkars. Unlike Delhi, Lahore thus lost all trace of its Ghaznavid and Ghorid past and has no monuments prior to those of the Mughals. That the Mongols did not then take advantage of Delhi's strife-torn predicament is largely thanks to Ghiyas-ud-din Balban, another Turkish slave who, while loyally dictating policy for the ineffectual Sultan Nasir-ud-din, was briefly disgraced but, eventually and allegedly, poisoned the sultan to secure his own succession.

During forty years as the effective (1246–65) and then actual (1265–87) ruler, the stern and merciless Balban held the Mongols at bay with a skilful mixture of force and diplomacy. Ghenghiz Khan was now dead, but his successors readily championed the cause of one of Sultan Nasir-ud-din's brothers plus other claimants to the Delhi throne; they frequently intervened in the tortuous affairs of Sind; and they advanced to the Beas river in the Panjab. This necessitated the diversion of the sultanate's best troops and most reliable commanders to patrolling the new frontier. 'If this anxiety . . . as guardian and protector of Mussulmans, were removed,' Balban is supposed to have said, 'I would not stay one day in my capital but would lead forth my army to capture treasures and valuables, elephants and horses, and would never allow the *Rais* and *Ranas* [i.e. the rajputs and other Hindus] to repose in quiet at a distance.'[19] While the Mongols threatened the very existence of the sultanate, even plundering raids into Hindu India, let alone conquests, were in abeyance.

Several Mongol incursions were indeed frustrated, but in 1260 Balban fêted an embassy from Hulagu, grandson of Ghenghiz Khan. Despite Balban's boast that up to fifteen ex-rulers of Turkestan, Khorasan, Iran and Iraq were enjoying asylum in Delhi, some sort of working relationship seems to have been established between the two neighbours. Balban could now concentrate on shoring up the status of the sultanate and securing his existing possessions. Perhaps influenced by all those royal refugees from the north-west, he introduced into his court an elaborate system of precedence and protocol modelled on Persian practice. The sultan being 'the shadow of God' and his vice-regent on earth, it was fitting that he be honoured as such. With drawn swords fearsome retainers now constantly attended the royal presence. Those who would approach the throne must abase themselves, performing *zaminbos* ('kissing the ground') and *paibos* ('kissing the [royal] feet') as they advanced. Any infringement of this rigid decorum brought instant and bloody punishment.

With an equally heavy hand, Balban's forces put down insurrections in the Ganga-Jamuna Doab and cleared the region round Delhi of both the marauding Mewatis and the scrub jungle in which they found sanctuary. A major expedition into Bengal, whose governor was again in revolt, took three years and was distinguished by more ferocious reprisals. But on the sultan's return, his most capable son and preferred successor was killed in a skirmish with the Mongols. Balban, now said to have been in his eighties, never recovered from this blow. When not presiding, grim-faced, over his terrified courtiers, he is said to have spent his nights howling with grief for the 'martyr-prince'. In 1287 death brought relief to the tortured sultan. Not, however, to his kingdom, which plunged into another bloodstained succession crisis.

A grandson, who quickly replaced the one Balban had nominated as his successor, celebrated his succession by renouncing the austerities of the previous reign and embarking on a riot of indulgence. The young sultan, says Ferishta, 'delighted in love and in the soft society of silver-bodied damsels with musky tresses'. Delhi welcomed the change; 'every shade was filled with ladies of pleasure and every street rung with music and mirth.'[20] But such was the young sultan's abandon, such the heavy inebriants and the musky tresses, that within three years the handsome and affable prince was reduced to a gibbering wreck. Meanwhile Balban's trusty lieutenants had been eliminated by the new sultan's self-appointed keeper, an evil genius who was himself then poisoned by jealous opponents. 'What little order had been maintained in the government was now entirely lost,' according to Ziau-ud-din Barani, the author of an important history, who was a boy about Delhi at the time. The still young but now paralysed and imbecilic sultan was replaced by his son, a three-year-old toddler. In his name cradle-snatching rivals continued to manoeuvre and fight for office.

The dénouement of this 1290 crisis saw the remnants of the Turkish 'Forty' outwitted by rivals belonging to the same Khalji tribe who had earlier conquered Bihar and Bengal. Despatching two sultans in quick succession – both the paralytic father and his wretched child – the Khaljis ended the so-called 'Slave dynasty' and proclaimed one of their seniors, Jalal-ud-din Feroz Khalji, as the new sultan. A kicking toddler was thus replaced by a grey-bearded patriarch as the Khalji dynasty began its thirty-year tenure of the throne of Delhi.

Jalal-ud-din Feroz, sometimes called Feroz Shah I, was an unlikely instrument of revolution. A Turk, though not exactly a young one, he also displayed a clemency unheard of in the annals of the sultanate. It even won him a certain popularity. Conciliating rivals and forgiving enemies, he 'weaned the citizens of Delhi from their attachment to the old family', says Ferishta. Such policies melted even Mongol hearts. The trickle of defectors from the Mongol khanates who were embracing Islam and trans-ferring their loyalties to the sultanate briefly became a flood. But such leniency also severely tested the loyalties of his Khalji supporters and offered much encouragement to potential opponents. Amongst the latter was the

THE DELHI SULTANATES (2) The Khalji Dynasty 1290–1320

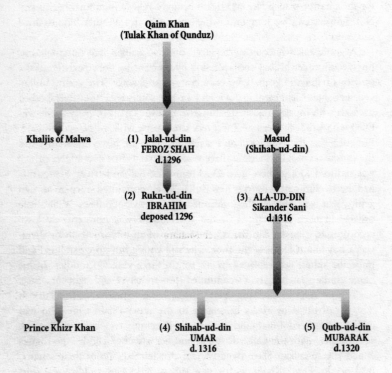

Qaim Khan
(Tulak Khan of Qunduz)

Khaljis of Malwa

(1) Jalal-ud-din
FEROZ SHAH
d.1296

Masud
(Shihab-ud-din)

(2) Rukn-ud-din
IBRAHIM
deposed 1296

(3) ALA-UD-DIN
Sikander Sani
d.1316

Prince Khizr Khan

(4) Shihab-ud-din
UMAR
d.1316

(5) Qutb-ud-din
MUBARAK
d.1320

sultan's nephew, who was also his son-in-law and a keen student of the earlier Khalji campaigns in Bengal.

This man was Ala-ud-din Khalji, and the lesson he drew from his kinsmen's experiences in Bengal was that plunder and conquests made at the expense of Hindu India could significantly enhance his challenge for the sultanate. After a lull of nearly a century during which the tide of 'Muslim conquest' in India had if anything receded, another giant surge was about to carry it deep into the peninsula.

ALADDIN'S CAVE

By now, the end of the thirteenth century, the still-Hindu Deccan and south had witnessed further dynastic change. Yet the pattern of struggle, modelled on the symmetry of the *mandala* and consummated in the compass-boxing *digvijaya*, remained the same. So too does our limited perception of it. Unenlivened by the gossipy narratives beloved of Muslim writers, the contemporary history of Hindu India has still to be laboriously extrapolated from the sterile phrasing and optimistic listings favoured by royal panegyrists and fortuitously preserved in a few literary compositions and numerous stone and copper-plate inscriptions. The formality of such sources drains their content of vitality and, without the labours lavished by the likes of Tod on the rajputs, the history of the Deccan is liable to appear as arid and confusing as its geography.

Lest this should prove to be the case, it must suffice to note that in the western Deccan the Western Chalukyas, those doughty opponents of the great Cholas of Tanjore, had succumbed, like their Rashtrakuta predecessors, to the rising power of two erstwhile feudatories, one of which now dominated Karnataka and the other Maharashtra. As Yadavas, both these new dynasties claimed descent from the Vedic Yadu lineage, once of Mathura and of Dwarka in Saurashtra. They were not 'Rajpoots' in the geographically-specific sense used by Tod, and not certainly even *ksatriya*, a caste that is practically unknown in peninsular India. Yet as befitted a lineage that could claim Lord Krishna as a Yadava, they too revered the martial ethic.

Of these two Yadava dynasties, the Hoysalas of Halebid are the more epigraphically articulate. Originally a hill-people from the Western Ghats just north of Coorg, they had carved out a small kingdom around Belur (two hundred kilometres west of modern Bangalore in southern Karnataka) in the tenth century. In the eleventh, as 'the rod in the right hand of the Chalukya king', Hoysala forces had served with distinction against both the Chola kings Rajaraja and Rajendra and against King Bhoj's Paramara successor in Malwa. More territory had been acquired, more scholars and adventurers attracted to the Hoysala court and, with the establishment of a new capital at Dorasamudra (now Halebid), twelve kilometres from Belur, the usual clustering of dynastic sites was under way. 'Striking hostile princes in a brilliant way as if they were balls in a game,' says an eleventh-century panegyrist (who must by now have been reborn as a cricket commentator), 'that famous [King] Vinayaditya ruled like Indra from the west as far as Talakad, until the circle of the Earth cried out "Well done, Sir!" in approval.'[21]

Imperial ambitions had first been entertained by the Hoysalas in the early twelfth century when the spectacularly ornate temples of Chenna Kesava at Belur and of Hoysalesvara at Dorasamudra-Halebid were designed to celebrate it. This bid for supremacy throughout Karnataka proved premature, but towards the end of the century, at about the same time as Prithviraj was succumbing to Muhammad of Ghor at Tarain, the Hoysalas successfully exploited a do-or-die struggle between the Western Chalukyas and the invading Kalachuris of Madhya Pradesh. Ballala II, the greatest of the Hoysala kings, thus added to his ancestral domains most of northern Karnataka and, by exploiting a similar conflict between the Chola and Pandya rulers in the Tamil country, also emerged with an important slice of the Kaveri plain around Srirangam (Trichy). A new chronological era was adopted by Ballala's royal bards, and so were the usual imperial titles, plus many besides. Gloriously if briefly the Hoysalas were paramount throughout most of the Kannada-speaking Deccan, and could pose as arbiters in the lusher lands below the Eastern Ghats.

There, in the Tamil country, their main rivals were the Pandyas of Madurai who in the 1250s under the great Sundara Pandya overthrew the Cholas and blunted the Hoysala thrust. The Pandyas also struck north deep into the Telugu-speaking Andhra country, where an important dynasty called the Kakatiyas had replaced the Eastern Chalukyas of Vengi. Thus it was the Pandyas from Madurai, the Hoysalas of Karnataka and these Kakatiyas of Warangal (their capital, near the later Hyderabad), together with their respective feudatories, who controlled most of the south when, as the thirteenth century drew to a close, Ala-ud-din Khalji began to formulate his plans.

North of the Hoysalas, and barring any access to the south via the western Deccan, there ruled those other beneficiaries of the Chalukyan decline who also claimed Yadava descent. Indeed they are often referred to as the 'Yadavas of Devagiri'. Since Maharashtra was their homeland they are also described as Marathas, although the correct name of the dynasty is Seuna, or Sevuna. These Seunas, then, once feudatories of the Rashtrakutas and then of the Chalukyas, had taken the latter's capital of Kalyana in c1190. Although boxed in on all sides – by the Hoysalas to the south, the Kakatiyas to the east, the Paramara rajputs of Malwa in the north and the Solanki rajputs of Gujarat in the west – they had yet carved out a substantial kingdom embracing most of what is now the state of Maharashtra. Very roughly, the Seuna kingdom therefore corresponded to the territory of the ancient Shatavahanas and the early Rashtrakutas.

Beset by so many aggressive neighbours, the Seunas had taken the

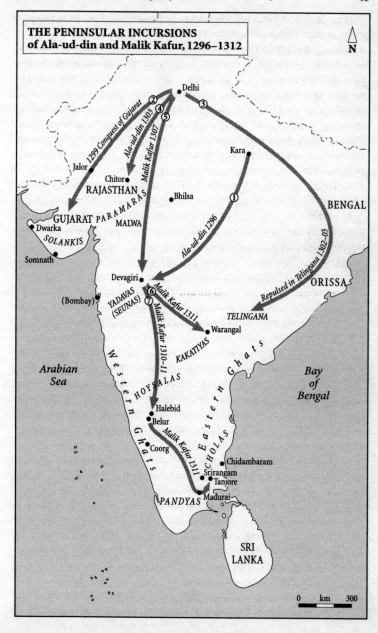

**THE PENINSULAR INCURSIONS
of Ala-ud-din and Malik Kafur, 1296–1312**

N

Delhi

② ④
⑤

③

1299 Conquest of Gujarat

Ala-ud-din 1303

Malik Kafur 1307

Kara

Jalor

Chitor

RAJASTHAN

Bhilsa

BENGAL

PARAMARAS

①

GUJARAT

Dwarka

MALWA

SOLANKIS

Somnath

Ala-ud-din 1296

Devagiri

ORISSA

(Bombay)

**YADAVAS
(SEUNAS)**

⑥ Malik Kafur 1311

⑦

Repulsed in Telingana 1302–03

TELINGANA

Warangal

Malik Kafur 1310–11

KAKATIYAS

*Arabian
Sea*

Western Ghats

HOYSALAS

*Bay
of
Bengal*

Halebid

Belur

Eastern Ghats

Coorg

Malik Kafur 1311

CHOLAS

Chidambaram

Srirangam

Tanjore

PANDYAS

Madurai

**SRI
LANKA**

0   km   300

sensible precaution of locating their capital at the base of the most impregnable citadel in western India. A fang of rock, mostly bare of vegetation, vertiginous, accessible only by a labyrinth of caves and shafts, and further strengthened by glowering fortifications plus a Stygian moat, the citadel rises three hundred metres above the plains at a place called Devagiri (Deogir), later Daulatabad, between the rock-city of Ellora and the garden-city of Aurangabad. Here the considerable fortune amassed by the Seunas from revenue, raiding and trade seemed secure. From his eyrie King Rama-chandra could survey the core of his kingdom on the upper Godavari river safe in the knowledge that, however his armies fared, his person and possessions were unlikely to be jeopardised.

In 1296 a dry-season offensive against the Hoysalas in Karnataka was being conducted by his son. Devagiri was therefore sparsely defended. But Rama-chandra, nearing the end of a successful reign that had already lasted twenty-five years, was not unduly anxious. A few Muslim troops were already serving as mercenaries in the Deccan. The rigidity of Islam was familiar from centuries of contact, and the aggressive forays of the Delhi sultans north of the Narmada must long have been matter for comment. Three years previously the young Ala-ud-din Khalji had led a plundering expedition from his base at Kara, near Allahabad, and pushed as far south as Bhilsa, near Bhopal in Madhya Pradesh. High-value booty had been secured from this ancient capital and from the neighbouring Buddhist centre of Sanchi. But Bhilsa was not halfway from the Ganga to the Godavari; there were still over three hundred kilometres of the ruggedest country between it and Devagiri. To Rama-chandra such barely authorised escapades by some unknown nephew of the remote and unusually pacific Feroz Shah I were scarcely cause for alarm. He was therefore taken completely by surprise when in the spring of 1296 Ala-ud-din suddenly materialised on his precipitous doorstep.

In the event, Rama-chandra was not the only one surprised. Ala-ud-din's eruption into the Deccan had been kept secret even from his uncle the sultan. In fact, surprising the latter was the higher priority; for as would soon appear, the real target was not Devagiri but Delhi. Ala-ud-din was acting without authority and with comparatively few troops. From Kara via Bhilsa he had stumbled on a secluded route to the rich kingdoms of the Deccan which avoided the still-defiant rajputs of Rajasthan and Malwa. But he needed to complete his mission before it was discovered and countermanded. Speed of movement was therefore essential; he had avoided towns, camping in the jungle and following previously reconnoitred routes. On what was essentially a quest for wealth and prestige, all that mattered was securing a quick submission plus a monumental ransom from the luckless Rama-chandra.

The Khalji's troops therefore sacked and plundered the town of Devagiri as soon as they reached it. Rama-chandra retired to his citadel and, to the invaders' distress, looked capable of holding out indefinitely. But after barely a week's defiance it was found that provisions within the citadel were already running low. With almost indecent haste the adversaries then concluded a pact which even the unexpected return of the Seuna army failed to compromise. Thus, after days rather than weeks, Ala-ud-din and Rama-chandra parted on the best of terms, the invader with a Seuna bride and treasure beyond his wildest dreams, and the invaded with his kingdom intact, his army undefeated, his beliefs uncompromised, and a powerful new *Turuska* ally.

As planned, news of Ala-ud-din's remarkable achievement reached the ears of his uncle in Delhi ahead of the reports about his original disobedience. All, if not forgiven, was now beyond reprehension. Ala-ud-din had rediscovered the predatory purpose behind Turkish rule in India; he had established himself as a resourceful and fortunate general; and he had acquired sufficient treasure, plus the possibility of more where that came from, to attract powerful support. Clearly he needed careful handling. The sultan therefore extended his congratulations and, ignoring advice to ambush his ambitious nephew *en route*, bade him return to Delhi with his plunder. In fact Ala-ud-din headed for the safety of his own fief at Kara on the Ganga. There he eventually inveigled his uncle into paying him a visit. Only a sultan as guileless as the aged Feroz would have accepted such an invitation and have then sailed downriver to the meeting with only a few unarmed attendants and no hope of escape. Needless to say, he had barely stepped ashore when he was cut down. 'While the head of the murdered sovereign was yet dripping with blood, the ferocious conspirators brought the royal canopy and elevated it over the head of Ala-ud-din.'[22]

The usurper then made his way to Delhi, gathering supporters as he went by showering the roadsides with coins fired as grapeshot from a specially-designed *manjanik*. His fellow conspirators were quickly disposed of; such men were obviously not to be trusted. But during a reign of twenty years (1296–1316) Ala-ud-din would not otherwise disappoint the high expectations he had aroused amongst the sultanate's supporters. Although an illiterate of unremarkable physique and unendearing presence, he combined the scruple-free instincts essential to survival with a paternal and even innovative concern for the welfare of his kingdom. Ala-ud-din's memory would transcend the eventful years of his reign and become something of a benchmark for later rulers. Much the most successful as well as the most unforgiving of the Delhi sultans, it was he who now directed the victorious progress of Turkish arms throughout India.

Conquest to any lasting purpose it was not. With the exception of Gujarat and parts of Rajasthan and Malwa, very little new territory was brought under direct Khalji rule. No pan-Indian empire under a Turkish or an Islamic dispensation resulted. Mass conversions were almost unknown. Existing rulers were mostly reinstated and, despite promptly acknowledging Delhi's suzerainty, they rarely fulfilled their tributary obligations unless compelled to do so by the threat of further armed intervention. Ala-ud-din's victories certainly conjured up amongst his supporters a vision of Islamic dominion throughout India. Perhaps they also reminded his Hindu subjects of those indigenous traditions of universal sovereignty associated with the concept of the *cakravartin*. But it would be another two hundred years before these ideals were fused into an effective reality; and the credit would then belong neither to the Turkish Khaljis nor their Afghan successors, but to the descendants of those hordes who continued to threaten the very existence of the Delhi sultanate and whom, though known to Europe as 'Mongols', contemporary Persian and Indian sources always called 'Mughals'.

From 1297 to 1303 Ala-ud-din faced almost annual Mongol onslaughts. Delhi itself was twice surrounded, the Doab was ravaged and what is now Pakistan suffered continual Mongol occupations. Whether even the stern Balban could have held the enemy at bay must be doubtful. But after a crushing victory in early 1300 and numerous other lesser triumphs, Ala-ud-din not only stemmed the tide but reversed it. Sind and the Panjab were regained and by the end of his reign Khalji forces were raiding Ghazni, Kabul and Kandahar in Afghanistan. It was by no means the end of the 'Mughal' threat. But Ala-ud-din's successes served as a temporary deterrent and provided a convincing demonstration of the military effectiveness of manoeuvrable Turkish cavalry in combination with a solid Indian elephant-phalanx.

Further demonstrations of military might were witnessed in Gujarat, Rajasthan, Malwa, the Deccan and even the extreme south. Although glossed over in contemporary accounts, there were also setbacks, most notably in Bengal and initially in Andhra. It is clear, too, that Tod's rajputs gave a good account of themselves, with the great hill-forts of Ranthambhor, Jalor and Chitor withstanding long sieges, occasioning heavy casualties, and inspiring posterity with their legendary *jauhars*. These *hara-kiri* rituals had been practised by other doughty patriots ever since Sind was first invaded in the eighth century, but the rajputs of Rajasthan now made them peculiarly their own. When all was lost, when the last scrap of food had been eaten, the last arrow fired, the last water-skin emptied, a pyre was lit and, as the womenfolk hurled themselves into the flames, the men rode out in a still brighter blaze of glory to kill until they were killed. Fanaticism was not an exclusively Islamic prerogative. The Khalji forces marvelled that principalities so agriculturally disadvantaged and forts so poorly endowed with treasure should occasion such passionate resistance.

Much less trouble and infinitely more rewarding were the conquests of Gujarat and then Malwa, from where the poet-king Bhoj's Paramara successors were finally removed. Gujarat, besides being extremely fertile and renowned for both its textiles and its cattle, was further enriched by the maritime trade of Cambay, which had now superseded Broach as north India's main port on the Arabian Sea. Prodigious spoils resulted from this campaign of 1298, including more gold and precious stones from the rebuilt, and now re-demolished, temple of Somnath; its replacement *lingam* was again hammered into fragments and reserved for trampling by the feet of the faithful, this time in Delhi. Amongst Cambay's seized assets the most prized was a Hindu captive who would add particular lustre to the Khalji sultanate. A eunuch and a slave, he quickly espoused Islam but retained the nickname 'Thousand-dinar Kafur', presumably a reference to his original valuation. 'His beauty,' says Barani, 'captivated Ala-ud-din' who thereafter trusted him implicitly and appointed him a *Malik-naib*, or senior commander.[23]

The king of Gujarat, meanwhile, had found sanctuary in the fortress of Devagiri where Rama-chandra's son, if not Rama-chandra himself, had been having second thoughts about the Seuna–Khalji alliance. In 1307, with the arrears of Seuna tribute mounting, Ala-ud-din sent an army to chastise the son and reoccupy the kingdom. Commanded by none other than 'Thousand-dinar Kafur' it quickly routed the Seuna forces and again ransacked the capital. Sangama, the Seuna heir, fled. Rama-chandra, however, was taken to Delhi and was there much fêted by the sultan, who reinstated him on his throne and showered him with favours in an unusually creditable display of magnanimity. As a result the Seuna king 'not only stood firm in his loyalty to the sultan but rendered valuable assistance to the officers whom he sent to subdue the Hindu kingdoms of the south'.[24]

Pre-eminent amongst these officers was again the inspirational *Malik-naib* Kafur. In 1309 he headed south for the second time and from Devagiri mounted an assault on the Kakatiyas of Andhra. About eighteen years earlier Marco Polo, while visiting Tamil Nadu by sea from China, had noted the rich diamond finds made in the Andhra country which, he reported, was then ruled by a formidable queen of Seuna birth. She had lost her Kakatiya husband and was acting as regent for her grandson. The grandson was Pratapa-rudra who, coming of age, had since succeeded to the Kakatiya throne, and now withdrew within the fortifications of Warangal as Malik Kafur approached. The siege proved lengthy but Pratapa-rudra eventually succumbed and was relieved of horses, elephants and the usual trunkloads of treasure before being reinstated on the promise of an annual tribute.

Next year Kafur was back in the Deccan, and from Devagiri he this time continued south. The Seunas, relishing the prospect of their Hoysala rivals being the next to be humbled, provided supplies, guides and covering forces. With the distant outline of the Western Ghats tracking his progress, Kafur pressed on south into the interminable Deccan horizon. Halebid, nestling amongst greener pastures, was reached and duly besieged. But Ballala III, the Hoysala king, then opted for terms under which he was to perform much the same escort service in respect of Kafur's onward march into the Pandya country. It did not mean that Halebid escaped the customary demands for treasure and elephants, but it did mean that Kafur's troops had traversed the entire Deccan without once having had to fight a battle.

Directed by Kafur, himself born a Hindu under rajput rule, 'the Muslim conquest of the south' was partaking more of the *digvijaya* than the *jihad*. Claims by Ferishta and others that Malik Kafur built a mosque in Halebid and established Islam throughout Karnataka are deemed a wishful fabrication. 'Though he served a master who bore the name of Ala-ud-din [i.e. Aladdin] he could not have worked, without the aid of the wonderful lamp, such miracles during a brief stay of less than two weeks.'[25]

From Halebid the Khalji forces, aided by the Hoysalas, descended into the Tamil country through elysian vales dotted with teak trees, their fallen leaves crackling underfoot like crisp papadums. They spent only a month amongst the rice fields of Tamil Nadu. Again no battles are recorded and the time seems to have been mainly spent in a fruitless pursuit of the elusive Pandyan ruler. It did, though, suffice to strip the temple cities of Madurai, Srirangam and Chidambaram of their solid-gold idols, to empty their gold-filled temple cavities, and to yield much other portable wealth. Such being the whole point of the exercise, 'Thousand-dinar Kafur' turned for home heavily laden and well satisfied.

Barani, who witnessed his ecstatic reception in Delhi, puts the campaign's haul at 612 elephants, twenty thousand horses, ninety-six thousand *man* of gold and countless boxes of jewels and pearls. Although modern equivalencies are notoriously difficult to work out, ninety-six thousand *man* is said to correspond to 241 tonnes.[26] 'The old inhabitants of Delhi remarked that so much gold had never before been brought into Delhi. No one could remember anything like it, nor was there anything like it recorded in history.'[27]

Yet in a thoughtful retrospect of Ala-ud-din's reign, Ziau-ud-din Barani would place 'constant succession of victories' no higher than second in his list of the sultan's most notable achievements. 'Rolling back the Mughals' came third, 'repairing mosques' eighth, while 'rooting out idolatry' or 'spreading the true religion' are not mentioned at all. The sultan was no Islamic bigot: 'there is no instance to show that Ala-ud-din oppressed some people simply because they were Hindus and favoured others just because they were Muslims.'[28] Indeed, if one may judge by his reported interest in founding a new religion centred on his own illustrious person, his faith was decidedly unorthodox. He did extend Aybak's Quwwat-ul-Islam mosque in Delhi, adding the great Alai Darwaza (Ala-ud-din's Gateway). He also planned a prodigious minaret which, if completed, would have dwarfed that of the Qutb. In fact it never rose much above its current stump height, and should be seen as the aberration of a sultan occasionally deluded by his own success. Like his assumption of the title 'The Second Alexander' on his coinage, it was a case of the megalomaniac getting the better of the Muslim.

In Barani's listing, the first and greatest of Ala-ud-din's achievements was, somewhat surprisingly, 'cheapness of grain, clothes and the necessaries of life'. Writing in an old age embittered by extreme poverty, Barani paid particular attention to such matters. His narrative, though coloured by an old-timer's recollection of palmier days, thus provides the first detailed account of the management of an Indian economy. From it we learn of Ala-ud-din's cancellation of all land grants and revenue assignments made by his predecessors and of his prohibition of the sale and consumption of alcohol. These measures affected mainly Muslim courtiers and were designed to cow dissent and quell conspiracy. The more draconian ordinances which followed – and which were designed to finance the vast armies required for his Mongol and Deccan campaigns, to eliminate profiteering and reduce the grievances of the Delhi populace – affected Hindus more directly. It is doubtful whether they were ever applied beyond the city of Delhi and its immediate environs. On the other hand, by concentrating on such a manageable entity, they could be enforced to dramatic effect.

Reasoning, apparently, that despite the expected yield of his 'Aladdin's cave' in the south, new troops could not be as handsomely paid nor as well equipped as rising costs and unflinching loyalty demanded, the sultan had hit on the idea of lowering prices. That meant, first and foremost, controlling the grain market. All foodgrains were listed, their prices duly fixed, and markets carefully and ruthlessly supervised. To guard against fluctuations in supply, the yield of the royal lands (*khalsa*) was stockpiled in city granaries, all transport was so heavily regulated as to be effectively nationalised, and provincial officials were bound to strict procurement targets. For the middleman the avoidance of penalties, invariably of the most barbaric nature, now replaced the accumulation of profits as his main incentive. Hoarding, even by the cultivator, kept a network of spies and torturers busy. Although a policy on paper, it became a purge in practice. Yet the results, according to Barani, were truly amazing. Grain prices plummeted, and stayed both cheap and unchanged even in years of drought. 'This was indeed the wonder of the age, and something which no other monarch was able to effect.'[29]

The success of this price-fixing policy resulted in its extension to just about every other commodity known to the Delhi bazaars. Textiles, groceries, slaves, whores, cattle, in fact everything 'from caps to shoes and from combs to needles' had its fixed price and its market regulators. It was not just one of the first recorded examples of planned economic management but also one of the most ambitious. And therein partly lay its undoing. 'A camel could be had for a *dang* [a farthing],' says Barani, 'but wherefrom the *dang*?' Purchasing power seemed to decline just as fast as prices; and urban sufficiency brought only chronic rural depression. There was no incentive to increase yields. Nor was there any chance of so ambitious a system surviving the heavy-handed authority which alone had made its imposition possible.

When Ala-ud-din succumbed to sickness and then death, both markets and prices simply reverted to the usual free-for-all. Most of his reforms, like most of his conquests, were temporary expedients and anything but proof against the internecine succession crises which now again overtook the sultanate. In the space of four years two of his sons, plus a Hindu convert, occupied the throne and quickly paid the price – a price which, though not fixed, was invariably lethal. So did 'Thousand-dinar Kafur', who briefly acted as king-maker; half a dozen other pretenders were either blinded or murdered. Mubarak, the son of Ala-ud-din who occupied the throne for longest, turned out to be what Ferishta calls 'a monster in the shape of a man'. Most of his indecencies were too gross to mention although not, strangely, his practice of 'leading a gang of abominable prostitutes, stark naked, along the terraces of the royal palaces, and obliging them to make water upon the nobles as they entered the court'.[30]

The Khaljis thus ended much as had the Slave kings. In 1320 Ghiyas-ud-din Tughluq, the son of one of Balban's slaves, emerged as the founder of a new dynasty. Briefly the Tughluqs would revive, and then fatally destroy, the fortunes of the sultanate, thereby surrendering Delhi's presumed hegemony to a host of powerful new rivals. Far from uniting India, early Islam's historic role would be to develop and entrench the subcontinent's so-called 'regional' identities.

Other Indias

1320–1525

THE TUGHLUQS

EAST OF THE QUTB MINAR, where the suburban sprawl of south Delhi finally peters out into scrub, lie six square kilometres of monumental desolation. This wilderness of cyclopean ramparts and dungeons is Tughluqabad (Tughlakabad), the most far-flung of the dozen-odd citadels which, originally some sultan's new Delhi, then his successors' old Delhi, are now decidedly dead Delhis; the howling jackals by night, and by day the mewing kites, could be ghouls at large.

Built by Sultan Ghiyas-ud-din Tughluq (Tughlak) in the early 1320s, Tughluqabad's parapeted walls and bastions march uncompromisingly along a low ridge which overlooks a wasteland of goat-grazed acacia and wind-borne litter. Jets scream low on a flightpath into the airport; in the distance isolated outcrops of many-storeyed housing rise from the ground-haze like the islands of an archipelago. Today's Delhi is still heading south, colonising the scrub with random developments and upgrading the goat tracks to feeder roads. The modern metropolis may yet reclaim Tughluqabad just as it already has the mosque of Qutb-ud-din Aybak, Iltumish's Lalkot and the Siri fort of the Khaljis.

Below the walls of his Tughluqabad, Sultan Ghiyas-ud-din Tughluq lies buried in a tomb of quite spectacular foreboding. Battlemented like the citadel, its steeply inward-sloping walls reminded James Fergusson, the nineteenth-century dilettante who first subjected India's architecture to systematic study, of an Egyptian pyramid; he much admired the structure's solidity, and memorably dubbed it 'an unrivalled model of a warrior's tomb'. But unlike the great grey citadel whose gigantic rough-cut stones fit so pleasingly in place, the squatly domed tomb is built with dressed precision from a rusty sandstone banded with off-white marble, both of them streaked and blackened by countless monsoons. The whole composition sits in a dusty bowl, sometimes a bog, which was once an artificial lake. It is reached across a causeway of many arches where a portcullis would not go amiss. 'Tughluq's Tomb' looks more like a place of detention than of repose.

Shaikh Nizam-ud-din Auliya, the Sufi saint and mystic after whom another bit of Delhi is named, must have rejoiced at the ghost of the first Tughluq sultan being committed to such secure confinement. Taking exception to what he saw as Ghiyas-ud-din's laxity in matters of religious observance, he had famously laid upon Tughluqabad the curse which still holds good: *Ya base Gujar, ya rahe ujar* ('Let it either belong to the Gujar [i.e. the herdsman], or let it remain in desolation'). He it was, too, who when warned to seek safety as the sultan drew near to the city at the end of a long campaign, still more famously gave the cryptic response 'Delhi is yet far off.' This proved to be an accurate forecast: the sultan never did reach Delhi. To Shaikh Nizam-ud-din's followers his premonition was proof of his exceptional powers. But such was the animosity between saint and sultan that more suspicious minds saw the prophecy as evidence of complicity. It all depended on whether the sultan's arrival was forestalled by accident or by design; and on this historians are still bitterly divided.

In 1320, emerging victorious from the five-year power struggle that followed Ala-ud-din Khalji's death, Ghiyas-ud-din Tughluq had skilfully combined the conciliation of rivals with the usual generosity towards supporters and kin. Prominent amongst the latter was his eldest son and designated heir, the future Muhammad bin Tughluq, who was despatched to the Deccan to deal with the ever-rebellious Kakatiya king, Pratapa-rudra of Warangal. Successful at his second attempt in taking Warangal, Muhammad had been recalled to Delhi in 1323 to act as viceroy while Ghiyas-ud-din himself ventured east. Affairs in Bengal had unexpectedly offered an opportunity for reasserting the sultanate's authority there, while recalcitrant Hindus in the Tirhut district of northern Bihar also required attention. Both these situations were addressed with remarkably little bloodshed during the course of 1324–5. It was only when nearing Delhi at the end of this highly successful campaign that Sultan Ghiyas-ud-din ran into trouble.

To prepare for his ceremonial entry into his new citadel of Tughluqabad, he had ordered his son Muhammad to construct a timbered pavilion by way of temporary accommodation at a place called Afghanpur, which was evidently nearby on the banks of the Jamuna. This was done, and there father and son were duly reunited. Barani says simply that they dined together and that when Muhammad and other notables had retired to wash

MUSLIM CONQUEST TO MUGHAL EMPIRE
The Dynasties of the Delhi Sultanate

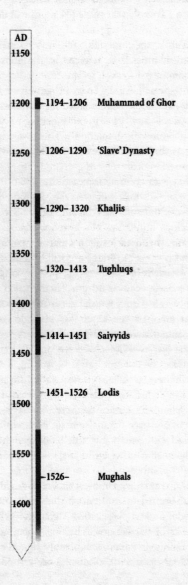

AD		
1150		
1200	1194–1206	Muhammad of Ghor
1250	1206–1290	'Slave' Dynasty
1300	1290–1320	Khaljis
1350	1320–1413	Tughluqs
1400		
1450	1414–1451	Saiyyids
1500	1451–1526	Lodis
1550		
1600	1526–	Mughals

their hands at the end of the meal 'a thunderbolt from the sky descended upon the earth, and the roof under which the sultan was seated fell down, crushing him and five or six other persons so that they died.'[1] It seems to have been July, a season of storms, and the pavilion was no doubt a conspicuous lightning conductor. But Barani is not usually so economical on affairs of magnitude. Perhaps, not having witnessed the disaster, he simply gave the official version; or perhaps the memory of those who stood by that version was not something he chose to ignore.

A very different account, though, was given by other writers, including Ibn Batuta, a distinguished Muslim scholar from Morocco whose twenty-eight years of adventure in three continents would make him not just 'the traveller of the age' but of most subsequent ages. Ibn Batuta began his long sojourn in India eight years after the Afghanpur tragedy, but his *Travels* would not be written until he was back in the safety of his native Fez, where neither fear nor favour can possibly have influenced him. Moreover, his version of the affair came from one who was actually present, in fact from another distinguished Delhi Sufi. Like Nizam-ud-din Auliya, this man had no love for the Tughluqs and may therefore have been happy to discredit them. On the other hand he offered a much more plausible account, insisting that the Afghanpur pavilion was meant to fall down, that Muhammad ordered up the ground-stamping elephants to make sure that it did fall down, that its collapse was carefully timed for the hour of prayer when the rest of the company would have moved outside, and that by design the shovels and pickaxes required to sift the rubble in the search for survivors did not arrive until too late. Additionally he thought it was no coincidence that amongst the other casualties was Mahmud, another of the sultan's sons and in fact his favourite.

None of this would normally trouble historians. After all, premature death was an occupational hazard for any contemporary ruler and parricide a fairly common cause; even when a ruler died in his bed, poison was invariably suspected. The debate over Ghiyas-ud-din Tughluq's untimely demise still rumbles on solely because of the light it supposedly throws on the character of the man who now automatically succeeded to the throne.

This was Muhammad bin Tughluq, the most complex and controversial figure ever to rule India. 'Muhammad Khuni' he is sometimes called, 'Muhammad the Bloody', Delhi's own Nero, India's Ivan the Terrible, the most autocratic, cold-blooded, power-crazed, and catastrophic of sultans who was yet also the most able, cultivated, philanthropic and even endearing. 'Was he a genius or a lunatic? An idealist or a visionary? A blood-

THE DELHI SULTANATES (3) The Tughluq Dynasty 1320–1413

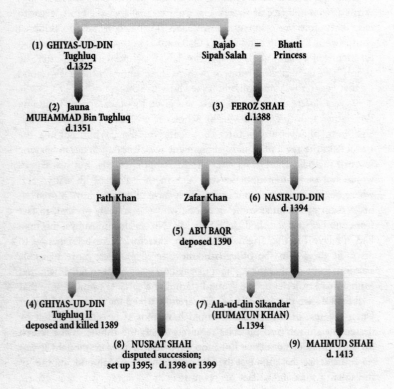

(1) **GHIYAS-UD-DIN**
Tughluq
d.1325

Rajab   =   Bhatti
Sipah Salah   Princess

(2) Jauna
MUHAMMAD Bin Tughluq
d.1351

(3) **FEROZ SHAH**
d.1388

Fath Khan

Zafar Khan

(6) **NASIR-UD-DIN**
d.1394

(5) **ABU BAQR**
deposed 1390

(4) **GHIYAS-UD-DIN**
Tughluq II
deposed and killed 1389

(7) **Ala-ud-din Sikandar**
(HUMAYUN KHAN)
d.1394

(8) **NUSRAT SHAH**
disputed succession;
set up 1395;   d.1398 or 1399

(9) **MAHMUD SHAH**
d.1413

thirsty tyrant or a benevolent king? A heretic or a devout Muslim?'[2] India's historians being divided by religious as well as ideological allegiances, he remains an enigma. Those of Hindu sympathies find Muhammad's excesses impossible to forgive and tend to accept Ibn Batuta's version of his accession. Those of Islamic sympathies favour the Barani version and regard Muhammad as an ill-starred and misunderstood philosopher-king whose gravest error was to antagonise and controvert the Muslim religio-academic establishment, or *ulema*.

To this influential class Ibn Batuta belonged. Muhammad would appoint him chief justice of Delhi and then one of his ambassadors. In between, the sultan also disgraced him and gave him cause to fear for his life. Yet throughout, Ibn Batuta remained fascinated by his master's personality, unable to decide between reverence and revulsion, seduced by the royal benevolence and appalled by the royal callousness. For Muhammad, he says, was pre-eminent for two things: 'giving presents and shedding blood'.

> At his gate there may always be seen some poor person becoming rich or some living one condemned to death. His generous and brave actions, and his cruel and violent deeds, have obtained notoriety amongst the people. In spite of this, he is the most humble of men, and the one who exhibits the greatest equity.[3]

For a tyrant Muhammad's lifestyle was simple, his libido restrained. Unusually amongst the conscience-ridden sultans he neither succumbed to inebriants nor vigorously proscribed them. He was exceptionally well-educated and of formidable intelligence, outwitting advisers so easily that he soon dispensed with them. He composed verses of outstanding merit; he was an authority on both medicine and mathematics; his penmanship was the envy of Islam's finest calligraphers; and as a patron of the arts he had no rival until the Great Mughals. 'But his distinguishing characteristic,' according to Ibn Batuta, 'was . . . a liberality so marvellous that the like has never been reported of any predecessor.'

For this liberality, as for his excessive severity, there would be ample scope although, since the order of events during his reign is uncertain, it is not always easy to trace their logic. The sultan was a relentless campaigner and seems initially to have enjoyed some success in consolidating Muslim rule in areas, like the Deccan, which had previously merely accepted Delhi's suzerainty. Arguably the sultanate more nearly approached the status of an Indian empire during the early years of his reign than it ever had under the Khaljis. This, however, only encouraged Muhammad to look further afield. A grandiose scheme to reverse Alexander the Great's march by conquering all Khorasan (including Afghanistan, Iran and what is now Uzbekistan) plus Iraq had to be abandoned in the face of mounting costs. Barani says vast sums were spent on buying up support in these countries and that a cavalry of 370,000 was raised and then maintained for a whole year before the project was dropped.

Another scheme, supposedly designed to afford flanking support for the Khorasan venture, went ahead. This time, explains Barani, the object was to 'bring under the dominion of Islam the mountain[s] which lie between the territories of Hind [India] and those of China'. An expedition of at least sixty thousand duly headed off into the western Himalayas. It probably got no further than the outer ranges in Kulu or Kumaon and was there heavily defeated by 'Hindus who closed the passes and cut off its retreat'. 'Only ten horsemen returned to Delhi to spread the news of its discomfiture.'[4]

Meanwhile revolts within India itself seem to have been more or less continuous but to have increased in both frequency and scale as Muhammad's policies took disastrous effect. Suppressing dissent, whether amongst Muslims or Hindus, he regarded as one of the main tasks of any sultan. It demanded energy and involved considerable expense but, since preserving the integrity of the state was deemed the only way of preventing civil war, he embraced the challenge with stern impartiality plus that awesome sense of duty which characterised all his actions. Justice demanded that rebels must die, and the more disagreeable their death the greater its deterrent effect. One of the first malcontents to fall into his hands was flayed alive; his skin was then stuffed and put on exhibition while its contents were minced, cooked with rice, and served up to the deceased's family. 'This revolting cruelty gave a foretaste,' says one of Muhammad's sterner critics, 'of the barbarous, if not fiendish, spirit which characterised the sultan, and it was not long before he displayed it on a massive scale.'[5] Muslims suffered quite as much as Hindus, innocent participants as much as guilty instigators. The sultan made no exceptions. Increasingly, though, he saw dissent less as a political challenge and more as a personal affront. A note of puzzlement is detectable in his dialogues with Barani. He dismissed the notion that the severity of his actions might actually engender disaffection, yet was genuinely wounded by what he took to be the obstinacy and ingratitude of so many of the beneficiaries of his rule.

As with Ala-ud-din, the high level of military spending also necessitated draconian fiscal measures. Additional taxes on the cultivators of the Ganga-Jamuna Doab are said to have driven the rich into rebellion and the poor into the jungles. Ferocious reprisals only made matters worse. The land went uncultivated and, when the rains failed, a catastrophic famine beset the whole of upper India, including Delhi. 'It continued for some years, and thousands upon thousands of people perished of want.'[6]

Following Barani, Muhammad's critics place the blame squarely on the sultan. Others see his additional taxes as negligible and certainly no worse than Ala-ud-din's exactions. The famine they attribute to drought; and the sultan's efforts to alleviate it become the most notable aspect of the disaster. Both Barani and Ibn Batuta acknowledge the depth of royal concern and note the measures taken to relieve distress by distributing existing grain stocks and arranging imports from further afield. Subsequently vast sums were disbursed to agents who undertook to bring wasteland into cultivation in an attempt to pre-empt future famines. This admirable initiative failed utterly. As Muhammad's reign degenerated into chaos, the agents simply pocketed the cash advances. His successor would be obliged to write them off.

Like Ala-ud-din, Muhammad bin Tughluq was attracted by more radical economic solutions. He did not resurrect the idea of managing the market, but instead conceived the yet more innovative expedient of bypassing the currency. The problem seems to have arisen not from the treasury's depletion but from a shortage of silver. Gold, thanks to hoards like those from the 'Aladdin's cave' in the south, was plentiful; but when it was released into circulation it strained the fixed monetary ratio between gold and silver. With a coinage that was 'more efficiently controlled than any Middle Eastern or European currency of the period',[7] the sultan was obliged to introduce gold coins of new weights plus heavily adulterated silver ones. Apparently influenced by reports of China's paper currency, he further introduced a token coinage of brass and copper to augment the silver coinage. 'The scheme was on the whole quite good and statesmanlike.'[8] It might even have worked had he been able to regulate the supply of these tokens and had the sultanate been reckoned credit-worthy. In the event the sultan's excesses, rather than the state of his treasury, undermined confidence, while smiths and metalworkers found the new coins absurdly easy to forge. Within two years the sultan was obliged to withdraw the lot, buying back both the real and the counterfeit at great expense until mountains of coins had accumulated within the walls of Tughluqabad.

This disastrous experiment seems to have been undertaken in the early years of his reign and to have been quickly followed by another: the removal of the capital from Delhi. In its stead Muhammad decreed that Devagiri, the city in Maharashtra from whose fang-like fortress the Seuna king Ramachandra had so dismally failed to defy Ala-ud-din, should henceforth be the hub of his realm. He knew the place well from having made it his headquarters while fighting against the Kakatiya king of Warangal during his father's reign. Now renamed Daulatabad, it was well sited for controlling the rich but troublesome provinces of Gujarat and Malwa and for making the sultanate's rule more effective in the peninsular kingdoms which had been overrun, but far from pacified, by Ala-ud-din, Malik Kafur and others.

But Devagiri/Daulatabad was all of fourteen hundred kilometres from Delhi, whose pampered citizens were disinclined to desert what Ibn Batuta judged 'one of the greatest cities in the universe'. They evinced no gratitude for the generous compensation given for their Delhi properties, nor for the elaborate arrangements made for their journey, nor for the comfortable reception being organised for them in Daulatabad. Once again the sultan was obliged to resort to force.

As well as sound strategic reasons for relocating his capital – like Daulatabad's greater security from Mongol attack – Ibn Batuta suggests that Muhammad had other reasons for evacuating Delhi. Its vulnerability to famine might have been one of them, but there was also a personal motive. In dealing severely even with Muslim miscreants, in refusing to heed the advice of established counsellors, and in promoting newcomers and Indian Muslims of low-caste origin, Muhammad had already alienated the city's Islamic intellectual elite of Turks, Persians and Afghans. A stream of anonymous poison-pen letters now confirmed his suspicions of the *ulema*, whose hostility may also account for the adverse criticism of chroniclers like Barani. Removal from Delhi was a convenient way of disrupting this opposition and, when the move was resisted, of punishing it.

Tales of the city being demolished and burnt, of a nonagenarian being turfed out of his deathbed, of a blind man being ordered onto the road tied to a horse's tail ('only one of his legs reached Daulatabad'[9]), and of a cripple being fired south by *manjanik* (catapult), sound like exaggerations. So may be the 'many who perished on the road'. But that Delhi was indeed deserted is attested by all. It may have been speedily repopulated. Ibn Batuta writes of other provinces being ordered to send people to reoccupy it. Moreover the whole scheme was soon abandoned, so that many of those who had reached Daulatabad, or were strung out along the road, were soon trailing back. Certainly Delhi had made something of a recovery by 1333 when Ibn Batuta first saw it. He found it magnificently appointed, although still somewhat thinly inhabited for a city of its size. Despite this renaissance, the disruption would not easily be forgotten, let alone forgiven. With his second monumental miscalculation, Muhammad had forfeited the trust of even loyal supporters. The swell of disaffection now exhibited itself in a crescendo of often simultaneous revolts.

Despite this overwhelming evidence of his unpopularity Muhammad remained on the throne until 1351, a reign of twenty-six years. Bengal had been virtually written off; the rajput princes of Rajasthan were reasserting their autonomy; in both Andhra and the Tamil country Muslim commanders established independent dynasties. Elsewhere lesser officers, mostly of Mongol and Afghan origin, repeatedly mutinied; Malwa and Gujarat heaved with dissent; the southern Deccan was experiencing a Hindu revival; something similar was underway in coastal Andhra; Sind revolted; civil war continued to flare up in the Ganga-Jamuna Doab – in all, Barani lists some twenty-two major rebellions. If in the early years of his reign Muhammad had won the sultanate's best chance of an Indian empire, in the latter years he lost it irrevocably.

Yet in Delhi his authority seems never to have been seriously challenged, and of the plots which dogged the reigns of other sultans little is heard. Far from incompetent, let alone insane, Muhammad bin Tughluq deserves credit less for his long-remembered experiments and more for his unquestioned ascendancy during a period of appalling turmoil, not all of it of his own making. An able commander who was rarely worsted in the field, and an effective administrator whose minor reforms and directives had genuine merit, he was also comparatively free of religious and ethnic bigotry. Perhaps he more than any of the sultans glimpsed the potential of an Indo–Islamic accommodation. Even his draconian severity seems to have had its desired effect. He died while pursuing rebels into the wastes of Sind. Although poison would later be suspected, from the contemporary accounts it seems certain that his labours were indeed crowned with that rare royal accolade of a natural death.

No less remarkable was the comparatively smooth succession which followed. Although a child, said to be his son, was briefly promoted as his successor, it was generally agreed that Muhammad bin Tughluq had no sons. The impostor was quickly retired to the nursery and Feroz Shah, Muhammad's cousin and designated heir, quietly succeeded. Already into his forties, Feroz yet managed to occupy the throne for thirty-seven years (1351–88). No less quietly, and with all the caution of advancing years, he endeavoured to preserve and pacify what remained of the sultanate's authority, proving to be a conservative in matters of religion and a consolidator in affairs of state. Although he received an exceptionally favourable press thanks to his deference to the *ulema*, even his eulogists fail to disguise the fact that he made no attempt to re-establish the sultanate's authority in the Deccan or the south, that two expeditions into Bengal were largely fruitless, and a six-year campaign in Gujarat and Sind nearly disastrous.

Only his leisurely excursion into Orissa in 1361, supposedly in search of elephants, can be claimed a success. Hitherto largely ignored, what Feroz's chronicler calls this 'happy and prosperous country'[10] received a rude awakening as the temple-building Ganga dynasty was routed and the great shrine of Lord Jagannath at Puri desecrated. Infidels received no favours from the orthodox Feroz, and there may be truth in the massacres allegedly inflicted on the local population. Yet in the end the country, now less happy, less prosperous, and less seventy-three elephants, was duly returned to its Hindu rulers. They, like others, soon neglected any tributary obligations to the Delhi invader.

Military manoeuvres apart, Feroz's record bears gentle scrutiny. He forswore the cruel excesses of his predecessor, showed a genuine regard for the welfare of his people and won wide support. Land revenue in those areas still administered by the sultanate was set at what seems to have been an equable rate and the *jizya* tax was extended to all non-Muslims, including the hitherto-exempt brahmans. Budgetary strains were further eased by abolishing the cash payment of the military and reverting to the system of remuneration by revenue grants. Since these grants often became hereditary, instant popularity was being bought at the price of eventual disarray. Large numbers of slaves, on the other hand, most of whom were Hindu captives, were rescued from penury and either enrolled as bodyguards or given productive work in the cities' *kharkhanas* (workshops). Thirty-six of these establishments, some with a workforce of thousands, were maintained by Feroz, mainly to supply the court with high-quality weapons, gems, robes and perfumes and to serve the sultan's ambitious building programmes.

Under the city-based dispensation of Islam, the buildings inevitably included another new Delhi. Erected several kilometres to the north of Tughluqabad, Feroz Shah's city and *kotla* (citadel) has long since been engulfed by more recent Delhis; below its ramparts, where once refreshingly flowed the Jamuna, heavy traffic now eddies in a sluggish fog of exhaust. Yet on its skyline there still protrudes one of the two Ashoka pillars which on Feroz's orders were so laboriously shipped downriver. Curious about their inscriptions, Feroz asked local brahmans for a translation; they expressed themselves mystified.

The sultan's tomb, 'an austere, plain block of grey sandstone',[11] stands in the urban oasis of Hauz Khas where, beside a reservoir built by Ala-ud-din Khalji, Feroz constructed gardens and one of many important *madrasseh* (colleges). Further afield he won acclaim for undertaking the first major irrigation projects with the construction of canals from both the Jamuna and the Sutlej. He also founded provincial cities, many of them called Ferozabad, including that which he later changed to Jaunpur. Jauna was the birth name of Muhammad bin Tughluq; Feroz, at least, continued to hold his predecessor in high regard.

Jaunpur, and the Awadh region of eastern Uttar Pradesh and Bihar which it commanded, was conferred on Malik Sowar, a eunuch-slave redeemed by Feroz and who, proving exceptionally able, was given the title of Sultan-ush Sharq. Taking advantage of the chaos which followed Feroz's death, it was this man who founded the Sharqi kingdom of Jaunpur and

DELHI – OLD AND NEW

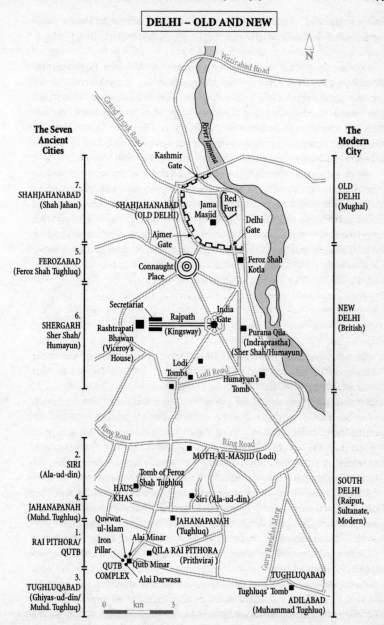

The Seven
Ancient
Cities

The
Modern
City

7.
SHAHJAHANABAD
(Shah Jahan)

5.
FEROZABAD
(Feroz Shah Tughluq)

6.
SHERGARH
Sher Shah/
Humayun)

2.
SIRI
(Ala-ud-din)

4.
JAHANAPANAH
(Muhd. Tughluq)

1.
RAI PITHORA/
QUTB

3.
TUGHLUQABAD
(Ghiyas-ud-din/
Muhd. Tughluq)

OLD
DELHI
(Mughal)

NEW
DELHI
(British)

SOUTH
DELHI
(Rajput,
Sultanate,
Modern)

N

Wazirabad Road

Grand Trunk Road

River Jamuna

Kashmir
Gate

SHAHJAHANABAD
(OLD DELHI)

Jama
Masjid

Red
Fort

Delhi
Gate

Ajmer
Gate

Connaught
Place

Feroz Shah
Kotla

Secretariat

Rajpath
(Kingsway)

India
Gate

Rashtrapati
Bhawan
(Viceroy's
House)

Purana Qila
(Indraprastha)
(Sher Shah/Humayun)

Lodi
Tombs

Lodi Road

Humayun's
Tomb

Ring Road

Ring Road

MOTH-KI-MASJID (Lodi)

Tomb of Feroz
Shah Tughluq

HAUS
KHAS

Siri (Ala-ud-din)

Quwwat-
ul-Islam
Iron
Pillar

Alai Minar

JAHANAPANAH
(Tughluq)

QILA RAI PITHORA
(Prithviraj)

QUTB
COMPLEX

Qutb Minar

Alai Darwaza

Guru Ravidas Marg

TUGHLUQABAD

Tughluqs' Tomb

ADILABAD
(Muhammad Tughluq)

0   km   3

whose successors – necessarily adopted and apparently of African origin – would soon defy and briefly eclipse the Delhi sultanate in the Gangetic plain.

Numerous other powers would wax brightly as the later Tughluqs presided over the contraction of the Delhi sultanate. In 1388 Feroz's long-awaited demise produced another long and bloody succession crisis which overturned Delhi's remaining authority. Ten years later, in 1398, the city itself was overturned when Mongol forces under Timur the Lame (Tamberlane), fresh from the conquests of Persia and Baghdad and now firm adherents of Islam, crossed the Jamuna just below Feroz's *kotla*.

With little difficulty the Mongols defeated the incumbent sultan and then for three days indulged in an orgy of rapine and killing. According to Timur's personal record, the gold, silver, jewels and precious brocades defied accounting. Exclusively Muslim quarters of the city were spared; everywhere else was sacked, and the entire Hindu population was either massacred or enslaved. 'Although I was desirous of sparing them,' wrote Timur in his unconvincing memoir, 'I could not succeed, for it was the will of God that this calamity should befall the city.'[12]

KAFTAN AND LOINCLOTH

It was not the end of the sultanate or of Delhi. Timur soon withdrew; the Tughluq sultan duly returned to his devastated capital; and two subsequent dynasties, the Saiyyids from 1414 and the Lodis from 1451, both Afghan in origin, continued to rule amidst the ruins throughout the fifteenth century. But under the Saiyyids an authority which had once embraced most of the subcontinent was so reduced that it barely extended beyond the village of Palam, now the site of one of Delhi's air terminals. The Lodis scarcely restored that authority, although they did restore some respectability by overcoming Jaunpur and overhauling the administration. Powerless to control erstwhile provinces and frequently under threat of invasion from them, Delhi was now just one of many, often more innovative and illustrious, power centres. If in pre-Islamic times the division of the subcontinent into strong independent states based on ancient identities of lineage, language, dynastic tradition and economic interest was the norm, then India was simply reverting to type.

Despite two centuries of dominance in most of northern and western India, the sultanate had failed to establish a pan-Indian supremacy, and had not even attempted an Indo–Islamic accommodation. True, in the cities the Hindu population had come to terms with their Muslim overlords: some enterprises, like the royal mints, remained exclusively in Hindu hands; many Muslims took Hindu wives; Indian captives often converted to Islam; and some converts had achieved high office. Yet in Delhi, as in the sultanate's provincial capitals, the court remained largely a preserve of the Turkish, Persian and Afghan elites. The same was true of membership of the *ulema*, of senior posts in the administration, and of much of the military. Ethnic as much as religious exclusivity made the Delhi regime totally alien to most of India's peoples.

Arriving at Multan, then the frontier city of Muhammad bin Tughluq's kingdom, in 1333, Ibn Batuta had observed how other new arrivals from west and central Asia all sought recruitment into the sultan's service. Most were mounted and, as *sowars* (troopers), they had to perform some equestrian manoeuvres before being enrolled in the armed forces. Others sought royal patronage as artisans, scholars, merchants or administrators. Very few looked beyond such patronage. Most trade, most industry and all financial services remained in Hindu hands. But as the English 'nabobs' of the eighteenth century would discover, this could be mutually advantageous. Ibn Batuta noted how Hindu banking houses in Multan grew wealthy by advancing to penniless hopefuls from central Asia such gifts as were suitable for presentation to the sultan –horses, slaves, brocades, jewels. The sultan invariably returned a far more valuable present from which the newcomer could repay with interest the Delhi agents of his Multani backer. It was official policy to encourage a stream of immigration; and such were the opportunities offered by India and such the turmoil elsewhere in Asia that the flood of adventurers from all over the Islamic world rarely dried up.

Ibn Batuta found that in Delhi most newcomers expected 'to gain riches and then return to their countries'[13] – again just like the eighteenth-century English 'nabobs'. As Delhi's authority declined, aggressive new sultanates on India's Islamic frontier in Bengal, Gujarat, Malwa and the Deccan boosted the market for military personnel and offered even better prospects for plunder, promotion and remunerative revenue assignments. In fact these independent sultanates had by the fifteenth century become the real lands of opportunity. Scholars, jurists and artisans gravitated towards the more generous patronage on offer. Merchants readily took to supplying and servicing the lucrative Arabian Sea trade from the peninsula's west coast ports. It was by way of sailings from the Red Sea that Gujarat acquired a large community of African Muslims. Meanwhile the influx of Persians and Afghans into the Deccan would give to the Bahmanid sultanate and

its successors a strongly Persian and Shi'ite flavour. This would survive
into the twentieth century in the case of Hyderabad, one of these successor
states.

If, as Ibn Batuta says of Delhi in the fourteenth century, many Muslim
fortune-seekers looked forward to a rich retirement in their original homelands, of elsewhere in the fifteenth century this seems not to have been the
case. Most stayed, prospered, married and settled. With the substantial
addition of Mongol recruits and Indian converts, the Muslim community
was not only growing but constantly renewing itself; as with horses so with
men – a steady stream of central Asian imports was seemingly vital to the
virility of Muslim rule.

The Muslim elite demanded of India's idolatrous natives no more than
occasional collaboration and no less than total submission. Islamic jurists
argued not over whether Hindus should be obliged to pay the *jizya* (the
tax on non-Muslims), but whether they should be allowed to pay it. Death
was the only penalty prescribed for idolaters by most Islamic schools of
law; only the daringly indulgent adherents of the Hanafi school argued
that the *jizya* was an acceptable alternative. Otherwise Hindus, although
occasionally serviceable and often diverting, were beneath contempt. Like
the white *sahibs* of European colonialism, the true believers of the sultanate
saw India simply as a source of wealth, a scene of adventure, and a subject
for moral indignation spiked with prurient fantasy. They too, indeed, were
colonialists. Compromise with the natives was as unthinkable as it was
preposterous.

For the tag of 'the greatest medieval traveller' Ibn Batuta's only rival
was Marco Polo. Arriving at India's opposite extremity when he called at
one of the Tamil ports *en route* from China in c1290, Marco Polo tells of
trying to have a coat made. To his surprise he found that in peninsular
India there were no tailors or seamstresses. In fact there was very little
clothing at all, and what there was was neither cut nor sewn. A single
length of cloth was simply tied or wrapped about the person, a custom
which still survives in the wearing of the sari, the shawl, the *lunghi* and
the *dhoti*. Bespoke apparel may not have been a Muslim innovation, but
it came late and from the colder north. Indeed, in many parts of India
tailoring remains a Muslim preserve.

Sailing on to Quilon in Kerala, a port which Ibn Batuta likened to
Alexandria as one of the busiest in the world, Polo noted how Hindu kings
were as scantily dressed as their poorest subjects; even soldiers, when riding
into battle, wore next to nothing. 'Men and women, they are all black, and
go naked, all save a fine cloth worn about the middle.' Even to one coming

from the East, so many bared chests and unbodiced breasts were a novelty. Like the international set who in the 1930s would be so charmed by the topless fashions still prevailing in Bali, the last outpost of Hindu society in south-east Asia, Marco Polo drew his own questionable conclusion: 'They look not on any sin of the flesh as a sin.'[14]

That Hindu society continued to challenge the austere morality of both Islam and Christendom well into the fifteenth century is clear from the account of a Russian merchant. Athanasius Nikitin, a native of Tver (Kalinin) on the Volga, reached India in c1470, so barely thirty years ahead of Vasco da Gama. He too arrived by sea, but from the Persian Gulf rather than round Africa, and like other Gulf traders he brought horses. According to Polo, the Pandyan ruler of Madurai imported two thousand horses a year 'and so do his four brothers'. They needed so many because of fatalities caused by the climate and unsuitable feeding; even if they bred, they produced 'nothing but wretched wry-legged weeds'. By land to the north and by sea to the south, the import of bloodstock was India's main extravagance.

Nikitin came ashore at the port of Chaul, about fifty kilometres south of modern Bombay (Mumbai). 'This is an Indian country,' he announces in his scatty but endearing memoir.

> People go about naked, with their heads uncovered and their breasts bare, the hair tressed into one tail, and thick bellies. They bring forth children every year and the children are many ... When I go out many people follow me and stare at the white man. Women who know you willingly concede their favours for they like white men.[15]

Abdu-r Razzak, another fifteenth-century visitor to the Deccan, noted that only Muslims wore trousers and kaftans (long coats). Heading an embassy from Shah Rukh of Samarkand, who was Timur's son and successor, Abdu-r Razzak found royal audiences in India a severe trial. The Zamorin of Calicut, another major port in Kerala, or the king of Vijayanagar would be coolly seated wearing little but pearls and a dazzling ensemble of gold jewellery while he, 'in consequence of the heat and the great number of robes in which he was dressed, drowned in perspiration'.[16] Whether admiring the intricate sculpture of the great Hoysala temple at Belur or ogling the courtesans of Vijayanagar, ambassador Razzak showed unusually catholic tastes. Such descriptions, though, merely point up the chasm of convention which separated Muslim and Hindu.

It was not just a question of ethnic or doctrinal differences. Two diametrically opposed codes of social behaviour had collided: one universal, inflexible, authoritarian and obligatory which upheld the equality of individual believers and theoretically promoted a strong sense of community; the other India-specific, sectional, discriminatory and hierarchical which denied equality and revelled in diversity. The social and cultural differences were as fundamental as they were obvious. To the Hindu the stiff brocade kaftan and the ankle-tight trouser must have seemed like some kind of confinement; to the Muslim the cotton loincloth – as finely woven, according to Polo, 'as a spider's web' – was disgustingly indecent. The veil and the zenana concealed Islam's womenfolk; the copious jewellery and the waist-level *lunghi* merely advertised Hindu femininity.

When that grim 'warrior tomb' of the Tughluqs was under construction below the ramparts of Tughluqabad in Delhi, a thousand kilometres away on the shore of the Bay of Bengal at Konarak the Ganga kings of Orissa had just completed one of the most elaborate and ambitious temples ever conceived. Dedicated to the sun-god Surya, it incorporated the idea, also associated with Apollo, of the sun being drawn by a chariot. Colossal stone wheels, each intricately carved, were positioned along its flanks and a team of massive draught horses, also stone-cut, reared seawards, apparently scuffing and snorting under the strain. Even in its partially reconstructed state, the conceptual scale of this temple is overwhelming, and so too the rich variety of its sculptural ornamentation which, as usual, includes many *mithuna* (intertwined couples) busy making ingenious love. To Muslims, for whom any representational art is anathema, it would have been the abomination of abominations. But then to Hindus the plain profile of the Tughluq tomb with its sloping sides and martial pretensions must have seemed pathetically primitive. Their aesthetics appeared irreconcilable. Mutual incomprehension seemingly precluded accommodation, let alone acculturation.

Nonetheless a gradual acceptance, which would eventually lead to a glorious synthesis, was underway. The process was not articulated. Muslim writers continued to tell of idolaters massacred and temples destroyed, Hindu eulogists of *mleccha* enemies humbled and *arya* heroes exalted. The evidence is often inferential, fragmentary and widely scattered. It is to be sought less amongst the literate elites – the largely foreign *ulema* and the staunchly orthodox brahmans – and more amongst artisans, cultivators and the commercial and secretarial classes, be they Indian Muslims or lesser-caste Hindus. At this level, wherever Hindu and Muslim lived and worked in close professional proximity, social exchange is evident. Hindus adopted a modified version of the Muslim *purdah* ('curtain', i.e.

the veil) to screen their women; Muslims adopted something approaching Hindu caste distinctions. Elements of ritual and popular devotion were also shared. Muslim *shaikhs* and *pirs* (Sufi saints) attracted Hindu followers; Hindu ascetics, dancers, musicians and craftsmen attracted Muslim patronage. In the arts and particularly architecture the results would soon be apparent.

But here again the evidence is diffuse and to be found not so much amongst the ruins of Delhi and in the chronicles of its sultans as in the records and remains of a dozen other capitals scattered across the subcontinent. From these places – Jaunpur, Ahmadabad, Mandu, Gulbarga, Chitor, Vijayanagar, Gaur – ruled the numerous sultans and kings who had succeeded in asserting their authority over particular regions – Awadh, Bengal, Gujarat, Malwa, the Deccan, Rajasthan, etc. – in the aftermath of the Tughluq decline and Timur's invasion.

The regions themselves encouraged a social consolidation which transcended religious allegiance. Based on core territories, each with a long dynastic pedigree, an economically important hinterland and a now distinct language, they were ready-made for statehood, whether under Muslim rule or Hindu. Location and circumstance also conspired to favour local integration. Here Muslim rulers, mostly far removed from the Islamic world, often at war with the sultan of Delhi or other co-religionists, and always dependent on the loyalty of a largely non-Muslim population, had perforce to compromise. Likewise their Hindu counterparts, isolated on the margins of an increasingly Islamic India, yet obliged to co-operate with Muslim allies, and eager to recruit Muslim troops, could ill afford to indulge ideas of a *dharma*-led defiance or a Hindu renaissance.

STILLBORN STATES

The number of states which emerged from the collapse of the Delhi sultanate, not to mention the complexity of their mutual relations, could warrant a long narrational stride onto the *terra firma* of Mughal India. But it would be wrong to diminish the political importance of the fifteenth and early sixteenth centuries. In Europe the period witnessed the emergence of those strong, centralised and mostly monarchical states which would become the basic units of European history. Something very similar appeared to be underway in India: Bengal, Gujarat, Kashmir, Orissa, the south and various parts of central India began to forge the territorial, political and cultural identities associated with the concept of a nation-state. But whereas not

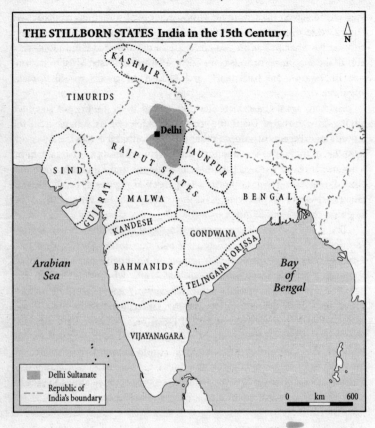

THE STILLBORN STATES India in the 15th Century

KASHMIR

TIMURIDS

Delhi

RAJPUT STATES

JAUNPUR

SIND

GUJARAT

MALWA

KANDESH

GONDWANA

BENGAL

Arabian
Sea

BAHMANIDS

TELINGANA

ORISSA

Bay
of
Bengal

VIJAYANAGARA

Delhi Sultanate
Republic of
India's boundary

0   km   600

even the most committed European federationist would dismiss Scotland
or the Netherlands, let alone France or Spain, as 'regional' aberrations,
such has been India's subsequent experience of subcontinental hegemonies,
and such today is Delhi's and Islamabad's paranoia about secessionist movements, that 'regions' is how these entities are designated. The recollection
of their independent status is not much promoted. The nation-state in
pre-colonial India would indeed be stillborn; yet the fact of its being born
at all is significant.

In the Deccan the Bahmanid kingdom and, further south, that of Vijayanagar, both emerged from the remains of the Khalji conquests in the
peninsula. Vijayanagar was founded in the late 1330s, the Bahmanid kingdom about ten years later. The kings of Vijayanagar were Hindus and are

often credited with spearheading Hindu resistance to the Islamisation of the peninsula. The Bahmanids, on the other hand, were Muslim sultans and their frequent wars with Vijayanagar are commonly seen as a continuation of the Islamising process begun by the Delhi sultanate. This, however, is certainly not the full story, and it may be no more than a gloss imparted by zealous writers, mostly of a later date.

Suspicions are aroused by legends which credit both states with highly ambiguous origins. The future founders of Vijayanagar, two brothers called Harihara and Bukka, were once feudatories of either the Hoysala king or the Kakatiya. In c1327 these brothers were supposedly captured by Muslim forces and taken to Delhi. There, legend has it, they adopted Islam before being allowed to return south as feudatories of Muhammad bin Tughluq. Only later, when a Hindu sage of high repute miraculously recognised them as embodiments of the god Virupaksha, was the sin of their apostasy cancelled and their right to erect a kingdom founded on *dharma* accepted. Whether this is true or not, the status of Vijayanagar's founders was obviously such that only elaborate mythologising and divine intervention could validate it.

Likewise, according to Ferishta, the Bahmanid sultans of the Deccan sprang from an unlikely alliance in Delhi. Hasan, who as Bahman Shah would become the first Bahmanid sultan, was once apparently the servant of a Delhi brahman called Gungu. By chance, while ploughing his patch of land, Hasan unearthed a cache of gold coins whereupon Gungu, in his capacity as an astrologer, predicted a great future for him. He also made him promise not to forget his one-time master. Encouraged by such predictions and by his evident good fortune, Hasan headed for the land of opportunity in the Deccan. There he rose rapidly in the service of Muhammad bin Tughluq; and when, at the end of the latter's reign, both Gujarat and the Deccan defied Delhi's authority, Hasan emerged from the subsequent confusion as the choice of his fellow commanders to assume the sultanate of the breakaway Deccani kingdom. Enthroned at Daulatabad, and now known as Bahman Shah, he remembered his promise to his brahman patron and duly summoned Gungu south to become finance minster of the new kingdom.

To be fair, Ferishta seems painfully aware of the implausibility of this story. It is thought that Hasan was of Afghan birth, and it seems most unlikely that a Muslim Afghan would ever have served a brahman. Ferishta was also surely wrong in suggesting that 'Gungu was the first brahman who accepted office in the service of a Muhammadan prince.'[17] Yet he adds that, in honour of the brahman, Hasan adopted the name Gungu as one of his titles, and that it was then used 'on all public documents and remained engraven on the royal seal of that dynasty until its extinction'. He further claims that the name 'Bahman' was of similar provenance, being an approximate rendering of 'brahman'. Others insist that the name derived from the ancient Persian King Bahman from whom the Bahmanids pretended descent. Howsoever, the willingness of a distinguished Muslim historian, who was writing within a century of the Bahmanids' demise, to credit such accounts is significant. In the eyes of the Delhi *ulema* the orthodoxy of the house of Hasan, alias Gungu Bahman Shah, was clearly compromised.

Ferishta's account of the Bahmanids is initially one of almost continuous conflict with their Hindu neighbours, most notably various rulers in what is now Andhra Pradesh plus the kings of Vijayanagar. Major wars with Vijayanagar's Bukka, who succeeded his brother Harihara, and then with Bukka's successors, Harihara II and Deva Raya I and II, are seen as triumphs for the Bahmanid sultans who repeatedly threatened the city of Vijayanagar itself. They also carried off hoards of treasure and massacred wholly incredible numbers of idolaters; as a noted authority on the Bahmanids has calculated, 'if we were to add together the casualties inflicted on the Hindus by the Muslims as given by our Indo-Persian chronicles, there would not have been a Hindu left alive in the Deccan.'[18] Rather fewer Muslim warriors 'drank the sherbet of martyrdom', as Ferishta puts it, but 'without an influx from overseas it was the Muslims', according to Professor Sherwani, 'who were in danger of dying out.' Mass conversions are not mentioned until the very end of Bahmanid rule, no doubt because Bahman Shah had rejected any idea of imposing the *jizya* on his Hindu subjects.

Significantly the great city of Vijayanagar (at Hampi in Karnataka), although repeatedly threatened, was never actually captured. No doubt its defences were as formidable as visitors reported and as its magnificent remains testify. Yet, according to Ferishta, it was in these wars of the fourteenth to fifteenth centuries that artillery was first deployed in India. The guns were operated by both Muslim and Christian mercenaries, the latter of whom also here make their Indian debut. Although this decidedly early instance of the new gunpowder technology might be attributed to peninsular India's maritime links with the Middle East and the Mediterranean, the casting of cannon would have presented no difficulty to India's highly skilled metalworkers.

If such firepower was indeed available, the destruction of Vijayanagar would have been possible. Annihilation, it seems, was not the object of the exercise. Nor, despite occasional mention of far-ranging ambitions, did either state entertain realistic expectations of bringing the other permanently under its sway. As with other warring neighbours of the period – Gujarat and Malwa, Malwa and the Bahmanids, Malwa and the rajputs of Chitor – victory invariably stopped short of conquest. Royal captives were released, defeated kings reinstated, and the victor's spoils regarded more as a one-off indemnity than as an annual tribute.

Conflict amongst the 'regional' kingdoms of the fifteenth century looks to have been not about sovereignty, only partly about plunder, and mostly about frontier demarcation. At issue between the Bahmanids and Vijayanagar was a rich tract of land between the Kistna and Tunghabhadra rivers known as the Raichur Doab. To command this tract the Bahmanids, like the Rashtrakutas many centuries earlier, soon moved their capital from Daulatabad (near the Rashtrakutas' Ellora) to Gulbarga and then Bidar (near the Rashtrakutas' Manyakheta). It was the perfect base from which to create a trans-peninsular kingdom and, as the Bahmanids duly expanded their domains to reach the west coast between Bombay and Goa and then the east coast between the Godavari and Madras, the importance of holding the Raichur Doab became immense. As if in recognition of such purely strategic imperatives, Ferishta reports that, despite the injunctions of religion, the two protagonists agreed to end the mindless slaughter of non-combatants and captives. And when in the late 1440s the issue of the Raichur Doab was settled by agreement, direct hostilities between the two neighbours ceased. Conflicting claims to the west coast ports, including Goa, continued, but elsewhere the protagonists avoided attacking one another and on one occasion actually collaborated against a common foe.

Territorial definition is fundamental to the formulation of a nation-state. A similar but shorter conflict between the Bahmanids and their northern rivals of the new sultanate of Malwa also revolved around a disputed frontier tract. When it was settled, this time not to the Bahmanids' advantage, the two neighbours resumed friendly relations. Parallel instances of the scimitar being readily sheathed once an outstanding territorial grievance had been resolved abound amongst the other powers of the period. When in the 1490s the Bahmanid kingdom suddenly plummeted from power as result of factional in-fighting, Vjayanagar would take advantage of the situation, and war over the status of the Raichur Doab would revive. But although Vijayanagar was left as much the most powerful of the Deccan states, it would soon find that a strong and territorially secure Muslim neighbour was infinitely preferable to the smaller, weaker but territorially ambitious sultanates into which the Bahmanid kingdom dissolved. The glorious heyday of Vijayanagar's supremacy would prove to be short-lived.

Thanks to the Russian Nikitin, who spent some months in Bidar and Gulbarga in 1470, a dazzling picture of Bahmanid power at its greatest has been preserved. Nikitin's military estimates, amounting to close on a million cavalry and infantry, must be wild guesswork but his first-hand evidence of both 'long muskets' and 'heavy guns' cannot be gainsaid. Nor can the almost unimaginable display of opulence. Sultan Shams-ud-din Muhammad, 'a little man, twenty years old, and in the power of the Khorasani [i.e. Afghano-Persian] nobles', rode forth to celebrate *Bairam* 'on a golden saddle, wearing a habit embroidered with sapphires and on his pointed head-dress a large diamond; he also carried a suit of gold armour inlaid with sapphires and three swords mounted in gold'. Ahead of him walked a huge elephant dressed in silk and brandishing from its trunk a heavy chain with which it cleared a path through the crowds. Behind followed the sultan's brother on a bed of gold, covered with velvet set with precious stones and carried by twenty men. Then came Mahmud Gawan, the able chief minister and mentor of successive sultans; he too reclined on a bed of solid gold which in this case was drawn by four horses in gilded harness. Hordes of riders in full armour followed, together with several hundred female singers and dancers. Some were practically naked but all were armed with shield and sabre, sword, lance or bow. Three hundred elephants 'clad in damask steel armour' completed the procession. Each elephant bore a 'citadel' which held six 'warriors with guns', and each had massive swords attached to its tusks plus 'large iron weights hanging from its trunk'. In Nikitin's mind there was no doubt that he was attending a potentate who, ranking above all others like a latter-day 'Balhara', was '*the* Muhammadan sultan of India'.[19]

SWINGING IN THE WIND

Such Bahmanid pre-eminence would not have been conceded by the sultans of Gujarat and Malwa. A latecomer compared with Vijayanagar or the Bahmanids, Gujarat became independent when its governor, the son of a rajput convert to Islam, assumed sovereignty after Timur's invasion in the early years of the fifteenth century. At about the same time Malwa followed suit under its erstwhile governor Dilawar Khan Ghori. Dilawar Khan was presumably a Turco-Afghan Ghorid but he quickly signified a more conciliatory attitude to idolaters by encouraging rajput settlement and creating what was in effect a Muslim–rajput condominium. Gujarat's sultans too, although more orthodox and credited with imposing the *jizya* and demolishing Hindu temples, habitually married rajput princesses, patronised Indian artists and Sanskrit scholars, and employed Hindus in the highest offices of state. Also prominent in both sultanates, and especially in their respective revenue departments, were Jains, whose survival in western India belied their near-extinction in the rest of the subcontinent.

Both Dilawar Khan of Malwa (or Amid Shah Daud, as he had become) and Ahmad Shah of Gujarat (who succeeded as sultan in 1411) signified their new status by establishing new capitals. Islam had provided a powerful stimulus to urbanisation. Muslims in India, as an elite minority largely dependent on royal patronage and united by the communal duties of prayer and mosque-attendance, were naturally drawn to city life. From Allahabad and Faizabad to Hyderabad and Aurangabad the map of India still betrays hundreds of Islamic urban foundations. In Gujarat Ahmad Shah's choice fell on a site beside the Sabarmati river. There he founded and heavily fortified the city of Ahmadabad which, rapidly populated by Gujarat's skilled craftsmen and commercially favoured by its location close to the Gulf of Cambay, had by the end of the sixteenth century become one of the largest and wealthiest cities in India, indeed in the world according to European visitors. It is still the capital of Gujarat, and in the midst of chaotic inner-city overcrowding there remain the many mosques, tombs and gateways of the Gujarati sultans and their usually rajput queens.

Were any proof needed of the eclectic Gujarati milieu, it is self-evident in the distinctive architectural style. Here elements and motifs from both Jain and Hindu tradition are incorporated not, as in the Delhi Quwwat-ul-Islam mosque, because dismembered temples were reassembled as mosques, but by gloriously intentional design. Gujarat's strong tradition of temple-building, together with its skilled masons, simply transferred to the Islamic architectural canon and thereby transformed *mihrab* and minaret into splendidly ornate features. Clichés of the Mughal style like the perforated screen (*jali*) and the cupola-ed pavilion (*chattri*) are anticipated. The Jami masjid of Ahmad Shah himself has been hailed as 'perhaps the most aesthetically satisfying [mosque] in the whole of India.'[20]

Very different was the new capital of Malwa. As if to challenge the lushly-sited and commercially-favoured city of Gujarat's sultans, Dilawar Khan and his successors of Malwa lit upon the rugged heights of Mandu. From nearby Dhar, the one-time capital of the good King Bhoj, a prodigious effort was directed to encircling with fortifications the already nigh-impregnable heights above the Narmada valley. At the same time they smothered the upland meadows not merely with the mosques and tombs of Islam but also with the airy palaces, the echoing courtyards and the lotus lakes so beloved of the rajputs and later of the Mughals. If one may judge by what neglect has so obligingly preserved, it was here at Mandu, and in the contemporary Man Singh palace at Gwalior, that India's secular architecture began to stake its claim as a serious rival to the religious tradition of temple, tomb and mosque.

No metropolis has succeeded to the site of Mandu. Deserted in the seventeenth century, it has remained so ever since, one of India's – or anywhere's – most wildly romantic sites. Malwa being landlocked with no very certain frontiers and a host of covetous neighbours, its sultans had frequent cause to congratulate themselves on the effort expended on their capital. Although repeatedly besieged by the Gujarati army and occasionally by expeditions from the Bahmanid sultanate and the rajputs of Mewar, Mandu stood firm throughout the fifteenth century. Under Sultan Mahmud Khalji (reigned 1431–69) Malwa took the offensive, with its forces penetrating deep into Gujarat, the Deccan and Rajasthan and briefly marching on Delhi. Mandu consequently basked in the splendours of lavish patronage. According to Ferishta, Mahmud's successor was able to assemble a harem of ten thousand maidens. To accommodate them, a self-contained 'city of women' was constituted whose inmates formed their own administration and militia, ran their own markets and set up their own manufactures.

What became of this feminist republic is not known. But in the early sixteenth century the Muslim–rajput balance on which the foundations of the Malwa state rested was overthrown. To offset the preponderance achieved by the rajputs, the incumbent sultan called in the forces of Gujarat, while the rajputs looked to their co-religionists in Mewar. In 1518 and then again in 1531 the Gujarati army would indeed take Mandu by storm, and its fall would presage that of the sultanate itself.

But if Malwa proved to be something of a failure in state-formation, Gujarat continued from strength to strength. In Mahmud Shah it enjoyed the services of an exceptionally able and long-reigning sultan (1459–1511) who completed the consolidation of the kingdom. Mercifully, given the innumerable other Mahmuds and Muhammads, he is usually remembered as Mahmud 'Begarha', a nickname which is variously explained. It may refer to his whiskers: according to European accounts his beard reached to below his waist, while his moustaches, long and grey like the horns of a buffalo (*begara*), were swept back to cross in a tie on the crown of his head. Alternatively it may refer to his capture of two vital fortresses (*garh*). One was Champaner near Baroda in eastern Gujarat, which became a subsidiary capital; the other was Girnar in Saurashtra, the great massif where Ashoka had left that famous rock inscription and where Rudradaman the satrap had once championed both irrigation and Sanskrit. 'Mahmud Two-Forts' in effect united mainland Gujarat with the Saurashtra peninsula to create a powerful maritime state enjoying a monopoly of those west coast ports which served upper India. It would prosper well into the seventeenth century and be finally overwhelmed only by a combination of Mughal might on land and Portuguese firepower at sea.

In the absence of obvious frontiers, fortifications were also the key to territorial aggrandisement in Rajasthan. The great plateau of Chitor, Mewar's equivalent of the heights of Mandu, had been refortified by the Sesodia rajputs following its partial destruction by Ala-ud-din Khalji. Under Rana, or Maharana (variants of Raja and Maharaja) Kumbha, who reigned from 1433 to 1468, another towering stronghold was ringed with battlemented walls at Kumbhalgarh. From these twin eyries the Sesodias extended their sway over the lesser rajput houses of Rajasthan and adventured deep into Gujarat and Malwa. 'Mewar was now in the middle path of her glory, and enjoying the legitimate triumph of seeing the foes of her religion captives on the rock of her power,' pronounces Colonel Tod.

At the other extremity of Rajasthan, Raja Jodha (reigned 1438–89), a rajput of the Rathor clan who had been instrumental in securing Rana Kumbha's throne, established his own hilltop stronghold at what became Jodhpur. 'Never capable of uniting, even for their own preservation,' as Colonel Tod put it, the rajputs scarcely constituted a state. They were, though, again about to give a good account of themselves. Famously if fortuitously it would be the boast of the Sesodias of Mewar that they alone never succumbed to the might of the Mughals.

In Orissa, Bengal and Awadh the same process of territorial definition and political consolidation might be traced. In Awadh (Oudh) the sultans of Jaunpur built Tughluq-esque mosques and fought with the Delhi sultans; in Orissa the Suryavamsha rajas built temples and warred with the rajas of Andhra and Vijayanagar. The success and liberality of the ruler, and the culture and language of the locality, created bonds which often transcended those of religion. In Bengal in 1418 a Hindu actually became sultan. This was too much for the Bengali *ulema*, who sought assistance from Jaunpur. Sultan Raja Ganesh was duly toppled, but only in favour of his son who, adopting Islam, changed his name from Jadusen to Jalal-ud-din and ruled under his father's direction until 1431. A successor, Ala-ud-din Husain Shah (reigned 1493–1519), is revered as an outstanding patron of Bengali scholarship and, though a Muslim, indeed an Arab, is said to have honoured Chaitanya, the leader of the Vaishnavite *bhakti* movement in Bengal. In return the Hindus 'went so far as to honour [the sultan] as an incarnation of Lord Krishna'.[21]

Husain's tolerance had its limitations. Like the sultans of Gujarat and Malwa he stands accused of destroying temples in time of war, most notably during an attack on Orissa. But temples were seldom exclusively places of worship. They were also depositories of treasure, political statements which embodied the ambitions of their royal patrons and, on occasion, even military strongholds. Desecration was not necessarily prompted by bigotry.

In Kashmir, where Muslim immigration and conversion had resulted in the installation of a Muslim dynasty in 1339, the normally cordial pattern of Hindu–Muslim relations was interrupted in the early fifteenth century. The great Sun temple of Martand was destroyed and heavy penalties imposed on the mainly brahman Hindus. But the persecution proved short-lived. In a fifty-year reign (1420–70) Sultan Zayn-ul-Abidin reversed such discriminatory policies and, fostering both scholarship and a variety of new crafts, transformed his Himalayan kingdom into a stable and thriving state. Canals and irrigation works were also undertaken and, with a reassertion of its authority over Ladakh and Baltistan, Kashmir aspired to the sovereign status which its distinct history had long promised and which the finest natural frontiers in India seemingly guaranteed.

It was a different story in the neighbouring Panjab. Here evidence of nation-state-building is notably lacking. Timur's Mongol descendants continued to nurse claims to the lands which he had traversed and conquered *en route* to Delhi in 1398. Meanwhile Afghan adventurers continued to migrate to and through the Panjab in large numbers. By the late fifteenth century the Afghan Lodis exercised desultory control from Delhi. But so heavily engaged was the Lodi sultan with rivals elsewhere that his governor in the Panjab enjoyed near independence. No obdurate dynasty like the Shahis stood between the undefended north-west frontier and the temptations of India. No champion like the later Ranjit Singh rose to rally Panjabi loyalty. The gates of Hind were swinging in the wind.

The Making of the Mughal Empire

1500–1605

BABUR GOES TO INDIA

ON 5 JULY IN THE YEAR 1505 a violent earthquake hit the city of Agra. According to Ferishta, 'so severe an earthquake was never experienced in India either before or since ... Lofty buildings were levelled with the ground [and] several thousand inhabitants were buried under the ruins.'[1] To the survivors it seemed like an omen. Sikander, the second and greatest of the three Lodi sultans of Delhi, had in the preceding year celebrated his recovery of some of the sultanate's erstwhile territories by designating Agra as his alternative capital. A small town of no previous importance, its elevation also signified Lodi ambitions to subdue rivals to the south of Jamuna. The town had been replanned round a grand fort and 'the foundations of the modern Agra were laid.'[2]

Their almost immediate destruction by the earthquake made no impression on Sikander Lodi. Heedless, he resumed the creation of his new capital and continued to hammer away at his nearest rajput rival. This was Raja Man Singh of Gwalior whose subsidiary fortress of Narwar was indeed taken. But before the beetling cliffs of the superbly fortified palace-citadel at Gwalior itself, the Lodi forces, lacking artillery, proved powerless. At enormous cost the siege dragged on for several years. Worse still, word of the Lodi's discomfiture reached the ear of a young and ambitious new Mongol ruler in Kabul.

Zahir-ud-din Muhammad, otherwise known as Babur or 'the Tiger', was already showing an unhealthy interest in the disturbed affairs of the Panjab, which province bordered his Afghan kingdom and was nominally under Lodi rule. In 1505, the year of the earthquake, he made his first foray across the north-west frontier. It was another omen which the Lodi sultan chose to ignore. Babur drew his own conclusion. As the Lodis' biographer puts it, 'Sikander Lodi, while fighting against the Tomars [i.e. the rajputs of Gwalior], was criminally neglecting the north-west frontier and the Panjab.'[3]

This state of affairs, if anything, worsened as the strife-torn Lodis squabbled amongst themselves. Twenty years and five exploratory incursions later, Babur would invade in earnest, topple Sikander's successor and, taking both Delhi and Agra, would inaugurate in India a Mongol, or Mughal, empire. Conventionally known in English as that of the Great Mughals, it would wax supreme for two centuries and engross most of the subcontinent. Through the agency of Babur, first of the Great Mughals, the multilateral history of the Indian subcontinent begins to jell into the monolithic history of India.

In his *Babur-nama*, a personal memoir-cum-diary of such disarming frankness that it was once reckoned 'amongst the most enthralling and romantic works in the literature of all time',[4] Babur leaps from the page with the zestful energy of a *sowar* (trooper) bounding into the saddle. Restless to the point of nomadism, he was a born adventurer to whom success was an ultimate certainty and failure but a temporary inconvenience. Publicly he never hesitated. Deliberation inspired decision; decision guaranteed action. Convivial and charismatic, he rejoiced in the adulation of his comrades much as did his adored English contemporary, the young Prince Hal. Yet while ambition and obesity would stifle all scruple in Henry VIII, Babur continued to nurse both a sensitive spirit and the rawest of consciences. In a career that speaks volumes for his courage and genius, it is this emotional frailty which is so remarkable. A succinct piece of versification seemingly gave him as much satisfaction as a well-worked cavalry manoeuvre. Ill health he often reckoned a penalty for past vanities and, though a mighty toper, long and often did he groan over the sinfulness of intoxicants. For his greatest battle he would prepare by finally forswearing alcohol and promoting prohibition. No less typically would the aroma of a musk melon, dewily redolent of his central Asian home, reduce him to a moist-eyed reverie of nostalgic abandon.

To such an adventurer direction was dictated as much by fate as by forebears. On his mother's side Babur was a distant descendant of Ghenghiz Khan, and on his father's he was a fifth-generation descendant of Timur, he who in 1398 had sacked the Tughluqs' Delhi. This latter conquest would furnish Babur with a cherished but highly dubious claim to legitimate sovereignty in northern India. But India was not his first choice. Nor was Kabul. His inheritance lay much further north beyond the Oxus in Ferghana, a minor kingdom to the east of the modern city of Tashkent. He had been born there in 1484 and, though of Mongol blood, it was in the Turkic and Islamic milieu of this subordinate kingdom of Timur's erstwhile empire that he was educated. Turki would remain his first language; he even wrote of himself and his followers as Turks. His Islam was a robust, workaday faith tempered more by the winds of circumstance and the exigencies of campaigning than by the niceties of theology. And it was to Samarkand, Timur's capital and the cultural focus of central Asia, that he aspired. Briefly, aged fifteen, he actually occupied it, but was quickly dispossessed by an Uzbeg rival. Twice more he would take the city and twice more he would lose it. Kabul, on the other hand, was just a distraction. Yet for a virtual fugitive it offered consolation. From Afghanistan Timur himself had launched his bid for Samarkand and had then gone on to conquer much of Asia. Babur could do worse. In 1504 he crossed the Oxus, then the Hindu Kush, and seized Kabul.

Apart from that one ominous raid across the Indian frontier in 1505, Babur spent the next fourteen years securing his position in Afghanistan and chasing the dream of sovereignty in Samarkand. In his memoir, which was written towards the end of his reign, he insists that 'my desire for Hindustan remained constant'. Yet it was not until 1519 that he resumed the quest and not until 1525 that he launched his successful bid. He did so with a highly mobile force which had shared his exploits in central Asia and which, as it was ferried across the Indus north of Attock, was carefully counted. 'Great and small, good and bad, retainer and non-retainer, [it] was written down as twelve thousand.' For the task in hand so modest a force must have seemed pitifully inadequate. But in the interim two factors had greatly emboldened him.

One was the acquisition and potential of firearms. In the new gun-powder technology, as in much else, Babur's Lodi adversaries lagged behind the kingdoms and sultanates of the Deccan and the south; there is no evidence to suggest that their forces were acquainted with either cannon or matchlocks. He, on the other hand, had both. Though personally more proficient at archery, he had studied the use of artillery in central Asia, had recruited Turkish gunners, and now took a close interest in the casting of siege-cannon and the transport of field guns. On a previous raid into the Panjab the sharp-shooting potential of matchlocks had also impressed him. For what his forces lacked in numbers they compensated with a capacity, terrifying alike to man, horse and elephant, for deafening and increasingly lethal bombardments.

The other consideration which worked in his favour was the now ter-minal rivalry amongst his enemies. Sikander Lodi had been succeeded by two sons who, on the insistence of the Lodis' fractious power-brokers, had divided the sultanate between them. Ibrahim, inheriting Delhi, had since overcome his brother in Jaunpur but had thereby alienated the most senior nobility and alarmed Indian rivals like the rajput chief, Rana Sangha of Mewar. The latter now encouraged Babur with offers of collaboration against the Lodis, while in 1523 it had been the Lodis' own governor in the Panjab who had invited Babur to capture Lahore and challenge for the sultanate. This man, Daulat Khan, had since changed his mind and now threatened to oppose the invasion, although other Lodis, including his own son, continued to back Babur.

In the event the twelve thousand Mughals advanced across the Panjab's rivers unopposed. Near the city of Lahore Daulat Khan, old though he was, donned a couple of swords and bragged about halting the invader. 'Was such a rustic blockhead possible!' scoffed Babur. 'With things as they were, he still made pretensions!'[5] When the old man then sheepishly surrendered, Babur ordered him to submit on bended knee with his ridiculous swords dangling round his neck. Milking the moment for mirth rather than vengeance, Babur then pressed on to Rupar, Ambala and Delhi.

> I put my foot in the stirrup of resolution, set my hand on the rein
> of trust in God, and moved forward against Sultan Ibrahim . . . in
> the possession of whose throne at that time were Delhi, the capital,
> and the dominions of Hindustan, whose standing army was rated
> at a *lakh* (100,000) and whose elephants and whose begs' [nobles']
> elephants were about 1000.[6]

The same figures are given for the host with which Ibrahim now moved out from Delhi to oppose him. Although Babur says that his own forces had, if anything, shrunk during their progress across the Panjab, they had also been supplemented by Lodi deserters. When in April 1526 the two armies met at Panipat, eighty kilometres due north of Delhi, Ibrahim is thought to have still enjoyed a numerical advantage of about ten to one.

Babur was not discouraged. For the Lodi he had nothing but contempt. Ibrahim was a novice who knew little of battle-craft, 'neither when to stand, nor move, nor fight'. After a week-long stand-off he had to be prodded into action by Mughal raiders; he then moved forward without guile or stratagem. Babur awaited him in a carefully chosen formation with the close-packed walls of Panipat on one flank and an ambuscade of brush on the other. Seven hundred carts, commandeered in the neighbourhood, were lashed together across his front with matchlock-men sheltering between them and gaps every hundred metres for the cavalry to charge from. Additional flying columns were held in reserve. As soon as battle was joined they swung round the enemy's flanks and pressed hard from the rear. Ibrahim had no room to manoeuvre. Despite repeated charges, he failed to break through the cordon of carts. His forces became ever more compacted, the wings falling back on the centre, unable either to advance or withdraw. That very numerical supremacy which should have overwhelmed the Mughals now overwhelmed the Lodis. 'By God's mercy and kindness this difficult affair was made easy for us,' recalled Babur. 'In one half-day that armed mass was laid upon the earth.' The most conservative estimate put the slain at fifteen thousand; amongst them was Ibrahim himself.

Hot in pursuit of survivors, Babur headed for Delhi while Humayun, his son, was 'to ride light and fast for Agra', there to secure the Lodi capital and treasury. Amongst those sheltering in Agra Humayun found Ibrahim's mother and also the family of raja Vikramaditya of Gwalior. Gwalior had finally submitted to the Lodis in 1519; Vikramaditya, Man Singh's successor, had thus become a Lodi feudatory and, fighting under Ibrahim at Panipat, had been duly 'sent to hell'. It was supposedly to curry favour with the conqueror that his family now made a 'voluntary offering [to Humayun] of a mass of jewels and valuables amongst which', notes Babur, 'was the famous diamond which Ala-ud-din must have brought'. The weight of this stone he gives as eight *misqals*, perhaps 186 carats, and its value as equivalent to 'two and a half days' food for the whole world'. If the Ala-ud-din in question was the Khalji sultan, the diamond had presumably been obtained during that 'Aladdin's' Deccan campaigns, since the main diamond fields were in Golconda (Hyderabad). How it came into the possession of the Gwalior rajas is not known; but many experts think that this notice in the *Babur-nama* constitutes the first reference to the famous Koh-i-Nur, 'the mountain of light', a gem credited with conferring on its owner either rulership of the world or imminent extinction, depending on how its erratic history is read. It is also sometimes called 'Babur's diamond', although the first Mughal never actually claimed it. Humayun did offer it to him but, perhaps wisely, Babur declined: 'I just gave it back to him.'[7]

For far from being any kind of world-ruler, Babur, although now possessed of the Panjab, Delhi and Agra, was in a critical situation. It was one thing to defeat the unloved Ibrahim, quite another to secure the submission of the unruly Afghan nobles who had poured into India at the invitation of the Lodi sultans and amongst whom the Lodi territories were now parcelled out. The populace of even Agra was openly hostile and, 'Delhi and Agra excepted, not a fortified town ... was in obedience.' The entire

Doab was in enemy hands; so were Aligarh, Bayana and Dholpur, all within easy striking distance of Agra.

Babur's situation was further worsened by growing dissatisfaction within the ranks of his own forces. India had few charms for a God-fearing Mughal *beg*. In a long inventory wherein he reveals as much enthusiasm for India's birds as for its revenues, Babur candidly lists the country's defects: 'no good horses, no good dogs, no grapes, musk-melons or first-rate fruits, no ice or cold water, no good bread or cooked food in the bazaars, no hot-baths, no colleges, no candles, no torches, and no candlesticks.' Perhaps his men could have managed without candlesticks, but amongst what Babur dubbed an unattractive, unsociable, uncouth and exceedingly numerous race of infidels they could never live at ease. In short, like Alexander's Macedonians, Babur's Mughals had had enough. It was May, one of the hottest and dustiest months of the north Indian year. Honours had been won, booty had been secured and vast amounts of treasure distributed. A more successful raid could scarcely have been hoped for. Now all they wanted was to return to their homes and families, to drink the cooler air of Kabul and in due course resume the struggle for Samarkand.

Babur, like Alexander, remonstrated with them. Sovereignty, he said, depended on the possession of resources, revenues and retainers. After long years of struggle and at appalling risk they had at last obtained such things: broad lands, infinite wealth and innumerable subjects were awaiting their command; who would seriously abandon such plenty for 'the harsh poverty of Kabul'? A close friend, who was also one of his most senior commanders, would do just that. Babur let him go, and took less exception to his departure than to the parting couplet he had daubed on his house: 'If safe and sound I cross the Sind,/Blacken my face ere I wish for Hind.' Most, however, stayed. Babur says they were swayed by his just and reasonable words. More probably they were shamed by his resolution. A few weeks later the monsoon brought relief from the heat. Then, in the campaigning season that followed, Humayun lead a force east to Awadh and Jaunpur, scattering the Lodis' recalcitrant feudatories and at last securing those broad lands and that infinite wealth. Greed could be gratified with spoils and ransoms, loyalty rewarded with offices, contracts, revenue assignments and landed fiefs.

There remained, though, one more obstacle to Mughal supremacy in the north. Listing the native powers of India in order of territory and forces, Babur placed first 'the Raja of Bijanagar'. This was Krishna-deva-raya, the greatest of the Vijayanagar kings; since his kingdom was more than a thousand kilometres from Agra he posed no threat. But the second, wrote

Babur, 'is Rana Sangha [of Mewar] who in these days has grown great by his own valour and sword'. Though contemptuous of the rajput's idolatry, Babur seems to have had a sneaking regard for Rana Sangha. It was not because Rana Sangha had originally encouraged him to invade. No treaty had ever been signed, and it was obvious that the rajput had simply hoped for a Lodi defeat and then a Mughal withdrawal which would leave the coast clear for his own ambitions. As it was, Rana Sangha had taken the opportunity to strengthen his hold over Rajasthan, and now, in early 1527, he swiftly advanced at the head of a largely rajput army to see off the invader who had so obligingly disposed of the Lodis.

By February the rajputs were at Bayana, seventy kilometres south-west of Agra and lately occupied by the Mughals. Babur moved out to give battle amidst news that his Bayana garrison had been heavily defeated and a reconnaissance party, a thousand strong, routed by 'the fierceness and valour of the pagan army'. It was an ominous beginning and brought gloom amongst the Mughal ranks. A soothsayer predicted disaster; subsidiary forts defected, Indian recruits deserted; 'every day bad news came from every side.' Once again Babur dug deep to rally his men, this time by appealing to their Islamic convictions. Since the rajputs were infidels, the war was designated a *jihad*. Cowardice thus became apostasy while death assumed the welcome guise of martyrdom. Better still, an acquisitive venture of doubtful legitimacy became the noblest possible of causes while any ambiguity in the minds of former Lodi retainers who were now under his command was dispelled. 'The plan was perfect,' confides Babur, 'it worked admirably . . .' All took an oath on the Quran to fight till they fell. Babur himself made what for him was the ultimate sacrifice by ostentatiously abjuring alcohol. Decanters and goblets were dashed to pieces, wine-skins emptied, and a quantity of the latest vintage from Ghazni salted for vinegar. At one, now, with both his men and his troublesome conscience, the born-again Babur prepared for battle.

Unfortunately the details of the great encounter at Khanua (just west of the later Fatehpur Sikri) are not altogether clear. For the forces available to Rana Sangha and his confederates a figure of 200,000 was calculated, but he probably never commanded half that number in battle. Babur, on the other hand, had far more troops than at Panipat; he had just received reinforcements from Kabul, and had now been joined by numerous ex-Lodi retainers including Ibrahim's son. Presumably there was nothing like the disparity of Panipat and, since the battle raged for a whole day, it seems to have been more evenly and much more fiercely contested. Babur again relied on a semi-fortified arrangement of ditches and fascines flanking the same chain of carts which were again interspersed with artillery and matchlock-men; and again he deployed his cavalry so that they early encircled the enemy. But the rajputs fought with the courage, if also with the lack of co-ordination, that was their wont. In the end, according to their annals as seen by Colonel Tod, defeat resulted not from tactical naivety but from treachery. 'The Tomar traitor who led the [rajput] van went over to Babur, and [Rana] Sangha was obliged to retreat.'[8] But if such a defection did indeed take place, it clearly came when the issue was already decided.

Khanua left the Mughals supreme in the heartland of northern India. Here mopping-up operations became something of a formality as Babur looked further afield. After the 1527 monsoon another expedition was sent east to Jaunpur. Meanwhile Babur himself struck south into Malwa territory and took the fortified town of Chanderi, whose rajput garrison re-enacted the suicidal ritual of *jauhar*. He planned to continue south, but rapidly changed his mind when news arrived that the eastern expedition had been defeated by Lodi sympathisers and other assorted Afghans.

Campaigns against these and other dissidents in Uttar Pradesh and Bihar kept him busy in 1528–9. It is clear from his memoir, however, that such challenges were not unwelcome; indeed the belligerence was often Babur's. 'The army must move . . . in whatever direction favours fortune,' he told his senior advisers; and again, 'To go to Bengal would be improper; but if the move be not on Bengal, where else on that side has treasure helpful for the army?'[9] Although 'boundless and infinite' was his declared desire to return to central Asia, it was not that easy to disengage from India; the appetite for broad lands and abundant revenues which he himself had aroused was proving insatiable. His now considerable forces and feudatories could best be held together only by the prospect of further conquests, plus the further treasure they would bring and the further emoluments they would afford. Babur, in effect, was confronting the challenge which would dog his successors: how to sustain an empire of conquest other than by making more conquests. When he died near Agra in 1530, the question remained unanswered.

INTERLUDE OR INSPIRATION

Of Babur's three sons, Humayun, the eldest and his favourite, had been designated his heir. After winning his spurs at Panipat and Khanua, Humayun had been sent back to Afghanistan to make another bid for Samarkand. This had failed through no fault of his own, and in 1529 he

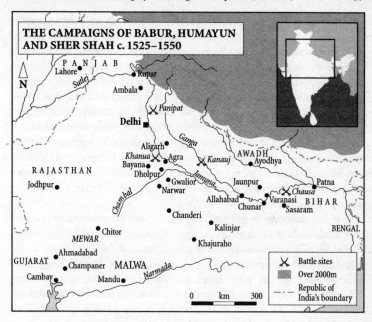

THE CAMPAIGNS OF BABUR, HUMAYUN
AND SHER SHAH c. 1525–1550

had reappeared in India, perhaps alerted by news of his father's failing health. In the event it was Humayun who suddenly sickened and looked as if he were about to die. Distraught, his father supposedly prayed by his sickbed that his own life be forfeit for Humayun's recovery. To a man who had traded abstinence for victory at Khanua, such dealings with the divine were second nature, and once again his piety was rewarded: the father faded as the son convalesced. Humayun was twenty-two when Babur was laid to rest in a parterred garden in Agra, one of many which the nature-loving Babur had himself planned and landscaped. (Later, in accordance with his final wishes, it was to another such retreat amidst the melons and vines of Kabul that his body was removed.)

Hankering for central Asia, Babur had won an empire in India; scorning central Asia, Humayun now lost the empire in India. Thus, though he reigned for twenty-six years, he ruled for barely ten. 'As remarkable for his wit as for his urbanity', says Ferishta, Humayun was 'for the most part disposed to spend his time in social intercourse and pleasure'.[10] Like his father he could be a formidable campaigner but, more wayward, more indulgent and much more indolent, he knew neither how to counter failure nor how to capitalise on success. Nor, unlike Babur, did he personally write any record which might explain his actions – or the lack of them. The long interludes of passivity which punctuated his campaigns are therefore ascribed to his addiction to opium, a drug which in various 'confections' Babur too had used and on which Humayun seemingly depended.

But his first mistake was to trust his three brothers; later Mughals would learn not to repeat it. Instead of eliminating them, he appointed each to the command of a part of the empire. Prince Kamran, who got Kabul, promptly added to it the Panjab, thus in effect severing Babur's legacy. Humayun simply accepted this situation and, in so doing, emboldened his two other brothers, Askari and Hindal. Both would support him only when it suited them; and when it did not, each would make a bid for the throne.

More pressing in Humayun's estimation was the situation in the east. Lodi warlords had again seized Jaunpur; Kalinjar, the great hill-fort of the Chandelas of Khajuraho which had defied Mahmud of Ghazni and almost every Delhi sultan, awaited its first Mughal assault; and in the neighbourhood of Varanasi one Sher Khan, an Afghan of the Sur clan who had followed the Lodis into India, was carving out a kingdom for himself based on the fortress of Chunar. Humayun abandoned his siege of Kalinjar to tackle the situation in Jaunpur; but he had scarcely focused on Sher Khan when news came of a threat to Agra from Ahmed Shah, the sultan of Gujarat. Operations in the east were therefore suspended, much to Sher Khan's advantage, as Humayun faced about. Pausing only to commission a palace which was meant to be the nucleus of another new Delhi, he led his forces south and west.

During the two-year (1534–6) campaign which followed, Humayun achieved in Rajasthan, Malwa and Gujarat conquests of which his father would have been proud and which his son (Akbar) would more famously emulate. The Gujarati sultan, though possessed of a formidable artillery, was roundly defeated, and the near-impregnable heights of both Mandu and Champaner were successfully stormed. At Champaner Humayun himself led the raiders and, with hammer and pitons, scaled the sheer rock-face in a wildly audacious assault which, says Ferishta, was 'equal in the opinion of military men to anything of the kind recorded in history'.[11] Ahmadabad was then occupied and so was Cambay, respectively the richest city and port in western India. It was a dazzling triumph which, carefully consolidated, could have provided the economic foundation of Humayun's empire as well as doubling its size. But he rejected the traditional solution of reinstating the defeated Ahmad Shah as a feudatory and, instead, installed the worthless Prince Askari. He then retired to Mandu whence, after several dazed months in the company of his favourites and his opium pipe, he headed home to Agra. As he did so, his conquests were simply rolled up behind him. Askari, seeing Gujarat primarily as a base whence to launch a bid for the throne, allowed Ahmad Shah to reoccupy his kingdom while he himself also hastened to Agra.

There Humayun forestalled him but, nothing if not conciliatory, again forgave the fraternal transgression. Then he returned to the familiar solace of pipe and playmates. 'Public business was neglected,' says Ferishta, 'and the governors of the surrounding districts, taking advantage of this state of affairs, . . . enlisted under the standard of Sher Khan Sur.' In July 1537 Humayun at last bestirred himself and marched east against the Afghan usurper. Chunar fell after a long siege but Sher Khan was not there; nor was he at Jaunpur or anywhere else in Awadh. For while Humayun had been conquering Gujarat, Sher Khan had been about the same business in Bihar and now Bengal. And unlike Humayun, he was taking great care to secure his newly-acquired conquests. Instead of another Afghan upstart, Humayun suddenly found himself faced by a well-prepared contender for sovereignty. The tussle between Mughal and Afghan was far from over.

In 1539, after much to-ing and fro-ing in Bengal, the rival armies finally met at Chausa between Varanasi and Patna. Humayun fell for an Afghan ruse and was defeated. He barely escaped with his life, his troops were decimated, and the myth of Mughal invincibility was badly dented.

A year later it was utterly exploded. Near Kanauj, the imperial city on the upper Ganga from which the Gurjara-Pratiharas had once obscurely reigned, the fate of the short-lived Mughal empire looked to have been decided. In a surprising reversal of Panipat, Humayun's army, forty thousand strong and well supplied with firepower, was overwhelmed by Sher Khan's fifteen thousand mainly Afghan cavalry. Humayun again escaped with his life – and with his monstrous diamond. But failing to win help or even sanctuary from his ungrateful brothers, he became a fugitive in the deserts of Sind and Rajasthan and then an exile at the court of Shah Tamasp, the Safavid ruler of Iran. Luckily Shah Tamasp liked diamonds. Humayun's fortunes would yet revive. Meanwhile Sher Khan Sur was supreme.

The Afghan Surs, dynastically sandwiched amongst the great and magnificently documented Mughals, easily elude the credit that is their due. Their fifteen-year supremacy is sometimes portrayed as a reactionary interlude or an impertinent interruption to the glorious Mughal succession. Yet the interlude was rich in inspiration. Sher Khan, who following victory at

Chausa had assumed the royal title of Sher Shah, was as able as any Mughal. If, fortuitously, the adventures of Babur the Mughal have a fictitious ring, no such complaint is heard of the stern and often devious doings of Sher Shah Sur. Where Babur's genius lay in the glamour of battle-craft, Sher Shah's lay in the minutiae of statecraft. To the sombre text of his short reign the empire which would soon embrace all India owes just as much as to the animated excitement of Babur's more colourful adventures.

Although embroidered by Afghan admirers, it is clear that Sher Shah's rise from an insignificant Lodi retainer with a couple of small fiefs near Varanasi was in itself remarkable. It took some time, and when he finally gained the throne he was already into his fifties. But to have overcome the rivalries of his fractious Afghan compeers was more than most Lodis had managed, while the conquest of Bengal, and his subsequent settlement of it, reduced that troublesome and previously independent kingdom to a subordinate status unknown since the Tughluq interventions of the four-teenth century.

Further Sur campaigns in the Panjab, Sind and Malwa followed the defeat of Humayun and duly secured those provinces. An expedition into the Deccan like that of Ala-ud-din Khalji, the sultan whom Sher Shah most admired, was also proposed. But, a devout if not fanatical Muslim, Sher Shah argued that the eradication of infidel authority within his existing domains was a higher priority. On the pretext that Muslim mothers and maidens were being abused in rajput households, he preferred first to reduce bastions of Hindu resistance like Jodhpur, Chitor and, fatefully, Kalinjar. There, too, he triumphed where so many others had failed, but at the cost of his life. A rocket aimed at the fort rebounded off its walls and, exploding, ignited the pile of rockets which were intended to follow it. Sher Shah, who was directing operations, was horribly burnt. He died a few hours later, just as news of the fort's surrender arrived.

In so short a reign (1540–5) a complete overhaul of the machinery of government had scarcely been possible. Yet 'during that brief period his energetic administration forecast many of the centralising measures in rev-enue assessment and military organisation that would be carried to com-pletion by the Mughals.'[12] These were particularly evident in his settlement of Bengal. Instead of appointing another all-powerful governor, who would assuredly cast off his allegiance at the first opportunity, he divided the province into districts, each directly responsible to himself, and then divided the exercise of authority amongst civil, military and religious officials who were themselves subject to rotation. There and elsewhere efforts were also made to rationalise the assessment and collection of revenue and to afford the cultivator a modicum of security; village headmen were made responsible for any unpunished crimes; corrupt officials were dismissed.

Corruption within the military was also tackled. The practice was revived of branding all cavalry horses so that on active service they could not be replaced by lesser mounts; and for similar reasons attempts were made to compile service rolls which identified and described each trooper. Military posts were established throughout the provinces; roads and caravanserais were built; illegal imposts and duties were removed to facilitate trade. Memorably Sher Shah also occupies an important place in the history of Indian coinage, in that he coined the first silver rupees which, together with his other coins of gold and copper, would form the basis of the Mughal currency.[13]

Something similar might be said of his architectural creations. Babur's only noteworthy additions to India's monuments had been three mosques of little stylistic distinction. One, at Panipat, celebrated his victory over the Lodi, although another, that at Ayodhya, has since upstaged it. Historians have of late been sorely taxed over this Ayodhya *Babur-i* (or *Babri*) *masjid*. Did it replace a Hindu temple which marked the spot where Lord Rama (of the *Ramayana*) was born? And what, if any, was Babur's role in its construction? Ever since Hindu fanatics laid into the mosque with pickaxes in 1992, thus provoking a more serious cave-in of modern India's secular credentials, more words have been written about this unimpressive site than about any other in India. Adding to them would be only to invite contradiction.

Happily, the much more stylish monuments of Sher Shah have fared better. In Delhi he added to the complex begun by Humayun on the supposed site of Indraprastha, the capital of the Pandavas in the *Mahabharata* and now known as Purana Qila. He also built there a mosque. Only parts of this Qila-i-Kuhna survive, but 'no sanctum and façade in India possesses quite such measured dignity allied to perfect taste in the rich but restrained decoration.' Making comparison with Brunelleschi, the master-builder of fifteenth-century Florence, J.C. Harle in the *Pelican History of Art* series finds here 'a strength, beauty and richness beyond anything achieved by the Mughals'.[14]

Still more arresting, although rarely visited, is the magnificent five-storey tomb at Sasaram (Sahasaram), midway between Varanasi and Gaya, to which Sher Shah's charred remains were carried from Kalinjar for interment. Octagonal like many of the Lodi tombs, and set upon a stepped plinth in the middle of a lake like that of Ghiyas-ud-din Tughluq, Sher Shah's mausoleum is yet wholly original. At the angles of three of its storeys, *chattris* (pillared and cupola-ed pavilions) of diminishing size recall the *amlakas* of a temple tower and contribute to a pyramidal profile of stunning beauty. The overall impression is as much of a palace as of a tomb and may owe something to Man Singh's great façade at Gwalior which Babur had much admired and where Sher Shah had stayed.

Nearly fifty metres high, the massive scale of Sher Shah's tomb is also remarkable. Dwarfing all previous Muslim tombs in India, it set another standard to which the greatest Mughal builders, Akbar, Jahangir and Shah Jahan, would dutifully strive. Nor was it their only challenge. The most ambitious structure of the seventeenth century would in fact be located neither in Agra nor Delhi but deep in the Deccan at Bijapur. Not far away, the sprawling stone metropolis of Vijayanagar, India's Angkor, offered further convincing proof that in the peninsula worthy rivals of Mughal and Sur yet flourished.

THE RISE AND FALL OF VIJAYANAGAR

When listing the native powers of what he called 'Hindustan', Babur had placed first 'the Raja of Bijanagar', that is Vijayanagar. From the great city beside the Tungabhadra river in northern Karnataka an erratic succession of Hindu kings had been extending its sway throughout the fifteenth century. With territories that now included much of Andhra Pradesh and Kerala and most of Karnataka and Tamil Nadu, the king of Vijayanagar, according to the *Babur-nama*, controlled the most extensive kingdom in the subcontinent. His forces were also the most numerous, although Babur knew nothing else worth recording of such a distant potentate.

He was better informed as to the plight of the Bahmanid sultans, Vijayanagar's one-time rivals in the Deccan. 'At the present time no independent authority is left them; their great *begs* have laid hands on the whole country, and must be asked for whatever is needed.'[15] In fact the great *begs*, or nobles, were in the process of carving up the Bahmanid kingdom. While Mahmud Shah, the last Bahmanid, yet reigned (1482–1518), four major power-centres, each with its own Muslim dynasty, laid claim to the Bahmanid dominions. One, based on the city of Ahmadnagar (two hundred kilometres east of Bombay in Maharashtra), occupied the north-western corner of the erstwhile sultanate and, adjacent to Malwa, would soon be of consuming interest to Babur's successors; another retained Bidar, the Bahmanid capital; to the south-east, the third was based on Golconda, the future Hyderabad; and the fourth, based on Bijapur, inherited the southern,

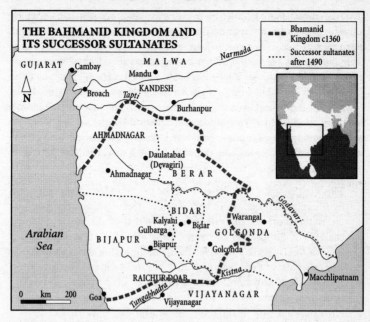

or Karnataka, part of the Bahmanid sultanate and, along with it, front-line status in respect of the Vijayanagar kings.

For Vijayanagar this gradual fragmentation of its ancient rival was timely. Following the death in 1446 of Deva Raya II, the last effective ruler of the Sangama dynasty, Vijayanagar too had been rent by internal strife. But territory lost in Andhra Pradesh and Tamil Nadu had been largely reclaimed by Narasimha, a general who eventually assumed the kingship and founded the Saluva dynasty. His death in 1491 led to another succession crisis from which emerged a second Narasimha who founded the Tuluva dynasty. It was this Narasimha Tuluva who in 1509 was gloriously succeeded by his half-brother, and Babur's contemporary, the great Krishna-deva-raya.

During the latter's twenty-year reign Vijayanagar soared to its spectacular zenith. Krishna-deva-raya's armies overran the strategic Raichur Doab, menaced the new Deccan sultanates, worsted even the Gajapati kings of Orissa and claimed extensive new territories in Andhra Pradesh. Tribute and plunder poured into Vijayanagar, there to be lavished on royal rituals, academic patronage and architectural extravaganzas. For his support of scholars Krishna-deva-raya was hailed as another King Bhoj. The city itself, covering thirty square kilometres, occasioned the sort of superlatives which a hundred years later would be showered on the Mughal capitals of Agra and Delhi. It 'seemed to me as large as Rome, and very beautiful', wrote Domingo Paes, a Portuguese visitor in the 1520s. Paes refrained from guessing at its population lest the improbable figure be taken to impugn the rest of his account, but from a check on its markets he was convinced that it was also 'the best provided city in the world'. Likewise the kingdom's resources, about which Paes was less reticent: 'the king has continually a million fighting troops [under arms].' And likewise Krishna-deva-raya himself, of whom Paes provides a thumbnail sketch as convincing as any in Mughal literature.

> This king is of medium height, and of fair complexion and good figure, rather fat than thin; he has on his face signs of small-pox. He is the most feared and perfect king that could possibly be, cheerful of disposition and very merry; he is one that seeks to honour foreigners, and receives them kindly, asking about all their affairs, whatever their condition may be. He is a great ruler and a man of much justice, but subject to sudden fits of rage, and this is his title 'Crisnarao Macacao, king of kings, lord of the greater lords of India, lord of the three seas and of the land'. He has this title because by rank he is a greater lord than any by reason of what he possesses ... but it seems that (in fact) he has nothing compared to what a man like him ought to have, so gallant and perfect is he in all things.[16]

Thanks to this paragon of kingly virtues, to the magnificence of his metropolis as evidenced by its still staggering ruins, and to the abrupt and imminent eclipse of both, Vijayanagar has attracted much scholarly attention. Typically the kingdom has been seen as the epitome of traditional Indian kingship and a spectacular finale to two thousand years of Hindu empire. 'It stood for the older religion and culture of the country and saved these from being engulfed by the rush of new ideas and forces.'[17] It was also 'the last bastion of Hinduism'; and when it fell, 'the South died'. All the city's monuments, its bazaars and streets, its temples and palaces, are constructed of massive stone blocks which have been hewn, dressed and sculpted from the rock-scape of monumental boulders amongst which they stand. Even the intervening hills are composed of these boulders, and so daringly are they stacked and balanced on top of one another that they too could be architecture and the city's monuments but an inspired elaboration of what nature has already ordained. Just so the kingdom has often been seen as a natural and climactic reordering of the ideals and achievements of all those earlier stone-whittling, elephant-trumpeting Deccan dynasties – Shatavahanas and Vakatakas, Chalukyas and Rashtrakutas. In particular the earliest Chalukyas seem to have inspired the kings of Vijayanagar, who modelled some of their temples on those of Badami and Aihole.

More recently, however, the Vijayanagar kingdom has been reinterpreted as very far from traditional and in fact a radical experiment in political and military organisation during a time of social and economic upheaval. The evidence, culled from accounts like that of Paes, from literary sources and from a painstaking analysis of thousands of inscriptions, suggests that by the sixteenth century the defence of Hindu *dharma* was not uppermost in the minds of the Vijayanagar kings (if it ever had been). Nor did they rely on the support of satellite kings or the impact of intoxicated elephants. Instead they looked to often Muslim cavalry and to a variety of new military structures including 'a system of royal fortresses under brahman commanders ... Portuguese and Muslim mercenary gunners ... foot-soldiers recruited from non-peasant, or forest, people ... and a new strata of lesser chiefs totally dependent on military service [the so-called 'Poligars']'.[18]

At the apex of this organisation the Vijayanagar kings, dispensing with the traditional notion of paramountcy implicit in the 'society of kings', had adopted a semi-feudal system of powerful military subordinates. It was amongst these subordinates, known as 'Nayaks' and numbering several hundred, that most of the kingdom was parcelled out. They were appointed by the sovereign and were responsible both for maintaining large military contingents at the service of the sovereign and for organising the collection and remission of revenue to the sovereign. In other words they performed somewhat the expected role of the mainly Afghan feudatories in the north. But whilst the latter, from a position of semi-independence, were coming under increasing pressure to submit to Mughal or Sur overlords, the Nayaks in the south, from a position of dependent commanders, were becoming king-makers whose standing with local religious and commercial institutions often eclipsed that of their sovereign.

Other factors beyond the control of Krishna-deva-raya and his successors also contributed to the growing instability of the kingdom. Amongst them was the new Portuguese presence on the peninsular seaboard. According to one authority, 'the Portuguese have the dubious distinction of introducing politics into the [Indian] ocean.'[19] Maritime trade had hitherto been considered as open to all and subject only to competitive pressures and local incentives. That Muslim traders and Islamic shipping interests had gained a near monopoly of the sea-routes to the west and to the east had not therefore been cause for alarm. But as of the early sixteenth century the freedom of the seas and of the monsoon winds was called in question. Thanks to developments in navigation and naval gunnery, oceanic trade was suddenly revealed as susceptible to state direction and subject to military control. By demonstrating that maritime empire was a paying and practical proposition, the Portuguese had indeed politicised the Indian Ocean. Land-based empires which in any way depended on overseas trade would have to come to terms with it.

Vasco da Gama's appearance at Calicut on the Kerala coast in 1498 had climaxed a century of Portuguese attempts to find a sea-route round Africa to the spice-producing Indies. He returned to Lisbon with a cargo of Indian pepper and his route was immediately followed by an annual armada of Portuguese shipping, much of it manned and armed for combat. In 1503 the first Portuguese fort was built at Cochin, whose raja then became something of a Portuguese puppet. Two years later the appointment of a viceroy for something which Lisbon now called its *Estado da India*, or 'State of India', betrayed the true nature of Portuguese ambition. Goa was taken in 1510, not from Vijayanagar but from the Bijapur sultanate, and was soon fortified as the hub of Portuguese maritime empire in Indian waters.

Stiffer resistance was offered to the Portuguese by the sultan of Gujarat and his distant allies, the Mameluke rulers of Egypt with whom Gujarati merchants traditionally traded. But in the 1530s the ports of Bassein (near Bombay) and Diu (in Saurastra) were incorporated into the *Estado da India* and effectively controlled access to Gujarat's outlets of Cambay, Surat and Broach. Portuguese ships and guns were demonstrably superior to those of either Indian or Arab, and Lisbon's claim to control the shipping of the entire west coast thus became effective.

To what extent the rulers of Vijayanagar had benefited from overseas trade is disputed. But the land-routes from the west coast ports up to Vijayanagar were evidently a high priority, and the city was a conspicuous consumer of foreign imports as well as a major market for their onward distribution. Crucially these imports included the desiderata of every Indian army, namely horses, mostly from the Persian Gulf, and some fire-arms. To encourage the supply of horses it was said that the Vijayanagar rulers would pay even for dead ones. The new Portuguese monopoly of the horse trade looks both to have deprived the kingdom of important revenues and to have prejudiced the supply of remounts when, as under Krishna-deva-raya's successor, Vijayanagar was at war with the Portuguese.

The war in question did not last long. Of far greater consequence was the rivalry between Achyuta-deva-raya, the brother and nominated successor of the great Krishna-deva-raya, and Rama Raja, Krishna's powerful son-in-law. Failing to secure the succession in 1529, Rama Raja tried again when Achyuta died in 1542. To advance his chances, he also sought the aid of the sultan of Bijapur. There were ample precedents for the involvement of the sultanates in the Vijayanagar succession (and vice versa). Rama Raja, a consummate intriguer, was merely taking advantage of the Deccan's fluid and opportunist rivalries. When, thanks to this alliance, he was safely ensconced as regent, he continued to pursue a tortuous policy of advancing Vijayanagar's frontiers by exploiting the rivalries between Bijapur, Golconda and the other Bahmanid successors.

In this Rama Raja succeeded, if anything, too well. During twenty years of complex intrigue he so provoked the sultanates that they came to fear for their very survival. It is possible that he also outraged their Islamic sensibilities. Ferishta makes this accusation so often that it smacks of pious convention; on the other hand religious sensitivity and sectarian solidarity may well have been heightened at a time when the neighbouring Portuguese were combining the anti-Muslim spirit of the Crusades with the excesses of the Inquisition.

Certainly, and fatally, Rama Raja also overstretched those frayed loyalties on which Vijayanagar's cohesion depended. This became apparent when in 1564 the four sultans at last patched up their differences and turned on him in concert. To meet this threat he summoned his Nayaks even from as far south as Madurai. Most did respond, but in January 1565 the Vijayanagar forces were catastrophically routed in the battle of Talikota. Rama Raja himself was beheaded, and casualties were colossal. Yet the great city of Vijayanagar, with its seven massive walls and its ingeniously designed gatehouses, might still have been defended. In the event, it was just deserted; Nayaks and Poligars withdrew to their individual territories. The 550 elephant-loads of treasure which they hastily 'rescued' from the city could just as well have been pillaged.

The battle had taken place on the banks of the Kistna river, about 120 kilometres north of Vijayanagar. But the victors did not immediately swoop on the city; local scavengers seem to have been the first to gain access. Nor is it self-evident that the Muslims' intention was to obliterate the place. Despite colourful descriptions of a five-month sack, wholesale slaughter, savage iconoclasm and such remorseless demolition that 'nothing now remains but a heap of ruins',[20] the impression these 'ruins' convey is less of wilful destruction and more of neglect, plus some random treasure-hunting and much casual pillage of building materials. Temples, the bigot's prime target, prove to be the least damaged structures; and in many of them the statuary, so invitingly vulnerable, remains miraculously intact. In short the city, like the kingdom, looks to have suffered less from conquering fanatics and more from that deepening internal crisis of authority.

Rid of Vijayanagar's supervision, Nayaks would continue to rule in many parts of the south just as would the quarrelsome sultans in the Deccan. In the extreme south the Nayaks of Madurai would evade even Mughal rule. Not so the others. Just when 'Vijaya-nagar' ('City of Victory' in Sanskrit) was disappearing from the map, a 'Fateh-pur' ('City of Victory' in the Persian of the Mughal court) was being built at Sikri near Agra. Urban triumphalism was passing from the Deccan to the north. Vijayanagar's collapse did indeed spell the end of the south as a separate political arena. As time would reveal, the real victors of Talikota were not Bijapur and Golconda but the Great Mughals.

ALLAHU-AKBAR

Twenty years earlier, in the summer of 1544 while Sher Shah Sur still ruled in northern India, the Mughal revival had begun near Sultaniyeh in north-western Iran. There Humayun, the fugitive from India, was entertained by Shah Tamasp. The two kings met in a tented city of silken pavilions dripping with pearls and lined with gold-embroidered velvet. Unlike that other 'Field of the Cloth of Gold' where Tudor and Valois had lately met, the encounter was beset with religious misgivings. They were resolved when Humayun briefly endorsed the Shi'ite teachings of his host. 'Fraternal unanimity' having been established, joint action was agreed and costly presents were exchanged, none more costly than that diamond, now said to be 'worth the revenue of countries and climes', which duly passed from Mughal to shah. Indeed its value was reckoned at four times the cost of the hospitality enjoyed by Humayun in Iran, and so may also have been sufficient to defray the military assistance which he now received. With twelve thousand Persian troops plus what remained of his own following, and with a train of Persian courtiers and artists whose influence at the Mughal court would be considerable, Humayun headed east to redeem his empire.

Again he was opposed by his brothers, one of whom still held Kandahar, the other Kabul. It took him eight years just to win back Afghanistan. The delay was not, however, disastrous. In India Sher Shah's brief but remarkable reign came to an end in 1545 just as Humayun entered Afghanistan. Sher Shah's less effective son, Islam Shah Sur, succeeded to the throne but himself died in 1553 whereupon the Sur dominions split into semi-independent provinces while famine and faction undid Sher Shah's reforms. Like the Lodis on the eve of Babur's invasion, the Surs on the eve of Humayun's attack were in terminal confusion.

Additionally, eight years in Afghanistan meant that Humayun's son, who had been born during the course of his father's flight from India, was now emerging from the seclusion of the seraglio. Akbar, or 'this nursling of Divine light' as his biographer calls him, was now twelve years old, hyperactive, and endowed, we are told, with 'a perfect understanding beyond computation'. Such judicious wording was designed to obscure the fact that the young 'World-Conqueror' had learned neither to read nor write. He never would; almost certainly he suffered from chronic dyslexia. But as a sportsman and a warrior he showed promise, and as a talisman of future Mughal rule he now accompanied his father on the march into India. In November 1554, continues Abu'l-Fazl, author of the imperial memoir known as the *Akbar-nama*, 'His Majesty [Humayun] laid firm hold of the strong hand of divine favour, grasped the stout cable of heavenly tidings, and set off with few men – they did not amount to three thousand – but with large help from the armies of Providence, which could not be calculated by intellectual accountants.'[21]

More troops soon joined him – to the relief, no doubt, of the intellectual accountants. They were seriously tested only once, when the Sur ruler of the Panjab was defeated at Sirhind. Otherwise it was a deceptively easy invasion. By August 1555 Humayun had reclaimed Delhi and was happily 'watering the rose-garden of sovereignty with the stream of justice' while planning the revival of Sher Shah's administrative reforms. Agra and adjacent areas were also secured. But their government and that of the Panjab had scarcely been settled when in January 1556 triumph turned to tragedy. A keen astronomer, Humayun tripped when descending from his makeshift observatory on the roof of Sher Shah's Delhi palace and fell to his death down the stone stairs. He thus, in the words of a less than generous scholar, 'stumbled out of this life as he had stumbled through it'.[22]

Once again Mughal rule was in jeopardy. Akbar was still only thirteen. He was not in Delhi but in the Panjab. And a formidable if unlikely adversary was mobilising to frustrate not only the Mughal succession but the whole Mughal presence.

Sometimes styling himself 'Raja Vikramaditya' in imitation of various Indian heroes, this new adversary was one Hemu, a Hindu of lowly parentage who had surmounted both the strictures of caste and the disadvantages of a wretchedly puny physique to rise from being a saltpetre pedlar in a provincial bazaar to chief minister to one of the principal Sur claimants. Yet more surprisingly for one who could not even ride a horse, he had acquired a reputation for inspired generalship. Twenty-two consecutive battles is Hemu said to have won against assorted adversaries. To this tally he now added a twenty-third when, soon after Humayun's death, he stormed Delhi and put its Mughal garrison to flight. Not surprisingly even his mainly Afghan, and so Muslim, troops regarded their 'Shah Hemu' as an inspirational commander and confidently sallied north to engage the main Mughal force in the Panjab.

Outnumbered and out-generaled, the Mughal commanders favoured a speedy retreat to Kabul. However Bayram Khan, the young emperor's guardian and virtual regent, stood firm – a decision which the chance capture of Hemu's artillery by a Mughal flying column seemed to support. Hemu's elephants were another matter. According to Abu'l-Fazl, the enemy had assembled a corps of fifteen hundred of the largest and most athletic beasts ever seen. 'How can the attributes of those rushing mountains be strung on the slender thread of words?' he asks. Swifter than the fleetest racehorses, they ran so fast 'that it could not be called running', while, 'mountain-like and dragon-mouthed ... they ruined lofty buildings by shaking them and sportively uprooted strong trees'.[23] In fanciful descriptions of pachyderms, as in panegyric invention, Abu'l-Fazl's Persian could challenge even the Sanskrit of ancient India's dynastic scribes.

At Panipat, the site of Babur's great victory, the two armies met on 5 November 1556. For once victory looked to be going the way of the elephants. 'The horses would not face the elephants,' which 'shook the left and right divisions' and 'dislodged many soldiers of the sublime army'. Hemu, to whose abilities even Abu'l-Fazl bears grudging testimony, commanded operations from a gigantic beast called 'Hawai' ('Windy', or possibly 'Rocket'). 'He made powerful onsets and performed many valorous acts.' Indeed the Mughals were wavering when 'suddenly an arrow from the bended bow of divine wrath reached Hemu's eye and, piercing the socket, came out at the back of his head.'[24] Seeing Hemu collapse into his howdah, his troops lost heart. It was now the sublime army, swords flashing and epithets flying, which closed for the kill. Hawai was captured; Hemu, extracted from his howdah and dragged before the young victor, was quickly beheaded. Next day a Mughal army entered Delhi in triumph yet again. Including Timur's assault, it was third time lucky. Not for another two hundred years would Delhi slip from Mughal rule.

Akbar's reign, begun amidst scenes of such dazzling portent, would outshine that of all Indian sovereigns. It helped that it lasted for all of half a century, during which time the emperor's energy scarcely flagged. It also helped that it was exceptionally well documented. Not even Elizabeth I of England, Akbar's exact contemporary, was so well served by annalists and artists. Akbar bestrides all accounts of the Great Mughals not just because without him there might not have been a Mughal empire but because without him it would certainly have been a much more obscure and controversial affair. In a manner which only Alexander and Ashoka had perhaps anticipated, Akbar was intensely aware of making history; reputation would vie with advantage at every turn of his reign; like the huntsman that he was, he sniffed the course of events, scenting the immortality which was his prey.

'Write with the pen of sincerity the account of the glorious events and of our dominion-increasing victories,'[25] he told Abu'l-Fazl. Others, painters as well as writers, were similarly bidden, then richly rewarded. Abu'l-Fazl himself wrote not only the *Akbar-nama*, a year-by-year account of the reign which in the printed English edition runs, with footnotes, to over 2500 pages, but also a compendious almanac and Domesday Book of the empire, the *Ain-i-Akbari*, which runs to another 1500 pages. In such works, commissioned by the emperor, 'the pen of sincerity' writes exclusively with the ink of adulation; Akbar can do no wrong, his enemies are written off as misguided scoundrels, his policies are wholly original, and his success is a foregone conclusion. Yet of all such 'dominion-increasing victories' and 'glorious events' Abu'l-Fazl speaks with an insight and authority which more critical accounts only substantiate.

Succeeding so young, Akbar's first years were necessarily of tutelage. In 1556–60 Bayram Khan, as regent, directed the defeat of Sur rivals in the Panjab, Awadh and Gwalior. A stern if devoted protector, the regent had earlier accompanied Humayun to Iran and was in fact a Shia of Persian tastes, if not birth. This provoked resentment amongst the mainly Sunni nobility and, when Akbar himself tired of his direction, Bayram Khan was first dismissed, then provoked into revolt and killed.

Those mainly responsible were a new clique centred round Akbar's erstwhile nurse and her son, Adham Khan. In 1561 the latter commanded an invasion of Malwa where Baz Bahadur, the last and most memorable of its much-restored sultans, had revived the Malwa tradition of Muslim–rajput amity. An outstanding musician and the subject of many popular verses, Baz Bahadur spent his days flitting from palace to palace across the heights of Mandu as he serenaded Rupmati, a rajput princess. This idyll now ended. Baz Bahadur was routed and put to flight, Rupmati poisoned herself rather than submit to Adham Khan's attentions, and their followers, Muslim as well as Hindu, were callously massacred.

Akbar took exception not to the massacre but to Adham Khan's with-holding the spoils of victory. A similar infringement by his commanders in Awadh brought the same response: Akbar personally rushed to the scene and secured abject protestations of homage. But although reconciled, in May 1562 Adham Khan again stepped on the royal prerogative when he made a fatal attempt on the life of the chief minister. The emperor was enjoying a siesta nearby at the time. Aroused by the tumult, he 'became nobly indignant' and, encountering the miscreant on the palace verandah, 'struck him such a blow on the face that that wicked monster turned a somersault and fell down insensible'.[26] Another account says that he was bowled over like a pigeon. Pigeon-like, he was then trussed and flung headlong from the top of the terrace.

With this exhibition of 'sublime justice' the personal reign of Akbar, now just nineteen, may be said to have begun. He assumed supreme civil and military authority, dispensing with the office of chief minister and thereby eliminating its potential for rivalry, while undertaking swift but vigorous campaigns against his sporadically dissident commanders in the east. Abu'l-Fazl notes that it was also about this time that he began to show an unconventional interest in his subjects and their beliefs. 'He sought for truth amongst the dust-stained denizens of the field of irreflection and consorted with every sort of wearers of patched garments such as *jogis*, *sanyasis* and *qalandars*, and other solitary sitters in the dust and insouciant recluses.'[27]

Sometimes Akbar slipped from the royal apartments to mingle unrecog-nised with bazaar folk and villagers. For one to whom the written word had to be read by others these contacts were a means to information and a method of verification. They were also the beginning of a lifelong enquiry into matters spiritual and religious. More obviously they made him uniquely aware of the diversity of his subjects and of the great gulf that separated them from their mainly foreign rulers. Unlike Babur or Humayun, Akbar had been born in India, in fact in an Indian village and under Hindu protection. (The place, now just in Pakistan, was Umarkot, a rajput fort in the great desert of Thar where in 1542 Humayun and his entourage had found temporary shelter during their flight from Sher Shah.) To Akbar Indians were not the uncultured mass of infidels who so horrified Babur; they were his countrymen. And whatever their religion, it was his duty not to oppress them. Discriminatory measures against Hindus, like a tax on pilgrims and the detested *jizya*, were lifted. He would even make a point of celebrating the Hindu festivals of Divali and Dussehra.

It was also at this time, 1562, that Akbar married the daughter of the Kacchwaha rajput raja of Amber (near Jaipur, which city later Kacchwahas would build, thus becoming the maharajas of Jaipur). The marriage was partly a reward for the family's loyalty to Humayun and partly a way of securing that loyalty to Akbar and his heirs. Additionally the raja, his son and his grandson were all inducted into the Mughal hierarchy as *amirs* (nobles), who in return for the retention of their ancestral lands, their Hindu beliefs and clan standing, would swear allegiance to the emperor and provide specified numbers of cavalry for service in the imperial forces. Both Bhagwant Das, the raja's son, and Man Singh, his grandson, eventually became amongst the most trusted of Akbar's lieutenants. In fact this formula, with or without a royal marriage, worked so well that it was steadily extended to numerous other rajput chiefs.

Rajasthan, so long a thicket of opposition combining the prickliest resistance with the least fruitful rewards, was thus incorporated piecemeal within the imperial system which itself became much more broad-based. In 1555 the Mughal nobility, or *omrah*, had numbered fifty-one, nearly all of them non-Indian Muslims (Turks, Afghans, Uzbeks, Persians). By 1580 the number had increased to 222, of whom nearly half were Indian, including forty-three rajputs. All benefited from this arrangement: the Mughals secured the services of a respected elite plus their warlike followers, while the rajputs gained access to high rank and wealth within a pan-Indian empire.

Not all rajput chiefs saw it that way. Some required the rougher persuasion of conquest while Udai Singh, the Sesodia Rana of Mewar, remained unpersuaded even in defeat. As a successor of Rana Sangha, Babur's opponent at Khanua, and as the scion of the most senior rajput clan, Udai Singh was an obvious focus for dissent. He had already afforded sanctuary to Baz Bahadur, the love-lorn fugitive of Malwa, and he was openly critical of the Kacchwahas' submission. The final straw came when Udai Singh's son, a hostage at the Mughal court, suddenly fled south. In 1567 Akbar himself marched south and, perhaps looking for a triumph to rival that just achieved by the Deccan sultans over Vijayanagar, personally set about the siege of Chitor.

The great Sesodia stronghold, although not the most inaccessible of hill forts, was difficult to approach and had tried the ingenuity of such redoubtable commanders as Ala-ud-din Khalji and Sher Shah. For Akbar, as operations dragged on into 1568, the investment of Chitor became much more

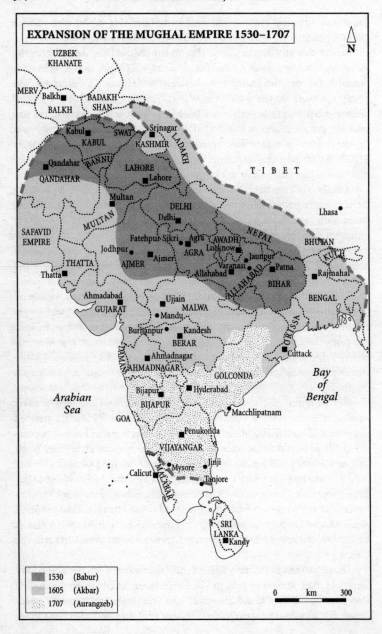

EXPANSION OF THE MUGHAL EMPIRE 1530–1707

N

UZBEK KHANATE

MERV
Balkh
BALKH
BADAKH SHAN

Kabul
KABUL
SWAT
Srinagar
KASHMIR
LADAKH

Qandahar
QANDAHAR
BANNU
LAHORE
Lahore

T I B E T

Lhasa

Multan
MULTAN
DELHI
Delhi

SAFAVID EMPIRE
Fatehpur Sikri
Agra
AGRA
AWADH
Lucknow
NEPAL
BHUTAN

Jodhpur
Ajmer
AJMER
Jaunpur
Varanasi
KUCH

THATTA
Allahabad
ALLAHABAD
Patna
Rajmahal

Thatta
BIHAR
BENGAL

Ahmadabad
GUJARAT
Ujjain
MALWA
Mandu

Burhanpur
Kandesh
BERAR
ORISSA

Ahmadnagar
AHMADNAGAR
GOLCONDA
Cuttack

DAMAN
Bijapur
BIJAPUR
Hyderabad

Arabian Sea

Bay of Bengal

GOA
Macchlipatnam

Penukonda
VIJAYANGAR

Calicut
MALABAR
Mysore
Jinji
Tanjore

SRI LANKA
Kandy

1530 (Babur)
1605 (Akbar)
1707 (Aurangzeb)

0   km   300

than a punitive siege. It was like a rite of passage, or a Herculean labour in which *izzat* (honour) was closely engaged. Udai Singh and his son had long since fled to sanctuary in the hills – an action so out of character for a rajput, let alone a Sesodia, that in Colonel Tod it would induce an apoplexy of indignation ('well had it been for Mewar . . . had the annals never recorded the name of Oody Singh in the catalogue of her princes'[28]). Akbar pressed the siege regardless of his enemy's absence. It became one of the great set-pieces of the age, avidly followed, gloriously recorded and in the end bloodily concluded. With flames engulfing their womenfolk, the defenders sallied forth in another suicidal *jauhar*. It was followed by Akbar's gratuitous massacre of some twenty thousand non-combatants.

Chitor was never reoccupied. Like Vijayanagar it remains much as the sixteenth century left it. But, about a hundred kilometres to the west, in a less conspicuous setting where the Sesodias had already created a lake, Udai Singh founded a smiling new capital. He died in 1572 but in his honour the place was named Udaipur and from there the house of Mewar would continue to defy the might of the Mughals and to delight connoisseurs of rajput romance.

Meanwhile Akbar was also founding a new capital. Hitherto the court had been based at Agra where, lining the right bank of the Jamuna, the walls of the great Red Fort had been completed by 1562. Other fortified complexes at Lahore, Allahabad and Ajmer were underway. Together with Agra, they framed the core of Mughal empire in northern India.[29] Ajmer, now the seat of the Mughal governor for Rajasthan, had once been the capital of Prithviraj Chahamana and contained the shrine of his contemporary, the Sufi saint Muin-ud-din Chishti. To this Chishti centre Akbar made a pilgrimage by way of thanksgiving for his success at Chitor. He then sought the intercession of a living member of the Chishti community, Shaikh Salim Chishti of Sikri near Agra. For the emperor, now twenty-six, was concerned for the succession. Although not for want of brides, he was still without an heir; reassurance was needed and the shaikh obliged, correctly foretelling three sons. Akbar's rajput bride gave birth to the first while she was lying-in at Sikri in 1569. The child was therefore named Salim (but later Jahangir) after the shaikh, the shaikh was heaped with honours, and Sikri – renamed Fatehpur Sikri – was deemed propitiously perfect as the site for a new capital.

Its construction, Akbar's wildest extravagance and his weirdest folly, began in 1571, the same year in which the great tomb of his father was completed in Delhi. Both are regarded as classics of Mughal architecture, being artfully staged compositions, mostly in a rose-to-ruddy sandstone, of monumental scale and majestic outline. Yet they could hardly be less alike in inspiration. Humayun's tomb was designed by a Persian architect, who had previously worked in Bukhara. The great white-marble dome, quite unlike anything previously built in the subcontinent (although the Taj would soon make it an Indian cliché), swells from a short 'neck' into the billowing, bulbous hemisphere typical of Timurid Samarkand and Safavid Iran. For Humayun, the Mughal emperor most closely associated with Persia, it was wholly suitable.

For an emperor more interested in India, Fatehpur Sikri provided an equivalent opportunity. The mosque and its *Buland* ('Lofty') gateway apart, Akbar's palatial complex in the middle of nowhere betrays some extravagant Persian planning but in its detail reads more like a textbook of existing Indian styles and motifs. Some had been anticipated in rajput creations like the palace of Man Singh Tomar at Gwalior. But more derive from Hindu and Jain temple architecture, especially that of Gujarat. Indeed Gujarat, won and lost by Humayun, was being reconquered and reincorporated into the Mughal empire even as the city was being built.

In an architectural setting of such blatant eclecticism Akbar's curiosity about his subjects and their beliefs also became markedly eclectic. From patronising a few Hindu practices he launched into a thorough investigation of the whole gamut of existing religions. At Fatehpur Sikri he installed a veritable bazaar of disputing divines and presided over their heated debates with something of the relish he usually reserved for elephant fights. To the Quranic arguments of Sunni, Shia and Ismaili were added the more mystical and populist appeals of numerous Sufi orders, the *bhakti* fervour of Saiva and Vaishnava devotees, the fastidious logic of naked Jains, and the varied insights of numerous wandering ascetics, saints and other 'insouciant recluses'.

Also welcome were representatives of several assertive new creeds. These included disciples of Kabir, the late-fifteenth-century poet and reformer, and probably those of Guru Nanak, the early-sixteenth-century founder of the Sikh faith. Kabir had spent most of his life in the vicinity of Varanasi, where he redirected the popular fervour of *bhakti* and *Sufi* devotionalism towards a supreme transcendental godhead which subsumed both Allah of Islam and brahman of Hinduism. Similar ideas of Hindu–Muslim accommodation and syncretism were explored by Guru Nanak as he travelled widely in India before eventually returning to his native Panjab, where he had once served as an accountant in the household of Daulat Khan Lodi, the two-sworded 'blockhead' who had opposed Babur's progress in 1526.

Like Kabir, Guru Nanak insisted on the unity of the godhead and on the equality of all believers regardless of community or caste. *Ulema* and brahmans alike were seen as conspiring to divide and appropriate an indivisible, infinite and unknowable God just as they divided His followers into Muslims and Hindus, Shia and Sunni, Vaishnava and Shaiva. By concentrating on this transcendent deity, on his Name and on his Word as revealed to the Guru, and by a neo-Buddhist attention to righteous conduct and truth, men might achieve the divine grace to overcome *karma* and attain salvation. Many from the trading and cultivating classes of the Panjab were drawn to this creed and formed a brotherhood (*panth*) under the nine Gurus who succeeded Nanak. To the third of these, Guru Amar Das, Akbar is said to have given the land at Amritsar on which the Sikh's Golden Temple would eventually be built. But as yet the *panth* remained a purely religious and social movement with no political or military dimension.

Definitely included in Akbar's theological *tournées* were Portuguese priests, of whose presence the emperor had become aware during the conquest of Gujarat. Interpreting the imperial summons as evidence of divine intervention, in 1580 the padres hastened from Goa confident of the most sensational conversion of all time. In the event they were disappointed – as were all the other disputants. Akbar's quest for spiritual enlightenment was undoubtedly sincere but it was not disinterested. He sought a faith which would satisfy the needs of his realm as well as those of his conscience, one based on irrefutable logic, composed (like Fatehpur Sikri) of the finest elements in existing practice, and endowed with a universal appeal, something monumental and sublime which would transcend all sectarian differences and unite his chronically disparate subjects. It was a tall order and one which even a bazaar-ful of theologians could not fulfil.

In its stead, and perhaps with something of the naivety and self-reliance of the unlettered genius, Akbar improvised an ideology based on the only element in which he had complete confidence, his imperial persona. The resultant *Din Ilahi* ('Divine Faith') was neither clearly formulated nor vigorously promulgated. It centred on himself, but whether as God or His representative is not certain; and it graded his disciples, all of whom were senior and uncritical courtiers, according to the degree to which they could supposedly perceive his divine distinction. By Abu'l-Fazl, who became the main exponent of the new creed, this distinction was represented as a mystical effulgence which beamed from the royal forehead as from a mirror. The *Akbar-nama* devotes whole chapters to the historical pedigree of the phenomenon.

The same work begins with what looks like the standard Muslim invo-

cation *Allahu Akbar!* ('God is Great!'). But given the coincidence of the
emperor's name, it could also be read as the blasphemous 'Akbar is God.'
The emperor claimed, even when the same phrase began appearing on his
coinage, that no unorthodox meaning was intended. But given that he was
assuming other religious prerogatives, including what some regarded as a
doctrinal authority amounting to infallibility, and given the announcement
of a new chronology to be known as the 'Divine Era' and to begin from
his own accession, his disclaimer must be suspect.

It certainly seemed so to his critics. To the orthodox, to the *ulema* of
whom Akbar was especially dismissive, indeed to all but royal sycophants,
it looked as if Islam was under threat. Thus in 1579–80 there materialised
the most serious challenge of the entire reign. Senior Islamic officials openly
condemned the new directives and so provided a focus for the rebellion
of mainly Afghan units in Bengal and Bihar plus a rising by Hakim, Akbar's
half-brother who held the governorship of Kabul. The latter had dynastic
ambitions, the former nursed military grievances; it was not a purely
religious protest. But with the promulgation in Jaunpur of a *fatwa* enjoining
all Muslims to rebel, and with the naming of Hakim as the legitimate
sovereign during the Friday congregational prayers, the emperor's authority
looked to be undermined.

Luckily Akbar's personal ascendancy was by now unquestioned; Hakim,
on the other hand, was acknowledged to be little more than an instrument
in the hands of others. Luckily, too, Akbar's reforms of both the administration and the military had created a nobility deeply interested in his
survival. Man Singh, the Kacchwaha rajput who held Lahore against the
invasion by Hakim, was typical; so too was Todar Mal, another Hindu
commander, who was sent east to deal with the Afghans in Bengal. Akbar
himself hastened to the Panjab and continued on to Kabul, which city, the
scene of his childhood, he entered in triumph in 1581. Although Bengal
would continue to be troublesome, the revolt was virtually over.

Four years later Akbar again forsook Fatehpur Sikri, this time for good,
as court and government shifted to Lahore. The litany of 'dominion-
increasing victories' had scarcely faltered throughout his reign; but with
the subjugation of Rajasthan, the reconquest of Gujarat in 1573, the annexation of Orissa in 1575 and now the latest and most successful of several
attempts to subdue Bengal, all the provinces held by his predecessors had
been secured and Akbar's gaze shifted back to the north-west. From Lahore
in the late 1580s the chant of victory continued. He imposed his authority
on the restless tribes of the frontier, then conquered Kashmir and next
Sind, both of which were incorporated into the empire. Kabul was again

secured; and in 1595 Kandahar, which had been awarded to the shah of Persia as part of Humayun's rescue package, was resumed.

Excluding quixotic adventures to China and central Asia like those envisaged by Muhammad bin Tughluq, there remained only the Deccan and the south. Akbar therefore returned to Agra in 1598 to pass the last and least rewarding years of his reign directing an assault on Ahmadnagar, the nearest of the Deccani sultanates. This conflict became inextricably confused with the struggle for the succession and the manoeuvres of his eldest son Salim. It was also possibly because of the threat posed by Salim that Akbar now preferred the security of Agra's Red Fort to the comparative isolation and vulnerability of Fatehpur Sikri. Popularly its desertion is attributed to the uncertainty of its water supply, although artificial reservoirs had previously been found adequate and could doubtless have been augmented. More convincingly it has been suggested that Akbar's ideology had outgrown the devotion to the Chishti saints which had prompted the choice of the site in the first place. A display of Islamic piety was no longer appropriate.[30] Moreover, disillusioned with his royal heirs, he had become disillusioned with the shaikh who had foretold them and with the site which celebrated that prophecy.

Agra with its cosmopolitan bazaars and its strategic location on the Jamuna was altogether a worthier setting for the focus of an empire. Some, like Babur, had accrued territories; others, like the Khaljis and the Tughluqs, had laid claim to far-flung feudatories. But Akbar had fashioned an empire. Arguably the imperial structures which he bequeathed to his successors would be more historically significant even than his roll-call of conquests.

Mughal Pomp, Indian Circumstance

1605–1682

In India as elsewhere economic indicators for the pre-modern period are hard to come by. But thanks to Abu'l-Fazl's *Ain-i-Akbari*, to the numerous accounts of the Mughal empire written by foreign visitors, and to the painstaking analysis recently undertaken by scholars like Irfan Habib,[1] some basic statistics are available from the late sixteenth century onwards. By combining different methods of calculation, the population of the Indian subcontinent in the year 1600 has been estimated at about 140 million, of whom about 100 million lived within the great band of territory between the Himalayas and the Deccan sultanates which comprised Akbar's empire. At a time when the population of the British Isles can have been barely five million, and that of all western Europe less than forty million, India was not short of manpower. Travellers, Asian as well as European, marvelled at the frequency of villages and at the dense crowds which thronged the cities. Even Babur, though unimpressed by the inventiveness of India's craftsmen, had been taken aback by their numbers. Timur had employed two hundred stone-cutters in Samarkand; Babur on the other hand employed nearly fifteen hundred, mostly at Agra. 'Men of every trade and occupation are numberless and without stint in Hindustan,' he reported.[2]

Nor was the country in any sense impoverished by having to support such a large population. Quite the contrary; it was this abundant labour force which generated the surplus on which the Great Mughals grew so great. Compared to central Asia, 'the chief excellency of Hindustan is that it is a large country and has abundance of gold and silver,' reckoned Babur. But neither gold nor silver were mined in very significant quantities anywhere in India: such wealth could be accumulated only from foreign trade. The largeness of the country, rather than the abundance of precious metals, represented its true 'excellency'. For a large country meant plenty of land and, given an average monsoon, plenty of land meant bounteous crops.

Land and labour generated the wealth of India; and on the success with which these resources could be commanded, and their surplus mobilised and distributed, depended the stability of every dynastic regime. It would be wrong, though, to conclude that land and labour were therefore considered the basic units of the economy. Possibly because they had always been comparatively abundant, ownership and input were usually subsumed in a calculation of their joint yield. In India, ever since the earliest evidence of a share of the crop being donated for ritual purposes, produce – not people, not property – was what mattered. On what a field, village, district or province could be expected to produce, or on the value placed on this product, were based all grants, taxes and other revenue rights.

These rights were the means by which the surplus was creamed off from the cultivator, and they varied enormously from one part of the country to another, from one period to another, and from one crop to another. Even in a single village at any given time there might be cultivators subject to three of four different kinds of surplus extraction; thus the yield of some lands might constitute the *jagir* (revenue assignment) of a great *amir* (noble), that of others might have been granted as income to some religious establishment, and that of yet others might have been reserved to the crown (*khalsa*). In addition to such grand and usually absent beneficiaries there were also various lesser and usually local intermediaries with a tenacious claim on the yield. These included those who facilitated or enforced its actual collection, amongst them powerful individuals and interests ranging from the village headman to the *zamindar* (literally 'landholder' but more generally a blanket term for any rural superior).

Although the theory was that all these beneficiaries were entitled to a certain percentage of the yield, leaving the remainder to the cultivator, the reality was that the entire yield, minus only what was deemed necessary for the cultivator's survival, was liable to appropriation. 'Amidst the complexity of the arrangements for assessment and collection [of the revenue], one major aim of the Mughal administration still stands out: the attempt at securing the bulk of the peasant's surplus.'[3]

In consequence the peasant's lot was not, even in good times, a happy one. François Bernier, a doctor who travelled widely in India in the 1660s and then reported his findings to Louis XIV's chief minister, described the lot of the Indian peasant as 'a debasing state of slavery'. *Jagirdars*, *zamindars* and the like exercised 'a tyranny often so excessive as to deprive the peasant and the artisan of the necessaries of life, and leave them to die of misery and exhaustion'. It was, moreover, 'a tyranny that drives the cultivator of the soil from his wretched home to some neighbouring state in hopes of milder treatment, or to the army where he becomes the servant of some trooper'.

> As the ground is seldom tilled otherwise than by compulsion, and as no person is found willing and able to repair the ditches and canals for the conveyance of water, it happens that the whole country is badly cultivated and a great part rendered unproductive for want of irrigation.[4]

Bernier thought the problem lay in the absence of individual property rights. Like most Europeans he mistook revenue rights for outright owner-ship and so considered the king, as the bestower of these rights, to be 'the sole proprietor of the land'. Since such rights, or in Bernier's estimation such land grants, were not heritable and could be resumed or swapped by the sovereign at will, the *jagirdars* who held them had no long-term interest in improving the yield by investing in wells and irrigation. '"Why should we spend time and money making [the land] fruitful," they asked, "when we may be deprived of it at any moment and our exertions will benefit neither ourselves nor our children?"' Likewise, according to Bernier, 'the peasant cannot avoid asking himself the question: "Why should I toil for a tyrant who may come tomorrow and lay his rapacious hands on all I possess without leaving me, if such be his humour, the means to drag on my miserable existence?"'

No doubt Bernier generalised. His India of the 1660s would be still recovering from a succession crisis which amounted to civil war. Large parts of the Deccan, through which he travelled, were in turmoil. An honest observer, he saw India as a parable in mismanagement which might be useful to France's chief minister, Jean-Baptiste Colbert, as he undertook the radical reform of Louis XIV's finances. Bernier also overlooked the fact that during the latter part of Akbar's reign and during those of his immedi-ate successors, Jahangir (1605–27) and Shah Jahan (1627–58), many parts of northern and central India had been enjoying a period of unprecedented political stability. Crop seizures and the requisitioning of transport and labour for military purposes had practically ceased. Markets functioned well, weights and measures were standardised, and cash circulated easily. The population was gradually increasing and so was productivity. Even the derelict villages noticed by the doctor may have been deserted simply because the cultivators had decamped to develop new lands on which the revenue assessment was lighter. Under such incentives much wasteland is thought to have been reclaimed for cultivation during the seventeenth century.

Industry and trade also boomed thanks to the settled conditions and safer communications. Roads, some still today with their Mughal *kos minar* (brick or stone watchtowers at regular intervals, like mile-posts), linked provincial capitals and trading centres to the imperial axis of Agra–Delhi–Lahore. Around the imperial court at all three of these cities grew up extensive service complexes housing costumiers, perfumiers, gold and silversmiths, jewellers, ivory-carvers, gunsmiths, saddlers, joiners and the army of architects, civil engineers, stonemasons and polishers needed for India's most ambitious building programme. Similar establishments catered for the nobility in the provincial capitals which, like Ahmadabad, rapidly grew into major cities under Islamic patronage. In the field a moveable bazaar of farriers, armourers, elephant-keepers, tent-makers and provisioners accompanied the imperial forces.

The advent of new European trading companies also stimulated industrial demand, especially for the cotton textiles – muslins, taffetas, brocades, batiks, ginghams – of Gujarat, Bengal, Golconda and the Tamil country. Founded respectively in 1600 and 1602, the East India Companies of London and the Netherlands had been intended to contest the Portuguese monopoly of the mainly Indonesian spice trade. They soon became equally interested in India's manufactures. During the reign of Jahangir, Akbar's immediate successor, both companies set up trading houses in Surat, which was by now the main port in Gujarat. They also began to tap into the ancient trade between India's east coast ports and south-east Asia. Politically the companies were an irrelevance and would long remain so. But by 1640 they had ended Portugal's monopoly of the eastern sea-routes; Europe's domestic markets were discovering the joys of cheaper soft-furnishings and more washable cotton apparel; and sailings, whether regulated by the companies or unregulated, were boosting demand in India and, since payment was usually made in bullion, providing a welcome influx of silver.

None of this alleviated the plight of the cultivator. In fact his situation may have been worsened by the prevailing *pax Mughala*. Unlike the nayaks of the Vijayanagar empire, office-holders and *jagirdars* under the Mughal dispensation were seldom left long enough in possession of their grants either to become acquainted with rural conditions or to attract local allegiance. Defiance of imperial directives was therefore rarer and, with the important exception of imperial claimants, the nobility were less inclined to revolt. The reforms undertaken by Akbar would indeed go a long way towards integrating most of the subcontinent into a strong, centralised political structure. But it was an integration from above which ignored the plight of the producer and sought increased productivity through increased exploitation. 'The Mughal state was an insatiable Leviathan,' writes Tapan Raychaudhuri in *The Cambridge Economic History of India*, 'its impact on the economy was defined above all by its unlimited appetite for resources.'[5]

Akbar's reforms focused on two distinct control mechanisms: the creation of a centralised bureaucracy, and the elaboration of a standard system of military grading. Each resulted in a separate hierarchy which overlapped only at the top. The bureaucracy sprang from his abolition of the office of chief minister. Instead there were to be four departments and four department heads, one for finance and revenue, one for the military and intelligence, one for religious affairs and the judiciary, and one for the royal household and public works. The same arrangement was duplicated in the provincial capitals of each of the main provinces (Lahore for the Panjab, Ajmer for Rajasthan, etc.), and was extended to other regions as they were incorporated into the empire. All departments were subject to audit; and most staff were salaried although the more senior office-holders were awarded *jagirs* (revenue assignments) and a ranking within the military hierarchy.

The system of military ranking, Akbar's other control mechanism, assigned to every senior military commander and office-holder a numerical rank which governed his status and remuneration. Additionally a second system was introduced to denote the number of armed cavalrymen, or *sowars*, which each had to maintain for service in the imperial army; extra horses, transport and elephants were stipulated for the most senior ranks. Thus all *amirs* (nobles) and many lesser *mansabdars* (rank-holders) had both a *zat* (personal) ranking and a *sowar* (trooper) ranking. All such rankings were in the emperor's gift, as were promotion, demotion and dismissal. The system was laden with incentives and duly produced some exceptionally able commanders and administrators. It also encouraged personal loyalty to the emperor while integrating into a single power-structure the assorted Turks, Persians, Afghans, rajputs and Indian Muslims who comprised the nobility.

Although the emperor maintained his own household troops, the recruitment and maintenance of most of his vast forces were thus in effect contracted out. Similarly, since all senior *mansabdars* were awarded *jagirs* by way of salaries, the responsibility for most revenue collection was also contracted out. Rates of remuneration, which included both the *mansabdar*'s salary and so much per *sowar*, were matched by *jagirs* affording a similar aggregate yield. If their specified yield came to more, the surplus was due to the imperial treasury; if the *jagirdar* extracted more than the specified yield, he kept it.

'Towards the end of [Akbar's] reign *mansabdars* and their followers consumed 82 percent of the total annual budget of the empire for their pay allowances.'[6] There were around two thousand *mansabdars* at the time and between them they commanded 150,000–200,000 cavalrymen. The emperor personally commanded a further seven thousand crack *sowars* plus eighty thousand infantry and gunners who together accounted for another 9 percent of the budget. In addition, according to Abu'l-Fazl, the locally-based *zamindars* could muster a colossal 4.5 million retainers, mostly infantrymen. These last, who were poorly paid if at all by their *zamindars*, did not feature in the imperial budget. But by aggregating all these troop numbers and then adding to them the likely horde of non-combatant military dependants – suppliers, servants, family members – it has been suggested that the figure for those who relied on the military for a living could have been as high as twenty-six million. That would be a quarter of the entire population. The Mughal empire, whether bearing the character of 'a patrimonial bureaucracy' as per the administrative hierarchy, or of 'a centralised autocracy' as per the ranking system, was essentially a coercive military machine.

Much of this coercive potential was deployed in campaigns against obdurate neighbours like the Deccan sultanates. But, excluding those units on active service or in attendance at the royal court, many *sowar* contingents were stationed in different parts of the empire where they could be called upon to maintain order and enforce the collection of revenue. In effect many regular troops, as well as all those *zamindari* retainers, were being used to extract the agricultural surplus which financed them. It was, as Raychaudhuri puts it, 'a vicious circle of coercion helping to maintain a machinery of coercion'.[7]

Such heavy-handed intervention on the part of the central government was necessary to overcome the resistance traditionally offered by local *zamindari* interests and so maximise the revenue yield due to the emperor or his *jagirdars*. Another way of maximising the revenue yield was to improve the means by which crops were assessed and the revenue calculated. During his brief reign Sher Shah had shown the way with new land surveys, new calculations of estimated yields, and collection in cash instead of kind. But it was Raja Todar Mal, a Colbert to Akbar's Louis XIV, who from 1560 onwards overhauled the whole revenue system. Standard weights and measurements were introduced, new revenue districts with similar soils and climate were formed, revenue officers were appointed for each such unit, more surveys were undertaken, more data on yields and prices collected, new assessments worked out for each crop and each area, written demands issued and accepted by the village headmen, and copious records kept and filed.

The introduction of these reforms necessitated a five-year period of direct administration during which all *jagirs* were cancelled. When they were reintroduced in 1585 the results were highly satisfactory. Revenue receipts were vastly increased and the state enjoyed a massive share of rural productivity amounting to 'one-third of all foodgrain production and perhaps one-fifth of other crops', much of it achieved 'at the expense of the older claims and perquisites of the *zamindars*'.[8]

NO MAN HIS RELATION

Drawing heavily on Bernier's account, in 1675 John Dryden's *Aureng-Zebe*, a highly romanticised verse epic, received its first performance in London. Through such works the 'Grand Mogul' became synonymous in English with autocratic rule and unimaginable opulence. All foreign visitors to the India of the six Great Mughals – Babur, Humayun, Akbar, Jahangir, Shah Jahan and Aurangzeb – found ample evidence of an awesome authority and were stunned by the magnificence of the imperial setting. This last was most obviously architectural, but not exclusively. The eye-catching profusion of solid gold and chased silver, precious silks and brocades, massive jewels, priceless carpets and inlaid marbles was probably without parallel in history. Sir Thomas Roe, an emissary from James I of England and a man usually more obsessed with his own dignity, was frankly amazed when he saw Jahangir in ceremonial attire. The emperor's belt was of gold, his buckler and sword 'sett all over with great diamonds and rubyes'.

> On his head he wore a rich turbant with a plume of herne tops, not many but long; on one syde hung a ruby unsett, as big as a walnutt; on the other syde a diamond as greate; in the middle an emeralld like a hart, [but] much bigger. His shash was wreathed about with a chaine of great pearles, rubyes and diamonds, drilld. About his neck he carried a chaine of most excellent pearle, three double (so great I never saw); at his elbowes, armletts set with diamonds; and on his wrists three rowes of several sorts.[9]

Bernier was equally impressed. 'I doubt whether any other monarch possesses more of this species of wealth [i.e. gold, silver and jewels] ..., and the enormous consumption of fine cloths of gold, and brocades, silks, embroideries, pearls, musk, amber and sweet essences is greater than can be conceived.'

Yet, despite all this show, there remained some doubt about the real prosperity of the Mughal emperors. Aurangzeb's income, reported Bernier in the 1660s, 'probably exceeds the joint revenues of the *Grand Seignior* [i.e. the Ottoman sultan] and of the King of Persia'. But so, continued the Frenchman, did his expenses. And although revenue receipts had doubled since Akbar's day (partly thanks to Todar Mal's reforms, partly as a result of the acquisition of new territories), so too had expenditure. The emperor was therefore to be considered wealthy 'only in the sense that a treasurer is to be considered wealthy who pays with one hand the large sums which he receives with the other'.[10] As for all the gems and gold, these represented not revenue but gifts, tribute and booty, 'the spoils of ancient princes'. Though valuable enough, they were not productive. India had long been 'an abyss for gold and silver', drawing to itself the world's bullion and then nullifying its economic potential by melting and spinning the precious metals into bracelets, brocades and other ostentatious heirlooms.

There was also doubt about the size of the imperial army. Jean de Thevenot, another French visitor to Aurangzeb's empire, had read that the emperor and his *mansabdars* could field 300,000 horse. This was what the records showed, and 'they say indeed that he pays so many'. But, *mansabdars* being notoriously lax in providing their full complement of troopers, 'it is certain that they hardly keep on foot one half of the men they are appointed to have; so that when the Great *Mogol* marches upon any expedition of war, his army exceeds not a hundred and fifty thousand horse, with very few foot, though he have betwixt 300,000 and 400,000 mouths in the army.'[11]

Worse still, the army, like the wealth, was not always being deployed to productive effect. Akbar's long reign (1556–1605) had been punctuated by a succession of brilliant and rewarding conquests, but as it drew to a close these were overshadowed by rivalry and rebellion. In 1600 Prince Salim, the future Jahangir, attempted to seize Agra during Akbar's absence in the Deccan; in 1602 he actually proclaimed himself emperor; and in 1605, a few weeks before Akbar's death, he re-erected that Ashoka pillar at Allahabad and, in a blatant assumption of Indian sovereignty, had his own genealogy inscribed alongside the Maurya's edicts and Samudra-Gupta's encomium. Abu'l-Fazl, by now a senior commander as well as Akbar's memorialist, was sent to deal with the prince but was coolly murdered on the latter's orders. Even when, after reconciliation with his father, Salim/Jahangir's succession seemed settled, he was opposed by sections of the nobility who preferred Prince Khusrau, his (Salim's) eldest son. When his father was duly installed as the Emperor Jahangir ('World-Conqueror'), Khusrau fled north, laid siege to Lahore, and had to be subdued in battle. Captured, he was eventually blinded on his father's instructions.

'Sovereignty does not regard the relation of father and son,' explained Jahangir in his enlightening but decidedly naive memoir. 'A king, it is said, should deem no man his relation.'[12] Distrust between father and son, as also between brothers, would be a recurring theme of the Mughal period, generating internal crises more serious and more costly than any external threat. Of another trouble-maker Jahangir quoted a Persian verse: 'The wolf's whelp will grow up a wolf, even though reared with man himself.' This proved unintentionally apposite. In 1622 Prince Khurram, Jahangir's second and best-loved son, on whom he had just bestowed the title 'Shah Jahan' ('King of the World'), would dispose of his elder brother (the blind Khusrau) and then himself rebel against his father. The whelp was indeed worthy of the wolf. In the field or on the run, Shah Jahan led the imperial forces a merry dance for four years. Father and son were only reconciled eighteen months before Jahangir's death in 1627. There then followed more blood-letting as Shah Jahan made good his claim to the throne by ordering the death of his one remaining brother, plus sundry cousins.

And so it went on. 'Deeming no man their relation', least of all their father, in due course each of Shah Jahan's four sons would mobilise separately against him as also against one another. When Aurangzeb won this contest and in 1658 deposed his father Shah Jahan and imprisoned him in Agra's fort for the rest of his days, he not unreasonably justified his conduct on the grounds that he was merely treating Shah Jahan as Shah Jahan had sought to treat Jahangir and as Jahangir had sought to treat Akbar. Unsurprisingly Aurangzeb would himself in turn be challenged by his progeny.

Such was the intensity of this internal strife that during much of the seventeenth century it obscured and even confounded attempts to expand Mughal rule. Jahangir's one notable success was achieved early in his reign when Prince Khurram (Shah Jahan), at that time still 'my dearest son' rather than 'the wretch' he later became, secured the submission of the Mewar rajputs. Since Rana Udai Singh's desertion of Chitor and its capture by Akbar, the Mewar Sesodias had recouped their forces and under Rana Amar Singh had successfully seen off several Mughal attempts to induce

THE GREAT MUGHALS

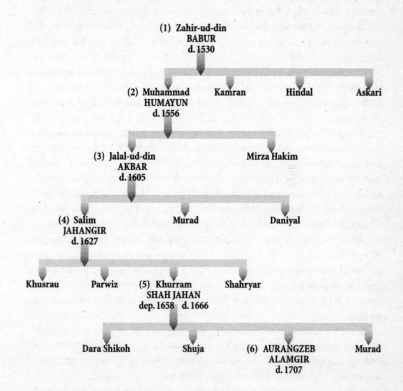

(1) Zahir-ud-din
BABUR
d. 1530

(2) Muhammad   Kamran   Hindal   Askari
HUMAYUN
d. 1556

(3) Jalal-ud-din   Mirza Hakim
AKBAR
d. 1605

(4) Salim   Murad   Daniyal
JAHANGIR
d. 1627

Khusrau   Parwiz   (5) Khurram   Shahryar
SHAH JAHAN
dep. 1658   d. 1666

Dara Shikoh   Shuja   (6) AURANGZEB   Murad
ALAMGIR
d. 1707

their submission. Khurram–Shah Jahan at the head of a vast army now concentrated on containment and attrition rather than epic sieges. There was no great battle; indeed Roe, the English ambassador, snidely remarked that the Rana had 'rather been bought than conquered', or 'won to own a superior by gifts and not by arms'.[13]

Nevertheless the arrival at court of the son of Rana Amar Singh was proof enough of Mewar's shame. Jahangir, content to have succeeded where Babur and Akbar had both failed, proved magnanimous in victory, while the young Mewar prince sought to save face by excusing himself from making personal submission; no reigning Rana ever would. Amar Singh's successors would remain on good terms with Khurram–Shah Jahan who received from them sanctuary when in revolt and support when in power.

It was during Shah Jahan's reign as emperor and Jagat Singh's as rana that the latter embellished his lake at Udaipur with the island, clad in white marble, which was later rebuilt as the famous Jagnivas or 'Lake Palace'.

But in the next Mughal succession crisis the rana was wrong-footed. A victorious Aurangzeb had no time for his father's allies nor for the half-loyalties of a Hindu princeling. Every rajput must now be a subservient Mughal *amir* (noble); either that or be outlawed as one of those 'Rashboots' (i.e. rajputs) whom, in the 1690s, the German traveller de Mandelso took to be 'Highway men or Tories'. Mughal–Mewar hostilities had yet to run their course.

Meanwhile on the frontiers of their empire Jahangir and Shah Jahan endeavoured to emulate Akbar. They rarely succeeded. In the east, although nearly all of what is now Bangladesh was by this time under Mughal rule, a Shan people from upper Burma, the Ahoms, pre-empted Mughal expansion in Assam and repeatedly rolled back Mughal incursions. In the north, along the foothills of the Himalaya, much was made of the capture by Khurram–Shah Jahan in 1618 of the great fort of Kangra (now in Himachal Pradesh). Again Jahangir, who was still emperor at the time, claimed the victory for himself; 'since the day when the sword of Islam and the glory of the Mohamedan religion have reigned in Hindustan' no sovereign, he boasted, had been able to reduce the place.[14] He was evidently unaware that, as Nagerkot, the fort had been ransacked by Mahmud of Ghazni six hundred years before. There followed minor conquests on the frontiers of Kashmir, whose willow-fringed lakes and cooler climate so enchanted Jahangir, plus another triumph for Khurram–Shah Jahan when at the very end of his father's reign he finally secured the submission of the raja of Garhwal, a minor hill state in Uttar Pradesh.

None of these places can have rewarded the expense of taking them, nor were they of any great strategic or prestige value. In a very different class, though, were the empire's two other land frontiers, that in the north-west and that in the Deccan. Invasion was possible from either, both were in the habit of welcoming and assisting Mughal dissidents, and both were arenas in which the Mughals had long-standing ancestral designs. A sovereign self-billed as a 'World-Conqueror' like *Jahan-gir*, or as a 'King of the World' like *Shah Jahan*, could ill afford to ignore either. But here again little real headway was made. In fact Kandahar, the commercially and strategically important capital of southern Afghanistan which Humayun had ceded to Persia and which Akbar had then won back, was again lost. As Persia's great Shah Abbas advanced on the city in 1622, Jahangir commanded Khurram–Shah Jahan to rush his troops to its defence. This

was the order which tipped the latter's suspicions of his being sidelined
for the succession into an open defiance. Jahangir had to switch his attention
to the more immediate challenge posed by his son, and Kandahar fell to the
shah. Although, as emperor, Shah Jahan launched numerous expeditions to
reclaim the city, all proved dismal and increasingly embarrassing failures.
So were Shah Jahan's two forays into northern Afghanistan. Neither of their
targets, Balkh and Badakshan, was secured and the dream of reinstating a
Timurid in Samarkand receded still further.

The Deccan should have offered a softer and more rewarding target.
In the early seventeenth century it was still divided amongst those successor
states of the Bahmanid sultanate – now principally Ahmadnagar (in Maharashtra), Golconda (later Hyderabad) and Bijapur (in Karnataka) – which
had briefly united for the conquest of Vijayanagar. Akbar, towards the end
of his reign, had made the first move by mounting several attacks on
Ahmadnagar which culminated with the capture of the city itself in 1600.
It also destabilised the Ahmadnagar sultanate, already shaken by rivalry
with Bijapur. In the confusion an unlikely but immensely able king-maker
emerged. Malik Ambar was an African *hubshi* (Negro) who had been sold
in Baghdad as a slave, brought to the Deccan and, after speedy advancement
as a result of numerous military exploits, now undertook the restoration
of the Ahmadnagar sultanate with himself as commander and policy-maker.
As an administrator he is said to have shown a fine impartiality as between
Hindus and Muslims and to have adopted most of the revenue reforms
pioneered in Mughal territory by Raja Todar Mal. As a commander he had
neither master nor equal and proved the most resourceful and resilient
campaigner of his day. Often obliged to use guerrilla tactics, he relied
heavily on highly mobile cavalry units which, raised from the martial Hindu
aristocracy of upland Maharashtra, were now known as Marathas. Other
Marathas served in the Bijapur and Golconda forces. In the increasingly
chaotic affairs of the Deccan these Maratha leaders, taking their cue from
Malik Ambar, would soon strike out on their own.

Throughout Jahangir's reign, 'the black-faced Ambar' harassed and
occasionally routed most of the many Mughal expeditions launched against
him. At one point he led his forces north as far as Mandu in Malwa, at
another he lay siege to Bijapur. Defeats were quickly reversed, losses recovered, submissions withdrawn. In 1624, at Bhatvadi near Ahmadnagar, Malik
Ambar inflicted such a crushing defeat on a combined Mughal–Bijapuri
force that he was able to recover virtually the whole of the erstwhile Ahmadnagar sultanate. Then in a final irony Khurram–Shah Jahan, a commander
at whose hands he had previously suffered, sought his alliance. This was

in 1625 when Khurram–Shah Jahan was in rebellion against his father. The African ex-slave welcomed the 'King of the World' and together their forces laid siege to the Mughal's Deccan headquarters at Burhanpur.

For Malik Ambar there was no such thing as defeat; only his death in 1626 proved irreversible. Thereafter the Ahmadnagar succession faltered and, despite the efforts of Shahji, a Maratha leader of some future consequence, the state barely survived until Shah Jahan, as emperor, formally incorporated it into the Mughal dominions in the mid-1630s. He followed this success by demanding, at the head of an army fifty thousand strong, the submission of Golconda and Bijapur as vassal states. Both eventually complied, the latter after a hard-fought resistance. This was undoubtedly Shah Jahan's greatest triumph and on paper it extended Mughal suzerainty deep into the peninsula.

But ironically it was also the making of the sultanates. Acceptance of Mughal overlordship scarcely limited their freedom of action and, with their northern frontiers now secure, both Bijapur and Golconda embarked on extensive conquests to the south in the domains of the Vijayanagar nayaks. Much of what is now northern Tamil Nadu – including a Portuguese settlement at San Thome plus a neighbouring stretch of deserted beach at Madras(patnam) where Francis Day of the English East India Company was about to petition the local nayak for building permission – passed under Golconda's rule. Bijapur secured southern Karnataka (the modern Mysore/Bangalore area) and a fat wedge of southern Tamil Nadu which included the Chola heartland.

In extending Muslim rule to the mouth of the Kaveri river, the Deccan sultanates had revived the successes of the Khalji and Tughluq sultans. Like these predecessors, they too were greatly enriched thereby and, together with the Marathas, they and their wealth would become a preoccupation of the redoubtable Aurangzeb. As Shah Jahan's governor in the Mughal Deccan and then as emperor, Aurangzeb would for long periods make the Deccan his home. Indeed Deccan policy would be a vital ingredient in his bid for power. Once again the interests of the empire would be subordinated to those of the succession.

It has to be said in defence of the chaotic Mughal successions that only the fittest could hope to survive. From the filial free-for-alls there emerged some of the ablest, most charismatic and most long-lived rulers India has ever known. Even Humayun and Jahangir, the one addicted to opium, the other to alcohol, yet had the sense to select extremely capable consorts and advisers. In 1611 Jahangir had married the thirty-year-old widow of one of his Afghan *amirs*. Her father, the Persian-born Itimad-ud-Daula,

INTERMARRIAGE OF THE GREAT MUGHALS WITH THE FAMILY OF ITIMAD-UD-DAULA

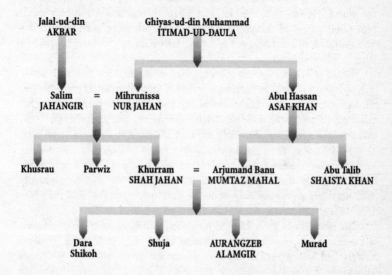

became his closest adviser-cum-minister; her brother Asaf Khan was one of his most successful generals; and the lady herself, eventually known as Nur Jahan ('Light of the World'), acted as co-ruler and, during periods of imperial incapacity, as the supreme sovereign. Public business 'sleepes', reported ambassador Roe, unless it was referred to her; she 'governs him [Jahangir] and wynds him up at her pleasure'.[15] In an unheard-of division of Islamic sovereignty, coins were even struck in her name. Were there any evidence that Jahangir could read the Gupta inscription on the pillar which he had so deliberately re-erected at Allahabad, one might infer that he derived the precedent from Chandra-Gupta I, whose Licchavi queen seems to have been the last consort to feature on north India's coinage.

Nur Jahan's influence should have extended into the next reign. Her brother Asaf Khan stood by Shah Jahan during his rebellion and duly became his closest adviser when he succeeded. Moreover Asaf Khan's daughter, the famous Mumtaz Mahal, was Shah Jahan's beloved consort. However Nur Jahan, nothing if not ambitious, came to doubt her chances of controlling her niece's wilful husband and preferred the idea of a less wilful son-in-law. This was Prince Shariyar, one of Shah Jahan's brothers and rivals, who was duly married to Nur Jahan's daughter by her first marriage. On Jahangir's death, Shariyar, aided by Nur Jahan, made his bid for power. He was outwitted by Asaf Khan, then defeated and murdered. Nur Jahan's days as the power behind the throne were over. Instead she concentrated on erecting a tomb for her father Itimad-ud-Daula, who had died just before Jahangir.

Itimad-ud-Daula's stately Agra tomb of white marble inlaid with semi-precious stones ushers in the classic period of Mughal architecture. Jahangir, though best remembered as an ardent and knowledgeable patron of Mughal painting, had not been uninterested in monuments, and under his direction Akbar's five-tiered but domeless tomb at Sikandra (near Agra) had been erected. Like Sher Shah's at Sassaram, its terraces and *chattris* seem to owe more to Indo-Muslim palace architecture than to the funerary conventions of Islam. Only the minarets which flank its gateway are determinedly Islamic; thirty years later they would be gloriously translated into the white marble sentinels which flank Shah Jahan's Taj Mahal.

Jahangir also built in Lahore, Allahabad and Agra itself, and endowed a variety of less obvious sites in Kashmir and the Panjab with gardens, towers and watercourses. But it is to his son Shah Jahan, to his lavish patronage, his grand imagination and his inspired example, that north India owes its most splendid monuments. Of the magnificence and the might of the Mughals, as also of their extravagance and oppression, there could be no more eloquent testimony.

Shah Jahan built both the black marble pavilion of his now forlorn Shalimar gardens in Kashmir and the white marble pavilions of his now unrecognisable palace in Ajmer. There and in Lahore he also built mosques and, although it is scarcely mentioned in memoirs of his reign, he was presumably responsible for Jahangir's tomb in Lahore. But it was in Agra and then Delhi that he most famously left his mark. Each in turn became the setting for the formal and increasingly rigid rituals of a self-conscious sovereignty which bordered on the divine. The informality of Babur's roving entourage and the outspoken animation of Akbar's symposia had given way to a more awesome ceremonial and a more exalted symbolism. Now the 'King of the World' ethereally presided from sun-drenched verandahs of the whitest marble; he was glimpsed through apertures of the richest inlay or framed by cusp-pecked arches; painted profiles showed his impeccable features within a glowing halo, a device adopted from Christian iconography; like the moon in the firmament he shone from the high-carat backdrop of his Peacock Throne wherein jewels to a value of ten million rupees humbly twinkled. The rituals of court and council and the conventions of costume and address were also set, as it were, in stone. Like the architecture, they were formulated to elevate and magnify the impossible grandeur of the greatest 'Grand Mogul'.

Shah Jahan's most ambitious creation was another new Delhi. Designed to supersede Agra as the imperial capital, it was not just a fort like Tughlaqabad and not just a sandstone fantasy like Fatehpur Sikri, but a whole new city with processional thoroughfares, bazaars, caravanserais, shaded waterways, spacious squares and massive stone walls. 'The new walls were punctuated with twenty-seven towers and eleven gates enclosing some 6,400 acres; about 400,000 people lived within them.'[16] Constructed in 1639–48 and called Shahjahanabad, this new Delhi was built to the north of the Khalji–Tughluq city and is now known as Old Delhi. Its rigid geometry has long since been blurred and its stately avenues obliterated, but some of the walls and gates remain as do the imperial complex known as the Red Fort and, hard by, the great Jama Masjid. The latter was then the largest mosque in India. From its slight eminence it still contrives to preside over the crowded chaos of one of India's most densely peopled inner cities. Likewise the Fort, though ravaged by subsequent occupants, including the British, remains an impressive ensemble and is still a focus for state occasions and political pronouncements.

Another Red Fort, that in Agra, retains more of the flavour of the age. Most of it is as Shah Jahan rebuilt it, including the great pillared hall of the *Diwan-i-Am* and the whole sequence of white marble chambers and pavilions which encrust the fort's upper storey. There, immured in his own creation and increasingly decrepit, the emperor would shuffle away his final years as Aurangzeb's prisoner. And thence, squinting into the morning sun, he would famously gaze down the Jamuna river to the great white cloud which, moored in marble on the riverbank, housed the remains of his beloved consort and wherein he would himself be laid to rest by her side.

The Taj Mahal was commissioned, and named, for Mumtaz (Mumtaj) Mahal (literally 'the Palace favourite'), who was the daughter of Asaf Khan and niece of Nur Jahan. She had shared the emperor's troubled years on the run and become his dearest associate in power. When she died in 1631 while giving birth to their fourteenth child, the emperor was distraught. Her tomb was begun in the following year. 'He intends it shall excell all other,' reported Peter Mundy, an employee of the English East India Company who passed through Agra in the 1630s. 'The building goes on with excessive labour and cost, prosecuted with extraordinary diligence, gold and silver [being] esteemed common metall, and marble but as ordinarie stone.'[17] Completed in 1643, it was instantly acknowledged as a masterpiece. Bernier thought it one of the wonders of the world, James Fergusson, the pioneer of architectural study in India, rated its combination of beauties 'unsurpassable', and both Kipling and Tagore ventured a stab at its profound emotional appeal; to the first it was 'the ivory gate through which all dreams pass', to the second 'a tear on the face of eternity'. Combining the bulb-like dome of Humayun's tomb and the marble and inlay of Itimad-ud-Daula's with the theatrical staging of Akbar's and the landscaping of Jahangir's gardens, it represented a triumphant summation of Mughal taste. Its symbolism, with a setting evocative of paradise and the great white tomb as an image of the Throne of God, is purely Islamic. But in its sculptural conception and in its execution many have recognised an essentially Indian aesthetic and ancient Indian skills.

The site on which the Taj stands was provided, at a price, by Raja Jai Singh, the Kacchwaha successor of that loyal rajput *amir*, Man Singh of Amber. From the Kacchwaha quarries at Makrana in Rajasthan also came its acres of white marble. The genius of the Mughals, in empire-building as in architecture, is often said to have lain in their synthesis of Indian and Islamic traditions and their eagerness to enlist the support of Hindu subjects, like the rajput princes, as well as that of fellow Muslims. Similarly, although the official language of the Mughal court was still Persian, *urdu* (literally 'camp'), a hybrid tongue which had developed in the military encampments of the empire, was winning a wider currency. Written in the Perso-Arabic script, much of its syntax and vocabulary was borrowed from the Sanskritic derivatives of northern India. Poetry, painting and music benefited from the same synthesis and flourished under the same catholic patronage.

Aurangzeb would not conform in this respect. Discrimination against Hindus and the active promotion of Islamic values were about to be revived. Simultaneously the great tradition of Mughal building virtually ceased. Aurangzeb would have little use for the worldly ostentation of his predecessors. Shah Jahan's expenditure on architecture is thought to have run to twenty-nine million rupees. Compared to the costs of war and the alienation of revenue to support the army, it was probably not significant.[18] But having inherited an empire crippled by the crisis of his own succession and beset by still greater military priorities, Aurangzeb would be reluctant to squander even the smallest portion of his colossal revenues on monumental extravagances.

CONQUEROR OF THE UNIVERSE

The popularity of the dome as an architectural feature in the sixteenth and seventeenth centuries extended beyond Mughal India. Far outspanning the Taj Mahal or Sir Christopher Wren's slightly later St Paul's, indeed second only to Michelangelo's somewhat earlier St Peter's, is an unsung edifice of still impressive integrity known as the Gol Gumbaz of Bijapur.

As if to match the Mughals mosque for mosque and tomb for tomb, the Deccani sultans of Bijapur – and to a slightly lesser extent their neighbours in Golconda – had been busy building since the 1570s; and just as Agra's architecture climaxed with the Taj so did Bijapur's with the Gol Gumbaz. Four-square with pagoda-like towers, seven storeys high, at each corner, the Gol Gumbaz ('Round Dome') displays a refreshing simplicity combined with extraordinary technical expertise. A finish of pale stucco imparts a certain warmth, but the emphasis is on strength, with the great dome in no way disparaging the sturdy castellate structure on which it sits. If the Taj, as befits the tomb of a queen, has a feminine delicacy, the Gol Gumbaz, the tomb of a sultan, is all masculine virility.

It was completed in 1659 for Sultan Muhammad Adil Shah who had died two years earlier after a reign of thirty years. His father, Ibrahim Adil Shah II, had reigned for forty-seven years (1580–1627) in the nearest thing to a golden age which strife-torn Bijapur would ever know. As a patron of the arts and a tolerant Sunni who allowed both his Shia and Hindu subjects to worship as they pleased, Ibrahim boosted the reputation of the Deccan sultanates for enlightened rule. 'Nor was he fond of unnecessary war,' says Ferishta, who under Ibrahim's protection wrote his great *History of the Rise of Mohammedan Power*. The *History* ends rather abruptly with Akbar's invasion of Ahmadnagar in 1600. Ibrahim had been drawn into this struggle, and wars, necessary and otherwise, now intensified. Under Muhammad Adil Shah, Bijapur had been obliged to acknowledge Mughal supremacy but found compensation in conquests in Mysore and Tamil Nadu. Bijapur's rule eventually spanned the peninsula from the Konkan and Malabar coasts in the west to the southern Coromandel coast in the east. There the triple fort of Jinji (Gingee, near Pondicherry) was taken and the nayaks of both Madurai and Tanjore acknowledged Muhammad Adil Shah.

It was, though, a fragile empire. The southern conquests had been achieved thanks to the tactical skills of Maratha units like that of Shahji Bhonsle, the latter-day champion of the Ahmadnagar sultanate who had since transferred his loyalties to Bijapur. Shahji, despite securing an extensive fief in the south, would remain loyal to Bijapur. But not so his son, the great Shivaji, the founder of the Maratha kingdom. As early as 1647 the seventeen-year-old Shivaji had begun subverting Bijapur's authority in the north-west of the state. With ingenuity and a cut-throat nonchalance he first stormed and tricked his way into the forts of neighbouring *deshmukhs* (landed nobles) in the Maratha homeland of the Western Ghats to carve out an independent Maratha zone around Pune (Poona). This was difficult terrain and with a status to match. It had previously been part of Ahmadnagar but was then transferred to Bijapur when the latter accepted Mughal suzerainty. It was also adjacent to the now directly-administered Mughal province of the Deccan. Maratha activities were therefore of as much concern to the Mughal emperor as to the Bijapur sultan. Equally, the ambiguity of the situation meant that the ever-plausible Shivaji could play off these Islamic superiors and rivals one against the other.

In 1652 Shah Jahan, still the reigning emperor, had reappointed his third son, Aurangzeb, to the governorship of the Deccan province. Aurangzeb, an able administrator and experienced commander who was already in his mid-thirties, quickly adopted a forward policy in respect of the Deccan sultanates. Twenty years of Mughal suzerainty over the sultanates had brought only disturbance and defiance. Additionally, their large Shi'ite communities and Hinduised ceremonial were deeply unacceptable to an orthodox Sunni as devout as Aurangzeb. Annexation rather than over-lordship was the only solution, and to this end Aurangzeb began intriguing with Mir Jumla, a Persian adventurer in the service of the Golconda sultanate who had risen to a position of immense power as the conqueror of the northern Tamil country. Becoming in the process something of a merchant-prince, Mir Jumla had latterly attracted the suspicions of the Golconda sultan. The mir therefore took little persuading that his wealth and authority would be better protected by Mughal recognition. In return for a guarantee of his territorial possessions and a top ranking in the Mughal military hierarchy he agreed to join Prince Aurangzeb in a two-pronged attack on Golconda.

This took place in 1656. Hyderabad was taken and the sultan was besieged behind the great walls of Golconda fort. Then orders arrived from Shah Jahan for a Mughal withdrawal. Apparently the Golconda sultan had appealed to Delhi where Dara Shikoh, Aurangzeb's eldest brother and deadly rival, had persuaded Shah Jahan to abort the campaign. Deeply disappointed, Aurangzeb extracted only territory and a hefty indemnity.

Next year almost exactly the same situation developed when Aurangzeb invaded Bijapur. Taking advantage of the death of Muhammad Adil Shah – he who was laid to rest in the mighty Gol Gumbaz – the Mughal–Mir

Jumla forces ravaged Bijapur's northern cities and were poised to tackle Bijapur itself when once more came the order to desist. Again Dara Shikoh, anxious to thwart his brother's chances of succeeding, had intervened; again a frustrated Aurangzeb had to be content with an indemnity plus territory. The latter in this case included the Maratha homeland and part of the Konkan coast. Shivaji was now very definitely a Mughal problem.

But it was a problem that would have to wait. Back in Delhi, in September 1657, Shah Jahan was suddenly taken ill with acute constipation. His limbs swelled, his palate dried, and fever developed.[19] Although he would partially recover, rumours of his death or incapacity spread, and the scare was enough to send potential successors rushing to arms. Aurangzeb bided his time. But as governor of Bengal Prince Shuja, another brother, was quickly in the field after a hasty coronation. And in Gujarat the fourth brother, Murad Baksh, followed suit. These two, Shuja and Murad, would prove to be the outsiders. Shuja's advance up the Ganga was halted by defeat near Varanasi at the hands of an imperial army under Jai Singh, the Kacchwaha rajput. Meanwhile Murad, the youngest and least effectual brother, rested his hopes on joint action with Aurangzeb. Garnering troops and plundering the port of Surat for funds, he waited impatiently for Aurangzeb to move north from the Deccan.

At this stage the front-runner was undoubtedly Dara Shikoh. As the eldest brother, Shah Jahan's favourite, his designated mouthpiece and heir, and the only Delhi-based contender with the reins of imperial patronage and power at his disposal, Dara looked unbeatable. His one fault was that, like Akbar, he inspired deep suspicion amongst orthodox Muslims and especially the religious *ulema*. A scholar of some repute, he consorted with Sufis, Hindus and Christians; he had translated the *Upanisads* into Persian; he even advanced the idea 'that the essential nature of Hinduism was identical with that of Islam'.[20] This was heresy by any orthodox standard. Aurangzeb's contention that in resorting to arms he was aiming to save the empire from idolatry and apostasy was no sanctimonious affectation. To a devout Muslim of simple habits, blameless lifestyle and sincere conviction Dara's free-thinking was anathema. The contest was therefore as much about ideology as power. Many saw Aurangzeb's cause as the more righteous and so his claim as the more legitimate.

In February 1658, having commandeered Mir Jumla's troops including a strong detachment of artillery under European direction, and having partially realised the cash indemnities outstanding from Golconda and Bijapur, Aurangzeb moved north into Malwa with a force of thirty thousand. There he met up with Murad and near Ujjain defeated an army sent

south to intercept him by Shah Jahan. Heavy rajput casualties in Shah
Jahan's army, but comparatively few amongst its Muslim component, suggest that Aurangzeb's cause already commanded sympathy across the filial
divide. The victors continued north. They were within eight miles of Agra
before they encountered Dara.

At the head of an impressive army somewhat larger than that of his
brothers, Dara still looked to hold the advantage. But the best Mughal
units had been sent east to oppose Shuja; Dara's dazzling array, in which
rajput contingents were again prominent, also included slippered courtiers
and bazaar recruits who quickly wilted in the furnace temperatures of late
May. They were no more a match for the dust-smothered veterans from
the Deccan than was the dilettante Dara for the resolute Aurangzeb. In
battle, despite more rajput heroics, Aurangzeb's Deccan army stood its
ground while the gunners did their work. Victory turned to rout when
Dara chose premature flight. Like Khusrau fleeing from Jahangir in 1605,
he paused in Agra only to gather funds and family, then took the loser's
well-worn road north through Delhi to Lahore. Aurangzeb occupied Agra.
The contest, if not the empire, was won. Dropping all pretence of rescuing
Shah Jahan from the infidel influence of Dara, he besieged and then confined the ailing emperor amongst the marble terraces of his Agra fort.
There he would remain, a semi-senile spectre of his former glory, until he
died eight years later.

Aurangzeb's victory would be complete only with the elimination of
his rivals. Each was now hunted down in turn. The feckless Murad, his
ally thus far, was easily dealt with. At Mathura, while heading north in
pursuit of Dara, Aurangzeb inveigled Murad into his camp and took him
prisoner; he would later be beheaded. Shuja, re-emerging from Bengal, was
a second time defeated and sent fleeing back to the east. But Dara continued
to elude capture as he flitted from the Panjab to Sind and from Sind to
Gujarat. At the head of a new army marching north from Gujarat, he was
eventually engaged near Ajmer. Again he escaped, but only to be betrayed
and turned over to Aurangzeb. Still a popular figure especially with Delhi's
non-Muslims, Dara's public humiliation was mercifully brief. After being
carried through the streets in chains, he was condemned and cut to pieces.
Some say that his body was then again paraded through the streets. 'So
once alive and once dead he was exposed to the eyes of all men, and many
wept over his fate.'[21]

Shuja, meanwhile, was fleeing east through Bengal with the redoubtable
Mir Jumla, Aurangzeb's ally from Golconda, hot in pursuit. In 1660 Shuja
took ship from Dacca (Dhaka) for the Arakan coast (now in northern

Left Statue of the Jain saint Gomateshwara, Sravana Belgola, Karnataka. The largest monolithic statue in the world, it faces the hill on which Chandragupta, founder of the Maurya empire, may have spent his declining years.

Below Relief medallion from the Bharhut stupa, originally in Madhya Pradesh. Such scenes from the *jataka* (birth) legends of the Buddha reveal the costumes, architecture and transport of the second century BC.

Above The Great Stupa (no. 1) of Sanchi, near Vidisha in Madhya Pradesh. The first-century BC stone stupa, with its balustrades and gateways, encases a brick stupa of Maurya times which enshrined a Buddhist relic.

Left Relief panel from the Amaravati stupa, originally in Andhra Pradesh, second–third century AD. As reconstructed from such illustrations of the original, the Amaravati stupa may have been the greatest monument in Buddhist Asia.

Left Relief panel from the Amaravati stupa. Early Buddhist narrative scenes do not depict the Buddha in human form but suggest his presence by symbols, like a throne, a footprint or, as here, the Boddhi tree.

Below Relief panel from the Amaravati stupa, second – third century AD. Musicians and dancers celebrate the descent to earth of a Bodhisattva, or Buddha incarnation.

Left Exterior of cave temple (no. 2), Badami, Karnataka, late sixth century AD. As Vatapi, Badami was adopted by the Chalukya dynasty as the core site of their seventh-to-eighth-century Deccan empire.

The Jyotirlinga group of temples, Aihole, Karnataka. An inscription here tells of the conquests of Pulakesin II, the Chalukya king who withstood the might of Harsha-vardhana.

Above The Rajarajeshwara temple at Tanjore, Tamil Nadu, early eleventh century. Largest and loveliest of temples, it was richly endowed by the Chola king Rajaraja I with booty from his peninsular and Sri Lankan conquests.

Right Sculptural panel from the Chenna Kesava temple, Belur, Karnataka, twelfth century. Traditions of ivory-carving are evident in the statuary of both Dorasamudra (Halebid) and Belur, the twin capitals of the Hoysala dynasty.

Right Jahaz Mahal ('Ship Palace'), Mandu, Madhya Pradesh, late fifteenth century. On the heights of Mandu, the sultans of Malwa built fancifully. With its moat full and access only by stepped 'gangplanks', this palace appeared to float.

Below Jaya Stambha ('Victory Tower') at Chitor(garh), Rajasthan, 1457–68. It was erected to commemorate the victory of the rajput Rana Kumbha of Mewar (later Udaipur) over Mahmud Khalji, the Muslim sultan of Malwa.

Opposite The tomb of Humayun in Delhi, completed 1565. The second of the Great Mughals spent much of his reign in exile in Afghanistan and Persia, whence came the architect of his tomb and its inspiration.

The tomb of Itimad-ud-Daula in Agra, completed 1628. Itimad-ud-Daula was Jahangir's minister, the father of Nur Jahan (Jahangir's wife), and the grandfather of both Shah Jahan and his wife Mumtaz Mahal.

Gol Gumbaz ('Great Tomb') of Muhammad Adil Shah II in Bijapur, Karnataka, *c.*1659. Contemporary with the Taj Mahal, but with a dome second only to St Peter's in Rome, the tomb epitomised the ambitions of the Bijapur sultanate.

Burma). He was never heard of again, although rumours that the king of Arakan had done Aurangzeb's killing for him sound plausible.

As the new governor of Bengal (which province included Bihar and Orissa), Mir Jumla moved the capital east to Dacca and is said to have revived the economic life of the region. He also continued in arms. His target was now Assam, whose Ahom rulers had taken advantage of the recent confusion to push down the Brahmaputra into Mughal territory. Mir Jumla pushed them back and in 1662, working upriver with a fleet of three hundred vessels, pressed on into the green unknown of the upper Brahmaputra until he reached the Ahom capital. This was situated at Garhgaon, between the modern Jorhat and Dibrugarh and just beneath the cloud-swept hills of Nagaland. Mir Jumla had added more than five hundred kilometres of the Brahmaputra valley to the Mughal possessions. But here Assam's torrential monsoon overtook him. Disease and starvation claimed even more victims than the Ahoms as the plight of the Mughal army came to resemble that of Mohammed Bakhtiyar's Khalji forces when Muslim arms first reached Assam in 1205. The remains of the army, plus boatloads of treasure, were eventually extracted, but Mir Jumla himself shared the Khaljis' fate. On the way back to Dacca he died of consumption. Four years later the Ahoms recovered most of their watery kingdom; they would retain it till an age when Mughal rule in Bengal was long since history.

Meanwhile Aurangzeb had had himself crowned emperor twice – once in a perfunctory ceremony in 1658 while chasing Dara, and then at a grand assembly in the Delhi *Diwan-i-Am* in 1659. On both occasions he adopted the title *Alamgir*, a name by which Muslim historians generally refer to him. It means 'Universe-Conqueror', and was obviously an improvement on mere *jehangir* ('world-conqueror'), although rather more onerous in terms of anticipated conquests. In addition to the Assam affair and several galling but eventually satisfactory campaigns against the tribes of the north-west frontier, in 1666 it was announced that the 'Universe-Conqueror' had secured the submission of 'Tibet'. To the Mughal agents who were sent there from Kashmir it may indeed have seemed like another planet, although it was probably only Ladakh, the western extremity of the Tibetan plateau. A contemporary chronicler well describes it as 'mostly a waste land' which, though bigger than any other *subah* (province) in the empire except Bijapur, produced a revenue yield no better than the average *pargana* (sub-district). 'No other useless place can be compared with it.' It was gratifying to know that its chief had been bullied into minting coins bearing the name of *Alamgir* and into building a mosque where the *khutba* would be read in the emperor's name, but it was no major triumph. 'Other kings, unwilling to incur expenditure, had not cared about the introduction of currency and *khutba* in such a place.'[22] Aurangzeb would have to do better in the way of meaningful conquests; and where else but in the rich and troubled peninsula? The Deccan beckoned.

Before personally intervening there, he had important reforms to put in hand. The war of succession had interrupted the work of government. Imperial authority needed to be reimposed in many areas, the vital flow of revenue restored, loyal servants rewarded, and reliable supporters enlisted. Many of the latter would be drawn from the ranks of the *ulema*, the religious and juridical establishment. Restoring the Muslim credentials of Mughal rule and so reinstating India in the world community of Islam remained Aurangzeb's priority. This was the God-given cause which had brought him success as a contender for the throne, and this alone could guarantee his further success as its incumbent.

An innovation at his second enthronement had been the appointment of a *muhtasib*, a 'censor' or guardian of public morality, whose duties included the supervision of bazaars and the suppression of such un-Islamic behaviour as gambling, blasphemy and the consumption of alcohol. Opium as well as liquor was totally forbidden, a prohibition which hit the convivial habits of the court as hard as it did the bazaars. In the same spirit, dancers, musicians and artists were dismissed from imperial employ. Their places were taken by bearded jurists and Quranic divines who laboured to produce a standard compilation of Hanafi jurisprudence. The emperor also discontinued his predecessors' practice of appearing on a palace balcony at sunrise, thus affording the public an apotheosised glimpse of their ruler. In the tenth year of his reign even the official chroniclers were ordered to lay down their simpering pens. Vanity, too, was un-Islamic. From such earnest endeavours to remodel his court in conformity with the precepts of his faith Aurangzeb emerges as a sincere believer untainted by hypocrisy.

Accusations of bigotry, on the other hand, are hard to counter. Although they invariably come from non-Muslim writers, they focus on a whole range of measures, introduced over a period of twenty years, which were indeed blatantly discriminatory. The tax on Hindu pilgrims, lifted by Akbar, was reimposed; revenue endowments enjoyed by temples and brahmans were rescinded; Hindu merchants were penalised by heavier duties; the provincial administrations were instructed to replace Hindu employees with Muslims; and most notoriously of all, newly built, or rebuilt, temples were to be destroyed. Amongst those temples razed and replaced with mosques were such high-profile and heavily patronised shrines as the great Vishvanatha temple in Varanasi – where now still stands (Hindu zealots permitting) the Great Mosque of Aurangzeb – and the new Keshava Deo temple at Mathura – where now still stands (ditto) another great Aurangzeb mosque. Finally, in 1679, came the heaviest blow of all with the reimposition of the detested *jizya* on non-Muslims.

One man's bigot may, however, be another man's saint. Aurangzeb's apologists argue that Shah Jahan had also discriminated against non-Muslims and targeted temples, that Aurangzeb in fact destroyed comparatively few temples, and that to others he even granted *jagirs*.[23] Moreover the sites which were indeed desecrated were chosen because they posed a direct political or ideological challenge. Hence Varanasi, 'the Athens of India' according to Bernier, was a prime target because it was 'the general school for Hindus'[24] as well as a major centre for what Muslims regarded as that most abominable form of idolatry, *lingam* worship. Even the *jizya* was not an unreasonable imposition. Although usually described as a poll tax, it was more like a commutation tax in that it applied only to male adults who, had they been Muslims, would have been liable to military service in a *jihad*; as non-Muslims they were excused this duty but must instead contribute to the protection they supposedly enjoyed by paying the *jizya*. The rate varied with the taxpayer's ability to pay. But the poorest were exempt and it seems unlikely that the tax was collected at all in the remoter regions of the empire.

Those hardest hit were those from whom it was easiest to collect, notably the commercial and artisanal classes in the cities. They were also the most vocal. When the order was first published, Shajahanabad–Delhi erupted in protest. Hordes of Hindus – 'money-changers and drapers, all kinds of shopkeepers from the Urdu bazaar, mechanics and workmen of all kinds' – jammed the roadway and barred the emperor's short progress from the Red Fort to the Jama Masjid.

> Every moment the crowd increased, and the emperor's equipage was brought to a standstill. At length an order was given to bring out the elephants and direct them against the mob. Many fell trodden to death ... For some days the Hindus continued to assemble in great numbers and complain, but at length they submitted to the *jizya*.[25]

Other protests are recorded and subsequent opponents of Mughal rule would cite the *jizya* as a major grievance. But the idea that Aurangzeb intentionally set about the persecution and forced conversion of his non-Muslim subjects is absurd. He was too shrewd; they too numerous. More reasonably he wanted to create a moral climate in which Muslims could live in accordance with the tenets of Islam and in which non-Muslims

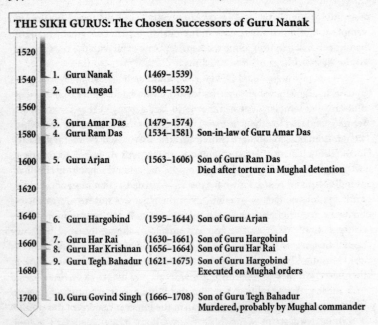

THE SIKH GURUS: The Chosen Successors of Guru Nanak

Year		Guru	Dates	Notes
1520				
1540	1.	Guru Nanak	(1469–1539)	
	2.	Guru Angad	(1504–1552)	
1560				
	3.	Guru Amar Das	(1479–1574)	
1580	4.	Guru Ram Das	(1534–1581)	Son-in-law of Guru Amar Das
1600	5.	Guru Arjan	(1563–1606)	Son of Guru Ram Das
				Died after torture in Mughal detention
1620				
1640	6.	Guru Hargobind	(1595–1644)	Son of Guru Arjan
1660	7.	Guru Har Rai	(1630–1661)	Son of Guru Hargobind
	8.	Guru Har Krishnan	(1656–1664)	Son of Guru Har Rai
	9.	Guru Tegh Bahadur	(1621–1675)	Son of Guru Hargobind
1680				Executed on Mughal orders
1700	10.	Guru Govind Singh	(1666–1708)	Son of Guru Tegh Bahadur
				Murdered, probably by Mughal commander

would be aware both of their subordinate status and of how they might improve it by conversion.

This general trend towards Islamic exclusivity was nevertheless a radical departure from the tolerant policies of Akbar and held potentially disastrous consequences for the Hindu–Muslim collaboration on which the empire depended. As a triumph for the *ulema* it alienated the brahmans and other literate castes who were the mainstay of the administration. It lent a religious dimension to the agrarian dissent of Hindu communities like the Jats of the Agra region who in the 1680s would virtually sever the vital supply-line between Delhi and the Deccan. And to non-Muslim groupings of a more martial disposition, like the Sikhs, rajputs and Marathas, it furnished both pretext and support for outright defiance.

In the Panjab the Sikh followers of Guru Nanak's successors now constituted a significant but still pacific and often divided minority. Arjan Singh, the fifth Guru, added his own compositions to the collected hymns and teachings of his predecessors, which also included compositions by non-Sikh *sufis* and *sants* like Kabir, and the whole became known as the *Adi Granth* ('Original Granth'). Revised and expanded by the tenth and last Guru, this would become the sacred Granth Sahib, itself enjoying the authority and respect of a Guru and so precluding any further human Gurus. But at about the same time as the *Adi Granth* was being compiled, the Sikh community fell foul of Jahangir when they supported Prince Khusrau in the 1605 succession crisis. Guru Arjan Singh is believed to have been martyred by Jahangir as a result. In the 1658 succession crisis Sikh hospitality to Prince Dara similarly angered Aurangzeb. The eighth Guru was summoned to court and his son and presumed heir was inducted into the Mughal hierarchy. This was not acceptable to most Sikhs who instead chose as their ninth Guru Tegh Bahadur, the brother of the seventh. He travelled throughout northern India, preaching to large crowds of followers and proselytising amongst Muslims as well as Hindus. Sikh *gurdwaras* became as much a target of imperial iconoclasm as Hindu temples. But it seems to have been the news of Muslim converts to Sikhism which most outraged Aurangzeb. Tegh Bahadur was brought to Delhi to defend himself and, failing either to convince the emperor or to apostasise, was condemned for blasphemy and executed (1675). 'At one stroke Aurangzeb earned the bitter hatred of thousands of Jat and Khatri Sikhs living in the north Indian plain.'[26] Under Guru Govind, the tenth and last Guru, Sikhism would retire to the fringes of Mughal rule in the Panjab hill states. There, not without ample provocation, it would transform itself from what had hitherto been a movement for religious and social reform into an embryonic political and military formation.

'Akbar [had] disrupted the Muslim community by recognising that India was not an Islamic country: Aurangzeb disrupted India by behaving as if it were.'[27] But it was one thing to antagonise a new sectarian group, like the Sikhs, of which even Hindu princes and *jagirdars* were suspicious, quite another to stir up the great rajput houses of Rajasthan. The trouble started when in 1678 the Rathor Maharaja of Marwar (Jodhpur) died without heir. Pending the selection of a successor, Aurangzeb's resumption of the Marwar *jagirs* was normal practice. The sequel, however, was highly provocative. The troops sent to oversee the takeover indulged in the gratuitous iconoclasm of Marwar's temples; and in the meantime, two of the deceased maharaja's widows gave birth to male heirs. One of these infants died but the other, Ajit Singh, immediately became a focus of anti-Mughal sentiment. When, therefore, Aurangzeb eventually conferred Marwar on an unpopular nephew of the deceased maharaja, revolt flared. In an episode beloved of the rajput bards, the infant was smuggled out of Delhi from under the emperor's nose and whisked away into the desert fastnesses of Rajasthan. There his mother, who happened to be a Sesodia princess of mighty Mewar, 'threw herself upon the Rana [of Mewar] as the natural guardian of [Ajit's] rights'.[28]

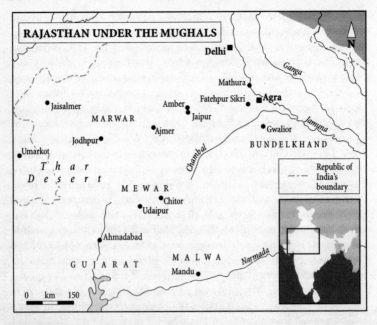

To her appeal Mewar's rana responded favourably. Welcoming the opportunity to voice Hindu opposition to the reimposed *jizya* and fearful of the iconoclasm in Marwar, he duly mobilised with strikes into Malwa and elsewhere. To resistance in Marwar (Jodhpur), Aurangzeb had thus added revolt in Mewar (Udaipur), a much more serious challenge. In 1680 a large Mughal army invaded Mewar, duly sacked the city of Udaipur and vandalised its temples. The rana, however, remained free; his forces scored some notable victories; and though peace without dishonour was eventually concluded, he maintained Mewar's proud record of never making personal submission to the emperor.

Mughal discomfiture can be judged from the reaction of Prince Akbar, one of Aurangzeb's sons. Akbar had commanded the Mewar campaign in its later phase but was now demoted to the Marwar command. It was not a good idea to humble an imperial contender. Inclined to the liberal views of his illustrious namesake, Prince Akbar had long been contemplating a challenge to his father. History sanctioned, indeed demanded, such conduct and rajput overtures and promises of support now emboldened him still further. In 1681 he therefore proclaimed himself emperor and marched against Aurangzeb. The latter was at Ajmer with very few troops. It was a contest which the prince should have won handsomely. But the emperor's adept intriguing roused the suspicions of Akbar's rajput allies and his own dilatoriness allowed for imperial reinforcement. Without his rajput allies, and then minus most of his own troops, Akbar fled south without giving battle. Narrowly escaping capture, he reached the Deccan, there to be warmly welcomed by an even more implacable Mughal foe. Prince Akbar became a protégé of the Marathas.

Aurangzeb soon followed him. Affairs in the Deccan had been crying out for his personal intervention for the past twenty years; now into his sixties, he may reasonably have supposed that time was running out. Moreover it was from the Deccan that he himself had challenged for the throne; Prince Akbar might do the same, possibly in alliance with both Marathas and rajputs. On the other hand a final solution in the Deccan could be the crowning glory of Aurangzeb's reign. New lands affording new sources of revenue in the form of *jagirs* were badly needed to meet the expectations of the ever-growing legion of *mansabdars*. Success in the Deccan would bring conquests to rival those of the great Akbar plus the resources to restore and sustain the imperial system which he had established.

Where the emperor went, the entire imperial court also went, plus, in this case, much of the army. The move to the south in 1681–2 meant that Shahjahanabad–Delhi was partially vacated. Like Sultan Muhammad bin Tughluq, Aurangzeb was shifting the whole apparatus of government to the Deccan. But this was not a move to a new capital, rather the launch of a campaign. For the purposes of travel, all moved into a tented city which was reconstituted with the same topography of bazaars, cantonments, administrative offices and imperial apartments at every halt. Once in the Deccan, they remained in camp. There they stayed, thus they lived, and thence the empire was ruled for the duration of the campaign. Akbar and Shah Jahan had campaigned in much the same style; no doubt it accorded with the semi-nomadic traditions of their Timurid-Mongol predecessors.

But what none realised was that this was a campaign without end. Many of those who went south in 1682 would never see Delhi again, including the emperor; and this was despite his having another twenty-six years to live. An active commander into his late eighties and for the most part a successful one, Aurangzeb would push Mughal rule to its greatest limits. Indeed the empire which he finally claimed exceeded that of any previous Indian ruler. But the price would far outweigh the prize. The emperor's dogged longevity, no doubt the reward of frugal habits and pious living, would prove to be a substantial contributor to his empire's undoing.

From Taj to Raj

1682–1750

'FRAUD AND FOX-PLAY'

EXCEPT FOR one ominous development, the Deccan to which Aurangzeb returned in 1682 differed little from the Deccan which he had left in 1658. In the north the Mughal province of that name still stretched across the upper peninsula like a waistband. Comprising the erstwhile Ahmadnagar sultanate along with the eastward territories of Kandesh and Berar, it was administered from Burhanpur in Kandesh. In the west of the province the city of Aurangabad – near the Seunas' fang-like fortress of Devagiri (Daulatabad) and the Rashtrakutas' cave city of Ellora – was also an important centre of Mughal power and would soon supersede Burhanpur; it had been the capital of the Ahmadnagar sultanate under 'black-faced' Ambar Malik but had been renamed Aurangabad during Aurangzeb's earlier governorship.

On the coast, the Europeans came and went. From their port of Bassein the Portuguese had acquired an adjacent trickle of islands which afforded good shelter for their shipping. Amongst the coconut groves on one of the islands they had built a small fort. They called it *Bon Bahia*, or Bombay. In the 1660s, following an Anglo–Portuguese alliance against their Dutch rivals, the place was transferred to Charles II as part of his Portuguese wife's dowry. Although Bombay itself was as yet of no commercial value, the English thus acquired a territorial toehold adjacent to the busy shipping lanes of the west coast.

To the south, Goa remained in Portuguese hands while Cochin, an important entrepôt for the spice trade, had been wrested from them by the Dutch, also in the 1660s. North of Bombay the Mughal port of Surat, superseding the now mud-silted Cambay as the main maritime outlet of northern India, hosted much the busiest Dutch and English trading estab-

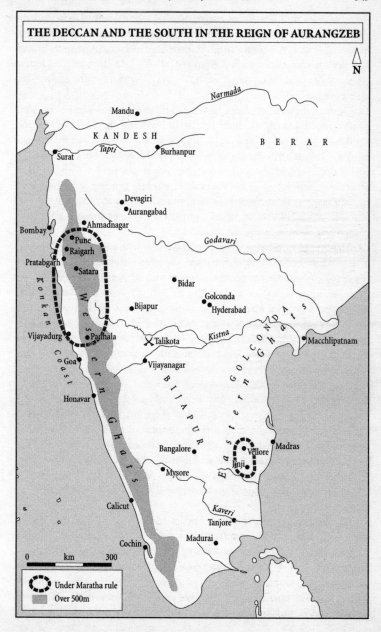

THE DECCAN AND THE SOUTH IN THE REIGN OF AURANGZEB

N

Narmada

Mandu

K A N D E S H

B E R A R

Tapti

Surat

Burhanpur

Devagiri

Aurangabad

Ahmadnagar

Bombay

Pune

Godavari

Raigarh

Pratabgarh

Satara

Bidar

Golconda

Bijapur

Hyderabad

Konkan Coast

Western Ghats

Vijayadurg

Panhala

Talikota

Kistna

Macchlipatnam

Goa

Vijayanagar

B I J A P U R

G O L C O N D A

Honavar

E a s t e r n   G h a t s

Bangalore

Vellore

Madras

Jinji

Mysore

Calicut

Kaveri

Tanjore

Cochin

Madurai

0   km   300

⬭ Under Maratha rule

▨ Over 500m

lishments. From Surat European purchasing agents fanned out into the cities and weaving centres of Gujarat and beyond to place their orders and oversee despatch. And down to Surat from Ahmadabad, Burhanpur, Broach and Baroda came the bundled cottons and silks and the barrelled indigo (in great demand for dyeing uniforms) which constituted the main items of export.

On the other side of the peninsula, all three European powers, plus the newly arrived French, retained similar toeholds on the Coromandel and Andhra coasts. Textiles were again the main item of trade, but there was a tendency here for the weavers to gravitate towards the European settlements which thus became zones of export-dependent prosperity. None of these settlements was yet of much political importance but the security offered by their heavy guns and well-built forts was proving an attraction. Additionally their stocks of powder, guns and gunners were eagerly sought by the contending powers in the hinterland.

The one obvious change which had overcome the Deccan during Aurangzeb's twenty-four-year absence was, however, momentous: whereas in the first half of the seventeenth century there had been two major powers in the peninsula, the Golconda sultanate and the Bijapur sultanate, there were now three. The Marathas had come of age. Having established their military credentials in the service of others and then, under Shivaji's inspirational leadership, having created an independent homeland in the Western Ghats, they had since elevated the homeland into a state and Shivaji into its king.

This revival of Hindu kingship at a time of awesome and markedly orthodox Muslim supremacy had been both unexpected and highly dramatic. As well as causing a sensation at the time, Shivaji's extraordinary exploits would transcend their immediate context to dazzle his successors, console Hindu pride during the looming years of British supremacy, and provide Indian nationalists with an inspiring example of indigenous revolt against alien rule. Latterly they have also served to encourage Hindu extremists in the belief that martial prowess is as much part of their tradition as non-violence.

Of Shivaji's exploits the most celebrated had occurred in 1659. In the words of Khafi Khan, an unofficial chronicler of Aurangzeb's reign, while in the north the emperor was 'beating off the crocodiles of the ocean of self-respect' (his brothers, in other words), Shivaji had 'become a master of dignity and resources'. In the previous years he had captured some forty forts in the Western Ghats and along the adjacent Konkan coast. But having 'openly and fearlessly raised the standard of revolt', when challenged, he revealed his true colours; 'he resorted to fraud and fox-play'. Afzal Khan, Bijapur's best general who had been sent to flush out 'the designing rascal', had run him to ground at the hill fort of Pratabgarh (near Mahabaleshwar). The Bijapuri army lacked the means to take such a strong position, while the Marathas stood no chance of driving them off. In time-honoured fashion the stalemate had therefore to be resolved by negotiation. Shivaji would have to make a token recognition of Bijapur's suzerainty; Afzal Khan would have to leave Shivaji in undisturbed possession of his forts. This much having been agreed, it remained only for Shivaji to make his personal submission.

In a clearing at the foot of the Pratabgarh hill the two men met. Each had supposedly dispensed with attendants and weapons. Nevertheless, 'both men came to the meeting armed'.[1] Amongst Shivaji's hidden arsenal was a small iron finger-grip with four curving talons, each as long and as sharp as a cut-throat razor.

> As soon as that experienced and perfect traitor [i.e. Shivaji] neared Afzal Khan, he threw himself at his feet weeping. When he [Afzal Khan] wanted to raise his [Shivaji's] head and put the hand of kindness on his back to embrace him, Shivaji with perfect dexterity thrust that hidden weapon into his abdomen in such a way that he [Afzal Khan] had not even time to sigh, and thus killed him.[2]

Shivaji then gave a signal to his men who were hidden in the surrounding scrub. Taking the Bijapuris by surprise, they 'destroyed the camp of the ill-fated Afzal Khan', captured his stores, treasure, horses and elephants, and enrolled many of his men. 'Thus Shivaji acquired dignity and force much larger than before.'

Since some of the Bijapuri troops were actually Marathas and some of Shivaji's were Muslims, it is clear that what Khafi Khan's translator renders as 'dignity' – or perhaps 'prestige' – mattered more than creed. The same translator, a Muslim, calls the affair 'one of the most notorious murders in the history of the subcontinent'; yet it seems that to contemporaries, as to most Hindu historians, it was testimony to Shivaji's resourceful genius as much as his 'designing turpitude'. Whilst the loyalties of kinsmen and co-religionists were vital, so were those of the assorted dissidents and adventurers who now recognised in him a leader of indomitable courage and assured fortune. Shivaji, says Khafi Khan, 'made it a rule ... not to desecrate mosques or the Book of Allah, nor to seize the women'.[3] Muslims as well as Hindus could comfortably serve under his standard.

Shivaji celebrated his success over Afzal Khan by grabbing more of the

Konkan coast between Bombay and Goa. There he assembled a small navy and began the fortification of the coves and estuaries from which it would operate. He also seized the pine-scented heights of Panhala, more a walled massif than a hill fort, just to the north of Kolhapur. A new Bijapuri army caught up with him there but, in another celebrated exploit, he gave the enemy the slip by escaping under cover of darkness with a few trusted followers.

By 1660 Aurangzeb had dealt with the 'crocodiles' and had sent to the Deccan a large army under Shaista Khan, the brother of Shah Jahan's beloved Mumtaz Mahal. Shaista Khan was to secure the territories ceded to the empire by Bijapur in 1657, which included the Maratha homeland in the Ghats. Shivaji thus faced a new and much more formidable foe whom he had even less chance of defeating. The Mughal army was relentlessly harried and every fort took a heavy toll of Mughal blood; yet Pune, Shivaji's capital, fell; then one by one the Maratha strongholds succumbed. By 1663 Shivaji was facing defeat. Another exploit was called for.

Shaista Khan had taken up residence in a house in the now Mughal city of Pune. No Marathas were allowed within the city walls and the house was heavily guarded. But special permission was obtained for a wedding party to enter the city and on the same day a more disconsolate group of Marathas were brought in as prisoners. Late that night the bridegroom, the wedding party, the prisoners and their guards met up as arranged. Discarding disguise, they produced their weapons, crawled into the compound of Shaista Khan's house through a kitchen window, and then smashed through a wall to reach the sleeping apartments. There 'they made everyone who was awake to sleep in death and everyone who was asleep they killed in bed.' Shaista Khan himself was lucky. He lost a thumb and seems to have fainted, whereupon 'his maid servants carried him from hand to hand and then took him to a safe place.' According to Khafi Khan, whose father was serving in Pune at the time, the Marathas then mistook their man and killed someone else thinking it was the Mughal commander. Also killed was Shaista Khan's son and one of his wives. No plunder was taken; the raiders withdrew as suddenly as they had emerged; and although Shivaji himself was not among them, it seems that he had organised the raid and had probably secured the collusion of one of the Mughal generals.

This affair, a great blow to Mughal pride, was followed by another of greater consequence for the Mughal purse. Breaking out of the hills in 1664, Shivaji personally led his forces north into Gujarat and headed for the great port of Surat. For forty days the Marathas then ransacked the place. Only the well-defended English 'factory' (a fortified warehouse-cum-counting-house-cum-hostel) was spared. Most embarrassingly Shivaji's 'dignity' was now eclipsing that of the empire.

Another Mughal army, fifteen thousand strong, headed for the Deccan under the great Jai Singh, the vanquisher of Prince Shuja. Once again the Maratha lands were ravaged as Jai Singh secured fort after fort and signed up their despairing defenders. By 1665 Shivaji himself was cornered near Purandhar and again sued for terms. The negotiations were protracted and complex. In the end, 'with the ring of submission in his ears and the mantle of devotion on his body', Shivaji agreed to the surrender of twenty forts, the payment of a substantial indemnity, the liability of his lands to assessment for Mughal military service, and the admission of his son as a Mughal *mansabdar*. He then made his personal submission to Jai Singh amidst security precautions which, understandably, were elaborate.

But the treaty of Purandhar had not been a surrender.[4] Shivaji retained twelve forts and he remained at the head of his depleted army which, consisting mostly of Maratha horse, could travel light and live off the countryside, and was thus infinitely more elusive and wide-ranging than its heavy Mughal counterpart. Indeed the treaty was as much about securing Maratha collaboration with the Mughal forces in an offensive against Bijapur as about neutralising Shivaji. A year later, in 1666, Mughal fears of Maratha defections in the course of this Bijapur offensive prompted a Mughal demand that Shivaji travel north to Agra to attend the emperor in person. This was not a success. At Aurangzeb's expense Shivaji assembled an impressive cavalcade of elephants, silver palanquins and gorgeously attired retainers only, on arrival, to be barely acknowledged by the imperial presence. He was then detained, amidst rumours of death or exile, in a situation that was little better than house arrest. True to form, the mortified Maratha escaped, although probably by bribery rather than buried in a basket of confectionery as per popular myth. Through the byways and backwoods he made his way undetected back to Maharashtra. 'It was the most thrilling exploit of all his most wonderful deeds,' opines a not impartial historian, 'which has for ever added a supernatural glow to his unique personality.'

> It immediately resounded throughout the country, making Shivaji an all-India figure, divinely ordained with extraordinary powers. The incident simultaneously exposed the emperor's craft, still further adding to his evil repute for cunning and cruelty. Shivaji's reputation, on the other hand, reached its zenith for having outwitted the cleverest and mightiest of the emperors.[5]

There followed a three-year lull before a Mughal demand seeking reimbursement for Shivaji's expenses in Agra provoked the Maratha leader into a new offensive. Several vital forts were recaptured, in 1670 the port of Surat was a second time pillaged, and Maratha units struck deep into the Kandesh and Berar districts of the Mughal Deccan. Pune was liberated and Panhala reclaimed along with much of the Konkan coast. Then in 1674, as it were to crown it all, Shivaji had himself elevated to kingship.

The assumption of kingship was less for Mughal edification than for domestic reasons. With an eye to the future, Shivaji sought to legitimise assumed rights to precedence, revenue and service from his Maratha peers which had hitherto depended largely on force of arms and his personal ascendancy. A basic machinery of government was also established and the kingdom's finances reorganised. The 'coronation' itself (no crown was actually used) presented the sort of problems which dynastic aspirants of old may have had to face. Marathas not being accounted as of *ksatriya* status, a bogus genealogy had to be fabricated which linked Shivaji's Bhonsle predecessors with the illustrious Sesodia rajputs of Mewar. This required a brahman of acknowledged repute who would sanction the arrangement, preside over Shivaji's penance for having hitherto lived as other than a *ksatriya*, and conduct the actual rituals of consecration. Such a man was found in Varanasi and triumphantly brought to Maharashtra; but the ritual, so long in abeyance, had to be laboriously deduced from ancient texts and adapted for current circumstances. It included much anointing with various liquids and, of course, lavish donations to brahmans. Additionally a new era was proclaimed and a new calendar drawn up. There was no horse-sacrifice but, to complete the traditional ceremony, Shivaji set off on a token *digvijaya* which included a raid on a Mughal encampment and more forays in Kandesh and Berar.

Now an independent sovereign and temporarily under no great threat from the Mughal forces, Shivaji turned south and, in alliance with the Golconda sultanate, made a joint attack on the distant Bijapur possessions in the south of Tamil Nadu. The campaign, his last, was conducted almost entirely by Maratha forces and resulted in the formation of a new Maratha military nucleus based on the captured forts of Vellore and Jinji (south-west of Madras). When in 1680 Shivaji died, dysentery having subverted 'dignity', he thus left a Maratha kingdom of great but ill-defined extent. Its territories were not contiguous and its subjects were still unaccustomed to other than personal allegiance to their remarkable leader.

Divisions amongst the Maratha leaders were further exacerbated by a disputed succession. But in 1681 Shambhaji, one of Shivaji's two competing sons, gained the upper hand, had himself crowned, and resumed his father's expansionist policies. It was to Shambhaji's court that Prince Akbar, Aurangzeb's rebellious son, had made his way after the failure of his rajput intrigues. And it was to nullify any possible rajput–Maratha alliance around the person of the prince, as well as to resume his long affair with the Deccan sultanates, that in 1682 the emperor himself headed south with the entire imperial court, the imperial administration, and something like 180,000 troops.

AURANGZEB'S LAST YEARS

The conjunction of Maratha and rajput resistance which Prince Akbar had hoped to engineer against his father never materialised. Shambhaji, with Mughal armies already swarming through the northern Maratha lands, preferred to ignore the prince's pleas for an all-India offensive and concentrated instead on his coastal neighbours, including a fierce little war with the Portuguese in Goa. In despair Prince Akbar took ship for Persia in 1687; like Humayun, he hoped to interest the shah in his ambitions but was disappointed.

Meanwhile Aurangzeb's armies were enjoying uninterrupted success although no decisive victories. 'The Mughal strategy toward Maharashtra was not subtle, just thorough.'[6] Maratha lands were ravaged and Maratha *deshmukhs* overawed and then enlisted in the imperial service as *mansabdars*. But the forts were rarely worth the immense effort of capturing them and the main enemy detachments proved too wily to be induced into battle. Already it was becoming clear that outright conquest of the Maratha kingdom would demand a greater commitment of imperial resources than Aurangzeb had realised.[7]

Badly in need of more tangible success, the emperor turned on Bijapur. In 1684 an army of eighty thousand invaded the sultanate. Not so much defeated as overwhelmed, both the city and its sultan surrendered after a desperate siege lasting over a year. The kingdom became a Mughal province, its chief nobles were co-opted into the Mughal hierarchy, and its sultan became a state prisoner in the imperial encampment. There he was soon joined by his opposite number of Golconda. First invaded and occupied in 1685, the Golconda sultanate finally fell, along with the great stronghold of that name, in 1687. It too was then incorporated into the empire.

Aurangzeb argued that both sultanates deserved their fate for having on occasion abetted the infidel Marathas. In Hyderabad especially, the revenge of the righteous was sweet; vast wealth was appropriated, temples were desecrated, brahmans killed and Hindus of all castes penalised by the *jizya*. But there also arose considerable disquiet, even amongst the *ulema*, over the emperor's cavalier treatment of such long-established Islamic states. Their non-Muslim subjects, especially those warrior aristocracies under their ex-Vijayanagar nayaks, would never become resigned to Mughal rule. And the 'Deccani' nobles, who though often of Persian origin and Shi'ite persuasion were now enrolled as ranking Mughal *amirs*, would retain a strong sense of regional and cultural identity. Within the Mughal military hierarchy they would constitute an influential clique on whom the 'Hindustani' *amirs* of the north looked with suspicion.

Aurangzeb's mission in the south seemingly soared to its glorious climax when in 1688 Shivaji's successor Shambhaji, together with his brahman chief minister, was captured in an ambush. Brought to the imperial encampment, Shambhaji managed to heap insult on both the emperor and the Prophet. He was duly tortured and then painfully dismembered, joint by joint, limb by limb. No doubt the procedure symbolised that by which Aurangzeb imagined himself dealing with the Maratha kingdom.

Rajaram, Shambhaji's brother and earlier rival, now assumed the mantle of Shivaji, but was himself besieged in the fort of Raigarh. He escaped and headed south to the Maratha possessions in Tamil Nadu. There, installed on the heights of Jinji, he was soon under siege from another Mughal army. The siege of Jinji lasted an amazing eight years (1689–97) and accounted for most of Rajaram's reign. At times Maratha units from elsewhere pressed the Mughals so hard, and cut off their supplies so successfully, that the besiegers became the besieged. At others the stalemate stemmed from collusion; when the fort finally fell Rajaram and most of his men were allowed to make their escape.

Aurangzeb himself never visited Jinji. Nor was Rajaram's protracted defence responsible for the emperor's remaining in the Deccan. The real difficulty lay in the intransigence of the Maratha bands in the Western Ghats. Here, well into his eighties, the emperor would continue to lead his weary armies on an expensive and increasingly futile round of fort-bagging. He saw the campaign as a *jihad* and, along with such pious works as transcribing the Quran and stitching skull-caps for the faithful, he regarded a visit to another doomed stronghold of idolatry as an appropriate way in which to end his days.

But such obsessive concentration on the minutiae of Maharashtrian resistance was not good for the empire as a whole, and it was hopelessly counter-productive in respect of the Marathas. The terrain was partly responsible. Anywhere less suited to the Mughal military machine than the mountain rockery of the Ghats would be hard to imagine. North-to-south perpendicular escarpments shield a chaotic land of wooded ravines and barren downs in which every hill is a natural fortress and every valley a potential death-trap. Between the Konkan coastline of baked rock and the Deccan hinterland of parched tundra, this same choppy configuration continues for hundreds of miles. Here the Mughals' superior artillery and heavily armoured cavalry were more a handicap than an asset.

When forts were taken it was rarely by storm. Their garrisons preferred to accept the best terms on offer, wait till the Mughal circus moved on, and then, renouncing their pledges, resume their lands and reoccupy the forts. Aurangzeb, in fact, was confronted with a new kind of insurgency which was partly of his own making. With Shambhaji dead and Rajaram cornered, each Maratha chief was now operating independently. The state was no longer susceptible to the systematic dismemberment meted out to Shambhaji. Aurangzeb's army was simply betraying its own impotence and, by devastating Maratha lands, positively obliging those whose livelihood derived from them to take up arms and redouble their raiding.

In 1700 Satara, to which place Shivaji had earlier moved the Maratha capital, came under siege and was eventually surrendered to the Mughals. At about the same time Rajaram died. His senior widow, Tarabai, assumed control in the name of her son, Shambhaji II, and offered terms to Aurangzeb which should have ended the war. Yet despite the fact that Satara had cost thousands of lives – two thousand Mughal troops died in a single misdirected mining attempt – the emperor rejected this overture. That same year Maratha raiders for the first time crossed the Narmada river. This was the traditional Rubicon between the Deccan and the north; Malwa was now in the Maratha sights. Two years later they turned east to launch an expedition fifty thousand strong against Hyderabad. The great city, still one of the richest in the peninsula, was ransacked. In 1704 it was ransacked again and the same fate befell even Machchlipatnam (Masulipatnam), its port on the Bay of Bengal. Maratha activities now extended to virtually the entire peninsula.

Meanwhile Tarabai as regent was insinuating into the Mughal province of the Deccan what amounted to a parallel administration. This was a new tactic based on a Maratha claim to a 25 percent share (*chauth*) of all revenues collected in the Deccan and a further 10 per cent for the hereditary Maratha *sardeshmukh*, or sovereign. Payment supposedly guaranteed protection, especially from Mughal revenue collectors; it also justified a shadow hierarchy of Maratha governors and deputies operating from their own

THE ROYAL HOUSE OF SHIVAJI (Bhonsle Chatrapatis)

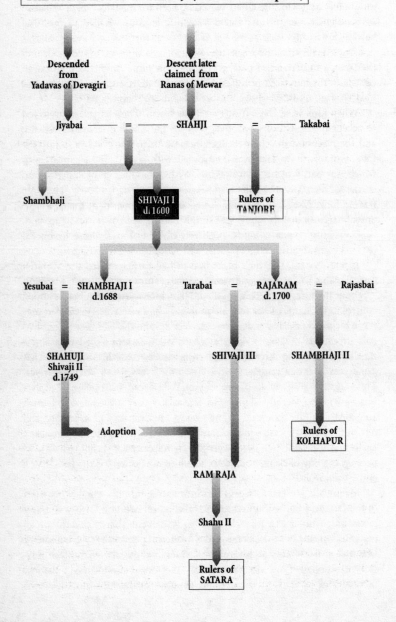

fortified bases within Mughal territory and levying additional tolls on the vital trade routes of the region. Non-payment, of course, whether by traders or *zamindars*, meant forcible expropriation or further raids. In practice it was little better than a protection racket. But it was not necessarily resisted. The emperor's extreme old age, the succession crisis which would inevitably follow his death, the resentment stirred up by his religious policies, the strain imposed on his military and financial resources by the incessant Maratha campaign, and the growing discontent amongst Mughal *mansabdars* whose Deccan *jagirs* either failed to materialise or failed to yield their expected revenue, were all taking their toll of Mughal authority.

In 1705 Aurangzeb fell seriously ill. A frail and shrouded spectre dressed 'all over white', as a visitor put it, with turban and beard of the same ghostly pallor, he was installed in a palanquin and carefully carried back to Ahmadnagar. Even then he was a long time dying. Embittered and isolated, he prayed hard, bemoaned the state of affairs, and found fault with his officials; he had already despaired of most of his progeny. As for himself, 'I am,' he wrote, 'forlorn and destitute, and misery is my ultimate lot.'[8] The misery ended in 1707, his ninetieth year. His funeral expenses were supposedly met from the sale of the Qurans he had copied and the caps he had stitched. True to his wishes, he was buried not beneath a stylish mountain of marble and sandstone at the heart of the empire but in a simple grave beside a village shrine dear to the Muslims of the Deccan. At Khuldabad, not far from Aurangabad, a neat little mosque now flanks the small courtyard in which stands the least pretentious of all the Mughal tombs. There is barely room for a vanload of pilgrims. And instead of a great white dome, a dainty but determined tree provides the only canopy.

TOWARDS A NEW ORDER

Considering that, by one calculation, Aurangzeb was survived by seventeen sons, grandsons and great-grandsons, all of an age in 1707 to lay claim to the throne, the war of succession passed off comparatively smoothly. Not, though, cheaply. Treasure was disbursed by the bucketload, *jagirs* doled out, armies mobilised, and about ten thousand soldiers butchered in the process.

The two main contenders clashed near Agra on nearly the same battle site as had Aurangzeb and his brother Dara Shikoh. Prince Muazzam (also known as Shah Alam), previously governor in Kabul, defeated and killed Prince Azam Shah, from the Deccan, and then assumed the title of Bahadur

Shah (or Shah Alam I). Another brother of doubtful sanity entered the fray a year later and was routed and killed in 1709. The new emperor promised well, despite his years. But whereas Aurangzeb's reign had lasted far too long for the good of his empire, Bahadur Shah's proved far too short. He died after five years. One succession war was barely over before the next began. And in between, major crises in Rajasthan and the Panjab, plus rural unrest just about everywhere, had fatally exposed the fragility of Mughal power.

The Rajasthan problem began with the eviction of Mughal troops from Marwar (Jodhpur) by Ajit Singh, the infant who had been sneaked out of Delhi in 1678. Now nearly thirty, Ajit was taking the long-awaited opportunity of Aurangzeb's death to avenge the earlier desecration of Marwar. Support came from other rajputs including the Kacchwahas of Amber (Jaipur) and the Sesodias of Mewar (Udaipur). But Bahadur Shah proved equal to the challenge. Overawing the Kacchwahas and ignoring the Sesodias, he re-invaded Marwar and reached a compromise settlement with Ajit Singh. A year later Ajit Singh and Jai Singh Kacchwaha again rose in revolt and attacked the provincial capital of Ajmer. Such repeated defiance would once have invited the direst of reprisals but now elicited only further clemency. As Bahadur Shah hastened away to the Panjab to deal with the Sikhs, it began to look as if imperial indulgence of the rajputs, once founded on strength and dictated by policy, was now beset by doubt and dictated by circumstance. Ten years later, after further rajput defiance and more abject Mughal concessions, the Jaipur and Udaipur rajas were said to hold 'all the country from 30 kos [about a hundred kilometres] of Delhi, where the native land of Jai Singh begins, to the shores of the sea at Surat'.[9]

The more pressing Sikh problem arose from the assassination in 1708 of Gobind Singh, the last of the Sikh Gurus. At the time the Guru had been attending the emperor in the hopes of winning back a Sikh base recently established at Anandpur Sahib (near Bilaspur in Himachal Pradesh) and of obtaining redress against the local Mughal commander who had been hounding the Sikhs. This same man, who had also murdered the Guru's two sons, was now widely regarded as having instigated the death of the Guru himself.

By the peace-loving disciples of Guru Nanak such provocation might once have been ignored. But under Guru Gobind the Sikh *panth* (brotherhood) had undergone a radical transformation. Retreating to the Panjab hills after Aurangzeb's execution of Guru Tegh Bahdur in 1676, Guru Gobind had been obliged to arm his followers so that they might hold their own against the hill rajas. Support arrived from Sikhs scattered

throughout north India. The claims of conscience were now to be maintained by force whenever necessary. Even Mughal contingents were successfully repulsed. In keeping with this more assertive stance, Guru Gobind
had also introduced a more rigid standard of orthodoxy. True Sikhs must
henceforth be inducted through a baptismal ceremony into the *khalsa*, 'the
pure'; and they must leave their hair uncut, carry arms and adopt the
epithet of 'Singh' ('Lion'). Clearly recognisable, more cohesive, more territorially aware, and much more militant, the *panth* was readying itself to
join the contest for power in the late Mughal period.

Within a year of the Guru's death a disciple calling himself Banda
Bahadur began collecting arms and followers in the eastern Panjab. The
Panjab, like other provinces, had prospered during the first half of the
seventeenth century, with revenue receipts increasing by two-thirds and
Lahore becoming a major commercial centre. This trend had since been
reversed, with both agricultural production and revenue falling despite
rising prices. Rural distress added to Banda Bahadur's appeal and turned
his protest into 'a millennial resistance movement'[10] with a strong element
of lower-caste revolt. Though poorly armed, the Sikh forces began systematically storming the mainly Muslim towns of the region.

Banda himself assumed a royal title, initiated a new calendar and began
minting the first Sikh coinage. In thus adding political autonomy to the
aspirations of the new brotherhood of the *khalsa*, he anticipated by nearly
a century the Sikh kingdom of Ranjit Singh. Although forced to retreat
into the hills by Bahadur Shah's massive onslaught, Banda and his many
sympathisers outlived the emperor and, when finally defeated in 1715, left
a legacy of defiant protest and sectarian militancy. 'Though Banda Bahadur,
. . . and along with him seven hundred other Sikhs, were captured and
slain in 1715, Sikh hostility continued to subvert the foundations of Mughal
power till the province was in total disarray in the middle of the eighteenth
century.'[11]

Despite such chronic subsidence, the Mughal edifice would stand for
another 150 years. During this period its legitimacy and authority were rarely
questioned. Well into the nineteenth century even the British acknowledged
Mughal supremacy and worked within its institutions. But the erosion of
its wealth and power in the early decades of the eighteenth century, and
the expropriation of the system through which they operated, was indeed
spectacular. Traditionally this is explained in dynastic terms. Disputed successions, imbecilic contenders, and short reigns resulted in a rapid depletion
of imperial resources, leading to administrative chaos and regional
secession. To these 'causes' of the 'decline' of the empire, historians with

Hindu sympathies add the alienation occasioned by Aurangzeb's religious policies, while those of Marxist sympathies emphasise rural desperation and peasant unrest as a result of the failure of an agrarian system founded on excessive exploitation and minimal investment. As so often, more historical data only generate less in the way of comforting certainty.

That local disturbances preceded Aurangzeb's death and then became widespread throughout the empire suggests that the Sikh and rajput troubles were symptomatic of a deeper problem. But whether this resulted directly from the sort of rural oppression so graphically described by Bernier is doubtful. 'It was not so much impoverished peasants but substantial yeomen and prosperous farmers already drawn into the Mughals' cash and service nexus, who revolted against Delhi in the late seventeenth and early eighteenth centuries.'[12] These yeomen and farmers were otherwise the vaguely defined, immensely various but always locally-based elites known as *zamindars*, the men at whose expense Todar Mal had set up his revenue system. Thanks to favourable trading conditions and increased yields during the first half of the seventeenth century they had evidently more than recouped their losses. In the *sarkars* (districts) and *parganas* (sub-districts) of northern India there was now a general flexing of *zamindari* muscle as such local caste- and kin-based groupings used new wealth to buy their way back into the revenue system or to acquire the troops and arms with which to defend existing privileges. The imperial edifice was being insidiously undermined from below even as, above ground, it was being converted and partitioned.

This unrest, it is argued, contributed to a *jagirs* crisis. Throughout the Mughal period *mansabs* had been subject to a bounteous inflation as more and more rank-holders were given higher and higher rankings. On the other hand, the supply of the *jagirs* which were supposed to support these rankings failed to keep pace, while their individual yields actually dwindled. A scale of differentials was drawn up to address this problem, but it seems that *jagirdars* now so dreaded ending up *jagir*-less that they defied orders to transfer from their *jagirs* and began to regard them as permanent perquisites which could be leased or farmed out at will and passed on to their heirs.

Office-holders felt the same way about their offices. At the highest level this meant that provincial governorships often came to be held for life and might, in the hands of a powerful and ambitious incumbent, become heritable. By the 1730s this would indeed be the case in respect of the governorships of the Panjab, Bengal, Awadh (Oudh) and the Deccan. The short step to genuine autonomy quickly followed, usually in the form of a refusal either to remit the provincial revenue to the imperial treasury or

to attend in person at the imperial court. In Bengal and Awadh two generations served to turn the provincial governor into an autonomous nawab;
in the Deccan the incumbent governor's title of Nizam-ul-Mulk simply
became analogous with 'nawab'.

This was not, however, outright secession – more like devolution or a
radical decentralisation. And in many ways the empire as represented by
the sum of its parts proved more prestigious and entrenched than when
all power rested with the emperor. The nawabs would continue to operate
through the officers and institutions inherited from Mughal administration.
Prayers continued to be said in the emperor's name; coins continued to
be struck in the emperor's name. His person and his authority gave to the
new order its only legitimacy. In effect the Mughal emperor was conforming
to the traditional pre-Islamic model of a *maharajadhiraja* or *shah-in-shah*.
The latter had actually become a Mughal title; 'a king of kings', it also
signified 'a king *among* kings'. However debilitated, the later Mughals stood
unchallenged at the pinnacle of 'a hierarchy of lesser sovereigns', presiding
over something not unlike that ancient 'society of kings'.

A COMMUNION OF INTEREST

Proof that the authority of the Mughal empire remained paramount came
most obviously from the willingness of even the Marathas to seek its sanction. For the Marathas the most important consequence of Aurangzeb's
death had been the release of Shahuji, son of the dismembered Shambhaji
(and so grandson of Shivaji). He had been brought up in the imperial
camp but had not been obliged to convert to Islam and, when freed by
Bahadur Shah, boldly claimed the Maratha throne. Tarabai, his aunt, contested this in the name of her own son, Shambhaji. The still spluttering
Mughal–Maratha war thus became a three-cornered affair, with Shahuji
also bidding for the loyalties of the Maratha leaders. Meanwhile governors
of the Mughal Deccan came and went, one favouring Shahuji and the next
Tarabai. Stalemate brought only chronic anarchy, until in 1713 Shahuji
began to listen to the councils of the redoubtable Balaji Vishvanath.

A brahman from the Konkan coast who had once worked as a clerk of
salt-pans, Balaji lacked the more obvious credentials of a rough-riding
Maratha. 'He did not particularly excel in the accomplishment of sitting
upon a horse and, at this time, required a man on each side to hold him.'[13]
Nevertheless he enjoyed a great reputation for that other essential Maratha
campaigning skill – negotiating. In 1714 he pulled off an unlikely coup by

winning for Shahuji the support of Kanhoji Angria, admiral of the Maratha fleet (or 'the Angrian Pirate' as the British in Bombay called him), who had been the mainstay of Tarabai's faction. Balaji was rewarded with the post of Shahuji's 'peshwa' or chief minister; his fellow brahmans assumed responsibility for the Maratha administration and also boosted its credit-worthiness; and Shahuji's situation immediately began to improve. In due course the office of peshwa would become hereditary in Balaji's family and the peshwas, rather than their royal patrons, would become the dispensers of Maratha power and patronage for the next sixty years.

Meanwhile in Delhi the succession crisis which followed Bahadur Shah's death in 1712 was taking its course. Although orchestrated more by senior Mughal officials than by the four contesting sons of Bahadur Shah, it proved no less costly in blood and treasure and it resulted in the accession of a man not unfairly described by Khafi Khan as a frivolous and drunken imbecile. Luckily this Jahandah Shah lasted only eleven months, a short reign if a long debauch. 'It was a time for minstrels and singers and all the tribes of dancers and actors ... Worthy, talented and learned men were driven away, and bold impudent wits and tellers of facetious anecdotes gathered round.' The anecdotes invariably concerned Lal Kunwar (or Kumari), the emperor's outrageous mistress, on whose fun-loving relatives were showered *jagirs*, *mansabs*, elephants and jewels. So infectious was the mood that 'it seemed *kazis* would turn toss-pots and *muftis* become tipplers.'[14]

The party ended, and decorum was temporarily restored, when in 1713 Farrukhsiyar, the son of one of Jahandah Shah's unsuccessful brothers, approached from Bihar with a sizeable army. Jahandah Shah's forces mostly melted away, and Farrukhsiyar, who had already declared himself emperor, began his six-year reign (1713–19). It was he who was responsible for the bloody repression of Banda Bahadur and his Sikhs, and it was he who would fatefully indulge the ambitions of the English East India Company.

But his bid for power, as now his rule, depended heavily on two very able brothers known as the Saiyids, one of whom had been governor of Allahabad and the other of Patna. The Saiyids were now rewarded with the highest offices, but soon fell out with an emperor whose ambition was exceeded only by his chronic indecision. Finding the Saiyids at first overbearing, then indispensable, then intolerable, Farrukhsiyar finally ordered the younger, Husain Ali Khan, to the Deccan. As governor of the Deccan he would be out of the way; better still, as per secret instructions given to the governor of Gujarat, he would be opposed and killed *en route*. In the event it was the Saiyid who disposed of his would-be assassin and who then, not surprisingly, began planning his revenge on the emperor.

THE LATER MUGHALS

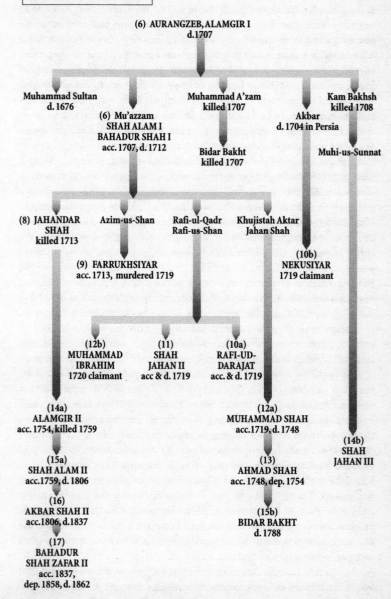

(6) AURANGZEB, ALAMGIR I
d.1707

Muhammad Sultan
d. 1676

(6) Mu'azzam
SHAH ALAM I
BAHADUR SHAH I
acc. 1707, d. 1712

Muhammad A'zam
killed 1707

Bidar Bakht
killed 1707

Akbar
d. 1704 in Persia

Kam Bakhsh
killed 1708

Muhi-us-Sunnat

(8) JAHANDAR
SHAH
killed 1713

Azim-us-Shan

Rafi-ul-Qadr
Rafi-us-Shan

Khujistah Aktar
Jahan Shah

(9) FARRUKHSIYAR
acc. 1713, murdered 1719

(10b)
NEKUSIYAR
1719 claimant

(12b)
MUHAMMAD
IBRAHIM
1720 claimant

(11)
SHAH
JAHAN II
acc & d. 1719

(10a)
RAFI-UD-
DARAJAT
acc. & d. 1719

(14a)
ALAMGIR II
acc. 1754, killed 1759

(12a)
MUHAMMAD SHAH
acc.1719, d. 1748

(14b)
SHAH
JAHAN III

(15a)
SHAH ALAM II
acc.1759, d. 1806

(13)
AHMAD SHAH
acc. 1748, dep. 1754

(16)
AKBAR SHAH II
acc.1806, d.1837

(15b)
BIDAR BAKHT
d. 1788

(17)
BAHADUR
SHAH ZAFAR II
acc. 1837,
dep. 1858, d. 1862

Into this vendetta the Marathas were drawn, and it was under cover of it that their forces would finally burst out of the Deccan and Gujarat to begin their long involvement in the affairs of northern India. Whether the initiative came from the Saiyid Husain Ali Khan or from the Peshwa Balaji Vishvanath is not clear; but in 1716 negotiations were opened between these two which ostensibly aimed at ending the Mughals' thirty-year war with the Marathas. Like Shivaji in 1665, Shahuji would have to accept Mughal rule in the Deccan, furnish forces for the imperial army and pay an annual tribute. But in return he demanded a *farman*, or imperial directive, guaranteeing him *swaraj*, or independence, in the Maratha homeland, plus rights to *chauth* and *sardeshmukh* (amounting to 35 percent of the total revenue) throughout Gujarat, Malwa, and the now six provinces of the Mughal Deccan (i.e. including the erstwhile territories of Bijapur and Golconda in Tamil Nadu). This was a very substantial demand and, although Husain Ali Khan agreed to the terms, they were flatly rejected by Emperor Farrukh-siyar, who realised that such a *farman* would effectively end Mughal power in the region.[15] Saiyid Husain Ali Khan, however, determined to press the treaty in person. His brother in Delhi was under constant threat from the intrigues of the vacillating emperor, and was urging his presence. Likewise Peshwa Balaji, in return for ratification of the treaty, was eager to support him. Accordingly, at the head of a joint army of Maratha and Mughal troops, the peshwa and the younger Saiyid headed north for Delhi in 1719.

Unopposed, they approached the city and pitched camp beside the Ashoka pillar re-erected by Feroz Shah II. The sound of their drums travelled up the Jamuna – which in those days still slid below the ramparts – and could be heard in the great Red Fort of Shahjahanabad. There Farrukhsiyar was quickly isolated and, with his guard surreptitiously replaced, fell an easy prey to the Saiyids. Blinded, caged, poisoned, garrotted and eventually stabbed, his death partook of the indecision which had characterised his life. He was replaced on the throne by a consumptive youth who lasted only six months, then by the latter's equally irrelevant brother, who rejoiced in the title of Shah Jahan II but died, says Khafi Khan, 'of dysentery and mental disorder after a reign of three months and some days'. 'Matters went on just as before . . .', continues the chronicler, 'he [Shah Jahan II] had no part in the government of the country.'[16] Under Saiyid scrutiny the first of these imperial nonentities did, however, sanction the Maratha treaty. Balaji Vishvanath and his men returned to the Deccan well pleased with their work.

Meanwhile Muhammad Shah, the third emperor in a year, was installed by the Saiyids. In an unexpectedly long reign (1719–48), his most notable achievement came early when in 1720 the younger Saiyid was murdered and the older defeated. But having freed himself of his minders, the emperor promptly fell a prey to other warring factions and seemingly despaired of actually ruling. 'Young, handsome and fond of all kinds of pleasures, he addicted himself to an inactive life.'[17] Catastrophic raids on Delhi by the Marathas (1737), by Nadir Shah of Persia (1739) and by the Afghan Ahmad Shah Abdali (1748 onwards) would fail to galvanise him. His reign, though long, would not be glorious.

Meanwhile Peshwa Balaji Vishvanath, the Saiyids' ally, had also died in 1720. His son, Baji Rao I, 'after Shivaji the most charismatic and dynamic leader in Maratha history',[18] duly inherited the office of peshwa. He also inherited the dazzling prospect opened by the new treaty plus his father's understandable contempt for the might, if not the mystique, of the Mughal emperor. Over the next two decades the Marathas would raid north, south, east and west with impunity. They reached Rajasthan in 1735, Delhi in 1737 and Orissa and Bengal by 1740. But the loose structure of Maratha sovereignty remained. Balaji's distribution of the ceded Deccan revenues amongst various Maratha commanders had produced what James Grant Duff, the first historian of the Marathas, called 'a communion of interest'.[19] Later distributions and partitions aimed at the same kind of harmonised commonwealth. It was susceptible to direction but fell well short of an imperial formation. Individual leaders at the head of their own armies operated independently. Sometimes they clashed and sometimes they collaborated but more typically each operated within a separate sphere which was determined by previous operations and existing outposts or sanctioned by the award of particular revenues. Baji Rao's exceptional talents ensured a degree of central control. But already the seventeenth-century Maratha 'state' had become the eighteenth-century Maratha 'confederacy'.

As with the devolving provincial governments of the Mughal empire, sovereignty itself could be an elusive concept. Maratha demands continued to focus more on revenue than territory, and to reflect the awesome mobility of the Maratha horse. Thus Maratha rule bubbled up wherever the existing revenue system was vulnerable or wherever trade arteries converged. Sometimes it circumvented existing rulers or even accommodated them. Although incomprehensible to writers schooled on the definable certainties of the nation-state, Maratha dominion often rejoiced in the character of a parallel, or counter, administration.

The great confederate families who emerged during this period would become the princely Marathas of British times. All distinguished themselves militarily in the 1720s, although they were not necessarily *deshmukhs* with ancestral lands in the Maratha homeland. Damaji Gaikwad for instance, the ancestor of the Gaikwads of Baroda, had served in Gujarat with a Maratha family that strongly opposed the peshwa and indeed fought against him in support of Nizam-ul-Mulk, the Mughal governor in the Deccan. Not till some years after the nizam's defeat at Palkhed in 1728 did Damaji, by then supreme in Gujarat, declare his loyalty to the peshwa. On the other hand, Malhar Rao Holkar and Ranoji Scindia (Sindia, Shinde) rose entirely in the peshwa's service, mostly in Malwa. Holkar performed with distinction at Palkhed and was rewarded with a large portion of Malwa including Indore, from where his descendants would rule as Maharajas of Indore. Scindia was awarded the ancient city of Ujjain although Gwalior, taken by his son Mahadji in 1766, would be the seat of future Scindia power and the most formidable Maratha maharaja-ship in northern India.

Likewise the Bhonsle supporters of Shahuji in his tussle with Tarabai were awarded revenue rights in Berar. These rights became the nucleus of Maratha power in eastern India whence raids were conducted deep into Orissa and Bengal. The Bhonsles adopted Nagpur as their capital, and it would be British annexation of this state of Nagpur, amongst others, which would contribute to the discontent which flared into the 1857 Uprising or 'Indian Mutiny'. As for the sidelined Tarabai and her own Bhonsle protégés, they were eventually bought off with the offer of Kolhapur in southern Maharashtra. As a separate state under its own Maratha maharajas, Kolhapur would outlive both the Mughals and the peshwas and survive even the British, only to surrender its autonomy at Independence. Like all the other princely houses it was finally disestablished by Indira Gandhi in the 1970s.

Meanwhile the peshwas remained in Pune. Baji Rao, the second peshwa, had correctly surmised that with the power of the Mughals devolving to the empire's provinces, the main challenge to Maratha expansion would come from regional regimes like those already emerging in Bengal and Awadh. Nizam-ul-Mulk, one of the most senior and able Mughal *amirs*, who had repeatedly rescued the imperial fortunes, reluctantly came to much the same conclusion. Instead of buttressing worthless emperors in Delhi, in 1723 he determined to carve out his own kingdom based on the Deccan province of which he was governor. Two formidable opponents, the Marathas, of course, and one Mubariz Khan, another Mughal functionary who had created a near-independent state based on Hyderabad, barred his way. In 1724 he defeated and killed Mubariz Khan but in 1728 and again in 1731 he was himself outmanoeuvred by the Marathas. Not surprisingly

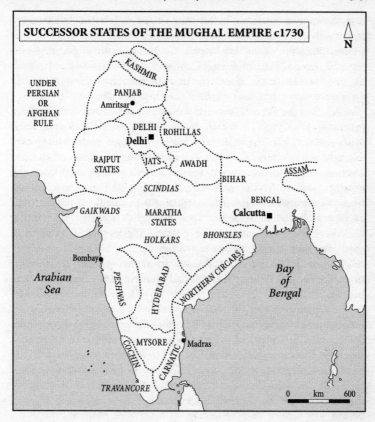

SUCCESSOR STATES OF THE MUGHAL EMPIRE c1730

N

UNDER PERSIAN OR AFGHAN RULE

KASHMIR

PANJAB
Amritsar

DELHI
Delhi   ROHILLAS

RAJPUT STATES   JATS   AWADH

ASSAM

BIHAR

SCINDIAS

BENGAL
Calcutta

GAIKWADS   MARATHA STATES

HOLKARS   BHONSLES

Bombay

Arabian Sea

PESHWAS   HYDERABAD   NORTHERN CIRCARS

Bay of Bengal

MYSORE   Madras

COCHIN   CARNATIC

TRAVANCORE

0   km   600

he eventually forsook his capital of Aurangabad and took his title, troops and aspirations east to Hyderabad. There he duly founded the strongest of all the newly devolved satellite states of the empire. It would also prove to be one of the most long-lived thanks to an eventual accommodation with the British.

FIRST THE *FARMAN* . . .

Farrukhsiyar, the protégé, scourge, and finally victim of the Saiyid brothers who in 1719 had rejected the agreement reached with Balaji Vishvanath, had in 1717 received another such request for imperial authorisation. It came from the opposite quarter of his tottering empire, in fact from Calcutta, and after much prevarication he did in this instance give his consent. But the consequences proved no less fateful. On the strength of Farrukhsiyar's imperial *farman*, 'The Honourable Company of Merchants of London trading into the East Indies' would line up with the Marathas and the nizam for a stake in the devolving might of the Great Mughals.

Ever since the days of Akbar the European trading companies had been petitioning the Mughal emperors for *farmans*, imperial directives. These would theoretically regularise their status, privileges and trading terms throughout the empire and would, as it were, trump the variety of vexatious exactions and demands imposed by local Mughal officials in the ports and provincial capitals. To an organisation like the English East India Company, whose very existence depended on a national monopoly of Eastern trade as solemnly conferred by charter from the English sovereign, the need for some such reciprocal authorisation guaranteeing favourable access to its most important trading partner was self-evident.

Within a decade of the English Company receiving its first royal charter in 1600, a Captain William Hawkins had journeyed from Surat to Agra to petition Jahangir for just such a *farman*. Provided with more lavish gifts or more impressive accreditation, a procession of hopefuls followed in his wake, amongst them Sir Thomas Roe, the first official ambassador from the Court of St James and the man who was so impressed by Jahangir's jewellery. With India as a whole Roe was less impressed, dismissing it in much the same terms as had Babur. Prickly to the point of apoplexy about his diplomatic status, Roe also pontificated to his countrymen in India and thus antagonised the Company's merchants, or 'factors', whose interests he was supposed to be representing. 'If he [Prince Khurram, the future Shah Jahan] should offer me ten [forts] I would not accept one,' he told the factors, '. . . for without controversy it is an errour to affect garrisons and land warrs in India . . . Let this be received as a rule, that if you will profitt, seek it at sea and in quiett trade.' Although Roe's idea of 'quiett trade' included a gratuitous attack on Mughal shipping once every four years – as he explained, 'we must chasten these people' – the directors of the East India Company had agreed with him about avoiding garrisons and wars. As a guarantee of favourable trading conditions an imperial *farman* looked to provide the perfect, because inexpensive, alternative.

But the *farman* had not been forthcoming, and garrisons and wars had followed. Madras had been acquired from the local nayak in 1640 and its foreshore immediately graced with the four-square Fort St George. Bombay, as noted, had passed to Charles II in 1661 as part of the dowry of his

Portuguese bride, Catherine of Braganza. After a disastrous attempt to install a royal garrison it had been leased to the Company, whose employees came to appreciate its greater security when Shivaji and his successors began their raids on Surat. The actual transfer from Crown to Company was by letters patent of 1668 which, presumably for reasons of bureaucratic convenience, described Bombay as being 'in the Manor of East Greenwich in the County of Kent'; the rent of £10 was to be paid 'in gold, on the 30th day of September, yearly, for ever'.

Calcutta had been founded twenty years later during the course of one of Aurangzeb's lesser-known wars. In 1664 Shaista Khan, fresh from the Deccan and minus the thumb lost during that audacious Maratha raid on his Pune home, had been appointed governor of Bengal in succession to Mir Jumla, the conqueror of Assam. When Aurangzeb himself moved to the Deccan in 1682, Shaista Khan was still in Bengal, and in that year he welcomed to his capital of Dacca one William Hedges, a director of the English East India Company. Hedges sought to persuade Shaista Khan to cancel a new tax on the imported bullion with which the Company paid for its Indian exports and to petition Aurangzeb for the long-sought *farman*. As the brother of Mumtaz Mahal of the Taj, and so Aurangzeb's uncle, Shaista Khan was believed to have considerable influence. At one point Hedges thought the *farman* was as good as signed. But in 1684 his diplomacy was undermined by a combination of the Company's bitching Bengal factors and Sir Josiah Child, its bellicose governor in London. Shaista Khan drew the obvious conclusion: 'the English are a company of base quarelling people and foul dealers.' Negotiations were broken off; and a couple of years later – it taking that long for recriminations to reach London and retribution to reach India – two ships carrying exactly 308 Company soldiers sailed up to Hughli to press the Company's suit and challenge an empire which had at the time at least 100,000 men in the field.[20]

The Company's Mughal War, also sometimes known as 'Child's War', figures no more prominently in histories of British India than it does in Mughal histories. It brought glory to no one. In Bengal, after a fracas in the Mughal port of Hughli, the English withdrew downriver, landed themselves at the spot which they later called Calcutta, then next year evacuated it. This performance was repeated in 1688–9 as the 'war' took a more serious turn elsewhere. In support of his Bengal brethren, the Company's senior official in Surat (who was also called Child) had removed to the comparative safety of Bombay. Thence, in accordance with ambassador Roe's long-remembered dictum, he began attacking Mughal shipping. Child in London applauded; within a year, he announced, 'the subjects of the

Mogoll [would be] starving and dying by thousands for want of our trade'. Meanwhile the Child in Bombay boasted that if Aurangzeb chose to send the admiral of his fleet against him he 'would blow him off with the wind of his bum'.[21] Aurangzeb did so choose, and 'Child's War' – or perhaps 'the Children's War' – thus spread from one extremity of the Mughal empire to the other. In early 1689 Sidi Yakub, the African who commanded a west coast fleet which served as the Mughal marine, took Bombay island completely by surprise. The English were besieged in Bombay Castle for most of the year and eventually capitulated.

The Company's 'envoys', who in 1690 journeyed up to the imperial encampment to plead for pardon, did so with their hands tied in more ways than one. As a further indignity they were made to prostrate themselves before the emperor. But Aurangzeb was not unaware of the value of their trade nor of the danger of their making common cause with the Marathas. For a massive indemnity and promises of better conduct in future, he graciously agreed to the restoration of their trading privileges and the withdrawal of his troops. In the same spirit of forgive and forget, the Company's Bengal establishment was allowed to return to the Hughli river where in 1690 it made a permanent settlement at Calcutta and began the fortifications of its 'Fort William'. With the first Anglo–Indian war having been so decisively won by the Mughal empire, there was no mention of the *farman*.

In the early eighteenth century Surat's trade revived while Bombay struggled to compete. Peace with Sidi Yakub and the Mughal emperor made the Company's shipping a natural target for the Mughals' inveterate enemy, Kanhoji Angria the Maratha admiral. A book entitled *A History of the Indian Wars* which was published in England in 1737, a decade before the British were generally thought to have become engaged in Indian wars, contains little mention of 'Child's War'. Instead it turns out to be a colourful account of the almost incessant attacks launched by Kanhoji Angria against ships flying the Company's colours and of the attempted British reprisals against Kanhoji's strongholds on the Konkan coast. These 'wars' would drag on until mid-century. Although in the 1720s and '30s neither side could be said to be winning, the advantage lay decidedly with Kanhoji. Bombay's trade suffered accordingly.

Madras and Calcutta, however, prospered. The Company's Indian 'investment', or purchases, of mainly cotton textiles but also silks, molasses and saltpetre from Bengal and of indigo from Gujarat were proving highly profitable. So, from an Indian point of view, was access to the silver of the Americas, with which the Company paid for its purchases. On arrival the silver was usually minted into rupees, thereby further monetising the Mughal economy which, if anything, grew more buoyant even as Mughal power declined. Indian bankers, entrepreneurs and officials benefited greatly from both the stability of the currency and the availability of capital. On the other hand, as the volume of trade increased, so did dependence on this seemingly unlimited source of treasure. In London too, as once in imperial Rome, there were other Jeremiahs who decried the haemorrhaging of their national reserves which resulted from such a one-sided trade. But with taffetas, muslins, chintzes and calicos taking over Europe's linen cupboards, crowding its wardrobes and smothering its furniture, the Company brushed aside such criticisms, confident in the support of stockholders whose handsome apparel mirrored their handsome dividends.

Of more immediate concern to the directors of the Company were the activities of its employees in a personal capacity. English fortunes were notoriously made in India not by loyal service in the purchase and despatch of the Company's piece-goods but by private investment in a variety of financial opportunities. Some were concerned with trade. Only over the 'out and back' traffic between England and the East was the Company able to enforce its monopoly. Within the East and within India itself, Company men took advantage of the decline in Indian-operated shipping which had begun during Portugal's sixteenth-century *Estado da India* to invest heavily in the Indian Ocean trade. They owned or leased ships, freighted cargoes, sold insurance, and above all took advantage of the security and protection of their employer's flag. Thus from Madras, as employees of the Company, the American-born Yale brothers amassed considerable fortunes in trade with Siam (Thailand) and Canton in China; part of Elihu Yale's earnings would endow the college, and later university, in Connecticut which bears his name. Some Company men also invested in, and often defected to, shipping interests which did not recognise even the Company's 'out and back' monopoly. These might be other European East India Companies like those of the Dutch or the French. They might be the 'illegal' English syndicates usually known as 'interlopers'. Or they might be a bit of both – English interlopers sailing under a flag of convenience. Up the Hughli river in search of Bengal produce there sailed in the early eighteenth century vessels which, though largely financed by Englishmen, flew the colours of the Ostend Company, the Swedish Company, the Prussian Company, the Royal Polish Company and the Royal Danish Company.

Thomas Pitt, once an interloper, then a Member of Parliament, had already made and spent one Indian fortune when in 1699 he returned to Madras as governor of its Fort St George. He stayed there for twelve years, amassing a second fortune which included the Pitt diamond (bought for £45,000 and sold to the Regent of France for £135,000); it would comfortably sustain the political careers of his prime ministerial grandson (Chatham) and great-grandson (William Pitt the Younger). Governor Pitt also jealously protected the Company's interests during the uncertain times before and after Aurangzeb's death. In 1701 another English ambassador, the first since Roe, had toiled up to the emperor's peripatetic court in the Deccan with a lavish presentation of cannons, horses and cartloads of glassware and crockery. But Aurangzeb would only entertain the idea of a *farman* if the English would undertake the expensive task of policing the Indian Ocean and suppressing the piratical activities of mainly European interlopers and renegades. No such undertaking was forthcoming, and nor was the *farman*. The embassy proved to be the expensive disaster which Pitt had predicted.

Aurangzeb's death in 1707 and the subsequent succession struggle opened new possibilities. On behalf of Prince Muazzam, an imperial inter-mediary asked for English assistance in cutting off the retreat of one of the prince's rivals; in return, Pitt was invited to draw up the terms of a *farman*. Although the prince's rival never reached Madras, Muazzam duly ascended the throne as Bahadur Shah and the Company began assembling the ele-phants, horses, clocks and musical boxes deemed suitable to accompany another mission to the imperial court. When Pitt left India in 1709 he was still sanguine of its prospects, and in 1710 overtures from the same intermediary, who had now been posted to Bengal, were renewed. The clocks and elephants were duly shipped to Calcutta and by 1712 the mission to the Mughal was ready to start. Then news came from Delhi that Bahadur Shah had died.

His 'imbecilic' successor barely lasted long enough for an exchange of letters, but with the accession of Farrukhsiyar the Company's hopes soared again. The new emperor had been brought up in Bengal, where his father had been governor after Shaista Khan. He was known to some of the English in Calcutta, and the Company had supplied his nursery with toys. Evidently the toys had been appreciated, for news that some forty tons of more adult exotica now awaited the emperor's orders brought an interim confirmation of the Company's existing privileges plus a request that the mission proceed to Delhi forthwith. In 1715, headed by the unexciting John Surman and guarded by some six hundred troops, a caravan consisting of 160 bullock carts, twelve hundred porters, and a choice assortment of carriages, cannons and camels headed west across the Gangetic plain.

'Considering the great pomp and state of the kings of Hindustan, we was very well received,' wrote Surman on arrival in Delhi. He relished the impressive ceremonial and was soon dispensing lavish bribes. Meanwhile the mission's doctor successfully treated some swellings in the imperial groin. He was handsomely rewarded, but as to the *farman* Farrukhsiyar remained infuriatingly indifferent. Only when threatened with the withdrawal of the Company from Surat and its other establishments in Gujarat did he relent. Losing the Company's bullion and trade for the price of a piece of paper was unthinkable. On New Year's Eve 1716, more than a century since Captain William Hawkins had first applied for it, the *farman* received the imperial signature.

Explicit as to the territorial and commercial rights enjoyed by the Company throughout India, the *farman* did indeed 'indicate such favour as has never before been granted to any European nation'. In Calcutta, Madras and Bombay celebrations were held, toasts were drunk, and salutes fired as the document was paraded through the streets and proclaimed at the cities' gates. 'Our dear bought *farman*' became 'the Magna Carta of the Company in India'. It provided imperial confirmation of a host of privileges, some of which had hitherto been more assumed than assured. It inducted the Company into the political hierarchy of Mughal India through a direct relationship with the emperor which bore comparison with that enjoyed by imperial office-holders. And in that it legitimised action against anyone supposedly infringing its terms, it offered great scope for future intervention. Thirty years later it would be on the strength of Farrukhsiyar's *farman* that Robert Clive would justify his advance to Plassey and the overthrow of Bengal's nawab.

But if the Company's direct participation in the emasculation of the empire was still a generation away, not so the participation of its employees in the Mughal economy nor of its troops in what has been called 'the all-India military bazaar'.[22] In a private capacity Company men invested not only in all those different forms of maritime trade but also in the whole range of monopolies, offices, franchises, revenue farms and commercial concessions which were now openly marketed within the empire. Office-holders and *jagirdars* had long since been in the habit of accepting cash advances against expected revenue receipts. But now, just as imperial authority was being devolved and farmed out, so were the constituent rights and revenues of nearly all subsidiary officials. Within the provinces of the empire, governors or autonomous nawabs increasingly leased their revenue rights to a handful of major *zamindars* who might, for a further consideration, be elevated to the status of subsidiary nawabs or rajas. Thus in Bengal 'by 1728 over a quarter of the nominal revenue depended on the *zamindars* [and later rajas] of Burdwan and Rajshahi alone. By end of the Nawab's

rule 60 per cent of the revenue came from fifteen *zamindars*.'[23] But these
major *zamindars* in turn farmed out most of their rights to lesser *zamindars*,
merchants, local warlords and substantial cultivators. Major Indian banking
houses and powerful mercantile interests helped to finance this market in
taxation rights and were amongst its principal beneficiaries. And, since the
realisation of revenues, and their conversion into coin, often depended on
a show of force, both local warrior aristocracies and freewheeling English
factors joined in.

Typically, every Company man had his local agent, known as a 'banian'
or 'dubash'. Surman's negotiations in Delhi had relied heavily on a mer-
curial Armenian; Pitt had employed 'the cursedest villain that ever was in
the world' because he was also 'the most dextrous indefatigable fellow in
business'.[24] Appreciating the *farman*-enhanced status of the Company and
the credit-worthiness of its employees, such agents placed a high value on
their English clients and readily arranged both their investments and the
loans needed to finance them. 'The British were sucked into the Indian
economy by the dynamic of its political economy as much as by their own
relentless drive for profit.'[25] Recent studies of colonialism emphasise the
crucial role played by native elites willing to collaborate with the colonial
power. Such were the dubashes and banians and, through them as intermediaries, British residents joined the new entrepreneurial class of later
Mughal India.

The dynamic of the Mughal political economy was as much about
troops as money. Military leaders financed their activities by engaging in
entrepreneurial ventures, and entrepreneurs secured their investments by
supporting military ventures. Thus, even before war broke out with the
French in the 1740s, the English Company, through its employees, was
already indirectly involved in the hire and maintenance of troops by neighbouring *zamindars* and revenue collectors. Encouraged by the *farman*'s
confirmation of certain local revenue rights, the Company had also significantly increased the number of troops deemed necessary to defend its own
establishments. The Madras garrison, for instance, increased from 360 in
1717 to some twelve hundred in 1742. Most were recruited locally, many
being from the Indo-Portuguese community. But Indian troops, known as
'peons' or 'sepoys' (*sipahis*, soldiers), were also hired, there being a ready
pool of professional soldiers – Marathas, Deccanis, Afghans, rajputs, Bak-
saris (from Awadh) – which Mughal rule had left stranded, and often
unpaid, throughout the subcontinent. The existence of this market in
troops, like that of the market in offices and revenue farms, positively
invited European participation.

. . . THEN THE *DIWAN*

But if the *farman* could be used to provide a legal basis for British interference, and if the lively market in commercial, fiscal and military opportunities encouraged such intervention, it was the Anglo–French wars which
precipitated it. They furnished the pretext, demonstrated the method and
inspired the confidence for the first British moves towards an Indian
dominion.

The French *Compagnie des Indes* was a latecomer compared to the Dutch
and English Companies. Founded by Bernier's correspondent Jean-Baptiste
Colbert in the 1660s, it had expanded rapidly in the early eighteenth century.
Pondicherry, the French headquarters, challenged Madras on the Coromandel coast, and Chandernagore aspired to rival Calcutta in Bengal. But the
rivalry had remained purely commercial even when England and France
were at war in Europe over the Spanish succession. In Bengal both Companies similarly elected to ignore the war over the Austrian succession in
the 1740s. Their colleagues in the south might have done likewise but for
the operations of British and French fleets in the Indian Ocean. In the
event prize-taking by the Royal Navy at sea provoked French reprisals on
land and led to the capture of Madras in 1746. Both fleets also offloaded
regular, or royal (as opposed to Company), troops and both Companies
recruited extra 'sepoys'; trained, drilled and uniformed, motley garrisons
grew swiftly into disciplined armies.

Additionally both Companies looked to their immediate neighbours
for support. Nizam-ul-Mulk, nominally Mughal governor of the Deccan
but in fact autonomous Nawab of Hyderabad, still firmly ruled most of
what is now Andhra Pradesh. But, to the south, the Tamil lands of the
erstwhile Golconda sultanate, though part of the nizam's *subah* (province),
were under a subsidiary nawab known either as the Nawab of Arcot (his
capital) or of 'the Carnatic'. (The word was an Anglicisation of 'Karnataka'
and had originally been used to designate both the southern half of modern
Karnataka state – e.g. the Mysore-Bangalore area – and the adjacent Tamil
lands, both having been acquired simultaneously from Vijayanagar's nayaks
by the Bijapur sultanate in the 1630s.)

It was this Nawab of the Carnatic whose territories lapped around
Madras and Pondicherry, and it was he who, while coming to the aid of
the British after their loss of Madras, unwittingly betrayed the superiority
of regular European troops. Twice his army of about ten thousand horse
was repulsed by barely five hundred well-trained French infantrymen and
gunners. European regulars, armed with muskets and drilled to load and

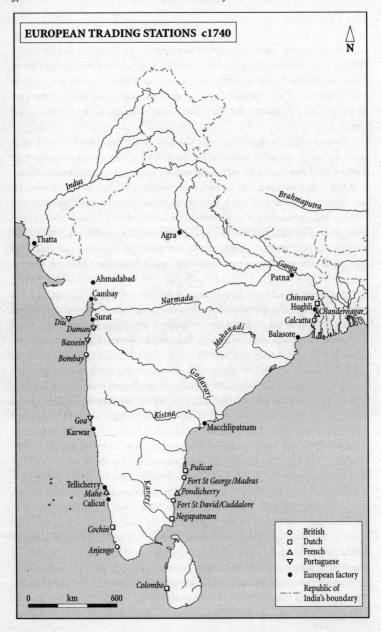

EUROPEAN TRADING STATIONS c1740

N

Indus

Brahmaputra

Thatta

Agra

Ganga

Patna

Ahmadabad

Cambay

Narmada

Chinsura
Hughli
Chandernagar

Diu
Daman
Surat

Calcutta

Bassein

Mahanadi

Balasore

Bombay

Godavari

Goa
Karwar

Kistna

Macchlipatnam

Pulicat
Fort St George/Madras

Tellicherry
Mahe
Calicut

Kaveri

Pondicherry

Fort St David/Cuddalore

Negapatnam

Cochin

Anjengo

Colombo

	British
	Dutch
	French
	Portuguese
●	European factory
---	Republic of India's boundary

0   km   600

fire with synchronised rapidity, could produce sufficient firepower to halt a conventional Indian cavalry charge. It was a sensational revelation. Cavalry, especially the well-mounted and heavily armoured *sowars* of the Mughals, epitomised Indian military might. If they were vulnerable to European infantry, then so was the military system which supported them, and so were the regimes which espoused it. To the Companies' long-acknowledged supremacy at sea was now added a potentially devastating capacity on land.

In 1748 news of peace in Europe brought the restoration of Madras to the British and a temporary lull in direct Anglo–French hostilities. But in the same year Nizam-ul-Mulk died and the Hyderabad succession was immediately disputed. One of the claimants ousted the Arcot nawab, whereupon both claimants for the throne of Hyderabad also fielded their own contenders for the subsidiary nawabship of Arcot. In such a situation it was inevitable that the European Companies would become involved. Their troops had just shown themselves the most effective in the peninsula, but were now without work and proving a heavy charge on their employers. Moreover Muhammad Ali, one of the Arcot contenders, had led the troops which had come to the aid of the British in the recent war; and Chanda Sahib, the other contender, kept his family in Pondicherry, spoke French, and was on close terms with Joseph Dupleix, the ambitious governor of Pondicherry.

Because he now supplied this Chanda Sahib with troops, Dupleix is often credited with introducing into India the use of political surrogates. Henceforth, when not officially at war, British and French could continue their hostilities under the aegis of competing Indian princes. Through these same princes they would extend their authority without seeming to acquire territories. But the idea of surrogate expansion was scarcely novel, least of all in India. 'The "subsidiary alliance system" was not a brilliant strategy developed by the French or the English, but a common and probably inevitable feature of post-Mughal, eighteenth-century politics.'[26] Moreover the British were already undertaking a similar exercise on behalf of the Maratha ruler of Tanjore. Dupleix's opportunism was not particularly original, just wholehearted.

The 'Carnatic War', ostensibly about the successions to the Arcot and Hyderabad nawabships but propelled by Anglo–French rivalry for hegemony in the south, spluttered on from 1749 to 1754. Dupleix's ambition plus the military genius of Charles de Bussy quickly carried the French beyond the Carnatic. In their wake Robert Clive, a 'writer' (junior merchant) and part-time soldier with the English Company, was able to claw back early British reverses and install Muhammad Ali, the British candidate,

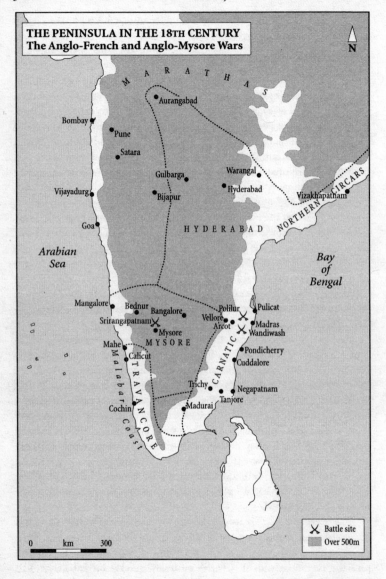

THE PENINSULA IN THE 18TH CENTURY
The Anglo-French and Anglo-Mysore Wars

N

M A R A T H A S

Aurangabad

Bombay

Pune

Satara

Gulbarga

Warangal

Vijayadurg

Bijapur

Hyderabad

Vizakhapatnam

NORTHERN CIRCARS

Goa

H Y D E R A B A D

Arabian
Sea

Bay
of
Bengal

Mangalore

Bednur

Bangalore

Polilur

Pulicat

Srirangapatnam

Vellore

Arcot

Madras

Wandiwash

Mysore

M Y S O R E

Mahe

Calicut

Pondicherry

Cuddalore

C A R N A T I C

Cochin

Trichy

Negapatnam

Madurai

Tanjore

T R A V A N C O R E

M
a
l
a
b
a
r

C
o
a
s
t

✕ Battle site

Over 500m

0   km   300

as Nawab of Arcot. But the greater prize of Hyderabad went to the French when Muzaffar Jang, their candidate, was installed as nizam. Both Companies, as well as enjoying the prospect of exercising further power by proxy, had profited hugely from the hostilities. To pay for their own and the Companies' troops, Muhammad Ali had ceded territory to Madras while Muzaffar Jang had awarded to the French the Northern Circars, comprising most of Andra Pradesh's coastline. Additionally the Companies' employees in a private capacity had invested heavily in their respective protégés. In fact the loans raised by Muhammad Ali made him as much a puppet of his English creditor-syndicate as of the East India Company.

With French troops under de Bussy now assisting the new nizam against other rivals like the Marathas and so penetrating deep into the Deccan, the British too were not averse to opening a new front. Robert Clive, returning from England after a hero's reception, reached Bombay in 1755 whence he expected to lead an Anglo-Maratha assault on de Bussy in the Deccan. This was called off. Instead, he joined a Royal Navy squadron under Admiral Charles Watson for an epic assault on what the British called the 'pirate stronghold of Gheriah'. The 'pirate' was Kanhoji Angria's successor as admiral of the Maratha fleet and 'Gheriah' was otherwise Vijayadurg, still today a spectacularly fortified promontory near Ratnagiri to the south of Bombay. Taken and pillaged, Vijayadurg's fall brought to an end both Maratha sea-power and those premature 'Indian Wars' which had so embarrassed Bombay. Clive then sailed on to Madras with Watson. Barely four months later, in July 1756, news reached Madras that Siraj-ud-daula, the Nawab of Bengal, had stormed Calcutta and ejected the British. With Watson, his squadron, a regiment of royal troops, and a thousand sepoys Clive sailed for Bengal.

The next seven months, or 'the Famous Two Hundred Days', would witness the British conquest of the richest and possibly the largest of the Mughal provinces. Bengal duly became the 'bridgehead', 'springboard' and 'foundation' of British rule in India. It was not the new front against the French which Clive had expected, but the French presence at Chander-nagore did provide a handy pretext for continuing his advance after Calcutta had been recaptured and all rights as per the *farman* restored. Chander-nagore itself would be stormed by Watson's ships in what was much the most ferocious engagement of the campaign. Thereafter it was the nawab's supposed intrigues with the French which justified a further advance to Plassey. In the battle which followed, the nawab would be toppled by intrigue and, following Arcot practice, the first of several puppet nawabs installed.

Nine years later rule by proxy in Bengal would become rule by *diwani*. In a decidedly tacky ceremony the Emperor Shah Alam II, Muhammad Shah's successor, formally inducted the Company, in the person of Clive, into the Mughal hierarchy. As *diwan*, or chancellor, for Bengal, the Company received a title which was now tantamount to sovereignty over a province that enjoyed virtual autonomy. Although the drama and scandals of 'the Famous Two Hundred Days' are often characterised as a 'revolution', no one could seriously contend that the Company had not observed the conventions of power-seeking under the later Mughal empire. Nor is it evident that most power-brokers in Bengal opposed their new superior. In fact many argued strongly in favour of British intervention. Foreign rule in India was seldom regarded as objectionable *per se*.

The British Conquest

1750–1820

THE BRITISH would often think of their conquests in India as fortuitous. It gratified a cherished conceit about the Englishman's amateurish innocence and it obviated the need to confront awkward questions – like how such aggression could be justified. Clive himself, normally neither temperate nor cautious, would agonise long and hard over whether to assume what he called 'the sovereignty of Bengal'. Twenty years later the polymath Sir William Jones would marvel at how Bengal had, like an over-ripe mango, 'fallen into England's lap while she was sleeping'. Even Warren Hastings, Jones's patron and the first British Governor-General of India, would shy from the idea of the all-India dominion with whose foundation he is rightly credited; it was something 'which I may not mention without adding that it is what I never wish to see'.[1]

Picking up on such breezy disclaimers, historians of the British Raj have generally explained its triumph less in terms of the push of conquest and more in terms of the pull of chaos. The Company was 'sucked into' the 'power vacuum' left by the declining Mughal empire. No native regime rose to fill this 'black hole', authority fragmented, and economic decline threatened. The 'lawlessness' of Afghans, Marathas and other 'warlords' brought cries for protection which necessitated an elaborate British-sponsored system of 'ring-fencing' based on subsidiary alliances which would embrace most of the subcontinent. Territorial acquisitions and local forms of resistance, as also administrative and fiscal anomalies, invited political, judicial and revenue 'settlements'. Suggestive of a pillowed repose, these 'settlements' were supposedly designed to restore a traditional order which, while advantageous to the British regime, would bring security and prosperity to all.

Such views have since been revised. It is argued that the 'chaos' and the 'vacuum' were in part of the Company's own making, in part an invention of its apologists, and in part the result of a misreading of India's history. Economic decline before the late eighteenth century cannot be substantiated. The vitality of the market in revenue rights and commercial concessions already noticed is taken as evidence of dynamism rather than decay. Regional regimes were not inconsistent with India's political and cultural traditions. And powerful successor states, like those of Bengal, Hyderabad (the Nizam), Pune (the Peshwa), Mysore (Haidar Ali) and Lahore (the Sikhs), were waxing impressively beneath the vault of Mughal authority until extinguished or suborned by the expansionist ambitions of the Company.

These expansionist ambitions, taken in the context of a global imperialism, are often explained simply in terms of greed. Much emphasis is laid on the fortunes acquired by individual Company men, the so-called 'nabobs', and on the exploitative character of the policies pursued by their employer. Testimony to personal fortunes is plentiful, especially amongst the condemnations of scandalised and jealous countrymen in England; systematic exploitation, although harder to quantify, is inferred from numerous examples of Indian protest and is linked with the great famine of 1770, which may have killed a quarter of Bengal's population.

But in an India where revenue extraction was the main business of government and where personal fortunes were not readily distinguished from official receipts, British rapacity attracted much less attention than it did in England. Under the later Mughals as under their 'Great' predecessors, power and prestige depended on conquests and access to revenue. Conversely conquests and access to revenue depended on power and prestige. Greed was as much the essence of government as it was of commerce. Merchants who became rulers happily adjusted their sights without experiencing any great conflict of interests. And although it would be hard to prove that either the Company or its servants espoused loftier ideals, it would also be hard to prove that any of their Indian rivals were motivated otherwise.

What did distinguish the British was their sense of being outsiders. Race, creed, culture and colour set them glaringly apart; so did their well-developed consciousness of a national identity. They might, and would, quarrel sensationally. Additionally, British government policy would often be at variance with that of the Company's London directors, London directives (if still relevant by the time they reached India) would often be ignored by the Company's senior administration in Calcutta, and Calcutta's interests were often flouted by the subsidiary administrations in Madras and Bombay. Coherent policies are hard to distinguish; it was the *ad hoc* and reactive nature of British expansion which convinced so many that dominion was fortuitous. But if coherence was lacking, cohesion was not. Despite the opportunities for personal enrichment and despite the Indophile interests of 'brahmanised' scholars like Sir William Jones, loyalties to regiment, service, Company, Crown and country would prove tenacious. British rule would be as impervious to India's powers of assimilation and as unsusceptible to fragmentation as it was unchallenged by succession crises. Authority was continuous, allegiance consistent. Herein lay a source of strength which was arguably more decisive than either economic advantage or military discipline. No other contender for power in India could present such a united front; no other foreign invader could maintain such a prolonged challenge.

The recapture of Calcutta by Clive and Watson in late 1756, their storming of nearby French Chandernagore in early 1757, and Clive's success at Plassey in June 1757, although later seen as milestones, would attract little contemporary comment in Mughal Delhi. Bengal had long since slipped from imperial control, and its quarrelsome European trading companies were still seen as peripheral and parasitic appendages in the great scheme of Mughal hierarchy. Moreover 'the Famous Two Hundred Days' so celebrated by the British happened to coincide with a winter of still greater infamy for the Mughal emperor, for in January the imperial capital was sacked by a more traditional predator in the shape of Ahmad Shah Abdali. An Afghan of the Durrani clan, Abdali was following in the hoofprints of earlier raiders from the skirts of the Hindu Kush like Mahmud of Ghazni and Muhammad of Ghor. The attack on Delhi was the climax of his fourth invasion of the Panjab, most of which province he had previously wrested from its Mughal governor and whence he had already conquered Kashmir.

Nor was his plunder of the capital itself unprecedented. Seventeen years earlier Abdali had served in the forces of Nadir Shah, a latterday Timur who, having usurped the throne of Persia and seized Kandahar and Kabul, had swept across the Panjab to rout an imperial army at Karnal. Thence, in 1739, Nadir had entered Delhi as the emperor's voracious guest. This amicable fiction lasted barely forty-eight hours. For some casual spilling of Persian blood Delhi's citizens paid a gruesome price as Nadir Shah ordered a general massacre. Twenty thousand may have been butchered in a single day, and further carnage followed as the Persians concentrated on the extortion of family heirlooms and hidden treasure. Muhammad Shah, the long-reigning emperor so celebrated for his inactivity, was ignominiously recrowned by his vanquisher. Then, following fifty-eight days of excess which would be remembered long after British 'nabobs' had become a bad joke, Nadir Shah departed Delhi with coin valued at eight or nine millions sterling plus a similar hoard in gold and silver objects. 'And this does not include the jewels, which were inestimable.'[2] Amongst them were Shah Jahan's Peacock Throne and the Koh-i-Nur diamond, which gem thus again passed into Persian possession. (How, if it was the same as Humayun's diamond, it had slipped from Persian possession in the first place is not certainly known. It may have been the stone reportedly gifted by Shah Tamasp of Persia to the Sultan of Golconda and then presented to Aurangzeb by Mir Jumla. Howsoever, it was soon on its way back towards India, having already passed from Nadir Shah's grandson to Ahmad Shah Abdali.)

In 1756 Abdali found the imperial treasury somewhat bare, 'but Delhi was plundered, and its unhappy people again subjected to pillage, and its daughters to pollution.'[3] The city of Mathura shared a like fate and Agra only narrowly avoided it. Confirmed in the possession of Sind as well as Kashmir and the Panjab, Abdali retired to Afghanistan. He would be back for more in 1760–1 and on that occasion would inflict a crushing defeat on the Marathas at Panipat. But suffice it here to note that in the late 1750s the rapacity of the British in Bengal was not exceptional. By contemporary standards it might even be described as restrained. As Clive would notoriously aver to a parliamentary committee which would eventually investigate his conduct in India, the opportunities which awaited him after Plassey had been almost unimaginable.

> A great prince was dependent on my pleasure; an opulent city lay at my mercy; its richest bankers bid against one another for my smiles; I walked through vaults which were thrown open to me alone, piled on either side with gold and jewels. Mr Chairman, at this moment I stand astonished at my own moderation![4]

Nor, by contemporary standards, was there anything particularly novel or outrageous about the means by which Clive and his men engineered their so-called 'revolution'. It has been argued that at the time Bengal, although 'not an oasis in a war torn India', remained more stable and prosperous than other provinces of the Mughal empire. 'For most of the [eighteenth] century the Nawabs and the British were able to maintain some kind of unity over an area extending hundreds of miles up the Ganges valley, at least as far as Patna. Beneath their umbrella the *zamindars* enforced a tolerably stable order.'[5] This was what made the region so attractive to foreign adventurers, and it was not something which they wanted to disturb.

Clive's 'revolution' was designed simply to replace an unsuitable nawab. It was not meant to subvert the existing order, rather to stabilise it.

Bengal's comparative prosperity, as also its autonomy, dated from the turn of the century and the appointment, a decade after Child's 'Mughal War', of a man later known as Murshid Quli Khan. Born a brahman in the Deccan, the much-renamed Murshid Quli Khan had been purchased, converted, adopted, and then inducted into Mughal service by one of Aurangzeb's Persian *amirs* in the Deccan. Exceptional ability won him the *diwani*, or chancellorship, of Hyderabad and from there in 1701 he had been sent to boost the revenues of Bengal. Like Sher Shah and Todar Mal before him, he compiled new revenue rolls, established an efficient system of collection run largely by Hindus (or farmed out to them), and ruthlessly enforced it. He also transferred most existing *jagirs* from the richer parts of Bengal to less-easily-taxed regions in Orissa. What are now West Bengal and Bangladesh thus became predominantly *khalsa*, their land revenues in other words being due directly to the emperor via the person of his brilliant *diwan*.

Receipts had immediately increased. Remitted to Aurangzeb in the Deccan, they helped to finance his vendetta against the Marathas. Indeed the emperor was so impressed that he now renamed his *diwan* as 'Murshid Quli Khan' after a revered official who had organised the revenues of the Deccan province following its conquest by Shah Jahan. Aurangzeb also upheld his *diwan*'s authority in the face of a challenge from the *subahdar*, or governor, of Bengal. In effect, Murshid Quli Khan thus came to exercise the rights of both offices. He removed from Dacca to found a new capital at 'Murshidabad' and for twenty years after Aurangzeb's death, as emperors rose and fell in Delhi, he continued to remit some ten million rupees a year to the imperial treasury. Farrukhsiyar, the emperor responsible for the Company's cherished *farman*, acknowledged him as governor, and Muhammad Shah confirmed his (Murshid Quli Khan's) son-in-law as his successor. In all but name, of which he had enough, Murshid Quli Khan was the first Nawab of Bengal and the founder of an autonomous kingdom.

His son-in-law 'reigned' from 1727 until 1739, 'an aera [sic] of good order and good government' according to a Company official.[6] The good government continued under Nawab Alivardi Khan (1740–56). But following Nadir Shah's humbling of the Mughal emperor, Bengal's revenues ceased to be sent to Delhi as matter of course. Moreover, since Alivardi Khan was a usurper, he faced other challenges, most notably from the Marathas. In the 1740s the Bhonsles of Nagpur mounted almost annual raids into Bengal's territories, ravaging to the gates of Murshidabad and persuading the British in Calcutta to dig a 'Maratha Ditch' round their settlement. In the event, the Marathas never crossed the Hughli river, let alone the Ditch, and in 1751 they were bought off by the nawab's cession of Orissa. But a taste of 'fiscal terrorism', first from the Marathas and then from the hard-pressed nawab as he mobilised against them, occasioned much hardship. This dislocation, plus the security supposedly afforded by Calcutta's defences and the concessionary tariffs and other favourable trading terms conferred by the *farman*, prompted rapid and unplanned growth within the Company's Calcutta enclave. The anchorage and settlement of 1690 had by 1750 become the busiest port-city in Bengal with a population of 120,000. Contemporary engravings show stately riverside mansions, town terraces and public buildings with pillars and pediments. Not shown are the less salubrious suburbs, known in Madras as 'Black Town', where the bulk of the population worked and lived.

To Alivardi Khan as Nawab of Bengal Calcutta's success was both irritating and tempting. But wisely preferring the golden eggs to the big white geese which laid them, he dealt as fairly with the British as with his other nesting colonies of French and Dutch merchants; he merely demanded of them additional, but always negotiable, subsidies. His successor and grandson, Siraj-ud-daula, proved less of a conservationist, indeed 'imprudent to the highest degree'. Within a year he had alienated his grandfather's officials, his greatest *zamindars*, his major bankers and all the European trading companies. 'His ultimate achievement was perhaps to make Frenchmen in Bengal hope that the English would defeat him.'[7] Considering that the Seven Years' War was about to pitch the European rivals into global confrontation, this was no mean feat. Siraj enjoys the distinction of having challenged not just one bumptious merchant community but seemingly the entire mercantilist presumption.

This should make him an obvious candidate for nationalist rehabilitation. But Siraj has found few champions amongst even Bengal's rabid revisionists, perhaps because his ejection of the British was not obviously intended. His demands – concerning the surrender of certain dissidents who had taken refuge in Calcutta, the demolition of unauthorised fortifications like the 'Maratha Ditch', and the withdrawal of trading concessions not clearly specified in the *farman* – were neither unreasonable nor original. A willingness to resolve them, or a cash offer to that effect, might well have satisfied him. But channels of communication between the new nawab and the European Companies had barely been opened, and Calcutta's governing council was exceptionally supine. It was also dangerously complacent. 'Such was the levity of the times,' recalled the

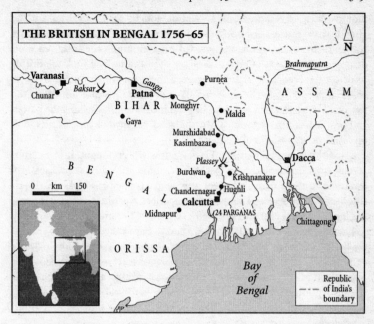

THE BRITISH IN BENGAL 1756–65

N

Brahmaputra

Varanasi   *Baksar*   *Ganga*   Purnea

Chunar   **Patna**   ASSAM

BIHAR   Monghyr

Gaya   Malda

Murshidabad
Kasimbazar

BENGAL   *Plassey*   **Dacca**

Burdwan   Krishnanagar

0   km   150   Chandernagar   Hughli

Calcutta

Midnapur   (24 PARGANAS)

Chittagong

ORISSA

Bay
of
Bengal

Republic
of India's
boundary

city's adjutant-general, 'that severe measures were not deemed necessary.'[8]
The city itself had long since engulfed the walls of Fort William and
was probably indefensible. When Siraj appeared on the other side of
the Maratha Ditch with a large army, British confusion positively invited
attack.

Although the fighting lasted five days, no serious attempt was made to
open the negotiations which might still have saved Calcutta. Successive
British withdrawals culminated in a panic-stricken dash to the ships, and
Siraj suddenly found himself master of the city. He also found himself
responsible for an assortment of European men, women and children who
had failed to get away. Unharmed, they were lodged overnight in the fort's
detention cell, otherwise 'the Black Hole'. How many went in is not certainly
known; but next morning only twenty-three staggered out. Dehydration
and suffocation had accounted for possibly fifty lives.

The tragedy seems to have been quite unintentional. Nevertheless, Siraj
was held responsible. Dramatised and magnified by the survivors, the Black
Hole greatly reduced the nawab's chances of restoring relations with the
British and lent to Clive's retaliation a self-righteous venom. When seven

months later Clive and Admiral Watson fought their way back up the Hughli river and easily retook the city, it was Clive who, against strong resistance from his colleagues, insisted on continuing the war. Peace on demeaning terms was offered to Siraj only for as long as it took the British to defeat the French at Chandernagore, a move for which the timely news of the outbreak of the Seven Years' War provided justification. With the risk of a French attack removed, Clive resumed hostilities against the nawab and proceeded upriver towards Murshidabad. Meanwhile Siraj's army took up a defensive position at Plassey.

Had the supposed battle of Plassey actually been fought, it is far from certain that Siraj would have lost it. The numerical odds, at perhaps fifty thousand to three thousand, were heavily in his favour; so was the disposition of his troops; and despite the superiority of the Company's guns, the initial artillery exchanges proved indecisive. Clive himself seems quickly to have despaired of a straight victory and to have rested his hopes entirely on the treachery of Mir Jafar and other dignitaries amongst the nawab's commanders with whom he had already signed a secret pact. When, after some delay, Mir Jafar opted to honour this pledge and duly made his hostile sentiments clear to Siraj, the nawab had little choice but to flee. Deserted by well over half his army, he was indeed as much the victim of a revolution as a rout.

Mir Jafar was related to Siraj as well as being his commander-in-chief. He had as good a claim to succeed him as anyone. It was in fact a standard palace revolution not unlike that which had resulted in Alivardi Khan's installation. Arrangements were swiftly made to have Mir Jafar's accession recognised by the emperor in Delhi, while Clive publicly insisted that the Company would not interfere in his government.

But in a significant move it was Clive who personally handed Mir Jafar to the throne. British arms had placed him there and British palms now awaited his greasing. The compensation promised to the Company for its recent losses and expenses, plus the massive cash 'presents' promised by Mir Jafar to Clive and his associates personally, left the new nawab heavily indebted to his British benefactors. 'Over £1,250,000 were eventually distributed to individuals'[9] from the Bengal treasury, of which Clive's share from this and subsequent pay-offs, and from an infamous *jagir* which he later secured, would come to over £400,000. Despite the 'moderation' at which he stood so amazed, it was 'much the greatest fortune ever made by a [British] individual in India'.[10]

Moneys due to the Company itself could be defrayed by the nawab's cession of revenue rights over convenient territories. A cluster of two dozen

districts (*parganas*) south of Calcutta which now passed to the Company
are still today officially known as the '24 Parganas'. Clive saw revenue rights
as much more remunerative than the profits of trade, and had promised
his employers that revenue receipts would quickly eliminate the need to
finance imports from India by the export of bullion from Britain. This
forecast proved over-optimistic, largely because of the Company's escalating
military expenses and its commitments elsewhere in India. But in Bengal
as around Madras, relieving a neighbouring nawab of revenue rights now
became a standard procedure whenever debts remained unserviced or
indemnities unpaid. No less important were the purely commercial concessions extracted from the nawab. In the wake of Plassey, Company men
fanned out into Bengal, Bihar and beyond to acquire a virtual monopoly
over choice export commodities like saltpetre, indigo and opium and over
the lucrative internal trade in sea-salt. More private fortunes were made;
more revenue was lost to the nawab.

The nawab's plight became critical when Company troops were
employed at his expense in repelling intruders. In 1759 and again in 1760–1
Bihar, still part of Bengal, was invaded by Shah Alam, the Mughal crown-
prince, supported by troops of the autonomous Nawab of Awadh (Oudh).
To defray the military costs, the Company demanded more revenue rights
from Mir Jafar; when he refused, the British simply replaced him in a
bloodless, but rewarding, coup. Mir Qasim (Kasim), the son-in-law of Mir
Jafar, had agreed to transfer to the British most of lower Bengal and was
duly installed as nawab.

This was in 1760, and during the next three years Mir Qasim made a
valiant effort to re-establish the viability of his truncated state. But whereas
the ageing Mir Jafar had been deemed ineffective, the young Mir Qasim
was soon deemed too effective. He dismissed officials suspected of collaboration with the British, greatly increased revenue demands, and began
reorganising and rearming his forces along European lines. In this he
anticipated the reforms which would be so successfully introduced in the
armies of Mysore, the Marathas and the Sikhs. Initially, however, they
proved of little avail and, following a dispute over the commercial liberties
being taken by private British traders in Bengal, Mir Qasim was defeated
and fled to Awadh. Plucked from a comfortable retirement in Calcutta,
Mir Jafar, now into his dotage, was again placed on the throne.

In 1764 the deposed Mir Qasim was back in Bihar, this time in a hostile
alliance with the now-emperor Shah Alam and his formidable ally, the
Nawab of Awadh. The war which ensued, and in particular the battle of
Baksar (Buxar), marked more convincingly than Plassey the true beginning

of British dominion in India. Despite five thousand veteran Afghan cavalry from Abdali's army, despite Mir Qasim's disciplined forces, the Mughals' prestige and the Awadh army of perhaps thirty thousand, it was Major Hector Munro's force of 7500 largely Indian sepoys which gained a hard-fought but decisive victory. All that separated Indian-led troops from British-led troops was 'regular discipline and strict obedience to orders', according to Munro. Just before the battle he had made his point by punishing twenty-four mutineers; they were fired from guns in front of their quaking colleagues. The enemy, on the other hand, was nearly as divided as at Plassey, with Mir Qasim's troops unpaid and Shah Alam sidelined by his allies and already engaged in overtures to the British.

'At Buxar all that still remained of Mogul power in northern India was shattered;'[11] it was 'perhaps the most important battle the British ever fought in south Asia'.[12] Mir Qasim fled into obscurity, the emperor transferred his vestigial prestige to the British, and next year (1765) he awarded to Clive and the Company the *diwani* of Bengal. Meanwhile Awadh had been largely overrun as Varanasi, Chunar and Allahabad all fell to the British. The Nawab of Awadh, although restored to his kingdom, then found himself saddled with the same combination of a crippling indemnity, a one-sided political alliance and a reduced revenue (the British detached the valuable territories of Varanasi and Allahabad) which had brought about the downfall of Bengal's nawabs.

Seven years later, armed with instructions to 'stand forth as *diwan*', Warren Hastings took full advantage of the changed situation. Until 1774 the Company's establishments in India were still administered as three separate 'presidencies' – Calcutta, Madras and Bombay – each under its own 'president' or 'governor'. As governor of Calcutta and now of all Bengal, Hastings assumed such residual powers, largely judicial, as remained to Mir Jafar's successor and thereby effectually terminated the nawabship. He also moved the Bengal treasury from Murshidabad to Calcutta and endeavoured to increase revenue receipts during a time of financial anxiety for the Company. First Company 'supervisors', then Indian agents and finally British 'collectors' were designated to oversee and enforce the demands of individual *zamindars*. Although the intention was to uphold the Mughal revenue system, the effect was to redistribute *zamindari* rights amongst a larger class of tax-farmers and, through the courts and police, to superimpose British ideas of enforcement. From such interventionist experiments, often disastrous and always oppressive, in late-eighteenth-century Bengal would emerge the administrative structures of the British Raj.

In 1773 the Company's directors, recognising the territorial responsibilities that had resulted from the conquest of Bengal, ordained that their Madras and Bombay administrations be subordinate to Calcutta, whose governor now became governor-general of all the Company's Indian establishments. Assuming this role in 1774, Hastings stayed on in Calcutta for another decade during which he would anticipate the spread of British rule throughout the subcontinent. On behalf of the now puppet-cum-buffer state of Awadh, Company troops penetrated to within two hundred kilometres of Delhi when in 1774 they invaded Rohilkand (now the Bareilly district). Its rulers, Afghan Rohillas, were defeated and their country attached to Awadh. Although the fiction of Awadh's independence would long be maintained, in effect the British were now supreme throughout the Gangetic plain. Between them and the Mughal capital there lay only the shifting sands of an encroaching Maratha hegemony. This obstacle would also be explored during Hastings' term of office. Meantime in the south a more direct and more obvious challenge to British supremacy demanded immediate attention.

MYSORE TAMED

Madras had paid a heavy price for Clive's 'Famous Two Hundred Days' in Bengal. When the Seven Years' War broke out in 1756, the city most vulnerable to French attack because of its proximity to Pondicherry had found itself without its most inspirational commander, without his troops and, worst of all, without his artillery. All the British possessions on the Coromandel coast were at risk and Fort St David (or Cuddalore), second only to Madras in importance, quickly fell. Madras itself was only saved thanks to visits by the Royal Navy.

But by 1759 the tide of French success was turning, most notably in neighbouring Hyderabad. It will be recalled that, following French support in the earlier Carnatic Wars, the Nizam of Hyderabad had been placed in much the same relationship to Pondicherry as Mir Jafar to Calcutta. Dupleix had installed him and de Bussy, in several brilliant campaigns, kept him there. But Dupleix had since returned to France and, with the outbreak of the war, de Bussy was recalled to Pondicherry. French troops still served in the nizam's army and more were based in the Northern Circars, the coastal regions of the Hyderabad state which had been earlier ceded to France by the nizam. In 1758–9 these Northern Circars were invaded by a small force sent by Clive from Bengal. It was meant to draw off French troops from Madras but resulted in an unexpected French defeat. Suddenly the nizam began to feel decidedly exposed. He now promised part of the Northern Circars to the British and began courting British support. From 1759 may be dated the brittle but long-lasting relationship between Hyderabad and Calcutta. To the British it would secure the collaboration of another of the Mughal successor states so that, just as Awadh 'ring-fenced' Bengal from Maratha attack, so Hyderabad would partially shield Madras.

Meanwhile Madras, besieged by the French in 1759, had been relieved. The arrival of more British troops also resulted in a hefty French defeat at Wandiwash, and in 1761 Pondicherry itself fell to the British. Although the city was later restored to French rule, the 1763 Treaty of Paris which ended the Seven Years' War also looked to have ended French ambitions in India.

But if the French *Compagnie* had lost its most important ally and surrogate in Hyderabad, the British soon credited it with another. During the siege of Pondicherry French hopes had briefly soared when a detachment of cavalry under the little-known Haidar Ali Khan had swept past the British to come to the aid of the hard-pressed defence. They departed a month later, dissatisfied; but it was a sign of things to come. From the Mysore region of the southern Deccan two formidable and ferociously anti-British dynasts in the persons of Haidar Ali and his son, Tipu Sultan, were about to pose a direct challenge to British hegemony in the Carnatic. Compared to these new challengers, the over-extended and seldom united Marathas were more an irritation than a threat; they could be 'ring-fenced' and then picked off as occasion offered. But in British eyes Mysore was a serious contender, a peninsular rival with the political and military credentials of genuine statehood. Whether or not Mysore was championed by France, it must be defeated.

The so-called 'kingdom' of Mysore had been one of the several dependent chieftancies and nayak-ships to survive from the ruins of the Vijayanagar empire. Although vulnerable to the expansionist ambitions of the Deccan sultanates in the seventeenth century and of the Marathas in the eighteenth century, its relations with the Mughal empire had been inconspicuous. Exceptionally, therefore, it was not a legatee of Mughal authority. Unlike, say, Hyderabad or Awadh, it did not correspond to a Mughal province; unlike the rajput and Maratha ruling families, its Wodeyar rulers had not been top-ranking *mansabdars*; and unlike the Nawab-Nizam of Hyderabad, the Nawab of Awadh or the Nawab of Bengal, the Mysore Wodeyars and their successors lacked the stature and legitimacy of high imperial office. If precedents be sought for the relationships on which their kingdom was based and for the economic and geographical factors which determined its expansion, they lurk in the history of earlier Hindu dynasties in southern Karnataka like the Hoysalas of Belur/Halebid or even the Chalukyas of Badami/Aihole.

Yet the Mysore which confronted the British was not a born-again Hindu kingdom like that which was so self-consciously reconstituted by Shivaji in Maharashtra. For in the 1730s the incumbent Wodeyar raja had been relieved of authority by two brothers, and it was in their service that Haidar Ali Khan, a devout Muslim whose ancestors had fought in the armies of the sultans of Bijapur, rose to prominence. In 1749, while participating in the succession struggle which followed the death of Nizam-ul-Mulk of Hyderabad (the first nizam), Haidar Ali had obtained both considerable wealth and the services of some French deserters. The first enabled him to increase his forces and the second helped train them in European tech-niques. During the Carnatic Wars he learned more about European tactics and acquired both artillery and French gunners. Thus in 1758, when Mysore was attacked by the Marathas, Haidar Ali was the obvious choice for com-mander of the Mysore forces. He acquitted himself well and, following a brief trial of strength with the incumbent brothers, had by 1761 become the undisputed ruler of Mysore.[13]

Meanwhile in Hyderabad the French-installed nizam had been deposed by his brother, Nizam Ali. The latter proposed an assault on Mysore to which the British in Madras, fearful that recent Mysore conquests in Kerala might be repeated in the Carnatic, readily agreed. Unconsciously treading the ancient trail of countless Pallava and Chola armies, an Anglo-Hyderabad expedition duly toiled up to the Deccan plateau and, with this piece of gratuit-ous and unashamed aggression, the First Mysore War got underway in 1767.

It was the first of four. No one could seriously maintain that the British conquest of India partook of the premeditated. The four Mysore wars, the three Maratha wars and the two Sikh wars, not to mention a host of lesser campaigns, hint at piecemeal policies and unco-ordinated direction. They also suggest a willingness on the part of Company officials to disown or disguise aggressive designs and on the part of subsequent British scholarship to diminish the scale of resistance. Where no long-term rationale for con-quest was available, the exigencies of the moment provided a compelling logic for only limited mischief. Moreover, many short wars attracted less attention than a few long ones; ideally they were fought and won before London's usually negative response could reach India. In retrospect they would seem so chronologically jumbled together as to throw all but the more dogged historians off the scent. Premeditation may indeed be dis-counted; yet a pattern of conquest, a progression of arms, does emerge.

The conquest of Bengal by the Company in Calcutta fuelled the ambitions of its Madras establishment in Mysore; Mysore's conquest opened the way to intervention in the Maratha territories; and the conquest of the Marathas brought the British up against the Sikhs.

The First Mysore War was chiefly notable as a demonstration of Haidar Ali's diplomatic and military skills. Having persuaded the nizam to defect, he drove the British back down to the Carnatic, sent his seventeen-year old son Tipu on a flying raid through the stately thoroughfares of Madras itself, and repeated this feat in person in the following year. Most unusually, when peace was concluded in 1769, no territories changed hands and no indemnity was mentioned. For the first time since Child's 'Mughal War' the British had been militarily checked by an Indian regime.

Included in the peace terms of 1769 was a defensive alliance which promised unequivocal British support in the event of an attack on Mysore by a third party. Haidar Ali set great store by this provision and soon had cause to invoke it. When Maratha forces swooped into southern Karnataka and laid siege to his great fort of Srirangapatnam (Seringapatam) near Mysore, he immediately turned to his British allies. They turned away. Haidar repeatedly invoked the defensive alliance, and Madras repeatedly prevaricated. Albion's perfidy, of which Haidar had no doubt heard from his French employees, was amply demonstrated. He damned the British as 'the most faithless and usurping of all mankind' and, if not already rabidly Anglophobe, both father and son now became so.

During the 1770s Haidar's reputation soared. The Marathas were pushed back and, excluding the nizam's territories and those of the British and their puppet Nawabs of Arcot and Tanjore, Mysore's sway came to embrace most of the peninsula south of the Kistna-Tungabhadra rivers. A revival of Anglo–French hostilities in the context of the American War of Independence distracted Madras's attention and brought Haidar more French arms and recruits. Meanwhile Governor-General Warren Hastings in Calcutta was preoccupied with Anglo–Maratha relations. It was a good moment to strike. Not without ample provocation, Haidar Ali launched the Second Mysore War with a pre-emptive assault on the Carnatic in 1780.

In a distinct escalation, this war involved far more troops, lasted twice as long (1780–4), and was fought on two fronts; while Haidar Ali engaged the Madras forces in the Carnatic, his son Tipu was detached to the Malabar coast in 1782 to oppose an expedition from Bombay. Again the Mysore army impressed, most notably at Polilur (near Kanchipuram) where in 1780 a British relieving force of about four thousand was practically annihilated. Only sixteen of its eighty-six European officers emerged unscathed;

even Hector Munro, the victor of Baksar, had to make an undignified dash for the safety of Madras, abandoning his artillery and baggage in the process. Polilur was the greatest defeat hitherto inflicted on the British by an Indian power. In his new summer palace beside the rushing Kaveri at Srirangapatnam, Tipu celebrated victory by commissioning a wall-to-wall painting of the engagement. It displays a tactical awareness more reminiscent of European battle-scenes than anything in Mughal art.

With Arcot captured and Haidar triumphant throughout the Carnatic, it was now Calcutta's turn to come to the rescue of Madras. A Company army of five thousand began the long march down the east coast from Bengal to Madras while a smaller force was sent by sea. There followed what Penderel Moon, author of the hefty *The British Conquest and Dominion of India* (1989), rightly calls 'three and a half years of profitless and uninteresting war'.[14] The British made gains on the west coast and then lost them. On the east coast, British victories were negated by the greater manoeuvrability of the Mysore forces. In 1782 Haidar Ali died, in 1783 Tipu was enthroned, and in 1784 the Peace of Mangalore again did little more than restore the situation as at the beginning of hostilities.

Tipu blamed his French allies for his failure to win a more convincing victory. Their support in the war had been negligible and their separate peace had been an act of treachery. To further overtures from Pondicherry he therefore replied by insisting on direct dealings with Versailles. In a refreshing reversal of roles, an Indian ruler was about to take the diplomatic game to the court of a European sovereign.

In 1785 an embassy had left Mysore for Constantinople. It was to alert the Islamic world to British designs on India's Muslim powers, to effect a political and commercial alliance, and to elicit from the Ottoman sultan, as the successor of the caliphs, recognition of Tipu's status as a legitimate Islamic sovereign, or *padshah*. This same mission was now ordered to proceed on to Paris. But, delayed in Iraq, it was superseded by a separate embassy sent direct to France in 1787.

All expenses were now to be paid by the French, who also provided a ship. Flying the flag of Mysore, this vessel eventually docked at Toulon in June 1788. Thence, after fireworks, receptions and visits to the theatre, Tipu's forty-five-man mission proceeded to Paris overland. The metropole turned out to greet its visitors in style, and the ambassadors were deluged with carriages, apartments and suitable clothes.

On the 10th of August, Louis XVI received the envoys with great pomp. The principal apartments of the Versailles palace were filled

with spectators, and the *salon d'Hercules*, where the audience was
to take place, was occupied by persons of rank of both sexes. The
Dauphin, being unwell, could not come. But the Queen, Marie
Antoinette, was seated in a private box at the side of the throne,
the envoys being required neither to look at her nor salute her.[15]

Whether Tipu's emissaries had any inkling that all was not well with
the Bourbons is unrecorded. But with the storming of the Bastille only a
year away and with London watching his every move, Louis XVI was in
no position to gratify his visitors with political and military support. In
fact France's domestic crisis meant that her ambitions in India were about to
be abandoned and all troops withdrawn. However, Tipu's less contentious
request for 'seeds of flowers and plants of various kinds, and for technicians,
workers and doctors' was entertained. When the mission left for home at
the end of the year it was accompanied by a veritable *atelier* of munitions
experts, gunsmiths, porcelain-workers, glass-makers, watchmakers, tap-
estry-makers and linen-weavers, plus 'two printers of oriental languages,
one physician, one surgeon, two engineers and two gardeners'.

Haidar Ali had turned Mysore's forces into a professional army, trained,
equipped and paid along European lines. Tipu was determined similarly
to modernise his state's economy. Where Haidar had been illiterate, Tipu
benefited from a good education and an extremely inquisitive mind. Alone
amongst his reigning contemporaries, he identified something of the
dynamic which lay behind the uniformed efficiency of the European regimes
and set about duplicating it. Trade was obviously important. To this end
he established a state trading company, encouraged investors to buy shares
in it, and organised a network of overseas 'factories' located around the
Arabian Sea and in the Persian Gulf. Modelled on those of the European
trading companies, they included both a commercial staff and a military
establishment. There is no mention of Louis XVI being petitioned for a
'factory' in France, but Tipu certainly urged the idea on the Ottoman
emperor and also approached the ruler of Pegu in Burma.

Command of the Malabar ports gave Mysore a ready outlet to the sea
plus control of their outward trade in pepper and timbers and of their
inward trade in mainly horses from the Gulf states; it was no coincidence
that the most effective cavalry in India belonged to the Marathas and to
Mysore, both of whom had ready access to the west coast ports. To increase
the variety of Mysore's exports Tipu sought new crops by experimenting
with seeds and plants from all over Asia as well as from France. Around
his summer palace at Srirangapatnam the ground was laid out in parterres

for botanical acclimatisation and propagation. The eighteenth century being the age of 'improvement', he took as close an interest in these schemes as any European 'improver', and was personally responsible for introducing sericulture into Mysore. The silkworms were obtained from Persia, mulberry-planting received official encouragement, and a factory for silk-processing and -weaving was set up. Other factories turned out sugar, paper, gunpowder, knives and scissors. 'The ammunition factories at Bednur produced twenty thousand muskets and guns every year.'[16] As Tipu boasted to a French correspondent, Mysore was self-sufficient in arms.

Testimony to the prosperity of his country and to the comparative leniency of his revenue demands comes mainly from the wide-eyed British officials and surveyors who would soon be swarming across Mysore to conduct its post-mortem; in victory the British prided themselves on magnanimity. But from the infrequency of protest and the failure of intrigues during his lifetime it would seem that Tipu's rule was indeed acceptable to most of his subjects, both Muslim and Hindu. 'Citoyen Tipu', as his revolutionary French contacts would soon call him, was no man of the people. A vindictive and sometimes cruel autocrat, he readily antagonised his enemies, both Indian and British, and was easily demonised by them. Yet, in his passion for reform and modernity some have seen parallels with the radicalism of the Paris revolutionaries. Thomas Munro, perhaps the most respected of all the British officials who later served in Mysore and a genuine admirer of Tipu's achievements, noted mainly his 'restless spirit and a wish to have everything originate from himself'.[17] The highly personalised nature of his rule was both its strength and its weakness. So long as he lived, there was little chance of the British reaching an accommodation with Mysore along the lines of those with Hyderabad or Awadh. Taming Tipu, 'the tiger of Mysore', meant destroying his entire habitat.

It was not a pretty story. If the conquest of Bengal had been partly dictated by a lust for personal gain, that of Mysore would owe much to a lust for personal glory. The Third Mysore War (1790–2) was declared and largely conducted by Lord Cornwallis, the general who had surrendered to George Washington at Yorktown during the American War of Independence. Upright and avowedly pacific, Cornwallis would wait three years before tackling Tipu. Once committed, however, he would pursue his quarry with a regard for his own dented military reputation that made anything less than Tipu's abject surrender unthinkable. By way of contrast Richard Wellesley, Earl of Mornington, the governor-general responsible for the Fourth Mysore War (1799), had barely touched Indian soil before he was preparing for battle. An uncompromising empire-builder whose annexations were anything but fortuitous, Wellesley immediately embarked on a veritable *digvijaya* in which a debilitated Mysore would offer easy pickings for a host of ardent officers including his brother Arthur, the future Duke of Wellington.

Tipu himself was no innocent. Far from avoiding contentious policies liable to unite and provoke his neighbours, he defiantly espoused them. The Third War was provoked by what Cornwallis regarded as an 'attack' on Travancore, the southernmost of the Malabar principalities. Tipu disclaimed responsibility but, instead of backing off, maintained his doubtful interests in the area and duly fuelled British paranoia with a full-scale invasion of Travancore. A tripartite alliance forged by Cornwallis with the Marathas and the Nizam of Hyderabad, which should have deterred him, merely antagonised him. The British then laboriously mobilised a force of twenty thousand for an invasion of Mysore. Initially they were outmanoeuvred by Tipu, who brought the war to the Carnatic. But Cornwallis eventually gained the Deccan, stormed Bangalore and advanced on Srirangapatnam. Meanwhile another British army had swept up from the Malabar coast, and Cornwallis had been joined by his Maratha and Hyderabad allies. Tipu, heavily outnumbered and outgunned, yet held out for the best part of a year before accepting terms which could hardly have been more humiliating. They included an eight-figure indemnity, the surrender of half his territories, and British custody of his two sons, one aged eight, the other ten, as surety.

Unexpectedly the indemnity was paid, the sons were reunited with their doting father, and Tipu's truncated kingdom was restored to an enviable prosperity. In that the Fourth War was so soon in progress, Cornwallis's boast of having 'deprived him [Tipu] of the power, and perhaps the inclination, to distract us for many years to come' would attract ridicule. In fact it was an understatement. Cornwallis's victory 'paved the way for British supremacy throughout India'.[18] Moreover it did indeed deprive Tipu of the power to challenge the British; the decision to reopen hostilities for a fourth and last time came entirely from Governor-General Wellesley.

In extenuation much was made of the fact that Napoleon had just landed in Egypt and made no secret of his designs on the British in India. When, therefore, Tipu was discovered to be in correspondence with the French commander at the Île de Bourbon in the Indian Ocean and to have recently received from there a few Jacobin recruits, Wellesley had the pretext he needed. Under cover of an exchange of letters protesting mutual amity between Calcutta and Mysore, he mobilised some forty thousand troops, who were joined by double that number of camp-followers plus the 100,000

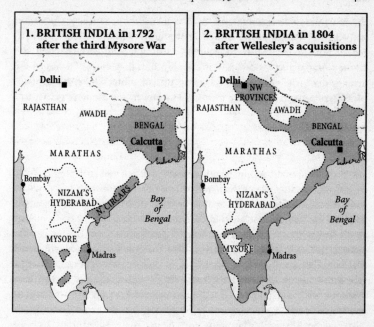

1. BRITISH INDIA in 1792 after the third Mysore War

Delhi

RAJASTHAN

AWADH

BENGAL

Calcutta

MARATHAS

Bombay

NIZAM'S HYDERABAD

N. CIRCARS

Bay of Bengal

MYSORE

Madras

2. BRITISH INDIA in 1804 after Wellesley's acquisitions

Delhi

NW PROVINCES

RAJASTHAN

AWADH

BENGAL

Calcutta

MARATHAS

Bombay

NIZAM'S HYDERABAD

Bay of Bengal

MYSORE

Madras

bullocks required for the largest ox-drawn baggage and munitions train ever organised.

Meanwhile Wellesley smugly recorded his satisfaction at having 'drawn the Beast of the jungle [i.e. Tipu] into the toils'. The 'toils' barely amounted to a campaign. Compared to the logistical problem of supplying such an invasion, the fighting was something of a formality. It was all over in three months. Srirangapatnam was stormed, then sacked with an ardour that would not have disgraced Attila. Amongst the perhaps nine thousand Mysore dead was found the body of Tipu Sultan. He had been cut about with bayonets, shot twice, and then robbed of his jewelled sword-belt. British casualties totalled fewer than four hundred, mostly just wounded.

The 'settlement' which followed left the British unchallenged throughout the peninsula. Mysore was pared down to something not much bigger than the statelet it had been before Haidar Ali's conquests. This was then awarded to a child of the old Wodeyar dynasty, assisted by a sufficient British presence, and burdened by sufficient British safeguards, to ensure subordination. The British helped themselves to more territory, including the coastline of Karnataka; and in 1800 the other beneficiary, the nizam, helped them to still more. In lieu of the subsidy he was expected to pay for the presence of British troops in his existing territories, he handed over to the Company all those lands awarded to him in Mysore. Thanks to this arrangement, the nizams would enjoy British protection at no expense, plus great personal affluence if rather less power, for the next 150 years.

THE MARATHAS MANAGED

India thus entered the nineteenth century with an unusual political configuration. Regions which had normally enjoyed immunity from outside interference, like the south and east, were directly or indirectly under foreign rule, while the usually more vulnerable west and north remained under indigenous regimes. These latter regimes were numerous. In another reversal of roles it was the playing fields of empire in the north which were now subdivided into a patchwork of political lots. They included the numerous rajput states in Rajasthan and elsewhere, various Indo-Afghan enclaves like Rohilkand, Muslim amirates and chieftaincies in Sind and on the frontier, and some newer caste-based hegemonies of uncertain extent like that established by Jat cultivators in the Agra region, plus a closely related tangle of Jat-Sikh and non-Sikh states in the Panjab.

Then there were the Marathas. Collectively they controlled much the most territory, the most revenue and the most forces. For a time in the early decades of the eighteenth century they had also acted collectively. But by 1740 the big Maratha families had begun to peel away. In a decentralising process similar to that which had overtaken the Mughal empire, the Holkars of Indore, Scindias of Gwalior, Gaikwads of Baroda and Bhonsles of Nagpur continued to recognise the authority of the peshwa-ship in Pune while treating individual peshwas as fellow leaders whose sanction, though desirable, was not an essential asset.

Given the loosely confederate nature of Maratha power and the spread of Maratha operations to practically the entire subcontinent, it was perhaps inevitable that each would in time respond more to local opportunities and challenges. The Maratha incursions into Orissa and Bengal which had so tested Nawab Alivardi Khan in the 1740s and had prompted construction of Calcutta's 'Maratha Ditch' were the work of the Bhonsles of Nagpur. The peshwa objected and even sent his own troops to Bengal to oppose the Bhonsle incursions. Thereafter Nagpur would often defy Pune and, much preoccupied with extorting revenue in Orissa and along its common frontier with the nizam, would play a marginal role in joint Maratha operations.

In the following decade other Marathas, particularly Malhar Rao Holkar of Indore and Jayappa Scindia soon of Gwalior, took advantage of succession disputes amongst the rajputs to extend their revenue claims in Rajasthan. In 1752–3 they again intervened in the chaotic affairs of Delhi and were a party to the blinding and removal of the then emperor. Further Maratha expansion saw Raghunath Rao, the brother of the peshwa Balaji Baji Rao (son of Baji Rao I), pushing into the Panjab in the wake of the Afghan withdrawal after Ahmed Shah Abdali's plunder of Delhi in 1756. In Lahore as in Delhi, the Marathas were now major players, while far away in the Deccan a defeat of the nizam in 1760 left the peshwas at Pune secure in possession of their Maharashtrian homeland.

Indeed 1760 is taken to mark 'the zenith of Mahratta power'. Freezing the moment for all its glory, James Grant Duff, author of the classic nineteenth-century *History of the Mahrattas*, seems to pay unintentional homage to the imagery of those fulsome dynastic inscriptions of an earlier age.

> The pre-eminence to which the Mahrattas had attained was animating and glorious; their right to tribute was acknowledged on the banks of the Coleroon [the lower Kaveri in Tamil Nadu], and the Deccan horse had quenched their thirst from the waters of the Indus. The Mahratta people felt a pride in the conquests of their countrymen . . .[19]

The moment was short-lived. Before the year was out the peshwa's general, fresh from his victory over the nizam, led the main Maratha army north to meet the threat posed by the reinvading Abdali. Abdali could count on the support of fellow Afghans, like the Rohillas, and had also won over the powerful (and then still independent) Nawab of Awadh. On the other hand Holkar, the Scindia family and other Maratha chiefs dutifully joined the swelling army of the peshwa. Well equipped with artillery, and with Duff's 'Deccan horse' looking especially splendid, this was the largest and most magnificent force ever assembled by the Marathas. In an age when sectarian loyalties rarely transcended political advantage, it might even have passed for a Hindu host had the hoped-for support of co-religionists like the rajputs and Jats materialised.

Notwithstanding, Delhi was retaken and the Marathas moved on up the Jamuna. On 14 January 1761 at Panipat, a hundred kilometres north of the capital and the scene, like nearby Karnal, Tarain and Kurukshetra, of so many decisive battles, they finally engaged the main Afghan army. For a few hours the Marathas seemed to prevail. Then in time-honoured fashion Abdali introduced his ten thousand reserve cavalry. As he told it in a letter to Raja Madho Singh of Jaipur, 'Suddenly the breeze of victory began to blow and, as willed by the Divine Lord, the wretched Deccanis suffered utter defeat ... Forty to fifty thousand troopers and infantrymen of the enemy became as grass before our pitiless swords.'[20]

As was his wont, Abdali soon withdrew again; as was their wont, bands of Sikh irregulars preyed on his treasure-laden convoys as they lumbered home across the Panjab. Such tactics had traditionally been those of the Marathas; had they preferred them to formal confrontation on the pitch of Panipat, they might have fared better. The Maratha leaders would quickly recoup their losses, reassert their authority in regions previously under their control, and reclaim their revenue rights in others, like the rajput states. But the prestige of the peshwa was seriously damaged by Panipat. The incumbent Balaji Baji Rao collapsed a few weeks later, supposedly of a broken heart. Although his young successor, Madhava Rao, briefly restored some authority, when he died prematurely in 1772 there began a succession crisis of mind-boggling complexity which lasted for a generation and would drain the office of much power. The Mughal emperor, his own office long since drained of power, had fared no better; Panipat left him a dependant of the Nawab of Awadh. And as for the nawab himself, the only Indian prince to emerge from the battle a winner, he was humbled five years later by the British at Baksar.

'Never was a defeat so complete and never was there a calamity which diffused so much consternation,' wrote Mountstuart Elphinstone of Panipat. It formed a fitting conclusion to his 1839 *History of India*; 'for the history of the Moghul empire here closes of itself.' The Maratha attempt to revive it had failed. Delhi was deserted, the emperor an exile. 'Meanwhile,' wrote Elphinstone in his grand finale, 'a new race of conquerors has already commenced its career which may again unite the empire under better auspices than before.'

In retrospect it is often asserted that the British were the real winners from the great tourney of Panipat. But this was not obvious at the time, and throughout the next two decades the Company's policy remained that of 'ring-fencing' Bengal and their other settlements with amenable buffer states capable of absorbing the still formidable impact of Maratha muscle. The Company's London directors had been deeply critical of the military expenditure incurred by the likes of Clive and Munro in Bengal and Awadh. Financial retrenchment was ordered, and to Warren Hastings in the 1770s the avoidance of Maratha attentions was crucial.

In a rare display of unanimity both the governor-general and his council therefore denounced the local alliance of 1775 which precipitated the First Anglo–Maratha War as 'unreasonable, impolitic, unjust and unauthorised'. It was unauthorised because the government of Bombay had concluded it without consulting its superior in Calcutta, unjust because it was no business of the British to blunder into the labyrinthine succession dispute over the peshwa-ship, impolitic because it flew in the face of Hastings' hands-off policy, and unreasonable because Bombay lacked the means to fulfil its share in the venture. The First Maratha War was not, then, a sequel to Panipat nor another assault on Maratha hegemony. An untidy affair with as many treaties as battles, it was more a piece of Bombay mischief.

Although of growing commercial importance, Bombay was still politically and territorially insignificant compared to Calcutta or Madras. Partly to redress this situation, successive governors had long coveted the two neighbouring enclaves of Salsette island and Bassein port, both once Portuguese but subsequently resumed by the Marathas (and nowadays absorbed within the sprawl of greater Bombay). An offer of the cession of these two places in return for the Bombay government assisting Raghunath Rao, now one of the contenders for the peshwa-ship, with a force of 2500 men, was too good to miss. After a treaty to this effect had been signed at Surat in 1775, a combined Anglo-Maratha force moved into Gujarat and enjoyed some success before being halted in its tracks by Calcutta's censure.

The Bombay troops were ordered back to camp and a British envoy was sent to negotiate with the Regency Council of the peshwa-ship in Pune. He agreed to abandon support of Raghunath in return for an indemnity and the cession of Salsette. But neither party honoured this treaty and in 1778 Bombay again rushed to Raghunath's aid. This time it mobilised a force of four thousand which marched inland from Bombay and was heavily defeated while climbing up the Western Ghats towards Pune.

The Convention of Wadgaon (1779), signed on the spot in the wake of this defeat, was about as near to a surrender as the British had come since Bombay's previous capitulation to Aurangzeb during the Childs' 'Mughal War'. In Pune the Regency Council, dominated by the redoubtable Nana Phadnavis (Farnavis), made much of this success and, on the strength of it, briefly enjoyed the support of Holkar, Scindia and the Gaikwad. By 1780 there was even talk of the grand alliance, so dreaded by the British, of the Marathas, the nizam, and Haidar Ali of Mysore. Against the background of the Second Mysore War and of the ongoing Anglo–French hostilities, Warren Hastings therefore repudiated the Wadgaon Convention and reopened direct negotiations with Pune. There was little chance of an accommodation with Phadnavis, but the possibility of detaching the other Maratha confederates had improved greatly thanks to the appearance on the west coast of a British force sent overland from Bengal.

By virtue of his office as governor-general for all the British possessions in India, Hastings was being drawn, not unwillingly, into all-India adventures. Bombay's plight, though richly deserved, could not be ignored; accordingly, in 1778 he had ordered six largely sepoy battalions to march right across the subcontinent to Gujarat. Starting from the Company's Bengal salient in Awadh, they had taken the best part of a year to reach the west coast but, as with the Bengal troops who were about to be sent overland to Madras following Haidar Ali's triumph at Polilur, their arrival changed the balance of power dramatically.

When the negotiations with Pune broke down, the Gaikwad, whose Gujarat base was particularly vulnerable, threw in his lot with the British. Meanwhile Mahadji Scindia received a rude shock when his core territories, hundreds of kilometres away to the north of Malwa, were threatened by another expedition from Bengal. Cragsmen from the latter even scaled the cliffs of Gwalior and captured what was still regarded as northern India's greatest stronghold. Nearer home, the Marathas fared better and, though defeated at Ahmadabad in early 1780, successfully repelled another British attempt to force a way up through the Ghats to Pune in 1781.

By now Scindia was trying to act as a peacemaker while Hastings, thoroughly alarmed by Haidar Ali's successes in the Carnatic, was also anxious to disengage. Hostilities therefore ceased in 1781 and a final treaty, that of Salbai, was ratified in 1782–3. Like the first two Mysore Wars, the First Maratha War had brought no significant territorial gains to either side. The Marathas, however, had retained their freedom of action and had obliged the British to relinquish their championship of Raghunath Rao. Hastings, on the other hand, could congratulate himself on having extricated Bombay, on having demonstrated the British potential to strike practically anywhere in India, and of having achieved what, since the treaty also regulated British and Maratha relations with the nizam, Mysore and the French, he took to be a general and lasting arrangement.

In that the peace lasted for a quarter of a century, Hastings' hopes were fulfilled. But this was mainly thanks to the survival into the mid-1790s of a remarkable generation of Maratha leaders. Nana Phadnavis, a brahman whom even the British acknowledged as the most astute political leader of his day, continued to control Pune until 1796. When the young peshwa in whose name he ruled came of age, his guardians simply became his gaolers and Phadnavis remained in command. He fought much with Tipu, including that half-hearted support of Cornwallis during the Third Mysore War, and he registered some territorial gains in northern Karnataka. More significantly, he managed to stave off the challenge of the other Maratha leaders.

These included the Holkars of Indore, whose core territory in Malwa now enjoyed something of a golden age under the regency of Ahalyabhai, daughter-in-law of Malhar Rao Holkar. Judging by their correspondence, Malhar Rao had relied heavily on the sage young Ahalyabhai during his lifetime. His death in 1766 was preceded by that of his useless son, who was Ahalyabhai's husband, and was followed by that of his equally useless grandson. Ahalyabhai was thus left with no obvious rivals. Her sex would still have disqualified her, had she not shown an extraordinary ability which won the regard of her subjects and of the other Maratha confederates, including Phadnavis. For some thirty years her firm and compassionate direction brought to southern Malwa a peace and prosperity which utterly belies the notion of Maratha administration as little better than legitimised extortion. 'Moderate assessment and an almost sacred respect for the native rights of village officers and proprietors' characterised her rule. Collecting oral memories of her in the 1820s, Sir John Malcolm, the British official most directly concerned with the 'settlement' of central India, seems to have become deeply enamoured of her.

> With the natives of Malwa ... her name is sainted and she is styled an *avatar* or Incarnation of the Divinity. In the most sober view that can be taken of her character, she certainly appears, within her limited sphere, to have been one of the purest and most exemplary rulers that ever existed.[21]

Her latest biographers call her 'the Philosopher Queen', a reference perhaps to the 'philosopher-king' Bhoj whose capital of Dhar lay just a short ride from Ahalyabhai's preferred residence beside the Narmada at the sacred site of Maheshwar. Her forts and roads brought a new security to Malwa and her patronage of temples and other religious establishments as far away as Varanasi and Dwarka (Gujarat) extended her fame throughout India. It has lasted. 'Her reputation in Malwa today is that of a saint,' reports a recent writer; 'such are the results of a good, honest administration.'[22]

By way of contrast Mahadji Scindia, Ahalyabhai's exact contemporary and her neighbour to the north, was rarely out of the saddle. Lamed by a wound at Panipat, he too reigned for over thirty years, during which he overran more of northern India than any other Maratha. Not without setbacks, he finally established Gwalior as the Scindia stronghold, retook Delhi and Agra, made the incumbent emperor a Maratha protégé, and stood as guarantor of the Treaty of Salbai on behalf of all the Marathas. Later he inflicted heavy defeats on the Rohilla Afghans, and in 1790 practically eliminated the rajputs of Jaipur and Jodhpur; indeed their territories were still reeling from his devastations when in the 1820s Colonel James Tod, pursuing the same sort of 'settlement' in Rajasthan as Thomas Munro had effected in Mysore and John Malcolm in central India, first encountered his beloved rajputs.

Mahadji's extraordinary success stemmed from his creation of a professional army. Under Count Benoît de Boigne, a Frenchman but a veteran of the English Company, he recruited several brigades of infantry and artillery officered by Europeans and composed of the largely Muslim and rajput mercenaries favoured by the Company. These proved immensely successful; but they were expensive and, when in arrears, unresponsive to appeals to their loyalty. Mahadji's supremacy in the north, as also amongst his fellow Marathas, was thus achieved at a price which his successors could scarcely afford and with an instrument that they could scarcely control.

When Mahadji died in 1794, he was at Pune negotiating with Phadnavis for the peshwa's recognition of his achievements and a contribution to the upkeep of his forces. It was the beginning of a rapid decline in Maratha fortunes. Ahalyabhai died in the following year, whereupon her Holkar successor would openly challenge Scindia's primacy. Then in 1796 the powerless but still pivotal peshwa committed suicide. He was without issue and the way was thus opened for a revival of the claim of Raghunath Rao's line as now represented by his sons. During four years of utter confusion at Pune, Nana Phadnavis arbitrated as best he could with the result that Baji Rao II, Raghunath's eldest son, was installed as peshwa with support from Mahadji's successor, Daulat Rao Scindia. But in 1800, when Phadnavis himself died, there 'departed all the wisdom and moderation of the [Pune] government'. War between Yaswant Rao Holkar and Daulat Rao Scindia for control of the new peshwa soon spread to Pune itself, and in a pitched battle Holkar came out the winner. Desperate to retain his independence, the new peshwa, Baji Rao II, fled across the Ghats, down to the coast, and into the open arms of the British.

Bombay had encouraged Baji Rao's hopes of British assistance and, with the bellicose Richard Wellesley as governor-general, the exiled peshwa was unlikely to be disappointed. By the Treaty of Bassein (1803) the British undertook to reinstate Baji Rao in return for his accepting, and paying for,

SUCCESSION OF THE PESHWAS OF PUNE

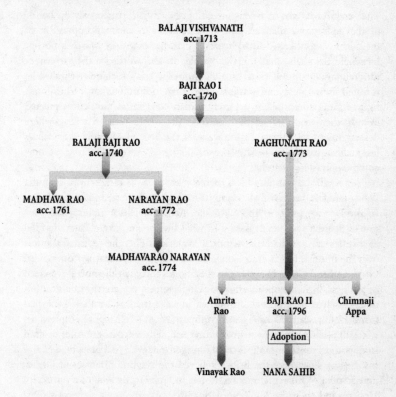

the presence of British troops in his territories, a British resident in his capital, and all the other restrictions associated with the now familiar role of a 'subsidiary ally'. Arthur Wellesley, fresh from the triumphs in Mysore, was sent north to prosecute this next phase of his brother's *digvijaya* and duly restored the peshwa to Pune. 'This act represented the end of the Maratha polity as an independent power. The rest of the story is one of British conquest, largely with funds from conquered territories.'[23]

THE FINAL PHASE

The Second Maratha War was waged by the British, supposedly on behalf of the peshwa, to silence Maratha opposition to their appropriation of the peshwa's authority. Such, however, was the extent of Maratha power, especially Scindia's, that the war would, in the words of the governor-general, lay 'the foundations of our Empire in Asia'. Richard Wellesley, be it noted, now foresaw an empire, rather than 'dominions' or 'possessions', in an Asian as opposed to a purely Indian context; as the British pushed ever further west and north it seemed that there was no telling where destiny might take them. In the wake of the Second Maratha War others less bullish, like Thomas Munro, would concede simply that 'we are now complete masters of India.'

Although the war lasted less than a year (1803–4) it destroyed Maratha power and left the British victorious throughout northern and central India. In the Deccan south of the Narmada, Arthur Wellesley triumphed over one of Scindia's armies at Assaye in what the future duke always regarded as a stiffer contest than his victory at Waterloo. Then he repeated the feat over the Bhonsle forces at Argaon. More sensationally, an army from Bengal under General Gerard Lake engaged Scindia's forces in the north. Deserted by most of their European officers, Scindia's men yet gave a good account of themselves in the final showdown at Laswari. But by then Lake had taken Delhi, stormed Agra, and commandeered the Mughal emperor (it was still Shah Alam, now a woebegone and sightless octogenarian dressed in rags and unrecognisable as the dashing prince who had once made Clive his *diwan*). Elsewhere the British relieved the Nagpur Bhonsles of Orissa, and Scindia of his remaining territories in Gujarat. By way of a postscript Holkar, and then the Jat Raja of Bharatpur (near Agra), were provoked into further defiance and severely embarrassed General Lake's forces before being brought to heel.

It was not quite the end of the Marathas. Richard Wellesley's expensive campaigning had greatly embarrassed his masters in London. His gratuitous swipe at Holkar was the last straw. He was recalled from India in disgrace and his planned 'settlement' of central and western India never materialised. Nevertheless Delhi, Agra and the Ganga-Jamuna Doab were retained as a new salient of British territory in the north-west.

The new British frontier supposedly ran north along the Jamuna, although some chiefs from the slice of territory between the Jamuna and the Satlej ('the Cis-Satlej states') had also tendered their allegiance to General Lake. This brought the British into potential conflict with Ranjit Singh, a young Sikh leader who had been prominent in repulsing Afghan attacks by Ahmed Shah Abdali's successors and who, since occupying Lahore in 1799, had been pursuing a policy of conquest and alliance that mirrored that of the British. By 1805 he had secured the Sikh centre of Amritsar together with its potential for converting religious patronage into political authority. He had also impressed his personal authority on much of the Panjab, including some of those 'Cis-Satlej chiefs' as the British called them. But whilst Ranjit's kingdom, like Tipu's, would incorporate some European features and represent a serious challenge to the British, Ranjit himself was too much of a realist to invite the risks of war. By the Treaty of Amritsar in 1809 he backed down over the Cis-Satlej chiefs and thus the Satlej, rather than the Jamuna, became the Anglo–Sikh frontier. In return Ranjit secured British recognition of his independent authority as 'Raja of Lahore'. Platitudes about friendship and non-interference would, for once, be respected and over the next thirty years the Raja of Lahore, comparatively free of British interference, would blossom into the Maharaja of the Panjab, creator of the most formidable non-colonial state in India.

Elsewhere the outcome of the Second Maratha War was less creditable. The British acquisition of the Ganga-Jamuna Doab was retained, mainly at the expense of Scindia whose ambitions were further constrained by a subsidiary alliance. But from central India and Rajasthan the British withdrew and disclaimed all authority, perhaps aghast at their own conquests and certainly alarmed by the high expenditure involved. The result was a predictable chaos. The Maratha leaders, impoverished, discredited and deeply resentful of the tightening British cordon, turned to indiscriminate plunder while many of their troops, despairing of payment, broke away to join bands of marauding adventurers, the so-called Pindaris. From Malwa, from the Bhonsles' Berar, and from Rajasthan the chronic lawlessness spilled into the Deccan, Hyderabad, and the now-British Doab. Here was a clear case of British policy, or the lack of it, having created an anarchy which did indeed cry out for further intervention.

It came in 1817 in the form of an ambitious military sweep designed to wipe out these Pindari bands. The Maratha leaders were pressured into supporting this operation. But as they observed the political preparations for it, and noted the massive mobilisation, they became convinced that they were as much the target as the Pindaris. Suspicions deepened when the terms of a new British treaty recently forced upon the peshwa became known. Much harsher than that of Bassein, it included a clause by which the peshwa renounced any claim to supremacy over the other Maratha leaders. Although traduced in practice, the authority of the peshwa as a

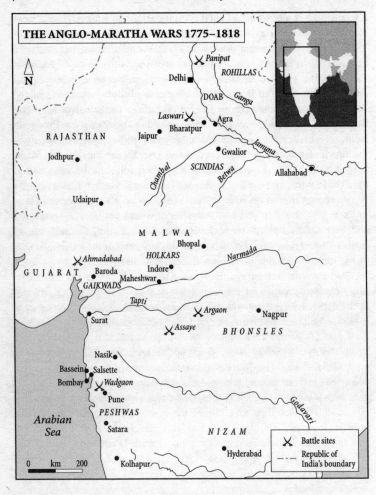

THE ANGLO-MARATHA WARS 1775–1818

N

Panipat
Delhi
ROHILLAS
DOAB
Ganga
Laswari
Bharatpur
Agra
RAJASTHAN
Jaipur
Jamuna
Jodhpur
Gwalior
SCINDIAS
Betwa
Allahabad
Chambal
Udaipur
MALWA
Bhopal
Ahmadabad
HOLKARS
Narmada
GUJARAT
Baroda
Indore
Maheshwar
GAIKWADS
Tapti
Argaon
Nagpur
Surat
Assaye
BHONSLES
Nasik
Bassein
Salsette
Bombay
Wadgaon
Pune
PESHWAS
Arabian
Sea
Satara
NIZAM
Hyderabad
Kolhapur
Godavari

✗ Battle sites
‐ ‐ ‐ Republic of India's boundary

0   km   200

focus of loyalty was precious to all the Maratha leaders, and especially so to Peshwa Baji Rao II himself. Ostensibly assembling forces to co-operate in the action against the Pindaris, Baji Rao suddenly turned on the British contingent in Pune. The British Residency was razed and the British Resident – it was the future historian Mountstuart Elphinstone – barely escaped. Then the peshwa's army marched against the British barracks nearby. It was repulsed and, when British reinforcements arrived, the peshwa fled.

He remained at large until mid-1818, during which time his territories were systematically conquered.

A similar rising at Nagpur by the Bhonsle incumbent resulted in a similar conquest. In a now clichéd procedure, a minor was installed as maharaja of the much-reduced Nagpur state and was then shackled with all the paraphernalia of British clientage. For the peshwa, already lumbered with the status of a subsidiary British ally, there could be no such soft landing. His lands were annexed and, when eventually he was captured, he was deposed and banished into a long but comfortable retirement in the British Doab. The place chosen was near Kanpur (Cawnpore). There he died in 1851, and thence his adopted son, known as Nana Sahib, would be plucked from obscurity to raise again the flag of the peshwas during the great conflagration of 1857.

The Pindari War and this Third Maratha War ended the long defiance of the Marathas. In Maharashtra only the small states of Kolhapur and Satara, where ruled the tamed descendants of Shivaji himself, were left with any vestige of autonomy. To the rajputs of Rajasthan, as to the Maratha survivors in central India, the status of subordinate allies or 'princely states' was extended. 'Except in Assam, Sind and the Panjab, British political supremacy was recognised throughout the whole subcontinent,' writes Penderel Moon. 'The Pax Britannica had begun.'[24]

Pax Britannica

1820–1880

SIKH TRANSIT GLORIA

IN MARKED CONTRAST to, say, Napoleon's adventure in Egypt, the British conquest of India was supposed to be self-financing. Although subject to increasing regulation and direction by the British government after 1776, the East India Company remained a business concern, run from stately offices in Leadenhall Street in the City of London, whose directors were primarily answerable to their stockholders. As with ships and cargoes, the recruitment and maintenance of troops had to be accounted for, and budgets had to be balanced. Before 1760 profits from trade had usually taken care of expenses. But as troop numbers and military overheads soared in the last decades of the eighteenth century, commercial receipts dwindled in significance. Now it was revenue in the form of indemnities, tribute and subventions from Indian states and of tax yields from directly administered territories which became the principal source of the Company's income and so the mainstay of the *Pax Britannica*.

Conquests and annexations could be justified in terms of the additional revenue which they would in time undoubtedly yield; but they were expensive in themselves. The banquet of British victories was thus interspersed with periods of retrenchment during which the diners, pulling back from the table, savoured their latest acquisitions and insisted they would eat no more. Central to such digestive interludes was the assessment and forceful imposition in newly acquired territories of revised and usually harsher fiscal demands, or 'revenue settlements'. The effect of these revenue settlements on India's rural economy would prove significant. Here it may simply be noted that the order and stability which British rule undeniably brought did not come cheap. In the experience of most Indians *Pax Britannica* meant mainly 'Tax Britannica'.

414

Nor, by any reasonable construction, could *Pax Britannica* be taken to mean actual peace, either in India or in the wider British empire. To maximise land revenue, frontiers had to be defended, marauding forest- and hill-peoples had to be excluded from taxable zones of settled cultivation, and these taxable zones had themselves to be extended into marginal areas of hill, forest and wetland. In that 'the century beginning 1780 saw the beginnings of extensive deforestation in the subcontinent',[1] the 'Axe Britannica' may bear as much responsibility as the 'Tax Britannica' for the desolated aspect of India's post-colonial rural economy. Armed conflict with those outside this economy, whether along external political frontiers or internal ecological frontiers, was a concomitant of empire. By one reckoning there was not a single year between the Napoleonic Wars and the First World War – the accepted duration of the *Pax Britannica* – when British-led forces were not engaged in hostilities somewhere in the world.

To this dismal record British India contributed substantially. Just before what the then governor-general was pleased to call 'the pacification of 1818' (that is the Pindari and Third Maratha Wars), British expeditions from India had invaded the East Indies (Indonesia) and Nepal. In the Indies a sharp little war (1811–12) involving twelve thousand Company troops relieved the Netherlands, then under Napoleonic control, of the island of Java and rewarded 'the insolence' of the island's senior sultan with the desecration of his far-flung 'Ayodhya', otherwise Jogjakarta. Thomas Stamford Raffles, appointed lieutenant-governor of the island, reckoned Java 'the Bengal of the East Indies' and, greatly encouraged by the discovery of those inscriptions and monuments advertising the island's ancient Indic associations, saw Java as the bridgehead for another British India. But it was not to be. Java was returned to the Dutch after Waterloo, and Raffles had to be content with a bridgehead on the south-east Asian mainland, namely Singapore.

The Gurkha War (1814–16) with Nepal went less smoothly but ultimately yielded some bracing Alpine territory in what are now Himachal Pradesh and north-west Uttar Pradesh. Unlike Java, these districts would be retained by the British; and although revenue yields would be disappointing, the amenity appeal of the outer Himalayas was quickly appreciated. Here in the 1820s and thirties were founded the choicest of hill-stations, including Naini Tal, Mussoorie, Dehra Dun and, above all, Simla, imminently to become what one of British India's greatest military historians candidly calls 'the cradle of more political insanity than any place within the limits of Hindustan'.[2]

Continuing the catalogue of conflict, six years after the 'pacification' of 1818, the First Burmese War was declared against Burman incursions into Assam. By way of diversion an expedition was also sent to Rangoon. Assam itself was annexed in sections between 1826 and 1838, throughout which period troops were kept busy dealing with a succession of minor revolts in the Brahmaputra valley and a campaign in the Khasi hills. Meanwhile, in 1825–6, the Jat stronghold of Bharatpur, near Agra, had to be besieged for a second time, then stormed; in 1830–3 the hill peoples of Orissa were in constant revolt; and further military intervention was required in Mysore in 1830 to wrest the government from the perceived incompetence of its restored Wodeyar maharaja and in Coorg in 1834 to end by annexation the ambiguous status of this hilly enclave in the south-west corner of Karnataka. And all this, be it noted, during a twenty-year period of vigorous British retrenchment which is usually accounted one of peace and consolidation.

It would indeed seem so in retrospect. The campaigns of the 1830s were mere spats compared to the major wars of the 1840s, not to mention the near-meltdown of the 1850s. Of the wars in the 1840s all would be waged in the north-west of the subcontinent. With most of what today comprises the Republic of India already subject to direct or indirect British rule, it was now the turn of those lands which have since come to comprise Pakistan.

When Ranjit Singh, the Sikh Raja of Lahore, had been deprived of the 'Cis-Satlej' states after the Second Maratha War, British expansion for the first time crossed the watershed between the Ganga and the Indus to touch the present-day Indo–Pakistan frontier. That was in 1809, and it was not until a generation later that the banquet of conquest in the north-west was resumed. By then, the 1840s, Bengal had been dominated by the British for ninety years, Mysore for fifty. The Panjab, Sind, Kashmir and the Frontier can scarcely be called afterthoughts, since Wellesley had had his eye on the Panjab at the turn of the century. But their experience of colonial rule would be very much briefer and perhaps less traumatic. Spared the early years of British 'rapacity' as in Clive's Bengal, spared the heady decades when the Company and its sepoy army competed with other Mughal successor states like the Marathas, and spared the deepening sense of military and religious betrayal which was about to flare into the conflagration of 1857, the peoples of the north-west would have a different perspective on British supremacy.

It was not more indulgent or collaborative, perhaps less so. But attitudes in the north-west were tempered by a historical experience in which alien conquest and migration had featured all too frequently. And amongst

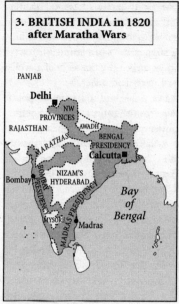

3. BRITISH INDIA in 1820 after Maratha Wars

PANJAB

Delhi

NW PROVINCES

RAJASTHAN

AWADH

MARATHAS

BENGAL PRESIDENCY

Calcutta

Bombay

NIZAM'S HYDERABAD

MYSORE

MADRAS PRESIDENCY

Madras

Bay of Bengal

4. BRITISH INDIA in 1856 after Dalhousie's annexations

JAMMU & KASHMIR

PANJAB

Delhi

RAJASTHAN

SIND

MARATHAS

AWADH

ASSAM

BENGAL PRESIDENCY

Calcutta

Bombay

SATARA

NIZAM'S HYDERABAD

MYSORE

MADRAS PRESIDENCY

Madras

TRAVANCORE

Bay of Bengal

peoples, mostly Muslim, with a greater awareness of nineteenth-century European supremacy elsewhere in the Islamic world, these attitudes may have been more pragmatic. In the north-west, Sikhs as well as Muslims would find it easier to come to terms with colonial rule. By the mainly Hindu peoples of the rest of India they would even be thought to enjoy preferential treatment. This, however, was not apparent in the 1840s. While substantial parts of what is now India had passed to the British by treaty and annexation, most of what is now Pakistan had to be physically conquered. The battles were more closely contested and the casualties proportionately heavier. This north-western addendum to British conquest would be both the most bloody and the most controversial.

In a provocative mix of commercial ambition and strategic paranoia, the British government had in 1830 urged on Lord William Bentinck, the then governor-general, the desirability of opening the river Indus for steam navigation and of simultaneously assessing the danger to British India of Tsarist Russian expansion into central Asia. There followed various missions upriver and overland into the Panjab, Afghanistan and the great beyond of the central Asian Khanates. Copious reports were written, colourful narratives published, and new geographical 'discoveries' bagged. Cooler heads insisted that the Indus, in so far as its erratic flow and shifting mudbanks allowed, was already 'open', that the idea of a Russian invasion of India was preposterous, and that such exploratory forays would only generate the hostility which they were supposed to pre-empt. But closer acquaintance with Afghan affairs obligingly fuelled the fantasies of alarmist bureaucrats and excited the ambitions of map-mad generals.

At the time Afghanistan's existence as a viable and independent polity, rather than just a turbulent Indo–Persian frontier zone, lacked conviction. Kabul had indeed been a Mughal frontier province, but much of what subsequently became Afghanistan was usually under Uzbek and Persian rule. More recently Ahmad Shah Abdali's fluctuating kingdom had relied heavily on its Indian conquests and anyway proved transitory; by 1814 his grandsons, one of them already blinded, had been ejected from Afghanistan. They repaired first to the Sikh kingdom of Lahore. There, from amongst the effects of Shah Shuja (the still-sighted grandson), Ranjit Singh extracted the Koh-i-Nur diamond as the price of his protection. Far from being a harbinger of misfortune, the gem was proving its worth as a life-saving talisman. In 1833 Ranjit Singh along with the British also assisted Shah Shuja in raising a force to reclaim his kingdom. It failed to do so and in the aftermath Dost Muhammad, the chief of a rival Pathan clan, established himself in Kabul.

Another British mission to Kabul in 1837 reported favourably of Dost Muhammad. British support of his claim to Peshawar, lately taken from Afghan rule by Ranjit Singh, was strongly urged; and in return Dost Muhammad was expected to prove a staunch ally against either Persian or Russian designs on India. To support this contention, the mission made much of the arrival in Kabul of a supposed Russian envoy who, if the British declined to take up Dost Muhammad's case against Ranjit Singh, might himself do so on behalf of his Tsarist master.

This and other such reports were turned on their head by the 'politically insane' coterie of advisers who surrounded Lord Auckland, the most vacillating of governors-general, during his 1838 summer sojourn in Simla. The mere suggestion of Dost Muhammad receiving Russian encouragement now became proof of 'his most unreasonable pretensions', indeed of 'schemes of aggrandisement and ambition injurious to the security and peace of the frontiers of India'. In great haste a tripartite alliance was arranged with Ranjit Singh and the exiled Shah Shuja. Dost Muhammad was to be ousted by force; Shah Shuja was to be installed in his place; the force itself was to be provided jointly by Ranjit Singh and Shah Shuja. But then, lest they prove half-hearted, a British expedition was organised to augment and, in the event, dwarf the Sikh and Afghan contributions. This was 'the Army of the Indus', some twenty thousand strong with perhaps double that number of camp-followers, which in early 1839 marched circuitously across 1500 kilometres of patchy desert and instantly denuded cultivation to climb through the Bolan Pass into Afghanistan and thence, for the most part, never to return.

The First Afghan War is usually ranked as the worst disaster to overtake the British in the East prior to Japan's World War II invasion of Malaya and capture of Singapore exactly a century later. In that in both campaigns most of the troops, and so most of the casualties, were Indian rather than British, this verdict conceals India's human tragedy beneath a mound of imperial hubris. Even sepoys who were lucky enough to survive the rout in Kabul often found themselves outcastes when they returned to India. 'This greatly mortified me,' recalled Sita Ram, a captured brahman sepoy who escaped back to India and may be regarded as 'a credible witness'.[3] In Afghanistan Sita Ram had been enslaved, some of his comrades had been forcibly converted to Islam, and all were deemed to have lost status by serving beyond the Indus, so contravening a high-caste taboo against travel outside India. The ostracism experienced by the survivors was so severe that 'I almost wished I had remained in Cabool where at any rate I was not treated unkindly.'[4] This same prejudice against 'overseas' service had led to a small mutiny at the time of the Burmese war. But in Afghanistan troubled caste consciences went unsoothed by the balm of victory, and the later expense of caste reinstatement went unpaid by the spoils of conquest. Suddenly employment in the Company's forces lost some of its popularity. Men thought less of unswerving loyalty to the Company and looked more closely at their terms of service.

Worse still, from the corpse-strewn gorges of the Kabul river, red-coated myths about the Company's invincibility, its armies' discipline and its officers' courage emerged in tatters. A quick reinvasion and heavy reprisals would to some extent restore British pride; but, since the country was ultimately evacuated, questions arose about the political wisdom, indeed sanity, of the 'tin gods' who from Simla or Calcutta ordained these affairs.

The conquest and annexation of Sind in 1843, a spin-off of the reinvasion of Afghanistan, did nothing to quell such doubts. Major-General Sir Charles Napier frankly admitted that 'we have no right to seize Scinde'; yet he actively 'bullied' (his own word) the Sindis into hostilities and then conducted what he called this 'very advantageous, useful, humane piece of rascality' with maximum brutality. It contravened a sheaf of treaties, themselves signed under duress, which had previously been concluded with the various rulers, or 'amirs', of Sind, and it incurred almost universal condemnation in Britain. The story that Napier, in one of the shortest telegraphs ever sent, announced his victory with a single Latin verb is apparently apocryphal. '*Peccavi*' (meaning 'I have sinned [i.e. Sind]'), was not unworthy of Napier's wit, but it was in fact the caption given him by the magazine *Punch*; 'and *Punch* represented him as confessing that he had sinned because the deposition of the Amirs and the seizure of their territories raised such a storm of criticism in England'.[5] Subsequently Sind, despite the development of Karachi as a major sea-port, failed to provide the revenue returns projected by Napier. Worse still, to the likes of sepoy Sita Ram it constituted another source of grievance in that, being for the most part beyond the pale of the Indus, garrison duty there carried the stigma of caste-loss without, since it was now British territory, the compensation of an 'overseas' allowance. Not unreasonably, Bengal troops posted to Sind were soon staging a succession of minor mutinies.

Mountstuart Elphinstone, who had led the first British diplomatic mission to Afghanistan in 1809, then been the last British Resident at the court of the peshwa in 1816 and later wrote that eminent history of India, likened Britain's post-Afghanistan conduct in Sind to that of 'a bully who had been kicked in the streets and went home to beat his wife'. But if the British were the bully, if Sind was the unfortunate wife and Afghanistan the lawless streets, it was Lahore which was the precinct boss. To avoid friction with Ranjit Singh, Dost Muhammad had been demonised; to avoid crossing his Sikh kingdom in the Panjab, the 'Army of the Indus' had marched to Afghanistan so circuitously; and to pre-empt a Sind–Sikh alliance, the amirs had been deposed. Novel though it was, the British were tiptoeing round the sensibilities of an Indian ruler. In Ranjit Singh it seemed as though the tide of British conquest had rolled up against a cliff of Panjabi granite.

Following his non-aggression Treaty of Amritsar with the British in 1809, Ranjit had by 1830 created a kingdom, nay an 'empire', rated by one visitor 'the most wonderful object in the whole world'.[6] In addition to uniting the Panjab, a phenomenal achievement in itself given the rivalries of its Muslim, Hindu and Sikh factions, and then reclaiming Multan and Peshawar, the 'Raja of Lahore' had also conquered most of the Panjab hill states and occupied Kashmir. In 1836 one of his Dogra vassals then overran neighbouring Ladakh at the western extremity of the Tibetan plateau; and from there in 1840, in one of those rare examples of Indian military aggression beyond its natural frontiers, Zorawar Singh, a Dogra general, actually invaded Tibet itself. Like the 'Army of the Indus' – and at almost exactly the same time (1840–1) – this expedition enjoyed initial success and then

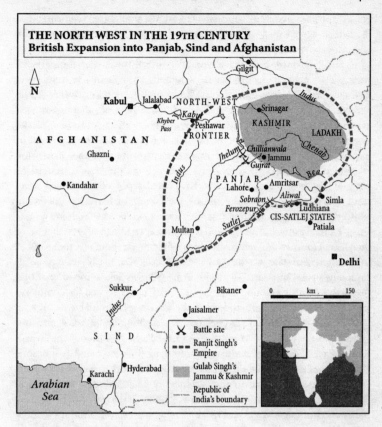

THE NORTH WEST IN THE 19TH CENTURY
British Expansion into Panjab, Sind and Afghanistan

sensational disaster. In mid-winter at five thousand metres above sea-level Zorawar's six thousand frostbitten Dogras were confronted by a Chinese host twice as numerous and infinitely better clad. 'On the last fatal day not half of his men could handle their arms.' Those who could, fled; the Chinese scarcely bothered to follow, 'knowing full well that the unrelenting frost would spare no one'.[7]

This, however, was a minor reverse and, bar the temperatures, not otherwise comparable to Napoleon's débâcle in Russia thirty years earlier. Defeat in central Tibet barely registered on the morale of the Lahore army; and like the long-forgotten empire of Kanishka, the Sikh realm still straddled the Himalayas. As contemporaries and, to the British, formidable opponents, Ranjit and Bonaparte invited more obvious comparisons. A

French traveller declared the misshapen Sikh 'a miniature Napoleon'; and
the British agreed that both were 'men of military genius'. Moreover 'the
Sikh monarchy was Napoleonic in the suddenness of its rise, the brilliancy
of its success, and the completeness of its overthrow.'[8] The comparisons
were particularly apposite because of Ranjit's enthusiasm for employing
distinguished ex-Napoleonic officers. Under his direction Generals Avitabile
and Ventura, Colonels Court and Allard and a host of others converted
his infantry and artillery into a sepoy army as effective as that of the
Company. 'In training, weapons, organisation, tactics, clothing, system of
pay, layout of camps, order of march, regular units of the Sikh army
resembled their [British] opponents as closely as they could; indeed in
battle it was possible to tell the scarlet-coated sepoy of the Bengal army
from the scarlet-coated Sikh only by the colour of his belt.'[9] Including
Muslims and Hindus of Dogra, Jat and rajput origin, the 'Sikh army' was
a pan-Panjabi army, but with a Sikh core. 'It may be safe to suggest that more
than half of the men . . . were Sikh, which would mean about fifty thousand.'[10]
In the councils of state and the rewards of office Sikhs similarly predominated.
To Ranjit's rule, and especially to his army, Sikhism lent something of that
distinctive identity and unity of purpose which characterised the command
structure of the Company and made the British so formidable.

With a healthy regard for one another's capabilities, both Calcutta and
Lahore did their utmost to avoid a head-on clash. To humour the British
Ranjit professed himself a sincere admirer of their rule, and to humour
Ranjit successive governors-general trailed up to Lahore to pay their respects
and solicit his assistance in the 'defence' of their frontier. But in 1839,
just as the joint Afghan enterprise was getting underway, Ranjit died. A
philanderer of many wives and more women, he was not without potential
successors. Yet so personal had been his rule and so absolute his authority
that the institutions of sovereignty and government through which a successor might establish himself scarcely existed. As rival court factions sought
support for their preferred candidates, authority drained back to its source,
the army.

When in 1843 the second maharaja since Ranjit's death was assassinated,
a veritable bloodbath ensued. It was no secret that the British were tempted
to intervene, and it is quite probable that they were already actively
fomenting the chaos. Certainly the massing of thirty-two thousand troops,
with boats, along the Satlej frontier, allegedly to prevent the trouble spreading to the British 'Cis-Satlej' states, was highly provocative. With the Sikh
army a law unto itself and the contenders for the throne competing for
outside support, including that of the British, the mere proximity of this

force was enough to ensure its involvement. The inevitable collision took place when in late 1845 word came that another British army was approaching from the east. To forestall it, the Sikh army crossed the Satlej.

The First Sikh War began with two ferocious battles in the vicinity of Ferozepur. From the jaws of defeat, the British edged towards a costly victory which, greatly assisted by the treacherous conduct of Sikh courtier-commanders at odds with their own army, was consummated at Aliwal and Sobraon in early 1846. In the latter battle Sikh losses were believed to total ten thousand and British 2400. A conclusive but expensive bid for Lahore itself was then ruled out as the British opted for the usual peace package consisting of an indemnity, partial annexation, a reduction in the Sikh army and other assorted safeguards.

The annexations included another tranche of the Panjab, which advanced the British frontier from the Satlej river to the Beas. Additionally, in lieu of part of the indemnity, Kashmir with all the hill country between the Beas and the Indus was ceded to the British. Though retaining suzerainty over this vast tract, the British then sold it on to Gulab Singh, the Dogra Raja of Jammu who had been one of Ranjit's feudatories. Having distanced himself from his nominal overlords in Lahore during the recent troubles and acted as intermediary in the peace negotiations, Gulab Singh now finally transferred from Sikh to British vassalage.

Thus was formed the princely state of Jammu and Kashmir, which would descend through Gulab Singh's successors as maharajas until 1947. The sale, for three-quarters of a million pounds, of an entire Indian state was criticised, particularly when its strategic importance at the apex of British India became more apparent. But the anomaly of a Hindu from the Panjab ruling a predominantly Muslim Himalayan kingdom was barely noted. Muslims ruled predominantly Hindu populations in Awadh, Hyderabad and elsewhere. There was no reason to assume that a Hindu ruling Muslims had explosive potential. Nor would it for nearly a century, during which time Kashmir enjoyed a peace and prosperity which had seldom been its lot under either Sikh or Afghan rule.

Rather as Cornwallis's triumph over Tipu in the Third Mysore War had proved to be but a prelude to Wellesley's 'tiger-shoot' in the Fourth, so the First Sikh War was quickly followed by the more conclusive Second. The circumstances were, however, very different. After the First Sikh War, some British troops, a British Resident and a very active staff had been left in the Panjab to uphold and direct the Regency Council operating in the name of the new Maharaja Dhalip Singh, another minor. Only thus, it was argued, could the Sikh court and Council hope to hold its own against still

restless elements in the Sikh army, not to mention the even more disgruntled troops who had been laid off as per the treaty.

In the event the British presence proved sufficiently interventionist to
provoke alarm but insufficiently supported to contain it. In 1848 the maharaja's garrison in the southern city of Multan mutinied and killed two
Englishmen who happened to be there at the time. The speedy despatch
of more British troops would no doubt have taken care of this situation;
but in 1848 India had a new governor-general. This was Lord Dalhousie,
a modernising and imperious workaholic who made no secret of his conviction that India's best interests would be served by the extension of British
rule wherever opportunity offered. The Multan affair was just such an
opportunity. Quickly quashed it would simply entrench the existing regime
but, ignored, it would spread to the rest of the Panjab. In the meantime
sufficient troops could be mobilised along the Sikh frontier for the full-scale
invasion that would assuredly become necessary. Annexation would then
follow as a matter of course.

And so it did. Within four months the mutiny had spread through
much of the Panjab; the mutineers were calling in Afghan assistance; and
the plight of the British staff and troops already in the Panjab was perilous
enough to awaken fears of another Kabul. Once again from Ferozepur a
large British army crossed the Satlaj, then the Ravi and the Chenab. In
early 1849 a major engagement at Chillianwala on the Jhelum was hailed
by the Sikhs as a victory. Although the British pretended otherwise, they
had lost three thousand men in a battle which now superseded Polilur as the
worst defeat suffered by the Company's forces in the Indian subcontinent.
Amends were made a month later at the battle of Gujrat. British victory
led to the surrender of the Sikh army and, with almost indecent haste, to
the arrival of Dalhousie's envoy with the instrument of annexation. 'On
29 March 1849, Maharaja Dhalip Singh held his court for the last time in
his life to sign the document of annexation in Roman letters and to become
a pensioner of the British. The "majestic fabric" raised by Maharaja Ranjit
Singh was a thing of the past.'[11]

Amongst the terms of this Treaty of Lahore was one to the effect that
'the gem called the Koh-i-noor which was taken from Shah Shuja-ul-Mulk
by Maharaja Ranjit Singh shall be surrendered by the Maharaja of Lahore
to the Queen of England.' Mislaid by John Lawrence, a member of the
triumvirate of British officials who now took over the administration of
the Panjab, but rediscovered by his valet, the diamond was entrusted to
Dalhousie, who personally conveyed it from Lahore to Bombay. 'It was
sewn and double sewn into a belt secured round my waist, one end of the

belt fastened to a chain round my neck. It never left me day or night . . .'[12] An unamused Queen Victoria took delivery at Buckingham Palace in 1850.

REFORM AND REACTION

Ahalyabhai Holkar, the 'philosopher-queen' of Malwa, had evidently been an acute observer of the wider political scene. In a letter to the peshwa in 1772 she had warned against association with the British, and likened their embrace to a bear-hug:

> Other beasts, like tigers, can be killed by might or contrivance, but to kill a bear it is very difficult. It will die only if you kill it straight in the face. Or else, once caught in its powerful hold, the bear will kill its prey by tickling. Such is the way of the English. And in view of this, it is difficult to triumph over them.[13]

Other foes made their intentions clear by denunciations of one's family or religion, and by ravaging the countryside and plundering the towns. The British, generally so restrained in their language and so disciplined in the field, were very different. They could make hostility look like friendship and conquest like a favour. It was difficult to rally support against such tactics.

Ahalyabhai's 'other beasts' would no doubt have included Afghans and Muslims in general. Muslim conquerors had been more open in their intentions than the British. In the context of Islam's triumphalism, dislodging infidels and demolishing shrines of idolatry were divinely-ordained activities. And if, for reasons of policy or compassion, these duties were neglected, Muslim historians could be relied on to invent them. Such things were expected of an Islamic ruler and were therefore conventions of Muslim history-writing.

The British, on the other hand, had been wont to disclaim aggression. Of religious zeal and dynastic ambition they had seemed refreshingly free. Indeed their respect for the traditions of Hindu and Muslim was laudable, and their regard for existing institutions of sovereignty positively gratifying. 'Tickled' into clientage, Indian rulers sustained a devastating loss of authority yet might also gain an increment in prestige. From the somewhat chaotic nomenclature of Indian potentates the British began distilling a competitive hierarchy of princely titles and perquisites. 'Rais' and 'rajas' were gratified to find their rank receiving official recognition way beyond its local parameters; some rajas, like the main Maratha and rajput lineages, became 'maharajas'. Amongst Muslims, an Indo-Afghan family was officially recognised as Nawabs – or more often Begums (lady nawabs) – of Bhopal, while the most notorious of the Pindari leaders was 'settled' as the Nawab of Tonk. In Mysore the young Wodeyar had been allowed to take as his regnant name that of 'Krishna-deva-raya III', thereby securing a cherished linkage with the first Krishna-deva-raya who from Vijayanagar had proudly ruled most of the peninsula.

Although sound political calculations underpinned such indulgence, it was not cynical. Company men had often displayed a genuine regard for India's institutions and were intrigued by what they could learn of their antiquity. Inquisitive minds and acquisitive habits had not unnaturally turned from trade-goods and revenue to other gainful pursuits like the mastery of India's languages and literature, the reconstruction of its history, the mapping of its geography, and the classification of its flora and fauna. Formidable dedication and a real sense of wonder made these 'Orientalist' researches more than just satisfying exercises in the intellectual appropriation of India. Informants, mostly brahmans and Jains, were flattered by the foreigners' interest and patronage; and from the 'discoveries' of people like Sir William Jones and James Prinsep, a wider class of educated Indians would imbibe a new awareness of their particularity and new pride in their past. Nehru would be one of several nationalists to concede 'to Jones and to many other European scholars ... a deep debt of gratitude'.[14] Not the least of Warren Hastings' achievements had been the foundation in 1784 of the Bengal Asiatic Society which, under the presidency of Jones, became a veritable clearing-house for intellectual data about India. Hastings, like Jones, was intrigued by India's antiquity and impressed by what he knew of its sacred literature and its legal codes. He hoped that, armed with such information, his fellow-countrymen might govern India in accordance with its own customs and so win the approbation of the governed.

Such idealism outlasted Hastings' era and influenced a generation of turn-of-the-century scholar-administrators. Men like Colin Mackenzie and Thomas Munro in the south, John Malcolm in central India, Mountstuart Elphinstone and his assistant James Grant Duff in Maharashtra, and James Tod in Rajasthan combined senior political or military office with outstanding contributions to the history and geography of their particular areas. As is the way, their scholarship sometimes slipped into active championship of the peoples and dynasts whom they studied, and their histories naturally made a strong case for British intervention. In fact the supposed acquiescence of all but a few Indians in their own conquest became as much a convention of early British history-writing as had the wholesale slaughter of Indians by Islamic conquerors in the chronicles of Muslim writers.

Thus Malcolm, from his experience of central India in the 1820s, insisted on 'the general opinion of the natives of our comparative superiority in good faith, wisdom and strength, to their own rulers'. True or false, this assumption had, in the case of Malcolm and others, something of a self-fulfilling effect. When challenged by a new and less cosy orthodoxy, he spelled out the *beau ideal* on which the good opinion of Indians rested.

> This important impression will be improved by the consideration we show to their habits, institutions and religions – by the moderation, temper and kindness, with which we conduct ourselves towards them; and [it will be] injured by every act which offends their belief or superstition, that shows disregard or neglect of individuals or communities, or evinces our having, with the arrogance of conquerors, forgotten those maxims by which this great empire has been established, and by which alone it can be preserved.[15]

Thomas Munro, more familiar with the realities of British rule in the long-settled districts around Madras, demurred from such self-satisfied paternalism. It was true that other foreign conquerors had treated Indians with greater violence and cruelty, 'but none has treated them with so much scorn as we, none has stigmatised the whole people as unworthy of trust, as incapable of honesty, and as fit to be employed only where we cannot do without them'. Justice and government should be dispensed 'through the natives themselves' for, as he told the Company's directors:

> Your rule is alien and it can never be popular. You have much to give your subjects but you cannot look for more than passive gratitude ... Work through, not in spite of, native systems and native ways with a prejudice in their favour rather than against them; and when in the fulness of time your subjects can frame and maintain a worthy Government for themselves, get out and take the glory of the achievement and the sense of having done your duty as the chief reward for your exertions.[16]

Whether patronising or pessimistic, such early-nineteenth-century attitudes had, however, become anathema by mid-century. A sea-change had come over British perceptions of responsible government. 'The general opinion of the natives' was no longer worthy of mention. The chance of any 'prejudice in their favour' had faded forever. And the 'Orientalist' ideal of a government conforming to Indian traditions, already tarnished by the rapacious nabobs, had been obliterated by a compound of cold utilitarian logic, cloying Christian ideology, and molten free-trade evangelism.

The free-trade lobby insisted that India's economy be opened to British investment and enterprise, and thus challenged the monopoly of eastern trade on which the East India Company had been founded. Subject to increasing supervision by the British government from the late 1770s and to direct management by a government Board of Control from 1785, the Company had already lost its political independence and much of its patronage. Its commercial assets were now stripped in the name of free trade. Backed by manufacturing interests in Britain anxious to obtain access to India's markets, and by British business houses in Asia keen to compete in the out-and-back carrying trade and exploit Indian production, the government made the periodic renewals of the Company's royal charter contingent on the surrender of its commercial privileges. In a wasting process not unlike that experienced by Mysore or the Maratha states, the Company was thus forced to make concessions in 1793, to surrender its monopoly of trade with India in 1813, and its monopoly of the even more valuable trade with China in 1833.

Stripped of its commercial assets, the Company's surviving function was mainly as a political front and a military scapegoat. London's ignorance and India's distance might commend the Company's continuance, but so did the fiction of its being less accountable than a government department; 'Company mismanagement', after all, sounded a lot less damaging than 'official maladministration'. Even, therefore, as its armies streamed triumphantly across the subcontinent, the Honourable Company's power and direction had drained away. The Afghan, Sind and Sikh campaigns were either prompted by the British government or provoked by its appointees. The Company acquiesced because it had, in effect, been nationalised. Like the Nawabs of Awadh living their extravagant pageant under British 'protection' at Lucknow, or like the ex-peshwa on his pension at Kanpur, or the Mughal himself rattling about the airless chambers of his Delhi fort, the Honourable Company had become just another of India's waxwork despots, dripping beneath the trappings of a defunct sovereignty.

Amongst other conditions of the Company's charter renewal in 1813 had been its reluctantly-given agreement to allow Christian missions to operate in India. The danger of Hindus and Muslims perceiving British rule as a threat to their religions had long been appreciated. But with the evangelical Clapham Sect in London making converts of a governor-general (Sir John Shore) and a leading Company director, as well as exercising a powerful influence in Westminster, the pressure from missionary enterprises became irresistible. William Wilberforce, the anti-slavery champion who was also a member of the Clapham Sect, declared missionary access to India to be 'that greatest of all causes, for I really place it before Abolition [of the slave trade]'.[17] It was so very important, he told the House of Commons in 1813, because 'our religion is sublime, pure and beneficent [while] theirs is mean, licentious and cruel.' Echoing the Muslim horror of idolatry, he declared the Hindu deities 'absolute monsters of lust, injustice, wickedness and cruelty', a sentiment with which James Mill, author of *The History of British India* (published in 1820), readily agreed. Since Hinduism was 'the most enormous and tormenting superstition that ever harassed and degraded any portion of mankind', Hindus were indeed 'the most enslaved portion of the human race'.[18] Emancipating them from this 'grand abomination' was as much the sacred duty of every Christian as emancipating Africans from slavery.

With Lord William Bentinck, an Evangelical sympathiser, as governor-general (1828–35) a start was made on India's 'reformation' with legislation to outlaw practices like widow-burning (*sati*, suttee) and ritualised highway killing (*thagi*, thuggee). Neither was particularly common, nor were they in any sense central or peculiar to Hindu orthodoxy. The effect of legislating against them, whilst it probably saved some lives, was principally to stigmatise Hinduism as indeed abominable to Christian consciences. Although Indian converts to Christianity were few and although Indians were shielded from the worst tirades of Evangelicalism, its assertive new ideology gained a degree of acceptance amongst the British in India. Their rule itself became increasingly imbued with a sense of divine mission, their earlier toleration and even support of Indian religions evaporated, their conviction of Christianity's moral superiority grew, and their solicitude for the taboos of their subjects was eroded by carelessness and ignorance. When an ambitious army chaplain or a well-meaning subaltern favoured the sepoys under his command with a homily on 'Christian values', they might once have indulged him. Now, apprised of a rumoured conversion or smarting under a caste affront, they fidgeted with apprehension.

Wilberforce had never been to India. Nor had James Mill who, as a historian and then as an influential employee of the Company in London, subjected the theory and practice of government in India to the scientific analysis of Utilitarian political thought. Inexperience of India's beguiling humanity and its bewildering diversity lent great clarity to such exercises. To Mill and his associates, including his son and successor in the employ of the Company, John Stuart Mill, it was axiomatic that 'the greatest happiness of the greatest number' depended on the formulation of laws whose 'utility' and morality were to be judged by simple, quantifiable criteria of maximum benefit. In Britain the Industrial Revolution had sparked expectations of a steady steam-driven progress towards ever greater prosperity and betterment, in which all would be entitled to participate through social and electoral reform. Although a pre-industrial society such as India's was clearly no candidate for enfranchisement, there too reform and modernisation were deemed the order of the day.

'Light taxes and good laws – nothing more is wanting for national and individual prosperity all over the globe,' declared the elder Mill. Bentinck concurred, and during his long governor-generalship he pruned expenditure, legislated furiously, and pushed through a variety of modernising reforms. But pruning expenditure was not without effect on the army, where allowances were reduced; nor did it lead to lighter taxes. Taxes being principally land revenue, a voluminous controversy was underway between advocates of the 'Permanent' revenue settlement introduced in Bengal by Cornwallis and those of the *ryotwari* system favoured by Munro in the south. The former, influenced by existing Bengali practice and by British ideas of a propertied aristocracy, made the major *zamindars* responsible for collection and payment; recognised as lords of the land, they became in effect landlords. The Munro system, influenced by the more self-sufficient traditions of south Indian villages, depended on direct collection from individual 'ryots', or peasant farmers, and regarded all superior intermediaries as parasites. Utilitarian thought naturally favoured the latter which, with considerable modification, was eventually applied in the Maratha lands and then in what the British called the 'North-West Provinces' around Delhi and Agra.

But in heated argument over the respective merits of the two systems, it was often overlooked that both rested on some novel assumptions of disturbing potential: revenue responsibility was taken to indicate actual ownership of the lands in question; default in payment was taken as grounds for dispossession by legal process; and enthusiasm for all such settlements presumed a maximum of assessment and a minimum of exception. The cultivator, unless he was also the revenue payer, thus became a mere tenant; and, by both tenant and landlord, security of tenure could no longer be taken for granted. Heavy assessments were no novelty, although they had usually been interspersed with periods of respite or relaxation. Under the British the demand was inelastic and inexorable. If debts incurred to meet the demand went unpaid, creditors foreclosed, and 'properties' were distrained by the courts, then sold on the open market. Although the accusation that the British Collector in alliance with the Indian moneylender undermined the country's rural economy may be an oversimplification, government intervention on a continuous and disruptive basis could not but attract such criticism and occasion deep hostility.

This was heightened by a flurry of legislation in the name of Mill's 'good laws'. To assist Bentinck in their formulation, Thomas Babington Macaulay, the son of an eminent Evangelical leader, was sent to India as Law Member on the Governor-General's Council. His model Penal Code was not introduced until two decades later, and his most telling contribution to the cause of reform proved to be in the field of education. The missionaries had identified literacy and education as essential to their promotion of Christianity. Macaulay, with a Utilitarian's belief in European science and culture as the epitome of modernity and enlightenment, insisted that it be English literacy and a Western curriculum. His object was, as he put it, to create 'a class of persons Indian in colour and blood, but English in tastes, in opinions, in morals, and in intellect . . . who may be interpreters between us and the millions we govern'.[19] The available funds were paltry but the principle was accepted and, as of 1835, for government as for education, English became the officially recognised language. Instead of the British essaying a slender command of Indian languages and then venturing across the cultural chasm to accommodate India's institutions and traditions, Indians were to be encouraged onto the rungs of Anglicisation and thence into the realms of Western thought and science.

It was a momentous decision which Indian opinion would eventually applaud. Demands for independence, when they materialised, would be couched in the language, and based on the principles, of Western liberal thought; the British would thus be hoist on their own petard. Arguably it also spared India the revolutions which would eventually overtake China and Russia. But it was not made without severing support for the study of Sanskrit and Persian, alienating those brahmans and *maulvis* (Muslim educators) who taught and cherished these languages, and savagely disparaging the arts, literature and traditions of ancient India. In arguing his case on the grounds that 'a single shelf of a good European library was worth the whole native literature of India and Arabia', Macaulay was betraying even the scholarship of his fellow-countrymen. His notorious tirade against 'medical doctrines which would disgrace an English farrier, astronomy which would move laughter in girls at an English boarding school, history abounding with kings thirty feet high and reigns thirty thousand years long, and geography made up of seas of treacle and seas of butter', though meant as ridicule, now reads as merely ridiculous.

Just as with the Evangelical condemnation of India's religions, so this assault on India's literary heritage affected the rulers as much as the ruled. For the British the cultural chasm was no longer a challenge. Secure in the conviction that their own intellectual achievements, artistic tastes and moral precepts were infinitely superior and would, if assiduously practised, soon be emulated, they increasingly withdrew into a way of life that owed as little as possible to India. As communications improved, wives and daughters opted to join their menfolk not just in the cities but also in the garrison towns of the upcountry '*mofussil*' (the hinterland, as opposed to the 'presidency', cities). Here gardens bloomed brightly behind thickets of prickly pear, amateur dramatics flourished, and the tailor turned dressmaker. But with memsahibs about, the servants had perforce to be removed to an outhouse; the club closed its doors to Indians; and the vicar often came to tea. The British were drawing apart, losing touch, becoming less approachable.

Although after Bentinck the cause of reform faltered as the Afghan, Sind and Sikh wars consumed the attentions of government, the conviction remained that British rule was indisputably the best on offer. That its benefits should therefore, in accordance with Christian duty and Utilitarian logic, be extended to as many Indians as possible seemed self-evident to Governor-General Lord Dalhousie. Under his vigorous direction, reform and modernisation were resumed in the 1850s. New laws protecting the rights of Hindu widows to remarry and of lapsed Hindus (mostly Christian converts) to retain their inheritance rights were eminently reasonable, but again ventured into the contentious domain of established practice. Meanwhile public works of undoubted utility, like surveys, roads, railways, telegraph lines and irrigation schemes, were bringing government into direct contact with the rural masses and dramatically demonstrating its power as an agency for change. On the new maps it looked as if India was about to be ensnared in a steel tangle of wires and railway tracks.

Caste taboos were not allowed to impede the march of progress, and there was much fuss over railway carriages not offering caste seclusion. To Dalhousie and his advisers it was equally obvious that the native states, or 'those petty intervening principalities' as he called them, should not interrupt the advance of the train and telegraph. Nor was there any reason why those who had had the misfortune to be born under a native dispensation should be excluded from the benefits of such progress and modernity. Hence Dalhousie's insistence on 'consolidating the territories which already belong to us by taking possession of States that may lapse in the midst of them'.

The doctrine of 'the right of lapse' held that the paramount power might assume the sovereignty of a state whose ruler was either manifestly incompetent or who died without a direct heir. Since the latter ignored the long-established right of an Indian sovereign to adopt an heir of his own choosing, and since the former was obviously a matter of opinion, the doctrine had hitherto been invoked rarely and with great caution. Now it abruptly became an obligation; the government, in Dalhousie's words, was 'bound to take that which is justly and rightly its due'. In fact he annexed seven states in as many years. They included Satara in the Maratha heartland, where Shivaji's direct descendants had long reigned; the Bhonsles' Nagpur, where insult was added to injury with a callous dispersal sale of the maharaja's effects; and Jhansi, another albeit minor Maratha raj whose youthful rani exhibited something of the character of Ahalyabhai Holkar but to whom widowhood now merely brought the added pain of deposition and dispossession.

Other rulers were greatly alarmed. The Mughal emperor had already been demoted to 'King of Delhi' and his image had been removed from the coinage. Now it was being suggested by Dalhousie that his successor be recognised as no more than a prince and that the Delhi Red Fort in which he held court be handed over to the British. Similarly Nana Sahib, the heir adopted by the Peshwa Baji Rao II while in exile near Kanpur, found himself not only stateless but pensionless and title-less. Like other disappointed princes and pensioners, he appealed to London but received no satisfaction. Several senior British political officers, including the Residents at Satara and Nagpur, also raised strong objections and insisted that the deposed dynasties enjoyed the affection of their subjects. But Dalhousie, never a man to welcome advice from subordinates, was unimpressed. In 1856, on the eve of his departure from India, he delivered his masterstroke by annexing Awadh – or Oudh as the British insistently spelled it.

Nearly the largest, probably the richest, and certainly the most senior and the most loyal of all the native states, Awadh's extinction seemed to call into question that good faith on which the British so prided themselves. Since the days of Clive, its rulers had been the Company's allies, graciously accepting a succession of territorial and financial demands and providing much of the manpower for the Company's Bengal army. It was true that latterly the nawabs – or 'kings' as the British now preferred, in a further blow to the Mughals' pride – had set something of a record in irresponsible government. Lucknow (Laknau), Awadh's adopted capital as of the turn of the century, had come to combine the monumental magnificence of Shah Jahan's Delhi with the scented allure of Scheherazade's Baghdad. In

BRITISH GOVERNORS-GENERAL

1770		
1780	HASTINGS, Warren	1773–1785
	* MACPHERSON, Sir John	1785–1786
1790	CORNWALLIS, Charles, 2nd Earl of Cornwallis	1786–1793
	SHORE, Sir John	1793–1798
1800	WELLESLEY, Richard, 2nd Earl of Mornington	1798–1805
	CORNWALLIS, Charles, 2nd Earl of Cornwallis	1805
	* BARLOW, Sir George	1805–1807
1810	Elliot, Sir Gilbert, 1st Earl of MINTO	1807–1813
1820	Hastings, Francis, 2nd Earl of MOIRA	1813–1823
	* ADAM, John	1823–1824
	AMHERST, William, 1st Earl of Amherst	1824–1828
1830	BENTINCK, Lord William	1828–1835
	* METCALF, Sir Charles	1835
1840	Eden, George, 1st Earl of AUCKLAND	1835–1841
	Law, Edward, 1st Earl of ELLENBOROUGH	1841–1844
	HARDINGE, Sir Henry	1844–1848
1850	Ramsay, Sir James, 10th Earl of DALHOUSIE	1848–1856
1860	CANNING, Charles, 1st Earl of Canning	1856–1862

* **Acting Governor-General**

a final outburst of what used to be called 'Indo-Saracenic' architecture, the nawabs endowed their city with palaces, gateways, halls and mosques of riotous profile. The Great Imambara, fifty metres long and fifteen high, may be the largest vaulted hall in the world and is certainly 'one of the most impressive buildings in India'.[20] But if it dates from 1780, it is old by Lucknow standards; most of the city's monuments are nineteenth-century and owe their distressed aspect simply to the intensity of the bombardment which Awadh was about to undergo, plus the chronic neglect which followed.

No less sensational was Lucknow's lavish lifestyle. As connoisseurs of the exquisite and the exotic, the nawabs supported the most celebrated Urdu poets, Persian calligraphers and Shi'ite divines. In the royal employ Hindu minstrels, dancers and impersonators mingled with English barbers, Scottish bagpipers and European clockmakers. Closer still to the royal person moved a swarm of eunuchs, courtesans, concubines and catamites. In short, to the best of their limited abilities the last nawabs fulfilled to the bejewelled hilt their role as the dissipated Oriental despots of European imagining.

But as the Company's own directors had admitted in 1828, it was the British government which was largely responsible; for 'such a state of disorganisation can nowhere attain permanence except where the short-sightedness and rapacity of such a barbarous government is armed with the military strength of a civilised one.'[21] British troops not only guaranteed Awadh's security; they also helped enforce the state's revenue demands. Its nawabs therefore had little to do but spend the proceeds. Nor was their extravagance always objectionable. Loans extracted from the Awadh government had part-financed several of the Company's wars, and in the case of the Gurkha War of 1814–16 had paid for the entire affair.

Under the terms of an 1801 treaty the nawabs were also bound to rule in the interests of their subjects and to accept British advice when tendered. In fact they did neither. Dalhousie's decision to annex followed repeated warnings and was prompted by genuine outrage over 'this disgrace to our empire'. Whether his decision was also 'just, practicable and right' as he contended is another matter. Legally it was doubtful, and the doubts were compounded first by the nawab's refusal to sign the instrument of accession and secondly by Dalhousie's decision to use limited force. There was also the question of Awadh's very desirable revenue. Had this played no part in British calculations, and had the spendthrift habits of the nawabs been the main reason for annexation, some of this revenue might reasonably have been earmarked for investment in Awadh. In fact it simply disappeared into the Company's coffers.

To the people of Awadh the whole affair was inexplicable, indeed indefensible.

> Few could really understand why their weak, harmless prince, who
> had done the British no injury, but like his ancestors, had ever
> been faithful to them, should be thrust aside. He was not a cruel
> tyrant and his self-indulgence and careless neglect of his subjects'
> welfare were not, in their eyes, such heinous offences as they were
> to the British.[22]

In place of 'careless neglect' and paternal exploitation the British signalled their arrival by introducing a radical hands-on reformation of the
revenue collection. Based on experience gained in the neighbouring North-
West Provinces of British India and informed by the principle of dealing
direct with the cultivator, it instantly alienated Awadh's influential aristocracy of rich hereditary revenue farmers, or *taluqdars*, while seemingly alarm-
ing the cultivating classes whom it was supposed to benefit.

Annexation also had the effect, as in the Panjab, of demobilising part
of the Awadh army and, worse still, of undermining the privileges enjoyed
by the forty thousand men of the Company's Bengal army who had been
recruited in Awadh. With their homeland reduced to the status of a British
province, these men lost rights of appeal and redress, previously exercised
through British influence with the nawab's government, which had guaranteed to their families and kinsmen a certain security and immunity. Now
they differed from all the other brahman and rajput sepoys recruited in
the neighbouring British districts of Bihar, Varanasi and Allahabad only in
the depth of their suspicions. They shared grievances over such matters as
serving outside India; they shared fears about the intent of alien rulers who
seemed increasingly indifferent to their religious beliefs; and they added
something very like a national grievance resulting from the faithless treatment meted out to their hereditary ruler in Lucknow. Any of these might
have provoked mutinous protests; some already had. Together they became
grounds for rebellion.

1857 AND ALL THAT

'The events of 1857 . . . have provoked more impassioned literature than any
other single event in Indian history.'[23] They generated much contemporary
documentation and they have since often been taken to mark a watershed
in both British rule and the Indian response to it. But the interpretation

Left Robert, Baron Clive of Plassey, engraving after a portrait by J. Drummond. While engineering British supremacy in Bengal, Clive realised a colossal fortune, yet, with reason, stood 'astonished at my own moderation'.

Below Warren Hastings, first British governor-general of India, from a painting by Sir Joshua Reynolds. A reluctant imperialist, Hastings found himself elevating the British presence in India to a position of paramountcy.

Previous page The City Palace, Udaipur, Rajasthan, from 1567. Udaipur was adopted by the (Maha)rana of Mewar after Akbar's sacking of Chitor. Here James Tod gathered the materials for his epic account of the rajput clans.

Lakshmi Bai, Rani of Jhansi. The Indian Joan of Arc, Lakshmi Bai's exploits during the Great Rebellion won her even British regard as 'the only man amongst the rebels'.

Opposite above The Indian National Congress at Allahabad, December 1888. George Yule, president (seated centre), with local convenor Pandit Ayodhia Nath (on his right), and William Wedderburn and secretary A.O. Hume (on his left).

Opposite below George Nathaniel, Lord Curzon (centre), on a tiger-shoot. Curzon, the most brilliant of British viceroys, precipitated the first great surge of nationalist resistance with his ill-judged partition of Bengal.

Above Lala Lajpat Rai, Bal Gangadhar Tilak and Bipin Chandra Pal. As 'Lal-Bal-Pal', the Panjabi *Arya Samaj* leader, the great Maharashtrian firebrand and the radical Bengali editor spearheaded *swadeshi* protest in 1907.

M. K. ('Mahatma') Gandhi leading the April 1930 Salt March. In the set-piece which launched the civil disobedience movement, Gandhi upheld man's inalienable right to the untaxed enjoyment of a common condiment.

Above Jawaharlal Nehru and Mohammed Ali Jinnah at the Simla Conference, 1945.
The Partition of British India into Jinna's Pakistan and Nehru's Republic of India
would provoke one of the twentieth century's greatest tragedies.

Opposite Protestors on the streets of Calcutta during the Quit India movement of
1942. In this wartime protest the British recognised the most violent phase of the
independence struggle and reacted accordingly.

Left Prime Minister Indira Gandhi. The most controversial of the Nehru-Gandhi dynasty, Mrs Gandhi dominated the political scene for nearly twenty years, but suborned the consensus on which it rested.

Below Rajiv Gandhi (third from left) at the cremation of his mother, Indira Gandhi. Mrs Gandhi's 1984 assassination by Sikh extremists, and a retaliatory massacre of Sikhs in Delhi, plunged India into crisis and precipitated Rajiv's elevation to office.

of these events remains controversial, and so does their title. Known to the British as 'the Sepoy', 'Bengal' or 'Indian Mutiny', to Indians as 'the National Uprising' or 'the First War of Independence', and to the less partisan of both nations simply as 'the Great Rebellion', what happened in 1857 defies simplistic analysis.

For example, equating the rebellion with a traditional, even 'feudal', form of reaction whose failure would usher in the new age of nationalism and politically organised protest is no longer completely acceptable. Many different groups with as many different grievances became aligned with either side in the Great Rebellion. The rights and wrongs of British rule were not always a decisive factor and the frontier between the two sides sliced through both agrarian and urban communities, both settled and nomadic peoples, both high caste and low, landlord and tenant, Muslim and Hindu. Paradoxically there was thus something of a national character in the composition of those who opposed the rebellion as well as in that of those who supported it.

Of the insurgents' various grievances, many were long-standing and had provoked earlier protests and mutinies. Some of these grievances had been, and continued to be, articulated in nationalist terms. But they lacked a pan-Indian dimension, and this mirrored the lack of overall cohesion in the British government of India itself, with each presidency (Calcutta/ Bengal, Madras, Bombay) still having its own army and its own administration. Thus, although the Rebellion commanded support amongst most communities in much of northern India, and although recognisably nationalist rhetoric contributed to it, large parts of the future nation, together with the most important centres of British rule, were quite unaffected. Moreover, if 'historians of the future will begin to define the content of nationalism much more widely and to date its origins much earlier',[24] no less surely will traditional forms of resistance based on hereditary leaders and local grievances be discerned long after 1857. The great 'watershed' of British–Indian relations, in other words, proves to be a broad plateau where the run of the rivulets is often contradictory.

But at least there is agreement that the Great Rebellion began as a rising within the Company's Bengal army. It was not the first. On the eve of Baksar, nearly a century earlier, the Company's Indian sepoys had refused orders and been horribly executed by Hector Munro. In 1806 at Vellore in Tamil Nadu new regulations about uniforms and the wearing of a cap-badge of leather (always repugnant to Hindus) had prompted a violent mutiny in the Madras army. And, as noted, during the Burmese, Sind and Panjab wars sepoys had staged several mutinies when denied compensation for the loss of caste involved in serving 'overseas'.

In 1857, soon after Dalhousie had fanned this still simmering discontent about 'overseas' service, the Bengal sepoys became aware of another development which would compromise their beliefs. A new rifle was being issued for which the cartridges, which had to be rammed down the barrel, were being greased with a tallow probably containing both pigs' fat and cows' fat. Moreover, the cartridges had first to be bitten open with the teeth. To cow-reverencing Hindus as to pig-paranoid Muslims the new ammunition could not have been more disgusting had it been smeared with excrement; nor, had it been dipped in hemlock, could it have been more deadly to their religious prospects.

Although the offending cartridges were quickly withdrawn, all existing cartridges immediately became suspect. So did other official issues like those of flour and cooking oil. Detected in such an underhand attempt, the British were deemed capable of adulterating anything whereby they might compromise the sepoy's religion and so advance his conversion to Christianity. In Bengal itself a serious mutiny over the cartridges was easily suppressed in February 1857, but as the rumours and the rancour spread upcountry they multiplied and were magnified.

The evidence for any organised incitement is unconvincing. Shared distrust was sufficient to concert action, British arrogance sufficient to incite it. At Meerut (Mirat), an important garrison town about sixty kilometres from Delhi, a particularly insensitive British command courtmartialled eighty-five troopers for refusing suspect cartridges and then publicly humiliated them in front of the entire garrison. Next day their comrades-in-arms at Meerut rose as one to free them. They also broke into the armoury and began massacring the local European community. It was early May, a hot month in a parched province. Tinder-dry, the wattle huts of the garrison and the thatched roofs of the officers' lines ignited at the kiss of a torch.

As a metaphor, spark and tinder would feature widely in contemporary British accounts. Meerut lit the 'conflagration' which then 'spread like wildfire' across the parched Gangetic plain and deep into the forest scrub of central India. There was no knowing where or when the 'flames of rebellion' would break out next; even when extinguished, they often 'flared up' again. By perceiving the mutiny as a natural disaster the British tried to come to terms with it. How else to explain an indiscriminate ferocity, their own as well as the enemy's, whereby innocents and onlookers, women and children, were routinely killed to no obvious purpose?

To the mutineers, however, the conflagration was not without purpose. From Meerut, the first insurgents headed immediately for Delhi, there to seek out the higher authority of the Mughal emperor. Bahadur Shah Zafar (or Bahadur Shah II) was eighty-two and had reigned from Shah Jahan's Red Fort for the past twenty years, a king with neither subjects nor troops. The sudden accession of both scarcely improved his position. With his local British sponsors outwitted, outnumbered and quickly evicted from the city, and with their sepoys joining the men from Meerut, he had little choice but to endorse the insurgents' cause. But if the insurgents did the Mughal no favours, the Mughal's co-option transformed the insurgency. Within hours of its outbreak, a regimental mutiny had acquired the character of a political revolt whose legitimacy arguably transcended that of the regime it challenged. 'For there is not the slightest doubt that the rebels wanted to get rid of the alien government and restore the old order of which the King of Delhi was the rightful representative.'[25]

If the example of Meerut prompted a host of other military mutinies, the sanction of the Mughal invited a swarm of civilian adherents. To all who sought redress for past grievances or reassurance over future fears the rebellion now provided a lawful focus. It was the British and their local allies, principally Sikhs, Gurkhas and others from beyond the margins of *arya-varta* (the Aryan homeland), who were regarded as the subversives. The Sikhs in particular, long hostile to Mughal rule and lately worsted by the now mutinous Bengal army, rallied to the British cause. Meanwhile in the Panjab and elsewhere hasty British disarmament and disbandment of suspect Bengal units contributed to the sense of a faith that had been broken and an authority transferred. The enemy was no longer the British government but the entire British presence plus all those who, unless they proved otherwise, had supported it or benefited by it. The old order was being restored, the clock set back; Bahadur Shah was appointing a governing council; Awadh had erupted; Kanpur had fallen; Agra, Allahabad, Varanasi and Gwalior seethed with dissent. Instead of a dry-season conflagration, to the insurgents their uprising partook of the green renewal heralded by the god-given monsoon which in late June duly blessed their struggle.

By then a force comprised of British, Sikh and Gurkha units had returned to the Ridge just north of Delhi. Although neither the British on the Ridge nor the insurgents in the city were actually besieged, for two months both sides engaged in the sallies, bombardments and reinforcements typical of a siege situation. Within the city, attempts to set up an administration floundered on the unruliness of the sepoys and the incompetence of the Mughal court. Many of the insurgents had dispersed elsewhere when in September the city finally fell to a British assault. The British, nevertheless, suffered heavy casualties which left them thirsting for revenge. Another indiscriminate massacre, another orgy of looting was added to Delhi's record of woe. Two of Bahadur Shah's sons and a grandson were shot while in custody, supposedly to thwart an escape. The emperor himself traded trial and ignominy for a few more months of an already wretched existence. Exiled to Rangoon, the last Mughal died 'a plaything of fortune, in a foreign land, far from the country of his ancestors, unhonoured and unsung, but maybe not altogether unwept'.[26]

Delhi, like the Mughal, had served its purpose. To the insurgents its loss was less disastrous than it had been to the British. Poorly armed compared to the British forces, lacking a command structure and hampered by weak communications, the rebels were ill-equipped to hold prestigious strongpoints or defend strategic frontiers. Their capabilities and their composition, now heavily diluted by irregular local militias, unruly bands of aggrieved cultivators and the firebrands of various religious and agrarian movements, were better suited to wide-ranging tactics of mobility, concentration and dispersal.

By September 1857 it was clear that south of the Narmada river the rebellion enjoyed little support; the Madras and Bombay armies remained loyal to the British. To the north-west Sind was indifferent, Kashmir's new maharaja supported the British, and the Panjab provided a steady stream of Sikh and Pathan recruits. In the east, Bengal itself and most of Bihar were neutralised by the prompt arrival of British troops redirected from imperial duties in China and the Persian Gulf. The rebellion thus became largely confined to the vast mid-Gangetic region which now comprises the states of Uttar Pradesh and Madhya Pradesh together with adjacent areas of Rajasthan and Bihar.

In the midst of this region Awadh – the recruiting ground whence a third of the mutinous Bengal army had traditionally been drawn, the erstwhile kingdom whose free-spending nawab had so recently been dispossessed, and the now-British province whose revenue system had just been so disastrously reorganised – became the main arena of revolt. Indeed in Awadh the rebellion transcended both its origin as an army mutiny and its transformation into a political revolt. It became, indeed, a genuinely populist uprising rooted in rural support. Amongst the Awadh insurgents armed retainers and rural militias outnumbered the Bengal mutineers. Lucknow now eclipsed Delhi as the military focus of the rising; and the Nana Sahib, the adopted heir of the last peshwa, emerged to replace the Mughal as its figurehead.

Amongst the British community in Kanpur the portly Nana Sahib had once been a popular figure. Although the loss of the peshwa's pension gave

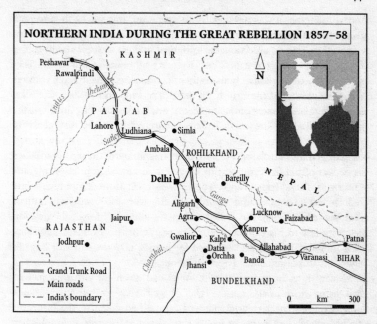

him a grudge against the British government, his support for the insurgents seems, like that of the Mughal, to have been given with some reluctance, and his authority over the mutineers remains doubtful. He nevertheless assumed the defunct peshwa-ship and took the surrender, after a three-week siege, of the four hundred British in Kanpur. For their massacre as they boarded boats to take them downriver to Allahabad, he was technically guilty as the guarantor of their safe-conduct. But at the time passions were running high. Reports of draconian British reprisals at Varanasi were followed by news of an avenue of gibbets along the road thence to Allahabad. Retribution was advancing up the Ganga; on the riverbank at Kanpur mercy must have seemed out of place. The first shots were probably mischievous. The Nana Sahib, far from ordering the massacre, organised the rescue of some British women who were abducted during the ensuing chaos.

They, along with other surviving women and children, perhaps two hundred in all, were then lodged under the Nana Sahib's protection. With the avenging British forces now fast approaching from Allahabad, the intention seems to have been to use these captives as hostages. But if that was indeed the plan, it was never put into operation. Instead, as the insurgent commanders debated escape, orders were issued for the captives' extermination. The task, so objectionable to trained soldiers, was eventually undertaken by five bazaar recruits. Two were actually butchers by trade. Their slaughterhouse methods, clumsy rather than sadistic, constituted an atrocity which would haunt the British till the end of their Indian days. For sheer barbarity this 'massacre of the innocents' was rivalled only by the disgusting deaths devised for dozens of equally innocent Indians by way of British reprisal.

The Nana Sahib claimed to have been as ignorant of the second massacre as he was of the first. Along with his ablest commander, a fellow Maratha known as Tatya Topi (Tantia Topi), he escaped from Kanpur, was later reported at Lucknow, and would continue with the insurgents until he disappeared in Nepal. But, noted mainly for a louche lifestyle, he owed his celebrity less to his exploits and more to the British need for scapegoats plus Indian nationalism's later need for heroes. Like the emperor Bahadur Shah, his importance was largely symbolic.

Meanwhile the recapture of Kanpur had given the British a forward base from which to attempt the relief of their fellow-countrymen in Lucknow. Awadh's spectacularly endowed capital had fallen to the insurgents at the end of June (1857), at which time about 750 European combatants, as many Indian soldiers, and about 1400 servants, women and children had taken refuge in a fortified area around the British Residency on the outskirts of the city. Here they made a defiant stand which developed into a remarkable siege. With the first relief effort in late September serving merely to reinforce the defence, the siege lasted nearly five months. It captured the imagination of India's entire British community, for whom Lucknow became a microcosm of the 'mutiny', and its saga of brave deeds, shattered hopes and ultimate redemption an enduring reminder.

> The little band in the Residency did more than make history. In a sense they made scripture, for their refuge became one of the holy places of British Imperialism and their struggle, reiterated in verse and prose, re-enacted on the stage and refought in spirit, summarised the Imperial ethos and furnished the Imperial dogma with all the apparatus of miracles and martyrs.[27]

The massacre at Kanpur, or rather 'Cawnpore' as it was known to the British, was too shocking for polite English mention; it was banished to the sweat-soaked realm of nightmares and high fevers. But Lucknow was a soaring triumph of the spirit, eminently worth mythologising, and defiantly commemorated by the Union Jack which would fly, night and day, above the ravaged Residency for the remaining ninety years of British rule.

To the insurgents too, Lucknow was important. The siege of the Residency provided a sustained focus for the revolt in Awadh. The longer it lasted, the more committed became both Hindu and Muslim participants and the more persuaded became the great rural *taluqdars*. Lucknow flourished again as a source of power and authority. A supposed son of the last nawab was enthroned, and a skeleton administration set up in his name. It lasted until March 1858 when the city finally fell to the largest British army, as opposed to Sepoy army, ever mustered in India. Suppressing the insurgency in the rest of Awadh took another year, plus a complete reversal of the 1856 land settlement. But with the fall of Lucknow and the ruthless sacking of this 'Babylon of India' the Great Rebellion lost all momentum.

The final scenes of defiance occurred to the south of the Jamuna in the wilder territory, mostly under princely rule, between the Chambal and Betwa rivers. This was Bundelkhand and amongst its states was that of Jhansi, a small Maratha principality south of Scindhia's Gwalior which had been annexed under Dalhousie's 'doctrine of lapse'. Lakshmi Bai, the last raja's widow, made a strong impression on those British who took over her state. She was 'of high character [and] much respected by everyone'; she was also comparatively young and possessed of 'many charms' and 'a remarkably fine figure'. Although, like the Mughal and the Nana Sahib, she had a strong grievance against the British, she too seems to have played no part in the mutiny of the Bengal troops stationed in Jhansi. There, in a carbon copy of events in Kanpur, the small British community had sought refuge in the local fort but soon accepted proposals for its evacuation. They then straggled out under what they thought was a safe-conduct and were promptly massacred. Again Lakshmi Bai may have been innocent. She blamed the mutinous troops and insisted that she too had been their victim, having been forced to part with funds and her few guns. The mutineers then marched off to Agra and Delhi leaving her implicated and defenceless.

No British troops were available to deal with this comparatively minor affair, but the rani soon found herself challenged both by a rival claimant to her husband's defunct title and by the neighbouring rajput rajas of Datia and Orchha. When the latter invaded Jhansi, supposedly on behalf of the British, she began raising troops and herself led them in repulsing the assault. This was in September and October 1857. It is notable that the rani's considerable military reputation was first acquired fighting not the British but local rivals and that, though her forces were drawn largely from elements who had aligned themselves with the Rebellion, in her correspon-

dence she continued to protest her fidelity to the British. In effect old
dynastic scores were being settled and new opportunities exploited under
cover of the Rebellion.

The situation changed in early 1858 with the northward advance of a
section of the British Bombay army. Having received no encouragement
from her various letters to the British, the rani and her advisers rightly
assumed that her reassertion of Jhansi's sovereignty was threatened and her
own safety in danger. Now, if not earlier, she definitely became reconciled to
rebellion and established contact with Tatya Topi, the Nana Sahib's protégé
who had established himself at Kalpi on the Jamuna. When the British laid
siege to Jhansi in March, Tatya came to her aid but was repulsed. After a
ferocious resistance led by Lakshmi Bai herself, Jhansi fell; but of its fearless
commander, 'the Jezebel of India' as a fanciful British writer called her,[28]
there was no sign. In one of those hair's-breadth escapes so dear to Maratha
folklore, she slipped out in disguise with a trusty band of followers and
rode hard for Kalpi.

Thereabouts the combined insurgents were again worsted, but on 1
June 1858 they responded with the boldest move of the whole Rebellion.
Just when the British thought they had finally dislodged them from Bundelkhand, Lakshmi Bai and Tatya Topi seized Gwalior. As Scindia's capital
and still the greatest natural stronghold in India, Gwalior was well-chosen
for a final stand. Scindia himself, while remaining loyal to the British, had
been pretending sympathy for the insurgents as a way of detaining the
large body of mutinous troops based in Gwalior. An appeal in the name
of the peshwa, Scindia's one-time superior in the Maratha hierarchy, failed
to sway him; but it did serve to disabuse his troops. With their collaboration,
Tatya Topi and the rani entered the city, paid their forces from its accumulated riches, and duly ensconced themselves on central India's 'Heights of
Abraham'.

This tableau, so dear to nationalist lore, lasted barely three weeks. It
ended when Lakshmi Bai died the death of the heroine she undoubtedly
was. While riding round the ramparts, she was hit by a spray of bullets as
the British launched their first assault. She was cremated nearby, 'the only
man among the rebels' according to one of her British adversaries. Three
days later the citadel fell and with it the last attempt at concerted action
by the insurgents. Tatya and his followers would roam through Rajasthan
and Madhya Pradesh for another year of improbable and much-embellished
escapades before he was betrayed, captured and executed. Meanwhile the
Nana Sahib and the rump of the Awadh insurgents were penned ever closer
to the Nepalese border. By 1860 even these 'embers' had been doused or

dispersed. Their cause was anyway hopeless, not least because many of the grievances on which it rested had by then been addressed.

Measured in terms of concessions the Great Rebellion was far from being a disaster for the insurgents. Obviously the British made sure that military vulnerability would never again be the undoing of the Raj. By 1863 the Indian component in the Bengal, Bombay and Madras armies had been reduced by about 40 per cent and the British component increased by nearly 50 per cent. This gave an Indian–British ratio of less than 3:1, which was henceforth considered the bare minimum; in 1857 it had been more like 9:1. No Indian troops were now given artillery training; recruitment was increasingly switched from Awadh and Bihar to the Panjab and marginal hill regions whose supposedly 'martial peoples' were deemed more reliable and less paranoid about caste-loss; at the same time deployment was so organised as to avoid a concentration anywhere of units with the same composition. Rapid expansion of the railway system and of the telegraph further precluded the danger of mutiny. The 250 kilometres of track laid by 1856 had become 6400 by 1870 and sixteen thousand by 1880. Moreover in 1869 the opening of the Suez Canal slashed journey times between Europe and India, while the 1870 completion of an overland telegraph link brought closer co-ordination of imperial policies and more supervision from London.

The issue of the offending cartridges had, of course, long since been resolved. The troops now greased them themselves with whatever lubricant they preferred; moreover in 1867 the whole procedure became unnecessary when the breech-loading rifle made its Indian debut. Other concessions which addressed the underlying causes of the 'mutiny' were much more significant. In recognition of the fact that the mutineers had genuinely feared conversion to Christianity, missionary activity was curtailed and the public funding of mission schools reduced. Queen Victoria's proclamation of 1858 specifically disclaimed any 'desire to impose Our convictions on any of Our subjects' and ordered British officials to abstain from interfering with Indian beliefs and rituals 'on the pain of Our highest displeasure'.

The reforming zeal of the Bentinck era was also repudiated. Already out of fashion in Britain, the presumed omniscience of Utilitarians and Benthamites was recognised as particularly inappropriate in India and the attempt to legislate away discriminatory traditions and eccentric practices was largely abandoned. An exception was made in respect of education; more schools were part-funded by government and the English language continued to be promoted. But the idea that extending the benefits of British rule to all Indians was a moral imperative lost favour. In particular the process of absorbing the Indian states and of eliminating hereditary revenue farmers was reversed. The *taluqdars* of Awadh, stigmatised as parasites in 1856 and rebels in 1857, had only to clear themselves of shedding British blood to emerge as faithful allies in 1858. Recognised as having a genuine hold on the loyalties as well as the remittances of their cultivating subordinates, they were confirmed in the hereditary possession of their rights and also co-opted into the British administration as local magistrates. Like Bengal's *zamindars* and other rural aristocracies they joined the British Indian hierarchy as rajas and rais and became some of its most stalwart supporters.

Likewise their princely brethren of the Indian states. Although annexed states like Awadh were not restored, there were to be no further annexations. Existing treaties with India's five hundred princes were now to be 'scrupulously maintained' while the detested 'doctrine of lapse' did just that; it lapsed. With few exceptions, the princes had remained loyal during the rebellion; in British eyes such loyalty now commanded a higher premium than enlightened rule.

The status of the princes was further enhanced by a new constitutional relationship between Britain and India. The royal proclamation of 1858 announced a decision of the British Parliament that all rights previously enjoyed by the East India Company in India were being resumed by the British Crown. Victoria thereby became Queen of India as well as of the United Kingdom, and India's governor-general became her viceroy as well as the British government's chief executive in India. The fiction of Company rule thus finally ended. Long as irrelevant as the Mughal, the Company now shared his fate as a casualty of the Rebellion. Instead of pining away in Rangoon, it would linger on for a few more years in a London office 'unhonoured and unsung, but maybe not altogether unwept'.

So India had a new sovereign; and just as in Britain the monarch's position was buttressed by a hierarchy of hereditary nobles and by the award of honours, so in India similar structures were created. The Star of India, a royal order of Indian knights, was introduced in 1861, and the first tour by a member of the British royal family took place in 1869. Meanwhile India's aristocracy of 'feudatory' princes, chiefs, rajas, nawabs and so on was being further stratified and grouped to conform to British ideas of hierarchy. The grading of gun salutes and other minutiae of protocol provided a ready reckoner of status, status itself being assessed on the basis of historical and territorial credentials, good governance, charitable activities and, of course, demonstrations of loyalty.

Only when this structuring was complete was the keystone installed. In

1876, on the advice of Disraeli, the Queen announced to the British Parliament that, satisfied that her Indian subjects were 'happy under My rule and loyal to My throne', she deemed the moment appropriate for her to assume a new 'Royal Style and Titles'. The style, it was later revealed, was to be imperial and the titles, in English, 'Empress of India' and, for the benefit of her Indian subjects, the rather unfortunate 'Kaiser-i-Hind'.

In January 1877, in a vast tented city around the Ridge whence British forces had recaptured Delhi twenty years earlier, the new imperium was solemnised at an Imperial Assemblage. The official attendance of eighty-four thousand included nearly all of India's 'sixty-three ruling princes' and 'three hundred titular chiefs and native gentlemen'. Lord Lytton, the presiding viceroy whose arrangements would provide a blueprint for all future imperial durbars, took some delight in listing those present. Here were the princes of Arcot and Tanjore from the deep south, the principal 'Talukdars of Oudh', 'Alor Chiefs of Sindh', Sikh Sardars, rajputs and Marathas, 'the semi-independent Chief of Amb', 'Arabs from Peshawar', 'Biluch Tommduis from Dera Ghazi Khan', and envoys from Chitral and Yassin in the high Hindu Kush 'who attended in the train of the Maharajah of Cashmere and Jammu'. Also included in Lytton's litany were quite a few ex-princes like the grandson of Tipu Sultan, the son of the last Nawab of Awadh and 'members of the ex-Royal family of Delhi'.

> The presence of these descendants of the former great ruling houses of India imparted some of the flavour of a Roman triumph to the assemblage. The British conception of Indian history thereby was realised as a kind of 'living museum', with the descendants of both the allies and the enemies of the English displaying the period of the conquest of India.[29]

Conservation was now the order of the day. The riot of privilege and particularism, once seen as an indictment of British rule, was to be preserved as imperial pageantry. And with the British apparently disclaiming plans for the rapid transformation of Indian society, the initiative now slowly passed from these hereditary representatives of the old dynastic order to a new elite, English-educated and city-based.

Awake the Nation

1880–1930

TRAINS AND DRAINS

INDIA'S RURAL LANDSCAPE looks rather different from that of most tropical ex-colonies. In particular it lacks those bold and regimented patterns of cultivation associated with large-scale agri-business. Tousled hectares of banana and coconut, rows of pineapples receding over the horizon, or gloomy ranks of regulation rubber trees are comparatively rare. There are exceptions: tea estates muffle the hills of Assam and Kerala in what are major enterprises by any standards, and cotton in the Deccan monopolises the black soil for mile upon featureless mile. But for the most part, rural India is a patchwork of more intimate fields, often eccentric in their layout, not over-capitalised in terms of machinery, and devoid of that plantation logic which is the usual legacy of colonial agrarian development.

It could have been otherwise. Expectations of white settlement and European enterprise transforming Indian agriculture had surfaced in the blueprints of early-nineteenth-century reformers. In respect of two highly valuable crops, the opium poppy and the indigo vetch, they had been partially realised. British investment in the processing necessary to produce China's favourite narcotic and to extract the blue dye for assorted European uniforms led to some contentious involvement in the supply and cultivation of these crops, particularly in Bengal and Bihar. But the East India Company had been generally opposed to European settlement, and the extortionate conduct of such quasi-planters had done nothing to change attitudes. In 1859–61, just as the British were congratulating themselves on having isolated Bengal itself from the traumas of the Great Rebellion (or sometimes the 'red mutiny'), serious riots (known as the 'indigo' or 'blue mutiny') had broken out amongst the oppressed indigo cultivators of west Bengal. Championed by Calcutta's press, which obligingly pointed out that the planters were mostly British, and not without some official sympathy, the rioting *ryots* duly won relief from their supply contracts. Thus by 1861 'the cultivation of indigo was virtually wiped out from the Bengal districts.'[1] Elsewhere indigo cultivators had a longer wait for redress. In neighbouring Bihar it would be over fifty years before their cause was adopted by an eccentric outsider, lately arrived from Africa, called Mohandas Karamchand Gandhi.

Also in 1861, while the 'blue mutiny' was in progress, Mr J.W.B. Money, a Calcutta-born Englishman with interests in indigo, returned from a trip to the Netherlands East Indies. Nursing new thoughts on India's colonial management, Money promptly wrote a book. The Dutch, according to his provocatively entitled *Java, or How to Manage a Colony*, had responded to the demise of their own East India Company by introducing a 'Cultivation System' whereby the cultivator was obliged to set aside part of his land and labour for the production of specified quantities of an export crop. These yields, usually of sugar or coffee, were then rendered to the government or its contractors in lieu of land rent. Natives, seemingly, did not want rights and legal redress. They wanted a chance to prosper, and that was precisely what the system offered in that it also guaranteed the purchase of any surplus. It thus encouraged the circulation of money, said Money, and improved native purchasing power.[2]

That the system was advantageous to the Netherlands was sensationally obvious. By 1860 a third of that state's annual revenue derived from its East Indies colony. Domestic taxation was reduced and the entire Dutch state railway network was built on the proceeds. Why could India, cowed by the suppression of the Great Rebellion, not now be managed to mutual advantage in the same way?

But Money's cheerful endorsement of the Dutch system overlooked the fact that most Javanese were not in fact enriched. Rather were they reduced to a state of rural bondage which was quite irreconcilable with either Munro-ite ideals of a sturdy peasantry or Cornwallis-ite ideals of a benign landed gentry. Mr Money also ignored the prevailing spirit of *laissez faire* which had earlier deprived the English East India Company of its trade monopolies and had since witnessed a steady withdrawal of government from many other areas of economic management. In the Americas and elsewhere, including even the Netherlands East Indies, British exporters and business houses were doing very well without the paraphernalia of empire; free trade, not state management, was the key.

Furthermore, and perhaps decisively, the idea of introducing a plantation economy was precluded by the extent to which in India land, and the extractive surplus/revenue rights to which it was subject, had become marketable assets. In Bengal, for example, the Raja of Burdwan had recently divided up part of his *zamindari* into lots, or *patnis*, on condition that the purchasers, or *patnidars*, paid the revenue on these lots. The *patnidars* then 'sometimes sold lots to others known as *dar-patnidars*, and they too sold lots to others below them, known as *das-dar-patnidars* . . . By 1855 it was estimated that some two-thirds of Bengal were held on tenures of this sort, and there is a presumption that many of the purchasers had urban connections.'[3] Inheritance laws encouraged a similar fragmentation; and city-based merchants, moneylenders and financiers were indeed prominent amongst the purchasers.

The 'commercialisation of agriculture', begun in late Mughal times, was thus an established fact by the mid-nineteenth century. Facilitated by the new railways, export booms in cotton during the 1860s (courtesy of the American Civil War) and in wheat from the 1870s onwards enriched and entrenched these middle-men as well as sustaining the mainly British business houses which handled overseas shipping and brokerage. Yet such was this superstructure of agents and rentiers, and such the extractive culture of the revenue system, that profits rarely found their way back into production other than as advances on the next crop. The actual cultivator thus became, if anything, even more indebted. Commercialisation only 'led to differentiation without genuine growth'. In effect India's rural economy was already experiencing the down-side of plantation economics, in terms of labour exploitation, without the usual up-side of capital investment. 'The point is not that so many peasants suffered (they would have suffered under capitalist modernisation, too) but that they suffered for nothing.'[4]

The British preferred to emphasise their investment in infrastructure, especially railways and irrigation works ('trains and drains'). They also pointed to the country's generally favourable balance of payments. Critics, though, were less impressed by India's theoretical prosperity and more exercised by Indians' actual poverty. As early as 1866 Dadabhai Naoroji, the future 'Grand Old Man of Congress', had begun to wonder whom the trains actually benefited and whither the drains actually led. In fact he developed a 'drain theory' which, with ramifications provided by his successors, would run like an undercurrent throughout the nationalist debate.

This 'drain theory' maintained that India's surplus, instead of being invested so as to create the modernised and industrialised economy needed to support a growing population, was being drained away by the ruling power. The main drain emptied in London with a flood of what the government called 'home charges'. These included salaries and pensions

for government and army officers, military purchases, India Office overheads, debt servicing, and the guaranteed interest payable to private investors in India's railways. Calculated in sterling at an increasingly
unfavourable rate of exchange, they came to something like a quarter of
the government of India's total revenue. With much of what remained
being squandered on administrative extravagances and military adventures
in Burma and Afghanistan, it was not surprising that Indians lived in such
abject poverty or that famines were so frequent.

The theory also included an analysis of how the drain actually worked.
The Secretary of State for India in London obtained sterling to meet his
'home charges' by selling bills of exchange to British importers. Presented
in India, these bills could be converted into rupees out of government
revenues and so used for the purchase of Indian produce. The private
sector therefore played an important part in the drain since its exports
from India constituted the drain's flow. By the same token the export
surplus was of little economic benefit to Indians; and worse still, since they
consisted mostly of raw materials, exports gave no encouragement to India's
industrialisation. The classic case was cotton. In the days of the Company,
British purchases had been mainly of finished piece-goods. Latterly, with
Lancashire's mills underselling India's handloom weavers, British purchases
switched to raw cotton and yarn. Now, when new and often Indian-owned
mills in Bombay were at last in a position to compete, they were repeatedly
frustrated by tariff policies which favoured British imports and by regulations which handicapped Indian production.

India's embryonic industries – principally jute, cotton, coir and coal –
needed protection; the British insisted on free trade. Their *laissez faire*
attitudes extended even to the land revenue, where rising prices meant that
fixed revenue assessments actually became somewhat less onerous during
the latter half of the nineteenth century. But rather than adjust such assessments the government now preferred to explore other sources of revenue,
like introducing an income tax. For the Great Rebellion, far from
emboldening the British to remodel India's agrarian economy along the
regimented plantation lines suggested by Money, was seen to have demonstrated the extreme danger of intervention.

Such governmental conservatism did not mean that Indians were
entirely spared the plantation experience. In regions of marginal cultivation,
and especially on the tea estates which proliferated in the Assam hills from
the 1850s onwards, indentured labour was widely employed. Further afield
the abolition of slavery and the introduction of new crops created more
exotic markets for indentured Indian labour in Sri Lanka, Burma, Malaya,

Fiji, Mauritius, south and east Africa and the Caribbean. Mortality rates amongst these migrants were so high in the nineteenth century, and the terms of indenture so oppressive, that critics saw only another form of slavery. The plight of emigrant Indian labour would feature prominently amongst early nationalist grievances, and in Africa M.K. Gandhi would find a challenging field for his first experiments in *satyagraha*.

The young Gandhi had found his way to Natal in south-east Africa in the employ of a Gujarati trading firm. India's maritime and mercantile contacts with south-east Asia had been sustained ever since the Pala and Chola periods, but under Muslim, Portuguese and British dispensations had been considerably extended. They now reached round the Indian Ocean and the Pacific rim to Aden, Zanzibar, east and south Africa, China, Japan and even the Pacific coast of North America. Latterly small communities of Indian clerks, police, dock-workers and other service personnel had become as sure a sign of a British presence in these places as the Union Jack. From as far afield as Vancouver and Singapore, as well as Gandhi's Natal, such expatriate groups would make a valuable contribution to the struggle for Indian independence. Conversely they, and the mass of indentured migrants, brought Indian issues to an international audience.

The accompanying diaspora of religious and social traditions established a score of 'Little Indias' from Singapore to Georgetown, Guyana, which were as much colonies of Indianisation as their parent settlements were colonies of Anglicisation. As in the long-forgotten days of Kanishka and the Karakoram route, India was successfully projecting its cultural influence just when politically it was in deepest eclipse. But, linked by the telegraph and the shipping line, such agents of outward acculturation now also served as antennae for inward politicisation. From Japan came word of Asian regeneration, from Europe came news of Ireland's struggle against British rule, and from the white settler colonies of Africa and Canada came ideas of autonomy and dominion status. India was not alone. British rule was not immutable. Nor was it invincible.

Augmented by a further exodus in the twentieth century, mainly to Europe, North America and the Gulf states, the diaspora would make the peoples of the subcontinent amongst the most numerous and recognisable of global societies. In Britain alone the number of immigrants from the subcontinent would eventually exceed the total of British civilian residents in India during the nearly two hundred years of British rule. Between 1880 and 1930 the average exodus was running at around a quarter of a million Indians a year, mainly from Tamil Nadu, Kerala and Gujarat. But although they made a significant impact on most of the receiving countries, they had little effect on India's teeming demography. This was in part because most indentured emigrants returned after the expiry of their five-year indenture. So did the troops of the British Indian army who were increasingly deployed on imperial service in China, south-east Asia, Persia and Africa. And so did the barristers, like Gandhi, the administrators, doctors and others who, bursting from India's universities in ever greater numbers, sometimes travelled abroad to complete their studies or pursue their professions. A few Indians were at last acquiring the first-hand experience of other cultures by which they would be enabled to judge their own identity as Indians rather than as members of a particular Indian community. It would be no coincidence that most of the giants of the independence movement, from Dadabhai Naoroji to M.A. Jinnah, Gandhi and Jawaharlal Nehru, were returnees.

Overseas study was an option only for the privileged. For most Indians an acquaintance with the traditions of Western thought depended on a university education, supported by access to newspapers and books. In the increasingly politicised and cosmopolitan atmosphere of the three main 'presidencies' – by which was now meant the cities of Calcutta, Bombay and Madras – the level of graduate debate was sophisticated and intense. Participants drew on a wide range of argument and ideology, and they avidly followed developments elsewhere in the world, especially Japan's modernisation and the course of Anglo–Irish disentanglement. Their enthusiasm for association and mutual collaboration over a range of political and social issues was equally impressive. But in cities where all manner of caste, professional, communal and linguistic groups were well represented, nationalism was perhaps seen more as the sum of its parts than as an indivisible whole. It was something to be laboriously constructed from within rather than being self-evidently defined from without.

Higher education was restricted to a minute elite; books and newspapers circulated sluggishly outside the main cities. The homespun nationalist in the *mofussil* had only the ubiquitous British presence against which to measure and define his identity. As in 1857, all manner of different definitions resulted. Yet recent studies, like that undertaken by Christopher Bayly in respect of Allahabad and other north Indian towns, discover a significant continuity between traditional urban groupings and the later 'nationalist' groups and interests which would subscribe to the National Congress. 'In all the major centres of Hindi-speaking north India, the new religious and political associations had links with existing shrines, *sabhas* [councils, societies] and commercial solidarities. In Allahabad, for instance, commercial and devotional relationships generated by the great bathing fair, the Magh [or Kumbh] Mela, contributed as much to the emergence of modern political associations as the camaraderies of the Bar Library.'[5]

Similar links are traced between Muslim associations of service gentry and membership of the later Muslim League. In Maharashtra the devotional allegiances of Pune's brahmans would see their festivals transformed into political protest gatherings and their cults being promoted as nationalist propaganda. Nor was this a passing phenomenon. 'The style of Hindu politics which emerged from the corporate urban life of the later nineteenth century remains vital . . . whether in the guise of the Hindu Mahasabha of the 1930s or of the Jana Sangh in the 1970s'[6] – or indeed of the Jana Sangh's later reincarnation, the Bharatiya Janata Party (BJP). Here, in short, was (and is) a third perspective, one by which nationalism was perceived, neither from without as an indivisible whole, nor from the metropolitan centres as the sum of its parts, but from deep within as a projection of entrenched sectional interests which were proud to owe very little to extraneous ideologies or a foreign-language education.

EVERYTHING IN MODERATION

Lord Lytton's 1877 Imperial Assemblage at Delhi was the sort of wasteful extravaganza to which Indians of almost every perspective took strong exception. That it happened to coincide with the worst famine of the century, which claimed perhaps 5.5 million lives in the Deccan and the south, added to the outrage. It may therefore be deeply unacceptable to suggest that the Assemblage provided the format, eight years later, for the first meeting of the Indian National Congress. But parallels have been noted. 'The early meetings of the All India Congress Committees were much like durbars, with processions and the centrality of leading figures and their speeches . . .' The sentiments expressed were not dissimilar either. The Congress leaders spoke of progressive government and the welfare and happiness of the Indian people, just like the viceroy; and when they demanded fair access to the civil service and greater representation in the councils of state they were merely reminding the Calcutta government of pledges already made, as for instance in the Queen's 1858 Proclamation which promised that all suitably qualified Indians would be 'freely and impartially admitted to office in Our service'. Indeed, some had already been admitted; but as the supply of qualified Indians increased, so did the government's reluctance to honour such pledges. Hence the reminders. Framed in the British 'idiom' of the great Delhi durbar, they 'set the terms of discourse of the national movement in its beginning phases. In effect, the early nationalists were claiming that they were more loyal to the true goals of the Indian empire than were their British rulers.'[7]

Nor was this claim obviously mischievous. Gandhi himself would invoke the 1858 Proclamation when demanding British redress against racial discrimination in Natal. Earlier in India, on the assumption – all too correct during Lytton's viceroyalty – that the Calcutta government was dragging its feet and was less receptive to Indian aspirations than were the British people, leading Indian protest groups despatched representatives to London and set up branches there. One of the earliest such organisations was the East India Association founded in 1866 by Dadabhai Naoroji, a successful businessman and a member of Bombay's small but immensely influential Parsi community (so-called because they subscribed to the Zoroastrian faith of pre-Islamic 'Pars', or Persia, whence their forebears had sought sanctuary in India). Much of Dadabhai Naoroji's career was spent in London, where he attracted a succession of high-flying Indian professionals who returned to India to lead many of the associations which eventually subscribed to Congress. He himself attended the first Indian National Congress and was elected president for the second. The better to represent Indian opinion in London he later became a Westminster MP. In 1893, while still sitting in the House of Commons, he would again return to India and the presidency of Congress.

The uncompromising imperialism of a Lytton (1876–80), or the temporising of a Dufferin (1884–8), encouraged such circumventory tactics. Conversely a Liberal viceroy like Lord Ripon (1880–4) was expected to be as sympathetic to Indian demands as was Gladstone to Irish demands, and could therefore expect nationalist support. Yet Ripon, repeatedly thwarted by the caution of the India Office in London and by the opposition of his own officials in India, delivered much less than he promised. He had the pleasure of repealing Lytton's draconian censorship of the vernacular press, and he introduced a degree of local self-government with the inauguration of municipal and rural boards whose members, partly elected, were to assume responsibility for such things as roads, schools and sewerage. Implementation proved more difficult, especially in Calcutta, Bombay and Madras, where the main deluge of suitably educated Indians met the high dam of greatest official suspicion. Moreover, highly qualified patriots who were exercised about the iniquities of Naoroji's drain theory found it hard to get excited about actual drains. Yet they liked Ripon's ideas, they appreciated the need for a political induction which started at the bottom of the ladder, and they eagerly awaited the invitation to climb to the next rung.

This prospect receded in 1883 when the innocuous-looking Ilbert Bill provoked a 'white backlash' from India's British residents. The bill, introduced by the Calcutta government to iron out a minor legal anomaly, was found on close examination to entitle a few Indian barristers who had now risen to the level of district magistrates and session judges to preside over trials of British as well as Indian subjects. This was too much for the planters and businessmen who made up the bulk of the European community. That there had to be Indian judges was one thing, but that an Indian judge might pronounce sentence on a member of the ruling race, perhaps even a female member of the ruling race, provoked the entire community into a hysterical and undisguisedly racist uproar. Memories of Kanpur and the 'red mutiny' were resurrected; Ripon was threatened; and, mindful of the 'indigo' or 'blue mutiny' of 1860, irate loyalists now promised a 'white mutiny' which would seal the fate of such a treacherous government. Their campaign 'gave Indians an object lesson in the arts of unprincipled, but highly organised, agitation';[8] it was also notably successful, emasculating Ilbert's bill and discrediting most of Ripon's other reforms. Here was another British 'idiom', another form of 'discourse', more raucous than that of the durbar and evidently more potent; it, too, would in due course be emulated.

The histrionics over the Ilbert Bill had come mainly from Bengal, whose British planters, industrialists and traders were much the most numerous. But Bengal also fielded much the largest body of Western-educated and articulate Indians. They rallied to Ripon's defence and, in loyal support of a cause which for once transcended creed, caste, class and locality, they were joined by fellow activists from all over India. Hailed as 'a constitutional combination to support the policy of . . . Government', this dignified and carefully orchestrated demonstration of all-India support found eloquent expression in the Bombay send-off arranged for Ripon in late 1884.

> From Madras and Mysore [reported the *Times of India*], from the Panjab and Gujarat, they came as an organised voice, from the communities where caste and race had merged their differences . . . waving their banners, rushing along with the carriages, crowding the roofs, and even filling the trees, and cheering their hero to the very echo . . . in order to express their appreciation of the new principles of government.[9]

In December 1885, exactly one year later, also in Bombay, and partly inspired by this demonstration of all-India action, the first Indian National Congress was convened. As yet Congress was just that – a congress, a gathering; not a movement, let alone a party. It was not unique; another national convention was meeting simultaneously in Calcutta (they would merge in the following year). Nor was it exclusively Indian. Its acknowledged founder, Allan Octavian Hume, was an ex-Secretary for Agriculture in the Calcutta government, a distinguished ornithologist and a Scot. Like his father, a Liberal radical who had spoken 'longer and oftener and probably worse than any other Member [of the Westminster Parliament]' in support of every imaginable reform, repeal and abolition, A.O. Hume had long been a thorn in the side of the authority he served. He had been particularly critical of 'the millions and millions of Indian money' squandered by Lytton, both on the Imperial Assemblage in Delhi and then on the Second Afghan War which in 1878 climaxed another confused passage of play in the interminable 'Great Game' between the British and Russian empires in central Asia.

After Lytton, in the happier times of Ripon's viceroyalty, Hume had come to see himself as a conduit between Government House and its Indian subjects. The role no doubt appealed to him, as an associate of the Theosophists who from their base in Madras energetically espoused Hindu revivalism while seeking ecstatic encounters with spiritualistic go-betweens; indeed, 'mystical mahatmas' seem to have figured prominently amongst Hume's anonymous Indian informants. There was nothing discreditable in such 'contacts'. Late Victorians relished spiritual experiments; and in India Theosophy was one of many revivalist movements which were significantly contributing to the climate of social reform and religious and cultural rehabilitation in which national regeneration would flourish.

To the British it seemed that many of these reform movements cancelled one another out. Social reformers who demanded, for instance, an end to child marriages were opposed by religious revivalists who resented any interference with existing custom; in the north, champions of the Hindi language antagonised the heirs of Urdu's literary heritage; and Marathas invoking the memory of Shivaji to sanction acts of violence were contradicted by universalist movements like the Brahmo Samaj whose adherents stressed the humanity and non-violence of Hinduism. In Bengal, as in Maharashtra, the literary and largely Hindu renaissance often bracketed British rule with that of the Muslim emperors and nawabs which had preceded it, both being deemed equally alien. Bankim Chandra Chatterjee went even further. In his immensely influential novel *Anandamath* (1882), Hindu leaders appeared to be struggling not against the British, who had supposedly come to India as liberators, but against Muslim tyranny and misrule.[10]

Needless to say, Muslims took exception to this as to much else about the predominantly Hindu character of many of these movements. In the north they responded both with a burst of fundamentalist activity which appealed to poorer Muslims and with a drive towards a more flexible and outward-looking orthodoxy which could accommodate a degree of Westernisation. The latter trend was well represented by Sir Sayyid Ahmed Khan who in 1875 founded the Anglo-Muhammadan Oriental College, later University, of Aligarh (between Delhi and Agra).

All these movements and associations would endow the political struggle with strong spiritual, cultural and social undertones. In the case of Vivekananda, the first of India's 'gurus' to address a world audience, they served to alert international opinion. In the case of the *Arya Samaj*, a reformist and aggressively Hindu 'Aryan Movement' which made spectacular advances in the Panjab, they drew on fashions in international scholarship, specifically the pan-Aryan enthusiasms of Max Muller, the Oxford Professor of Sanskrit. Additionally the high-profile Theosophists set a useful organisational example with their annual conventions. But it was the mainstream political groupings of Calcutta, Bombay and Pune, heavily influenced by Dadabhai Naoroji and his associates, which first urged the need for a national congress; the organisation for such a gathering had come into existence at the time of Ripon's send-off demonstrations in the winter of 1884;[11] and Allan Hume was regarded by the British authorities as the prime instigator. Additionally, by the seventy-two delegates who attended the first Congress, he was seen as an able organiser and, because unaligned as to caste and community, as the most suitable secretary and spokesman.

Hume also had more time and money than most to devote to the Congress. For the next decade it existed as an annual gathering, organised by a local committee in whichever city had been chosen to host it, and presided over by a president chosen for that one occasion. 'There were no paying members, no permanent organisation, no officials other than a general secretary [usually Hume], no central offices and no funds.'[12] It met over the Christmas break, thereby ensuring that the professional careers of the principally lawyers, journalists and civil servants who attended were not unduly disrupted. Proceedings were conducted in English, the only language shared by all delegates; and given the Congress's pan-Indian character, resolutions focused on those national, as opposed to local or communal, issues around which delegates could be expected to unite.

Not surprisingly, the first years of Congress would therefore come to be seen as years of caution and moderation. Dufferin would sneer that it represented only 'a microscropic minority'. Lord Curzon (viceroy 1899–1905), though conceding that its semi-permanent committees now made it a 'party', insisted that it was 'tottering towards its fall'. Frustration led even supporters to decry the Congress's 'mendicancy' when in the 1890s its ritual demands for political, administrative, and economic concessions, as also its pitiful funds, were re-routed through its London subsidiary. Although Congress continued to aspire to the status of an embryonic Indian parliament, its hopes lay with the Westminster Parliament, with allies in the British Liberal Party, and with the London lobbying of the likes of Dadabhai Naoroji.

An 1892 India Councils Act was accounted a notable Congress triumph. It broadened the remit of the Legislative Councils which advised the viceroy and his provincial governors and to which Indians were already being nominated. It also increased the membership of these councils and conceded that in principle some members might be elected, albeit indirectly. This was a far cry from *swaraj* (self-rule), the avowed objective of many Congress speakers, but it did ensure more Indian representation at the political level. Access to the higher grades of the administration also looked to have been secured when in 1893 the Westminster Parliament acceded to Congress demands for entrance examinations into the elite Indian Civil Service to be held in India as well as England. In the event this measure was aborted by the government in India on the grounds that free and accessible competition would be discriminatory. It would favour, they said, the educated and mainly Hindu elite, so alienating less academic communities like the Muslims and Sikhs of the north-west on whose loyalty the Indian army, and so the British Raj, particularly relied.

Muslim attendances at Congress were already falling away. Hume had assiduously wooed Muslim support but, with his retirement to Britain in 1892, the opposition of Sir Sayyid Ahmed Khan became more pronounced. Anticipating the arguments which would eventually lead to the genesis of Pakistan, Khan insisted that representative government might work in societies 'united by ties of race, religion, manners, customs, culture and historical traditions [but] in their absence would only injure the well-being and tranquillity of the land.' The land in question he liked to portray as a bright-eyed bride, one eye being Hindu, the other Muslim, and each equally brilliant. Any cosmetic enhancement which had the effect of favouring one over the other would ruin the whole countenance.

Resentment of Congress, and especially the elitist, 'mendicant' and Anglophone tone of its leadership, came also from non-Muslims. In the late 1890s, against a background of industrial unrest, more appalling famines

BRITISH VICEROYS

1850	
1860	CANNING, Charles, 1st Earl of Canning 1856–1862
	Bruce, James, 8th Earl of ELGIN 1862–1863
	LAWRENCE, Sir John 1863–1869
1870	Bourke, Richard, 6th Earl of MAYO 1869–1872
	Baring, Thomas, 1st Earl of NORTHBROOK 1872–1876
	LYTTON, Edward, 1st Earl of Lytton 1876–1880
1880	Robinson, George, 1st Marquess of RIPON 1880–1884
	Blackwood, Frederick, 1st Marquess of DUFFERIN & Ava 1884–1888
1890	Petty-Fitzmaurice, Henry, 5th Marquess of LANSDOWNE 1888–1894
	Bruce, Victor, 9th Earl of ELGIN 1894–1898
1900	CURZON, George, 1st Marquess Curzon of Keddleston 1898–1905
	Elliot, Gilbert, 4th Earl of MINTO 1905–1910
1910	HARDINGE, Charles, 1st Baron of Penshurst 1910–1916
	Thesiger, Frederic, 1st Viscount CHELMSFORD 1916–1921
1920	Isaacs, Rufus, 1st Marquess of READING 1921–1926
	Wood, Edward, Lord IRWIN & 1st Earl of Halifax 1926–1931
1930	Freeman-Thomas, Freeman, 1st Marquess of WILLINGDON 1931–1936
1940	Hope, Victor, 2nd Marquess of LINLITHGOW 1936–1943
	WAVELL, Archibald, 1st Viscount & Earl Wavell 1943–1947
	MOUNTBATTEN, Louis, 1st Viscount & Earl Mountbatten 1947
1950	

and an outbreak of plague, the first signs of a polarisation in the Congress ranks began to appear in Maharashtra. Moderates who favoured constitutional methods, albeit backed by trenchant economic and political critiques, became identified with Ferozeshah Mehta and Gopal Krishna Gokhale, whose power base was amongst the Bombay intelligentsia. Meanwhile radicals gravitated towards the Marathi populism and the more experimental methods urged by Bal Gangadhar Tilak from his power base around Pune.

Gokhale, a lecturer at Bombay University, and Mehta, a Parsi lawyer, accepted the need for patience and moved easily between the presidency of Congress and membership of the viceroy's council. Tilak, on the other hand, from the same brahman community which had furnished the Maratha state with its peshwas, experimented with a variety of mass-focus appeals through his editorship of a Marathi newspaper. They included the politicisation of fairs and festivals associated with the local cult of Ganapati (Ganesh) and a patriotic crusade based on the defiance of Shivaji. Tentative boycotts and exhortations to civil disobedience were also tried. In 1897 Tilak's exposition of Shivaji's most famous exploit, the disembowelling of the Bijapuri general Afzal Khan with those fearsome steel talons, was taken to have incited the assassination of a British official. Sentenced to prison, Tilak, the scapegoat for this first successful act of terrorism, duly became Tilak, the martyr for the nationalist cause. A repeat performance in 1908 would galvanise all Bombay. Tilak had made the important discovery that the consequences of extremist rhetoric could transcend its appeal.

Bengali luminaries, including Aurobindo Ghose, the social and religious reformer, and Rabindranath Tagore, the poet, philosopher, educationalist and first Indian Nobel laureate for literature, also sought to broaden the base of the struggle. The former's advocacy of passive resistance and the latter's of psychological, educational and economic self-reliance were both, however, dramatically subsumed in the explosion that greeted the partition of Bengal in 1905. Courtesy of the British and the greatest of their proconsuls, rather than of the stridency of Congress, the first phase of the national struggle was about to peak.

DIVIDE AND UNITE

George Nathaniel Curzon, Baron of Kedleston, had equipped himself for viceregal authority like no other British viceroy. He had had India on the brain since his schooldays at Eton, and 'as early as 1890 he had admitted at a dinner in the House of Commons that [the viceroyalty] was the greatest of his various ambitions'.[13] Perhaps it had something to do with the familiar aspect of Government House in Calcutta. The viceregal residence, built by Wellesley a century earlier, had been modelled on the Curzon family's Kedleston Hall. By design, as it were, a home from home awaited him in India.

But characteristically he had recommended himself for the job by travelling and writing extensively not about India itself but about its landward frontiers and the central Asian wastes beyond. For to Curzon, India's appeal resided in its status as the proverbial jewel in the imperial crown. 'For as long as we rule India,' he told Prime Minister Arthur Balfour, 'we are the greatest power in the world.' That made the viceroyalty the jewel of imperial patronage; and who better to wear it than George Nathaniel Curzon, that 'most superior person' (as one rhymester had put it)? By common consent Curzon was not only the most brilliant scholar-administrator of his day but also the soundest of imperialists. In words which would have dashed a few hopes in Congress, he told Balfour that it would 'be well for England, better for India and best of all for the cause of progressive civilisation if it be clearly understood that ... we have not the smallest intention of abandoning our Indian possessions and that it is highly improbable that any such intention will be entertained by our posterity'.[14]

As viceroy, one of Curzon's less controversial achievements would be the establishment of India's Archaeological Survey, set up to revive the work of recording and preserving what he rightly hailed as 'the greatest galaxy of monuments in the world'. India's history fascinated him, and he was probably better informed about its languages and customs than any British ruler since Warren Hastings. But of its people as other than an administrative commodity and the decadent heirs of an interesting past he knew, and perhaps cared, little. Like the Taj Mahal to which he devoted much attention, India was a great imperial edifice which posed a challenge of presentation and preservation. It needed firm direction, not gentle persuasion. History, by whose verdict Curzon set great store, would judge him by how he secured this magnificent construction, both externally against all conceivable threats and internally against all possible decay. To this end he worked heroically and unselfishly; but his example terrorised rather than inspired, his caustic wit devastated rather than delighted. Even the British in India found him quite impossible.

To the troublesome north-west frontier, where British India petered out amongst mountains swept by gusts of Afghan disquiet and strewn with the debris of unsatisfactory campaigns, Curzon did indeed bring order.

British troops were withdrawn from the Afghan frontier and a buffer zone was created within which tribal levies under British command were to keep the peace. Responsibility for this zone and for the whole area west of the Indus was in 1901 transferred from the Panjab province to a newly-created North-West Frontier Province. Further north, in the high Hindu Kush, British expeditions operating in the name of the Maharaja of Jammu and Kashmir had already pushed the frontier up to that of Chinese Sinkiang. This practically doubled the size of Kashmir and pre-empted any Russian approach by way of the Karakoram route. It also established the near physical impossibility of any such 'invasion'. Nevertheless, by way of a lookout post over this 'roof of the world', the Gilgit Agency was retained, nominally as part of Kashmir territory.

East of Kashmir, the politically uncharted wastes of Tibet had frustrated repeated British overtures. To a mind as orderly as Curzon's, the uncertainties posed by Tibet's status and by the naivety and indifference of its monkish rulers were anathema. Doubtful rumours about a doubtful Russian spy in Lhasa were made into an imperative for intervention. With exasperation masquerading as policy, a military expedition commanded by Sir Francis Younghusband was despatched across the frontier in 1904. Militarily it fared better than Zorawar Singh's frost-blighted invasion thanks largely to death-dealing inventions like the Gatling machine-gun. But the reports and, worse, the photographs of robed monks being mown down amongst the glaciers as they brandished hoes and fumbled with their flintlocks was a poor advertisement for imperialism. So much, noted nationalist critics, for 'the cause of progressive civilisation'.

If civilisation was supposed to be progressive, government was supposed to be efficient. More railways were built and ambitious irrigation projects were undertaken, especially in the Panjab. The drive for greater efficiency lay behind most of Curzon's internal reforms, and nowhere to greater effect than with the bureaucratic leviathan that was the government of India itself. Famously in 1901 he ridiculed the year-long odyssey of a particularly important proposal. 'Round and round, like the diurnal revolution of the earth, went the file, stately, solemn, sure, and slow; and now, in due season, it has completed its orbit, and I am invited to register the concluding stage.'[15] The file in question concerned another bit of territorial repackaging like the creation of the North-West Frontier Province. That alone was important enough to merit the viceroy's early attention. But the file also mooted other such adjustments, including the break-up of Bengal.

The partition of Bengal would be Curzon's nemesis. It fatally discredited the unyielding imperialism for which he stood, it sparked the first nationwide protest movement, and it introduced direct confrontation, plus a limited recourse to violence, into the repertoire of British–Indian 'discourse'. Only the tidiest of minds would have tackled such a thorny project, only the most arrogant of autocrats have persisted with it. But as the largest, most populous and most troublesome administrative unit in British India, Bengal posed a worthy challenge. With a population, twice that of Great Britain, which was predominantly Hindu in the west and Muslim in the east, the administrative case for a division of the two brooked little argument. Curzon therefore pushed ahead.

He was not unimpressed by the view that Bengal's highly vocal critics would also thereby be partitioned. 'The best guarantee of the political advantage of our proposal is its dislike by the Congress Party,' he told the secretary of state. But whether he understood the grounds for this dislike, or its intensity, may be doubted. In a 1904 speech in Dacca, the capital of the proposed new province of 'East Bengal and Assam', he assured Muslims that the new arrangement would restore a unity not seen since 'the days of the Mussulman viceroys and kings'. This was presumably a reference to the heavily Persianised courts of the eighteenth-century nawabs; it may not, therefore, have had much resonance for East Bengal's mainly low-caste converts to Islam. On the other hand it was certainly offensive to the mainly Hindu *zamindars*, *patnidars*, and their innumerable diminutives who were so well represented amongst the vocal Anglophone agitators of Calcutta.

Stock accusations of a wider Macchiavellian intent to 'divide and rule' and to 'stir up Hindu–Muslim animosity' assume some premonition of a later partition. They make little sense in the contemporary context. 'Divide and rule' as a governing precept supposes the pre-existence of an integrated entity. In an India politically united only by British rule – and not yet even by the opposition which it generated – such a thing did not exist. Division was a fact of life. As Maulana Muhammad Ali would later put it, 'We divide and you rule.' Without recognising, exploring and accommodating such division, British dominion in India would have been impossible to establish, let alone sustain. Provoking sectarian conflict, on the other hand, was rarely in the British interest.

Only ten years earlier the armies of Bengal, Bombay and Madras, which had been kept separate as a safeguard against another mutiny, had been quietly amalgamated. It was thought to be a more efficient arrangement; in that efficiency meant more effective deployment, this could be seen as a case of 'unite and rule'. For similar reasons of imperial convenience the North-West Frontier Province had been carved out of the Panjab, and Bengal and Assam were now rearranged as West Bengal (with Orissa and

Bihar) and East Bengal (with Assam). Arguably this partition should have reduced sectarian rivalry. More certainly, under a viceroy as committed to indefinite British rule as Curzon, there was no logic in stirring up conflict. At the time the nationalist challenge was being comfortably contained and Muslims were already boycotting Congress. More discord would merely defeat efficiency. It was costly to contain, it damaged British business interests, and it taxed the loyalties of the princely states and the now-united Indian army.

Such reasoning would duly surface when in 1911 it was announced that Curzon's partition had been reversed and Bengal was to be reunited. Instead, Bihar and Orissa would be detached to form a separate province, and likewise Assam. The 'unity' promised to East Bengal's Muslims thus lasted just six years. Their resentment was understandable. Nor was it soothed by the simultaneous announcement that Delhi, the erstwhile seat of a Muslim empire to which Bengalis had rarely been reconciled, was to replace Calcutta as British India's capital (and be graced with a new New Delhi). If this was an acceptable idea to the Muslim gentry of northern India, it was meaningless to the Muslim peasantry of what is now Bangladesh. More obviously, Bengali Muslim resentment over the reversal of partition scarcely squares with the popular idea that it was Bengali patriotism which forced this reversal. All communities in Bengal did indeed share the same language, the same rich literature, the same distinctive history and the same passionate attachment to a delightfully mellow land. But the explosion of protest which had greeted Curzon's partition and which had rocked much of India while the partition lasted had other causes.

Many related to the disadvantaged status and lost job opportunities which Bengali Hindus anticipated within a divided Bengal. In 'East Bengal and Assam' they would be a religious minority in a predominantly Muslim province; in 'West Bengal with Orissa and Bihar' they would be a linguistic minority amongst a non-Bengali-speaking majority. Wherever they lived they stood to lose by partition. Other grievances drew on the catalogue of demands being submitted by Congress and the negligible progress being made in their redress. But one outstanding objection, for which Curzon must be held directly responsible, was the appalling insensitivity with which the scheme had been imposed. As Gokhale apprised Congress at the end of 1905, no Bengali had been consulted, no objections entertained.

> The scheme of partition, concocted in the dark and carried out in the face of the fiercest opposition that any government measure has encountered in the last half-a-century, will always stand as a

complete illustration of the worst features of the present system of bureaucratic rule – its utter contempt for public opinion, its arrogant pretensions to superior wisdom, its reckless disregard of the most cherished feelings of the people, the mockery of an appeal to its sense of justice, [and] its cold preference of Service interests to those of the governed.[16]

Gokhale's, it will be remembered, was the voice of moderation. Others preferred action to words. Mass rallies clogged the thoroughfares of Calcutta, Dacca and other Bengali towns. Pamphlets and petitions outcirculated the newspapers. Within a month of the government decree a popular proclamation had announced the extension of *swadeshi* protest to the whole of India. *Swadeshi*, meaning 'of our own country' or 'home-produced', expressed a determination to be self-reliant and included a strict boycott of imported products, most obviously British textiles. Those on sale were publicly destroyed and existing stocks became practically valueless; while Indian mills prospered and some hand-loom weavers resumed production, Lancashire manufacturers fumed.

Significantly it was in 1907 and as a result of enthusiastic *swadeshi* investment that Jamshed Tata, a Parsi mill-owner, diversified into foundry work with the launch of his Tata Iron and Steel Company based at what became the 'steel-city' of Jamshedpur in Bihar. The plant would become one of the largest in the world and the Tatas the greatest of India's, and Congress's, industrialist backers. Reversing dependence on imported manufactures and developing indigenous production had entered the nationalist soul. Whether as Gandhian self-suffiency or Nehruvian 'import-substitution', it would continue to inform economic thinking long after independence.

By pamphlet, press and word of mouth *swadeshi* protest was extended throughout India in a remarkable display of united and effective action which soon obscured the partition which had provoked it. The coincidence of Japan's sensational victory over a major European power in the 1905 Russo–Japanese war fanned the movement and persuaded some that victory was nigh. In Bengal a more extreme form of boycott extending to government institutions, colleges and offices was widely urged, fitfully adopted, and brutally suppressed by cane-wielding security forces. It was also disowned by the rump of Congress, whose gradualism now appeared outdated. At the 1906 Congress a split was avoided by inviting the octogenarian Dadabhai Naoroji to take the chair for the third time and by some not very ingenious fudging; one resolution boldly but nonsensically called for

'*Swaraj* [self-rule] like that of the United Kingdom or the colonies'. In 1907 at Surat the divisions between 'extremists' like Tilak and 'moderates' like Gokhale could no longer be contained. The Surat Congress dissolved into chaos and was aborted.

Briefly an 'extremist' splinter group known as 'Lal, Bal and Pal' now made most of the running – as well as providing its youthful followers with a head-banging mantra. 'Lal' was otherwise Lala Lajpat Rai, the militant *Arya Samaj* leader from the Panjab; 'Bal' was the fiery Maratha revivalist Bal Gangadhar Tilak; and 'Pal' the radical Bengali leader Bipin Chandra Pal. Pal also edited the journal *Bande Mataram*, itself named after the patriotic Bengali anthem which, written by Bankim Chandra Chatterjee, had been set to music by Tagore. *Swadeshi* ideals were extended to educational reform, labour organisation, self-help programmes and cultural activities. But in advocating a total boycott amounting to non-co-operation and including non-payment of taxes, 'Lal, Bal and Pal' invited a ferocious government clampdown. In 1907, fifty years after the last Mughal had been packed off to Burma, an untried 'Lal' trod the deportee's road to Mandalay, and in 1908 he was followed by 'Bal'. Tilak's trial for incitement had brought Bombay's industries to a standstill; for leftist nationalists this 'massive outburst of proletarian anger ... remains a major landmark in our history'.[17] The even more explosive response to his six-year sentence brought troops onto the streets and sixteen reported deaths. In a quieter Mandalay, Tilak consulted his traditional inspiration. While awaiting the dawn 'like thunder outer China 'crost the Bay', he wrote a commentary on the *Bhagavad Gita*.

His offence had been that of apparently condoning terrorism. 'The sound of the bomb', a spontaneous response to government repression according to Tilak, was first heard in Bengal in 1907 when the lieutenant-governor's train was derailed. More tragically two Kennedys, a mother and daughter, were killed at Muzaffarapur in Bihar in 1908; a bomb had been lobbed into their carriage in the mistaken belief that it was that of an unpopular magistrate. The apprehending of the culprits led to the discovery of a munitions factory in the garden of the Calcutta home of the Ghose brothers. Aurobindo Ghose was amongst those brought to trial. Disillusioned, he, like Tilak, then found in religion a 'royal road for an honourable retreat'.[18] In Pondicherry (still under French rule) he also found a sanctuary from British rule and a site for his proposed 'Auroville', an urban experiment in internationalism and cross-cultural collaboration. Unlike Tilak in Mandalay, he would stay there.

Sporadic assassinations and '*swadeshi* dacoities' (political crimes) continued, notably in Maharashtra and Bengal. Clandestine revolutionary groupings headed by V.D. Savarkar, Rashbehari Bose and others also made contacts outside India. In 1909 London itself witnessed its first Indian atrocity when Sir Curzon Wyllie, an India Office official, was gunned down by a Panjabi, Madanlal Dhingra.

Such assassination attempts, many of them botched, remained a threat to both British and Indian officials. The only viceroy to die in a terrorist attack would be the last – Lord Louis Mountbatten – and the nationalists responsible would be Irish rather than Indian. But in 1913 Lord Hardinge, one of Mountbatten's viceregal predecessors, would have a bomb tossed into his howdah while making his ceremonial entry into Delhi to mark its adoption as the new capital; severely wounded, both viceroy and elephant yet survived. The culprit proved to be one of Rashbehari Bose's Bengali followers. 'They gave us back the pride of our manhood,' writes an irresponsible but not untypical apologist for these first 'revolutionaries'.[19] Happily by 1910 their threat was being contained and the 'moderate' Congress rump, headed by Gokhale and Mehta, at last had something to show for its moderation.

Curzon had resigned as viceroy within days of the Bengal partition, although not as a result of it; the affront to his dignity from a petty row with his notorious commander-in-chief, Lord Kitchener, proved a more fatal wound than *swadeshi*. His successor, Lord Minto, reached India in late 1905 just as a Liberal ministry was taking over in London. With the appointment of the Liberal scholar John Morley as Secretary of State for India a new programme of reforms/concessions had soon come under consideration. These did not materialise till 1909, but knowledge of their preparation, plus *swadeshi*'s assertion of mainly Hindu demands, prompted a Muslim deputation to the viceroy at Simla in late 1906.

Not without British encouragement, the Muslim deputees cited the under-representation of Muslims amongst those Indians already elected to official bodies and demanded that any future reforms include separate electorates for Muslims. They also wanted a weighted system of representation which would reflect the size of the Muslim population and the value of its 'contribution to the defence of the empire'. Headed by the Aga Khan and heavily supported by mainly landed and commercial Muslim interests in the United Provinces (which were the same as the early-nineteenth-century North-West Provinces and the future Uttar Pradesh), the deputees had inherited Sir Sayyid Ahmed Khan's distrust of Congress. In early 1907 they duly consummated this distrust by forming the All India Muslim League. Not all Muslim interests supported them, however. Some groups continued to subscribe to Congress, amongst them one headed by a brilliant young Bombay lawyer, Mohammed Ali Jinnah.

The Morley–Minto Indian Councils Act, when it at last materialised in 1909, was the first major reform package since the 1892 Councils Act and apparently did no more than, as Minto put it, 'prudently extend' the principle of representative institutions. The councils in question were those attached to the central government, still in Calcutta but about to remove to Delhi, and to the now numerous provincial governments in Madras, Bombay, Agra (for the United Provinces), Lahore (for the Panjab and North-West Frontier provinces) and so on. Known as Legislative Councils, all were now increased in size; more seats were to go to non-officials and more of these non-officials were to be indirectly elected. With up to sixty members the Legislative Councils would thus accommodate more Indians, some of whom would represent a wider spectrum of Indian opinion. They became in effect chambers rather than councils and, although Minto disclaimed the very idea, could be seen to foreshadow a parliamentary system.

But they were not legislatures and had no power to initiate or frustrate legislation, merely to question and criticise it; India remained a British autocracy, albeit a consultative one. Additionally, an Indian member, Satyendra Sinha, was co-opted onto the viceroy's Executive Council, and in London two Indians served on the council which advised the Secretary of State for India.

The reforms were initially welcomed by Congress, but not by the Muslim League. When supplementary regulations later revealed that some seats were indeed to be reserved for Muslims and elected only by Muslims, the situation was reversed; Congress complained and the League rejoiced. Other seats were reserved for other sectional interests. It was not the principle of reservation which caused controversy but that of a separate electorate for the perhaps 20 per cent of the population, distributed throughout the subcontinent, who happened to adhere to Islam. Fairly in the subsequent view of Pakistanis, fatally in that of most citizens of the Republic of India, the principle of a separate electorate along sectarian lines had been conceded to a fifth of all Indians.

It would be impossible to deny that the arrangement suited British interests. But once again it was hardly an insidious application of 'divide and rule'. It neither fractured an existing consensus nor prejudiced any future consensus. No division had been created that did not already exist, no demand created which could not subsequently be accommodated. In fact, seven years later, Congress would itself accept the principle of separate electorates. The 1916 Lucknow Pact, by which Congress and the League agreed a joint programme, would see the League accept Muslim under-representation in Muslim majority areas (like East Bengal) in return for Congress's acceptance of Hindu under-representation in Hindu majority areas (like the United Provinces). Here was precisely the political horse-trading essential to the working of a plural society. Both sides embraced it; so even did an 'extremist' like the lately returned Tilak. At this stage, with one partition having just failed, another was not only unthinkable; it was eminently avoidable.

AN AFTERNOON IN AMRITSAR

Steeped in the gradualist traditions of their own constitutional evolution, the British assumed that India's induction into the practice of representative government would be a protracted business. Ripon's minimalist pro-gramme had sufficed for a decade, and the first Indian Councils Act (1892) for rather more. The Morley–Minto reforms were expected to stem the tide for at least as long. Congress demands for *swaraj* were not yet accom-panied by an ultimatum, and their objective was not that dissimilar to the 'responsible government' envisaged by the more enlightened amongst the British. In what the latter often characterised as a doctor–patient relation-ship, it looked as if India could be retained on a drip-feed of concessions until the sacred cows came home.

The First World War changed all that. With the imperial medico coming under severe strain, the Indian patient was co-opted onto the nursing staff. He was fitter, evidently, and the doctor frailer than had been supposed. Doing the rounds he heard tell of an American panacea called self-determination and of a more revolutionary cure being pioneered in Russia. It was doubtful whether he should be in hospital at all. If the doctor was so obviously fallible, why should the patient be patient?

News of war had been greeted in India with a demonstration. For once it was not of dissent but of enthusiastic support. British hearts warmed at the protestations of loyalty and the offers of support which poured in not only from the predictably sycophantic princely states but also from the Muslim League and Congress. With recruitment exceeding all expectations, Indian troops were soon sailing for novel destinations like Flanders, Gal-lipoli and Mesopotamia. Over two million Indian combatants and support staff would eventually serve overseas, dwarfing all other imperial contri-butions to the war effort. 'It was the performance of India which took the world by surprise and thrilled every British heart,' reported John Buchan, then writing his *Thirty-Nine Steps*.[20]

While the troopships sailed forth, other Indians headed home. From Africa by way of Britain and a failed attempt to enlist in the ambulance corps came Mohandas Karamchand Gandhi. Already forty-six, his twenty years in Africa had transformed a gawky and rather unsuccessful London-trained lawyer into a wiry social activist with a formidable record of unconventional protest. In India he continued to support the war effort and encourage enlistment. He retained a strong belief in British justice and he acknowledged as his mentor Gokhale, the Bombay Congressman who epitomised 'moderate' opinion.

But Gandhi did not, therefore, launch into conventional politics. On behalf of the racially disadvantaged Indian community in Natal, mostly end-of-indenture settlers, he had developed a form of protest which he called *satyagraha*, or 'truth-force'. To most observers it was just 'passive resistance' but to Gandhi it was something much more constructive and much more demanding. Drawing on the non-violent Jain and Vaishnava traditions of his native Gujarat, it elevated suffering and denial into a quasi-religious discipline, like yoga or meditation. The realising 'force' for truth and selflessness which could be released by such self-discipline transcended the forms of protest through which it might be manifest. In fact, such outward demonstrations (petitions, boycotts, etc.), without the inward sanction of *satyagraha*, would merely encourage the violence and intolerance which it was supposed to negate. Like a secret weapon, therefore, *satyagraha* needed careful study and the deftest of handling; it was only to be invoked selectively and in carefully controlled doses.

Instead of making it available to the Western-educated intelligentsia of Congress, Gandhi spent a year sizing up the situation and then two years experimenting with limited and unfashionable campaigns well away from the presidency cities. A *satyagraha* in the remote north of Bihar won redress for its wretched indigo cultivators, whose status reminded him of Natal's indentured labourers. In Gujarat in 1917 he led a *satyagraha* on behalf of farmers unable to meet the revenue demand, and another on behalf of underpaid mill-workers in Ahmadabad's cotton industry. Not all were successful, but the support they mobilised amongst groups hitherto considered as politically irrelevant greatly enhanced both Gandhi's reputation and his following. To one who so readily identified with the underprivileged and who in dress and lifestyle resembled a religious *sadhu* more than a political activist the epithet *mahatma* ('great soul') was first applied by Tagore and then widely adopted. Amongst Gandhi's Bihar recruits from this period was the lawyer Rajendra Prasad, a future President of India, and from Gujarat Vallabhai Patel, a landlord and lawyer who would become the Congress power-broker at the time of independence. In short, Gandhi's homecoming, though low-key, glinted with novel purpose.

Other returnees to India at the beginning of the war fared less well. In September 1914 a Japanese steamer disembarked over three hundred Panjabis, mostly Sikhs, at Budge Budge, a port on the Hughli river below Calcutta. The ship had originally been chartered by a Sikh businessman in Singapore to convey its immigrant passengers from various places of Indian settlement in east and south-east Asia to a new life in Vancouver. But the Canadian authorities had refused permission to land and now at Budge Budge, after recrossing the Pacific (during which time war was declared), the ship had attracted the suspicions of the British authorities in India. Troops escorted the passengers ashore and, when some attempted to reach Calcutta, they opened fire. Twenty-two were killed; the rest, sent by train to the Panjab, were kept under the closest surveillance. To the British, if the returning Gandhi represented the acceptable face of Indian protest, these not so 'Pacific Panjabis' represented its unacceptable obverse, mutiny.

Ghadr, or 'Mutiny', was indeed the title of a weekly newspaper which had been circulating widely amongst expatriate Indians in the Far East and North America. Lest any doubt remain about its politics, its subtitle boldly declared it the 'Enemy of the British Government'. A party of the same name, founded in the USA but now operating from British Columbia, was responsible for the paper's publication, and it was one of the party's Singapore adherents who had chartered the Japanese steamer. With the outbreak of war other ships from North America and east Asia brought back to India more returning migrants of 'Ghadrite' sympathies. Committed to the violent overthrow of British rule, the Ghadrites had identified the war as a golden opportunity to foment rebellion. Already a German cruiser, the *Emden*, was loose in the Indian Ocean and playing havoc with British shipping. In September 1914, tearing a leaf from the annals of the French *Compagnie des Indes*, it even shelled Madras. For a minute it looked as if the world war might engulf India itself.

But the *Emden*'s bombardment would not be repeated, and the Ghadrites soon found that they had badly miscalculated. Many never reached the Panjab; others were betrayed by their own disorganisation or by the pro-British loyalties of most Panjabis. Additionally the war had strengthened the British capacity to deal with them thanks to the newly-imposed Defence of India Act. A few murders and robberies were carried out, but a planned uprising was foiled and by 1916 most of the perhaps five thousand

Ghadrite activists had been rounded up. Of those who stood trial in the Panjab, forty-six were hanged and two hundred transported or jailed. The only actual mutiny was that staged by sympathisers, both Muslim and Sikh, amongst Indian troops in Singapore in early 1915; after courts-martial, thirty-seven of the Singapore mutineers faced a firing squad. According to one of the finest of India's twentieth-century historians, 'these lowly Ghadr peasant and sepoy heroes have been much less remembered than the *bhadralok* [gentleman] Bengal terrorists – yet surely they deserve a better fate.'[21] The British would certainly remember them. Insurrection was a far more serious affair in the recruiting grounds of the Panjab than in Bengal. With consequences which, come 1919, Gandhi would rightly call 'diabolical', the Panjab would now be policed with exceptional vigilance and rigour.

While Gandhi stalked the *mofussil* and evaded institutional politics, while Ghadrites blundered into police traps, and while Indian troops tasted the horror of the trenches and the appalling mismanagement of the Meso-potamian campaign, government and politicians continued their centre-stage recitative of agonised complaint and trumpeted concession. To encourage wartime support, to compensate for its economic hardships, and to allay the dangers of a necessarily reduced British military presence, the government let it be known that a new package of reforms was under consideration. This was in 1915. In 1916 the new viceroy Lord Chelmsford and the Liberal secretary of state Edwin Montagu began active discussions. In 1917 they issued a public statement of intent. In 1918 they toured India collecting representations from every conceivable interest group. In 1919 they finally announced the Montagu–Chelmsford (or 'Mont-ford') reforms. And in 1921 the reforms finally came into effect. 'The motto I would ask you to place before yourselves is *Festina lente*,' said Chelmsford.

'Hastening slowly' themselves, Congress 'moderates' had kept up their genteel demands for greater representation and equal access to the civil service while outlawing tactics which under wartime restrictions might be construed as seditious. This left the field clear for Bal Tilak, who returned from his Burma exile in 1914, and for another ageing but formidable cam-paigner in the person of Mrs Annie Besant. A professional patron of radical causes, Besant's Theosophical interests had brought her to Madras in 1907 where her Irish parentage, Fabian principles and bustling energy converted her to active championship of Indian home-rule. In 1916 both she and Tilak founded Home Rule Leagues outside the control of Congress and campaigned energetically for them.

Tilak concentrated on his old stamping grounds in the Deccan. There he adopted, as well as the national campaign, a local home-rule agenda

which included the promotion of the Deccan's regional languages –
Marathi, Kannada and Telugu – as media of education and as criteria
for the creation of distinct language-based states (the future Maharashtra,
Karnataka and Andhra Pradesh). Other leaders, Muslim as well as Hindu,
invariably espoused similarly non-national issues which were dear to particular religious communities, castes, language groups, economic interests
or labour organisations. Politicisation, while heightening national awareness, was also heightening sectional competition. In fact the frantic behind-
the-scenes activity at the 1916 Lucknow Congress brings to mind
post-independence politics with its mass of 'parties' engaged in fickle alliances for the advancement of particular interests. Not only did Congress
and the Muslim League agree a joint programme at Lucknow but, with
the deaths of the moderate Gokhale and Ferozeshah Mehta in 1915, both
Tilak and Besant negotiated their way back into the Congress fold.

It did not mean that they eschewed 'extremism'. Six months later
Besant's rhetoric became so outspoken that she was arrested. Howls of
protest from the whole spectrum of nationalist opinion greeted this affront.
Even Gandhi, who had no liking for either Besant or her Westernised
methods, threatened a *satyagraha*. But Montagu and Chelmsford remained
in conciliatory mood. In what amounted to a milestone in British policy
they declared the goal of their proposed reform package to be 'the gradual
development of self-governing institutions with a view to the progressive
realisation of responsible government in India as an integral part of the
British Empire'.

This constitutional mouthful, once its jaw-breaking roughage about
'gradual' development and 'progressive' realisation had been spat out, tasted
much like home-rule. Moreover, as Congress gulped, Montagu and Chelmsford made a sincere effort to secure the widest possible co-operation in
the consultation process which was to precede the final package. Annie
Besant was therefore released after just three months' detention and in
December 1917 was elected president of Congress. The consultations went
on throughout 1918. Meanwhile the war ended and, to replace the wartime
Defence of India Act which had proved so effective against the Ghadrites,
the government opted for preventative powers of summary trial and detention. Embodied in the Rowlatt Bills, this package of 'no charge, no trial,
no appeal' proved decidedly unpalatable. It belied the spirit of the imminent
reforms, it insulted a people who had lately made such heavy sacrifices for
the empire, and it foreshadowed British readiness to resort to further
repression. Even those Indians who now sat on the viceroy's council unani-
mously rejected the bills. The Home Rule Leagues of Besant and Tilak

mobilised for defiance. More significantly they deferred to Gandhi, who now forsook his lofty detachment to declare the first national *satyagraha*. Though many nationalists had gulped down the 'Montford' promise, all gagged on the Rowlatt repression.

A nationwide *hartal* ('lock-out') scheduled for 6 April 1919 had mixed results. Delhi got the date wrong and shut down on 30 March; there were violent protests and some shooting. Bombay was brought to a complete standstill on schedule; most other cities witnessed some disruption; and Gandhi, while travelling north to supervise *satyagraha* in Delhi and the Panjab, was removed from the train and informed of his confinement to the Bombay presidency. This 'arrest' sparked more protests, especially in Bombay and Gujarat. But it was in the Panjab, still mindful of the Ghadrites and heavily policed under an uncompromising lieutenant-governor called Sir Michael O'Dwyer, that tragedy struck.

Although most Panjabis had little understanding of *satyagraha* – some were reportedly unsure whether Gandhi was 'a person or a thing'[22] – his call was respected even in the Sikhs' holy city of Amritsar. There, on 10 April, two of those who had addressed the 6 April protest were arrested for incitement. This brought their supporters out onto the streets on the eleventh. They were stopped, fired on by troops, and then took revenge in an orgy of arson and violence which left five Europeans dead. According to an admirably dispassionate assessment, 'it is difficult, given the clear difference in Panjab methods [of dealing with protesters] and the unmistakable evidence about crowd reactions, not to conclude that the violence was largely due to government action.'[23] In the same uncompromising spirit and without apparently attempting any form of consultation, O'Dwyer also sent for more troops. They arrived next day under Brigadier-General Reginald Dyer who, for pig-headedness as well as a nearly identical surname, is easily confused with the governor. Dyer stationed pickets throughout the city of Amritsar and issued orders prohibiting all meetings and demonstrations.

On the thirteenth, a Sunday, word came of an assembly at the Jallianwala Bagh, an open space hemmed in by houses. It was also the feast-day of *Baisakhi*, and many of the several thousand in the Bagh are thought to have been villagers from outside Amritsar who had come into the city to celebrate this popular spring festival. Dyer probably knew nothing of this. Arrived at the Bagh, he was disappointed to find that there was no access for his armoured car. He left it outside, marched in with a mixed force of Indian and Gurkha troops, and immediately ordered them to fire into the crowd. He gave the order to cease firing only when their ammunition was nearly exhausted. Then he withdrew.

The crowd had offered no threat, Dyer had given no warning; communication was by bullet alone. Because Dyer's men were occupying the main exit, the crowd obligingly formed a dense scrum round the only other way out. It was impossible for the troops to miss; nor did they. After the firing stopped, they shouldered arms and turned about. The wounded were left untended, the dead uncounted. Dyer simply drove away, mission completed.

The official inquiry would later conclude that 1650 rounds had been fired inside the Jallianwala Bagh, that over 1200 men, women and children had been seriously wounded, and that 379 had died (an equally reliable but unofficial source gave the latter figure as 530). There were other casualties, too. On an April afternoon in Amritsar, in a few minutes of vindictive folly, the moral pretence for British rule had been riddled into transparency, and all hope of peaceful post-war collaboration blown away in the maelstrom of killing.

There was no excuse for it. The massacre had occurred before the imposition of martial rule; even if it had occurred afterwards, Dyer's conduct would have been indefensible under any military code. To make matters worse, when later questioned, Dyer seemed if anything proud of his action. His intention, he said, had been to exact revenge for the previous killings and to make an example which would deter further defiance anywhere in the Panjab. To this end he had also had prisoners beaten, sometimes in public, and had made Indians crawl the street where an English missionary lady had been attacked. Nor was he alone. Equally provocative methods were employed in Lahore, where there had also been arson attacks. At Gujranwala, when the situation appeared to be getting out of control, Governor O'Dwyer had simply ordered up aircraft and had the city bombed.

Dyer came from a British family long-resident in India. They ran a brewery near Simla and there the general had perhaps imbibed the racial fears which had haunted his countrymen ever since 1857. Certainly he knew his history. His punishments reeked of the Kanpur reprisals, and his behaviour looks to have been conditioned by 1857 ideas of 'saving the Panjab' when, as now, Delhi was already wracked by disturbances. Moreover it soon became apparent that many other British people felt the same way. Although relieved of his command, Dyer was never formally punished. To have done so, it was argued, would have provoked a white backlash like that which had greeted the Ilbert Bill. On the contrary, in England he was rewarded. As the 'Saviour of the Panjab', a *Morning Post* subscription was raised on his behalf; it realised £26,000. Designated 'Defender of the Empire' he was also presented with a gilt sword.

This lionising of Dyer was as offensive to Indian opinion as was the repressive conduct of the Panjab authorities. Details of the Amritsar mass-acre emerged only slowly as government and Congress inquiries got under-way. The gasps of Indian horror thus coincided with the grunts of Indo-British approval. For many hitherto 'moderate' nationalists it was the turning point. Tagore, for instance, renounced his knighthood. The December 1919 Congress was switched to Amritsar to highlight the sense of betrayal; and it was presided over by Motilal Nehru, an immensely successful Allahabad lawyer who had previously been denied permission to enter the Panjab in order to defend one of the Amritsar protesters.

Up till now no family could have been more staunchly pro-British than Motilal's. Such was his admiration for British ideals of legality and human-ity, and such his expectations of British–Indian collaboration, that he had sent Jawaharlal, his only son, to school at Harrow and university at Cam-bridge. On Jawaharlal's return he had censured his radical outbursts. Now he began to endorse them. The British were no longer worthy of respect. Anand Bhawan, the Nehrus' palatial residence in Allahabad, was stripped of its European furniture. Motilal abandoned his Savile Row suits and took to wearing the homespun cottons recommended by Gandhi. A great bonfire of the dresses, ties, boas and homburgs discarded by the Nehru clan would be the earliest memory of granddaughter Indira, born in 1917. Although still opposed to any action outside the law, Motilal would join the imminent non-co-operation movement and make the considerable sacrifice involved in withdrawing from legal practice.

PURNA SWARAJ

In 1920–2 India was convulsed by a crescendo of *satyagrahas*, *swadeshi* boycotts, strikes and disturbances in the greatest display of mass non-co-operation and organised protest yet witnessed. Gandhi at last emerged as its inspiration and, with the death of Tilak in 1920, he also became the dominant figure in Congress. At his instigation the organisation was trans-formed into a more permanent, representative and effective institution, with the subscription reduced to attract a mass membership, a new structure of committees headed by a standing 'working committee', and more fre-quent meetings at national and provincial level. As well as repeal of the Rowlatt Acts and redress for the subsequent atrocities, protest focused on two other issues: the political opportunities opened by the Montagu–Chelmsford reforms, and a wild-card grievance dear to Muslim opinion concerning the plight of the caliphate, or *khilafat*.

COUNTDOWN TO INDEPENDENCE

Nationalist Demand / Protest	Year	British Concession / Reform
	1880	Viceroy Ripon introduces Rural and Municipal Boards
	1881	Judicial reforms spark British backlash against Ilbert bill
	1882	
	1883	
Rapturous send-off for Ripon	1884	
FIRST INDIAN NATIONAL CONGRESS	1885	
	1892	INDIA COUNCILS ACT. Indirect elections to Legislative Councils conceded
	1893	
	1894	
[Serious famines 1895–1900]	1895	
[Plague 1896–98]	1896	
SWADESHI MOVEMENT against Bengal partition	1905	Curzon's partition of Bengal
	1906	Partition reversed
	1907	
Tilak's re-arrest sparks more trouble in Maharastra	1908	
First bombs and assassinations	1909	MORLEY-MINTO reforms; more elected members on Legislative
	1910	Councils; Separate Hindu and Muslim electorates
	1911	
	1912	
	1913	
Ghadr Movement	1914	
	1915	
Lucknow Pact. Home Rule League	1916	
Gandhi's first *satyagrahas*	1917	Montague 'Statement of Intent'
	1918	
AMRITSAR MASSACRE	1919	MONTAGUE-CHELMSFORD REFORMS
KHILAFAT MOVEMENT 1920–23	**1920**	
Gandhi promises *swaraj*	1921	Fiscal autonomy conceded
	1922	Opportunities for Indian officers in ICS improved
Congress boycotts Simon; demands *purna swaraj*;	1928	Simon Commission
hails independence	1929	Irwin offers Dominion Status
SALT MARCH CIVIL DISOBEDIENCE CAMPAIGN	**1930**	ROUND TABLE CONFERENCE
1930–31 and 1932–33	1931	Gandhi-Irwin Pact; Federation proposal attracts Princes
	1932	
	1933	
	1934	
	1935	GOVERNMENT OF INDIA ACT gives provincial autonomy
	1936	
Elections – Congress governments in 7 provinces	1937	
League condemns 'Congress Raj'	1938	
Congress ministries resign	1939	
League adopts 'Pakistan Resolution'	**1940**	
Anti-War *satyagraha*	1941	
QUIT INDIA MOVEMENT	1942	CRIPPS MISSION offers virtual independence but
	1943	fails to discountenance 'Pakistan'
Gandhi–Jinnah talks fail	1944	
	1945	SIMLA CONFERENCE; Jinnah holds to ransom
Elections; Congress triumphs but League progresses	1946	Atlee declares end of British rule in 1948
Direct Action Day and Calcutta killings	**1947**	MOUNTBATTEN concedes Pakistan;
Nehru interim Prime Minister		advances date to:
INDEPENDENCE / PARTITION		**14–15 AUGUST 1947**

FIRST WORLD WAR

SECOND WORLD WAR

The office of caliph, the supreme political and religious institution according to many exponents of Muslim law, had long since passed from Baghdad to Cairo and then on to Constantinople and the Ottoman sultans of Turkey. It had therefore been to Constantinople that in the 1780s Tipu Sultan had appealed for recognition of his Mysore sovereignty. When Turkey entered the First World War as a German ally, some Indian Muslims had raised objections to Muslim troops being used against their 'spiritual leader'. The British had largely allayed these by insisting that the caliphate would be respected in any eventual peace treaty. Some Khilafatist supporters had nevertheless been interned during the war. Released in 1919, and fearing that the government of India would prove unwilling and perhaps unable to influence the peace process, these activists immediately began to apply what pressure they could.

Gandhi had worked closely with Muslims in Natal. He realised the importance of Hindu–Muslim collaboration in the struggle for *swaraj*, and adopted the Khilafatist cause as a means to that end. A non-co-operation programme was organised and, when the 1920 Treaty of Sèvres revealed that the caliph would indeed lose out to the extent of ceding control over the holy places of Islam to the Arabs, it swung into action. Medals were to be returned, appointments declined, schools and government institutions boycotted.

Additionally a *hijra*, or 'flight' like that of the Prophet from Mecca to Medina, saw about thirty thousand Muslims flee from infidel rule in the Panjab to Islamic brotherhood in Afghanistan. Most soon trailed back, penniless and exceedingly bitter. In India those of their brethren who urged Muslim sepoys to disobey orders were quickly arrested. The movement served to unite many shades of Islamic opinion and to politicise some of the poorer sections of Muslim society. Thanks to Gandhi's leadership, it also gave the impression of a united Hindu–Muslim front against the British. But in reality 'Hindus and Muslims were fairly launched not upon a common struggle but upon a joint struggle; they worked together but not as one.'[24]

The chosen issue of the caliphate emphasised the allegiance of Muslims not to Indian sovereignty but to an external sovereignty of the *dar-ul-Islam*, the 'world of Islam'. Gandhi hoped that joint action would create its own bond; and for a time it did. The non-co-operation movement, started by Gandhi and the Khilafatists in mid-1920, had quickly spread to Congress, whose members, already in an uproar over the Panjab atrocities, were at last examining the implications of the long-delayed Montagu–Chelmsford reforms.

These significantly increased Indian representation at all levels of government; they also introduced a new principle, known as dyarchy, whereby certain subjects – agriculture, health, education, local government – were devolved from the central government to the provincial governments. Since the provincial governments were now to have ministers who would be chosen from, and responsible to, the provincial legislative councils which themselves now consisted mainly of elected Indian members, dyarchy meant that the devolved subjects passed into Indian control – save, that is, for the casting veto of the governor. Additionally, Indian representation in the viceroy's Executive Council was increased from one to three members, while his central Legislative Council became two chambers, one a Legislative Assembly, the other a Council of State; both were to have a majority of elected members but, again, the viceroy retained a superior prerogative.

Before the war these provisions would have caused a sensation, but by 1921 they were barely acceptable. In recognition of her wartime contribution, India had sent representatives to the peace conference at Versailles and had been enrolled in the League of Nations. The appetite for full nationhood could no longer be met by the drip-feed of heavily diluted constitutional concessions. It was only browbeating by Gandhi which wrung from Congress a grudging vote of thanks for the new reforms, and this was more from policy than gratitude. To him, as to most Congress members in the aftermath of Amritsar, dyarchy sounded too much like a lame apology for 'Dyer-archy'. Moreover the powers reserved to the governors and viceroy clearly negated the veneer of self-rule. As for the new seats and offices on offer, they became simply targets for renunciation as Congress endorsed the new wave of non-co-operation.

At its Calcutta meeting in September 1920 Gandhi narrowly won a trial of strength in persuading the majority of Congress to endorse the new programme of boycott. By December, when elections under the new dispensation had nevertheless been held and various dissident groupings had successfully contested them, Congress was ready to take a much sterner line. Support for non-co-operation at every level was now overwhelming as Gandhi, not without a sense of triumphalism, promised *swaraj* within one year.

On a state visit in 1921 the Prince of Wales (the future Edward VIII) processed through streets that were empty and silent as the boycott took effect. Cultivators rallied to the cause in UP and elsewhere to form *kisan sabhas*, 'peasant societies', pressing agrarian grievances. Industrial workers from Bombay to Bengal organised strikes and formed themselves into unions. Amongst the tens of thousands arrested and sentenced to short gaol terms were both Nehrus.

But 1921 ended with Gandhi's promised *swaraj* still unattained. Indeed he looked to be losing control of the situation. Like *satyagraha*, he interpreted *swaraj* in a personal as well as a national sense. It could as well be translated as 'self-control' or 'self-reliance' as 'self-rule'. Political emancipation lay through economic emancipation from dependency on manufactured and imported products, through ideological emancipation from the materialism of the West, and through individual emancipation from the tyranny of self and the violence of desire. His obsession with spinning, with the nationwide distribution of spinning wheels, and with the wearing of homespun *khadi* looked to many like a wildly eccentric distraction at this time of national upheaval. Gandhi, though, saw in it the discipline and the dignity of a more profound and universal resurgence. In short, like everyone else, he had his own agenda. While Khilafatists looked to the crescent of international Islam, India's first communists brandished the Marxist hammer and socialists like Jawaharlal Nehru took up the *kisan*'s sickle. Hindu revivalists saw *swaraj* as *Ram-raj* (the utopia of the *Ramayana*), Sikhs as a return to the rule of the *khalsa* (the 'pure'), and practically every caste and language group as a chance for self-promotion. Meanwhile Gandhi fixed his gaze on human redemption.

In early 1922, in a bid to refocus the movement, he announced a new phase of civil disobedience which was to start at Bardoli in Gujarat and to include the ultimate defiance of refusing to pay taxes. Imprisoned activists sensed a climax; India braced itself for the great showdown. Then Gandhi called it all off. Hindu–Muslim collaboration was already crumbling at the edges. M.A. Jinnah had walked out on Congress over the boycotting of the new reforms and what he regarded as Gandhi's rabble-rousing techniques; in distant Kerala the *moplahs* of Calicut and Cannanore (Muslims who claimed descent from the first Arab traders to settle on the Malabar coast) had taken up arms against Hindus as well as Europeans; and in the north Madan Mohan Malaviya's *Mahasabha*, a Hindu revivalist movement like the *Arya Samaj*, stood accused of forcibly converting Muslims with a form of Hindu baptism. Then came news from UP of mob violence in which twenty-two Indian constables had been burnt to death in their own police station. For Gandhi it was the last straw. India was obviously not ready for 'self-rule'. He retired to his spinning wheel, was promptly arrested for past incitements, pleaded guilty, and successfully secured the maximum six-year sentence; he thought of it more as a penance.

Partly out of frustration, partly out of ambition, in that same year

Motilal Nehru and others successfully argued in Congress that the limitations of the new reforms could be more effectively exposed, and *swaraj* promoted, from within the system. Known as the 'Swarajists', these Congress members then stood for election, assumed office, and fitfully suborned the operation of government. But since they were always overruled by the powers reserved to the governors and viceroy, their ardour soon cooled and they lapsed into a more collaborative mode.

Thus by 1923 many Congress members had ceased their protest, and Muslim Khilafatists were already feeling betrayed by their Hindu colleagues. A worse betrayal awaited them from the caliphate itself. In 1924 it was, of all people, a Turk, in fact Kemal Ataturk, who simply abolished the whole institution when he overthrew the last Ottoman sultan. Indian Muslims now felt more isolated than ever. They were left, in the words of a noted authority, 'politically "all dressed up with nowhere to go" . . . [They] had hitched their wagon to the crescent of the caliphate and it had dragged them "up the garden path".'[25] After this bitter experience it would be more than a decade before pan-Indian Muslim sentiment would again unite on a single issue. By then Jinnah would have joined the Muslim League, and the ideal of an Indian *dar-ul-Islam* would have replaced that of the caliphate.

While Gandhi languished in gaol some of his disciples, like Rajendra Prasad, continued to boycott government office and to concentrate on the social programmes dear to their leader. From 1925 onwards these programmes included the support and education of those downtrodden members of Hindu society who were conventionally regarded as 'untouchable' but whom Gandhi renamed as 'Harijans' ('Children of God'). Jinnah, meanwhile, stood aloof from both Congress groups. And 'communal strife', the Indian euphemism for Hindu–Muslim conflict, worsened; in 1926 riots in Calcutta left over a hundred dead.

The British, not unhappy about this evidence of nationalist disarray, quietly removed two long-standing grievances: access to the elite Indian Civil Service (the senior administrative cadre) and to officer-training in the army was made less difficult for Indian applicants; and by establishing India's fiscal autonomy, much of the 'drain theory' critique was negated. Duties on imported cloth were soon raised, thus removing the preferential status enjoyed by Lancashire's products. 'The British still had a great economic interest in India, but the principle of tariff autonomy was established and the days of the old economic imperialism were over.'[26]

Political advances remained much more contentious. The Montagu–Chelmsford reforms had contained provision for a review and further progress towards 'responsible government' within ten years. In 1928, therefore, a parliamentary commission under Sir John Simon arrived to assess the situation and make proposals. By what is sometimes described as an 'oversight', it contained not a single Indian. Moreover Baldwin's Conservative government was known to be out of sympathy even with the 'Montford' reforms, let alone any advance on them. Massive demonstrations greeted the wretched commissioners throughout India. Congress united around a strict boycott of them, and Gandhi, released on medical grounds, at last returned to the political fray.

Where all else had failed, British pig-headedness had again provided India with an issue on which most nationalists were in agreement. Anticipating the Simon Report, Congress had already called an All Parties Convention which demanded a dominion status for the 'Commonwealth of India' equivalent to that enjoyed by Canada or Australia. In late 1928 the young Jawaharlal Nehru went one better, piloting through Congress a resolution demanding *purna swaraj*, 'complete self-rule'. This meant independence. At the December 1929 Congress the green, saffron and white flag was unfurled to shouts of 'Long Live the Revolution'; the first Independence Day, when all endorsed a long pledge to resist British rule and assert *purna swaraj*, was celebrated on 26 January 1930.

The tricolour is still India's flag and, although independence had to wait another seventeen years, 26 January is still commemorated. But ironically this historic meeting of Congress, whence the Republic of India traces its genesis, took place in Lahore, a city which today belongs to Pakistan and which, but for strategic reasons, would probably be its capital. The green in the new flag was for Islam, just as the saffron was for Hinduism. But the Muslim League had had nothing to do with it. Jinnah had walked out of the All Parties Convention following its rejection of separate Muslim electorates. Without these safeguards, he said, there would be 'revolution and civil war'. Meant as a threat, his words contained a prophecy. The ensuing decades would be as much about trying to decide the future political composition of the subcontinent as about evicting the British and adjusting to a post-colonial world.

At the Stroke of the Midnight Hour

1930–1948

SWADDLED IN JUST a shawl and a *dhoti*, with a long thin arm clutching a long thin staff, Mahatma Gandhi had quickly become the most recognisable symbol of anti-colonial protest. His flimsy cottons epitomised the defence-less apostle of non-violence, his stout staff declared the unbending champion of national rights. But if it was the near-naked Gandhi who alerted the world to India's struggle, it was Jawaharlal Nehru, always impeccable even in homespun, who alerted India to world struggle.

During a European tour in 1927 Nehru had attended the Congress of Oppressed Nationalities in Brussels, been elected to the executive committee of the League Against Imperialism and been invited to Moscow for the tenth-anniversary celebrations of the Russian Revolution. A socialist since his Cambridge days, he was already in close touch with the British Labour Party and looked a promising recruit to international Marxism. By making 1930 the year in which Congress ratcheted up its demand to full indepen-dence, then backed it with a new programme of civil disobedience, the brooding Nehru showed a keen awareness of how the international scene was changing.

Elsewhere in Asia the struggle against colonialism was also entering its final phase. Sukarno, another young leader of undoubted charisma, was challenging the Netherlands in their East Indies or, as he preferred, 'Indo-nesia'. Like the Indian National Congress, the Indonesian Nationalist Party (PNI) had lately gained enormous support by demanding full indepen-dence. When in 1930 Sukarno stood trial for incitement he used the occasion to deliver one of the keynote speeches of the age. 'The sun does not rise because the cock crows,' he declared, 'the cock crows because the sun rises.' Emancipation from colonial rule was historically inevitable, the awakening of Asia's peoples an irresistible phenomenon, not an invention of their leaders. Nehru could not have put it better. On the banks of the Ravi outside Lahore he had saluted India's new flag at the midnight hour on New Year's Night 1930. The dawn of the decade presaged a dazzling era of liberation and fulfilment all over Asia. 'We can just hear the promise it holds,' Sukarno told his supporters, 'like the melody of a distant gamelan on a moonlit night.'

In Manchuria it was already daybreak. The 'Rising Sun' flew over the start of a southward trail of Japanese acquisitions on the Asian mainland which would eventually engross Sukarno's Indonesia and reach even Nehru's India. Also in northern China and also in 1930, the first rehearsal for decolonisation took place when, with minimum publicity, the British hauled down the Union Jack at Weihaiwei, a coastal outpost sometimes known as 'the other Hong Kong'. It was the first time since the American War of Independence that they had surrendered territory to a nationalist government. In the same year, in Hong Kong itself a group of Vietnamese exiles headed by Nguyen Ai Quoc founded the Indo-Chinese Communist Party. The party would eventually become the main component in the anti-French Viet Minh, and Nguyen Ai Quoc, after ten years underground, would re-emerge with the sobriquet of 'Ho Chi Minh'.

A year of high hopes for nationalists, for the imperial powers 1930 was darkened by grave doubts about the whole world order which they represented. In Malaya recession so reduced the demand for rubber that indentured Tamil labourers were being repatriated to India and European plantation-managers were said to be begging their passage money home. India's capitalists were also badly hit, with Bengal's export-dependent jute industry a notable casualty. Nor were things any better in London and New York. The markets had crashed in 1929; in 1930 the Great Depression bit hard. Dance-halls became soup-kitchens and the streets of the industrialised world filled with the angry armies of the unemployed. Elected governments took heed. Social spending at home assumed a higher priority; and those who championed it, like the Labour Party in Britain, criticised global defence expenditure and warmed to the idea of imperial disengagement. Western capitalism was in crisis, and so too was the colonial system which (according to the imperialists) it supported, or which (according to the Marxists) supported it. Either way, after 1930 the Western empires in Asia began to back off. Gears crashed as the great imperial juggernauts of the nineteenth century shuddered into reverse. Within three decades, but for a bogged American vehicle in Vietnam, all would have pulled out of Asia.

Internationalists like Nehru itched to scale the barricades, but the other-worldly Gandhi seemed indifferent to the march of history and increasingly out of touch with these tumultuous times. For him, if 1920 had meant spinning, 1930 meant salt. Nehru was in despair. 'Salt suddenly became a mysterious word, a word of power ... We were bewildered and could not quite fit in a national struggle with common salt.'[1] The Simon Commission had recommended no changes in the central government and had made no mention even of dominion status as demanded by the All Parties Convention and by a constitutional report prepared by Motilal Nehru. It seemed that even the drip-feed of concessions was drying up; hence the new Congress demand for full independence, or *purna swaraj*, and the *carte blanche* given to Gandhi and Jawaharlal Nehru to implement another programme of action.

But first Gandhi made a final appeal direct to the viceroy Lord Irwin. He wanted the land revenue halved, the rupee pegged, alcohol prohibited, Indian cloth protected, the salt tax abolished, political prisoners released and much else besides. No one expected Irwin to deliver on such a package. The Mahatma, whose twinkle of compassion concealed a steely-eyed cunning, was testing the mass appeal of the weapons at his disposal. In late February 1930 he announced the winner, and therefore the focus of the new campaign, to be salt. Massive civil disobedience was to be launched in the name of man's inalienable right to the untaxed enjoyment of a common condiment.

Salt had traditionally been produced in coastal salt-pans whence it was traded inland. Since at least Mughal times production had been regarded as a state monopoly and a suitable subject for taxation. In the eighteenth century, East India Company employees had claimed that Emperor Farrukhsiyar's *farman* entitled them to exemption from local salt duties. By extending this exemption to their agents, they had acquired a monopoly of the salt trade in Bengal even before Plassey. Clive had reclaimed this monopoly for the Company itself and, ever since, the government had enjoyed a salt revenue. The rate of tax was low; Curzon had tried to reduce it further and, although recently increased, it still came to less than a quarter of a rupee per head per year. The yield accounted for no more than 4 percent of government revenue. But its application was wide; everyone ate salt. And it was deeply resented. As Gandhi explained, 'there is no article like salt, outside water, by taxing which the state can reach even the starving millions, the sick, the maimed and the utterly helpless. The tax constitutes therefore the most inhuman poll tax the ingenuity of man can devise.' Long a dispensable anachronism, it had suddenly become a deliberate iniquity; and since the salt monopoly had legal sanction, all who flouted it could expect to be prosecuted.

With this in mind, Gandhi assembled his followers, alerted the press, and in one of the great set-pieces of the independence struggle staged a month-long salt march from his Sabarmati ashram near Ahmadabad to Dandi on the Gujarat coast. There, 'on 6 April 1930, by picking up a handful of salt, Gandhiji inaugurated the Civil Disobedience Movement, a movement that was to remain unsurpassed in the history of the Indian national movement for the country-wide mass participation which it unleashed.'[2]

Other marches were staged all over the country, from the north-west frontier to East Bengal and Tamil Nadu; some concentrated on industrial salt plants, where protesters in their thousands were beaten back by police and arrested. The government, pleasantly surprised that something as innocuous as the salt tax had been singled out, had at first responded cautiously. But active civil disobedience, as opposed to passive non-co-operation, directly challenged the law. As the movement spread to the non-payment of rents, of revenue and of taxes, distraints on land and property became commonplace and were bitterly contested. The movement also coincided with a startling revival of terrorist activity in places as far-flung as Chittagong and Peshawar. Less sensationally but much more effectively, there was mass participation in a host of non-violent activities like picketing liquor shops, *swadeshi* boycotts, commercial *hartals*, and rural *satyagrahas* (designed to contest forest restrictions). Jawaharlal Nehru later reckoned the number of those gaoled in 1930 at over ninety-two thousand (the official figure was nearer sixty thousand). He, Motilal, the rest of the Congress leadership and eventually Gandhi himself were amongst the detainees. Congress committees were declared unlawful, and special ordinances muzzled the press and restricted picketing.

However, the campaign was comparatively short-lived; it barely lasted into 1931 and, although revived in 1932–4, would never regain its full momentum. Moreover, if 'primarily designed to strengthen and unite Indians [and] to influence *them* rather than in a direct way to weaken the administration',[3] its success was limited. Unlike the 1919–22 Rowlatt-Khilafat protests, the 1930–1 protests did not enjoy Muslim support. The common condiment proved to be of less universal appeal than Gandhi had hoped, and Muslims seemingly preferred to take the government's salt to that of Congress. In fact in late 1930 Jinnah and other Muslim leaders were amongst those heading for London. There, as with the 'Montford' reforms in 1919–20, protest was lending urgency to a new cycle of constitutional discussion.

To offset the negative effect of the Simon Report, Viceroy Irwin had reinterpreted the goal of the 'Montford' reforms as eventual dominion status, and had proposed a Round Table Conference at which all parties and interests would be represented. Its discussions were not to be limited by the Simon Report. In fact the British hope was that it would lift critical Indian eyes from the contentious scrutiny of minor reforms to the nobler prospect of India's future status and constitution as an autonomous member of, and dominion within, the British empire. In effect the participants were being invited to forget the trees and, standing back, to map out the shape of the whole wood.

Congress, with most of its leading lights in gaol, declined to participate; it regarded dominion status as an unacceptable alternative to *purna swaraj*, and would remain deeply suspicious of all else that emerged from the Round Table Conference. The first session was thus, as Gandhi put it, much like *Hamlet* without the prince. But when the conference reconvened for its second session in 1931, Gandhi had undergone another of his sudden changes of heart. Following personal discussions with the viceroy – which prompted a piqued Winston Churchill to sneer at the King-Emperor's representative stooping to parley with a 'half-naked fakir' – Gandhi and Irwin had signed a pact which brought the release of detainees and other concessions. Gandhi now trusted Irwin and was ready to join the Round Table Conference when it reconvened in late 1931.

The first session had been attended by representatives of various Muslim parties including the League, and by those of the Hindu revivalist *Mahasabha*, the Sikh and Christian communities, the Harijans, the Anglo-Indians, various liberal nationalists, numerous professional groups and a strong contingent of British parliamentarians. It was an impressive cast even without the prince. There were, besides, other princes, plus a veritable army of Round Table knights. For it was at this point that representatives of India's princely states, most of whom held honours from the British Crown as well as Indian titles, were for the first time brought into the constitutional equation – and thereby greatly complicated it.

FEDERATION FIASCO

Hyderabad, Jammu-and-Kashmir, Mysore, Travancore, the great Maratha states of central India, the phalanx of rajput states in Rajasthan, and the other princely archipelagos in Gujarat, Orissa, Bengal, Assam, UP and the Panjab were united only in their relationship with the imperial government. Like the vassal states of old they represented that 'society of kings' which had legitimised and gratified the pretensions of more traditional imperial-isms. But together they still accounted for over a third of the subcontinent's population and nearly half of its land-mass. An India without them would have been so moth-eaten as to disintegrate at the touch.

So long as the British ruled the provinces which constituted the rest of India directly, it had hardly mattered that the princely states enjoyed internal autonomy, since they were subject to individual treaties with the British, to supervision by a political cadre of British officials, and to a vague doctrine of British paramountcy. But once the British began to devolve power to their provinces, to share it at the centre, and even to consider transferring it altogether, the anxieties of the princely states became acute. Would they become free agents if the British withdrew? Or would the British continue to uphold their treaty responsibilities after ceding power? Was paramountcy also transferable? And would its likely claimant, an increasingly left-wing Congress, be disposed to safeguard the autonomy, the territorial integrity and the dynastic rights of unregenerated feudal autocrats with a poor record for social justice and a far from hostile attitude to the British?

In February 1931, at the height of the London talks, the British formally inaugurated their New Delhi capital. As a last imperial extravaganza, it smothered in bungalows and bougainvillaea the wasteland between Shah Jahan's metropolis and the bat-infested battlements of all those other old Delhis. It also embodied the imperial thinking of the day. At the ceremonial heart of the city, on a ruddy acropolis atop Raisina Hill, flanked by Herbert Baker's classical secretariats and the domed temple of Edwin Lutyens' Vice-regal House, there had been erected four columns representing Canada, South Africa, Australia and New Zealand. The columns supposedly wel-comed India into the brotherhood of the British dominions. But it was noteworthy that each of these dominions comprised a federation of various provinces and protectorates which had subscribed to a single central government. For India's patchwork of provinces and princely states, federa-tion also looked to be the way forward.

To progressive sections of British opinion and to moderate sections of Indian opinion, federation also appealed as a way of opening up central government (as opposed to the provincial governments) to greater Indian participation. When, unexpectedly, the idea also found favour with a major-ity of the princes, federal proposals suddenly soared like the Raisina col-umns to the top of the Round Table's agenda. But they were not to everyone's taste. By diehard imperialists like Churchill any infringement of British sovereignty, federal or otherwise, had to be resisted; they would fight federation tooth and nail. So would most sections of Congress, which saw in it an attempt not to unite British India with the princely states but rather to divide – and, of course, rule – an emerging entity which transcended both British and princely India, namely the Indian nation.

Nor were such suspicions unjustified. For if the central government became a federal government representing both the provinces and the princely states, the British might expect to play a lasting supervisory role. The princes would continue to look to the British authorities for support against any encroachment on their autonomy. And with this support, plus that of the minorities (Muslims, Sikhs, etc.), the British would be able to command a majority at the federal centre. Given such a scenario, the arrangements whereby defence and foreign affairs were to remain under British control during a transitional period might be prolonged indefinitely; likewise a residual British presence which would ensure to the empire the services of the Indian army at minimal cost might also be preserved indefinitely. In short, federation, though a highway to integration and independence elsewhere, might in India become a congested thoroughfare leading to the exact opposite – disintegration and continued dependence.

Compared to this contentious prospect, the other vista opened during the Round Table discussions and incorporated into the monumental Government of India Act of 1935 was comparatively uncontroversial. Yet because federation would never actually be implemented, it would be much the most significant part of the Act; and it would have a considerable bearing on the Partition of 1947 and on the different constitutions of the two states that resulted.

As a package of reforms which advanced the long-running process of Indianisation and democratisation in the provincial assemblies, this other component of the 1935 India Act looked unexciting. But in effect it made the provinces autonomous. The franchise, although still restricted by property and gender criteria, was increased from seven million to about thirty-five million, or one-sixth of the potential adult suffrage; the number of provinces was also increased, with Sind being separated from Bombay and Orissa from Bihar; and all the provincial assemblies were reorganised and their memberships greatly enlarged so that elected Indian representatives could command majorities and form governments. Many subjects remained the preserve of the central government, and some important powers of intervention and supersession remained reserved to the mostly British governors. But from 1937, when the first elections under this scheme were held, the provincial governments of British India were no longer necessarily run by the British.

Nehru nevertheless characterised the India Act as 'a new charter of slavery'; it was, after all, a long way short of *purna swaraj*. He embraced the opportunity of the 1937 elections to show the strength of Congress but expected all those elected to resign as a protest. With much the best organisation Congress duly swept the polls, capturing 70 per cent of the popular vote and, despite the system of separate electorates, nearly half of all seats. Then, after much heart-searching, indeed a near-thrombosis, and in contravention of Nehru's wishes, the party's leaders reluctantly agreed to let its successful candidates participate in government.

The agreeable business of allocating ministries and rewarding supporters was readily embraced. In every province, elected Indian members now formed Indian governments, appointed Indian ministers, and legislated in Indian interests. 'The province became the most important arena in political life,' and, more than ever, provincial leadership and identity became entrenched components of national politics. In the run-up to Independence, and thereafter when the provinces became the component states of independent India and the constituent provinces of Pakistan, this would 'affect profoundly the nature of all-India [and all-Pakistan] "national" leadership and power'.[4] Against well-organised and intransigent provincial leaderships even a Congress-run national government would not be able to make much headway.

In 1937 seven of the now eleven provinces ended up with Congress governments. The outstanding exceptions were Bengal and the Panjab, both with slim Muslim majority populations and both future subjects of partition. But there the similarity ended. In Bengal a predominantly Muslim government was formed. For the first time Calcutta's influential, English-speaking Hindu *bhadralok*, the landed 'gentlemen' or 'babus' who had made so much of the running in the early days of Congress, experienced the harsh realities of democracy and found themselves out in the cold. They condemned the system of separate minority electorates which had made their electoral chances even more hopeless, then they increasingly turned on those whom they saw as the main beneficiaries, the Muslims. Thus, 'while the rest of nationalist India was rejecting the "autonomy" outlined in the Government's White Paper as a sham, the Bengali bhadralok – Congress-men and non-Congress-men alike – were concerned only with its disregard of their own provincial political ambitions.'[5] Having pilloried the system of separate electorates as a 'shameless surrender to [Muslim] communalists', they now shamelessly demanded just such a surrender to Hindu communalism by insisting that, as a minority, they too were entitled to electoral safeguards.

There was, though, another way: the political arithmetic could be revised by changing the units to which it applied. Curzon's partition of Bengal, against which the *bhadralok* had fought so successfully in 1905, began to look less 'utterly contemptuous of public opinion'.

In the Panjab, landed interests were also vocal but, instead of sundering the different communities, they actually cemented sectarian relations. Under the aegis of a Unionist Party, Muslims, Hindus and Sikhs all participated in government together. British dependence on the Panjab's agricultural communities for three-fifths of its army recruitment, plus the availability and potential of newly irrigated land there, had created a markedly prosperous province in which the agriculturalist enjoyed a privileged position. Whether Hindu, Sikh or Muslim, his main interest was in protecting this position, particularly against the encroachment of urban moneylenders. The principal division was thus not between Muslim and Sikh or Hindu, but between landed interests and commercial interests. Legislation which afforded the landowner security against the alienation of his land and which ensured that the agricultural vote was maximised had 'institutionalised the political division between the rural and urban populations', and now provided the Unionist Party with its ideology.[6]

In 1937 the Unionist Party won well over half the seats in the Panjab, and neither Congress nor the Muslim League gained a significant foothold. In striking contrast to Bengal, the Panjab thus looked a most improbable candidate for sectarian partition, let alone for its later tripartite reincarnation as a hotbed of Hindu communalism (Haryana), a stronghold of Sikh separatism (Indian Panjab) and the cornerstone of an Islamic state (Pakistani Panjab).

Other ambiguities haunted the new constitutional set-up. The system of separate electorates for the minority communities was bitterly contested in principle by Congress and in its details by almost everyone. Gandhi had taken particular exception to Harijans being considered a non-Hindu community and embarked on a fast to get their agreement to the removal of this provision. He succeeded; separate Harijan electorates were abolished but more seats were reserved exclusively for Harijan members. The 'Communal Awards' which enumerated the seats reserved for the other separate electorates were decided by the British, no agreed scheme being forthcoming from Indian sources. Naturally this endeared the awards to no one. In Bengal the provincial Congress, representing the disillusioned Hindu *bhadralok*, very nearly split away from the national Congress as firebrands like Subhas Chandra Bose demanded direct action against the awards. This would have alienated the substantial Muslim support which

Congress still enjoyed nationally, and was therefore unacceptable to the central leadership.

Far more serious was the fate of the federation. It was to have come into operation as soon as a majority of the princes had signed Instruments of Accession. But partly because of lobbying by diehard empire dinosaurs like Churchill, and partly thanks to the intense rivalries amongst the princes themselves, the process was delayed. In the interim the princes began to have second thoughts. Some were worried about the financial implications of federation, others about the continuation of paramountcy. But what made them dig in their heels most was Congress triumphalism following the 1937 elections.

Congress's national leadership had hitherto discouraged the party's involvement in the princely states. But its provincial leaders, many of them now in government, were not so particular. In arguments redolent of those used by Dalhousie to support British annexations in the 1850s, they stigmatised princely rule as a corrupt anachronism. How could they remain deaf to the unenfranchised plight of close colleagues and neighbours who happened to live under such autocratic dispensations? Financial and organisational support was offered to populist movements in the states; activists and agitators were allowed to drift across state borders. Suddenly, unexpected demands for more accountable government and more popular representation brought disturbances in Kashmir, Hyderabad, Mysore and elsewhere. Where a Hindu prince ruled a predominantly Muslim state, as in Kashmir – or vice versa as in Hyderabad – the situation was exacerbated by sectarian tension. Not surprisingly nawabs and nizams, rajas and maharajas alike took fright. If provincial Congress governments could so threaten their prerogatives, what chance would they stand against a Congress-dominated federal government?

Congress-men saw it rather differently. Under a federation the two central chambers were to be indirectly elected, candidates being chosen by the provincial assemblies (in the case of British India) and by the princes (in the case of the states). Congress had done well enough in the 1937 elections to look forward to a substantial bloc of seats under this arrangement. It would, however, only be able to achieve a governing majority if it also commanded some of the seats allocated to the princes. This in turn would only be possible if some of the princes could be pressured into sending candidates who enjoyed a popular mandate. 'Here, then, I would argue,' writes Ian Copland in a detailed study of princely attitudes, 'was the crux of [Congress's] new strategy in the states: to pressure the princes into returning only popularly elected representatives . . . to the federal legislature.'[7]

If the princes were thus panicked out of their support for federation, so too were Muslims. The attitude of Muhammad Ali Jinnah and the Muslim League to the new constitution had at first been equivocal: as nationalists they condemned it as falling short of independence, while as a minority they were tempted by its apparent safeguards. But in 1938, as Congress pressure on the princely states mounted and as Congress governments in the provinces rejected Muslim overtures for power-sharing, Jinnah too foresaw the danger of a 'Congress Raj' at the federal centre. Accusations of Hindu discrimination against Muslims in the already Congress-run provinces were probably much exaggerated, but they received wide publicity. To the call of 'Islam in Danger' the League began a drive for the mass support which had hitherto eluded it. Bengal's governing Muslim party joined the League, most of UP's Muslims did likewise, and in the Panjab the first cracks began to appear in the Unionist Party consensus. The League's claim to represent the majority of Muslims at last began to acquire some substance.

With the princes and the Muslims, supposedly the beneficiaries of federation, now backing off, the scheme was probably doomed; the outbreak of the Second World War merely gave it a plausible burial. As well as polarising communal opinion and leaving the princes in the constitutional wilderness, the federation débâcle had also left its mark on Congress. In accepting power in the provinces, Congress-men had soon found themselves having to compromise on some of their principles. Plans for agrarian reform were diluted and links with the trade unions were strained by loyalties to industrialists, like the Tata and Birla families, who had substantially funded Congress. The responsibility for law and order meant a more cautious approach to radical causes. 'A steady shift to the Right, occasionally veiled by Left rhetoric, increasingly characterised the functioning of the Congress ministries as well as of the party High Command.' Even Nehru, whom the British regarded as little better than a communist, 'increasingly sought in internationalist gestures [like a trip to war-torn Spain] a kind of surrogate for effective Left action at home'.[8]

The resulting discontent in the socialist and communist wings of Congress provided the radical Bengali leader, Subhas Chandra Bose, with his chance. A vehement *bhadralok* opponent of the entire 1935 constitution, in 1938 he secured re-election as Congress president on a platform of uncompromising opposition to the new constitution, to the communal awards and in particular to the federation. Congress was to withdraw its collaboration in the provinces and a new wave of *satyagraha* was to be launched in support of immediate independence. Gandhi had virtually retired from Congress in 1934, but, deeply distrustful of Bose, he again returned to the fray and, with the support of Nehru and others, engineered Bose's downfall in 1939. Bose, or 'Netaji' ('Leader') as he would soon be known, responded by setting up a radical party known as the Forward Bloc and espousing terrorist tactics. In 1940 he was arrested. He escaped on the eve of his trial, fled to Afghanistan and thence to Moscow and Berlin.

It was under Tokyo's auspices that Bose next surfaced, literally, when he landed from a submarine in Japanese-held Singapore in 1943. Like Sukarno in Indonesia, and despite the same left-wing reservations, Bose admired Japan's disciplined and defiant emergence as a world power and was encouraged by her championship of Asian emancipation and of regional co-prosperity. Forced to choose between two imperialisms, he plumped for what looked at the time to be the more amenable and dynamic.

By late 1943 he was installed on Indian soil as the head of state in Azad Hind ('Free India') and commander-in-chief of the Indian National Army (INA), a twenty-thousand-strong force recruited from Indian prisoners of war in Japanese hands. Azad Hind comprised just the Andaman Islands in the Bay of Bengal, they being the only Indian territory under Japanese occupation. Previously the Andamans had served as a British detention centre for those convicted of political crimes. Ironically, after an odyssey of some twenty thousand kilometres, Bose had ended up exactly where he would have been sent had he never fled India.

'A BLESSING IN DISGUISE'

India entered the Second World War much as it had the First. Without consultation, let alone consent, the viceroy simply informed its people that they were at war. The response, though, was less 'heart-warming' than on the previous occasion. As well as telegrams of support and a rush to the recruiting stations, there was a howl of protest and, in late 1939, a mass Congress exodus from provincial government. In those provinces where Congress had formed an administration the boycott cleared the way for direct British rule and for the rapid imposition of wartime restrictions. Elsewhere the princes breathed a sigh of relief while the Muslim League provocatively declared a Day of Deliverance from the oppression of 'Congress Raj'.

The League would be one of the few beneficiaries of Nazi aggression. As Jinnah would later put it, 'the war which nobody welcomed proved to be a blessing in disguise.' It would enable the League to make good its claim to represent the majority of Muslims and Jinnah, its leader since 1936, to make good his claim to a principal role in the transference of power. Although lacking the charm of Nehru, let alone the fire of Bose or the popular appeal of Gandhi, Jinnah possessed a formidable mind in which intimidating resolve combined with unequalled skills as a tactician. No leader of the twentieth century has a greater claim to have fathered a nation. Schooled in the adversarial techniques of the bar and, as a Bombay Ismaili, comparatively unencumbered by the taboos and concerns of more orthodox Muslims, he soared above both colleagues and adversaries, a lofty and awesome figure immaculately suited for direction rather than incitement. But when he stooped to strike, he did so with effect. Choosing a date and a venue calculated to point up the failure of Nehru's 1930 proclamation of *purna swaraj*, in early 1940 also in Lahore he secured the League's endorsement of a very different resolution which changed the whole substance of the independence debate.

Although known as the 'Pakistan Resolution', the Lahore text made no mention of 'Pakistan' as such. The term was still an academic fiction. It had first been adopted by a group of Muslims at Cambridge in the early 1930s as a wishful acronym for a greater Muslim homeland consisting of P(unjab), A(fghania, i.e. the North-West Frontier), K(ashmir), I(ran), S(ind), T(urkharistan), A(fghanistan) and (Baluchista)N. It also meant, according to its inventor, 'the land of the *paks* – the spiritually pure and clean'. Since there was no 'B' for Bengal in 'PAKISTAN' it was presumably in this latter sense that it was subsequently applied to the Lahore Resolution.

The Resolution itself stemmed from a shuffling of various constitutional proposals evolved by Muslims anxious about the federation proposal and unhappy with the experience of provincial Congress government, or 'Hindu Raj'. Some of these proposals included a Muslim homeland in the south (an 'Usmanistan' based on the nizam's Hyderabad) as well as homelands in the north-west and the east. But the final Resolution was both more realistic and more vague. In recognition of the fact that Muslims represented a separate 'nation' it called for a constitution whereby 'areas in which Muslims are numerically in a majority, as in the North-Western and Eastern zones of India, should be grouped to constitute "Independent States" in which the constituent elements shall be autonomous and sovereign.'

Whether these 'states' were to be linked in a federation, either with one another or with the rest of India, was left unclear. Bengalis who eventually found themselves in East Pakistan could thus reasonably claim that under the terms of the Lahore Resolution they should have been independent. Also unclear was the geography of the 'areas' and 'zones' to be so 'grouped'.

Existing provinces were not mentioned by name, partly because the League could as yet lay no claim to overwhelming support in any of them, and partly because Jinnah was keeping his options open. Indeed it may be that the whole Resolution represented a tactical ploy or, as the viceroy thought, 'a bargaining position'. It would soon become something much less negotiable, but the hint of a separate Muslim sovereignty certainly had the effect of uniting Muslims behind the League and significantly empowering Jinnah in his negotiations with the Congress leadership and the British.

British attitudes were now heavily conditioned by the war effort. To secure India's military support and its political acquiescence, initiatives and incentives came thick and fast. Schemes for party representation in the central government and in the conduct of the war, as well as offers of a constituent assembly and dominion status, climaxed with a mission by Sir Stafford Cripps in March 1942. By then Singapore had fallen, 100,000 imperial troops, mostly Indian, were in Japanese detention, and Japanese forces were rapidly advancing through Burma on India itself. It was a moment for closing ranks, for the bold gesture and the magnanimous response. The Cripps Mission, brainchild of the Labour leader Clement Attlee and headed by a man known to be sympathetic to Indian independence, was seen by the British as just such a move. To previous offers it added a clear pledge, as soon as the war was over, of a dominion status which, as recently redefined, amounted to full independence.

Two years earlier such terms might have been welcomed. But, as so often in the past, London was advancing what India already banked on. By now the issue was not so much independence, or even when, but whose; and in this the Cripps offer was deeply disappointing. Gandhi mischievously likened it to a post-dated cheque on a failing bank. But the real problem lay not with the bank or the date but the name of the payee. For the Cripps offer, like all the others, betrayed a British willingness to appease Muslim nationalism and princely autonomy by endorsing the possibility that some provinces and states might eventually secede. This was anathema to all shades of Congress opinion. It challenged the idea of a single and indivisible Indian nation on which claims for independence had always rested; it contradicted the idea of Congress as a secular party representing all of India's communities and transcending all religious differences; and it denied the primacy of democratic representation on which both the national consensus and Congress's supremacy relied.

'It is possible, though by no means certain, that if from the outset the British had made it clear that they would never countenance the partition of India, the demand for Pakistan would have been dropped.'[9] Like many other British Indian officials, Penderel Moon, himself a key figure in the Partition saga, would see the break-up of India not just as a colossal human tragedy but as an enduring political tragedy. Had Linlithgow, the wartime viceroy, been less 'casual' about the demand, and had he tried 'to heal the breach between Congress and the League', Jinnah might have been forced to compromise. But the priority for Linlithgow, as for all his beleaguered countrymen, was the war. Post-imperial strategies were an indulgence which the desperate battle for survival, in Asia as in Europe, as yet precluded. Confronting Jinnah over Pakistan and so inviting the League's hostility at a time when Congress was already refusing to co-operate with the war effort was unthinkable. It could in fact be argued that it was Congress which badly miscalculated; by withholding its support, indeed endeavouring to exploit Britain's wartime predicament, it practically obliged the British to play along with the Pakistan idea.

Personally both Gandhi and Nehru wished the Allies well. But to Gandhi the pacifist, all wars were anathema; and to Nehru the socialist, this particular war between rival imperialisms should never have involved India. Prior to the Cripps Mission a limited form of anti-war protest had already landed Nehru and some twenty thousand other *satyagrahis* in gaol. They had since been released but, after the disappointment of the Cripps Mission, and at a time when the first Japanese bombs were falling on Indian installations, Gandhi in particular lost patience. Arguing first that only immediate British withdrawal and a declaration of Indian neutrality could save India from Japanese attack, then that only immediate independence would ensure whole-hearted resistance to the Japanese, he secured support for what he called a final 'do or die' challenge to British rule.

It was, of course, to be non-violent, but his pre-emptive arrest, and that of other Congress leaders, in August 1942 made this 'Quit India' movement a more random, spontaneous and violent outburst than any of its predecessors. As well as strikes and boycotts, telegraph and railway lines were sabotaged, police and railway stations blown up, and in large areas of Bihar and eastern UP the government temporarily ceased to function. Viceroy Linlithgow reckoned it 'the most serious rebellion since 1857'. Given the wartime paranoia, he ordered massive repression, which involved the deployment of tens of thousands of troops, a like number of arrests and perhaps a thousand deaths.

Although the worst violence was all over within a matter of weeks, and although a few misty-eyed imperialists like Churchill and Linlithgow were thereby confirmed in the belief that Britain still had a vital peace-keeping role in India, most British politicians now concurred with international, especially American, opinion in dismissing the possibility of a post-war British Raj. 'Quit' they now must, for repression on such a scale in peacetime would be unthinkable and probably impractical; Gandhi's point had been made, if not in the manner he approved. However, for the Congress Party the 1942 Quit India movement was much less successful than the Rowlatt-Khilafat protests of 1919–21 or the salt-and-civil-disobedience campaign of 1930–1. The arrest of its leaders meant that the party was unable to direct the movement or to profit from it, and their detention for most of what remained of the war meant that the party would be singularly ill-prepared for the post-war endgame. The League on the other hand, unchallenged by either the British or Congress, continued to proselytise, organise and mobilise.

THE TRYSTING HOUR

Three years of intensive negotiations led up to the final transfer of power from the British Crown to the two successor states of India and Pakistan in 1947. The peaceful conclusion of these negotiations was hailed as a triumph. It was celebrated as such even by the British, and it appeared all the more remarkable in the light of the armed confrontations then getting underway in Indonesia and Indo-China. But the triumph was compounded of failures and betrayals.

For Nehru, Congress and most citizens of the Republic of India, Pakistan itself was just such a failure – historically indefensible as well as humanly catastrophic. Many British officials agreed, seeing it as a betrayal of the united India which they liked to think of as their own creation. The British in turn stood accused of having failed the princes who, without the umbrella of federation, were left to negotiate entry into the successor states with a nationalist leadership they had long distrusted. The League for its part had obviously failed those of its supporters who lived in Muslim minority areas which would not be included in Pakistan. Similarly Congress stood accused of betraying its supporters in what became Pakistan, most notably the Pathans of the North-West Frontier Province who had consistently opposed the League and Partition. More obviously, in the two partitioned provinces of Bengal and Panjab, all parties to the negotiations had failed those Muslims, Sikhs and Hindus who would experience death and dispossession on an unprecedented scale as their homelands were divided, their economic links severed and their shared cultures dismembered.

Not surprisingly, the negotiations which produced this catalogue of failures have been closely scrutinised. Gandhi's 1944 initiative of direct talks with Jinnah, the first move towards a post-war settlement, has been criticised as a well-meaning blunder which served only to enhance Jinnah's standing and to entrench his demands. The Simla Conference of 1945 had a similar effect. Convened by Lord Wavell, Linlithgow's successor as viceroy, it proposed transforming his Executive Council into something like a national government. But it floundered on a Congress insistence on its right to nominate amongst its representatives the odd Muslim and on Jinnah's insistence that all Muslim representatives must be nominated by the League. Jinnah was allowed in effect to veto the initiative.

New elections in India, called by the incoming British Labour government of Clement Attlee and held in early 1946, confirmed the sectarian polarisation. As the first since 1937, a poll was long overdue and was a necessary prelude to further negotiations. But it was based on the existing, very limited franchise, and on the existing system of reserved electorates and seats as per the communal awards of 1936. With the League sweeping the reserved constituencies as convincingly as did Congress the unreserved, it deepened the religious divide. Except in the North-West Frontier Province – where tribal loyalties and the Pakhtun (Pathan) language underpinned a sub-separatist allegiance to Congress – and the Panjab, where some Muslims still adhered to the rural and non-sectarian Unionist Party, Jinnah's claim to speak for Muslim India seemed vindicated; his demand for Pakistan began to look correspondingly irresistible. Conversely Congress, though enjoying a colossal majority, could no longer claim to represent all communities. Critics, principally from the left, maintained that had elections been based on universal suffrage the results would have been different. The League's pretensions to represent all Muslims would have been exposed and, capitalising on industrial and agrarian grievances, a third force of cross-communal pedigree and impeccably socialist ideology would have emerged. The elections, in short, were yet another missed opportunity, another failure.

Wavell's alarm at the outcome brought a top-level British Cabinet Mission to India in March–June 1946. The tortuous negotiations which followed were designed to set up both a Constituent Assembly (which would decide on a new constitution) and a transitional government to handle matters in the interim. Not for want of ingenious ideas, both bodies also proved to be failures. Jinnah seemed to back away from Pakistan when confronted with the proposition that, by the terms of the League's own Pakistan Resolution, 'Muslim majority areas' must mean that Hindu majority areas in the Panjab and Bengal would have to be excluded from Pakistan.

Instead he joined Congress in endorsing a complicated system of provincial groupings whence the Constituent Assembly was to be elected. This was hailed as a breakthrough. In fact the system was so complicated that each side had interpreted it differently. Recriminations followed, including an August 1946 call by the League to the 'Muslim nation' to institute 'direct action'; its results, though unforeseen, would be horrifying. As for the interim government, this also materialised, but only through viceregal appointment. With Nehru as prime minister and Liaqat Ali Khan of the League as a late-joining finance minister, it served to give a convincing demonstration of why a power-sharing coalition would not work.

In despair over London's erratic support as well as India's irreconcilable leaders, the well-meaning Wavell had earlier advocated as a last resort a 'Breakdown Plan'. The 'breakdown' – which could well have been his own – in fact referred to the failure of Congress and the League to work together in the bodies proposed by the Cabinet Mission. This being now amply demonstrated, the British government examined the 'Breakdown Plan'. As the supreme commander who in 1942 had overseen the Allied retreat from south-east Asia, Wavell was proposing a similar retreat in India, in fact a phased withdrawal of British troops and officials, first from the south to the north, then from the Congress-dominated provinces to those of the League. He also proposed an announcement that the withdrawal would be completed by 31 March 1948.

Although militarily sound, the political consequences of such a retreat were rightly deemed unthinkable. The 'Breakdown Plan' was revealed as more like a 'break-up' plan. Besides inviting a fragmentation of late-Mughal proportions, it looked like a safe bet for civil war. Only the idea of announcing a withdrawal date was adopted. In February 1947 Attlee declared that British rule would end by June 1948.

For once both Congress and League applauded. Urgency was thus injected into the discussions. But far from conjuring a spirit of compromise it fuelled Congress demands for the dismissal of unco-operative League ministers in the interim government, and fanned League attempts to topple the non-League governments in the Panjab and the North-West Frontier Province.

In March 1947, to meet its new deadline, the Attlee government replaced Wavell with Lord Louis Mountbatten and, more importantly, empowered him to obtain a settlement without the usual interference from London. Mountbatten looked to be a good choice. As a cousin of the King-Emperor he enjoyed a regard which transcended politics, and as commander-in-chief in south-east Asia at the end of the war he had shown some sympathy for Indonesia's nationalists. He had no preconceptions where India was concerned, and for the task in hand his insatiable ego looked no bad thing; before the credit could be claimed or blame evaded, something had to have been achieved. The appointment of Mountbatten was in fact as much an earnest of British intentions as the setting of a deadline. Nehru appreciated this. He got on well with Lord Louis and famously with his wife Edwina. Mountbatten's legendary charm would ensure that two hundred years of colonial exploitation ended with warm smiles and hearty handshakes.

To all, including the disillusioned Wavell, it had by now become glaringly obvious that Jinnah would accept, and most Muslims would settle for, nothing short of a Pakistan to which sovereignty and power were directly transferred by the British. Mountbatten nevertheless pursued a proposal whereby power would be transferred to the provinces and the princely states, who might then choose whether to join India, Pakistan or neither. This was quite unacceptable to Nehru, who foresaw a 'Balkanisation' of India. His protestations persuaded some hasty British revision and led Mountbatten to adopt the inevitable Partition.

Thus in June 1947 the viceroy proudly announced Congress–League agreement to a formula whereby power would be transferred to two successor states. The option of provinces or states choosing independence was dropped; Bengal and the Panjab were to be partitioned along sectarian lines; and the princely states were to be urged to join either India or Pakistan. To speed up the constitutional formalities, ensure third-party supervision over the division of assets, and leave the British with a fig-leaf of imperial pride, it was also agreed that power should be transferred on the basis of dominion status; this would require only the amendment of the 1935 India Act, which could subsequently be repudiated or endorsed by the successor states. To preserve the tottering interim government, Mountbatten also brought forward the deadline to 15 August 1947. Ten weeks would suffice for the constitutional, social, military and infrastructural vivisection of a subcontinent.

Jinnah, anxious to emphasise that Pakistan was succeeding the British Raj and not seceding from an independent India, celebrated Independence in Karachi on 14 August. Mountbatten attended the ceremonies despite a bomb scare, then left in haste. Unlike Nehru, Jinnah had never buckled before Mountbatten's boyish charm offensives. Rejecting the viceroy's wish to be accepted as governor-general of both successor states, he now himself assumed the role of Pakistan's first governor-general and president of its Constituent Assembly. As the officially titled *Quaid-i-Azam*, or 'Supreme Leader', the Friday prayers were read in his name. He was not just head of state and father of the nation but its constitutional caliph. There was no room for a representative, however well-connected, of the House of Windsor.

From Karachi on the night of 14 August Mountbatten flew straight to Delhi, where the celebrations would prove much more gratifying. There the appreciative Nehru was that night intoning his most famous oration. Its style was unashamedly Churchillian, and the quaint suggestion of a 'tryst with destiny' echoed the 'trysting hour' in 'Horatius', a much-loved poem by the man who had once savaged Indian scholarship, Thomas Babington Macaulay. The speech, in short, was a performance for history's consumption.

> Long years ago we made a tryst with destiny, and now the time comes when we shall redeem our pledge, not wholly or in full measure but very substantially. At the stroke of the midnight hour, when the world sleeps, India will awake to life and freedom. A moment comes, which comes but rarely in history, when we step out from the old to the new, when an age ends, and when the soul of a nation, long suppressed, finds utterance. It is fitting that at this solemn moment we take the pledge of dedication to the service of India and her people and to the still larger cause of humanity.

'A MADNESS HAS SEIZED THE PEOPLE'

Nehru, Mountbatten and many of their associates were acutely conscious of making history. In speeches, memoirs and personalised chronicles they confidently wrote themselves into it. Historians are grateful. But there is a danger of the record reading like conference minutes or a Government House diary of who said what and when and why. Far from the dappled lawns of New Delhi, out of range of the loudspeakers on the municipal maidan, other agendas were being followed, and never more determinedly than in the heady days before and after Independence.

In a land of limited opportunity but boundless importunity the keeping of trysts and the redeeming of pledges could seem irrelevant; so could the sudden switch from bitter antagonism to mutual applause. Elsewhere a less self-conscious history was being made. Often more instructive and always more harrowing, it had a way of sabotaging noble sentiments and exploding grand creations, showing scant regard for the old or the new, let alone that 'rare moment' which distinguishes them.

In 1943, like an uninvited guest from the past, famine had swept through large parts of lower Bengal. Scarcity during this bleakest period of the war had been expected. Rice imports from Burma had ceased with that country's occupation by the Japanese; domestic food-grains were in great demand for the military build-up in eastern India; and hoarding had resulted. Additionally, rail freight was being commandeered by the armed forces while Bengal's riverine shipping had been largely requisitioned for fear of its use by Japanese infiltrators. Yet the shortfall in food-grains was not great, and with foresight, rationing, better distribution and vigorous action against black-market hoarding, it should never have come to famine. It was a failure of personnel as much as anything. When in July the walking dead began straggling into Calcutta to expire on the streets, Linlithgow was looking forward to England, leaving India, as he rashly put it, 'in pretty good shape'. Bengal, too, had just had a change of government; the returning Muslim League ministry was shaky and inexperienced. Worst of all, the British governor of the province, to whom ample powers were reserved for just such a crisis, was supine and very sick.

Between July and November the famine raged almost unchecked. When in October the just-installed Wavell visited the affected areas, he acknowledged 'one of the worst disasters that has befallen any people under British rule'. He was not exaggerating. Famine fatalities are notoriously unreliable; in this case the totals range from two million to four million. But even if the lower figure is accepted, the famine still killed more Indians than did two world wars, the entire Independence struggle, plus the communal holocaust which accompanied Partition. 'Direct British rule had begun with a Bengal famine in 1770; it was now drawing to a close with a comparable calamity.'[10]

At the time, with Congress banned and its leaders in gaol following the 'Quit India' movement, many of Bengal's Hindu *bhadralok* had temporarily switched their support to the extremist Hindu party known as the *Mahasabha*. For the famine the *Mahasabha*, as was its wont, unhesitatingly blamed the Muslim League, accusing it of exploiting the disaster to obtain a monopoly of the lucrative distribution of relief. The League, on the other hand, blamed the hoarding and profiteering of the mainly Hindu grain-dealers. Out of famine, as out of other forms of agrarian and industrial distress (like recession in the jute industry), communal hatred was born.

But Hindu–Muslim, or 'communal', violence was not inevitable. According to leftist historians, had the Congress leadership been less bent on a quick transfer of power at any price, both Partition and the communal massacres which it prompted might have been avoided. In November 1945 the British had brought to trial in Delhi three members of Subhas Chandra Bose's INA. (Bose himself had died in a plane crash a few weeks earlier.) One of the accused was a Sikh, the second a Muslim and the third a Hindu, the idea being to avoid the accusation of discriminating against any particular community. The nationalist response partook of the same even-handedness. On behalf of the accused, student protesters in Calcutta, then mutineers from ships of the Royal Indian Navy at Bombay and Karachi, rallied beneath the green flags of Islam, the red of the communists and socialists, and the tricolour of Congress. It was a fine display of communal harmony to which labour unions and other civilian groups enthusiastically lent their support.

Confrontations with police and troops followed. The naval mutiny was particularly menacing and brought British threats to bomb the disaffected ships, plus a high-level Congress mission under Vallabhai Patel to talk sense to the mutineers. Congress leaders, although strident in their support of the INA men, had been taken by surprise and were severely embarrassed. As the prospect of a negotiated settlement neared, militant protest was no longer welcome. It undermined the authority of the negotiators and destabilised the institutions of the state to which they expected to succeed.

More of what nationalist histories call 'these upsurges' had followed. In Bengal in April 1946, following a period of direct rule by the governor, new provincial elections returned another Muslim League ministry in Calcutta. It was headed by Huseyn Shaheed Suhrawardy, who as Minister for Civil Supplies in 1943 had been held principally responsible for the inept famine relief programme. In August Suhrawardy responded to Jinnah's call for a Direct Action Day (following the collapse of the Cabinet Mission proposals) and proclaimed a public holiday. The police too, he implied, would take the day off. Muslims, rallying *en masse* for speeches and processions, saw this as an invitation; they began looting and burning such Hindu shops as remained open. Arson gave way to murder, and the victims struck back. During three days of unchecked mayhem some four thousand Muslims, Sikhs and Hindus died in what became known as the Calcutta Killings. In October the riots spread to parts of East Bengal and also to UP and Bihar, where the death toll was even higher. Nehru wrung his hands in horror; 'a madness has seized the people,' he reported. Gandhi rushed to the scene, heroically progressing through the devastated communities to preach reconciliation and to 'wipe every tear from every eye'. There followed a lull, but by March 1947 the first signs of a new 'madness' were detected in both Calcutta and, much more ominously, in the Panjab.

Although for Nehru the Partition of India was a tragedy, for Jinnah it was a necessity. The tragedy in Jinnah's eyes lay in the partition of Bengal and the Panjab. To connect these two provinces he had once argued for a Pakistan corridor running right through UP and Bihar. Failing that, he had insisted that Bengal and Panjab must be transferred to Pakistan in their entirety, since a Pakistan which, as well as being divided by UP and Bihar, excluded Hindu-majority areas in the eastern Panjab and western Bengal (Calcutta itself amongst them) would be but 'a shadow and a husk'. In the final negotiations, when the choice left to him was indeed between this 'maimed, mutilated and moth-eaten Pakistan' or no Pakistan at all, he still could not bring himself to accept it. At the crucial meeting, unable to say yes, he had just inclined his head. It was taken to be a nod of assent, but he could as well have been placing his head on the block.

In Bengal the job of dissecting majority Muslim areas from majority non-Muslim areas was comparatively straightforward. Curzon had already shown the way; and Gandhi, following the Calcutta Killings of 1946, continued to make Bengal his personal responsibility. There would be a massive exodus of refugees in both directions, and great economic dislocation. Without Calcutta and the more industrialised regions of West Bengal, East Bengal looked like what one British official had called 'a rural slum'; without the agricultural yield of East Bengal, Calcutta's mills fell silent. But, as if exhausted by the earlier killings, there was comparatively little blood-letting.

It was otherwise in the Panjab. Here, thanks to British recruitment preferences, all communities had strong military connections and cherished martial traditions. The Muslims of the Panjab, unlike the mostly lower-caste converts of East Bengal, included descendants of long-converted rajput tribes (Bhatti, Ghakkar, etc.) and of the Turks, Mongols and Afghans who had so often traversed the region. The Hindus of the Panjab, mostly Jats and Dogras, were reckoned no less 'sturdy', whether as aggressive agriculturalists or indomitable infantrymen. And the Sikhs, the third dimension in the Panjab's communal equation, provided some two-fifths of the entire Indian army and constituted the most militant religious brotherhood on the subcontinent. Though a majority in very few areas, the Sikhs were fairly evenly spread throughout the province which they regarded both as their religious homeland and as the core of Sikh 'empire'.

The first troubles in the Panjab broke out in early 1947. Although the Muslim League had made sensational gains in the 1946 elections, a coalition ministry cobbled together by remnants of the old Unionist Party with Sikh and Congress support denied it power. The League therefore launched a programme of civil disobedience and brought down the ministry in March 1947. Sikhs, who had most to lose from the Panjab becoming Pakistani,

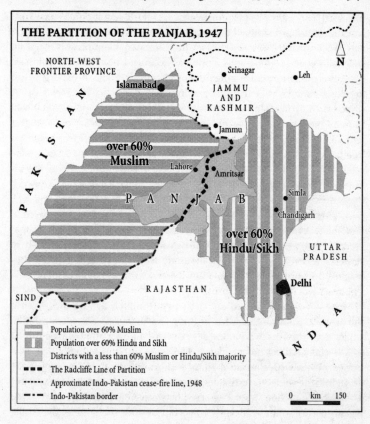

THE PARTITION OF THE PANJAB, 1947

NORTH-WEST
FRONTIER PROVINCE

Islamabad

Srinagar   Leh

JAMMU
AND
KASHMIR

Jammu

over 60%
Muslim   Lahore   Amritsar

P A N J A B   Simla
Chandigarh

over 60%
Hindu/Sikh

UTTAR
PRADESH

RAJASTHAN   Delhi

SIND

PAKISTAN

INDIA

N

	Population over 60% Muslim
	Population over 60% Hindu and Sikh
	Districts with a less than 60% Muslim or Hindu/Sikh majority
■ ■ ■	The Radcliffe Line of Partition
------	Approximate Indo-Pakistan cease-fire line, 1948
─ ■ ─	Indo-Pakistan border

0   km   150

responded by demanding their own 'Sikhistan'. There were riots in many
of the main cities and by August the death toll had risen to about five
thousand. But by then the Sikhs, following reassurances from Congress
about their status within what would become India's slice of the Panjab,
had accepted the inevitability of partition. There was no lull in the violence,
but official anxieties, British as well as Indian, were seemingly allayed.

The new boundary, drawn up in great haste by a League–Congress
commission under the chairmanship of an English judge (Sir Cyril Radcliffe), was not announced until after the Independence celebrations. The
Sikhs had demanded that the line of Partition, whilst dividing the majority
non-Muslim East Panjab from the majority Muslim West Panjab, make
exceptions for sites and shrines important to them by virtue of religious and

historical associations. Thus, for instance, Lahore, Ranjit Singh's erstwhile capital, should not simply be allocated to Pakistan because its population was predominantly Muslim. In fact the Boundary Commission made no such allowances. Demography alone was decisive; Lahore went to Pakistan.

Anticipating a massive influx of co-religionists, Sikhs in the east began expelling non-Sikhs and appropriating their lands in early August. A response to earlier Muslim expulsions in the west, this merely provoked more of the same. The announcement of the actual boundary on 17 August lent a cut-throat urgency to the tit-for-tat. The flow of refugees became a flood; word of atrocities, rapes and mass killings brought the inevitable retaliations. As the violence escalated, ghost trains chuffed silently across the new frontier carrying nothing but corpses. In the 'land of the five rivers' the waters ran with blood and the roads ran with mangled migrants. The twenty thousand troops who materialised to police the transfer proved at best ineffective, at worst infected by the madness. 'Of one convoy that recently arrived,' reported the still-British governor of West Panjab to readers of *The Times*, 'over one thousand who had struggled on till they reached the frontier-post just laid down and died. They could go no further. The road was littered with corpses for miles.'[11]

East to west and west to east perhaps ten million fled for their lives in the greatest exodus in recorded history. The killings spread even to Delhi, where non-Muslims, who a few days earlier had been amongst the throng so cheerfully hailing Independence, hailing Nehru and Mountbatten, now turned on their Muslim neighbours with knife and club. The higher the death toll, the wilder the estimates. Two hundred thousand at least, possibly as many as a million, were massacred between August and October in the Panjab partition and associated riots. But as with the famine, the earlier killings in Bengal and Bihar, and other such 'upsurges', the names of the victims went unrecorded, their numbers uncounted. Unprepared and overwhelmed, neither of the new nations could do more than feed the living. Meanwhile Mountbatten, 'determined to keep clear of the whole business',[12] as he put it, had washed his hands of the Panjab and headed for the hills. The history-makers looked the other way.

Crossing the Tracks

1948–

THE KASHMIR CONTENTION

FOR THE INDIAN SUBCONTINENT, as for the rest of the colonial world, the twentieth century peaked at Independence. Triumph duly brought its rewards in terms of national self-determination, international recognition and, for India, representative government. But the subsequent enjoyment of these rewards, the means taken to safeguard them and the constraints encountered in their exercise, have produced a second half-century of erratic progress marred by internal discord and vicious encounters. Looking back, the years of struggle and sacrifice, of concerted endeavour and supreme achievement seem much the more admirable. What followed has not lacked purpose; it is just that, with the direction less clear, the record easily degenerates into a year-by-year recitation of events and statistics.

For somewhere in mid-twentieth century, perhaps indeed at the very moment of Independence, history at last blends into the clamorous world of current affairs. Time's locomotive slows and the broad horizons of the past are obscured as the starker shapes of a high-rise foreground press close. Gathering up his cherished omniscience, the historian must get down from the air-conditioned express with its tinted windows, cross the tracks, and elbow his way aboard a slower, noisier train whose windows have no glass and whose doors are never closed. Here, where single-seat occupancy is unknown and the luggage is all sacks and bundles, uninterrupted views are rare. The comfortable generalisations come less readily, less confidently.

With nose pressed hard against a knobbly reality, the historian soon makes a disconcerting discovery: he has been downgraded to the role of a participating observer, just another of those contemporary chroniclers whose testimony he has so often found wanting. Nor are their failings now a matter of surprise. It's not easy, one finds, to make sense of what is happening before one's eyes. Until distance lends depth and time clarity, there is much to be said for hanging back. Impressions now look a safer bet than narrative, and the thumbnail sketch must serve as illustration.

Limited perspective is only part of the problem; a further complication may simply be the result of dividing the century into two halves. Such was the impact of the 1947 Partition, both psychologically and politically, that it came to be regarded as a major historical feature, a periodising landmark worthy of a capital letter just like 'Independence'. Indeed, in the currency of a phrase like 'post-Partition India' the prominence of Partition seems to have come to overshadow that of Independence. It is as if an experience so catastrophic and contradictory must, like the Jewish Holocaust, be constantly re-emphasised if it is not to be re-enacted.

But 'there are no full stops in India,' declares a character in Mark Tully's 1991 collection of contemporary Indian parables.[1] In a land better known for continuities and commas, partition and secession were not laid to rest in 1947. They continue to obsess the governments of both countries. The consequences of the first Partition have dictated the foreign relations and slewed the economic development of both India and Pakistan. Similarly the danger of further internal partition has largely governed domestic politics and dominated the language of dissent. Pakistan would experience a second partition in 1971; both countries have been lurching from one supposed secession crisis to the next for fifty years. No sooner was the horror of the Panjab beginning to subside in October 1947 than the two successor states found themselves at war with one another over the princely state of Jammu and Kashmir. Its outcome too would be tantamount to another Partition.

In the weeks prior to Independence most of the princely states had been bundled into digestible entities, like Rajasthan, and incorporated into an Indian union with the new republic in Delhi. The princes accepted this situation reluctantly and in return for generous personal allowances and privileges. Technically they could opt for either Pakistan or India; and the few states lying west of the new India's frontier with Pakistan did join Pakistan. But the vast majority were within or contiguous to India and they duly became a part of it.

Serious problems arose only in respect of three states. One, Junagadh in the Saurashtra peninsula of Gujarat, was too small to provoke a major crisis. Predominantly Hindu, proudly possessed of that Ashoka rock at Girnar, and once the home of the Sanskrit-loving Rudradaman and of the brightly-toed Maitrakas, little Junagadh was always going to be part of India. Moreover Junagadh's ruler, aside from being a Muslim, was not the sort to give Congress or Vallabhai Patel, its chief negotiator, any misgivings. At the time an estimated 11 percent of the state's income was earmarked for the upkeep of the royal kennels, wherein some eight hundred canine pensioners lived in a luxury denied to most of Junagadh's other subjects. To the nuptials of a favourite golden retriever the prince is said to have invited fifty thousand guests, including the viceroy. His decision to declare allegiance to Pakistan had, though, nothing to do with dogs. It was made on the grounds of religion, for which piety his only reward was a show of strength from Delhi which sent him winging his way to Pakistan with just four canine companions, plus a like number of wives. Pakistan, of course, protested. Although unwilling to go to war over Junagadh, it continued to regard the accession of the state as legal – which it was – and on Pakistani maps a little patch of green in the midst of Indian Gujarat continues to record the fact.

An identical situation, but of vastly greater import, developed in Hyderabad. The nizam and his court, though notable patrons of Muslim culture and legatees of the illustrious Deccan sultanates, held sway over an extensive chunk of the now wholly Indian peninsula and a large population which was overwhelmingly Hindu. To Nehru and Patel it was therefore unthinkable that Hyderabad should do other than join India. But the nizam's advisers prevaricated, not so much over joining Pakistan or India as over whether to join either or to opt for independence. In the face of international attention, Delhi offered a year's grace in which Hyderabad was to decide. It proved to be but a stay of execution. In September 1948, no decision having been forthcoming, Indian troops unceremoniously rolled across the state borders. Pakistan again protested; but in the face of this 'police action', a decision favourable to Delhi was a formality. The nizam duly signed on the dotted line.

A precedent for such strong-arm Indian tactics had already been set in the state of Jammu and Kashmir. There, however, the situation was reversed: the Dogra (Hindu) maharaja ruled a mainly non-Hindu state. Parts, like Ladakh, were predominantly Buddhist; others, as around Jammu, included a sizeable Hindu component; but the vast mountain territories awarded to the maharajas for Britain's strategic convenience were overwhelmingly Muslim, and so was the densely populated Kashmir valley itself. Pakistanis therefore assumed that Jammu and Kashmir's future lay with them, as per the 'K' in the acronym that was 'PaKistan'. Since there was no 'J' for Jammu, and since the state was contiguous to both Pakistan and India, a *prima facie* case could perhaps have been made for an early dismemberment.

There were, though, other complications. Kashmir itself had a special resonance both for the Nehru family, who as Kashmiri *pandits* (teachers) originally hailed from the valley, and for Congress, which regarded Kashmir's accession as essential confirmation of its and India's secular stance. Additionally Congress had forged links with a secularist state party known as the Jammu and Kashmir National Conference. This was a political front which, under the leadership of Sheikh Muhammad Abdullah, had been demanding of the maharaja greater popular representation ever since the 1930s. Like Nehru, Sheikh Abdullah, an imposing figure otherwise known as 'the Lion of Kashmir', combined leftist rhetoric with secular leanings which reflected the rather easy-going Islam of most Kashmiri Muslims. He, if anyone, could claim to speak for Kashmiris, and popular support (where such a thing could be ascertained) being a desideratum of accession, his role in deciding the state's future was as crucial as that of the maharaja.

Independence found Sheikh Abdullah in a state gaol. His National Conference was in trouble from a rival party with close links to Jinnah's League. And Maharaja Hari Singh, now facing both popular and sectarian dissent, was in a dilemma. The case of Switzerland was often cited, and arguably all these parties would individually have preferred a neutral and independent Kashmir. But legally this was a doubtful option, and certainly not one to which either India or Pakistan would agree. Nor was it one around which the communally divided and faction-ridden peoples of the state would unite.

For two months the state and its ruler teetered on the crest of their Himalayan dilemma. Then on 22 October 1947 a truck-mounted incursion of Islamic partisans from the neighbouring tribal regions of Pakistan rumbled up the only road into the Kashmir valley, thereby pitching the maharaja into the open arms of India. Fearing that his rule was about to be overthrown, he released Sheikh Abdullah and sent him post-haste to treat with Nehru in Delhi. Four days later the state's accession to India, as signified by the maharaja's decision and the sheikh's support, brought its reward. Indian planes began airlifting troops into the state capital of Srinagar to resist the intruders. The first Indo–Pak war had begun.

From all over northern Pakistan more volunteers poured across the Kashmir frontier. Neither side officially declared war, and regular Pakistani units were not deployed. But there were enough zealous irregulars in the Pakistani Panjab and the North-West Frontier to make a fight of it. There were also enough ambiguities about the actual extent of the maharaja's territories to give each side a share of the spoils. When in 1948 the United

Nations brokered a ceasefire, Pakistan had secured an arc of mountains round the Kashmir valley (henceforth known as the 'Northern Areas') plus the western end of the valley itself (known as Azad – 'Free' – Kashmir). India held the rest, and immediately began building a road link into the Kashmir valley, which was otherwise accessible only via Pakistan, and another into Ladakh.

The ceasefire line remained – and remains – just that, the line at which the firing was supposed to have ceased. It obeys no geographic or strategic logic, let alone economic or social convenience. Although it in effect partitions Jammu and Kashmir state, neither India nor Pakistan recognises it as a frontier. Nor, therefore, do they have any compunction about transgressing it. The UN corps in Kashmir, perhaps the longest-serving on record, has no peace-keeping responsibilities; it merely 'observes and monitors' violations.

Legally the problem appears insoluble. India rests its case on the fact of the maharaja's accession to India and on the popular endorsement supposedly afforded by Sheikh Abdullah. The first, the maharaja's decision, would have been conclusive but for India's having ignored princely preference in the cases of Junagadh and Hyderabad. As for the sheikh, somewhat shaky were his then credentials as an elected representative and even more shaky was his subsequent attitude towards integration with India. Retaining the support of most Kashmiris for another quarter of a century, he would spend more of it in Indian detention as a separatist than in government as an integrationist.

Pakistan's case rests on the surer, but not decisive, fact of the state's Muslim majority and on Nehru's refusal to hold a plebiscite. The latter contravenes a UN resolution and Nehru's own promise, given at the time of accession, to ascertain the wishes of the people. Delhi argues that the assent of the sheikh and his subsequent success in the polls is proof enough of the wishes of the people. There are also good reasons to suppose that in 1948 a plebiscite involving the whole of the erstwhile Jammu and Kashmir state would have strained to breaking point both the resources of the UN and the good faith of the interested parties. On the other hand a plebiscite which in 1948 might conceivably have gone in India's favour would subsequently almost certainly have gone against India.

None of these tired legal arguments need have precluded a negotiated settlement had it been possible to isolate the Kashmir problem. But it was not possible. Like a fuse-box, Kashmir was soon discovered to lie at a point where the delicate internal wiring of two new and complex polities met a number of high-voltage external polarities. Throughout the 1960s and

seventies the Chinese and the Americans vied for Pakistan's favour and the
Russians and the Americans for India's. Then in the late eighties pan-Islamic
revivalists, fired by their success in Afghanistan, saw in Kashmir another
incipient *jihad*. To this challenge both India's security forces and its
resurgent Hindu 'nationalists' obligingly responded.

'Who has not heard of the Vale of Cashmere?' the poet Thomas Moore
had asked in his 1826 'oriental romance', *Lalla Rookh*. Seemingly by the
1990s everyone had, although not for 'its temples and grottoes and fountains
so clear'. 'The Happy Valley' as the tourist brochures called it, Jahangir's
scented 'paradise' and the white sahibs' sporting estate, where spring gilds
the willow-fringed waterways and autumn encrimsons the lofty chenars, now
became a drab and fearful war zone churned by gratuitous politicisation,
militarisation and religious extremism. Fifty years on, the once-welcomed
Indian security forces had become identified with appalling brutality, the
placid Kashmiris had espoused various brands of fanatical Islam, more
people were dying annually in terrorist attacks and security sweeps than
in the first Indo–Pak war, and the tourism industry to which Kashmiris
had once taken as hungry ducks to weedy water had become a sick joke.

THE NEHRU YEARS

By an unhappy coincidence many of those most closely involved with
Independence and Partition had died in the months immediately afterwards. *Quaid-i-Azam* Jinnah, who alone of Pakistan's various leaders has
commanded that nation's whole-hearted support, succumbed to cancer a
year after Independence; his close associate in the Muslim League and then
successor, Liaqat Ali Khan, was assassinated in 1951; and Vallabhai Patel,
the Congress strong-man and latterly India's deputy prime minister, died
in 1950. Worst of all for the cause of reconciliation, Mahatma Gandhi had
been gunned down on 30 January 1948. His killer, Nathuram Godse, was
a Pune brahman who has been linked to the paramilitary RSS (*Rashtriya
Swayamsevak Sangh*, 'Association of National Volunteers'), an extreme offshoot of the Hindu communalist *Mahasabha*. In the eyes of such organisations, Gandhi stood condemned by his insistence that, despite war over
Kashmir, India must honour its commitments in the division of reserves
and resources with Pakistan.

Jawaharlal Nehru remained. Chosen by Gandhi as his political heir, he
was now India's undisputed leader. As prime minister and as president of
Congress, which party won massive majorities on a universal suffrage in

the general election of 1952 and repeated this success in 1957 and 1962, he led the world's largest democracy and so enjoyed the world's largest mandate. A strong internationalist from his youth, in his Independence oration he had dedicated himself to the service of 'the still larger cause of humanity'. Now, from a platform of such global stature, he championed the anti-colonial struggles of others, including the Vietnamese and the Indonesians, and began to project India's experience onto a world screen. Socialism and democracy became international panaceas while secularism, the third god-head in the Congress trinity, underwent an extension from non-discrimination as between Hindu and Muslim to non-alignment as between communism and capitalism. In 1955, as guests of the now President Sukarno of the Indonesian Republic, Jawaharlal and daughter Indira attended the Bandung Conference of Afro-Asian countries at which the Non-Aligned Movement was born. A year previously he had signed a treaty with China which enshrined the *panchsila*, 'the five principles' of non-interference and peaceful co-existence. They became the cornerstones of the Non-Aligned Movement as also of both Nehru's and Sukarno's state ideologies. Sino–Indian friendship, or *Hindi–Chini Bhai Bhai*, was celebrated throughout India as the key to peace in Asia.

Non-interference meant respecting one another's territorial integrity. Its application was, however, selective. The 1950 Chinese invasion of Tibet had gone uncondemned by the Indian government on the grounds that it was an internal affair. An existing convention whereby India guaranteed Tibetan autonomy was thus 'totally disregarded'.[2] In equally cavalier style Nehru justified his own 1961 annexation of Portuguese Goa as a legitimate act of reclamation. Fifteen years later, for overrunning an equivalent Portuguese enclave in East Timor, the Indonesian government would be internationally pilloried. Nehru's action attracted less criticism because it was not obviously resisted and because India, as a democracy, got the benefit of Western doubt.

But its legality was highly questionable; and if Goa was India's internal affair, what was the status of, say, East Pakistan (otherwise East Bengal), which was also surrounded by Indian territory, or indeed the rest of Pakistan? Not surprisingly General Ayub Khan, who in 1958 had ended Pakistan's first unhappy decade of civilian rule by imposing martial law, sought out the best guarantees on offer, namely membership of the US-sponsored Central Treaty Organisation (CENTO) and South-East Asia Treaty Organisation (SEATO), plus the ready access which these offered to the US tanks and jet-fighters deemed necessary to America's global policy of 'containing' communism.

In 1959 the flight into India of the Dalai Lama with up to 100,000 Tibetans finally ended the fiction of Tibetan autonomy. To the annoyance of Beijing, Nehru afforded them sanctuary. There was now no disguising the fact that India's longest land frontier was shared with a hegemonist People's Republic of China. The silence of the Himalayan passes was rudely shattered by the loudspeakers and labour gangs of the People's Liberation Army (PLA). As any student of the political *mandala* could have predicted, contiguity was not conducive to harmony.

Two years later, Chinese military traffic was found to be taking a short-cut from Tibet to Sinkiang (Xinjiang) by way of a new and unsuspected highway across the Aksai Chin, an uninhabited salient of Ladakh's (and so Indian Kashmir's) territory. Political protests were registered and border skirmishes followed. China responded by questioning the legality of the Sino–Indian frontier at its other extremity to the east of Nepal. Here in September 1962 Nehru tried to pre-empt the situation by establishing occupation of the existing border as laid down by the British. This was a bad idea; Mao's China did not accept imperialist demarcations of its territory. Toughened PLA units easily repelled the Indian forces and then swept down towards the strategic corridor which linked West Bengal with Assam.

The 'invasion' turned out to be more in the nature of a demonstration, or perhaps a diversion from the contentious Aksai Chin. Either way, it was goodbye *Hindi–Chini Bhai Bhai*. Frantic Indian appeals for military hardware were promptly answered by the United States, which still regarded Mao's China as a Soviet ally and therefore an American foe. Nehru, the high priest of non-alignment, had hitherto shunned 'the Great Satan' in Washington. Now the Indian premier found himself shamefacedly composing a shopping list for President Kennedy which was to include a radar communications network, fighters (twelve squadrons, supersonic, all-weather) and bombers (two squadrons, B-47s). Although *Hindi–Yankee Bhai Bhai* was never an officially endorsed slogan, non-alignment was clearly in tatters. Nehru had been visibly shaken by Mao's rude rejection of his utopian internationalism, and never fully recovered. Already suffering from a liver complaint, he collapsed in early 1964 and died in May of that year.

Meanwhile Pakistan's General Ayub Khan, emboldened by the Chinese success, had in 1963 despatched Zulfikar Ali Bhutto to forge a new Sino–Pakistani entente which would further embarrass New Delhi. He had then, from what seemed a position of strength, renewed his efforts to reopen the Kashmir issue with a diplomatic offensive. Communal troubles sparked by the theft of a Muslim relic were rocking the 'Happy Valley' and Nehru, in one of his last public actions, had responded by having Sheikh Abdullah released from another gaol sentence. Nothing came of these initiatives: Bhutto got no joy over his demands for the long-promised plebiscite; the 'Lion of Kashmir' was soon back behind bars; and most Kashmiris remained as unreconciled to Indian rule as ever.

In Lal Bahadur Shastri, Nehru's pacific, diminutive and untried successor, General Ayub Khan saw the chance for a different kind of initiative. Early in 1965 Pakistani tanks rolled across the salt-flats of the Rann of Kutch to push Indian forces back from a disputed section of the Sind–Gujarat border. Although a ceasefire was quickly arranged, Ayub Khan celebrated the Kutch affair as a success. He and the Pakistani army, to whom he was alone responsible, felt confident enough to organise a Kashmir offensive as soon as the monsoon was over.

The 1965 Indo–Pak war lasted barely a month. Pakistan made gains in the Rajasthan desert but its main push against India's Jammu–Srinagar road link was repulsed and Indian tanks then advanced to within sight of Lahore. Both sides claimed victory but India had most to celebrate. In the peace negotiations conducted under Soviet auspices in Tashkent, the status quo was restored, the use of force was rejected, and non-interference and the normalisation of relations were pledged. But the 'Kashmir Problem' itself was scarcely addressed, let alone solved. In Islamabad, Pakistan's new capital, support was now increasingly sought in a closer alliance with Beijing. Some Chinese weaponry replaced the American tanks lost in the 1965 war and agreement was reached for the construction of the first China–Pakistan road link. This was the Karakoram Highway which, though scarcely an important commercial artery, would be strategically symbolic. It would also yield all that impressive evidence of an earlier era of trans-Himalayan contacts between the north-west corner of the subcontinent and China.

Islamabad remained obsessed with the Kashmir problem, but Delhi, during the nearly two decades (1966–84) of Indira Gandhi's almost continuous leadership, refused to acknowledge that there was any such problem. Accession was taken as fact and secession as the only threat. It was a threat which Mrs Gandhi readily perceived in many of the other constituent states of the Republic of India. A determined centralist, she would confront it with consummate opportunism. But like her father she misconstrued the nature of the threat. It was not the integrity of the nation that was in danger but the national credentials of the Congress Party.

THE CENTRE CANNOT HOLD

At the time of Independence Mahatma Gandhi had urged that the Congress Party be disbanded. It had served its organisational purpose in the rout of colonialism but, according to the Mahatma, its capacity for moral regeneration had been compromised in the process. India must abandon the confrontational terminology of Western politics like majority/minority, socialist/capitalist, public sector/private sector, centre/regions, all of which figured prominently in Congress debate. Instead it must rediscover basic values of self-help and service, and rebuild a community-based consensus from the village level upwards. As usual Gandhi had a word for this: *sarvodaya* meant 'the uplift of all' and, like *swadeshi* homespun and *satyagraha* truth-force, it inspired those of his disciples who would continue to work the byways of rural India. It did not persuade Nehru to disband Congress but, like so many of the Mahatma's homeo-political remedies, it did prove prescient. The first fifty years of the Indian Republic may be seen as the story of the fragmentation and decline of the mighty Congress in the face of a reassertion of regional and sectional interests.

In the 1950s the most obvious challenge to Congress looked to be ideological. However, the left in India was seldom united. As well as Bose's Forward Bloc, a Congress Socialist Party had split from the moderately socialist Congress before the war. After Hitler's invasion of Russia, India's communists, in their support for the fight against fascism, were at variance with the socialists who, like Congress, boycotted the war effort. Later, following Nehru's Chinese débâcle and the Sino–Soviet split, the communists themselves would divide as between the pro-Beijing CPM (Communist Party (Marxist)) and the pro-Moscow CPI (Communist Party of India).

Chronically divided, the left was further handicapped by Nehru stealing its thunder. A sincere admirer of Soviet Russia's social and economic progress, he duly emulated it by espousing public ownership and the break-up of landed holdings, adopting the panacea of a Planning Commission and a system of five-year plans, and concentrating investment in heavy industry and infrastructure. India's communist parties, with little to offer at the national level, concentrated increasingly on local grievances and local power centres. Calcutta and its industrial hinterland in West Bengal would become a CPM stronghold while, more surprisingly, in Kerala, the most literate and Christian of India's states, state elections in 1957 returned one of the first-ever elected communist governments.

Thanks to Nehru's personal charisma, and thanks to a Westminster-style 'first-past-the-post' voting system which leaves minority parties under-represented, Congress remained unassailable in the central government throughout the Nehru years. It was also successful in provincial or 'state' elections, but less so and, as before Independence, only by permitting the local Congress parties a good deal of latitude. Comprising the erstwhile provinces of British India plus the larger of the erstwhile princely states, most of the Republic of India's constituent units, or states, had longer traditions of self-government and responsible political activity than did the centre. Against the Unionist Party in the Panjab, the well-entrenched Justice Party in Madras, and other such local alignments, Congress had never had it all its own way. Nor, under the terms of the new Indian constitution, could the ruling party at the centre presume on supremacy in the states, although it enjoyed considerable powers for intervention.

As hammered out by the Constituent Assembly originally convened by Wavell, the new constitution was but a revised version of that introduced by the 1935 Government of India Act. Since the latter had been designed to safeguard the ultimate authority of the imperial power, its adapted form contained fewer democratic safeguards than most liberal constitutions and was 'not altogether free from authoritarian trends'.[3] As officially adopted in 1950, it continued to reserve to the centre obvious responsibilities like defence, foreign affairs and communications but also included various sweeping emergency powers, plus a device known as 'President's Rule' whereby state governments could be rather easily suspended. Other areas of government, like public health, agriculture, education and police were reserved to the states; but another long list comprehending most aspects of economic planning and management, trade and industry was 'concurrent', that is 'shared'.

Nehru, whose five-year plans and socialist reforms necessitated strong central direction, looked to Congress bosses in the states to ensure state-level collaboration. But even at a time when Congress controlled most states, this was not a foregone conclusion. In matters like educational reform and the introduction of a 'ceiling' on the size of land holdings, the rights reserved to the states enabled them to delay and frustrate change. In many sectors a yawning gap between central legislative intention and actual local implementation characterised the Nehru years.

With the opposition in the Delhi parliament hopelessly outnumbered, the states, whether or not Congress-run, also acted as channels for dissent. This might be ideological but was usually prompted by a sense of regional or sectional disadvantage. For states whose configuration and composition stemmed originally from Mughal convenience and the progress of British arms, a high priority was a more logical alignment with ethnic and linguistic realities. In the south a Dravida movement played on the ethnic and non-brahman identity of the mainly Tamil-speaking, and so Dravidian, people of the Madras state. The likelihood of Hindi, as spoken throughout the densely populated Gangetic basin, being adopted as India's official language was particularly feared in the south and became a prime target of the Dravida Munnetra Kazhagham (DMK), founded in 1949.

At the same time there resurfaced demands for greater recognition of other major vernacular languages, along with greater opportunities for those who spoke them. Tilak had urged reorganisation of the provinces along linguistic lines at the beginning of the century, and the Congress Party had since adopted this principle in its internal organisation. But Nehru feared the fragmentation which would result from such reorganisation, and continued to oppose it. Then in 1953 a Telugu activist, climaxing a long campaign for a Telugu-language state to be known as Andhra, fasted unto death. Assailed by the arguments of the already language-based state Congress parties, Nehru was finally convinced. Later in 1953 he duly set up a States Reorganisation Commission.

As a result of this and later commissions, Madras state was reorganised into the Tamil-speaking Tamil Nadu, the Kannada-speaking Karnataka, the Telugu-speaking Andhra Pradesh, and the Malayalam-speaking Kerala. Likewise in 1960 Bombay state was split into a Gujarati-speaking Gujarat and a Marathi-speaking Maharashtra. On the other hand, to appease the now deafening demands from what was easily India's largest language-group, Hindi was indeed declared India's 'official language'. But it was not the 'national language' nor, as soon transpired when other languages secured a similar status, was it the 'official language'; it was *an* 'official language'.

At first glance Nehru's fears of fragmentation would seem to have had some justification. Instead of about a dozen states, by 1990 there were twenty-seven, with several more in the pipeline. It was also clear that establishing a linguistic identity could lead to other forms of particularism. The uneven distribution of caste, religious and professional groups throughout India meant that the concentration of any one group in any one of the now much smaller states could slew its whole ideology. The classic example would be the Panjab, although similar weightings would promote caste and cultivator interests in Karnataka, Gujarat, Andhra and elsewhere.

On the basis of linguistic identity many of the new states also set about projecting a distinct cultural identity and rediscovering the historical pedigree of their territory. Maharashtra, for instance, as well as promoting Marathi-language education, media and literature, vigorously championed

the historical achievements of the Marathas and identified with their perceived role as the seventeenth- and eighteenth-century pioneers of a
resurgent and militant Hinduism. This in turn helps to explain the rise of
an organisation like the Shiv Sena or 'Army of Shiv' (Shiv being identified
with both the divine Lord Shiva and the historical Shivaji). From modest
beginnings as a social pressure group in Bombay, the Sena rocketed to
electoral success first in the metropolitan area and then, in the 1990s,
throughout the state. Elsewhere other state, as opposed to national, parties
have followed a similar trajectory. And by electing members to the Delhi
parliament as well as to the state assemblies, they have been steadily eating
into the unassailable majority once enjoyed by Congress at the centre. Mrs
Gandhi's alarm was well-founded. But, misinterpreting the nature of the
threat as secessionist, she badly miscalculated how to handle it.

GREEN REVOLUTION AND BLUESTAR

Although Nehru had set up the States Reorganisation Commission, he
had been adamant about not extending its remit to the Panjab. After
Independence India's share of the old Panjab province had rejoiced in the
title of 'The Panjab and East Panjab States Union' (PEPSU). It included
Urdu-, Hindi- and Panjabi-speakers. The last proved to be the most vocal
when they demanded that PEPSU, the product of Partition, itself be partitioned into Panjabi and non-Panjabi-speaking states. The demand, however, was championed by an exclusively Sikh party, the Akali Dal, and
Nehru rightly judged that this was not in fact a linguistic issue but a
sectarian one. Because Panjabi was spoken by nearly all Sikhs, and because
the script they favoured was that of the Sikh Granth, the Akalis were actually
demanding what would in effect be a Sikh state. In a determinedly secular
India this was anathema. The government therefore remained firm in the
face of fasts and clamped down hard on agitators. In 1955 police actually
raided Akali offices within the precincts of the Golden Temple in Amritsar.
A sacrilege in Sikh eyes, the action would later be seen as a precedent for
intervention by the government. It would not be forgotten either in
Amritsar or in Delhi.

Centre–state relations underwent further strain as a result of the leadership crisis which followed the sudden death of Lal Bahadur Shastri. (He
had collapsed in Tashkent within hours of signing the 1966 agreement
which ended the second Indo–Pak war.) Since no provision had been made
for a successor, it fell to the Congress leadership in the form of a powerful

THE NEHRU-GANDHI DYNASTY

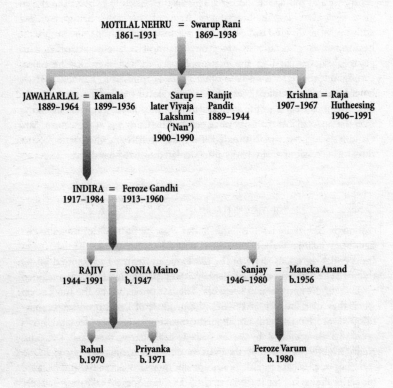

cabal of provincial leaders to nominate a candidate. They chose Indira
Gandhi, Nehru's only surviving daughter. Despite her patriotic first name,
despite her marriage to a Parsi who just happened to be called Gandhi,
and despite her having been co-opted as her father's political amanuensis
and as a Congress official, Nehru tradition insists that Indira had not been
groomed for leadership. The Congress bosses who chose her evidently felt
the same way; while anticipating the electoral bonus to be expected of a
third-generation Nehru, they saw her as a malleable and disposable
figurehead.

She had other ideas. Scouring the political spectrum for support from
any quarter, she reversed her father's policy towards the Sikh Akali Dal
and conceded the creation of a Punjabi-speaking, and so mainly Sikh, state.

Accordingly in 1966 PEPSU was divided into three, its hill states becoming Himachal Pradesh, its Hindi-speaking belt immediately north of Delhi becoming Haryana, and the Panjabi-speaking remainder remaining as Panjab. The Akali Dal, having won a state, promptly demanded exclusive possession of Chandigarh, the Le Corbusier-designed capital of PEPSU which was now shared with Haryana. This too Mrs Gandhi conceded when in 1969 she was in still greater need of support. But the award was contingent on Panjab ceding two districts to Haryana. It refused to do so. The settlement therefore remained a dead letter, the status of Chandigarh continued to provide a focus for Sikh resentment, and sections of the Akali Dal began to have second thoughts about Mrs Gandhi.

Following a disappointingly small victory in the 1967 general election and heavy Congress losses in the states, Mrs Gandhi had meanwhile turned on the Congress cabal which had chosen her. In a series of combative manoeuvres which climaxed in 1969 over the selection of the Republic's next president (the mainly titular head of state), the Congress 'Old Guard' were sidelined as she split the party into two factions. Heading her own Congress (R) – for 'Requisition' (or the requisitioning of a Congress committee to choose the new president) – and later Congress (I) – for 'Indira' – she then revived the radical agenda of the 1950s and announced the nationalisation of banks, the cancellation of the privileges and stipends guaranteed to the princes when they opted to join the Indian union, and new legislation on land holdings, corporate profits and personal incomes. The rhetoric was socialist; it duly secured her the support of most socialist and communist parties while her rivals, the Congress (O) – for 'Organisation' but later just 'Old' – turned to right-wing parties. But the intention was unashamedly populist. In the 1971 elections, under the slogan '*Gharibi hatao*', 'Out with Poverty', she trounced both Congress and non-Congress opponents.

Before, during, and particularly after these elections she further secured her position by unprecedented use of the patronage and powers of office. With any hostility to her Congress (I) being interpreted as anti-national or secessionist, state governments, whether run by her Congress opponents or non-Congress parties, were routinely dismissed by the device of President's Rule. In the two decades before 1966, President's Rule had been invoked ten times; over the next two decades it was invoked seventy times. The hierarchies of party and government were ignored as appointments were increasingly made on the basis of personal loyalty to an increasingly personalised leadership. Mrs Gandhi's Congress itself 'swiftly degenerated into an unaudited company for winning elections'.

In the past, its factional conflicts had borne some relation to real ideological differences; now they became crudely instrumental, and the party simply acted as a mechanism for collecting funds, distributing 'tickets' or nominations for seats, and conducting campaigns ... The subtle routines of politics between elections – when support must be nurtured, promises delivered on, things actually done – were neglected.[4]

Polls were heavily weighted in favour of the governing incumbent as official facilities, funds and transport were brazenly deployed for electioneering purposes. For Mrs Gandhi this would have serious repercussions. Raj Narain, a battle-scarred socialist who in 1971 unsuccessfully opposed the prime minister in her own Rae Bareli constituency, filed a protest about these irregularities. After a leisurely five-year progress through the courts, it would return to haunt her.

In the interim, although poverty was not banished, Mrs Gandhi was presiding over some sensational successes and achieving near-divine status in the eyes of her supporters. Courtesy of new high-yield grain varieties and more irrigation, the country edged from local famine in 1965 to national self-sufficiency in food-grains by the early 1970s. This was a major achievement, especially in the context of an exponential increase in population and of the low priority given to agricultural investment during the Nehru years. Officially, and perhaps for the first time, India could feed itself. Farming incomes in the more productive regions, especially in the northwest, also improved. And so did the expectations of those who enjoyed them.

One 'green revolution' nicely coincided with another. The green in this case was that of Islam across the border in East Pakistan. There, championing those secessionist forces which in India she so vehemently opposed, Mrs Gandhi contrived a success which was even more nationally gratifying.

East Pakistan, with its capital at Dacca (Dhaka), was what had previously been East Bengal. Although constituting a single province on a par with the several provinces of West Pakistan (Sind, Panjab, North-West Frontier, etc.), East Pakistan's population was such that it exceeded the combined total of all the other provinces. Moreover, in a nation not blessed with export potential, its jute industry was the main foreign-exchange earner. To East Bengalis it therefore seemed reasonable that their language should be treated as a national medium, like West Pakistan's officially recognised Urdu, and that they should command a generous share of such political

THE POST-INDEPENDENCE LEADERSHIP

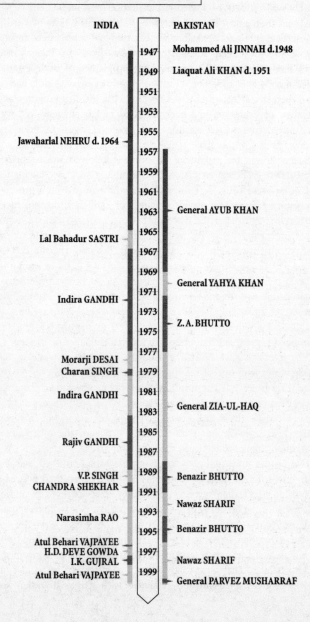

INDIA | PAKISTAN

	1947	Mohammed Ali JINNAH d.1948
	1949	Liaquat Ali KHAN d. 1951
	1951	
	1953	
	1955	
Jawaharlal NEHRU d. 1964	1957	
	1959	
	1961	
	1963	General AYUB KHAN
Lal Bahadur SASTRI	1965	
	1967	
	1969	
	1971	General YAHYA KHAN
Indira GANDHI	1973	
	1975	Z. A. BHUTTO
	1977	
Morarji DESAI		
Charan SINGH	1979	
Indira GANDHI	1981	
	1983	General ZIA-UL-HAQ
	1985	
Rajiv GANDHI	1987	
V.P. SINGH	1989	Benazir BHUTTO
CHANDRA SHEKHAR	1991	
		Nawaz SHARIF
Narasimha RAO	1993	
	1995	Benazir BHUTTO
Atul Behari VAJPAYEE		
H.D. DEVE GOWDA	1997	Nawaz SHARIF
I.K. GUJRAL		
Atul Behari VAJPAYEE	1999	General PARVEZ MUSHARRAF

representation, government investment and employment opportunities as Pakistan's admittedly straitened circumstances permitted.

In fact they enjoyed none of these things. At the time of Partition in 1947, departing Hindu Bengali administrators had simply been replaced by arriving Muslim Panjabi administrators. As early as 1948 Bengali members of Pakistan's Constituent Assembly had complained of neglect and 'being treated merely as a colony of Western Pakistan'. Language riots had broken out in the early 1950s, and in 1954 elections the Muslim League, Pakistan's equivalent of Congress, had been defeated in East Bengal. Victory went to a united front which included the Awami League, founded by H.S. Suhrawardy and whose general secretary was Sheikh Mujibur Rahman.

Suspension of the provincial government followed, much as under the Indian device of President's Rule. It remained in abeyance during General Ayub Khan's era of 'basic democracy', a euphemism which proved to be basic military dictatorship with a veneer of civilian endorsement. It was not therefore until after the discomfiture of Pakistan's Panjabi-dominated military in the 1965 Indo–Pak war that demands for a return to representative government reopened the issue of East Pakistan. In 1966 Z.A. Bhutto formed a Pakistan People's Party in West Pakistan, and at the same time in the East Sheikh Mujibur launched a six-point programme demanding virtual autonomy for his province. Both leaders were arrested. But the protests continued until Ayub's successor, General Yahya Khan, having reimposed martial law, suddenly responded to mainly US pressure and announced general elections plus a return to civilian rule in 1970.

The elections gave Bhutto a majority in the West while in the East Sheikh Mujib won one of the most impressive mandates ever recorded in a genuinely free vote. The implications for the cohesion of Pakistan were grim. The meeting of the National Assembly was postponed; talks between Mujib, Bhutto and Yahya Khan ended in failure; and in March 1971, as the Awami League made good its threat to proclaim the independence of 'Bangladesh', tanks rolled onto the streets of Dacca.

During the previous monsoon Bangladesh had suffered one of its all too frequent floods. Tens of thousands of flood victims had poured across the border into Indian territory. Now they were followed by millions of refugees from the butchery of the Pakistani army. Not without cause, India cited the influx to announce that it could no longer view the crisis as Pakistan's domestic affair. Refugees were in fact being armed and trained by the Indian army, and then returned to their homeland as freedom-fighting 'Mukhti Bahini'. They were followed in November 1971 by regular units of the Indian army. Pakistani jets retaliated with strikes at Indian airports,

INDIA'S GENERAL ELECTIONS 1947–1999

Year	Most seats won by	Prime Minister
1952	Congress	Jawaharlal Nehru
1957	Congress	Jawaharlal Nehru
1962	Congress	Jawaharlal Nehru
1967	Congress	Indira Gandhi
1971	Congress (R)	Indira Gandhi
1977	Janata	Morarji Desai
1980	Congress (I)	Indira Gandhi
1984	Congress (I)	Rajiv Gandhi
1989	National Front / Janata Dal	V.P. Singh
1991	Congress (I)	Narasimha Rao
1996	(BJP) United Front	(Atul Behari Vajpayee) H.D. Deve Gowda
1998	BJP	Atul Behari Vajpayee
1999	BJP	Atul Behari Vajpayee

and India's airforce hit back in West Pakistan. But in Bengal it was all over within days. Supported by a delirious civilian population, Indian divisions took the surrender of the Pakistani forces on 15 December. In the West, Yahya Khan and his traumatised military command stepped down in favour of Bhutto. And in January 1972 Sheikh Mujibur Rahman was installed as the first prime minister of an independent Bangladesh.

Pakistan's defeat was a victory for India as much as for Bangladesh. Indira Gandhi had swept the polls in the 1971 elections and her cup of triumph seemed now to run over. To cap it all, in 1974 India successfully tested a nuclear device. Earlier her father had espoused non-proliferation and insisted that India's only nuclear interest was in power-generation; now Indira insisted that a nuclear device was not a nuclear weapon. But in refusing to sign the self-denying nuclear ordinance she made it clear that, like non-violence and non-alignment, non-proliferation was no longer Indian policy. The nuclear programme continued while in Pakistan Bhutto sought Chinese assistance with an equivalent Pakistani deterrent.

Replacing a hostile East Pakistan with a friendly Bangladesh opened the way to a reorganisation of India's eastern territories. Assam was divided into two states (Assam and Meghalaya), and statehood was conferred on Tripura, Mizoram and Arunachal Pradesh. Sporadic outbreaks of violence continued in the region, especially in Nagaland and Assam. But in 1974 a more serious threat came again from Panjab state, where the Akali Dal adopted a programme known as the Anandpur Sahib Resolution. This, while ostensibly demanding for all the states the autonomy guaranteed to them under the constitution, could also be read as a demand for greater autonomy for Panjab and so for the Sikhs.

Mrs Gandhi's suborning of the political process brought its reward a year later as enemies old and new, Akalis and Dravidians, princes and communists, Old Congress and new Hindu communalists, rallied in support of a mass protest movement led by the veteran Gandhian and socialist J.P. Narayan. Excluded from the political process, dissent had taken an extra-constitutional form. Protesting against corruption and the severe economic hardship occasioned by rampant inflation, itself the result of the recent hike in OPEC oil prices, Narayan's bandwagon rolled up the Gangetic plain and into Delhi in June 1975. There it conveniently coincided with a decision of the Allahabad High Court in favour of Raj Narain, Mrs Gandhi's lame but dogged opponent in the 1971 elections. Convicted of electioneering malpractice, she was automatically banned from office.

Instead of resigning, she promptly declared a national emergency, thereby suspending the constitution. Troops appeared on the streets; perhaps twenty thousand political leaders, journalists, lawyers and students were gaoled without trial. The press was heavily censored and the courts silenced. Whether or not there had been a civil emergency to justify this action, there was now very definitely a constitutional emergency. The world's largest democracy had bombed.

The eighteen-month 'Emergency' itself, the strong-arm methods used during it by Sanjay, Mrs Gandhi's younger son, in the promotion of slum clearance and birth control, and the resounding defeat that followed her attempt to secure democratic endorsement by calling elections in 1977, caused a sensation at the time. In 1975, for imposing what she preferred to call 'Disciplined Democracy', Mrs Gandhi was congratulated by some but condemned by most. In 1977, for calling elections, she was applauded for her democratic commitment and blamed for her poor judgement in almost equal measure. Obituaries for Indian democracy in 1975 were followed by euphoric appraisals of its 'maturity' in 1977.

Two years later the tables were turned again. The lionised heroes of *Janata morcha* (the 'popular front' which had supported Narayan's protest) became the petty villains of the Janata government which, having won the 1977 elections and restored democratic practices, disintegrated in an orgy of in-fighting. By 1980 Mrs Gandhi and her Congress (I) were back in power with a fresh mandate and a backlog of scores to be settled. State governments were soon toppling like nine-pins as the raps of President's Rule replaced the concussion of 'Emergency' dictatorship.

Amongst scores outstanding was that against the Sikh Akali Dal. To maximise the divisions to which Sikhs in general and the Akali Dal in particular were notoriously prone, Mrs Gandhi encouraged the extremist rantings of a young religious leader, Sant Jarnail Singh Bhindranwale. Bhindranwale took up residence beside the Golden Temple in Amritsar and from there, defying both his prime ministerial patron and his enemies, conducted a terrorist campaign designed to eliminate non-Sikhs in Panjab state and secure autonomy, if not an independent Sikh state ('Khalistan'). In late 1983, with killings and bomb-blasts becoming a daily occurrence, Panjab was duly taken under President's Rule. Paramilitary units under central government direction moved into the state; and Bhindranwale moved into the precincts of the Golden Temple itself. An ex-general, now one of Bhindranwale's disciples, who had once trained the Bangladeshi *Mukti Bahini*, organised the defence of the shrine and positioned sharp-shooters in neighbouring buildings. When in June 1984 the Indian army finally launched 'Operation Bluestar' and stormed the place, heavy casualties were suffered by both sides and the Sikhs' holiest shrine was severely damaged as well as defiled.

Bhindranwale died in the attack. He was promptly hailed as a martyr. Blood cried out for blood. Four months later, amidst extraordinarily relaxed security, Indira Gandhi was assassinated by two of her bodyguards, both Sikhs, as she took the early-morning air in her Delhi garden.

As during Partition in 1947, the citizens of Delhi joined in the carnage, with Hindu mobs taking their revenge on the capital's large Sikh population. In this they were undistracted by police intervention, and used electoral registers, allegedly provided by Congress politicians, to identify the homes of their victims. The killing and burning was methodical. Fifteen years later few of those responsible had been brought to justice.

THE SAFFRON REVOLUTION

The assassination of Mrs Gandhi looked to have ended the Nehru-Gandhi dynasty. Sanjay, her politically ambitious son and presumed successor, had been killed four years earlier in 1980 while performing aerial stunts in his private plane. Rajiv, his quieter elder brother, also flew planes but as an airline pilot. Soaring above the political mêlée, he had made no secret of his distaste for party antics and was genuinely reluctant to enter the fray. But Sanjay's death had obliged him to support his mother more prominently, and her assassination plus the explosion of communal violence was now deemed to have generated such severe turbulence that only another Nehru-Gandhi could be entrusted with the controls of state. On the insistence of the then president of the republic, Rajiv was hoisted into the prime minister's office and expected to steady the trajectory of the nation.

In this he was surprisingly successful. With little more than a youthful image and a flawless reputation as 'Mr Clean' he won an impressive mandate in the late-1984 elections and then defused the crisis in the Panjab, plus another in Assam. Elsewhere intervention by central government in the affairs of the states was reined back. The federal principles which underlay the original constitution were reaffirmed by a less ready recourse to the suspension of state governments and the imposition of President's Rule. At the same time the leverage exercised by all governments, including that at the centre, was somewhat reduced by new legislation to discourage elected representatives from changing their party allegiance whenever the inducements of office, cash or concessions so dictated.

For if Rajiv had a big idea it was not, like his mother, to engross all authority but to liberate its exercise from the day-to-day detail of its implementation. He conceived that government had become too interventionist and politicians too glib with their promises. A scathing attack was made on the time-serving conduct of his own Congress hierarchy. Politicians, like the people as a whole, were no longer to look to government for every imaginable facility, provision and assistance, but to rediscover the potential of private initiative, personal responsibility and local endeavour.

In terms of the economy this represented a radical departure from the Nehru years with their state directives, five-year plans and 'permit-raj'. The enterprise culture was hailed and socialist rhetoric discredited. Although the impact was limited, some taxes were cut, quotas freed, licensing requirements reduced or simplified, and private investment from both Indian and foreign sources encouraged. Passionate about gadgetry, Rajiv scorned the state-run industries churning out their high-cost megawatts and low-quality tonnages; instead he extolled the merits of the personal computer, satellite communication and multi-media education.

His several successors in the prime ministerial office during the 1990s would not reverse this trend. Rajiv lost the 1989 election and then succumbed to assassination in 1991, the victim not of a Sikh bullet but of a Tamil bomb. It had been primed by the war in Sri Lanka to which he had sent troops at the request of the Sri Lankan government. Although Rajiv had headed only one government, it was the last of the twentieth century to enjoy a clear majority. Thereafter alliances of convenience formed and fell apart in the *bhawans* of New Delhi with bewildering rapidity. The decade saw four general elections, eight new prime ministers, and perhaps twice that number of coalition changes. Only one government, a Congress one led by P.V. Narasimha Rao, lasted its full term (1991–6). Under Rao's distinguished finance minister Manmohan Singh, economic liberalisation gathered pace. For its beneficiaries, principally the urban middle classes, lifestyles changed dramatically. The shoddy goods and drab austerities of the Nehru age gave way to conspicuous expenditure on consumer durables, imported luxuries and foreign travel.

Rao lost the election in 1996, as had Rajiv in 1989, amidst allegations of financial corruption. Liberating the economy and encouraging private enterprise had spawned a rich crop of pecuniary scandals, one of which rocked the Bombay stock exchange in 1992, and had left the rupee unusually volatile. Devaluation helped exporters, but farmers producing foodgrains largely for domestic consumption felt themselves excluded from the new wealth. Yields no longer increased as they had during the years of the Green Revolution, and the impact of new irrigation in one area was offset by the falling water table in another. If the 'New Economic Policy' was meant to have a trickle-down effect, it had yet to moisten most of rural India.

What part a sense of rural disadvantage played in the rise of Hindu nationalism and of its principal advocate, the Bharatiya Janata Party (BJP), is debatable. In some states the farming lobby had thrown its weight behind the stranded representatives of other once-national groupings. Thus, just as the Communist Party (Marxist) had become a largely regional phenomenon with its power base in West Bengal, so the Janata Party became increasingly marginalised in Karnataka and Gujarat. A similar fate looked to be awaiting the once-mighty Congress. As the century drew to a close the BJP and its affiliates and rivals successfully staked their claim to the core regions of the Gangetic plain and Maharashtra, precisely those areas whence Congress had once drawn its staunchest support and whence, because of their population densities, nearly half of all MPs are returned.

The BJP, the 'Bharat [i.e. India] People's Party', had been formed from the relics of the Jan Sangh (itself a legatee of the Hindu *Mahasabha* of pre-Independence days) after the Sangh's unhappy participation in the Janata government of 1977–80. It emerged as a major contender in the 1989 elections which ended Rajiv's term of office. Rajiv had himself placated Hindu revivalist opinion by caving in to demands for access to the hitherto locked Babri masjid in Ayodhya – the unused mosque which the Emperor Babur was supposed to have built on the site of a supposed temple at the supposed birthplace of Lord Rama. What others supposed, the fundamentalists of the BJP passionately believed. Equating Indian identity with Hindu identity – a logical but not a valid equation for a nation with large Muslim, Sikh and Christian components – the party urged the promotion of *hindutwa* ('Hindu-ness') in all aspects of national life, and hit upon Babur's unremarkable mosque in the city sacred to Lord Rama as a classic example of *hindutwa* affronted.

Agitation for access to the site and its reclamation for Hindu worship coincided with the television screening of serialised dramatisations of the *Mahabharata* and *Ramayana*. In a society profoundly attached to its epic heritage, already peculiarly susceptible to the magic of the movies, and now rapidly discovering the more socially congenial habit of home-viewing, these long-running sagas took the nation by storm. Espousing their props, indeed leaping aboard their bandwagon, in 1990 L.K. Advani, the BJP president, donned saffron garb and posed with bow and arrows atop a truck decked out in imitation of Lord Rama's chariot. His cavalcade, swelling prodigiously, headed for Ayodhya but was arrested, as was Advani himself, on the orders of the then government under the leadership of Vishwanath Pratap Singh.

V.P. Singh, once Rajiv's finance minister and now the leader of a leftist front within the incumbent coalition, had been endeavouring to match the BJP's appeal to Hindus of upper and middling caste by wooing those of lower and no caste. To this end he promised to implement the recommendations of the 1980 Mandal Commission which would reserve nearly half of all government and educational places for the underprivileged castes. Encouraged by such commitments, the once-despised sections of Indian society became much more politically conscious and, by voting for a variety of populist mavericks with unashamedly local and communitarian loyalties, contributed significantly to the electoral volatility of the 1990s.

Bihar and UP witnessed the main struggle between these caste championships, although similar tinkering with the definition of 'Backward Classes' and the professional and educational rights reserved for such groups occurred in most other states. Ironically, in pursuit of caste equality, caste identity was not being eroded but actively promoted. It was precisely the outcome which Gandhi had feared when he insisted that Harijans decline the chance of being a separate electorate. Some brahman youths burned themselves to death in protest over the Mandal recommendations. Elsewhere castes not obviously disadvantaged in any way secured their reclassification as 'backward' so as to win a share of the opportunities on offer.

In 1992, after P.V. Narasimha Rao had been installed at the head of a minority Congress government, the BJP's supporters and affiliates returned to the Babri masjid. Elections in the previous year had given the party control of the state government of UP. As in Amritsar a decade earlier, when Bhindranwale had enjoyed local immunity, this placed the state police in an ambivalent position. Confronted by a mob of fanatical Hindu 'volunteers' and aware that their claims on the site were supported by the state government, the police proved unable or unwilling to hold the line. The 'volunteers' clambered onto the mosque and began its demolition.

We are told by Khafi Khan that Shivaji, the Maratha leader whose example is so cherished by Hindu nationalists, had 'made it a rule not to desecrate mosques'. But Khafi Khan's words were ignored by the new breed of zealots, and the BJP's attempts to disclaim authority lacked conviction. A hit-list of other Muslim sites was known to exist; bomb blasts in Bombay, supposedly by way of Muslim retaliation, unleashed the stormtroopers of the Shiv Sena, whose Muslim massacres, like those of the Sikhs in Delhi in 1984, were assisted by access to the electoral registers. When, in alliance with the Shiv Sena, the BJP came to power in Delhi (1998–9), Christian churches and missionaries were also targeted.

Under the BJP's dispensation, if not its direction, India's carefully nurtured secularism looked to have been as irrevocably demolished as the Ayodhya mosque. Peaceful co-existence as per the principles of *panchshila* had earlier been laid to rest by Mrs Gandhi; but to a party and a government dedicated to reviving Hindu pride and prowess even the pretence of Gandhian non-violence was now anathema. Within weeks of coming to office in 1998 the BJP government detonated India's first nuclear weapons at Pokharan in Rajasthan, then tested the missile which would deliver them. Pakistan promptly followed suit. Lest anyone doubt either the proud nationalisms which had produced these weapons or the targets for which they were intended, the Indian missile was named 'Agni', after the Vedic god of fire, and the Pakistani missile 'Ghorid', after Muhammad of

Ghor, he who had breached the gates of *arya-varta* at the battle of Tarain.

Both nations fêted their scientists and acclaimed the blasts with equally impressive explosions of nationalistic triumphalism. It was as if a trophy had been won, an impossible victory recorded. Even those pale liberal hands lately wrung in despair over Ayodhya flapped and clapped uncontrollably for Pokharan. Caution, let alone dissent, was deemed unpatriotic. Before daring to speak out against the tests, India's prize-winning novelist Arundhati Roy was advised to check carefully that her taxes were paid and her papers in order.

Calling the tests 'the final act of betrayal by a ruling class that has failed its people',[5] Roy was particularly horrified by the demonstrations of approval. Here was a nation so poorly educated and so starved of achievement that most of its citizens imagined a nuclear capacity to be cause for riotous celebration. The betrayal was not just that of the BJP government but of all its predecessors. How could a people, many of whom were still illiterate, begin to comprehend the horror of nuclear warfare? Jawaharlal, Indira and Rajiv had all failed the nation, all neglected basic social provisions, all sanctioned the nuclear programme. Prime Minster Atul Behari Vajpayee of the BJP had merely pushed the button.

Yet while socialism has been discarded, secularism demolished, and non-violence exploded, democratic practices remain firmly entrenched. More parties, new ideologies, unstable governments and frequent polls have only increased the popularity of the great electoral bazaar. Participants, even those credited with outrageous personalities or offensive programmes, may be said to observe the norms of Indian electoral conduct. Arguably elections have become too popular, obscuring their deeper purpose of providing a government that actually governs rather than one which simply readies itself for the next poll.

It might also be claimed that the integrity of the Indian Republic is no longer open to question. The devolution of responsibilities back to the states and the proliferation of regional and communitarian parties has certainly reduced the threat of secession. Federalism seems at last to be working while commitment to the electoral process presumes an acceptance of the parameters of the Indian state. But there is an exception. So long as Pakistan continues to dispute the status of Jammu and Kashmir, and so long as India continues to deem the Kashmir problem a purely domestic issue, the integrity of neither nation can be confidently taken for granted.

SOURCE NOTES

Publication details of most of the cited works will be found in the bibliography.

The following abbreviations refer to works listed in the General section of the bibliography:

CEHI – *The Cambridge Economic History of India*, vol.1, *c1200–c1750* (ed. Raychaudhuri, T. and Habib, I.)

HCIP – *The History and Culture of the Indian People* (ed. Majumdar, R.C. et al)

HOIBIOH – *The History of India as Told by its Own Historians* (ed. Elliot, H.M. and Dowson, J.)

NCHI – *The New Cambridge History of India* (ed. Johnson, G. et al)

INTRODUCTION

1 Majumdar, R.C., in HCIP, vol.1, 'The Vedic Age' p.47
2 Keay, J., *India Discovered*, HarperCollins, London, 1988
3 Stein, B., *A History of India*, Blackwell, Oxford, 1998, p.5
4 Braudel, F. (trans. Maine, R.), *A History of Civilisations*, Penguin, New York, 1993, p.217

CHAPTER 1

1 Adapted from the *Satapatha Brahmana* as rendered by A.D. Pusalkar, in HCIP, vol.1, 'The Vedic Age', pp.271–2
2 Thapar, R., 'The Study of Society in Ancient India', in *Ancient Indian Social History*, p.212
3 Bhandarkar, D.R., quoted in Possehl, G. (ed.), *Harappan Civilisation*, p.405
4 Allchin, B. and F.R., *Birth of Indian Civilisation*, p.131

5 *Ibid*, p.132
6 Ghosh, A., *The City in Early Historical India*, p.83
7 Lal, B.B., 'The Indus Civilisation', in Basham, A.L. (ed.), *A Cultural History of India*, p.16
8 Pusalker, A.D., in HCIP, vol.1, 'The Vedic Age', p.181
9 Ratnagar, S., *Enquiries into the Political Organisation of Harappan Society*, p.152
10 Ratnagar, S., *Encounters: The Westerly Trade of the Harappan Civilisation*, p.247

CHAPTER 2

1 Thapar, R., 'The Image of the Barbarian in Early India', repr. in *Ancient Indian Social History*, p.140
2 Thapar, R., 'The Study of Society in Ancient India', repr. in *ibid*, p.190
3 *Asiatick Researches*, vol.1, 1788, quoted in Keay, John, *India Discovered*, p.30

4 Muller, F. Max, *Chips from a German Workshop*, vol.1, 1867, p.63

5 Wheeler, R.E. Mortimer, 'Harappan Chronology and the *Rig Veda*', repr. in Possehl, G.L. (ed.), *Ancient Cities of the Indus*, p.291

6 Dales, G.F., 'The Mythical Massacre at Mohenjo Daro', repr. in *ibid*, p.293

7 Elphinstone, Mountstuart, *The History Of India* etc., p.54

8 Majumdar, R.C., *Ancient India*, p.30

9 Ghosh, B.K., 'Language and Literature', in 'The Age of the Rik-Samhita', bk v in HCIP, vol.1, 'The Vedic Age', pp.347–8

10 Rig Veda, Mandala I, 175

CHAPTER 3

1 Kosambi, D.D., *The Culture and Civilisation of Ancient India in Historical Outline*, p.89

2 Kosambi, D.D., *An Introduction to the Study of Indian History*, p.2

3 *Ibid*, p.146

4 Ghosh, A., *The City in Early Historical India*, p.34

5 Thapar, R., *From Lineage to State*, pp.16–17

6 Quoted in Meyer, J.T., *Sexual Life in Ancient India*

7 Thapar, R., *From Lineage to State*, p.22

8 *Ibid*, p.134

9 Sharma, J.P., *Republics in Ancient India*, p.9

10 Thapar, R., *From Lineage to State*, p.73

11 Ghosh A., *The City in Early Historical India*, p.64

12 Thapar, R., *From Lineage to State*, pp.102–3

13 *Rig Veda*, X, 90

14 Thapar, R., *From Lineage to State*, p.170

15 Spelman, J.W., *Political Theory of Ancient India*, p.69

CHAPTER 4

1 Mountbatten, quoted in Collins, L. and Lapierre, D., *Mountbatten and the Partition of India*, p.70

2 Lane Fox, R., *Alexander the Great*, p.56

3 Marshall, J., *Taxila*, vol.1, p.12

4 Basham, A.L., *The Wonder that was India*, p.390

5 Bechert, H., in *When did the Buddha Live?: The Controversy of the Dating of the Historical Buddha* (ed. Bechert, H.), p.286

6 Sharma, J.P., *The Republics in Ancient India*, pp.123–4

7 Mookerji, R.K., in HCIP, vol.2, 'The Age of Imperial Unity', p.25

8 Thapar, R., *A History of India*, vol.1, p.59

9 Majumdar, R.C., *Ancient India*, p.101

10 Lane Fox, R., *Alexander the Great*, p.331

11 Mookerji, R.K., in HCIP, vol.2, 'The Age of Imperial Unity', p.44

CHAPTER 5

1 *Asiatick Researches*, 1793, quoted in Keay, J., *India Discovered*, p.35

2 Wells, H.G., *A Short History of the World*, 1922, repr. Penguin, Harmondsworth, 1946, p.114

3 Kautilya (ed. and trans. Rangarajan, L.N. etc.), *The Arthasastra*, p.21

4 Trautmann, Thomas R., *Kautilya and the Arthasastra*, p.186

5 Fergusson, J., *A History of Indian Architecture*, London, 1897

6 Yazdani, G., *The Early History of the Deccan*, vol.1, p.69

7 Kosambi, D.D., *An Introduction to the Study of Indian History . . .*, 1975, preface and pp.17–53

8 Tod, James, *Travels in Western India*, W.H. Allen, London, 1839, p.76

9 Prinsep, James, in *Journal of the Asiatic Society of Bengal*, vol.8, 1838, quoted in Keay, John, *India Discovered*, p.53

10 As trans. in Thapar, Romila, *Asoka and the Decline of the Mauryas*, p.256

11 Mookerji, R.K., 'Asoka the Great', in HCIP, vol.2, 'The Age of Imperial Unity', p.74

12 Wells, H.G., *A Short History of the World*, 1922, repr. Penguin, Harmondsworth, 1946, p.115

13 Kautilya (ed. and trans. Rangarajan, L.N. etc.), *The Arthasastra*, p.741
14 McCrindle, J.W., *Ancient India as Described by Megasthenes and Arrian*, Trübner, London, 1877, p.84
15 As trans. in Thapar, Romila, *Asoka and the Decline of the Mauryas*, p.254
16 *Ibid*, p.266
17 Thapar, R., 'Asokan India and the Gupta Age', in Basham, A.L. (ed.), *A Cultural History of India*, p.42

CHAPTER 6

1 Narain, A.K., *The Indo-Greeks*, p.viii
2 Kulke, H. and Rothermund, D., *A History of India*, p.83
3 S[h]astri, K.A. Nilakantha, *A Comprehensive History of India*, vol.2, *The Mauryas and the Satavahanas*, p.102
4 Thapar, Romila, *A History of India*, vol.1, p.93
5 Narain, A.K., *The Indo-Greeks*, p.11
6 Harle, J.C., *The Art and Architecture of the Indian Subcontinent*, p.70
7 Bagchi, P.C., *India and China: A Thousand Years of Cultural Relations*, p.10
8 Dani, A.H., *Human Records on the Karakoram Highway*, p.49
9 *Ibid*, p.77
10 S[h]astri, K.A. Nilakantha, *A History of South India from Prehistoric Times to the Fall of Vjayanagar*, 1955, p.130
11 Hart, George L., 'Ancient Tamil Literature: Its Scholarly Past and Future', in Stein, Burton (ed.), *Essays on South India*, pp.41–2
12 Maloney, Clarence, 'Archaeology in South India: Accomplishments and Prospects', in *ibid*, p.24
13 Wheeler, R.E. Mortimer, *Rome Beyond the Imperial Frontiers*, p.147
14 Glover, I.C., *Early Trade Relations Between India and South East Asia*, pp.47–8
15 Coedes, G., *The Indianised States of Southeast Asia*, p.18
16 Quoted in Sarkar, H.B., *Cultural Relations Between India and Southeast Asian Countries*, p.87
17 Quoted in Coedes, G., *The Indianised States* etc., p.37
18 Ray, Himanshu Prabha, *Monastery and Guild: Commerce Under the Satavahanas*, p.108

CHAPTER 7

1 Williams, L.F. Rushbrook (ed.), *A Handbook for Travellers in India, Pakistan, Nepal, Bangladesh and Sri Lanka*, p.278
2 Banerjea, J.N., 'The Satraps of Northern and Western India', in S[h]astri, K.A. Nilakantha (ed.), *A Comprehensive History of India*, vol.2, p.283
3 Ghoshal, U.N., 'Political Organisation (Post-Mauryan)', in *ibid*, p.350
4 Kosambi, D.D., *An Introduction to the Study of Indian History*, p.285
5 *Ibid*, p.279
6 *Ibid*, p.286
7 Bagchi, P.C. and Raghavan, V., 'Language and Literature', in S[h]astri, K.A. Nilakantha (ed), *A Comprehensive History of India*, vol.2, pp.632–3
8 Smith, V.A., *The Early History of India*, p.266
9 Majumdar, R.C., 'The Rise of the Guptas', in HCIP, vol.3, 'The Classical Age', p.4
10 Fleet, J.F., *Corpus Inscriptionum Indicarum*, vol.3, 'Inscriptions of Early Gupta Kings and their Successors', pp.10–17
11 Smith, V.A., *The Early History of India*, p.274
12 Kosambi, D.D., *An Introduction* etc., p.313
13 Mookerji, R.K., *The Gupta Empire*, p.38
14 Inden, R., *Imagining India*, pp.239–40
15 See Williams, J.G., *The Art of Gupta India*, p.25
16 Beal, S., in H[i]euen Tsang, *Si-Yu-Ki, Buddhist Records of the Western World*, vol.1, pp.xxxvii–xxxviii
17 *Ibid*, p.lvii

18 Altekar, A.S., 'Religion and
Philosophy', in *The Vakataka-Gupta
Age* (ed. Majumdar, R.C. and Altekar,
A.S.), p.341

19 Devahuti, D., *Harsha, A Political Study*,
pp.114–15

20 Quoted in Keay, J., *India Discovered*,
pp.151–2

21 Williams, J.G., *The Art of Gupta India*,
p.3

22 Harle, J.C., *Art and Architecture* etc.,
p.87

23 Basham. A.L., *The Wonder that was
India*, p.442

24 Keith, A.B., *A History of Sanskrit
Literature*, p.94

25 Kosambi, D.D., *An Introduction* etc.,
p.284

CHAPTER 8

1 Kosambi, D.D., *The Culture and
Civilisation of Ancient India*, p.191

2 Gaur, A., *Indian Charters on Copper
Plates in the Department of Oriental
Manuscripts and Books*, p.viii

3 Fleet, J.F., *Corpus Inscriptionum
Indicum* etc., p.169

4 H[i]euen Tsang (trans. Beal, S.),
Si-Yu-Ki, Buddhist Records etc., vol.1,
pp.120, 137

5 See Sudhir Ranjan Das, 'Types of Land
in North-Eastern India (from the
Fourth Century to the Seventh
Century)', in Chattopadhyaya, B. (ed.)
*Essays in Ancient Indian Economic
History*, pp.62–3

6 Basham, A.L., *The Wonder that was
India*, p.449

7 Devahuti, D., *Harsha* etc., p.71

8 Bana (trans. Cowell, E.R. and Thomas,
F.W.), *Harsa-Carita*

9 H[i]euen Tsang (trans. Beal, S.), *Si-Yu-
Ki: Buddhist Records* etc., vol.1, p.213

10 *Ibid*, vol.2, p.256

11 Michell, G., *Monuments of India*, vol.1,
p.332

12 Satianathaier, R., 'Dynasties of South
India', in HCIP, vol.4, 'The Classical
Age', p.262

13 Coedes, G., *The Indianised States of
South East Asia*, p.66

14 Lamb, A., 'Indian Influence in South
East Asia', in *A Cultural History of
India* (ed. Basham, A.L.), p.446

15 Smithies, M., *Yogyakarta*, p.60

16 Dumarcay, J., *The Temples of Java*, p.5

17 Inden, R., *Imagining India*, p.230

CHAPTER 9

1 H[i]euen Tsang, *Si-Yu-Ki, Buddhist
Records* etc., vol.2, pp.272–3

2 *Chach-nama* or *Tarikh-i Hind wa Sind*,
in HOIBIOH (ed. Elliot, H.M. and
Dowson, J.), vol.1, pp.142–4

3 Al-Biladuri, in HOIBIOH, vol.1, p.119

4 Majumdar, R.C., 'Northern India
during AD 650–750', in HCIP, vol.3
'The Classical Age', p.170

5 *Chach-nama* etc., as above, pp.209–11

6 Al-Biladuri quoted in Ray, H.C., *The
Dynastic History of Northern India*,
vol.1, p.12

7 See Puri, B.N., *The History of the
Gurjara-Pratiharas*, pp.445–6

8 Quoted in Thapar, R., *A History of
India*, vol.1, p.239

9 See Inden, R., *Imagining India*,
pp.217–28

10 Suleiman, in HOIBIOH, vol.1, p.7

11 Altekar, A.S., 'The Rashtrakutas', in
The Early History of the Deccan (ed.
Yazdani, G.), vol.1, p.256

12 As rendered in Inden, R., *Imagining
India*, p.260

13 Puri, B.N., *The History of the
Gurjara-Pratiharas*, p.94

14 Majumdar, R.C., 'The Palas', in HCIP,
vol.4, 'The Imperial Age of Kanauj',
p.53

15 Williams, L.F. Rushbrook (ed.), *A
Handbook for Travellers* etc., p.698

16 Munshi, K.M., in HCIP, vol.4, *The
Imperial Age of Kanauj*, p.xiv

17 Majumdar, R.C., *Ancient India*, p.266

18 See Altekar, A.S., 'The Rashtrakutas', in
The Early History of the Deccan etc.,
vol.1, p.273

19 Inden, R., *Imagining India*, p.259

CHAPTER 10

1 Sulaiman, as quoted in HOIBIOH, vol.1, p.4
2 *Tabaqat-i-Akbari*, as quoted in Ray, H.C., *The Dynastic History of Northern India*, vol.1, p.81
3 Al-Utbi, *Shahr-i Tarikhi Yamini*, as quoted in HOIBIOH, vol.2, p.20
4 Ferishta (trans. Dow, A.), *The History of Hindoostan*, vol.1, p.34
5 Al-Utbi, as above, p.48
6 Ibn Asir, *Kamilu-t Tawarikh*, quoted in HOIBIOH, vol.2, p.470
7 Ferishta, *The History of Hindoostan* etc., vol.1, pp.33–4
8 Al-Biruni, quoted in Ganguly, D.C., 'Ghaznavid Invasion', in HCIP, vol.5, p.17
9 Keay, J., *India Discovered*, pp.98–9
10 See Punja, S., *Divine Ecstasy: The Story of Khajuraho*
11 Harle, J.C., *Art and Architecture* etc., p.311
12 Champakalakshmi, R., 'State and Economy: South India c.AD 400–1300', in *Recent Perspectives of Early Indian History* (ed. Thapar, R.), p.282
13 Duby, G. (trans. Clarke, H.B.), *The Early Growth of the European Economy: Warriors and Peasants from the Seventh to the Twelfth Century*, Ithaca, 1974, pp.51–2
14 Spencer, G.W., *The Politics of Expansion: The Chola Conquest of Sri Lanka and Sri Vijaya*, p.11
15 Karashima, N., *South Indian History and Society: Studies from Inscriptions AD 850–1800*, pp.37–40
16 Narayanan, M.G.S. and Kesuvan Veluthat, 'Bhakti Movement in South India', in *Indian Movements: Some Aspects of Dissent, Protest and Reform* (ed. Malik, S.), p.37
17 Champakalakshmi, R., 'State and Economy', as above, p.298
18 Spencer, G.W., *The Politics of Expansion* etc., p.39
19 S[h]astri, K.A. Nilakantha, *The Colas*
20 Harle, J.C., *Art and Architecture* etc., pp.321–5

21 Verma, H.C., 'The Ghaznavid Invasions, Part 2', in The Indian History Congress, *A Comprehensive History of India*, vol.4, pt 1 (ed. Sharma, R.S.), p.365
22 Sharma, R.S., *Indian Feudalism*, pp.195–6
23 Quoted in Ray, H.C., *The Dynastic History of Northern India*, vol.2, p.857
24 Keith, A.B., *A History of Sanskrit Literature*, p.53
25 Sharma, D., 'The Paramaras of Malwa', in Indian History Congress, *A Comprehensive History of India*', vol.5, pp.420–2

CHAPTER 11

1 Yule, H. and Burnell, A.C., *Hobson-Jobson: A Glossary of Colloquial Anglo-Indian Words and Phrases*, p.754
2 Ferishta (trans. Briggs, J.), *The History of the Rise of Mohammedan Power in India*, vol.1, p.xx and e.g. p.175
3 Tod, J., *Annals and Antiquities of Rajas'than*, vol.1, p.155
4 Ray, H.C., *Dynastic History of Northern India*, vol.2, p.1086
5 Elliot, H.M. and Dowson, J. (eds), HOIBIOH, vol.2, p.251
6 Nizami, K.A., *Some Aspects of Religion and Politics in India during the Thirteenth Century*, pp.76–7
7 Ferishta (trans. Briggs), *History of the Rise* etc., vol.1, p.177
8 Tod, J., *Annals and Antiquities* etc., vol.1, p.210
9 Nizami, Khaliq Ahmed, *Some Aspects* etc., p.91
10 Munshi, K.M., in HCIP, vol.5, *The Struggle for Empire*, p.xv
11 Minhaju-s Siraj, *Tabakat-i Nasiri*, in HOIBIOH, vol.2, p.329
12 Habib, I., in CEHI, p.67
13 Nizami, K.A., *Some Aspects* etc., p.90
14 Nigam, S.B.P., *The Nobility Under the Sultans*, p.183
15 Minhaju-s Siraj, *Tabakat-i Nasiri*, in HOIBIOH, vol.2, p.306
16 Abu Imam, 'Bengal in History', in

India: History and Thought (ed.
Mukherjee, S.N.), pp.76–7
17 Minhaju-s Siraj etc., as above, p.332
18 Habib, I., as above, p.78
19 Ziau-u Din Barani, *Tarikh-i Feroz
Shahi*, in HOIBIOH, vol.3, p.103
20 Ferishta (trans. Dow), *The History of
Hindoostan*, vol.1, p.197
21 Derrett, J.D.M., *The Hoysalas*, p.33
22 Ziau-d Din Barani, *Tarikh-i-Feroz
Shahi* etc., p.155
23 *Ibid*, p.163
24 Venkataramanyya, N., *The Early
Muslim Expansion in South India*, p.31
25 *Ibid*, p.57
26 Digby, S., in CEHI, p.97
27 Ziau-d Din Barani, *Tarikh-i-Feroz
Shahi* etc., p.204
28 Lal, K.S., *History of the Khaljis*, p.275
29 Ziau-d Din Barani, *Tarikh-i-Feroz
Shahi* etc., p.195
30 Ferishta (trans. Dow), *The History of
Hindoostan*, vol.1, p.267

CHAPTER 12

1 Ziau-d Din Barani, *Tarikh-i-Feroz
Shahi* etc., p.235
2 Majumdar, R.C. et al, *An Advanced
History of India*, p.317
3 Ibn Batuta (Muhammad ibn 'Abd
Allah) (trans. Gibb, H.A.R.), *Travels in
Africa and Asia*, p.196
4 Ziau-d Din Barani, *Tarikh-i-Feroz
Shahi* etc., pp.241–2
5 Majumdar, R.C., 'Muhammad Bin
Tughluq', in HCIP, vol.6, *The Delhi
Sultanate*, p.64
6 Ziau-d Din Barani, *Tarikh-i-Feroz
Shahi* etc., p.238
7 Digby, S., in CEHI, p.97
8 Husain, A.M., *The Rise and Fall of
Muhammad Bin Tughluq*, p.134
9 Ibn Batuta etc., *Travels* etc., p.204
10 Shams-i Siraj Afif, *Tarikh-i Firoz Shahi*,
in HOIBIOH, vol.3, p.312
11 Davies, P., *The Penguin Guide to the
Monuments of India*, vol.2, p.138
12 *Malfuzat-i Timuri* (Autobiography of
Timur), in HOIBIOH, vol.3, p.446

13 Ibn Batuta etc., *Travels* etc., p.207
14 Polo, Marco (trans. and ed. Yule, H.),
The Book of Ser Marco Polo, vol.2, p.313
15 'The Travels of Athanasius Nikitin', in
India in the Fifteenth Century (ed.
Major, R.H.), p.8
16 'Narrative of the Journey of
Abd-er-Razzak', in *ibid*, p.31
17 Ferishta (trans. Dow), *The History of
Hindoostan*, vol.2, p.292
18 Haroon Khan Sherwani, 'The Bahmani
Kingdom', in The Indian History
Congress, *A Comprehensive History of
India*, vol.5, pt ii, p.974
19 'The Travels of Athanasius Nikitin', in
India in the Fifteenth Century etc.,
pp.23–8
20 Harle, J.C., *Art and Architecture* etc.,
p.429
21 Tod, J., *Annals* etc., vol.1, p.231

CHAPTER 13

1 Ferishta (trans. Briggs), *History of the
Rise* etc., vol.1, p.579
2 Lal, K.S., *Twilight of the Sultanate*, p.176
3 *Ibid*, p.180
4 Ross, D., *Cambridge History of India*,
vol.5, p.236
5 Babur (trans. Beveridge, A.S.),
Babur-nama, vol.2, p.459
6 *Ibid*, p.463
7 *Ibid*, p.477
8 Tod, J., *Annals* etc., vol.1, p.245
9 Babur, *Babur-nama* etc., vol.2, pp.628,
637
10 Ferishta (trans. Briggs), *History of the
Rise* etc., vol.2, p.70
11 *Ibid*, p.79
12 Richards, J.F., 'The Mughal Empire', in
NCHI, Pt 1, vol.5, p.11
13 Habib, I., 'Monetary System and
Prices', in CEHI, p.360
14 Harle J.C., *Art and Architecture* etc.,
p.427
15 Babur, *Babur-nama* etc., vol.2, p.482
16 Stein, B., *Vijayanagara*, in NCHI, pt 1,
vol.2, p.30
17 Paes, D., in Sewell, R., *A Forgotten
Empire*, pp.246–7

18 Majumdar, R.C. et al, *An Advanced History of India*, p.366
19 Stein, B., *Vijayanagara* etc., p.43
20 Pearson, M.N., *The Portuguese in India*, in NCHI, pt 1, vol.1, p.29
21 Sewell, R., *A Forgotten Empire*, p.207
22 Abu'l-Fazl (trans. Beveridge, H.), *Akbar-nama*, vol.1, pp.620–1
23 Lane-Poole, S., *The History of the Moghul Emperors of Hindustan Illustrated by their Coins*, Constable, London, 1892, p.lii
24 Abu'l-Fazl, *Akbar-nama* etc., vol.2, p.59
25 *Ibid*, pp.62–4
26 *Ibid*, vol.1, pp.27–8
27 *Ibid*, vol.2, pp.271–2
28 *Ibid*, p.236
29 Richards, J.F., *The Mughal Empire* etc., p.23
30 Tod, J., *Annals and Antiquities* etc., vol.1, p.253

CHAPTER 14

1 See especially CEHI
2 Babur, *Tuzak-i Babari (Babur-nama)*, in HOIBIOH, vol.4, p.223
3 Habib, I., 'North India', in 'Agrarian Relations and Land Revenue', CEHI, p.238
4 Bernier, F. (trans. Constable, A.), *Travels in the Mogol Empire AD 1656–1668*, pp.225–7
5 Raychaudhuri, T., 'The Mughal Empire', in 'The State and the Economy', CEHI, p.173
6 Richards, J.F., *The Mughal Empire* etc., p.63
7 Raychaudhuri, T., in CEHI, p.179
8 Richards, J.F., *The Mughal Empire* etc., p.86
9 Roe, Sir T. (ed. Foster, W.), *The Embassy of Sir Thomas Roe to India, 1615–19*, pp.283–4
10 Bernier, F., *Travels* etc., p.222
11 Thevenot, J. de, 'The Third Part of the Travels', in *Indian Travels of Thevenot and Careri* (ed. Surendranath Sen), p.7

12 Jehangir, *Waki'at-i Jahangiri*, in HOIBIOH, vol.6, pp.292, 385
13 See Tod, J., *Annals and Antiquities*, vol.1, pp.278–92
14 Jehangir, *Waki'at-i Jahangiri* etc., p.374
15 Roe, Sir T., *The Embassy* etc., pp.270, 337
16 Asher, C.B., *Architecture of Mughal India*, in NCHI Pt 1, vol.4, p.200
17 Mundy, P., *The Travels of Peter Mundy in Europe and Asia, 1608–67*, vol.2, p.213
18 Richards, J.F., *The Mughal Empire* etc., p.127
19 Sarkar, J., *History of Aurangzib*, vol.1, p.302
20 Richards, J.F., *The Mughal Empire* etc., p.152
21 Khafi Khan, *Muntakhabu-l Lubab*, in HOIBIOH, vol.7, p.246
22 Khafi Khan (ed. and trans. Moinul Haq, S.), *History of Alamgir*, p.159
23 See Moinul Haq, S., introduction to *ibid*, p.xxvii
24 Bernier, F., *Travels* etc., p.334
25 Khafi Khan, *Muntakhabu-l* etc., p.296
26 Richards, J.F., *The Mughal Empire* etc., p.178
27 Gascoigne, B., *The Great Moghuls*, p.227
28 Tod, J., *Annals and Antiquities*, vol.1, p.302

CHAPTER 15

1 Gordon, S., *The Marathas 1600–1818*, in NCHI, pt 2, vol.4, p.67
2 Khafi Khan, *History of Alamgir* etc., pp.122–4
3 *Ibid*, p.125
4 Gordon, S., *The Marathas* etc., p.74
5 Sardesai, G., 'Shivaji', in HCIP, vol.7, *The Mughal Empire*, p.264
6 Gordon, S., *The Marathas* etc., p.92
7 Richards, J.F., *The Mughal Empire* etc., p.220
8 As quoted in Gascoigne, B., *The Great Moghuls*, p.238
9 Khafi Khan, *Muntakhubu-l Lulab*, in HOIBIOH, vol.7, p.485

10 Richards, J.F., *The Mughal Empire* etc., p.256

11 Muzaffar Alam, *The Crisis of Empire in Mughal North India: Awadh and the Punjab, 1707–48*, p.134

12 Bayly, C.A., *Indian Society and the Making of the British Empire*, in NCHI, pt 2, vol.1, p.3

13 'The Mahratta Manuscripts', as quoted in Duff, J.C. Grant, *A History of the Mahrattas*, vol.1, p.322

14 Khafi Khan, *Muntakhubu-l Lubab*, in HOIBIOH, vol.7, p.432

15 Gordon, Stewart, *The Marathas* etc., p.110

16 Khafi Khan, *Muntakhubu-l Lubab* etc., p.483

17 Ghulam Husain, *Siyar-ul-Mutakherin*, as quoted in Majumdar, R.C. et al, *An Advanced History of India*, p.529

18 Gordon, S., *The Marathas* etc., p.114

19 Duff, J.C. Grant, *History of the Mahrattas*, vol.1, p.354

20 Hunter, W.W., *History of India*, vol.7, p.284

21 As quoted in Keay, J., *The Honourable Company*, pp.145–7

22 Bayly, C.A., *Indian Society and the Making of the British Empire* etc., p.48

23 Marshall, P.J., *Bengal: The British Bridgehead*, in NCHI, pt 2, vol.2, p.55

24 As quoted in Keay, J., *The Honourable Company*, p.215

25 Bayly, C.A., *Indian Society* etc., p.46

26 Gordon, S., *The Marathas* etc., p.138

CHAPTER 16

1 See Keay, John, *The Honourable Company*, p.398

2 Elphinstone, Mountstuart, *History of India* etc., p.720

3 Duff, J.C. Grant, *A History of the Mahrattas* etc., vol.1, p.511

4 Quoted in Chaudhuri, Nirad C., *Clive of India*, p.465

5 Marshall, P.J, *East Indian Fortunes: The British in Bengal in the Eighteenth Century*, pp.32–3

6 As quoted in Marshall, P.J., *East Indian Fortunes* etc., p.30

7 Marshall, P.J., *Bengal: The British Bridgehead*, pt 2, vol.2 of NCHI, p.75

8 As quoted in Keay, J., *The Honourable Company*, p.303

9 Marshall, P.J., *Bengal: The British Bridgehead*, p.77

10 Marshall, P.J., *East Indian Fortunes* etc., p.235

11 Moon, P., *The British Conquest and Dominion of India*, p.114

12 Barnett, R.B., *North India Between Empires: Awadh, the Mughals and the British 1720–1801*, p.64

13 Mohibbul Hasan, *The History of Tipu Sultan*, p.6

14 Moon, P., *The British Conquest* etc., p.203

15 Mohibbul Hasan, *The History* etc., p.120

16 *Ibid*, p.349

17 As quoted in Majumdar, R.C. et al, *Advanced History of India*, p.715

18 Moon, P., *The British Conquest* etc., p.261

19 Duff, J.C. Grant, *A History of the Mahrattas*, vol.1, p.507

20 Ahmad Shah Abdali to Madho Singh, letter (trans. Jadunath Sarkar), in *Modern Review*, May 1946, quoted in HCIP, vol.8, *The Maratha Supremacy*, p.199

21 Malcom, J., *A Memoir of Central India*, quoted in Kamath, M.B. and Kher, V.B., *Devi Ahalyabhai Holkar: The Philosopher Queen*, p.85

22 Gordon, S., *The Marathas* etc., p.162

23 *Ibid*, pp.172–3

24 Moon, P., *The British Conquest* etc., p.409

CHAPTER 17

1 Bayly, C.A., *Indian Society and the Making of the British Empire* etc., p.138

2 Kaye, Sir J., as quoted in Moon, P., *The British Conquest* etc., p.497

3 Mason, P., *A Matter of Honour: An*

Account of the Indian Army, its Officers and Men, p.210

4 Sita Ram (trans. Norgate, J.T.), *From Sepoy to Subedar: Being the Life and Adventures of a Native Officer in the Bengal Army*, p.68

5 Moon, P., *The British Conquest* etc., pp.567–75

6 Hugel, Baron C. von, *Travels in Kashmir and the Punjab*, London, 1845, p.293

7 Cunningham, A., *Ladak, Physical, Statistical and Historical*, London, 1854, quoted in Keay, J., *When Men and Mountains Meet*, John Murray, London, 1977, p.170

8 Griffin, Lepel, *Ranjit Singh and the Sikh Barrier between Our Growing Empire and Central Asia*, pp.9–10

9 Mason, P., *A Matter of Honour* etc., p.229

10 Grewal, J.S., *The Sikhs of the Punjab*, pt 2, vol.3 of NCHI, p.115

11 *Ibid*, p.127

12 Quoted in Balfour, I., *Famous Diamonds*, 3rd edn, London, 1997, p.168

13 Sardesai, G.S., *Marathi Riyasat*, Bombay, 1925, quoted in Kamath, M.V. and Kher, V.B., *Ahalyabai Holkar* etc., p.126

14 Nehru, Jawaharlal, *The Discovery Of India*, p.266

15 Malcolm, Sir J., *The Political History of India, 1784–1823*, London, 1826, vol.2, pp.cclxiii–iv, quoted in Cohn, B.S., *Colonialism and its Forms of Knowledge: The British in India*, pp.41–2

16 Munro, Sir T., quoted in Moon, P., *The British Conquest* etc., p.427

17 Quoted in Stokes, E., *The English Utilitarians in India*, p.28

18 Mill, J., *The History of British India*, vol.2, pp.166–7, cited in Metcalf, T.R., *The Aftermath of Revolt: India 1857–70*, pp.8–9

19 Trevelyan, G.O., *The Life and Letters of Lord Macaulay*, London, 1908 edn, pp.329–30

20 Davies, P., *The Penguin Guide to the Monuments of India*, vol.2, *Islamic, Rajput and European*, p.243

21 As quoted in Pemble, J., *The Raj, the Indian Mutiny and the Kingdom of Oudh 1801–1859*, p.59

22 Moon, P., *The British Conquest* etc., p.652

23 Metcalf, T.R., *The Aftermath* etc., p.46

24 Bayly, C.A., *Indian Society and the Making of the British Empire* etc., p.196

25 Sen, Surendra Nath, *Eighteen Fifty-Seven*, p.411

26 *Ibid*, p.113

27 Pemble, John, *The Raj, the Indian Mutiny and the Kingdom of Oudh, 1801–59* etc., p.215

28 Lowe, T., *Central India During the Rebellion of 1857 and 1858: A Narrative of Operations . . .* , London, 1860, p.236

29 Cohn, B.S., 'Representing Authority in Victorian India', in *The Invention of Tradition* (ed. Hobsbawn, E. and Ranger, T.), p.193

CHAPTER 18

1 Chandra, B. et al, *India's Struggle for Independence 1857–1947*, p.52

2 Keay, J., *Last Post: The End of Empire in the Far East*, John Murray, London, 1997, p.23

3 Seal, A., *The Emergence of Indian Nationalism: Competition and Collaboration in the Late Nineteenth Century*, p.52

4 Sumit Sarkar, *Modern India*, pp.30–2

5 Bayly, C.A., *Rulers, Townsmen and Bazaars: North Indian Society in the Age of British Expansion 1770–1870*, p.450

6 *Ibid*, p.450

7 Cohn, B.S., 'Representing Authority' etc., p.209

8 Seal, A., *The Emergence* etc., p.165

9 Quoted in *ibid*, p.265

10 Sayid, K.B., *Pakistan: The Formative Phase 1857–1948*, p.5

11 Seal, A., *The Emergence* etc., p.276

12 *Ibid*, p.278

13 Gilmour, D., *Curzon*, John Murray, London, 1994, p.135

14 Moon, P., *The British Conquest* etc., p.912
15 Quoted in Gilmour, D., *Curzon*, p.271
16 Quoted in Wolpert, S., *A New History of India*, p.273
17 Sarkar, S., *Modern India*, p.134
18 *Ibid*, p.125
19 Mukherjee, H., *India Struggles for Freedom*, Bombay, 1948, p.96, quoted in Chandra, B. et al, *India's Struggle for Independence 1857–1947*, p.145
20 Quoted in Moon, P., *The British Conquest* etc p.968
21 Sarkar, S., *Modern India*, p.148
22 Brown, J.M., *Gandhi's Rise to Power: Indian Politics 1915–1922*, p.184
23 Robb, P.G., *The Government of India and Reform: Policies Towards Politics and the Constitution 1916–21*, p.179
24 Hardy, P., *The Muslims of British India*, p.198
25 *Ibid*, p.198
26 Moon, P., *The British Conquest* etc., p.1012

CHAPTER 19

1 Moon, P., *The British Conquest* etc., p.1039
2 Quoted in Chandra, B. et al, *India's Struggle* etc., p.270
3 Brown, J.M, *Modern India: The Origins of an Asian Democracy*, p.265
4 *Ibid*, p.277

5 Chatterji, J., *Bengal Divided: Hindu Communalism and Partition, 1932–47*, p.24
6 Talbot, I., 'The Unionist Party and Punjabi Politics', in *The Political Inheritance of Pakistan* (ed. Low, D.A.), pp.89–90
7 Copland, I., *The Princes of India in the Endgame of Empire, 1917–47*, pp.166–7
8 Sarkar, S., *Modern India*, pp.351, 371
9 Moon, P., *The British Conquest* etc., pp.1092–3
10 Sarkar, S., *Modern India*, p.406
11 *The Times*, London, 4 September 1947
12 Viceroy's Personal Report No.17, 16 August 1947, quoted in Collins, L. and Lapierre, D., *Mountbatten and the Partition of India*, p.177

CHAPTER 20

1 Tully, Mark, *No Full Stops in India*
2 Amar Kaur Jasbir Singh, *Himalayan Triangle*, British Library, London, 1988, p.139
3 Chanda, A., *Federalism in India: A Study of Union–State Relations*, p.67
4 Khilnani, S., *The Idea of India*, pp.45, 51
5 Roy, Arundhati, 'The End of Imagination', in the *Guardian*, 1 August 1998 (reprinted from *Frontline & Outlook*, 24 July 1998)

BIBLIOGRAPHY

The bibliography lists only those works which have proved of most help in writing the text. It is divided into seven sections. The first section lists mainly general histories, and the remaining six correspond to groups of chapters. The periodisation of Indian history into 'classical', 'medieval' and so on has not been used in the text but, since much extant scholarship falls into these categories, they have been resurrected for the chapter groupings in the bibliography.

The following abbreviations are used in the chapter groupings and refer to works specified in full in the General section:

HCIP = *The History and Culture of the Indian People* (ed. Majumdar, R.C. et al)

HOIBIOH – *The History of India as Told by its Own Historians* (ed. Elliot, H.M. and Dowson, J.)

NCHI – *New Cambridge History of India* (ed. Johnson, G. et al)

GENERAL

Basham, A.L., *The Wonder that was India*, 1967, repr. Rupa, New Delhi, 1981
Basham, A.L. (ed.), *A Cultural History of India*, OUP, Oxford, 1975
Davies, Philip, *The Penguin Guide to the Monuments of India*, vol.2, *Islamic, Rajput, European*, Penguin, London, 1989
Dodwell, H.H. et al (eds), *Cambridge History of India*, 6 vols, CUP, Cambridge, 1922–37 (no vol.2)
Elliot, H.M. and Dowson, J. (eds.), *The History of India as Told by its Own Historians* (HOIBIOH), 7 vols, Trubner, London, 1867–
Elphinstone, Mountstuart, *The History of India: The Hindu and Mahometan Periods*, 6th edn, John Murray, London, 1874
Harle, J.C., *The Art and Architecture of the Indian Subcontinent*, Penguin, Harmondsworth, 1986
Hunter, W.W., *The History of India*, London, 1899–1900
Hunter, W.W., *A History of British India*, London, 1912
Johnson, Gordon, Bayly, C.A., Richards, John F. (eds), *The New Cambridge History of India* (NCHI), 4 pts, numerous vols, CUP, Cambridge, 1987–

Keay, John, *India Discovered*, Windward, London, 1984, repr. HarperCollins, London, 1988

Kulke, H. and Rothermund, D., *A History of India*, Routledge & Kegan Paul, London, 1990

Kumar, Dharma (ed.), *The Cambridge Economic History of India*, vol.2, *c1757–c1970*, CUP, Cambridge, 1963

Majumdar, R.C. et al, *The History and Culture of the Indian People* (HCIP), 11 vols, Bharatiya Vidya Bhavan, Bombay, 1950–

Majumdar, R.C., Raychaudhuri, H.C., Datta, K.K. (eds), *An Advanced History of India*, Macmillan, London, 1961

Michel, George, *The Penguin Guide to the Monuments of India*, vol.1, *Buddhist, Jain, Hindu*, Penguin, London, 1989

Mill, James, *The History of British India*, London, 1826

Panikkar, K.M., *Survey of Indian History*, London, 1960

Raychaudhuri, Tapan and Habib, Irfan (eds), *The Cambridge Economic History of India*, vol.1, *c1200–1750*, CUP, Cambridge, 1982

Rizvi, S.A.A., *The Wonder that was India*, vol.2, London, 1987, repr. Rupa, New Delhi, 1993

S[h]astri, K.A. Nilakant[h]a, *A History of South India from Prehistoric Times to the Fall of Vijayanagar*, 1955, repr. OUP, Delhi, 1975

Smith, V.A., *Oxford History of India*, OUP, London, 1919

Smith, V.A., *The Early History of India from 600BC to the Muhammadan Conquest*, OUP, Oxford, 1924

Spear, Percival, *A History of India* (vol.2), Penguin, Harmondsworth, 1965

Stein, Burton, *A History of India*, Blackwell, Oxford, 1998

Thapar, Romila, *A History of India* (vol.1), Penguin, Harmondsworth, 1966

Tod, James, *Annals and Antiquities of Rajasthan*, London, 1960

Watson, Francis, *A Concise History of India*, Thames & Hudson, London, 1979

Williams, L.F. Rushbrook (ed.), *A Handbook for Travellers in India, Pakistan, Nepal, Bangladesh and Sri Lanka*, 22nd edn, John Murray, London, 1975

Wolpert, Stanley, *A New History of India*, OUP, New York, 1982

Yule, H. and Burnell, A.C., *Hobson-Jobson: A Glossary of Colloquial Anglo-Indian Words and Phrases*, 1886, repr. Routledge & Kegan Paul, London, 1985

CHAPTERS 1–4

Prehistory

Allchin, B. and F.R., *The Birth of Indian Civilisation: India and Pakistan Before 500 BC*, Penguin, Harmondsworth, 1968

Allchin, B. and F.R., *The Rise of Civilisation in India and Pakistan*, Cambridge, 1982

Basham, A.L., *History and Doctrine of the Ajivikas: A Vanished Indian Religion*, Luzac, London, 1951

Bechert, Heinz (ed.), *When did the Buddha Live?: The Controversy of the Dating of the Historical Buddha*, Sri Satguru Publications, Delhi, 1994

Dani, A.H. (ed.), *Indus Civilisation: New Perspectives*, Islamabad, 1984

Deshpande, M.M. and Hook, P.E. (eds), *Aryan and Non-Aryan in India*, University of Michigan, 1979

Drekmeier, C., *Kingship and Community in Early India*, Stanford, 1962

Dutt, N., *Early Buddhist Monasticism*, Calcutta, 1973

Edwardes, M., *In the Blowing out of a Flame: The World of the Buddha and the World of Man*, George Allen & Unwin, London, 1976

Fick, R., *Social Organisation of North Eastern India in the Buddha's Time*, Calcutta, 1920

Ghosh, A., *The City in Early Historical India*, Indian Institute of Advanced Studies, Simla, 1973

Ghosh, B.K., in HCIP, vol.1, *The Vedic Age*, Allen & Unwin, London, 1951

Kautilya (ed. Rangarajan, L.N.), *The Arthasastra*, Penguin India, Delhi, 1992

Kosambi, D.D., *The Culture and Civilisation of Ancient India in Historical Outline*, 1950, repr. Vikas, New Delhi, 1996

Kosambi, D.D., *An Introduction to the Study of Indian History*, 1956, repr. Popular Prakarshan, Bombay, 1975

Lal, B.B. and Gupta, S.P. (eds), *Frontiers of the Indus Civilisation*, Books & Books, Delhi, 1984

Lane Fox, R., *Alexander the Great*, Allen Lane, London, 1973

McCrindle, J.W., *The Invasion of India by Alexander the Great as Described by Arrian* etc., Constable, London, 1893

Majumdar, R.C., *Ancient India*, repr. Motilal Banarsidass, Delhi, 1994

Marshall, J., *Mohenjo-daro and the Indus Civilisation*, Probsthain, London, 1931

Marshall, J., *Taxila*, CUP, Cambridge, 1951

Meyer, J.T., *Sexual Life in Ancient India*, London, 1952

Mookerji, R.K., in HCIP, vol.2, *The Age of Imperial Unity*, Bharatiya Vidya Bhavan, Bombay, 1951

Mukerjee, S.N. (ed.), *India: History and Thought*, Subarnarekha, Calcutta, 1982

Piggott, S., *Prehistoric India*, Penguin, Harmondsworth, 1962

Possehl, G.L. (ed.), *Ancient Cities of the Indus*, Vikas, New Delhi, 1979

Possehl, G.L. (ed.), *Harappan Civilisation: A Contemporary Perspective*, New Delhi, 1982

Pusalker, A.D., in HCIP, vol.1, *The Vedic Age*, George Allen & Unwin, London, 1951

Ratnagar, Shireen, *Encounters: The Westerly Trade of the Harappan Civilisation*, OUP, Delhi, 1981

Ratnagar, Shireen, *Enquiries into the Political Organisation of Harappan Society*, Ravish, Pune, 1991

Sankalia, H.D., *The Prehistory and Protohistory of India and Pakistan*, Bombay, 1963

Sharma, J.P., *The Republics in Ancient India*, E.J. Brill, Leiden, 1968

Spellman, J.W., *Political Theory of Ancient India*, Clarendon Press, Oxford, 1964

Thapar, R., 'Asokan India and the Gupta Age', in *A Cultural History of India* (ed. Basham, A.L.), OUP, Oxford, 1975

Thapar, R., 'The Historian and the Epic', in *Annals of the Bhandarka Oriental Research Institute*, LX, 1979

Thapar, R., 'The Ramayana: Theme and Variations', in Mukherjee, S.N., *India: History and Thought*, Calcutta, 1982

Thapar, R., *From Lineage to State*, OUP, Bombay, 1984

Thapar, R., *Cultural Transaction and Early India*, Delhi, 1987

Thapar, R., *Interpreting Early India*, OUP, Delhi, 1992

Thapar, R. (ed.), *Recent Perspectives of Early Indian History*, Popular Prakarshan, Bombay, 1995

Thapar, R., *Ancient Indian Social History: Some Interpretations*, repr. Sangam, London, 1996

Varma, V.P., *Early Buddhism and its Origins*, Munshiram Manoharlal, New Delhi, 1972

Wagle, K.N., *Society in the Time of the Buddha*, Bombay, 1966

Wheeler, R.E. Mortimer, *Early India and Pakistan*, London, 1959

Wheeler, R.E. Mortimer, *Civilisation of the Indus Valley and Beyond*, Thames & Hudson, London, 1966

CHAPTERS 5–8

'The Classical Age'

Ahir, D.C., *Ashoka the Great*, BR Publishing, Delhi, 1995

Altekar, A.S., in *The Gupta-Vakataka Age* (ed. Majumdar, R.C. and Altekar, A.S.), Motilal Banarsidass, Varanasi, Benares, 1946

Bagchi, P.C., *India and China*, 1944, repr. Hindi Kitabs, Bombay, 1950

Bana (trans. Cowell, E.R. and Thomas, S.W.), *Harsa-Carita*, Royal Asiatic Society, London, 1897

Burrow, T., *The Sanskrit Language*, London, 1965

Chattopadhyaya, B.D. (ed.), *Essays in Ancient Indian Economic History*, Munshiram Manoharlal, New Delhi, 1987

Chattopadhyaya, B.D., *Aspects of Rural Settlements and Rural Society in Early Medieval India*, Calcutta, 1990

Coedes, G. (trans. Wright, H.M.), *The Making of South East Asia*, Routledge & Kegan Paul, London, 1966

Coedes, G. (trans. Cowing, S.B.), *The Indianised States of South-East Asia*, East-West Center Press, Honolulu, 1968

Dani, A.H., *Human Records on the Karakoram Highway*, Islamabad, 1983

Devahuti, R., *Harsha: A Political Study*, OUP, Delhi, 1983

Dumarcay, Jacques (trans. Smithies, M.), *The Temples of Java*, OUP, Singapore, 1986

Fa Hian, in Hiuen Tsang (trans. Beal, S.), *Si-Yu-Ki, Buddhist Records of the Western World*, vol.1, Trubner, London, 1884

Fleet, J.F., *Corpus Inscriptionum Indicarum*, vol.3, *Inscriptions of the Early Gupta Kings and their Successors*, Government of India, Calcutta, 1888

Gaur, A., *Indian Charters on Copper Plates in the Department of Oriental Manuscripts and Books*, British Library, London, 1975

Glover, I.C., 'Early Trade Relations Between India and South East Asia', in *Occasional Papers No.16*, Centre for Southeast Asian Studies, University of Hull, 1983

H[i]euen Tsang, see Fa Hian

Inden, Ronald, *Imagining India*, Blackwell, Oxford, 1990

Kautilya (ed. Rangarajan, L.N.), *The Arthasastra*, Penguin India, Delhi, 1992

Keith, A.B., *History of Sanskrit Literature*, OUP, Oxford, 1920

Kosambi, D.D., *An Introduction to the Study of Indian History*, 1956, repr. Popular Prakarshan, Bombay, 1975

Kosambi, D.D., *The Culture and Civilisation of Ancient India in Historical Outline*, 1950, repr. Vikas, New Delhi, 1996

McCrindle, J.W., *Ancient India as Described by Megasthenes and Arrian*, Calcutta, 1877

Majumdar, R.C., *Ancient Indian Colonies in the Far East*, Lahore, Dacca, Madras, 1927–44

Majumdar, R.C., 'The Rise of the Guptas', in HCIP, vol.3, *The Classical Age*, Bharatiya Vidya Bhavan, Bombay, 1954

Mookerji, R.K., *The Gupta Empire*, Hind Kitabs, Bombay, 1947

Mookerji, R.K., 'Ashoka the Great', in HCIP, vol.2, *The Age of Imperial Unity*, Bharatiya Vidya Bhavan, Bombay, 1951

Morton-Smith, R., *Dates and Dynasties in Earliest India*, Delhi, 1975

Narain, A.K., *The Indo-Greeks*, OUP, Oxford, 1957

Ray, H.P., *Monastery and Guild: Commerce Under the Satavahana*, OUP, Delhi, 1986

Raychaudhuri, H.C., *The Political History of Ancient India*, Calcutta, 1953

Sarkar, H.B., *Cultural Relations Between India and South East Asian*

Countries, Indian Council for Cultural Relations and Motilal Banarsidass, New Delhi, 1985

Satianathaier, R., 'Dynasties of South India', in HCIP, vol.4, *The Classical Age*, Bharatiya Vidya Bhavan, Bombay, 1954

Sharma, R.S., *Indian Feudalism*, Calcutta, 1965

S[h]astri, K.A. Nilakantha (ed.), *A Comprehensive History of India*, vol.2, *The Mauryas and the Satavahanas*, Orient Longmans, Calcutta, 1957

S[h]astri, K.A. Nilakantha, *A History of South India from Prehistoric Times to the Fall of Vijayanagar*, 1955, repr. OUP, Oxford, 1975

Sircar, D.C., *Successors of the Satavahanas*, University of Calcutta, 1939

Smithies, Michael, *Yogyakarta*, OUP, Singapore, 1986

Stein, B. (ed.), *Essays on South India*, Asian Studies Program, University of Hawaii, 1975

Subramaniam, N., *Sangam Polity*, Asia Publishing, London, 1966

Thapar, R., *Ashoka and the Decline of the Mauryas*, OUP, Oxford, 1961

Thapar, R., 'Asokan India and the Gupta Age', in *A Cultural History of India* (ed. Basham, A.L.), OUP, Oxford, 1975

Trautmann, T.R., *Kautilya and the Arthasastra*, E.J. Brill, Leiden, 1971

Trautmann, T.R., *Kinship and History in South Asia*, Michigan, 1974

Warmington, E.H., *The Commerce Between the Roman Empire and India*, CUP, 1928, repr. Curzon Press, London, 1974

Wheeler, R.E. Mortimer, *Rome Beyond the Imperial Frontiers*, G. Bell, London, 1954

Williams, J.G., *The Art of Gupta India*, Princeton University Press, Princeton, 1983

Yazdani, G. (ed.), *The Early History of the Deccan*, 2 vols, OUP, London, 1960

Chapters 9–12

'The Medieval Period'

Abd-er-Razzak, 'Narrative of the Journey of Abd-er-Razzak', in *India in the Fifteenth Century* (ed. Major, R.H.), Hackluyt Society, London, 1857

Abraham, Meera, *Two Medieval Merchant Guilds of South India*, Munshiram Manoharlal, New Delhi, 1988

Aiyangar, S. Krishnaswami, *South India and her Muhammadan Invaders*, OUP, Madras, 1921

Al-Biladuri, in HOIBIOH, vol.1, Trubner, London, 1867

Altekar, A.S., 'The Rashtrakutas', in *The Early History of the Deccan* (ed. Yazdani, G.), OUP, London, 1960

Al-Utbi, *Shahr-i Tarikhi Yamini*, in HOIBIOH, vol.2, Trubner, London, 1867

Bosworth, C.E., *The Ghaznavids*, 2nd edn, Librairie du Liban, Beirut, 1993

Chach-nama or *Tarikh-i Hind wa Sind*, in HOIBIOH, vol.1, Trubner, London, 1867

Champakalakshmi, R., 'Urbanisation in Medieval Tamil Nadu', in *Situating Indian History* (eds Bhattarcharya, S. and Thapar, R.), OUP, Delhi, 1986

Champakalakshmi, R., 'Urbanisation in South India: The Role of Ideology and Polity', in Indian History Congress, *Proceedings of 47th Session*, Srinagar, 1986

Champakalakshmi, R., 'State and Economy: South India c400–1300', in *Recent Perspectives of Early Indian History* (ed. Thapar, R.), Popular Prakarshan, Bombay, 1995

Coedes, G. (trans. Cowing, S.B.), *The Indianised States of South East Asia*, East-West Center Press, Honolulu, 1968

Derrett, J.D.M., *The Hoysalas*, OUP, London, 1957

Digby, S., in *The Cambridge Economic History of India*, vol.1, c1200–1750 (eds Raychaudhuri, T. and Habib, I.), CUP, Cambridge, 1982

Ferishta (trans. Dow, A.), *The History of Hindoostan*, Walker, J. et al, London, 1812

Ferishta (trans. Briggs, J.), *History of the Rise of Mohammedan Power in India*, Longman, London, 1829

Ganguly, D.C., 'Ghaznavid Invasion', in HCIP, vol.5, *The Struggle for Empire*, Bharatiya Vidya Bhavan, Bombay, 1957

Habib, Irfan, in *The Cambridge Economic History of India*, vol.1, c1200–1750 (eds Raychaudhuri, T. and Habib, I.), CUP, Cambridge, 1982

Hall, K.R., *Trade and Statecraft in the Age of the Colas*, Abhinav, New Delhi, 1980

H[i]uen Tsang (trans. Beal, S.), *Si-Yu-Ki, Buddhist Records of the Western World*, 2 vols, Trubner, London, 1884

Husain, A.H., *The Rise and Fall of Muhammad bin Tughluq*, Luzac, London, 1938

Ibn Asir, *Kamilu-t Tawarikh*, in HOIBIOH, vol.2, Trubner, 1867

Ibn Batuta (Mohamed ibn 'Abd Allah) (trans. Gibb, H.A.R.), *Travels in Africa and Asia*, Routledge & Kegan Paul, London, 1929

Imam, Abu, 'Bengal in History', in *India: History and Thought* (ed. Mukherjee, S.N.), Subaranarekha, Calcutta, 1984

Inden, Ronald, *Imagining India*, Blackwell, Oxford, 1990

Karashima, Noboru, *South Indian History and Society: Studies from Inscriptions AD 850–1800*, OUP, Delhi, 1984

Keith, A.B., *History of Sanskrit Literature*, OUP, Oxford, 1920

Lal, K.S., *History of the Khaljis*, Asia Publishing, London, 1967

Majumdar, R.C. et al, *An Advanced History of India*, Macmillan, London, 1946

Majumdar, R.C., 'The Palas', in HCIP, vol.4, *The Imperial Age of Kanauj*, Bharatiya Vidya Bhavan, Bombay, 1957

Majumdar, R.C., 'Muhammad bin Tughluq', in HCIP, vol.6, *The Delhi Sultanate*, Bharatiya Vidya Bhavan, Bombay, 1960

Majumdar, R.C., *Ancient India*, repr. Motilal Banarsidass, Delhi, 1994

Minhaju-s Siraj, *Tabakat-i Nasiri*, in HOIBIOH, vol.2, Trubner, London, 1867

Narayanan, M.G.S., and Veluthat Kesavan, 'Bhakti Movement in South India', in *Indian Movements: Some Aspects of Dissent, Protest and Reform* (ed. Malik, S.), Indian Institute of Advanced Studies, Simla, 1976

Nigam, S.B.P., *The Nobility Under the Sultans*, Munshiram Manoharlal, New Delhi, 1968

Nikitin, Athanasius, 'Travels of Athanasius Nikitin', in *India in the Fifteenth Century* (ed. Major, R.H.), Hackluyt Society, London, 1857

Nizami, Khaliq Ahmed, *Some Aspects of Religion and Politics in India During the Thirteenth Century*, Asia Publishing, New Delhi, 1961

Polo, Marco (trans. and ed. Yule, H.), *The Book of Ser Marco Polo*, John Murray, London, 1871

Punja, Shobita, *Divine Ecstasy: The Story of Khajuraho*, Viking, New Delhi, 1992

Puri, B.N., *The History of the Gurjara-Pratiharas*, Munshiram Manoharlal, New Delhi, 1986

Ray, H.P., *The Dynastic History of Northern India*, 2 vols, Calcutta University Press, Calcutta, 1931

Sewell, R., *A Forgotten Empire (Vijayanagar)*, Swan Sonnenschein, London, 1900, repr. Asia Education Services, New Delhi, 1980

Shams-i Siraj Afif, *Tarikh-i Firoz Shahi*, in HOIBIOH, vol.3, Trubner, London, 1871

Sharma, Dasharata, 'The Paramaras of Malwa', in Indian History Congress, *A Comprehensive History of India*, vol.5 (ed. Sharma, R.S.), People's Publishing House, New Delhi, 1992

Sharma, R.S., *Indian Feudalism*, Calcutta, 1965

S[h]astri, K.A. Nilakantha, *The Colas*, 2nd edn, University of Madras, Madras, 1955

S[h]astri, K.A. Nilakantha, *A History of South India from Prehistoric Times to the Fall of Vijayanagar*, 1955, repr. OUP, Oxford, 1975

Sherwani, H.K., 'The Bahmani Kingdom', in Indian History Congress, *A Comprehensive History of India* (ed. Sharma, R.S.), vol.5, pt 2, People's Publishing House, New Delhi, 1992

Spencer, G.W., *The Politics of Expansion: The Chola Conquest of Sri Lanka and Sri Vijaya*, New Era, Madras, 1983

Stein, B., *Peasant, State and Society in Medieval South India*, New Delhi, 1980

Stein, B., *Vijayanagara*, in NCHI, pt 2, vol.1, Cambridge, 1994

Sulieman, in HOIBIOH, vol.1, Trubner, London, 1867

Venkataramanyya, N., *The Early Muslim Expansion in South India*, University of Madras, Madras, 1942

Verma, H.C., 'The Ghaznavid Invasions, Part 2', in Indian History Congress, *A Comprehensive History of India*, vol.4, pt 1 (ed. Sharma, R.S.), People's Publishing House, New Delhi, 1992

Yazdani, G. (ed.), *The Early History of the Deccan*, 2 vols, OUP, London, 1960

Ziau-d Din Barani, *Tarikh-i-Feroz Shahi*, in HOIBIOH, vol.3, Trubner, London, 1871

CHAPTERS 13–15

Mughal Rule

Abu'l-Fazl (trans. Beveridge, A.S.), *Akbar-nama*, Baptist Mission Press, Calcutta, 1907

Alam, Muzaffar, *The Crisis of Empire in Mughal North India: Awadh and the Punjab 1707–48*, OUP, Delhi, 1997

Asher, Catherine B., *The Architecture of Mughal India*, in NCHI, pt 1, vol.4, Cambridge, 1992

Babur, *Tuzak-i Baburi (Babur-nama)*, in HOIBIOH, vol.4, Trubner, London, 1872

Babur (trans. Beveridge, A.S.), *Babur-nama*, Luzac, London, 1921

Bayly, C.A., *Indian Society and the Making of the British Empire*, in NCHI, pt 2, vol.1, Cambridge, 1987

Bernier, François (trans. Constable, A.), *Travels in the Mogol Empire AD 1656–68*, OUP, London, 1914

Duff, J.C. Grant, *A History of the Mahrattas*, 3 vols, 1826, repr. OUP, London, 1921

Eraly, A., *The Great Mughals*, Viking, New Delhi, 1997

Ferishta (trans. Dow, A.), *The History of Hindoostan*, Walker, J. et al, London, 1812

Ferishta (trans. Briggs, J.), *History of the Rise of Mohammedan Power in India*, Longman, London, 1829

Gascoigne, B., *The Great Moghuls*, Jonathan Cape, London, 1971

Grewal, J.S., *The Sikhs of the Punjab* in NCHI, pt 2, vol.3, Cambridge, 1990

Habib, Irfan, 'Monetary System and Prices', in *The Cambridge Economic History of India* (eds Raychaudhuri, T. and Habib, I.), vol.1, *c1200–1750*, CUP, Cambridge, 1982

Jehangir, *Waki'at-i Jahangiri*, in HOIBIOH, vol.6, Trubner, London, 1875

Karashima, Noboru, *Towards a New Formation: South Indian Society under Vijayanagar Rule*, OUP, Delhi, 1992

Keay, John, *The Honourable Company: A History of the English East India Company*, HarperCollins, London, 1991

Khafi Khan (ed. and trans. Moinul Haq, S.), *History of Alamgir*, Pakistan Historical Society, Karachi, 1975

Khafi Khan, *Muntakhabu-i Lulab*, in HOIBIOH, vol.7, Trubner, London, 1977

Lal, K.S., *The Twilight of the Sultanate*, Asia Publishing House, London, 1963

Lane-Poole, S., *The History of the Moghul Emperors of Hindoostan Illustrated by their Coins*, London, 1892

Majumdar, R.C. et al, *An Advanced History of India*, Macmillan, London, 1946

Marshall, P.J., *Bengal: The British Bridgehead*, in NCHI, pt 2, vol.2, Cambridge, 1987

Mundy, P., *The Travels of Peter Mundy in Europe and Asia, 1608–67*, 2 vols, Hackluyt Society, London, 1914

Paes, D., 'Narrative of', in Sewell, R., *A Forgotten Empire (Vijayanagar)*, Swan Sonnenschein, London, 1900, repr. Asia Education Services, New Delhi, 1980

Pearson, M.N., *The Portuguese in India*, in NCHI, pt 1, vol.1, Cambridge, 1987

Qanungo, K.R., *Sher Shah*, Calcutta, 1921

Qureshi, I.H., *Administration of the Moghul Empire*, Karachi, 1966

Raychaudhuri, T., 'The Mughal Empire', in 'The State and the Economy', *The Cambridge Economic History of India*, vol.1, *c1200–1750* (eds Raychaudhuri, T. and Habib, I.), Cambridge, 1982

Richards, John F., *The Mughal Empire*, in NCHI, pt 1, vol.5, Cambridge, 1993

Roe, Thomas (ed. Foster, W.), *The Embassy of Sir Thomas Roe to India, 1615–19*, Hackluyt Society, London, 1926

Ross, D., in *Cambridge History of India*, vol. 5, Cambridge, 1929

Sardesai, G.S., *New History of the Marathas*, Bombay, 1946

Sardesai, G.S., 'Shivaji', in HCIP, vol.7, *The Mughal Empire*, Bharatiya Vidya Bhavan, Bombay, 1974

Sarkar, Jadunath, *History of Aurangzib*, 4 vols, Sarkar & Sons, Calcutta, 1912

Sewell, R., *A Forgotten Empire (Vijayanagar)*, Swan Sonnenschein, London, 1900, repr. Asia Education Services, New Delhi, 1980

Spear, Percival, *Twilight of the Moghuls*, Cambridge, 1951

Stein, B., *Vijayanagara*, in NCHI, pt 2, vol.1, Cambridge, 1994

Stewart, Gordon, *The Marathas 1600–1818*, in NCHI, pt 2, vol.4, Cambridge, 1993

Thevenot, J. de, 'The Third Part of the Travels', in *Indian Travels of Thevenot and Carreri* (ed. Sen, S.), National Archives of India, Delhi, 1949

CHAPTERS 16–17

British Rule

Barnett, Richard B, *North India Between Empires: Awadh, the Mughals and the British 1720–1801*, University of California, Berkeley, 1980

Bayly, C.A., *Indian Society and the Making of the British Empire*, in NCHI, pt 2, vol.1, Cambridge, 1987

Chaudhuri, Nirad, *Clive of India*, London, 1975, repr. Jaico, Bombay, 1977

Cohn, Bernard S., 'Representing Authority in Victorian India', in *The Invention of Tradition* (ed. Hobsbawm, E. and Ranger, T.), CUP, Cambridge, 1983

Cohn, Bernard S., *Colonialism and its Forms of Knowledge: The British in India*, Princeton University Press, Princeton, 1996

Duff, J.C. Grant, *A History of the Mahrattas*, 3 vols, repr. OUP, London, 1921

Grewal, J.S., *The Sikhs of the Punjab*, in NCHI, pt 2, vol.3, Cambridge, 1990

Griffin, Lepel, *Ranjit Singh and the Sikh Barrier Between our Growing Empire and Central Asia*, Clarendon, Oxford, 1905

Gupta, P.C., *Baji Rao II and the East India Company 1796–1818*, OUP, Oxford, 1939

Hasan, Mohibul, *The History of Tipu Sultan*, World Press Pvt Ltd, Calcutta, 1951

Hibbert, Christopher, *The Great Mutiny: India 1857*, Allen Lane, London, 1978

Kamath, M.B. and Kher, V., *Devi Ahalyabhai Holkar: The Philosopher Queen*, Bharatiya Vidya Bhavan, Bombay, 1995

Keay, John, *The Honourable Company: A History of the English East India Company*, HarperCollins, London, 1991

Majumdar, R.C. et al, *An Advanced History of India*, Macmillan, London, 1946

Malcolm, John, *A Memoir of Central India Including Malwa and Adjoining Provinces*, Murray, London, 1824

Malcolm, John, *The Political History of India 1784–1823*, London, 1826

Marshall, P.J., *East Indian Fortunes: The British in Bengal in the Eighteenth Century*, OUP, London, 1976

Marshall, P.J., *Bengal: The British Bridgehead*, in NCHI, pt 2, vol.2, Cambridge, 1987

Mason, Philip, *A Matter of Honour: An Account of the Indian Army, its Officers and Men*, Jonathan Cape, London, 1974

Metcalf, Thomas R., *The Aftermath of Revolt: India 1857–70*, Princeton University Press, Princeton, 1964

Moon, Penderel, *The British Conquest and Dominion of India*, Duckworth, London, 1989

Moorhouse, Geoffrey, *India Britannica*, Harvill, London, 1983

Nehru, Jawaharlal, *The Discovery of India*, Meridian Books, London, 1946

Pemble, John, *The Raj, the Indian Mutiny and the Kingdom of Oudh 1801–59*, Associated University Press, Cranbury, NJ, 1977

Sen, Surendra Nath, *Eighteen Fifty-Seven*, Publications Division, Government of India, Delhi, 1957

Sita Ram (trans. Norgate, J.T.), *From Sepoy to Subedar: Being the Life and Adventures of a Native Officer in the Bengal Army*, 1873, 3rd edn, London, 1911

Spear, Percival, *Twilight of the Moghuls*, CUP, Cambridge, 1951

Stewart, Gordon, *The Marathas 1600–1818*, in NCHI, pt 2, vol.4, Cambridge, 1993

Stokes, Eric, *The English Utilitarians in India*, OUP, Oxford, 1939

Stokes, Eric, *The Peasant and the Raj: Studies in Agrarian Society and Peasant Rebellion in Colonial India*, CUP, Cambridge, 1978

Stokes, Eric, *The Peasant Armed* (ed. Bayly, C.A.), Clarendon, Oxford, 1986

Chapters 18–20

To Independence and After

Adams, J. and Whitehead, P., *The Dynasty: The Nehru-Gandhi Story*, Penguin/BBC, London, 1997

Bayly, C.A., *Rulers, Townsmen and Bazaars: North Indian Society in the Age of British Expansion 1770–1870*, CUP, Cambridge, 1983

Brass, Paul, *The Politics of India since Independence*, in NCHI, pt 4, vol.1, Cambridge, 1990

Brown, Judith M., *Gandhi's Rise to Power: Indian Politics 1915–22*, CUP, Cambridge, 1972

Brown, Judith M., *Modern India: The Origins of an Asian Democracy*, OUP, Oxford, 1985

Chanda, Ashok, *Federalism in India: A Study of Union–State Relations*, Allen & Unwin, London, 1965

Chandra, Bipan et al, *India's Struggle for Independence 1857–1947*, Viking, London, 1988; Penguin, New Delhi, 1989

Chatterjee, Partha (ed.), *State and Politics in India*, OUP, Delhi, 1998

Chatterji, Joya, *Bengal Divided: Hindu Communalism and Partition, 1932–47*, CUP, Cambridge, 1994

Cohn, Bernard S., 'Representing Authority in Victorian India', in *The Invention of Tradition* (ed. Hobsbawm, E. and Ranger, T.), CUP, Cambridge, 1983

Collins, Larry and Lapierre, Dominique, *Mountbatten and the Partition of India*, Vikas, Delhi, 1982

Copland, Ian, *The Princes of India in the Endgame of Empire, 1917–47*, CUP, Cambridge, 1997

Gilmour, David, *Curzon*, John Murray, London, 1994

Grewal, J.S., *The Sikhs of the Punjab*, in NCHI, pt 2, vol.3, CUP, Cambridge, 1990

Hardy, P., *The Muslims of British India*, CUP, Cambridge, 1972

Khilnani, Sunil, *The Idea of India*, Hamish Hamilton, London, 1997

Low, D.A. (ed.), *Congress and the Raj*, London, 1977

Low, D.A. (ed.), *The Political Inheritance of Pakistan*, Macmillan, London, 1991

Moon, Penderel, *The British Conquest and Dominion of India*, Duckworth, London, 1989

Philips, C.H. and Wainwright, M.D. (eds), *The Partition of India: Policies and Perspectives 1935–47*, Allen & Unwin, London, 1970

Robb, P.G., *The Government of India and Reform: Policies Toward Politics and the Constitution, 1916–21*, OUP, Oxford, 1976

Sarkar, Sumit, *Modern India*, Macmillan (India), Delhi, 1983

Sayid, Khalid B., *Pakistan: The Formative Phase 1857–1948*, OUP, London, 1968

Seal, Anil, *The Emergence of Indian Nationalism: Competition and Collaboration in the Late Nineteenth Century*, CUP, Cambridge, 1968

Tully, Mark and Jacob, Satish, *Amritsar: Mrs Gandhi's Last Battle*, Jonathan Cape, London, 1985

Tully, Mark, *No Full Stops in India*, Viking, London, 1991

Wolpert, Stanley, *A New History of India*, OUP, New York, 1982

INDEX

Abbasid Caliphate of Baghdad, 180, 187
Abdullah, Shaikh Muhammad, Kashmiri
  patriot, 512, 513, 517
Abdu-r Razzak, 15th c ambassador, 277
Abu'l-Fazl, Mughal chronicler, 309, 310, 311,
  312, 317, 320, 325, 327
Achaemenids, kings of Persia, 57–9, 60–2,
  71, 88
Achyuta-Deva-Raya, 16th c Vijayanagar
  ruler, 307
Adham Khan, Mughal general, 310–12
Aditya, 9–10th c Chola king, 215
Adivasis, 'Aboriginals', 28
Advani, L.K., BJP leader, 532
Afghanistan 15, 21, 26, 71, 84, 96, 104, 106,
  180, 203–5, 225–6, 291, 308–9, 417–20,
  451, 479
Afzal Khan, Bijapur general, 351, 461
Aga Khan, Ismaili leader, 468
Agni, Vedic deity, 21, 25, 40, 43
Agra, Uttar Pradesh, 289, 293, 296, 315, 319,
  334–6, 340, 353, 410, 439
Ahalyabhai Holkar, 'Philosopher Queen' of
  Malwa, 407, 408, 425
Ahmad Shah Abdali (Durrani), 18th c
  Afghan adventurer, 367, 385–6, 403–4,
  418
Ahmad Shah, 15th c Sultan of Gujarat, 285,
  298–9
Ahmadabad, Gujarat, 279, 285, 298, 406,
  471, 487
Ahmadnagar, Maharashtra, 302, 319, 331,
  348, 359
Aihole, Karnataka, 3, 169, 174, 195, 222
Ajanta, Maharashtra, 125, 149–51, 153
Ajatashatru, 5th c BC king of Magada, 66–70
Ajaya-Raja, Chahamana rajput king of
  Ajmer, 233
Ajit Singh, Rathor rajput ruler of Marwar,
  345, 360
Ajivikas, sect, 64, 89, 99, 104
Ajmer, Rajasthan, 206, 233, 235, 239, 241,
  315, 334, 347
Akali Dal, Sikh political party, 521, 522,
  528–9

Akbar, Mughal emperor, 136–7, 309–19,
  325, 327, 331, 334
Akbar, Prince, son of Aurangzeb, 346–7,
  355
Akbar-nama see Abu'l-Fazl
Aksai Chin, Ladakh, 516
Alamgirpur, Harappan site, 10
Ala-ud-din Husain Shah, 15–16th c Sultan
  of Bengal, 287–8
Ala-ud-din Khalji, 13–14th c Delhi Sultan,
  250, 254–60, 293
Al-Biladuri, Muslim chronicler of Sind, 184,
  185, 187
Al-Biruni, ('Alberuni') 15th c scholar, 188,
  189, 203, 210, 212
Alexander the Great of Macedonia, 59, 63,
  70–7, 78–9, 82, 83, 106
Al-Hajjaj ibn Yusuf, 8th c governor of Iraq,
  183, 185
Aligarh, Uttar Pradesh, 239, 294, 458
Alivardi Khan, 18th c Nawab of Bengal,
  387–8
Aliwal, Battle of (1846), 423
Allahabad, Uttar Pradesh, 136–7, 153, 327,
  334, 392, 439, 441, 453–4, 477
Allard, Colonel, Napoleonic officer, 422
Al-Masudi, 10th c Muslim chronicler, 196
Alor (Rohri), Sind, 185
Alptigin, Turkish general, 204
Al-Utbi, 11th c Muslim chronicler, 205, 206,
  207, 208
Amar Das, Sikh Guru, 317
Amar Singh, Rana of Mewar, 328–30
Amaravati Stupa, 102, 125
Amber, Rajasthan, 313
Ambhi, 4th c BC ruler of Taxila, 71, 82
Amir, a member of the Mughal nobility, a
  Muslim prince, 313, 321, 324, 356
Amrapali (Ambarapali), courtesan, 67–8
Amritsar, Panjab, 317, 411, 475–7, 521,
  529
Amyntas, Bactrian Greek king, 107
Anandapala, 11th c Shahi king, 207–8
Anandpur Sahib, Sikh shrine, 360, 528
Andaman Islands, 495

Andhra Pradesh, 105, 118, 125, 170, 220, 252, 303, 377, 474, 520

Anga Kingdom, Bengal, 50, 65, 68, 83

Angkor, Cambodia, 124, 176, 214

Anglo-French Wars, 377–82, 388, 393–4, 396

Anhilwara (Patan), Gujarat, 239

Antialcidas, Bactrian Greek king, 108

Anuradhapura, Sri Lanka, 215

Aornos, Battle of (326 BC), 71

Arabs, 167, 172, 180–7, 196, 202

Aranya, forest, wilderness, 40

Archaeological Survey of India, 7, 9, 462

Architecture, xviii-xix, 24; Buddhist 51, 102–3, 125, 178–9, 194; Gupta, 141, 169; Harappan, 8–9, 12, 13–14; Jain, 241; Mughal, 315–6, 334–6; Muslim, 240–1, 259, 262–3, 272, 285–6, 301–2, 337, 433–5; Temples, 168–9, 173–4, 178–9, 200–1, 213, 216–7, 223–5, 252, 278

Arcot, Tamil Nadu, 377, 379

Argaon, Battle of (1803), 410

Arikamedu, Tamil Nadu, 121–3

Arjan Singh, Sikh Guru, 344, 345

Arjuna, hero, 4, 39, 73

Arrian, Romano-Greek historian, 73, 78

Arthasastra, Sanskrit manual of statecraft attrib. to Kautilya, xx, 60, 63, 80–2, 83, 92, 94, 97–8, 103, 119, 170–1

Artillery, 282, 284, 291, 310, 339, 350, 395

Arunachal Pradesh, 528

Arya, ('Aryans'), 19–29

Arya Samaj, Hindu revivalist movement, 458, 467, 481

Arya-varta, 'land of the arya', 26, 159, 233

Aryanisation, xxvi-xxvii, 28–9, 42, 43, 44, 46–7, 49, 53, 120–1, 127–8, 132, 176–7, 200, 233

Asaf Khan, Mughal general, 333

Ashoka, 3rd c BC Maurya emperor, 63, 88–100, 106, 114, 119, 127, 129, 136, 140, 233, 272

Asiatic Society of Bengal, 79, 426

Askari, Prince, brother of Humayun, 298, 299

Assam, 137, 163, 193, 239, 244, 330, 341, 416, 448, 464–5, 520, 528, 530

Assaye, Battle of (1803), 410

Asvaghosha, Buddhist writer, 103, 104

Aswamedha, Vedic horse-sacrifice, 32–3, 139, 147, 168

Atlee, Clement, British Prime Minister 497, 500

Auckland, Lord, British Governor-General, 418

Augustus, Roman Emperor 121

Aurangabad, Maharashtra, 348, 359, 369

Aurangzeb, Mughal Emperor, 327, 328, 330, 332, 336, 338–47, 355–9, 362, 371–2, 387

Avanti, ancient name for Malwa, 42, 50, 84, 90

Avatar, descent, incarnation or manifestation as with Vishnu's (*q.v.*) nine *avatars*

Avitabile, General, Napoleonic officer, 422

Awadh (Oudh), Uttar Pradesh, 242, 272, 287, 294, 362, 391–2, 393, 404, 433–6, 439, 440–3, 446

Awami League, Bangladeshi political party 526

Ayanar, deity, xxvii

Ayodhya, Uttar Pradesh, 44, 45, 46–7, 102, 165, 202, 301, 532–3

Ayuthia, Thailand, 47

Azad Hind ('Free India'), 495

Azes, Shaka king, 109, 130

Babri (Baburi) Masjid, Ayodhya, Babur's mosque which became 1990s Hindu/Muslim flashpoint, 301, 532–3

Babur, Mughal emperor, 289–96, 297–8, 301, 302, 320

Bactria, Northern Afghanistan, 84, 102, 106–9, 114, 117, 143

Badami, Karnataka, xx, 168–9, 170, 172, 191

Bahadur Shah (Muazzam, Shah Alam) Mughal emperor, 359–60, 361, 364, 374

Bahadur Shah Zafar, the last Mughal, 439–40

Bahman Shah (Hasan), founder of Bahman dynasty, 281–2

Bahmanid Kingdom, 275–6, 280–2, 302–3

Baji Rao I, Maratha peshwa, 367, 368

Baji Rao II, Maratha peshwa, 408–9, 412–3

Bakhtiyar, Muhammad – *see* Muhammad

Baksar (Buxar), battle of (1765), 391–2, 404, 437

Balaji Baji Rao, Maratha peshwa, 403, 404

Balaji Vishvanath, Maratha peshwa, 363–4, 366, 367

Balban, Ghiyas-ud-Din, Delhi sultan, 242, 248–9

Balfour, Arthur, British prime minister, 462

'Balhara', The, Muslim rendering of *Vallabha*, a title of the Rashtrakuta kings (*q.v.*)

Bali, Indonesia, 172, 277

Balkh, Afghanistan, 206

Ballala II, 13th c Hoysala king, 252

Ballala III, 14th c Hoysala king, 258

Baluchistan, 118, 181

Bamiyan, Afghanistan, 114

Bana, biographer of Harsha, 161–4, 167

Banda Bahadur, 18th c Sikh leader, 361, 364

Bandung Conference (1955), 515

Banerji, R.D., archaeologist, 9

Bangalore, Karnataka, 400
Bangladesh, 7, 193, 330, 465, 524–8
Barani, Ziau-ud-Din, 14th c Muslim chronicler, 249, 257, 258–9, 260, 263–5, 266–7, 268, 271
Bareilly, Uttar Pradesh, 137
Baroda, Gujarat, 368
Bartuh, 13th c Hindu leader, 242
Basham, A.L., historian, 151
Bassein, Maharashtra, 306, 348, 405, 408
Bayana, near Agra, 294, 295
Bayly, Christopher, historian, 453–4
Bayram Khan, Akbar's guardian, 310, 311
Baz Bahadur, 16th c sultan of Malwa, 311–2, 313
Beas River, 73, 423
Belur, Karnataka, 251
Benares *see* Varanasi
Bengal xxiv, 43, 50, 65, 137, 140, 143, 165, 176, 192–4, 220, 239, 243–5, 248, 263, 270, 275, 287–8, 300, 318, 341, 362, 371, 375–6, 381–2, 385, 386–93, 448–9, 456, 463–6, 491–2, 499, 504, 505, 506, *see also* Bangladesh
Bentinck, Lord William, British governor-general, 417, 429–31
Berar, Maharashtra, 348, 354
Bernier, François, 17th c French traveller, 321–2, 326–7, 336
Besant, Annie, freedom fighter, 473–4
Betwa River, xxv, 90
Bhadralok, the Bengali Hindu intelligentsia, 473, 504
Bhagavad Gita, ethical and devotional Sanskrit text, 42, 148
Bhagwant Das, Kacchwaha rajput, 313
Bhaja, cave site in Maharashtra, 125
Bhakti, Hindu devotional movement, 148, 194, 219–10, 287–8, 316
Bhandarkar, D.R., archaeologist, 7–8
Bharat, Bharatas, Vedic lineage whence alternative for 'India' derives, 35, 56, 61
Bharata-varsha ('Kingdom of the Bharatas') *see* Bharat
Bharatiya Janata Party (BJP) ('Indian People's Party'), 454, 532–4
Bharatpur, Rajasthan, 416
Bharhut Stupa, 68, 102
Bhasa, Sanskrit playwright, 103
Bhaskara-varman, 7th c ruler of Assam, 163
Bhatia, Panjab, 207
Bhatvadi, battle of (1624), 331
Bhilsa, Madhya Pradesh, 254
Bhima, hero, 39, 42
Bhimpal, Pratihara rajput, 208
Bhindranwale, Sant Jarnail Singh, Sikh activist, 529

Bhoj of Dhar, 11th c 'philosopher king' 226–30
Bhoja of Kanauj, 9th c Pratihara king, 199, 202
Bhonsles of Nagpur, Maratha family, 368, 387–8, 402, 410
Bhopal, Madhya Pradesh, 426
Bhutan, 244
Bhutto, Zulfiqar Ali, prime minister of Pakistan, 516, 526–7, 528
Bhuvaneshwar, Orissa, 213, 220
Bidar, Karnataka, 283, 284, 302
Bihar, 40, 41, 43, 49, 61–70, 134, 193, 239, 243–4, 263, 296, 391–2, 449, 465, 471
Bijapur, Karnataka, 216, 302–3, 307, 331, 332, 337–9, 351, 355
Bimbisara, king of Magada, 65, 66, 67–8
Bindusara, Maurya emperor, 80, 89, 90, 91
'Black Hole of Calcutta', 389–90
Boigne, Count Benoit de, general, 408
Bombay (Mumbai), 126, 348, 370–1, 372, 381, 393, 405, 456, 461, 521
Borobudur, Java, 177–8
Bose, Rashbehari, nationalist revolutionary, 468
Bose, Subash Chandra, Congress radical & 'Azad Hind' leader, 492, 494–5, 505, 518
Brahma, deity, 33
Brahmadeya, land or revenue grant made to brahmans, 159, 219
Brahmanabad, Sind, 185, 186
Brahmanas, Sanskrit texts dealing with sacrificial ritual, 2, 26, 30, 40, 43
Brahmans, members of the priestly/scholarly caste, 28, 31, 32, 38, 47, 52–4, 86, 97, 99, 105, 120, 124, 146–7, 148–9, 152, 159–60, 166, 219, 344, 364, 454
Brahmaputra River, 341
Brahmo Samaj, Hindu reformist movement, 457
Braudel, F., historian xxiv
Brhadratha, last Maurya emperor, 104
Briggs, John, scholar, 231–2, 236
British perceptions of India, xxviii, 22, 426–32
Broach, Gujarat, 90, 126, 130, 187
Buchan, John, writer, 471
Buddh Gaya, Bihar, 65, 146, 169
Buddha (Siddhartha Gautama), 39, 47, 62–7, 102, 117, 125, 145, 150–1, 194
Buddhism, 47, 62–70, 87, 89, 97, 99, 105, 120, 124, 146–7, 148–9, 152, 158, 166, 182, 193–4, 223
Budha-Gupta, 5th c Gupta king, 144
Bukka, 14th c founder of Vijayanagar kingdom, 281, 282
Bulandshahr, Uttar Pradesh, 239

Burdwan, Bengal, 450
Burhanpur, Maharashtra, 332, 348
Burma, 123, 194, 416, 451
Burt, Captain, antiquarian, 214
Bussy, Charles de, French commander, 357–81, 393

Cakravartin, Buddhist ideal of universal emperor or cosmic 'wheel-turner', 70, 139, 140, 159, 170
Calanus, renunciate, 76–7
Calcutta (Kolkata), 370, 371, 372, 374, 381, 388–9, 392–3, 482, 505, 518
Calicut, Kerala, 277, 306, 481
Cambay, Gujarat, 257, 298, 348
Cambodia, 176–7
Candala, Harijan community, 54, 145
Cannanore, Kerala, 481
Cape Comorin (Kanya Kumari), Kerala, 122
Carnatic Wars, 377–81
Caste, 28, 34, 52–5, 120, 145, 189, 279, 419, 432, 533
Catherine of Braganza, 371
Ceraman Perumal, Tamil saint, 219
Chach, 7th c ruler of Sind, 182–3
Chahamanas, rajput lineage, 206, 233–8
Chaitanya, Bengali religious leader, 287–8
Chalukyas, 7–8th c Deccan dynasty, 168–70, 172–6, 181, 190–1, 305
Chalukyas, Later Western, 11–12th c Deccan dynasty, 216, 220, 223, 227, 251, *see also* Eastern Chalukyas
Chambal River, xxv, 192
Champa, Bengal, 65
Cham-pa, Indian kingdom in Vietnam, 124, 177
Champaner, Gujarat, 286, 298
Chand, rajput bard, 233, 234
Chanda Sahib, 18th c claimant to Arcot, 379
Chandelas, rajput rulers of Bundelkhand, 199, 206, 209, 213–4, 227, 234
Chanderi, Uttar Pradesh, 296
Chandernagore, Bengal, 377, 381, 390
Chandigarh, Panjab/Haryana, 523
Chandra-Gupta I, Gupta emperor, 134–6
Chandra-Gupta II, Gupta emperor, 134, 141–3, 145
Chandragupta, Maurya emperor, 69, 79–80, 81, 82–6, 130, 134
Charles II of England/Scotland, 348
Charsadda, Panjab, 51
Chashtana, 2nd c Shaka satrap, 131
Chatterjee, Bankim Chandra, writer, 457, 467
Chaul, Maharashtra, 277
Chausa, battle of (1529), 299

Chauth, Maratha claim to 25% of revenue, 357, 366
Chedi, district & dynasty in central India, 50, 227
Chelmsford, Lord, British Viceroy, 473
Chenab River, 72, 73
Chennai, xxviii, *see* Madras
Cheras, people & dynasty of Kerala, 170, 173, 181, 199, 215, 218, 220
Chidambaram, Tamil Nadu, 223–5, 258
Chilas, Jammu & Kashmir, 115
Child, John, East India Company merchant, 371–2
Child, Sir Josiah, East India Company governor, 371–2
Chillianwala, battle of (1849) 424
China, 104, 110, 113–7, 123, 134, 146, 161, 167, 176, 177, 221, 223, 421, 514, 515–6, 517
Chishti, Shaikh Salim, Sufi saint, 315
Chishti, Shaikh Muin-ud-Din, Sufi saint, 235, 315
Chitor, Rajasthan, 256, 279, 287, 300, 313–5
Chola dynasty of Tanjore, xix, xxviii, 119, 121, 170, 201, 214–23, 225, 252
Christians, Indian, 122, 429, 432, Missions, 428–9, 438, 445
Chunar, Uttar Pradesh, 298, 299, 392
Churchill, Winston, British Prime Minister, 488, 489, 493
Clive, Robert, Colonel & Governor of Bengal, 375, 379–82, 383, 386, 393, 486
Cochin, Kerala, 306, 348
Coinage, 52, 61, 101, 105, 106–7, 111, 131, 135, 139, 144, 269, 275, 301, 317, 333, 342, 361, 373, 433
Colbert, Jean-Baptiste, French finance minister, 322, 377
Communist Party (CPI & CPM), 481, 518, 531
Compagnie des Indes, 350, 373, 376, 377, 393–4
Congress Party, 453, 454, 455, 456–61, 464, 465, 466–7, 470, 477, 480–3, 491, 493–5, 500–2, 518–21, 523, 531
Constitutional Reform & Representation (1880–1947), 455, 459, 468, 469, 480, 489–90, 490–1
Coorg, Mysore, 416
Copland, Ian, historian, 493
Cornwallis, Lord, British Governor-General, 399–400, 430
Cotton & Textiles, 13, 85, 119, 245–7, 276, 323, 350, 372–3, 448, 450, 451
Court, Colonel, Napoleonic officer, 422
Crafts & Industry, xxvi, 10, 13, 55, 127, 145, 272, 323, 451, 466
Cranganore, Kerala, 122

Cripps, Sir Stafford, British politician, 497, 498

Cuddalore, Tamil Nadu, 393

Cults, 14, 31–2, 53, 96, 147–8, 194

Cunningham, Alexander, archaeological surveyor, 136

Curzon, Lord, Viceroy, xviii, 459, 461–4, 468

Cyrus, Achaemenid king, 58

Dacca (Dhaka), Bangladesh, 340, 341, 371, 464, 466, 524

Dahar (Dahir), 8th c ruler of Sind, 183–5

Daksinapatha, 'the southern route' – hence 'Deccan', 43, 90, 119, 169

Dalai Lama, 516

Dales, George F., archaeologist, 23

Dalhousie, Lord, Governor-General, 424, 432–5

Damaji Gaikwad, Maratha leader, 368

Danda, 'force', 'coercion', 149

Dandi, Gujarat, 487

Dani, Dr Ahmad Hassan, archaeologist, 114–7

Dantidurga, 8th c founder of the Rashtrakuta dynasty, 190–1, 200

Dara Shikoh, Mughal prince, son of Shah Jahan, 338, 339, 340, 345

Darius I, Achaemenid king, 57–8, 60

Dasa, pre-*Arya* peoples of India, 21, 23, 24, 28, 29, 35, 53–4

Dasaratha, Maurya emperor, 104

Dasyu, interchangeable with *dasa* (*q.v.*)

Datia, Madhya Pradesh, 443

Daulat Khan, governor of Panjab under Lodi sultanate, 292, 316

Daulat Rao Scindia, Maratha leader, 408

Daulatabad *see* Devagiri

Day, Francis, East India Company merchant, 332

Debal, Sind, 183–4, 234

Dehra Dun, Uttar Pradesh, 415

Delhi, 42, 131, 136, 142–3, 206, 233, 239, 240, 247–8, 259–61, 262–6, 292, 301, 309, 310, 335, 340, 366, 374–5, 385–6, 403, 410, 439–40, 447, 465, 489, 503, 508, 529

Delhi Sultanate, 213, 240–50, 262–276

Demetrius II, Bactrian Greek king, 107

Deshmukhs, landed nobles of Maharashtra, 338, 355

Deva Raya I, 15th c king of Vijayanagar, 282

Deva Raya II, 15th c king of Vijayanagar, 282, 303

Devagiri (Daulatabad), Maharashtra, 252–5, 257, 269, 270, 281, 283

Devapala, 9th c Pala king, 193, 195

Devnimori, Gujarat, 141

Dhaka *see* Dacca

Dhalip Singh, last Maharaja of Panjab, 423, 424

Dhamma see *Dharma*

Dhanga, 10–11th c Chandela king, 213

Dhar, Madhya Pradesh, 226–30, 285

Dharma, 'religion', 'duty', 'order', 46, 94–100, 131, 147, 149, 171, 225

Dharmapala, 8th c Pala king, 192–3, 195

Dhingra, Madanlal, patriot & assassin, 468

Dholpur, Rajasthan, 294

Dhruva, 8th c Rashtrakuta king, 192, 197, 199, 201

Dhruvadevi, Gupta queen, 141

Digvijaya, 'conquest of the four quarters' of the globe, 160, 171, 182, 191, 192, 199, 215, 217, 235, 258, 409

Dilawar Khan Ghori, 15th c founder of Malwa sultanate, 284–5

Disraeli, Benjamin, British prime minister, 447

Diu, Gujarat, 306

Divodasa, ancient king of Varanasi, 33, 35

Diwan, finance minister of a Muslim ruler, or the office of same, 382, 387, 392

Doab, region between rivers Jamuna & Ganga in Uttar Pradesh, xxiv, 26, 41–2, 44, 256, 268, 294, 413

Dorasamudra *see* Halebid

Dost Muhammad, 19th c Amir of Kabul, 418, 420

Dow, Alexander, historian, 232

Draupadi, heroine, 39, 46

Dravida Munnetra Kazhaghan (DMK) Tamil political party, 520

Dravidian languages, xxvii, 6, 28, 118–9

Dryden, John, playwright, 326

Duby, Georges, historian, 218

Duff, James Grant, administrator & historian, 367, 403, 426

Dufferin, Lord, Viceroy, 455, 458–95

Dupleix, Joseph, Governor of Pondicherry, 379, 393

Dyer, Brigadier-General Reginald, soldier & butcher, 475–7

East India Company, Dutch, (*Vereenigde Oostindische Compagnie*) 323, 348, 373

East India Company, English, 323, 332, 350, 361, 364, 370–82, 383–5, 404–8, 414, 419, 427–31, 446, 448, 486

Eastern Chalukyas, 7–11th c dynasty, 170, 191, 216

Economy, 259–60, 269, 320–4, 384, 448–51, 482, 518

Egypt, 121

Elections (1937) 491, 493, (1946) 500, (1952, 1957, 1962) 515, (1967, 1971) 523, (1977, 1980) 528–9, (1989) 531, 532, (1996) 531
Elephanta Island, Maharashtra, 169
Elephants, 27, 58, 65, 70, 73, 84, 109, 168, 185, 189–90, 220, 237, 271, 284, 310
Ellora, Maharashtra, xx, xxviii, 125, 191, 200–1
Elphinstone, Mountstuart, administrator & historian, 26–7, 404, 412, 420, 426
'Emergency', The, constitutional suspension of 1975–7, 528
Emigration, 451–3
Epic of Gilgamesh, 3
Eran, Madhya Pradesh, 148
Eucratides, Bactrian Greek king, 107
Euthydemus, Bactrian Greek king, 106

Fa Hian (Fa Hsien), 5th c Chinese visitor, 145–7, 152, 158, 160, 176
Famine, 86, 268, 454, 459, 504
Farman, Mughal imperial directive, 366, 369–77
Farrukhsiyar, Mughal emperor, 364–6, 369–70, 375
Fatehpur Sikri, Uttar Pradesh, 308, 315–6, 319
Federation, aborted constitutional proposal, 488–95, 499
Fergusson, James, architectural historian, 262, 336
Ferishta, Muslim historian, 204, 206, 207, 210, 231–2, 236–7, 240, 241, 249, 258, 260, 281, 282, 286, 289, 297, 299, 307, 337
Feroz Shah I Khalji (Jalal-ud-Din), 13th c Delhi sultan, 249–50, 254–5
Feroz Shah II Tughluq, 14th c Delhi sultan, 136, 242, 271–4
Ferozepur, battle of (1845), 423
Feudalism, 132, 159–60, 226, 232, 305
Firdausi, poet, 210
Flood, The, 1–5
Fort Derawar, Harappan site, 9
Funan, Indic kingdom in Vietnam, 124, 128, 176

Gama, Vasco da, 306
Gana-Sangha (early republic) 47–8, 49, 51, 64, 67
Gandak River, 43
Gandhara, people, region & artistic genre of the north-west, 50, 58–62, 71, 84, 103, 117, 121, 143
Gandhi, Indira, prime minister, 477, 517, 521, 522–4, 527–9
Gandhi, M.K.,'Mahatma', 100, 247, 449, 452,

453, 455, 471–2, 475, 477, 479–83, 484, 486, 492, 497, 498, 514, 518
Gandhi, Rajiv, prime minister, 530–2
Gandhi, Sanjay, younger son of Indira, 530
Ganesh, Sultan Raja of Bengal, 287
Ganga dynasty of Mysore, 169, 191, 192, 199
Ganga dynasty of Orissa, 220, 271, 278
Ganga River, xxiv, 26, 36, 40, 43, 44, 61, 70, 73–5, 106, 135, 164, 192, 201, 208, 220–1
Gangaikondacholapuram, Tamil Nadu, 221
Garhgaon, Assam, 341
Garhwal, Uttar Pradesh, 330
Gauda, Bengal, 162, 163
Gaur, Bengal, 244, 279
Gautamiputra Satakarni, 1st–2nd c AD Shatavahana ruler, 131
'Ghadr', 'Mutiny' movement of c1914, 472–3
Ghaggar River, 13
Ghakkars, warrior community in Panjab, 240, 247
Ghatotkacha Gupta, early Gupta ruler, 134
Ghazni, Afghanistan, 204, 207, 209, 210, 225–6, 235–6, 239, 256
Ghenghiz Khan, Mongol leader, 239, 243, 248
Gheriah *see* Vijayadurg
Ghiyas-ud-Din Tughluq, 14th c Delhi sultan, 261, 262–5
Ghor, Afghanistan, 225, 284
Ghose (Ghosh), Aurobindo, nationalist & reformer, 461, 467
Ghosh, Dr B.K., scholar, 29, 30
Gilgit, Northern Areas of Pakistan, 115, 463
Girnar, Gujarat, 84, 88, 129–30, 144, 286–7
Goa, 169, 283, 306, 348, 355, 515
Gobind, last Sikh Guru, 345, 360–1
Godavari River, 149, 190, 200
Godse, Nathuram, assassin, 514
Gokhale, Gopal Krishna, teacher & Congress leader, 461, 465–6, 468, 471, 474
Gol Gumbaz *see* Bijapur
Golconda, Andhra Pradesh, 293, 302, 332, 337, 338, 355
Gomateshwara, Jain saint, 85
Gondophares, 1st c AD Parthian king, 109–10, 115
Gopala, 8th c founder of Pala dynasty, 192, 195
Gosala, Ajivika founder, 64
Government of India Act (1935), 490–1, 502, 519
Govinda III, 8–9th c Rashtrakuta king 199
Govinda-Raja, 12th c ruler of Delhi, 235, 237
Graeco-Roman perceptions of India, 58–9, 76–7, 78, 85

Great Rebellion (Indian Mutiny) of 1857–8, 436–47
Greeks, Ancient, 59, 70–77, 78–9, 104, 106–9, 117, *see also* Graeco-Roman
'Green Revolution', 524
Gresley, Captain, explorer of Ajanta, 149–50
Grhpatis, 'house-holders', 30, 53
Guhasena, 6th c Maitraka ruler of Saurashtra, 157
Gujarat, 36, 42, 84, 88, 129–33, 141–2, 195–6, 209, 231, 234, 256–7, 275, 284–7, 298–9, 306, 316, 352, 368, 405, 520
Gujars, community of herdsmen, 195, 263
Gujranwala, Panjab, 476
Gujrat, Panjab, 424
Gulab Singh, first Maharaja of Jammu & Kashmir, 423
Gulbarga, Karnataka, 279, 283, 284
Gungu, brahman minister, 281
Guptas, 4th–5th c dynasty, 104, 132, 133, 134–54, 157
Gurjara-Pratiharas, composite rajput dynasty of 8–10th c Kanauj, 169, 187, 195–9, 202–3, 206, 231, 233
Gurkha War of 1814–16, 415, 435
Gwalior, Madhya Pradesh, 144, 199, 211, 239, 286, 289, 293, 368, 406, 408, 439, 444

Habib, Irfan, historian, 245, 320
Haidar Ali Khan, 18th c sultan of Mysore, 394–7
Hakim, half-brother of Akbar, 318
Halebid, Karnataka, 251–2, 258
Hampi, Karnataka, 282
Harappa, Panjab, 9, 13, 15, 23, 24
Harappan Civilisation, 5–18, 19, 22–4
Hardinge, Lord, Viceroy, 468
Hari Singh, Maharaja of Jammu & Kashmir, 512
Harihara I, 14th c founder of Vijayanagar kingdom, 281
Harihara II, 14th c king of Vijayanagar, 282
'Harijans', 'children of God', 'untouchables', 'Dalits', 482, 492
Harisena, Gupta minister & panegyrist, 151
Harsha-vardhana, 7th c emperor, 159, 160–7, 168, 169–70, 182
Haryana, 233, 523
Hastinapura, Uttar Pradesh, 4, 40, 42, 44
Hastings, Warren, Governor-General, 383, 392–3, 396, 404–6, 426
Hawkins, Captain William, East India Company emissary, 370
Hedges, William, East India Company director, 371
Heliocles, Bactrian Greek king, 107

Heliodorus, Bactrian Greek ambassador, 108
Hemu, 'raja Vikramaditya', 16th c adventurer, 309–10
Herodotus, historian, 58, 59, 60, 78
Himachal Pradesh, 208, 415, 523
Himalayas, xxii, 27, 113–7, 182, 244, 267–8, 421
Hinayana School of Buddhism, 115–7, 182
Hindal, Mughal prince, brother of Humayun, 298
Hindi Language 44, 132, 457, 520
'Hindu', 'Hindustan', 57–8
Hindu Kush, 113–7
Hinduism, 133, 147–8, 189, 304
History & Culture of the Indian People, 3, 155
Ho Chi Minh, 485
Horses, 25, 29, 32, 70, 109, 158, 181, 211, 276–7, 306, 398
Hoysalas, 10–13th c dynasty in Karnataka, 251–2, 258
Hsuan Tsang, 7th c Chinese visitor, 158, 161, 162, 164–7, 168, 170, 182, 195, 203
Hughli, river & town in Bengal, 371, 372, 390
Hulagu, Mongol leader, 248
Humayun, Mughal emperor, 293, 294, 296–9, 308–9, 316, 332
Hume, Allan, Congress leader, 457–8
Hund (Ohind), Panjab, 203
Huns, 110, 117, 143–4, 158–9, 167
Hunza, Pakistan's Northern Areas, 114, 115
Husain Ali Khan *see* Saiyid
Hyderabad, Andhra Pradesh, 276, 338, 355–6, 357, 369–70, 377, 379, 381, 393–4, 395, 400–1, 488, 496, 511
Hyderabad, Sind, 184
Hydrography, xxiii-xxv

I'Tsing (I'Ching) 7th c Chinese visitor, 177
Ibn Asir, 11th c scholar, 235
Ibn Batuta, 14th c traveller, 265, 266–7, 270, 275–6
Ibrahim Adil Shah, 16–17th c sultan of Bijapur, 337
Ibrahim Lodi, 16th c sultan of Delhi, 292–3
Ilbert Bill (1883), 456
Iltumish, Shams-ud-Din, 13th c sultan of Delhi, 240–1, 243–4
Independence, (of India, Pakistan, Bangladesh), 483, 497, 502–3, 509, 526
'India', etymology of, 56–9
India Councils Acts of 1892 & 1909, 459, 469
India Office, 455
India, Republic of, 7, 56–7, 89, 112, 510*ff passim*

'Indian Mutiny' *see* Great Rebellion
'Indian National Army', (INA) 495, 505
Indian National Congress *see* Congress
Indigo, 350, 372, 391, 448, 471
Indo-Aryans, xxvi-xxvii, 19-36, 42, *see also arya* & Aryanisation
Indo-European languages, 21
Indonesia, 20, 176, 177-8, 415, 515
Indo-Pakistan Wars, 512-3, 517, 526-7
Indore, Madhya Pradesh, 368
Indra III, 10th c Rashtrakuta king, 199
Indra, Vedic deity, 21, 23, 25, 26
Indraprastra, Delhi, 41-2, 301
Indus River, xxiv, 4-5, 56-60, 71, 75-6, 107, 114-7, 143, 180-7, 417-8
Indus Valley Civilisation – *see* Harappan Civilisation
Industry *see* Crafts & Industry
Inscriptions, xx-xxi, 84, 87-9, 91-6, 101-2, 111, 114-7, 129-30, 136-7, 144-5, 169, 216-8, 222-3, 305
Iqta, a military fief, 244, *see also Jagir*
Iron, 41, 142, 154, 466
Irrigation, xxiv-vi, 118, 130, 144, 272, 288, 450, 463
Irwin, Lord, Viceroy, 486, 487-8
Isami, historian, 245, 247
Islam Shah Sur, son & successor of Sher Shah, 309
Islamabad, Pakistan, 517
Itimad-ud-Daula, Jahangir's minister, 332-4

Jagat Singh, 17th c Rana of Mewar, 330
Jagir, a revenue right over specified lands as granted by a Mughal ruler to one of his *amirs* for the maintenance of troops, 321-6, 345, 346, 359, 362, 364, 387, 390
Jagirdar, the holder of a *jagir* (*q.v.*)
Jahandah Shah, 18th c Mughal emperor, 364
Jahangir, Mughal emperor, 136-7, 315, 319, 326, 328, 332-3, 334, 345, 370
Jai Singh, Kacchwaha rajput of Amber, 9, 336, 339, 353, 360
Jains, 47, 64, 76, 85-6, 99, 120, 129, 219, 285, 316
Jaipur, Rajasthan, 9, 313
Jalalabad, Afghanistan, 203
Jalal-ud-Din (Jadusen), 15th c sultan of Bengal, 287
Jalal-ud-Din Feroz *see* Feroz Shah I Khalji
Jallianwala Bagh, site of 1919 Amritsar massacre, 475-7
Jamal-ud-Din Yakut, African companion of Raziya, 245
Jammu & Kashmir, 423, 463, 488, 511-4, 534
Jamshedpur, Bihar, 466

Jamuna River, xxv, 26, 136, 164, 263
Jan Sangh, Hindu nationalist party, 454, 532
Janapada, a post-Vedic clan (*jana*) territory, 35, 43, 44, 48, 50, 58, 143
Janata Party, 'People's' party & front, 529, 532
Jati, family & profession-based caste (*cp. varna*) 54, 55, 98, 145, 189
Jats, caste of cultivators in Panjab, Rajasthan, UP, 344, 410, 415
Jauhar, the ritualised abandonment of a fortress or palace, 256, 296, 315
Jaunpur, Uttar Pradesh, 272-4, 279, 287, 292, 294, 298, 318
Java, Indonesia, 28, 47, 120, 133, 152, 177-9, 194, 415, 449
Jaxartes River, 71
Jayapala (Jaipal), 10-11th c Shahi king, 204-6, 207
Jayappa Scindia, 18th c Maratha leader, 403
Jhansi, Uttar Pradesh, 433, 443-4
Jhelum River, 72, 75
Jinji, Tamil Nadu, 337, 354, 356
Jinnah, Mohammed Ali, Quaid-i-Azam of Pakistan, 56-7, 453, 469, 481, 482, 483, 487, 494, 495-6, 501-3, 506, 514
Jizya, a tax imposed by Muslim rulers on non-Muslims, 185, 242, 274, 282, 343, 356
Jodha, Raja, Rathor rajput ruler of Marwar, 287
Jodhpur, Rajasthan, 287, 300, 345, 360
Jogjakarta, Java, 47, 177, 415
Jones, Sir William, scholar & judge, 20-21, 79, 86, 151, 383, 385, 426
Joshi, J.P., archaeologist, 9
Junagadh, Gujarat, 84, 129-30, 131, 144, 145, 510-2
Junaid ibn Abdur Rahman al-Marri, 8th c governor of Sind, 186, 187
Junnar, Maharashtra, 131
Jurz, probably Gujarat, 195-6 *see* Gurjara-Pratiharas
Jute, 451, 485

Kabir, 15th c poet & reformer, 316, 344
Kabul, Afghanistan, 71, 158, 181, 203-4, 205, 256, 290-1, 308, 318, 418-9
Kacchwahas, rajput clan of Amber/Jaipur, 199, 313, 318, 336, 360
Kadamba kings of Mysore 168, 169
Kadaram (Kedah), Malaya, 222, 223
Kafur, Malik, 14th c general, 257-9, 260
Kakatiyas, 12-14th c dynasty in Andhra Pradesh, 252, 257-8
Kakshivant, Vedic brahman, 30, 32, 35
Kalachuris, 10-13th c dynasty in Madhya Pradesh, 227, 252

Kalhana, historian, 203, 211, 212
Kali Yug, ('the Dark Era') 2, 46, 48, 102
Kalibangan, Harappan site, 13
Kalidasa, poet & playwright, xx, 103–4, 151–2, 153, 169, 170
Kalinga (Orissa), 50, 84, 91–2, 94, 106, 108, 109, 220
Kalinjar, Madhya Pradesh, 206, 211, 213, 239, 298, 300
Kalyan, Karnataka, 126, 130
Kalyana, Maharashtra, 216, 252
Kamarapura *see* Assam
Kamasutra, 81, 103
Kambujas/Kamboja, ancient lineage & territory, 50, 176–7
Kamran, Prince, brother of Humayun, 298
Kanauj, Uttar Pradesh, xx, 159, 162, 164, 181, 192–201, 206, 208, 234, 239, 299
Kanchipuram, Tamil Nadu, xx, 110, 137, 156, 170, 172, 173–4, 199, 215
Kandahar, Afghanistan, 96, 256, 308, 319, 330–1
Kangra, Himachal Pradesh, 208, 330
Kanheri, Maharashtra, 150
Kanhoji Angria, Maratha naval commander, 364, 372, 381
Kanishka, Kushana emperor, 103, 111–2, 114, 115, 203
Kannada language, xxvii, 118
Kanpur, Uttar Pradesh, 413, 428, 439, 440–2
Kanva Dynasty of Magadha, 105–6, 125
Kapilavastu, Nepal, Buddha's birthplace, 64, 146
Kara, Uttar Pradesh, 254, 255
Karachi, Sind, 183, 420, 502
Karakoram Highway, 113–7, 134, 145, 158, 463, 517
Karli, cave site, Maharashtra, 125, 150
Karma, 'deed', 'fate', the causal effect of conduct in one life on status in the next, 189
Karnal, Haryana, 385
Karnataka, xxvii, 85–6, 105, 118, 168, 191, 251–2, 302–8, 474, 517
Kashmir, 97, 107, 111, 144, 158, 166, 182, 202–3, 211–12, 288, 318, 330, 334, 341, 385, 420, 423, 493, 516–7, *see also* Jammu & Kashmir
Kaundinya, brahman adventurer, 124, 177
Kauravas, descendents of Kuru (*q.v.*)
Kaushambi, Uttar Pradesh, 51, 69, 136
Kautilya, supposed author of the *Arthasastra*, xx, 60, 63, 80–3, 92, 103, 119, 170–1
Kaveri River, xix, 118, 122, 214–5
Kerala, 28, 118, 119, 120, 121, 122, 170, 277, 396, 398, 448, 481, 518, 520

Khadi, homespun cotton textiles, 481
Khafi Khan, Muslim chronicler, 350–1, 352, 364, 366, 533
Khajuraho, Madhya Pradesh, 151, 213–4
Khaljis (Khiljis), Afghan lineage & Delhi dynasty, 243–5, 249, 253–61
Khalsa, (1) land revenues reserved to the king, 321, 387; (2) the Sikh brotherhood of 'the pure', 361
Khan, General Ayub, President of Pakistan, 515, 516–7, 526
Khan, General Yahya, President of Pakistan, 526, 527
Khan, Liaqat Ali, prime minister of Pakistan, 501, 514
Khan, Sir Sayyid Ahmad, Muslim reformer & educationalist, 458, 459
Khanua, battle of (1526), 295–6
Kharavela, King of Kalinga, 106, 108, 119
Khilafat Movement in support of Ottoman caliphate, 477–9, 482
Khizrabad, Haryana, 136.
Khmers, Cambodian dynasty & people, 124, 176, 223
Khunjerab Pass, between Pakistan & China on Karakoram Highway, 113, 115
Khurram, Prince, *see* Shah Jahan
Khusrau, Prince, son of Jahangir, 328, 345
Khyber Pass, between Pakistan & Afghanistan, 71, 181, 206
Kingship, 32–3, 39, 47, 48–9, 70, 111, 131, 139, 140, 159, 170–2, 220, 248, 350, 354
Kipling, Rudyard, 336
Kistna River, 200, 283
Kitchener, Lord, Commander-in-chief of Indian army 468
Koh-i-Nur Diamond, 293, 299, 308, 386, 418, 424–5
Kolhapur, Maharashtra, 368, 413
Kolkota, xxviii, *see* Calcutta
Konarak, Orissa, 213, 275
Kosambi, D.D., historian, xvii, 38–9, 86, 132, 133, 134, 154, 159
Koshala, ancient kingdom in Uttar Pradesh, 44, 50, 66, 67–9
Krishna I, 8th c Rashtrakuta king, 191, 200
Krishna III, 10th c Rashtrakuta king, 215
Krishna, deity, 42, 46, 73, 147, 208
Krishna-Deva-Raya I, 16th c king of Vijayanagar, 294, 303–5
Krishna-Deva-Raya III, 18th c Maharaja of Mysore, 425
Ksatriya, the warrior & ruling caste, 52, 70, 120, 131, 197, 231, 345
Kshtrapas, 'satraps', subordinate rulers, *see* esp. Western Satraps
Kujula Kadphises, Kushana king, 111, 115

Kumaradevi, 4th c queen, consort of Chandra-Gupta I, 135
Kumara-Gupta, 5th c Gupta emperor, 142, 143–4
Kumbalgarh, Rajasthan, 287
Kumbha, 15th c Rana of Mewar, 287
Kuru, Vedic clan, 41, 42, 46, 50
Kurukshetra, battle of (c950BC), 46
Kushanas, 1–2nd c AD dynasty, 110–12, 113–4, 115–6, 117, 130, 137

Ladakh, Jammu & Kashmir, 288, 341–2, 420, 511, 516
Lahore, Panjab, 73, 203, 225, 226, 233, 247, 292, 318, 334, 403, 411, 422, 476, 483, 508
Lake, Gerard, British general, 410
Lakhnauti, Bengal, 244
Lakshmana, hero, xxvii, 39
Lakshmanasena, 12–13th c Sena king of Bengal, 244
Lakshmi Bai, 19th c Rani of Jhansi, 443–4
Lal Kunwar, 18th c mistress of Jahandah Shah, 364
Lal, B.B., historian, 9
Lalliya, 9th c king of Kabul, 203
Lamghan (Lughman), Afghanistan, 203, 205
Laswari, battle of (1803), 410
Lawrence, John, Governor-General, 424
Licchavis, tribe & republic, 48, 49–50, 52, 67–70, 135–6
Lingam, the phallic icon of Shiva, 209, 216, 343
Linlithgow, Lord, Viceroy, 498, 504
Literature, 103, 119–20, 151–2, 161, 229
Lodi, Afghan tribe & Delhi dynasty, 274, 288, 289–90, 298
Lohara, 11th c Kashmiri dynasty, 212
Lokayats, sect, 64
Lop Nor, China, 114
Lothal, Harappan site, 10, 13
Louis XVI, French king, 397–8
Lucknow, Uttar Pradesh, 428, 435, 440–3
Lucknow Pact (1916), 470, 474
Lytton, Lord, Viceroy, 447, 454, 455

Macaulay, Thomas, author, statesman & legal adviser in India, 171, 431, 503
Machchlipatnam, Andhra Pradesh, 357
Mackay, Ernest, archaeologist, 9
Mackenzie, Colin, surveyor & antiquarian, 426
Madhava Rao, Maratha Peshwa, 404
Madho Singh, Raja of Jaipur, 404
Madhya Pradesh, 130, 227
Madras, 121, 122, 156, 332, 370, 373, 376, 377–9, 393–4, 396, 472

Madurai, Tamil Nadu, 119, 120, 172, 215, 252, 258, 308, 337
Magadha, Bihar, 50, 61–70, 73, 79, 82–3, 90–100, 105, 106, 111, 134, 135, 147, 165
Mahabharata, Sanskrit epic, xxvii, 2, 3, 4, 34, 37–46, 54, 60, 73, 120
Mahadji Scindia, 18th c Maratha leader, 368, 406–9
Maha-janapada, 'great clan-territories', embryonic states, 50, 58
Maha-kshtrapa, 'great satrap', see esp. Western Satraps
Mahapadma Nanda, 4th c BC king, 70, 78
Maharajadhiraja, 'great king of kings', 134, 137, 140, 160, 169, 195, 197
Maharashtra, 118, 125–8, 168, 191, 252–5, 338, 454, 474, 520
Mahasabha, Hindu revivalist party, 454, 481, 504, 514
Maha-samanta, 'great vassal', 'great neighbour', 160
Mahavira Nataputta, Jain founder, 47, 62, 64, 86
Mahayana school of Buddhism, 115–7, 194
Mahendrapala, 9–10th c Gurjara-Pratihara king, 199
Maheshwar, Madhya Pradesh, 407
Mahinda, son of Ashoka & Buddhist missionary to Sri Lanka, 90, 96
Mahipala I, 11th c Pala king of Bengal, 220
Mahmud Gawan, chief minister in Bahmanid sultanate, 284
Mahmud Khalji, 15th c Sultan of Malwa, 286
Mahmud of Ghazni, 11th c invader, 205–12, 213, 235
Mahmud Shah, 15–16th c Bahmanid Sultan, 302
Mahmud Shah Begarha, 15–16th c Sultan of Gujarat, 286–7
Maitrakas, 6–8th c dynasty in Gujarat, 157, 166, 181, 187
Majumdar, Prof R.C., historian, xvi, 28
Makran, coastal region of Baluchistan, 10, 76, 182, 183
Malaviya, Madan Mohan, founder of Hindu *mahasabha*, 481
Malaya, 104, 123, 124, 152, 176, 222
Malayalam language, 118
Malcolm, Sir John, British administrator, 407, 408, 426–7
Maldive Islands, 215
Malhar Rao Holkar, 18th c Maratha leader, 368, 403, 407
Malik Ambar, 17th c general, 331–2, 348
Malik Sowar, 14th c founder of Sharqi sultanate of Jaunpur, 272–4

Malla, early tribe & republic, 50, 66

Malwa, western half of Madhya Pradesh, 130, 131, 137, 141, 148, 152, 162, 169, 192, 197, 243, 256–7, 283, 284–6, 296, 311–2, 368, 407, *see also* Avanti

Mamallapuram, Tamil Nadu, 156, 174, 176

Man Singh, Kacchwaha ruler of Amber, 313, 318

Man Singh, Tomar rajput ruler of Gwalior, 289, 316

Mandala, concentric diagram of geo-political & cosmic relations, 170–2, 179, 225

Mandelso, Albert de, 17th c German visitor, 231

Mandu, Madhya Pradesh, 227, 279, 285–6, 298, 311, 331

Mangalore, Karnataka, 397

Manjanik, catapult-like siege-engine, 184, 255, 270

Mansabdars, those with a ranking (*mansab*) in the Mughal hierarchy, 324–5, 327, 347, 353, 355

Mansehra, Panjab, 96, 114

Mansurah, Sind, 185, 187, 202, 234

Manu, royal progenitor & law-giver, 1–2, 27, 49, 103, 164, 169

Manyakheta, Maharashtra, 200, 216

Mao Tse Tung, Chinese leader, 516

Marathas, people, kingdom & confederacy from upland Maharashtra, xxii, 331, 338, 347, 350–59, 363–4, 367–9, 388, 394, 396, 402–13, 521

Marathi language, xxvii, 132, 461, 520

Marco Polo, Venetian traveller, 257–8, 276–7, 278

Marshall, Sir John, archaeologist, 9, 60

Martand, Kashmir, 288

Marwar, rajput kingdom based round Jodhpur, 346

Masud of Ghazni, successor of Mahmud (*q.v.*), 225

Mathura, Uttar Pradesh, xx, 42, 103, 111, 137, 151, 208, 219, 343, 386

Matsya-nyaya, state of anarchy, 2, 49, 171, 225

Maues, 1st c BC Shaka king, 109, 115, 130

Maukharis, 6–7th c Kanauj dynasty, 159, 162, 163

Mauryas, 4–3rd c BC imperial dynasty of Magadha, 69, 78–100, 101, 104–5, 120, 139–40

Meds, piratical tribe, 183

Meerut, Uttar Pradesh, 239, 438–9

Megasthenes, Greek ambassador to Magadha, 79, 80, 85, 92–4, 97, 98, 119, 190

Meghalaya, 528

Mehrauli Pillar, 'Iron pillar', 142–3, 154

Mehta, Ferozeshah, Congress leader, 461, 468, 474

Meluhha, possible name of Harappan country, 16, 23

Menander, 2nd c BC Bactrian Greek king, 107–8

Mewar, Rajput kingdom based round Chitor & Udaipur, 286, 313–5, 328–30, 345

Mewatis, elusive tribe of Delhi region, 248

Mihirakula, 6th c Hun leader, 158

Mill, James, historian, 429–30

Mill, John Stuart, philosopher & political economist, 429

Minhaju-s Siraj, Muslim chronicler, 244, 245

Minto, Lord, Governor-General, 468, 469

Mir Jafar, 18th c Nawab of Bengal, 390–1

Mir Jumla, 17th c adventurer & general, 338, 339, 341, 386

Mir Qasim (Kasim), 18th c Nawab of Bengal, 391–2

Mizoram, 528

Mlechha, disparaging name for non-*arya* peoples, 24, 43, 59, 143, 187–8, 211, 233

Mofussil, hinterland, upcountry provinces, 432, 453, 471

Mohenjo-daro, Sind, 7, 8, 9, 13, 15, 22–3, 182

Money, J.W.B., businessman & author, 449

Mongols, 239, 242–3, 247–8, 249, 256, 270, 274, 288

Montagu, Edwin, Secretary of State for India, 473

Mont-Ford Reforms (1921), 473, 474, 480, 483

Mookerji, R.K., historian, 92

Moon, Penderel, administrator & historian, 397, 413, 497–8

Moore, Thomas, poet, 514

Morley, John, Secretary of State for India, 468

Mouhot, Henri, French explorer & naturalist, 214

Mount Abu, Rajasthan, 197, 233, 239, 241

Mount Kailas, Tibet, 200–1

Mount Meru, mythical axis of the world, 170–1

Mountbatten, Lord, Viceroy, 57, 468, 501–3, 508

Muazzam, Prince *see* Bahadur Shah

Mubarak Khalji, son and successor, briefly, of Ala-ud-Din Khalji, 260

Mughal empire, xxviii, 256, 289–363 *passim*, 382, 385, 387, 391, 439–40

Mughal, M. Rafique, archaeologist, 9

Muhammad Adil Shah, 17th c sultan of Bijapur, 337, 338

Muhammad Ali, 18th c ruler of Arcot, 379, 381

Muhammad Ali, Maulana, 464

Muhammad Bakhtiyar Khalji, 13th c conqueror of Bengal, 243–4

Muhammad bin Tughluq, 14th c sultan of Delhi, 263–71, 281, 319

Muhammad ibn Qasim, 8th c conqueror of Sind, 183–6, 187

Muhammad of Ghor, 12th c invader & conqueror, 213, 226, 233, 234–8, 239–40

Muhammad Shah, 18th c Mughal emperor, 366–7, 385–6

Muhammad, The Prophet, 157, 180

Muizzudin Muhammad bin Sam *see* Muhammad of Gaur

Muller, Friedrich Max, scholar, 21, 458

Multan, Sind, now Pakistan, 185, 187, 196, 202, 207–8, 234, 275, 420, 424

Mumbai, xxviii, *see* Bombay

Mumtaz Mahal, wife of Shah Jahan, 333–4, 335, 352

Mundy, Peter, East India Company merchant, 335–6

Munro, Hector, British officer, 392, 397, 437

Munro, Thomas, administrator, 399, 410, 426, 427, 430, 437

Murad Baksh, Mughal prince, son of Shah Jahan, 339, 340

Murshid Quli Khan, Mughal governor of Bengal, 387

Murshidabad, Bengal, 387, 392

Muslim Conquests 180–7, 187–9, 202–12, 232–3, 234–8, 243–4, 354–6, 254–9, 271–2, 295–6, 341–2

Muslim League, 454, 468–9, 470, 483, 494, 495–7, 500–2, 504, 526

Muslim perceptions of India, 188–9, 207–10, 241–3, 244, 275–9, 294, 312

Mussoorie, Uttar Pradesh, 415

Muttra *see* Mathura

Muzaffar Jang, 18th c Nawab/Nizam of Hyderabad, 381

Mysore, 337, 394–401, 416, 488

Nabobs, British officials & officers personally enriched by their service in India, 384, 390, 428

Nadia, Bengal, 244

Nadir Shah of Persia, 367, 385–6

Nagaland, 528

Nagas, tribe, 40

Nagasena, Buddhist philosopher, 108

Naghabhata II, 8–9th c Gurjara-Pratihara king, 199

Nagpur, Madhya Pradesh, 190, 368, 413, 433

Nahapana, 1st c AD Shaka satrap, 131

Naini Tal, Uttar Pradesh, 415

Nalanda, Bihar, 167, 169, 176, 193

Namazga Culture of Turkestan, 15

Nana Phadnavis, 18th c minister of several Pune peshwas, 405–6, 407, 408

Nana Sahib, adopted son of peshwa Baji Rao II, 413, 433, 440–2, 444

Nanak, Guru, first Sikh guru, 100, 316

Nandas, 4th c BC dynasty of Magadha, 70, 73, 78–9, 80, 82, 83, 102, 120

Nandangarh, Bengal, 179

Naoroji, Dadabhai, Congress president, 450, 453, 455, 459, 466

Napier, Major-General Sir Charles, British conqueror of Sind, 419–20

Napoleon, 400, 414, 421–2

Narain, Raj, socialist politician, 524, 528

Narasimha Tuluva, 15–16th c Vijayanagar king, 303

Narasimha-varman I, 7th c Pallava king, 172, 174

Narasimha-varman II, 8th c Pallava king, 174

Narayan J.P., Gandhian activist & reformer, 528

Narmada River, xxv, 84, 90, 126, 192, 227, 357

Narwar, Madhya Pradesh, 239, 289

Nasik, Maharashtra, 125, 131

Nasir-ud-Din, son of Slave Sultan Iltumish, 244

Natal, S. Africa, 452

Nayaks, military commanders of the Vijayanagar kingdom & later independent rulers, 305, 307, 308, 337

Negapatnam, Tamil Nadu, 223

Nehru, Jawaharlal, Prime Minister, 56–7, 89, 137, 426, 453, 481, 483, 484–6, 491, 494, 498, 501, 502–3, 512, 513, 514–7

Nehru, Motilal, President of Congress Party, 477, 482, 486

Nepal, 64, 97, 135, 137, 194, 415

Nicobar Islands, 222

Nikitin, Athanasius, 15th c Russian visitor, 277, 284

Nizam Ali, 18th c Nawab/Nizam of Hyderabad, 395

Nizam-ud-Din Auliya, Delhi Shaikh, 263

Nizam-ul-Mulk, Mughal governor & then Nawab in the Deccan, 363, 368–70, 377, 379, 395

Northern Circars, coastal belt in Andhra Pradesh, 381, 393–4

North-West Frontier Province, Pakistan, 462–3, 499, 500

Nur Jahan, Jahangir's queen, 332–4

Oc-Eo, Indian site in Vietnam, 124

Odantapuri, Bihar, 244

O'Dwyer, Sir Michael, Lieutenant-Governor of Panjab, 475

Omrah, the nobility, the class of *amirs*, 313

Opium, 448

Orchha, Madhya Pradesh, 443

Orissa, 50, 70, 91, 106, 166, 170, 176, 220, 271–2, 287–8, 303, 318, 388, 416, 464, 490

Oudh, *see* Awadh

Oxus River, 10, 71

Paes, Domingo, 16th c Portuguese visitor to Vijayanagar, 304

Pagan, Burma, 194

Paharpur, Bengal, 179, 193

Pahlavas, 'Parthians', 109

Paithan, Maharashtra, 127

Pakistan, 7, 56–7, 113–7, 183, 234, 416, 459, 496–7, 499, 500, 502–3, 506, 510, 512, 515, 524–8

Pal, Bipin Chandra, radical Bengali journalist, 467

Palas, 8–11th c dynasty in Bengal, 192–4, 199, 220

Pali language, 87

Palkhed, battle of (1728), 368

Pallavas, 5–9th c dynasty of Tamil Nadu, 110, 137, 156, 170, 172–7, 190, 192, 215

Panchala, tribe & territory in the Doab, 108

Pandavas, sons of Pandu, heroes of *Mahabharata*, 39, 41, 42, 44, 46

Pandyas, long-lasting dynasty of Madurai, 119, 120, 121, 170, 172, 199, 215, 218, 220, 223, 252, 258

Panhala, Maharashtra, 352, 354

Panini, Sanskrit grammarian, 60–1, 71, 103, 153

Panipat, battles of (1526, 1556 & 1761), 292–3, 301, 310, 386, 403–4

Panjab, xxiv, 21, 26, 43, 57–61, 70–7, 82, 84–5, 106–12, 144, 202–5, 225–6, 233–5, 247, 256, 288, 289–90, 316–7, 361, 362, 385, 417, 420–4, 445, 472, 473, 475–7, 492, 499, 505–8, 521, 528–30

Panth, the Sikh brotherhood, 317, 360–1

Paramaharajadhiraja, 'king of all other great kings', 134

Paramaras, rajput lineage & rulers of Malwa, 201, 226–30, 257

Paramesvara, 'lord of other [lords]', 169, 195, 197

Parantaka, 10th c Chola king, 215

Parsees, Zoroastrian community, 455

Parthia, eastern Iran, 102, 109, 110

Partition, of India in 1947 & Pakistan in 1971, 56–7, 502, 506–8, 510, 526–7

Pataligrama *see* Pataliputra

Pataliputra, Bihar, xx, 68–9, 79, 80, 82–3, 85, 90, 96, 97, 100, 104–5, 108, 135, 146

Patan *see* Anhilwara

Patanjali, Sanskrit grammarian, 103, 153

Patel, Vallabhai, Congress leader, 472, 505, 511, 514

Patna, Bihar, 69, 386

Pattadakal, Karnataka, 169, 174

Periplus of the Erythraean Sea, The, 1st c AD description of Indian Ocean, 121, 126, 127, 130

Persepolis, Iran, 57, 71

Peshawar, North-West Frontier, 26–7, 95, 114, 158, 206, 419, 420

Peshwas of Pune, Maratha ministers & rulers, *see* Baji Rao, Balaji Vishvanath, etc.

Pindaris, 19th c freebooters, 411–3

Pir Panjal, outer range of Himalayas (*q.v.*)

Pitt, Thomas, Governor of Madras, 373–4, 376

Plantations, 448–9

Plassey, battle of (1757), 381, 390

Pliny the Elder, Roman author, 121

Plutarch, Greek historian, 78, 79

Polilur, Tamil Nadu, battle of (1780), 172, 396–7

Pondicherry, Tamil Nadu, 121, 377, 379, 393, 394, 467

Poona *see* Pune

Population, 320

Portuguese, 287, 305–6, 317, 323, 348, 355, 373

Porus, king, adversary of Alexander the Great, 72–3, 82

Pottery: Black and Red Ware, 42, 43; Harappan, 8, 12, 13, 14; Northern Black Polished, 51–2; Ochre Glazed, 37; Painted Grey Ware, 42, 43; Roman, 121–3

Prabhakara-Vardhana, father of Harsha, 162

Prabhavati, daughter of Chandra-Gupta II & Vakataka queen, 142

Prambanam, Java, 194

Prasad, Rajendra, President, 472, 482

Prasenajit, 5th c BC king of Koshala, 66, 67

Pratabgarh, Maharashtra, 351

Pratapa-Rudra, 14th c Kakatiya king, 258, 263

Pratihara, 'gate-keeper', a rajput dynasty, 202, & *see* Gurjara-Pratiharas

Prayaga (Allahabad), Uttar Pradesh, 135, 165

President's Rule, constitutional device, 519, 523, 529, 530

Prinsep, James, antiquarian, 87–9, 136

Prithviraj III, 12th c Chahamana ruler of Ajmer, 233–8, 241

Ptolemy, Egyptian geographer, 121

Pudukottai, Tamil Nadu, xxvii

Pulakesin I, founder of Chalukya dynasty, 168

Pulakesin II, 7th c Chalukya king, 168–70, 172

Pundra, Bengal, 165

Pune (Poona), Maharashtra, 86, 338, 352, 354, 368, 402, 405–6, 409, 412, 461

Purana Qila, Delhi, 301

Puranas, ancient Sanskrit texts dealing with genealogies & traditions, 3, 38–9, 42, 46, 79, 89, 135, 148, 152

Purandhar, Treaty of (1665), 353

Puri, Orissa, 213, 219, 271

Purushpura (Peshawar), iii

Pushyamitra of Malwa, 5th c opponent of Guptas, 143

Pushyamitra, 2nd c BC, founder of Shunga dynasty, 105

Quetta, Baluchistan, 181

Quilon, Kerala, 276

Quit India Movement of 1942, 498–9, 504

Qutb Minar, Delhi, 142, 240–1

Qutb-ud-din Aybak, first Delhi sultan, 240, 244

Quwwat-ul-Islam mosque, Delhi, 240–1, 259

Radcliffe, Sir Cyril, judge, 507–8

Raffles, Thomas Stamford, Lieut-Governor of Java, 415

Raghu, King of Ayodhya, 152, 170

Raghunath Rao, 18th c Maratha peshwa, 403, 405–6, 408

Rahman, Shaikh Mujibur, Prime Minister of Bangladesh, 526, 527

Rai Dynasty of Sind, 182

Rai, Lala Lajpat, *Arya Samaj* leader, 467

Raichur Doab, between Kistna & Tungabhadra Rivers in Andhra Pradesh, 283, 303

Rajanya, clan leadership, 32, 35, 36, 52

Rajaraja I, 10th c Chola king, 215–9, 220, 222

Rajaram, 17th c Maratha ruler, 356, 357

Rajasthan, 130, 131, 137, 169, 196–7, 231–4, 233, 238, 270, 287, 295, 313–5, 345–6, 360, 411

Rajasuya, royal consecration ritual, 46

Rajendra I, 11th c Chola king, 214, 216–23

Rajgir (Rajagriha), Bihar, 51, 62, 64, 66, 67

rajputs, 53, 196–7, 206, 227–30, 231–4, 237–8, 256–7, 284, 295, 313–5, 329–30, 345–6, 360, 408, 413

Rajya-Sri, sister of Harsha, queen of Maukharis, 162–4

Rajya-vardhana, brother of Harsha, 162

Ralph, Mr, explorer of Ajanta, 149–50

Ram Lila see *Ramayana*

Rama Raja, 17th c Vijayanagar king, 307

Rama, King of Ayodhya, xxvii, 39, 44, 45, 46, 102

Rama-Chandra, 13–14th c Seuna king of Devagiri, 254–5, 257

Rama-Gupta, 4th c Gupta king, 141

Rama-rajya (Ram-raj), the utopian government of Rama, 46

Ramayana, Sanskrit epic, xxvii, 2, 37–8, 44–7, 60

Ranjit Singh, Maharaja of Panjab, 410–11, 418–9, 420–3, 424

Ranoji Scindia, 18th c Maratha leader, 368

Ranthambor, Rajasthan, 239, 256

Rao, P.V. Narasimha, Prime Minister, 531, 533

Rao, S.R., archaeologist, 9

Rashtrakutas, 8–10th c Deccan dynasty, xxviii, 157, 190–2, 196, 199–201, 202, 215

Rathors, rajput lineage of Marwar, 345

Ratnagar, Shireen, historian, 17

Ratnins, 'jewels' or ministers of early kings, 55

Ratri, Vedic deity, 30

Ravi River, 73

Ravikirti, poet, 169

Ray, Hemachandra, historian, 155, 233

Raychaudhuri, Tapan, historian, 324, 325

Raziya, 13th c Delhi Sultan(ess), 245–7

Reinaud, M., French historian, 109

Rig Veda, the earliest & most revered collection of Vedas, 23, 25, 26, 29, 31, 32, 35, 53

Ripon, Lord, Viceroy, 455–6

Risis (rishis), 'seers', 52

Roe, Sir Thomas, English Ambassador in 17th c, 326, 329, 333, 370

Rohilkand, district in NW Uttar Pradesh, 393

Rome, contacts with India, 104, 111, 117, 121–3, 124–5, 126

Round Table Conference (1930–1), 488, 489–90

Rowlatt Bills (1918–19), 474

Roy, Arundhati, novelist, 534

Rudra, Vedic deity, 142

Rudrabhuti, brahman, 159

Rudradaman, 2nd c Western Satrap (Shaka), 130–3, 144
Rudrasena II, 4th c Vakataka king, 142
Rupmati, rajput princess beloved of Baz Bahadur, 311–12
Russia, 417–9, 457, 463
Russo-Japanese War (1905), 466

Sabuktigin, 9th c Sultan of Ghazni, 204–5, 206
Sacrifice, 29–34, 46
Sailendra, Javanese dynasty, 177
Saiyyid Husain Ali Khan, one of the Saiyyid brothers, 364–6, 367
Saiyyids, king-making brothers in early 17th c, 274
Sakyas, tribe & territory to which the Buddha belonged, 48, 64, 66
Salbai, Anglo-Maratha treaty (1782), 406, 408
Salim *see* Jahangir
Salsette, Maharashtra, 405
Salt, 486–7
Samarkand, Uzbekistan, 291, 296, 316
Samatasimha, Guhila rajput ruler of Mewar, 237
Samgramaraja, 11th c king of Kashmir, 211, 212
Samrat, over-lord, 'emperor', 139
Samudra-Gupta, 4th c Gupta emperor, 134, 136–41, 146, 151, 152
San Tomé, Portuguese settlement in Madras, 332
Sanchi, Madhya Pradesh, xx, 87, 90, 102, 108, 141, 169, 254
Sangam, 'assembly' of Tamil poets & collections of their verses, 119–20
Sangha, Rana, 16th c rajput ruler of Mewar, 292, 295–6
Sangha, the Buddhist monastic community, 65, 99, 115, 166, 194
Sangharama, a Buddhist monastery, 182
Sanjaya, Javanese dynasty, 177
Sankara, 9th c philosopher & theologian, 194–5
Sanskrit, language, xxvi–xxvii, 2, 19–21, 24–5, 28, 57, 61, 103, 120–1, 132–3, 149, 151–4, 157, 161, 431
Saraswati River, 26
Sardeshmukh, Maratha leader's claim to 10% of revenue, 357, 366
Sargon the Great, Sumerian king, 16
Sarnath, Varanasi, 65, 151
Sasana, charters or grants recorded in stone or on copper plates, 156–7, 160, 164, 171, 187, 191
Sasanka, 7th c king of Gauda, 162, 163, 165

Sasaram, Uttar Pradesh, 301–2
Sastri, Prof Nilakantha, historian, 221
Satapatha Brahmana, one of the Brahmana texts, 2, 40
Satara, Maharashtra, 357, 413, 433
Sati, the cremation of a widow on the death of her husband, 429
Satiyaputras, South Indian people or tribe, 119
Satlej River, 410–11, 423
Satyagraha, Gandhian 'truth force' or passive resistance, 471, 475, 477, 487
Saurashtra, Gujarat, 111, 129, 157, 209, 287
Savarkar, V.D., revolutionary nationalist, 468
Science, 33, 131, 153–4, 188, 228
Scripts: 336; Aramaic, 60; Ashoka Brahmi, 6, 87–8, 104, 120, 121, 129–30; Gupta Brahmi, 136–8, 152; Harappan, 6, 13, 16; Kharosthi, 96, 104; South-East Asian, 124, 152
Sculpture: Buddhist, 103, 104, 112, 114, 117, 125, 147, 194; Gupta, 141, 148, 150–1, 176; Harappan, 14–15, 16; Hindu, 200–1; Mauryan, 88
Seleucus Nikator, Alexander the Great's successor in his eastern conquests, 84, 106
Senas, 11–12th c dynasty in Bengal, 244
Sesodias, rajput lineage of Mewar (Udaipur), 287, 313–5, 328–30, 354, 360
Seunas, 12–13th c Yadava dynasty of Devagiri, 252–5, 257
Shah Alam I, *see* Bahadur Shah
Shah Alam II, 18th c Mughal emperor, 382, 391–2, 410
Shah Jahan, Mughal emperor, 328–30, 331, 332, 333–6, 338–40, 343, 370
Shah Jahan II, 18th c Mughal emperor, 366
Shah Shuja, 19th c claimant to throne of Kabul, 418–19, 424
Shahbazgarhi, North West Frontier Province, 95
Shahis, 9–11th c dynasty in Kabul & Panjab, 202–7, 211–2
Shahjahanabad, i.e. Old Delhi, 335, 343, 366
Shahji Bhonsle, 17th c Maratha leader, father of Shivaji, 332, 337
Shahuji, 18th c Maratha leader, grandson of Shivaji, 363, 364, 366
Shaista Khan, Mughal commander, brother of Mumtaz Mahal, 352, 371
Shaiva, Shaivite, 'pertaining to Shiva' (*q.v.*)
Shakas, 'Scythian' dynasty of kings & satraps, 109, 110, 111, 130–3
Shamasastry, Dr R., scholar, 81

Shambhaji I, Maratha king, son of Shivaji, 354–5, 356

Shambhaji II, 18th c Maratha leader, grandson of Shivaji, 357, 363

Shams-ud-Din, Muhammad, 15th c Bahmanid Sultan, 284

Shariyar, Mughal Prince, son of Jahangir, 334

Sharqi Kings, 14–15th c dynasty of Jaunpur, 272–4

Shastri, Lal Bahadur, Prime Minister, 517, 521

Shatavahana, 1st–3rd c Deccan dynasty, 106, 125–8, 130, 133

Sher Shah Sur, 16th c Afghan rival of Mughals, 298, 299–302, 308–9, 325

Sherwani, Prof, historian, 282

Shiv Sena, militant Hindu nationalist party, 521, 533

Shiva, deity, xxvii, 14, 33, 109, 147, 151, 200–1, 209, 212, 216

Shivaji, 17th c Maratha king & patriot, 338, 339, 350–4, 457, 461, 533

Shore, Sir John, Governor-General, 428

Shortughai, Afghanistan, 10

Shuja, Mughal Prince, son of Shah Jahan, 339, 340–1

Shunga Dynasty, 2nd–1st c BC rulers of Magadha, 105, 106, 108

Siddhartha Gautama, *see* Buddha

Sidi Yakub, naval commander in alliance with Aurangzeb, 372

Sikander Lodi, 15th c Delhi Sultan, 289, 291–2

Sikhs, 316–7, 344–5, 360–1, 404, 411, 417, 418–19, 420–5, 439, 472, 506–8, 521, 528–9

Simla Conference (1945), 500

Simla, Himachal Pradesh, 415

Simon, Sir John, UK politician & chairman of 1927 Commission, 483

Sind, 58, 131, 166, 167, 180–7, 202, 210, 256, 271, 318, 419–20, 490

Singapore, 415, 452, 472, 473, 495

Singh, Manmohan, finance minister, 531

Singh, Vishwanath Pratap, prime minister, 532

Sinkiang, 104, 112, 114

Siraj-ud-Daula, 18th c nawab of Bengal, 381, 388–90

Sircar, D.C., historian, 155

Sirhind, Panjab, 235, 309

Sita Ram, brahman NCO in Bengal army, 419

Sita, deity, xxvii

Skanda-Gupta, 5th c Gupta emperor, 130, 144, 145

'Slave' Dynasty, the first Delhi sultanate founded by Qutb-ud-Din Aybak, 240–50

Sobraon, battle of (1846), 423

Solankis of Gujarat, rajput dynasty of 11th–13th c, 227, 234, 241

Somapura (Paharpur), Bengal, 193

Somnath, Gujarat, 209, 257

Sopara, Maharashtra, 126, 127

Sowars, mounted soldiers, troopers, 275, 324, 325, 379

Spices, 122–3, 188, 306

Sramanas, renunciates, members of heterodox sects, 97, 184

Sravana Belgola, Karnataka, 85–6

Sravasti, capital of Koshala, 51, 64, 66, 165

Sreni, guilds of urban artisans, 125–6, 145

Sri Gupta, 3rd c precursor of imperial Guptas, 134

Sri Lanka, 89, 90, 119, 121, 137, 146, 172–3, 177, 215, 220, 223, 531

Srirangam, Tamil Nadu, 252, 258

Srirangapatnam, Karnataka, 396, 397, 398–9

Srivijaya, SE Asian naval kingdom, 222

Stupa, a hemispherical mound, often clad in stone, commemorating the Buddha & containing Buddhist relics – *see* esp. Amaravati, Barhut, Sanchi

Suddhodana, father of Buddha, 64

Sudraka, playwright, 151

Sudras, the labouring caste, 53, 182

Sufis, Islamic saints & miracle workers, 279, 316

Sukarno, President of Indonesia, 484–5, 515

Suleiman, merchant, 190, 191, 195

Sultaniyeh, Iran, 308

Sumatra, Indonesia, 104, 123, 133, 177, 222

Sumeria, ancient Mesopotamian kingdom, 3, 9, 16

Sundara Pandya, 13th c Pandya king of Madurai, 252

Sundramurti, Tamil saint, 219

Surat, Gujarat, 323, 339, 348–50, 352, 354, 371–2, 375

Surhawardy, Husayn Shaheed, Bengali politician & founder of Bangladesh's Awami League, 505, 526

Surman, John, East India Company factor, 374–5, 376

Suryadevi, princess of Sind, 185–6

Sutkagen-dor, Makran, 10

Suvarnagiri, Andhra Pradesh, 98, 100

Suvisakha, Rudradaman's minister, 130, 133

Swadeshi, nationalist focus on 'home-produced' goods & the boycott of imported manufactures, 466, 467, 477, 487

Swaraj, 'self-rule', 467, 470, 479, 480, 481, 483, 486
Swat, Pakistan, 71, 107, 108, 114, 158

Tagore, Rabindranath, Bengali philosopher & poet, 336, 461, 467, 471, 477
Taj Mahal, xxviii, 241, 335–6
Takla Makan, Sinkiang, 104, 114
Talikota, Battle of (1565), 307–8
Tamasp, Shah of Persia, 299, 308, 386
Tamil Nadu, xxv, 118, 172, 212, 214–23, 252, 258, 332, 337, 354, 520
Tamil language, 106, 118, 119–20, 121–2, 219–20, 520
Tamluk (Tamralipti), Bengal, 65, 145, 176
Tamralipti *see* Tamluk
Tanjore, Tamil Nadu, xix, 215, 216–7, 218, 222–3, 337, 379
Tantras, Hindu-Buddhist texts on the rites of supernatural communion, 194
Tarabai, Maratha consort & regent, 357, 363, 368
Tarain, Battles of (1191 & 1192), 235–7
Tashkurgan, Sinkiang, 115
Tata, Jamshed, industrialist, 466
Tatya Topi (Tantia Topi), military leader in 1857 Rebellion, 442, 444
Taxation, 50, 97–8, 185, 218–9, 235, 242, 268, 272, 276, 313, 321–4, 325, 342–3, 357–9, 375–6, 387, 390, 414, 430, 436
Taxila, Panjab, 51, 60–2, 71, 79, 90, 96, 98, 100, 103, 107, 114, 158
Tea, 448
Tegh Bahadur, Sikh Guru, 345
Telugu language, 118
Thailand, 123
Thanesar, Haryana, 159, 160, 162, 208, 235
Thapar, Romila, historian, 4, 19, 38–9, 99
Thar Desert, Sind/Rajasthan, 182
Theosophy, 457, 458, 473
Thevenot, Jean de, 17th c French visitor, 327
Thomas, St, apostle, 109–10, 115, 122
Tibet, 194, 420–1, 463, 515, 516
Tilak, Bal Gangadhar, radical nationalist, 461, 467, 470, 473–4
Timur 'the Lame', Mongol leader, 274, 290, 320
Tipu Sultan, 18th c ruler of Mysore, 394, 396, 397–401, 407
Tod, James, officer & antiquarian, 88, 196, 231–3, 237–8, 287, 296, 315, 408, 426
Todar Mal, Akbar's finance minister, 318, 325–6, 331
Tomars, rajput lineage of Delhi & Gwalior, 199, 206

Tondaimandalam, district in Tamil Nadu, 156, 215
Toramana, Hun leader, 144, 158
Tosali, Orissa, 98, 100
Trade & Commerce, xxvi, 52, 55, 60, 84, 90, 117, 118–28, 145–6, 158, 181, 188, 275, 305–6, 323, 370, 372–3, 391, 398, 414, 428–9, 449, 451, Harappan, 12, 15–17
Trautman, Thomas, historian, 81
Travancore, southern Kerala, 400, 488
Trilochanapala, 11th c Shaka king, 211–2
Tripura, 528
Tughluq Dynasty, Delhi sultans, 261
Tughluqabad, 262–5, 269
Tully, Mark, journalist & author, 510
Tulsi Das, Hindi poet, 44
Tunga, 11th c Kashmiri commander, 211–2
Tungabhadra River, 283
Turfan, China, 104
Turks (Turuskas) 203–4, 234, 235, 238, 240, 243, 247, 249, 255, 291

Udai Singh, rajput rana of Mewar, 313–5
Udaipur, Rajasthan, 315, 330, 346
Udayagiri, Orissa, 148
Ujjain, Madhya Pradesh, 42, 51, 90, 98, 100, 105, 111, 130, 146, 187, 227, 339, 368
Ulema, the legal, academic & religious 'establishment' in Muslim society, 231, 275, 282, 287, 316, 318, 342, 344
Uma, deity, 109
Umarkot, Sind, 312
Umayyad Caliphate, 180, 186
Unionist Party of Panjab, 492, 500, 506
Upanisads, ancient Sanskrit texts concerned with metaphysics & mysticism, 26, 30, 66, 147, 339
Urdu language, 336, 435, 457
Ushas, Vedic deity, 30
Utkala, kingdom in Orissa, 193
Uttar Pradesh, 40, 135, 159, 296, 415
Uttarapatha, the 'northern route' of *arya* settlement or traffic, 43, 44, 61, 169

Vaishnava, Vaishnavite, 'pertaining to Vishnu' (*q.v.*)
Vaisali, capital of the Licchavi republic, 52, 64, 67–8, 69
Vaisya, the wealth-creating & mercantile caste, 52–3, 82, 120
Vajpayee, Atul Behari, prime minister, 534
Vakatakas, 3rd–5th c Deccan dynasty, 142, 150
Vallabhi, Gujarat, 144, 157, 159, 166
Vanga, kingdom in Bengal, 142, 193
Varanasi, Uttar Pradesh, xx, 33, 44–5, 51, 67, 157, 239, 241, 244, 342, 392, 439, 441

Vardhanas, 7th c dynasty of Thanesar & Kanauj, 159, 160–7

Varna, the fourfold division of post-Vedic society into classes or castes, 54, 64, 98, 145, 189, see also *brahmans, ksatriya, vaisya, sudras*

Varnaramadharma, social order based on *varna* and on the ages of man, 64

Varuna, Vedic deity, 25

Vasudeva, deity, 108

Vasudeva, 1st c BC Kanva king, 105

Vatsaraja, 8th c Gurjara-Pratihara ruler, 197

Vatsyana, supposed author of *Kamasutra*, 103

Vedas, collections of early Sanskrit hymns, 1, 6, 19, 21–2, 23, 24, 27, 29–34, 37, 52, 148, 149

Vellore, Tamil Nadu, 354, 437

Ventura, General, Napoleonic officer, 422

Vengi, kingdom in Andhra Pradesh, 170, 216, 220

Victoria, Queen, 446–7

Videha, clan & territory in Bihar, 43, 48

Vidisha, Andhra Pradesh, 90, 108

Vietnam, 104, 123, 124, 133, 177, 515

Vigraha-raja, 12th c Chahamana king of Ajmer, 233

Vijayaditya, 8th c Chalukya king, 174

Vijayadurg, Maharashtra, 381

Vijayanagar (Hampi), Karnataka, 277, 279, 280–3, 294, 302–8

Vikramaditya, 16th c Tomar ruler of Gwalior, 293

Vikramaditya I, 7th c Chalukya king, 172, 174

Vikramaditya II, 8th c Chalukya king, 173–4, 190

Vikramashila, Bihar, 193

Vinayaditya, 11th c Hoysala king, 251

Vindhya Hills, 43, 84, 163

Vishnu, deity, xvii, 2, 49, 108, 124, 139, 147–8, 191

Vishnugopa, 4th c Pallava king, 137

Vitashoka, brother of Ashoka, 91

Vivekananda, 19th c Hindu reformist & teacher, 458

Vratya, 'degenerate' or quasi, as in *vratya ksatriya*, 59

Wadgaon, Battle & Convention of (1779), 405

Walid, Caliph, 185–6

Wandiwash, Battle of (1760), 394

Warangal, Andhra Pradesh, 252, 258, 263

Watson, Admiral Charles, 381, 390

Wavell, Lord, Viceroy, 500–1, 504

Wellesley, Arthur, Duke of Wellington, 400, 409–10

Wellesley, Richard, Governor-General, 399–400, 401, 408, 410, 416

Wells, H.G., writer, 92

Western Ghats, xxii, 127, 168, 338, 350, 356–7

Western Satraps, Shaka rulers of Gujarat/Malwa, 111, 126, 130–3, 137, 141

Wheeler, Sir Mortimer, archaeologist, 9, 14, 22–3

Wilberforce, William, philanthropist & propagandist, 429

Wima Kadphises, Kushana king, 111, 115

Wodeyars, Mysore dynasty, 394–5, 401, 426

World War I, 470–1

World War II, 495, 498, 504

Wyllie, Sir Curzon, political secretary to Secretary of State for India, 468

Xenophon, historian, 58

Xerxes, Achaemenid king, 58–9

Yadavas, *arya* lineage descended from Yada, 35, 42–3, 147, 251, 252

Yale, Elihu, American-born employee of East India Company, 373

Yasodharman of Malwa, 6th c victor over the Huns, 158

Yaswant Rao Holkar, 18th c Maratha leader, 408

Yaudheyas, tribe of Rajasthan, 131, 137

Yavanas, Sanskrit term for Greeks & other western foreigners, 59, 106, 107, 108, 121, 127, 187, 193

Younghusband, Francis, officer & explorer, 463

Yudhisthira, one of the five Pandava heroes, 39, 46

Yueh-chi, Central Asian tribe, 110, 113

Zahir-ud-Din Mohammed *see* Babur

Zamindars, 'land-holders', rural magnates & revenue officers, 321, 325, 362, 376, 386, 392, 430, 450

Zayn-ul-Abidin, 15th c Kashmiri sultan, 288

Zorawar Singh, 19th c Dogra general, 420–1